1 MONTH OF
FREE
READING

at

www.ForgottenBooks.com

By purchasing this book you are eligible for one month membership to ForgottenBooks.com, giving you unlimited access to our entire collection of over 1,000,000 titles via our web site and mobile apps.

To claim your free month visit: www.forgottenbooks.com/free793572

ISBN 978-0-483-75180-4
PIBN 10793572

THE
LAYS AND POEMS
OF
WILLIAM SHAKSPEARE.

VOLUME THE NINTH.

THE

PLAYS AND POEMS

OF

WILLIAM SHAKSPEARE.

VOLUME THE NINTH.

CONTAINING

KING HENRY VI. PART FIRST.
KING HENRY VI. PART SECOND.
KING HENRY VI. PART THIRD.
A DISSERTATION ON THE THREE PARTS
OF KING HENRY VI.

D U B L I N:

PRINTED BY JOHN EXSHAW, No. 98, GRAFTON-STREET.

1794.

KING HENRY VI.

PART I.

B

Perfons Reprefented.

King Henry *the Sixth.*
Duke of Glofter, *uncle to the king, and Protector.*
Duke of Bedford, *uncle to the king, and Regent of* France.
Thomas Beaufort, *Duke of* Exeter, *great uncle to the king.*
Henry Beaufort, *great uncle to the king, Bifhop of* Winchefter,
  and afterwards Cardinal.
John Beaufort, *Earl of* Somerfet; *afterwards, Duke.*
Richard Plantagenet, *eldeft fon of* Richard *late Earl of* Cam-
  bridge; *afterwards Duke of* York.
Earl of Warwick. *Earl of* Salifbury. *Earl of* Suffolk.
Lord Talbot, *afterwards Earl of* Shrewfbury:
John Talbot, *his fon.*
Edmund Mortimer, *Earl of* March.
Mortimer's *Keeper, and a Lawyer.*
Sir John Faftolfe. Sir William Lucy.
Sir William Glanfdale. Sir Thomas Gargrave.
Mayor of London. Woodville, *Lieutenant of the Tower.*
Vernon, *of the White Rofe, or* York *faction.*
Baffet, *of the Red Rofe, or* Lancafter *faction.*

Charles, *Dauphin, and afterwards king of* France.
Reignier, *Duke of* Anjou, *and titular king of* Naples.
Duke of Burgundy. *Duke of* Alençon.
Governor of Paris. Baftard *of* Orleans.
Mafter-Gunner of Orleans, *and his fon.*
General of the French *forces in* Bourdeaux.
A French *Serjeant. A* Porter.
An old Shepherd, father to Joan la Pucelle.

Margaret, *daughter to* Reignier; *afterwards married to* King
  Henry.
Countefs of Auvergne.
Joan la Pucelle, *commonly called,* Joan *of* Arc.

Fiends appearing to La Pucelle, Lords, *Warders of the Tower,*
  Heralds, Officers, Soldiers, Meffengers, *and feveral Attend-*
  ants *both on the* Englifh *and* French.

SCENE, *partly in* England, *and partly in* France.

ACT I. SCENE I.

Weſtminſter Abbey.

Dead march. The corpſe of King Henry the Fifth diſcovered, lying in ſtate: attended on by the dukes of BEDFORD, GLOS-TER, *and* EXETER; *the earl of* WARWICK; *the Biſhop of* Wincheſter, *heralds,* &c.

Bed. Hung be the heavens with black, yield day to night!
Comets, importing change of times and ſtates,

Brandiſh

---

¹ The hiſtorical tranſactions contained in this play, take in the com-paſs of above thirty years. I muſt obſerve, however, that our author, in the three parts of *K Henry VI.* has not been very preciſe to the date and diſpoſition of his facts; but ſhuffled them, backwards and for-wards, out of time. For inſtance; the lord Talbot is killed at the end of the fourth act of this play, who in reality did not fall till the 13th of July 1453: and *The Second Part of Henry VI.* opens with the mar-riage of the king, which was ſolemnized eight years before Talbot's death, in the year 1445. Again, in the ſecond part, dame Eleanor Cobham is introduced to inſult queen Margaret; though her penance and baniſhment, for ſorcery happened three years before the princeſs came over to England. I could point out many other tranſgreſſions againſt hiſtory, as far as the order of time is concerned. Indeed, though there are ſeveral maſter-ſtrokes in theſe three plays, which inconte-ably betray the workmanſhip of Shakſpeare; yet I am almoſt doubtful, whether they were entirely of his writing. And unleſs they were wrote by him very early, I ſhould rather imagine them to have been brought to him as a director of the ſtage; and ſo have received ſome finiſhing beauties at his hand. An accurate obſerver will eaſily ſee, the diction of them is more obſolete, and the numbers more mean and proſaical, than in the generality of his genuine compoſitions. THEOBALD.

Having given my opinion very fully relative to theſe plays at the end of the third part of *King Henry VI.*, it is here only neceſſary to apprize the reader what my hypotheſis is, that he may be the better enabled, as he proceeds, to judge concerning its probability. Like many others, I was long ſtruck with the many evident *Slakſpearianiſms* in theſe plays, which appeared to me to carry ſuch deciſive weight, that I could ſcarce-ly bring myſelf to examine with attention any of the arguments that have been urged againſt his being the author of them. I am now ſur-priſed, (and my readers perhaps may ſay the ſame thing of themſelves,) that I ſhould never have adverted to a very ſtriking circumſtance which diſtinguiſhes this *firſt* part from the other parts of *King Henry VI.* This circumſtance is, that none of theſe Shakſpearian paſſages are to be found here, though ſeveral are ſcattered through the two other parts. I am therefore deciſively of opinion that *this* play was not written by Shakſpeare. The reaſons on which that opinion is founded, are ſtated

Brandiſh your cryſtal treſſes [2] in the ſky;
And with them ſcourge the bad revolting ſtars,
That have conſented [3] unto Henry's death!

King

at large in the Diſſertation above referred to. But I would here requeſt the reader to attend particularly to the verſification of this piece, (of which almoſt every line has a pauſe at the end,) which is ſo different from that of Shakſpeare's undoubted plays, and of the greater part of the two ſucceeding pieces as *altered* by him, and ſo exactly correſponds with that of the tragedies written by others before and about the time of his firſt commencing author, that this alone might decide the queſtion, without taking into the account the numerous claſſical alluſions which are found in this firſt part. The reader will be enabled to judge how far this argument deſerves attention, from the ſeveral extracts from thoſe ancient pieces which he will find in the Eſſay on this ſubject.

With reſpect to the *ſecond* and *third* parts of *K. Henry VI.* or, as they were originally called, *The Contention of the two famous houſes of Yorke and Lancaſter*, they ſtand, in my apprehenſion, on a very different ground from that of this firſt part, or, as I believe it was anciently called, *The Play of K. Henry VI.*—The *Contention*, &c. printed in two parts, in quaito, 1600, was, I conceive, the production of ſome playwright who preceded, or was contemporary with, Shakſpeare; and out of that piece he formed the two plays which are now denominated the *Second* and *Third* Parts of *King Henry VI.*; as, out of the old plays of *King John* and *the Taming of a Shrew*, he formed the two other plays with the ſame titles. For the reaſons on which this opinion is formed, I muſt again refer to my Eſſay on this ſubject.

This old play of *King Henry VI.* now before us, or as our author's editors have called it, the *firſt* part of *King Henry VI.* I ſuppoſe, to have been written in 1589, or before. See *An Attempt to aſcertain the order of Shakſpeare's plays*, Vol. I. The diſpoſition of facts in theſe three plays, not always correſponding with the dates, which Mr. Theobald mentions, and the want of uniformity and conſiſtency in the ſeries of events exhibited, may perhaps be in ſome meaſure accounted for by the hypotheſis now ſtated. As to our author's having accepted theſe pieces as a *Director* of the ſtage, he had, I fear, no pretenſions to ſuch a ſituation at ſo early a period. MALONE.

[2] *Brandiſh your* cryſtal *treſſes*—] *Chryſtal* is an epithet repeatedly beſtowed on comets by our ancient writers. So, in a *Sonnet* by Lord Sterline, 1604:
     " When as thoſe *chryſtal* comets whiles appear."
" There is alſo a *white comet* with ſilver haires," ſays *Pliny*, as tranſlated by P. Holland, 1601. STEEVENS.

[3] *That have* conſented—] If this expreſſion means no more than that the ſtars gave a bare *conſent*, or *agreed* to let king Henry die, it does no great honour to its author. I believe to *conſent*, in this inſtance, means to act in concert. *Concentus*, Lat. Thus *Erato* the muſe applauding the ſong of Apollo, in Lylly's *Midas*, 1592, cries out, " O ſweet *conſent!*" i. e. ſweet union of ſounds. Again, in Spenſer's *Faery Queen*, B. IV. c. ii.
     " Such muſick his wiſe words with time *conſented*."
Again, in his tranſlation of Virgil's *Culex*:
     " Chaunted their ſundry notes with ſweet *concent*."
and in many other places. *Conſented*, or as it ſhould be ſpelt, *concented*, means, *have thrown themſelves into a malignant configuration, to pro-*

King Henry the fifth, too famous to live long!
England ne'er loft a king of fo much worth.
- *Glo.* England ne'er had a king, until his time.
Virtue he had, deferving to command:
His brandifh'd fword did blind men with his beams;
His arms fpread wider than a dragon's wings;
His fparkling eyes, replete with wrathful fire,
More dazzled and drove back his enemies,
Than mid-day fun, fierce bent againft their faces.
What fhould I fay? his deeds exceed all fpeech:
He ne'er lift up his hand, but conquered.
　　Exe. We mourn in black; Why mourn we not in blood?
Henry is dead, and never fhall revive:
Upon a wooden coffin we attend;
And death's difhonourable victory
We with our ftately prefence glorify,
Like captives bound to a triumphant car.
What? fhall we curfe the planets of mifhap,
That plotted thus our glory's overthrow?
Or fhall we think the fubtle-witted French [4]
Conjurers and forcerers, that, afraid of him,
By magick verfes have contriv'd his end?
　　Win. He was a king bleft of the King of kings.
Unto the French the dreadful judgment-day
So dreadful will not be, as was his fight.

The

---

mote the death of Henry. Spenfer, in more than one inftance, fpells this word as it appears in the text of Shakfpeare; as does Ben Jonfon, in his *Epithalamion on Mr. Wefton.* The following lines,

"—— fhall we curfe the planets of mifhap,
" That *plotted* thus, &c.

feem to countenance my explanation; and Falftaff fays of Shallow's fervants, that—" they flock together in *confent*, like fo many wild geefe." STEEVENS.
　　Confent, in all the books of the age of Elizabeth, and long afterwards, is the ufual fpelling of the word *concent.* In other places I have adopted the modern and more proper fpelling; but, in the prefent inftance, I apprehend, the word was ufed in its ordinary fenfe. In the fecond act, p. 25, Talbot, reproaching the foldiery, ufes the fame expreffion, certainly without any idea of a *malignant configuration:*
　　" You all *confented* unto Salifbury's *death.*" MALONE.
　　4 — *the fubtle-witted French,* &c.] There was a notion prevalent a long time, that life might be taken away by metrical charms. As fuperftition grew weaker, thefe charms were imagined only to have power on irrational animals. In our author's time it was fuppofed that the Irifh could kill rats by a fong. JOHNSON.
　　So, in Reginald Scot's *Difcoverie of Witchcraft,* 1584: " The Irifhmen addict themfelves, &c. yea they will not fticke to affirme that they can *rime* either man or beaft to death." STEEVENS.

The battles of the Lord of hofts he fought :
The church's prayers made him fo profperous.

   Glo. The church! where is it ? Had not churchmen pray'd,
His thread of life had not fo foon decay'd :
None do you like but an effeminate prince,
Whom, like a fchool-boy, you may over-awe.

   Win. Glofter, whate'er we like, thou art protector ;
And lookeft to command the prince, and realm.
Thy wife is proud ; fhe holdeth thee in awe,
More than God, or religious church men, may.

   Glo. Name not religion, for thou lov'ft the flefh ;
And ne'er throughout the year to church thou go'ft,
Except it be to pray againft thy foes.

   Bed. Ceafe, ceafe thefe jars, and reft your minds in peace !
Let's to the altar :—Heralds, wait on us :—
Inftead of gold, we'll offer up our arms ;
Since arms avail not, now that Henry's dead.—
Pofterity, await for wretched years,
When at their mothers' moiften'd eyes babes fhall fuck ;
Our ifle be made a nourifh of falt tears [5],
And none but women left to wail the dead.—
Henry the fifth ! thy ghoft I invocate ;
Profper this realm, keep it from civil broils !
Combat with adverfe planets in the heavens !
A far more glorious ftar thy foul will make,
Than Julius Cæfar, or bright [6]—

                                        Enter

---

[5] *Our ifle be made a nourifh of falt tears.*] It feems very probable
that our author wrote, a *nourice*; i. e. that the whole ifle fhould be one
common *nurfe*, or *nou-ifher*, of tears : and thofe be the nourifhment of
its miferable iffue. THEOBALD.

   I have been informed, that what we call at prefent a *ftew*, in which
fifh are preferved alive, was anciently called a *nourifh*. *Nourice*, however, Fr. a *nurfe*, was anciently fpelt many different ways, among
which *nourifh* was one. So, in *Syr Eglamour of Artois*, bl. l. no date:
     "Of that chylde fhe was blythe,
     "After *noryfhes* fhe fent believe."
A *nourifh* therefore in this paffage of our author fignifies a *nurfe*, as it
apparently does in the *Tragedies of John Bochas*, by Lydgate, B. I. c. 12:
     "Athenes whan it was in his floures
     "Was called *nourifh* of philofophers wife."
     " —— Jubæ tellus generat, leonum
          " Arida *nutrix*." STEEVENS.

   [6] *Than Julius Cæfar, or bright*—] It might have been written,—
or bright Berenice. JOHNSON.

   This blank undoubtedly arofe from the tranfcribers or compofitors
not being able to make out the name. So, in a fubfequent paffage the
word *Nero* was omitted for the fame reafon. See the Differtation at the
end of the third part of *King Henry VI.* MALONE.

Enter a Meffenger.

Meff. My honourable lords, health to you all!
Sad tidings bring I to you out of France,
Of lofs, of flaughter, and difcomfiture:
Guienne, Champaigne, Rheims, Orleans[7],
Paris, Guyfors, Poictiers, are all quite loft.

Bed. What fay'ft thou, man, before dead Henry's corfe?
Speak foftly; or the lofs of thofe great towns
Will make him burft his lead, and rife from death.

Glo. Is Paris loft? is Roüen yielded up?
If Henry were recall'd to life again,
Thefe news would caufe him once more yield the ghoft.

Exe. How were they loft? what treachery was us'd?

Meff. No treachery; but want of men, and money.
Among the foldiers this is muttered,—
That here you maintain feveral factions;
And, whilft a field fhould be difpatch'd and fought,
You are difputing of your generals.
One would have ling'ring wars, with little coft;
Another would fly fwift, but wanteth wings;
A third thinks, without expence at all,
By guileful fair words peace may be obtain'd.
Awake, awake, Englifh nobility!
Let not floth dim your honours, new-begot:
Cropp'd are the flower-de-luces in your arms;
Of England's coat one half is cut away.

Exe. Were our tears wanting to this funeral,
Thefe tidings would call forth her flowing tides.*

Bed. Me they concern; regent I am of France:—
Give me my fteeled coat, I'll fight for France.—
Away with thefe difgraceful wailing robes!
Wounds I will lend the French, inftead of eyes,
To weep their intermiffive miferies[8].

Enter another Meffenger.

2. *Mef.* Lords, view thefe letters, full of bad mifchance.
France is revolted from the Englifh quite;
Except fome petty towns of no import:

7 *Guienne, Champagne, Rheims, Orleans,*] This verfe might be completed by the infertion of *Roüen* among the places loft, as Glofter in his next fpeech infers that it had been mentioned with the reft. STEEVENS.

* — *her flowing tides.*] i. e. England's flowing tides. MALONE.

8 — *their intermiffive miferies.*] i. e. their miferies, which have had only a fhort intermiffion from Henry the Fifth's death to my coming amongft them. WARBURTON.

The

The Dauphin Charles is crowned king in Rheims ;
The baſtard of Orleans with him is join'd :
Reignier, duke of Anjou, doth take his part ;
The duke of Alençon flieth to his ſide,

Exe. The Dauphin crowned king ! all fly to him !
O, whither ſhall we fly from this reproach ?

Glo. We will not fly, but to our enemies' throats :—
Bedford, if thou be ſlack, I'll fight it out.

Bed. Gloſter, why doubt'ſt thou of my forwardneſs ?
An army have I muſter'd in my thoughts,
Wherewith already France is over-run.

Enter a third Meſſenger.

3. *Meſſ.* My gracious lords,—to add to your laments,
Wherewith you now bedew king Henry's hearſe,—
I muſt inform you of a diſmal fight,
Betwixt the ſtout lord Talbot and the French.

Win. What ! wherein Talbot overcame ? is't ſo ?

3. *Meſſ.* O, no ; wherein lord Talbot was o'erthrown :
The circumſtance I'll tell you more at large.
The tenth of Auguſt laſt, this dreadful lord,
Retiring from the ſiege of Orleans,
Having full ſcarce [9] ſix thouſand in his troop,
By three and twenty thouſand of the French
Was round encompaſſed and ſet upon :
No leiſure had he to enrank his men ;
He wanted pikes to ſet before his archers ;
Inſtead whereof, ſharp ſtakes, pluck'd out of hedges,
They pitched in the ground confuſedly,
To keep the horſemen off from breaking in.
More than three hours the fight continued ;
Where valiant Talbot, above human thought,
Enacted wonders with his ſword and lance.
Hundreds he ſent to hell, and none durſt ſtand him ;
Here, there, and every where, enrag'd he flew[*] :
The French exclaim'd, The devil was in arms ;
All the whole army ſtood agaz'd on him :
His ſoldiers, ſpying his undaunted ſpirit,
A Talbot ! a Talbot ! cried out amain,
And ruſh'd into the bowels of the battle.
Here had the conqueſt fully been ſeal'd up,

If

---

9. *Having full ſcarce*, &c.] The modern editors read,—*ſcarce full*,
but, I think unneceſſarily. So, in the *Tempeſt* :
   " —Proſpero, maſter of a *full* poor cell." STEEVENS.
* —*he flew* :] I ſuſpect the author wrote—*ſlew*. MALONE.

If Sir John Faftolfe had not play'd the coward[1] ;
He being in the vaward, (plac'd behind[2],
With purpofe to relieve and follow them,)
Cowardly fled, not having ftruck one ftroke.
Hence grew the general wreck and maffacre ;
Enclofed were they with their enemies :
A bafe Walloon, to win the Dauphin's grace,
Thruft Talbot with a fpear into the back ;
Whom all France, with their chief affembled ftrength,
Durft not prefume to look once in the face.

Bed. Is Talbot flain ? then I will flay mfelf,
For living idly here, in pomp and eafe,
Whilft fuch a worthy leader, wanting aid,
Unto his daftard foe-men is betray'd.

3. *Meff.* O no, he lives ; but is took prifoner,
And lord Scales with him, and lord Hungerford :
Moft of the reft flaughter'd, or took, likewife.

Bed.

---

[1] *If Sir John Faftolfe, &c.*] Mr. Pope has taken notice, " That Falftaff is here introduced again, who was dead in *K Henry V.* The occafion whereof is, that this play was written before *K Henry IV.* or *K. Henry V.*" But it is the hiftorical Sir John Faftolfe (for fo he is called by both our Chroniclers) that is here mentioned ; who was a lieutenant general, deputy regent to the duke of Bedford in Normandy, and a knight of the garter ; and not the comic character afterwards, introduced by our author, and which was a creature merely of his own brain. Nor when he named him *Falftaff* do I believe he had any intention of throwing a flur on the memory of this renowned old warrior.— THEOBALD.

Mr. Theobald might have feen his notion contradicted in the very line he quotes from. *Faftolfe,* whether truly or not, is faid by Hall and Holinfhed to have been degraded for cowardice Dr. Heylin in his *St. George for England,* tells us, that " he was afterwards, upon good reafon by him alledged in his defence, reftored to his honour."—" This Sir *John Falftoff,*" continues he, " was without doubt, a valiant and wife captain, notwithftanding the ftage hath made merry with him."— FARMER.

See Oldys's Life of Sir John Faftolfe in the GENERAL DICTIONARY. MALONE.

In the 18th fong of Drayton's *Polyolbion* is the following character of this Sir *John Faftolph :*
" Strong *Faftolph* with this man compare we juftly may ;
" By Salfbury who oft being ferioufly imploy'd
" In many a brave attempt the general foe annoy'd ;
" With excellent fucceffe in Main and Anjou fought,
" And many a bulwarke there into our keeping brought ;
" And chofen to go forth with Vadamont in warre,
" Moft refolutely tooke proud Renate duke of Barre." STEEV.

[2] *He being in the vaward* [*plac'd behind,*] Some of the editors feem to have confidered this as a contradiction in terms, and have propofed to read—the *rerewward* —but without neceffity. Some part of the van muft have been behind the foremoft line of it. We often fay the *back-front* of a houfe. STEEVENS.

B 5

Bed. His ranfom there is none but I fhall pay :
I'll hale the Dauphin headlong from his throne,
His crown fhall be the ranfom of my friend ;
Four of their lords I'll change for one of our's.—
Farewell, my mafters ; to my tafk will I ;
Bonfires in France forthwith I am to make,
To keep our great faint George's feaft withal :
Ten thoufand foldiers with me I will take,
Whofe bloody deeds fhall make all Europe quake.

 3. Mef. So you had need ; for Orleans is befieg'd ;
The Englifh army is grown weak and faint :
The earl of Salifbury craveth fupply,
And hardly keeps his men from mutiny,
Since they, fo few, watch fuch a multitude.

 Exe. Remember, lords, your oaths to Henry fworn ;
Either to quell the Dauphin utterly,
Or bring him in obedience to your yoke.

 Bed. I do remember it ; and here take my leave,
To go about my preparation.   [*Exit.*

 Clo. I'll to the Tower with all the hafte I can,
To view the artillery and munition ;
And then I will proclaim young Henry king.   [*Exit.*

 Exe. To Eltham will I, where the young king is,
Being ordain'd his fpecial governor ;
And for his fafety there I'll beft devife.   [*Exit.*

 Win. Each hath his place and function to attend :
I am left out ; for me nothing remains.
But long I will not be Jack-out-of-office ;
The king from Eltham I intend to fend *,
And fit at chiefeft ftern of publick weal. [*Exit. Scene clofes.*

SCENE II.

France. *Before* Orleans.

Enter CHARLES, *with his forces* ; ALENÇON, REIGNIER,
   and Others.

 Char. Mars his true moving [3], even as in the heavens,
So in the earth, to this day is not known :
Late, did he fhine upon the Englifh fide ;

---

 * — *to* fend,] Mr Mafon, with fome probability conjectures that we
fhould read—to *fteal.* The fecond charge in the *Articles of accufation*
preferred by the Duke of Glofter againft the Bifhop, (Hall's *Chron.*
Hen y VI. f. 12. b.) countenances this conjecture. MALONE.

 3 *Mars his true moving,* &c] So, Nafh in one of his prefaces before
Gabriel Harvey's Hunt is up, 1596 :—" You are as ignorant in the true
movings of my mufe, as the aftronomers are in the *true movings of
Mars,* which to this day they could never attain to." STEEVENS.

               Now

Now we are victors, upon us he smiles.
What towns of any moment, but we have ?
At pleasure here we lie, near Orleans ;
Otherwhiles, the famish'd English, like pale ghosts,
Faintly besiege us one hour in a month.

Alen. They want their porridge, and their fat bull-beeves :
Either they must be dieted, like mules,
And have their provender ty'd to their mouths,
Or piteous they will look, like drowned mice.

Reig. Let's raise the siege ; Why live we idly here ?
Talbot is taken, whom we wont to fear :
Remaineth none, but mad-brain'd Salisbury ;
And he may well in fretting spend his gall,
Nor men, nor money, hath he to make war.

Char. Sound, sound alarum ; we will rush on them.
Now for the honour of the forlorn French :—
Him I forgive my death, that killeth me,
When he sees me go back one foot, or fly.   [*Exeunt.*

Alarums ; Excursions ; afterwards a Retreat.

Re-enter CHARLES, ALENÇON, REIGNIER, *and others.*

Char. Who ever saw the like ? what men have I ?—
Dogs ! cowards ! dastards !—I would ne'er have fled,
But that they left me 'midst my enemies.

Reig. Salisbury is a desperate homicide ;
He fighteth as one weary of his life.
The other lords, like lions wanting food,
Do rush upon us as their hungry prey.

Alen. Froisard, a countryman of ours, records,
England all Olivers and Rowlands bred +,
During the time Edward the third did reign.
More truly now may this be verified ;
For none but Sampsons, and Goliasses,
It sendeth forth to skirmish.   One to ten !
Lean raw-bon'd rascals ! who would e'er suppose
They had such courage and audacity ?

Char. Let's leave this town ; for they are hair-brain'd slaves,
And hunger will enforce them to be more eager :

---

4 *England all Olivers and Rowlands* bred,] These were two of the
most famous in the list of Charlemagne's twelve peers ; and their exploits are rendered so ridiculously and equally extravagant by the old ro-
mancers, that from thence arose that saying amongst our plain and sensi-
ble ancestors, of *giving one a Rowland for his Oliver*, to signify the
matching one incredible lie with another.   WARBURTON.

Rather, to oppose one hero to another, i. e. *to give a person as good as
one as he brings.*   STEEVENS.

The old copy has—*breed.* Corrected by Mr. Rowe.   MALONE.

Of old I know them; rather with their teeth
The walls they'll tear down, than forsake the siege.

   Reig. I think, by some odd gimmals [5] or device,
Their arms are set, like clocks [6], still to strike on;
Else ne'er could they hold out so, as they do.
By my consent, we'll e'en let them alone.

   Alen. Be it so.

         Enter the BASTARD *of* Orleans.

   Baſt. Where's the prince Dauphin? I have news for him.
   Char. Baſtard of Orleans, thrice welcome to us.
   Baſt. Methinks, your looks are sad, your cheer [7] appall'd;
Hath the late overthrow wrought this offence?
Be not dismay'd, for succour is at hand:
A holy maid hither with me I bring,
Which, by a vision sent to her from heaven,
Ordained is to raise this tedious siege,
And drive the English forth the bounds of France.
The spirit of deep prophecy she hath,
Exceeding the nine sibyls of old Rome [8];
What's paſt, and what's to come, she can descry.
Speak, shall I call her in? Believe my words [9],
For they are certain and infallible.

   Char. Go, call her in: [*Exit* Baſt.] But firſt to try her
      skill,
Reignier, ſtand thou as Dauphin in my place:
Queſtion her proudly, let thy looks be ſtern;—
By this means shall we found what skill she hath.   [*Retires.*

---

   5 — *gimmals*—] A *gimmal* is a piece of jointed work, where one
piece moves within another, whence it is taken at large for an *engine*.
It is now by the vulgar called a *gimcrack.* JOHNSON.

   In the inventory of the jewels, *&c.* belonging to Saliſbury Cathedral,
taken in 1536, 28th of Henry VIII, is—" A faire cheſt with *gimmals*
and key." Again, " Three other cheſts with *gimmals* of ſilver and
gilt." Again, in the *View-Breaker,* or the *Faire Maide of Clifton,* 1636:
     " My acts are like the motionall *gymmals*
     " Fixt in a watch." STEEVENS.

   6 *Their arms are set, like clocks,*] Perhaps the author was thinking
of the clocks in which figures in the shape of men ſtruck the hours. Of
these there were many in his time. MALONE.

   7 — *your cheer*—] *Chear* is countenance, appearance. STEEVENS.

   8 — *nine sibyls of old Rome*;] There were no *nine sibyls* of Rome;
but he confounds things, and miſtakes this for the nine books of Sibylline
oracles, brought to one of the Tarquins. WARBURTON.

   9 *Believe my words,*] It should be read—believe *her* words.
                           JOHNSON.

   I perceive no need of change. The baſtard calls upon the Dauphin to
believe the extraordinary account he has juſt given of the prophetick
ſpirit and proweſs of the Maid of Orleans. MALONE.

                                Enter

Enter LA PUCELLE, BASTARD *of* Orleans, *and others.*

Reig. Fair maid, is't thou wilt do thofe wond'rous feats?

Puc. Reignier, is't thou that thinkeft to beguile me?—
Where is the Dauphin?—come, come from behind;
I know thee well, though never feen before.
Be not amaz'd, there's nothing hid from me:
In private will I talk with thee apart;—
Stand back, you lords, and give us leave awhile.

Reig. She takes upon her bravely at firft dafh.

Puc. Dauphin, I am by birth a fhepherd's daughter,
My wit untrain'd in any kind of art.
Heaven, and our Lady gracious, hath it pleas'd
To fhine on my contemptible eftate:
Lo, whilft I waited on my tender lambs,
And to fun's parching heat difplay'd my cheeks,
God's mother deigned to appear to me;
And, in a vifion full of Majefty,
Will'd me to leave my bafe vocation,
And free my country from calamity:
Her aid fhe promis'd, and affur'd fuccefs:
In complete glory fhe reveal'd herfelf;
And, whereas I was black and fwart before,
With thofe clear rays which fhe infus'd on me,
That beauty am I bleft with, which you may fee.
Afk me what queftion thou canft poffible,
And I will anfwer unpremeditated:
My courage try by combat, if thou dar'ft,
And thou fhalt find that I exceed my fex.
Refolve on this: Thou fhalt be fortunate,
If thou receive me for thy warlike mate.

Char. Thou haft aftonifh'd me with thy high terms;
Only this proof I'll of thy valour make,—
In fingle combat thou fhalt buckle with me;
And, if thou vanquifheft, thy words are true;
Otherwife, I renounce all confidence.

Puc. I am prepar'd: here is my keen edg'd fword,
Deck'd with five flower-de-luces on each fide [1];

---

[1] *Deck'd with* five *flower-de-luces*, &c.] The old copy reads—*fine.*
The fame miftake having happened in *A Midfummer Night's Dream*
and in other places, I have not hefitated to reform the text, according
to Mr. Steevens's fuggeftion. In the Mfs. of the age of Queen Elizabeth
u and n are undiftinguifhable. MALONE.

We fhould read, a cording to Holinfhed, *five* flower-de luces. " —in
a fecret place there among old iron, appointed fhe hir fword to be fought
out and brought her, that with *five* floure delices was graven on both
fides," &c. STEEVENS.

The which, at Touraine in saint Catharine's churchyard,
Out of a great deal of old iron I chose forth.

Char. Then come o'God's name, I fear no woman.

Puc. And, while I live, I'll ne'er fly from a man.

                      [*They fight.*

Char. Stay, stay thy hands; thou art an Amazon,
And fightest with the sword of Debora.

Puc. Christ's mother helps me, else I were too weak.

Char. Whoe'er helps thee, 'tis thou that must help me:
Impatiently I burn with thy desire [2];
My heart and hands thou hast at once subdu'd.
Excellent Pucelle, if thy name be so,
Let me thy servant, and not sovereign, be;
'Tis the French Dauphin sueth to thee thus.

Puc. I must not yield to any rites of love,
For my profession's sacred from above:
When I have chased all thy foes from hence,
Then will I think upon a recompence.

Char. Mean time, look gracious on thy prostrate thrall.

Reig. My lord, methinks, is very long in talk.

Alen. Doubtless, he shrives this woman to her smock;
Else ne'er could he so long protract his speech.

Reig. Shall we disturb him, since he keeps no mean?

Alen. He may mean more than we poor men do know:
These women are shrewd tempters with their tongues.

Reig. My lord, where are you? what devise you on?
Shall we give over Orleans, or no?

Puc. Why, no, I say, distrustful recreants!
Fight till the last gasp; I will be your guard.

Char. What she says, I'll confirm; we'll fight it out.

Puc. Assign'd am I to be the English scourge.
This night the siege assuredly I'll raise:
Expect saint Martin's summer [3], halcyon days,
Since I have entered into these wars.
Glory is like a circle in the water,
Which never ceaseth to enlarge itself,
Till, by broad spreading, it disperse to nought [4].

                            With

---

2 *Impatiently I burn with thy desire;*] The amorous constitution of the Dauphin has been mentioned in the preceding play:

     " *Doing* is activity and he will still be *doing*." COLLINS.

3 *Expect saint Martin's summer,*] That is, expect *prosperity* after *misfortune*, like fair weather at Martlemas, after winter has begun.

                               JOHNSON.

4 *Glory is like a circle in the water,*
    Which never ceaseth to enlarge itself,
    Till, by broad spreading, it disperse to nought.] So, in Nosce TEIPSUM, a poem by Sir John Davies, 1599.

                           " As

With Henry's death, the Englifh circle ends ;
Difperfed are the glories it included.
Now am I like that proud infulting fhip,
Which Cæfar and his fortune bare at once [5].

Char. Was Mahomet infpired with a dove [6] ?
Thou with an eagle art infpired then.
Helen, the mother of great Conftantine,
Nor yet faint Philip's daughters [7], were like thee.
Bright ftar of Venus, fall'n down on the earth,
How may I reverently worfhip thee enough ?

Alen. Leave off delays, and let us raife the fiege.

Reig. Woman, do what thou canft to fave our honours ;
Drive them from Orleans, and be immortaliz'd.

Char. Prefently we'll try :—Come, let's away about it :
No prophet will I truft, if fhe proves falfe.   [*Exeunt.*

SCENE III.

London. *Hill before the Tower.*

Enter, at the gates, the Duke of GLOSTER, *with his ferving-men in blue coats.*

Glo. I am come to furvey the Tower this day ;
Since Henry's death, I fear, there is conveyance [8].—

" As when a ftone is into water caft,
" One circle doth another circle make,
" Till the laft circle reach the bank at laft."
The fame image, without the particular application, may be found in Silius Italicus, Lib. xiii.
Sic ubi perrumpfit ftagnantem calculus undam,
Exiguos format per prima volumina gyros,
Mox tremulum vibrans motu glifcente liquorem
Multiplicat crebros finuati gurgitis orbes;
Donec poftremo laxatis circulus oris
Contingat geminas patulo curvamine ripas. MALONE.

[5] *Like that proud infulting fhip,*
Which Cæfar and his fortune bare at once.] This alludes to a paffage in Plutarch's *Life of Julius Cæfar,* thus tranflated by Sir T. North. " Cæfar hearing that, ftraight difcovered himfelfe unto the maifter of the pynnafe, who at the firft was amazed when he faw him, but Cæfar, &c. laid unto him, Good fellow, be of good cheere, &c and fear not, for *thou haft Cæfar and his fortune with thee.*" STEEVENS

[6] *Was* Mahomet *infpired with a dove?*] *Mahomet* had a dove, " which he ufed to feed with wheat out of his ear; which dove when it was hungry, lighted on Mahomet's fhoulder, and thruft its bill in to find its breakfaft; *Mahomet* perfuading the rude and fimple Arabians, that it was the Holy Ghoft that gave him advice." See Sir *Walter Raleigh's Hiftory of the World,* Book 1. Part 1. ch. vi. *Life of Mahomet,* by Dr Prideaux. GREY.

[7] *No, yet faint Philip's daughters,*] Meaning the four daughters of Philip mentioned in the *Acts.* HANMER.

[8] *— there is conveyance.*] *Conveyance* means *theft.* HANMER.

Where

Where be thefe warders, that they wait not here ?
Open the gates ; it is Glofter that calls. [Servants *knock*.

  1. *Ward* [*within*.] Who is there, that knocks fo imperi-
    oufly ?

  1. *Serv.* It is the noble Duke of Glofter.

  2. *Ward.* [*within*.] Whoe'er he be, you may not be let in.

  1. *Serv.* Villains, anfwer you fo the lord protector ?

  1. *Ward.* [*within*.] The lord protect him ! fo we anfwer
    him :

We do no otherwife than we are will'd.

  Glo. Who willed you ? or whofe will ftands, but mine ?
There's none protector of the realm, but I.—
Break up the gates [9], I'll be your warrantize :
Shall I be flouted thus by dunghill grooms ?.

Servants rufh at the Tower gates. *Enter, to the gates,* WOOD-
VILLE, *the lieutenant.*

  Wood. [*within*.] What noife is this ? what traitors have we
    here ?

  Glo. Lieutenant, is it you, whofe voice I hear ?
Open the gates ; here's Glofter, that would enter.

  Wood. [*within*.] Have patience, noble duke ; I may not
    open ;
The cardinal of Winchefter forbids :
From him I have exprefs commandment,
That thou, nor none of thine, fhall be let in.

  Glo. Faint-hearted Woodville, prizeft him 'fore me ?
Arrogant Winchefter ? that haughty prelate,
Whom Henry, our late fovereign, ne'er could brook ?
Thou art no friend to God, or to the king :
Open the gates, or I'll fhut thee out fhortly.

  1. *Serv.* Open the gates unto the lord protector ;
Or we'll burft them open, if that you come not quickly.

Enter WINCHESTER, *attended by a train of fervants in tawny
coats* [1].

  Win. How now, ambitious Humphry [2] ? what means this ?
    Glo.

---

  9 Break up *the gates*,] I fuppofe to break up the gate is to force up
the portcullis, or by the application of petards to blow up the gates
themfelves. STEEVENS.

  Some one has propofed to read—break *ope* the gates ; but the old copy
is right. So Hall, *Henry VI.* folio 78, b. " The lufty Kentifhmen
hoping on more friends, *brake up* the gaytes of the King's Bench and
Marfhalfea," &c. MALONE.

  1 — *tawny coats.*] A tawny coat was the drefs of a *fumpner*, i. e. an
apparitor, an officer whofe bufinefs it was to fummon offenders to an
               .ecelefiaftical

Glo. Piel'd prieft [3], doft thou command me to be fhut out.?

Win. I do, thou moft ufurping proditor,.
And not protector of the king or realm.

Glo. Stand back, thou manifeft confpirator ;
Thou, that contriv'dft to murder our dead lord ;
Thou, that giv'ft whores indulgences to fin [4] :
I'll canvafs thee in thy broad cardinal's hat [5],

If

ecclefiaftical court. Thefe are the proper attendants therefore on the bifhop of Winchefter. So, in Stowe's *Chronicle*, p. 822 : " —and by the way the *bifhop* of London met him, attended on by a goodly company of gentlemen in *tawny coats*," &c.

Tawny was a colour worn for mourning, as well as *black* ; and was therefore the proper and fober habit of any perfon employed in an ecclefiaftical court.

    " A crowne of baies fhall that man weare
    " That triumphes over me ;
    " For *blacke* and *tawnie* will I weare,
    " Which *mourning colours be*."

The Complaint of a Lover wearing *blacke* and *tawnie* ; by E. O. *Paradife of Dainty Devifes*, 1596. STEEVENS.

[2] — Humphry ?] Old Copy—*Umpheir*. Corrected by Mr. Theobald. MALONE.

[3] *Piel'd Prieft*,] Alluding to his fhaven crown. POPE.

In Skinner (to whofe dictionary I was directed by Mr. Edwards) I find that it means more : *Pill'd* or *peel'd garlick, cui pellis, vel pili omnes ex morbo aliquo, præfertim e lue venerea, defluxerunt*. In Ben Jonfon's *Bartholomew Fair* the following inftances occurs : " I'll fee them p—'d firft, and *pil'd* and double *pil'd*." STEEVENS.

The old copy has—*piel'd* prieft. *Piel'd* and *pil'd* were only the old fpelling of *peel'd*. So, in our poet's *Rape of Lucrece*, 4to. 1594:
    " His leaves will wither, and his fap decay,
    " So muft my foul, her bark being *pil'd* away."

See alfo Florio's Italian Dictionary, 1598 : " *Pelare*. To *pill* or pluck, as they do the feathers of fowle ; to *pull off the hair* or *fkin*." MALONE.

In Weever's *Funeral Monuments*, p. 154, Robert Baldocke, bifhop of London, is called a *peeled* prieft, *pilde* clerk, feemingly in allufion to his fhaven crown alone. So, *bald head* was a term of fcorn and mockery. TOLLET.

[4] *Thou, that giv'ft whores indulgences to fin :*] The publick ftews were formerly under the diftrict of the bifhop of Winchefter. POPE.

There is now extant an old manufcript (formerly the office book of the court leet held under the jurifdiction of the bifhop of Winchefter in Southwark) in which are mentioned the feveral fees arifing from the brothel-houfes allowed to be kept in the bifhop's manor, with the cuftoms and regu'ations of them. One of the articles is, " *De his, qui cuftodiunt mulieres habentes nefandam infirmitatem.*"

" *Item*, That no ftewholder keep any woman within his houfe, that hath any ficknefs of brenning, but that fhe be put out upon pain of making a fyne unto the lord of C fhillings. UPTON.

[5] *I'll canvafs thee in thy broad cardinal's hat*,] This means, I believe, I'll tumble thee into thy great hat, and fhake thee, as bran and meal are fhaken in a fieve." So, Sir William D'Avenant, in the *Cruel Brother*, 1630:

" I'll

If thou proceed in this thy insolence.

Win. Nay, stand thou back, I will not budge a foot ;
This be Damascus, be thou cursed Cain [6],
To slay thy brother Abel, if thou wilt.

Glo. I will not slay thee, but I'll drive thee back :
Thy scarlet robes, as a child's bearing-cloth
I'll use, to carry thee out of this place.

Win. Do what thou dar'st ; I beard thee to thy face.

Glo. What ? am I dar'd, and bearded to my face ?
Draw, men, for all this privileged place ;
Blue-coats to tawny-coats. Priest, beware your beard ;

　　　　　[Gloster *and his men attack the Bishop.*

I mean to tug it, and to cuff you soundly :
Under my feet I stamp thy cardinal's hat ;
In spite of pope, or dignities of church,
Here by the cheeks I'll drag thee up and down.

Win. Gloster, thou'lt answer this before the pope.

Glo. Winchester goose [7], I cry—A rope ! a rope [8] !—
Now beat them hence, Why do you let them stay ?—
Thee I'll chase hence, thou wolf in sheep's array.—
Out, tawny coats !—out, scarlet hypocrite !

*Here a great tumult. In the midst of it, Enter the Mayor of
London, and officers.*

May. Fie, lords ! that you, being supreme magistrates,
Thus contumeliously should break the peace !

Glo. Peace, mayor ; thou know'st little of my wrongs :
Here's Beaufort, that regards nor God nor king,
Hath here distrain'd the Tower to his use.

Win. Here is Gloster, a foe to citizens ;

" I'll sift and winnow him in an old hat."
To *canvas* was anciently used for *to sift.* STEEVENS.

Probably from the materials of which the bottom of a *sieve* is made. In
K. *Henry IV.* P. II. Doll tells Falstaff, that she will " *canvass* him between a pair of sheets.

Perhaps, however, in the passage before us Gloster means, that he will
toss the cardinal in a sheet, even while he was invested with the peculiar badge of his ecclesiastical dignity.—Coarse sheets were formerly
termed *canvass sheets.* MALONE.

6 *This be Damascus, be thou cursed Cain,*] About four miles from Damascus is a high-hill, reported to be the same on which Cain slew his
brother Abel. Maundrel's *Travels,* p. 131. POPE.

Sir John Maundeville says, " And in that place where *Damascus* was
founded *Kaym* sloughe *Abel* his brother." *Travels,* edit. 1725, p. 148.
REED.

7 *Winchester goose*] A strumpet, or the consequences of her love,
was a Winchester goose. JOHNSON.

8 *—A rope ! a rope !—*] See the *Comedy of Errors.* MALONE.

One that ftill motions war, and never peace,
O'er-charging your free purfes with large fines ;
'I hat feeks to overthrow religion,
Becaufe he is protector of the realm ;
And would have armour here out of the Tower,
To crown himfelf king, and fupprefs the prince.

Glo. I will not anfwer thee with words, but blows.

[*Here they fkirmifh again.*

May. Nought refts for me, in this tumultuous ftrife,
But to make open proclamation :—
Come, officer ; as loud as e'er thou canft.

Off. All manner of men, affembled here in arms this day, againft God's peace and the king's, we charge and command you, in his highnefs' name, to repair to your feveral dwelling-places ; and not to wear, handle, or ufe, any fword, weapon, or dagger, henceforward, upon pain of death.

Glo. Cardinal, I'll be no breaker of the law :
But we fhall meet, and break our minds at large.

Win Glofter, we'll meet ; to thy coft, be fure 9 :
Thy heart-blood I will have for this day's work.

May. I'll call for clubs 1, if you will not away :—
This cardinal is more haughty than the devil.

Glo. Mayor, farewell : thou doft but what thou may'ft.

Win. Abominable Glofter ! guard thy head ;
For I intend to have it, ere long. [*Exeunt.*

May. See the coaft clear'd, and then we will depart.—
Good God ! that nobles 2 fhould fuch ftomachs bear !
I myfelf fight not once in forty year. [*Exeunt.*

SCENE IV.

France. *Before* Orleans.

Enter, on the walls, the Mafter-Gunner and his Son.

M. Gun. Sirrah, thou know'ft how Orleans is befieg'd ;
And how the Englifh have the fuburbs won.

Son. Father, I know ; and oft have fhot at them,
Howe'er, unfortunate, I mifs'd my aim.

M. Gun. But now thou fhalt not. Be thou rul'd by me :
Chief mafter-gunner am I of this town !

---

9 —*be fure :*] The latter word is here ufed as a diffyllable. MALONE.
1 *I'll call for clubs, &c.*] That is, for peace-officers armed with clubs or ftaves. In affrays, it was cuftomary in this author's time to call out, *clubs, clubs! See As you like it.* MALONE.
2 —*that nobles—*] Old copy—*thefe* nobles. Corrected by Mr. Rowe.
MALONE.

Something

Something I muſt do, to procure me grace.
The prince's eſpials [3] have informed me,
How the Engliſh, in the ſuburbs cloſe entrench'd,
Wont, through a ſecret grate of iron bars [4]
In yonder tower, to over-peer the city ;
And thence diſcover, how, with moſt advantage,
They may vex us, with ſhot, or with aſſault.
To intercept this inconvenience, .
A piece of ordnance 'gainſt it I have plac'd ;
And even theſe three days have I watched,
If I could ſee them.
Now do thou watch, for I can ſtay no longer [5].
If thou ſpy'ſt any, run and bring me word ; .
And thou ſhalt find me at the governor's.   [*Exit.*

  Son. Father, I warrant you ; take you no care ;
I'll ne'er trouble you, if I may ſpy them.

Enter, in an upper chamber of a tower, the Lords SALISBURY
  and TALBOT [6], *Sir.* William GLANSDALE, *Sir* Thomas
  GARGRAVE, *and others.*

  Sal. Talbot, my life, my joy, again return'd !
How wert thou handled, being priſoner ?
Or by what means got'ſt thou to be releaſ'd ?

                  Diſcourſe,

---

3 *The prince's* eſpials—] *Eſpials* are ſpies. So, in Chaucer's *Freres
Tale :*
  - " For ſubtilly he had his *eſpiaille.*" STEEVENS.
  The word is often uſed by Hall and Holinſhed. MALONE.
  4 Wont, *through a ſecret grate of iron bars,* &c.] . The old copy
reads—*Went.* I have not heſitated to adopt the emendation propoſed
by Mr. Tyrwhitt, which is fully ſupported by the paſſage in Hall's Chronicle, on which this ſpeech is formed.
  So, in *The Arraignment of Paris,* 1384 :
    " —— the uſual time is nie,
    " When *wont* the dames of fate and deſtinie
    " In robes of cheerfull colour to repair,—" MALONE.
  I believe, inſtead of *went,* we ſhould read—*wont,* the third perſon
plural of the old verb *wont.* " *The Engliſh—wont,* that is, *are accuſ-
tomed to overpeer the city.*" The word is very frequently uſed by Spenſer, and ſeveral times by Milton. TYRWHITT.
  . 5 *Now do thou watch, for I can ſtay no longer.*] Part of this line being in the old copy by a miſtake of the tranſcriber connected with the
preceding hemiſtich, the editor of the ſecond folio ſupplied the metre
by adding the word *boy,* in which he has been followed in all the ſubſequent editions. The regulation now made ſhews that ſuch addition was
unneceſſary. MALONE.
  6 —Talbot.] Though the three parts of *K. Henry VI.* are deſervedly
numbered among the feebleſt performances of Shakſpeare, this firſt of
them appears to have been received with the greateſt applauſe. So, in
Pierce Pennyleſi's Supplication to the Devil, by Naſh, 1592 : " How
                          would

Difcourfe, I pry'thee, on this turret's top.

Tal. The duke of Bedford had a prifoner,
Called—the brave lord Ponton de Santrailles;
For him was I exchang'd and ranfomed.
But with a bafer man of arms by far,
Once, in contempt, they would have barter'd me :
Which I, difdaining, fcorn'd : and craved death
Rather than I would be fo pil'd efteem'd [7].
In fine, redeem'd I was as I defir'd.
But, O ! the treacherous Faftolffe wounds my heart !
Whom with my bare fifts I would execute,
If I now had him brought into my power.

Sal. Yet tell'ft thou not, how thou wert entertain'd.

Tal. With fcoffs, and fcorns, and contumelious taunts.
In open market-place produc'd they me,
To a be a publick fpectacle to all ;
Here, faid they, is the terror of the French,
The fcare-crow that affrights our children fo [8].
Then broke I from the officers that led me ;
And with my nails digg'd ftones out of the ground,
To hurl at the beholders of my fhame.
My grifly countenance made others fly ;
None durft come near, for fear of fudden death.
In iron walls they deem'd me not fecure ;
So great fear of my name 'mongft them was fpread,
That they fuppos'd, I could rend bars of fteel,

would it have joyed brave *Talbot* (the terror of the French) to thinke that after he had lien two hundred yeares in his tombe, he fhould triumph againe on the ftage, and have his bones new embalmed with the teares of ten thoufand fpectators at leaft, (at feveral times,) who in the tragedian that reprefents his perfon, imagine they behold him frefh bleeding." STEEVENS.

[7] —*fo pil'd efteem'd.*] I have no doubt that we fhould read—*fo pile-efteem'd* : a latini m, for which the author of this play had, I believe, no occafion to go to Lilly's grammar. " Flocci, nauci, nibili, *pili,* &c. his verbis, *æftimo,* pendo, peculiariter adjiciuntur ; ut,—*Nec hujus facio, qui me pili æftimat.*" Even if we fuppofe no change to be neceffary, this furely was the meaning intended to be conveyed. In one of Shakfpeare's plays we have the fame phrafe, in *Englifh,*—vile-efteem'd. MALONE.

[8] — *the* terror *of the* French,
The fcare-crow that affrights our children fo.] From Hall's *Chronicle :* " This man [Talbot] was to the French people a very fcourge and a daily *terror,* infomuch that as his perfon was fearful, and terrible to his adverfaries prefent, fo his name and fame was fpiteful and dreadful to the common people abfent ; infomuch that women in France to feare their young children, would crye, the *Talboth* commeth, the *Talbot* commeth." The fame thing is faid of King Richard I. when he was in the Holy Land. See Camden's *Remaines,* 4to. 1614, p. 267. MALONE.

And

And spurn in pieces posts of adamant :
Wherefore a guard of chosen shot I had,
That walk'd about me every minute while ;
And if I did but stir out of my bed,
Ready they were to shoot me to the heart.

Sal. I grieve to hear what torments you endur'd ;
But we will be reveng'd sufficiently.
Now it is supper-time in Orleans :
Here thorough this grate, I count each one,
And view the Frenchmen how they fortify ;
Let us look in, the sight will much delight thee.—
Sir Thomas Gargrave, and Sir William Glansdale,
Let me have your express opinions,
Where is best place to make our battery next.

Gar. I think, at the north gate : for there stand lords.

Glan. And I, here, at the bulwark of the bridge.

Tal. For aught I see, this city must be famish'd ;
Or with light skirmishes enfeebled [9].

[*Shot from the town.* SAL. *and Sir* Tho. GAR. *fall.*

Sal. O Lord, have mercy on us, wretched sinners !

Gar. O Lord, have mercy on me, woful man !

Tal. What chance is this, that suddenly hath cross'd us ?—
Speak, Salisbury ; at least, if thou canst speak ;
How far'st thou, mirror of all martial men ?
One of thy eyes, and thy cheek's side struck off [1] !—
Accursed tower ! accursed fatal hand,
That hath contriv'd this woful tragedy !
In thirteen battles Salisbury o'ercame ;
Henry the fifth he first train'd to the wars :
Whilst any trump did sound, or drum struck up,
His sword did ne'er leave striking in the field.—
Yet liv'st thou, Salisbury ? though thy speech doth fail,
One eye thou hast [2] to look to heaven for grace :
The sun with one eye vieweth all the world.—
Heaven, be thou gracious to none alive,
If Salisbury wants mercy at thy hands !—
Bear hence his body, I will help to bury it.—
Sir Thomas Gargrave, hast thou any life ?

9 — *enfeebled*] This word is here used as a quadrisyllable. MALONE.
1 —*thy cheek's side struck off !*—] Camden says in his *Remains* that
the French scarce knew the use of great ordnance, till the siege of Mans
in 1425, when a breach was made in the walls of that town by the English, under the conduct of this Earl of Salisbury ; and that he was the
first English gentleman that was slain by a cannon ball. MALONE.
2 *One eye thou hast*, &c.] A similar thought occurs in *King Lear* :
" —— my lord, you have one eye left,
" To see some mischief on him." STEEVENS.

Speak

Speak unto Talbot; nay, look up to him.
Salisbury, cheer thy spirit with this comfort;
Thou shalt not die, whiles—
He beckons with his hand, and smiles on me;
As who should say, *When I am dead and gone,*
Remember to avenge me on the French.—
Plantagenet, I will; and like thee, Nero [3],
Play on the lute, beholding the towns burn:
Wretched shall France be only in my name.

[*Thunder heard; afterwards an alarum.*

What stir is this? What tumult's in the heavens?
Whence cometh this alarum, and the noise?

Enter a Messenger.

Mess. My lord, my lord, the French have gather'd head:
The Dauphin, with one Joan la Pucelle join'd,—
A holy prophetess, new risen up,—
Is come with a great power to raise the siege.

[*Salisbury groans.*

Tal. Hear, hear, how dying Salisbury doth groan!
It irks his heart, he cannot be reveng'd.—
Frenchmen, I'll be a Salisbury to you:
Pucelle or puzzel [4], dolphin or dogfish,
Your hearts I'll stamp out with my horse's heels,
And make a quagmire of your mingled brains.—
Convey me Salisbury into his tent,
And then we'll try what these dastard Frenchmen dare.

[*Exeunt, bearing out the bodies.*

3 — *and like thee*, Nero,] In the old copy, the word *Nero* is wanting, owing probably to the transcriber's not being able to make out the name. The editor of the second folio, with his usual freedom, alter'd the line thus:—and *Nero-like will—*. MALONE.

4 *Pucelle or* Puzzel,] *Puzzel* means *a dirty wench* or *a drab*, from *puzza*, i. e. *malus fætor*, says Minsheu. In a translation from Steephens's *Apology for Herodotus*, in 1608, p. 98, we read,—" Some filthy queans, especially our *puzzles* of Paris, use this other theft. TOLLET.

Again, in Ben Jonson's *Commendatory Verses*, prefix'd to the works of Beaumont and Fletcher:

" Lady or *Pusill*, that wears mask or fan "

As for the conceit, miserable as it is, it may be countenanced by that of James I. who looking at the statue of Sir Thomas *Bodley* in the library at Oxford, " — Pii Thomæ *Godly* nomine insignivit, eoque potius nomine quam *Bodly*, deinceps merito nominandum esse censuit." See *Rex Platonicus*, &c. edit. quint. Oxon. 1635, p. 187.

It should be remembered, that in Shakspeare's time the word *dauphin* was always written *dolphin*. STEEVENS.

There are frequent references to Pucelle's name in this play:

" — I scar'd the dauphin and his *trull.*"

Again:

" Scoff on, vile fiend, and shameless *courtezan!*" MALONE.

SCENE

SCENE V.

The same. Before one of the gates.

Alarum. Skirmishings. TALBOT *pursueth the* Dauphin, *and driveth him in: then enter* JOAN LA PUCELLE, *driving Englishmen before her. Then enter* TALBOT.

Tal. Where is my strength, my valour, and my force ?
Our English troops retire, I cannot stay them ;
A woman, clad in armour, chaseth them.

Enter LA PUCELLE.

Here, here she comes :—I'll have a bout with thee ;
Devil, or devil's dam, I'll conjure thee :
Blood will I draw on thee [5], thou art a witch,
And straightway give thy soul to him thou serv'st.

Puc. Come, come, 'tis only I that must disgrace thee.
                                            [*They fight.*

Tal. Heavens, can you suffer hell so to prevail ?
My breast I'll burst with straining of my courage,
And from my shoulders crack my arms asunder,
But I will chastise this high-minded strumpet.

Puc. Talbot, farewell ; thy hour is not yet come :
I must go victual Orleans forthwith.
O'ertake me, if thou canst ; I scorn thy strength.
Go, go, cheer up thy hunger-starved [6] men ;
Help Salisbury to make his testament :
This day is ours, as many more shall be.
                          [PUCELLE *enters the town, with soldiers.*

Tal. My thoughts are whirled like a potter's wheel ;
I know not where I am, nor what I do :
A witch, by fear, not force, like Hannibal,
Drives back our troops, and conquers as she lists :
So bees with smoke, and doves with noisome stench,
Are from their hives, and houses, driven away.
They call'd us, for our fierceness, English dogs ;
Now, like to whelps, we crying run away.
                                      [*A short alarum.*

Hark, countrymen ! either renew the fight,
Or tear the lions out of England's coat ;

5 *Blood will I draw on thee,*] The superstition of those times taught that he that could draw the witch's blood, was free from her power.
                                                      JOHNSON.

6 —*hunger-starved—*] The same epithet is, I think, used by Shakspeare. The old copy has *hungry*-starved. Corrected by Mr. Rowe.
                                                      MALONE.

                                        Renounce

Renounce your foil, give fheep in lions' ftead :
Sheep run not half fo timorous [7] from the wolf,
Or horfe, or oxen, from the leopard,
As you fly from your oft-fubdued flaves.—

[*Alarum. Another fkirmifh.*

It will not be :—Retire into your trenches :
You all confented unto Salifbury's death,
For none would ftrike a ftroke in his revenge.—
Pucelle is enter'd into Orleans,
In fpite of us, or aught that we could do.
O, would I were to die with Salifbury !
The fhame hereof will make me hide my head.

[*Alarum. Retreat. Exeunt* TALBOT *and his forces*, &c.

SCENE VI.

The fame.

Enter, on the walls, PUCELLE, CHARLES, REIGNIER, ALEN-
ÇON, *and foldiers.*

Puc. Advance our waving colours on the walls ;
Refcu'd is Orleans from the Englifh [8] :
Thus Joan la Pucelle hath perform'd her word.

Char. Divineft creature, Aftræa's daughter,
How fhall I honour thee for this fuccefs ?
Thy promifes are like Adonis' gardens [9],
That one day bloom'd, and fruitful were the next.—

7 —*fo timorous*—] Old copy—*treacherous.* Corrected by Mr. Pope.

MALONE.

8 — *from the Englifh :*] Thus the old copy. The editor of the fecond folio, not perceiving that *Englifh* was ufed as a trifyllable, arbitrari-
ly reads—Englifh *wolves* ; in which he has been followed by all the
fubfequent editors So, in the next line but one, he reads *bright
Aftræa*, not obferving that *Aftræa*, by a licentious pronunciation, was
ufed by the author of this play, as if written *Afteræa.* So *monftrous* is
made a trifyllable ;—*monftereus.* See Mr. Tyrwhitt's note, *Two Gentlemen of Verona.* MALONE.

9 — *like Adonis' gardens*,] " The Greeks (fays Dr. Pearce, in a
note on the following lines of Milton,

" Spot more delicious than thofe gardens feign'd,
" Or of reviv'd Adonis, or—"

had a *tradition* that Adonis, when he was alive, delighted in gardens,
and had a magnificent one ; for proof of this we have Pliny's words,
xix. 4. " Antiquitas nihil priùs mirata eft quàm Hefperidum hortos,
ac regum *Adonidis* et Alcinoi." Hence it was (he adds) that the Grecian women ufed to carry about fmall portable pots with lettuce, or fennel
growing in them, on the annual feftival of Adonis.

On this fubject Dr. Warburton has written a long note, of which no
part but the foregoing quotation appears to me worth preferving.

MALONE.

France, triumph in thy glorious prophetefs !—
Recover'd is the town of Orleans :
More bleffed hap did ne'er befall our ftate.

   Reig. Why ring not out the bells aloud throughout the
     town ?
Dauphin, command the citizens make bonfires,
And feaft and banquet in the open ftreets,
To celebrate the joy that God hath given us.

   Alen. All France will be replete with mirth and joy,
When they fhall hear how we have play'd the men.

   Char. 'Tis Joan, not we, by whom the day is won ;
For which, I will divide my crown with her :
And all the priefts and friars in my realm
Shall, in proceffion, fing her endlefs praife.
A ftatelier pyramis to her I'll rear,
Than Rhodope's [1], or Memphis' ever was :
In memory of her, when fhe is dead,
Her afhes, in an urn more precious
Than the rich-jewel'd coffer of Darius [2],
Tranfported fhall be at high feftivals
Before the kings and queens of France.
No longer on faint Dennis will we cry,

---

[1] *Than* Rhodope's] *Rhodope* was a famous ftrumpet, who acquired
great riches by her trade. The leaft but moft finifhed of the Egyptian
pyramids (fays Pliny in the 36th book of his *Natural Hiftory*, ch. xii)
was built by her. She is faid afterwards to have married Pfammeti-
chus, king of Egypt Dr. Johnfon thinks that the Dauphin means to
call *Joan of Arc* a ftrumpet, all the while he is making this loud praife
of her.—I would read :
    " Than *Rhodope's of* Memphis, ever was." STEEVENS.
   The brother of Sappho, was in love with *Rhodope*, and purchafed her
freedom (for fhe was a flave in the fame houfe with Æfop the fabulift)
at a great price. Rhodope was of Thrace, not of Memphis. Memphis
a city of Egypt, was celebrated for its pyramids :
    " Barbara *Pyramidum* fileat miracula *Memphis*."
            MART. De fpectaculis Libel. Ep. i. MALONE.
   [2] —*coffer of Darius;*] When Alexander the Great took the city of
Gaza, the metropolis of Syria, amidft the other fpoils and wealth of Darius treafur'd up there, he found an exceeding rich and beautiful little
cheft or cafket, and afked thofe about him what they thought fitteft to be
laid up in it. When they had feverally delivered their opinions, he
told them, he efteemed nothing fo worthy to be preferved in it as
Homer's Iliad. Vide *Plutarchum* in Vitâ *Alexandri Magni.*
                THEOBALD.
   The very words of the text are found in Puttenham's *Arte of Englifh
Poefie*, 1589 : " In what price the noble poems of Homer were holden
with Alexander the Great, infomuch as everie night they were layd under his pillow, and by day were carried in *the rich jewel cofer of Darius*,
lately before vanquifhed by him in battaile." MALONE.

                                                  But

But Joan la Pucelle fhall be France's faint.
Come in ; and let us banquet royally,
After this golden day of victory.   [*Flourifh. Exeunt.*

ACT II. SCENE I.

The fame.

Enter to the gates, a French Serjeant, *and two* Sentinels.

Serj. Sirs, take your places, and be vigilant :
If any noife, or foldier, you perceive,
Near to the walls, by fome apparent fign,
Let us have knowledge at the court of guard.

   1. *Sent.* Serjeant, you fhall. [*Exit* Serjeant.] Thus are
      poor fervitors
(When others fleep upon their quiet beds)
Conftrain'd to watch in darknefs, rain, and cold.

Enter TALBOT, BEDFORD, BURGUNDY, *and forces, with
   fcaling ladders ; their drums beating a dead march.*

Tal. Lord regent,—and redoubted Burgundy,—
By whofe approach, the regions of Artois,
Walloon, and Picardy, are friends to us,—
This happy night the Frenchmen are fecure,
Having all day carous'd and banqueted :
Embrace we then this opportunity ;
As fitting beft to quittance their deceit,
Contriv'd by art, and baleful forcery.

Bed. Coward of France !—how much he wrongs his fame,
Defpairing of his own arm's fortitude,
To join with witches, and the help of hell.

Bur. Traitors have never other company.—
But what's that Pucelle, whom they term fo pure ?

Tal. A maid, they fay.

Bed. A maid ! and be fo martial !

Bur. Pray God, fhe prove not mafculine ere long ;
If underneath the ftandard of the French,
She carry armour, as fhe hath begun.

Tal. Well, let them practife and converfe with fpirits :
God is our fortrefs ; in whofe conquering name,
Let us refolve to fcale our flinty bulwarks.

   Bed. Afcend, brave Talbot ; we will follow thee.

Tal. Not all together : better far, I guefs,
That we do make our entrance feveral ways ;
That, if it chance the one of us do fail,
The other yet may rife againft their force.

Bed. Agreed ; I'll to yon corner.

Bur. And I to this.

Tal. And here will Talbot mount, or make his grave.—
Now, Salisbury ! for thee, and for the right
Of English Henry, shall this night appear
How much in duty I am bound to both.

[*The English scale the walls, crying St.* George ! *a Talbot ! and all enter by the town.*

Sent. [*within.*] Arm, arm! the enemy doth make af-
sault !

The French *leap over the walls in their shirts. Enter several
ways* BASTARD, ALENÇON, REIGNIER, *half ready, and
half unready.*

Alen. How now, my lords ? what, all unready so [3] ?

Bast. Unready ? ay, and glad we 'scap'd so well.

Reig. 'Twas mine, I trow, to wake, and leave our beds,
Hearing alarums at our chamber doors.

Alen. Of all exploits, since first I follow'd arms,
Ne'er heard I of a warlike enterprize
More venturous, or desperate, than this.

Bast. I think, this Talbot be a fiend of hell.

Reig. If not of hell, the heavens, sure, favour him.

Alen. Here cometh Charles ; I marvel, how he sped.

Enter CHARLES, *and* LA PUCELLE.

Bast. Tut ! holy Joan was his defensive guard.

Char. Is this thy cunning, thou deceitful dame ?
Didst thou at first, to flatter us withal,
Make us partakers of a little gain,
That now our loss might be ten times so much ?

Puc. Wherefore is Charles impatient with his friend ?
At all times will you have my power alike ?
Sleeping, or waking, must I still prevail,
Or will you blame and lay the fault on me ?—
Improvident soldiers ! had your watch been good,
This sudden mischief never could have fall'n.

Char. Duke of Alençon, this was your default ;
That, being captain of the watch to-night,
Did look no better to that weighty charge.

---

3 —unready so ?] *Unready* was the current word in those times for
undress'd. JOHNSON.

So, in Haywood's *Rape of Lucrece,* 1638 : " Enter Sixtus, and
Lucrece *unready.*" Again, in *The two Maids of More-clacke,* 1609 :
" Enter James *unready,* in his night-cap, garterless " &c. STEEVENS.

Alen.

Alen. Had all your quarters been as fafely kept.
As that whereof I had the government,
We had not been thus fhamefully furpriz'd.

Baft. Mine was fecure.

Reig. And fo was mine, my lord.

Char. And, for myfelf, moft part of all this night,
Within her quarter, and mine own precinct,
I was employ'd in paffing to and fro,
About relieving of the fentinels :
Then how, or which way, fhould they firft break in ?

Puc. Queftion, my lords, no further of the cafe,
How, or which way ; 'tis fure, they found fome place
But weakly guarded, where the breach was made.
And now there refts no other fhift but this,——
To gather our foldiers, fcatter'd and difpers'd,
And lay new platforms to endamage them.

Alarum. Enter an Englifh Soldier *crying, a* Talbot ! *a* Talbot [4] ! *They fly, leaving their cloaths behind.*

Sol. I'll be fo bold to take what they have left.
The cry of Talbot ferves me for a fword ;
For I have loaden me with many fpoils,
Ufing no other weapon but his name.   *Exit.*]

---

4 *Enter an* Englifh *foldier crying,* a Talbot ! a Talbot !] And after-
wards :
  " The cry of *Talbot* ferves me for a fword."
Here a popular tradition, exclufive o any chronicle evidence, was in
Shakfpeare's mind. Edward Kerke, the old commentator on Spenfer's
Paftorals, firft publifhed in 1579, obferves in his notes on *June*, that
lord Talbot's " nobleneffe bred fuch a terrour in the hearts of the
French, that oftimes great armies were defeated and put to flight, at
the only hearing of his name : infomuch that the French women to affray
their children, would tell them, that the TALBOT *cometh*." See alfo
Sc. iii. T. WARTON.
  In a note on a former paffage, p 21, n 8, I have quoted a paffage
from Hall's Chronicle, which probably furnifhed the author of this
play with this circumftance It is not mentioned by Holinfhed, (Shakfpeare's hiftorian,) and is one of the numerous proofs that have convinced
me that this play was not the production of our author. See the Effay
at the end of the third part of *King Henry VI.* It is furely more probable that the writer of this play fhould have taken this circumftance from
the chronicle which furnifhed him with this plot, than from the Comment on Spenfer's paftorals. MALONE.

S C E N E II.

Orleans.   *Within the town.*

Enter Talbot, Bedford, Burgundy, *a Captain, and*
Others:

Bed. The day begins to break, and night is fled,
Whose pitchy mantle over-veil'd the earth.
Here found retreat, and cease our hot pursuit.
[*Retreat founded.*

Tal. Bring forth the body of old Salisbury;
And here advance it in the market-place,
The middle centre of this cursed town.——
Now have I pay'd my vow unto his soul;
For every drop of blood was drawn from him,
There hath at least five Frenchmen dy'd to-night.
And, that hereafter ages may behold
What ruin happen'd in revenge of him,
Within their chiefest temple I'll erect
A tomb, wherein his corpse shall be interr'd:
Upon the which that every one may read,
Shall be engrav'd the sack of Orleans;
The treacherous manner of his mournful death,
And what a terror he had been to France.
But, lords, in all our bloody massacre,
I muse, we met not with the Dauphin's grace;
His new-companion, virtuous Joan of Arc;
Nor any of his false confederates.
Bed. 'Tis thought, lord Talbot, when the fight began,
Rous'd on the sudden from their drowsy beds,
They did, amongst the troops of armed men,
Leap o'er the walls for refuge in the field.
Bur. Myself (as far as I could well discern,
For smoke, and dusky vapours of the night)
Am sure, I scar'd the Dauphin, and his trull [5];
When arm in arm they both came swiftly running,
Like to a pair of loving turtle doves,
That could not live asunder day or night.
After that things are set in order here,
We'll follow them with all the power we have.

[5] —*and his* trull;] So afterwards:
    " Scoff on, vile fiend, and shameless *courtezan.*"
See also p. 23, n. 4. Malone.

                                        Enter

Enter a Meſſenger.

Meſſ. All hail, my lords ! which of this princely train
Call ye the warlike Talbot, for his acts
So much applauded through the realm of France ?
  Tal. Here is the Talbot ; Who would ſpeak with him ?
  Meſſ. The virtuous lady, counteſs of Auvergne,
With modeſty admiring thy renown,
By me entreats, great lord, thou wouldſt vouchſafe
To viſit her poor caſtle where ſhè lies [6] ;
That ſhe may boaſt, ſhe hath beheld the man
Whoſe glory fills the world with loud report.
  Bur. Is it even ſo ? Nay, then, I ſee, our wars
Will turn unto a peaceful comick ſport,
When ladies crave to be encounter'd with.—
You may not, my lord, deſpiſe her gentle ſuit.
  Tal. Ne'er truſt me then ; for, when a world of men
Could not prevail with all their oratory,
Yet hath a woman's kindneſs over-rul'd :—
And therefore tell her, I return great thanks ;
And in ſubmiſſion will attend on her.—
Will not your honours bear me company ?
  Bed. No, truly ; it is more than manners will :
And I have heard it ſaid,—Unbidden gueſts
Are often welcomeſt when they are gone.
  Tal. Well then, alone, ſince there's no remedy,
I mean to prove this lady's courteſy.
Come   hither,   captain.   [*Whiſpers.*]—You   perceive   my
          mind.
  Capt. I do, my lord ; and mean accordingly.   [*Exeunt.*

SCENE III.

Auvergne.   *Court of the Caſtle.*

Enter the Counteſs, *and her Porter.*

  Count. Porter, remember what I gave in charge ;
And, when you have done ſo, bring the keys to me.
  Port. Madam, I will.   [*Exit.*
  Count. The plot is laid : if all things fall out right,
I ſhall as famous be by this exploit,
As Scythian Tomyris by Cyrus' death.

---

[6] —*where ſhe lies ;*] i. e. where ſhe dwells.   MALONE.

Great is the rumour of this dreadful knight,
And his atchievements of no lefs account :
Fain would mine eyes be witnefs with mine ears,
To give their cenfure of thefe rare reports.

Enter Meffenger, and TALBOT.

Meff. Madam, according as your ladyfhip defir'd,
By meffage crav'd, fo is lord Talbot come.
Count. And he is welcome. What! is this the man?
Meff. Madam, it is.
Count. Is this the fcourge of France?
Is this the Talbot, fo much fear'd abroad,
That with his name the mothers ftill their babes?
I fee, report is fabulous and falfe :
I thought, I fhould have feen fome Hercules,
A fecond Hector, for his grim afpect,
And large proportion of his ftrong-knit limbs.
Alas! this is a child, a filly dwarf:
It cannot be, this weak and writhled [7] fhrimp
Should ftrike fuch terror to his enemies.
Tal. Madam, I have been bold to trouble you :
But, fince your ladyfhip is not at leifure,
I'll fort fome other time to vifit you.
Count. What means he now?—Go afk him, whither he
   goes.
Meff. Stay, my lord Talbot; for my lady craves
To know the caufe of your abrupt departure.
Tal. Marry, for that fhe's in a wrong belief,
I go to certify her, Talbot's here.

Re-enter Porter, with keys.

Count. If thou be he, then art thou prifoner.
Tal. Prifoner! to whom?
Count. To me, blood-thirfty lord;
And for that caufe I train'd thee to my houfe.
Long time thy fhadow hath been thrall to me,
For in my gallery thy picture hangs :
But now the fubftance fhall endure the like ;
And I will chain thefe legs and arms of thine,
That haft by tyranny, thefe many years,
Wafted our country, flain our citizens,

---

7 — *writhled*—] i. e. *wrinkled.* The word is ufed by Spenfer. Sir
Thomas Hanmer reads—*wrizled*, which has been followed in fubfequent editions. MALONE.

And fent our fons and hufbands captivate[8].

Tal. Ha, ha, ha!

Count. Laugheft thou, wretch? thy mirth fhall turn to moan.

Tal. I laugh to fee your ladyfhip fo fond[9],
To think that you have aught but Talbot's fhadow,
Whereon to practife your feverity.

Count. Why, art not thou the man?

Tal. I am, indeed.

Count. Then have I fubftance too.

Tal. No, no, I am but fhadow of myfelf:
You are deceiv'd, my fubftance is not here;
For what you fee, is but the fmalleft part
And leaft proportion of humanity:
I tell you, madam, were the whole frame here,
It is of fuch a fpacious lofty pitch,
Your roof were not fufficient to contain it.

Count. This is a riddling merchant for the nonce[1];
He will be here, and yet he is not here:
How can thefe contrarieties agree?

Tal. That will I fhew you prefently.

*He winds a horn. Drums heard; then a peal of ordnance.
The gates being forced, enter* Soldiers.

How fay you, madam? are you now perfuaded,
That Talbot is but fhadow of himfelf?
Thefe are his fubftance, finews, arms, and ftrength,
With which he yoketh your rebellious necks;
Razeth your cities, and fubverts your towns,
And in a moment makes them defolate.

Count. Victorious Talbot! pardon my abufe:
I find, thou art no lefs than fame hath bruited,
And more than may be gather'd by thy fhape.
Let my prefumption not provoke thy wrath;
For I am forry, that with reverence
I did not entértain thee as thou art.

Tal. Be not difmay'd, fair lady; nor mifconftrue
The mind of Talbot, as you did miftake

---

[8] —captivate] So, in *Soliman and Perfeda*, 1599:
" If not deftroy'd and bound, and *captivate*,
" If *captivate*, then forc'd from holy faith." STEEVENS.
[9] —*fo* fond.] i. e.] fo foolifh. So, in *K Henry VI.* Part II.
" *Fondly* brought h re, and fo lifhly fent hence.," STEE FN.
[1] *This is a riddling merchant*, &c.] So, in *Romeo and Juliet*:
" What faucy *merchant* was this." See a note on this paffage, Act II.
fc. iv. STEEVENS.

The

The outward composition of his body.
What you have done, hath not offended me:
Nor other satisfaction do I crave,
But only (with your patience) that we may
Taste of your wine, and see what cates you have;
For soldiers' stomachs always serve them well.
   Count. With all my heart; and think me honoured
To feast so great a warrior in my house.   [*Exeunt.*

SCENE IV.

London. *The Temple Garden.*

Enter the Earls of SOMERSET, SUFFOLK, *and* WARWICK;
Richard PLANTAGENET, VERNON, *and another* Lawyer.

   Plan. Great lords, and gentlemen, what means this
        silence?
Dare no man answer in a case of truth?
   Suf. Within the Temple hall we were too loud;
The garden here is more convenient.
   Plan. Then say at once, If I maintain'd the truth;
Or, else, was wrangling Somerset in the error [2]?
   Suf. 'Faith, I have been a truant in the law;
And never yet could frame my will to it;
And, therefore, frame the law unto my will.
   Som. Judge you, my lord of Warwick, then between us.
   War. Between two hawks, which flies the higher pitch,
Between two dogs, which hath the deeper mouth,
Between two blades, which bears the better temper,
Between two horses, which doth bear him best,
Between two girls, which hath the merriest eye,
I have, perhaps, some shallow spirit of judgment:
But in these nice sharp quillets of the law.
Good faith, I am no wiser than a daw.
   Plan. Tut, tut, here is a mannerly forbearance:
The truth appears so naked on my side,
That any purblind eye may find it out.
   Som. And on my side it is so well apparell'd,
So clear, so shining, and so evident,
That it will glimmer through a blind man's eye.
   Plan. Since you are tongue-ty'd, and so loth to speak,

<hr>

   [2] *Or, else was wrangling Somerset in the error?*] So all the editions.
There is apparently a want of opposition between the two questions. I
once read,
      Or else was wrangling Somerset i'th' right? JOHNSON.
   Sir T. Hanmer would read—*And was not—.* STEEVENS.

                                               In

In dumb fignificants [3] proclaim your thoughts:
Let him, that is a true-born gentleman,
And ftands upon the honour of his birth,
If he fuppofes that I have pleaded truth,
From off this briar pluck a white rofe with me [4].

Som. Let him that is no coward, nor no flatterer,
But dare maintain the party of the truth,
Pluck a red rofe from off this thorn with me.

War. I love no colours [5]; and, without all colour
Of bafe infinuating flattery,
I pluck this white rofe, with Plantagenet.

Suf. I pluck this red rofe, with young Somerfet;
And fay withal, I think he held the right.

Ver. Stay, lords, and gentlemen; and pluck no more,
Till you conclude—that he, upon whofe fide
The feweft rofes are cropp'd from the tree,
Shall yield the other in the right opinion.

Som. Good mafter Vernon, it is well objected [6];
If I have feweft, I fubfcribe in filence.

Plan. And I.

Ver. Then, for the truth and plainnefs of the cafe,
I pluck this pale and maiden bloffom here,
Giving my verdict on the white rofe fide.

Som. Prick not your finger as you pluck it off;
Left, bleeding, you do paint the white rofe red,
And fall on my fide fo againft your will.

Ver. If I, my lord, for my opinion bleed,
Opinion fhall be furgeon to my hurt,
And keep me on the fide where ftill I am.

Som. Well, well, come on: Who elfe?

Law. Unlefs my ftudy and my books be falfe,
The argument you held, was wrong in you;   [*To* Som.
In fign whereof, I pluck a white rofe too.

Plan. Now, Somerfet; where is your argument?

Som. Here, in my fcabbard; meditating that,

---

3 *In dumb* fignificants—] I fufpect, we fhould read—*fignificance.*
MALONE.

4 *From off this briar pluck a white rofe with me.*] This is given as
the original of the two badges of the houfes of York and Lancafter,
whether truly or not, is no great matter. WARBURTON.

5 *I love no colours;*] *Colours* is here ufed ambiguoufly for *tints* and
deceits. JOHNSON.

6 — *well objected;*] Properly thrown in our way, juftly propofed.
JOHNSON.

So, in Chapman's Verfion of the 21ft Book of Homer's *Odyffey:*
" Excites Penelope t' *object* the prize
" (The bow and bright fteeles) to the woer's ftrength. STEEV.

C 3   Shall

Shall dye your white rose in a bloody red.

Plan. Mean time, your cheeks do counterfeit our roses;
For pale they look with fear, as witnessing
The truth on our side.

Som. No, Plantagenet,
'Tis not for fear; but anger,—that thy cheeks[7]
Blush for pure shame, to counterfeit our roses;
And yet thy tongue will not confess thy error.

Plan. Hath not thy rose a canker, Somerset?

Som. Hath not thy rose a thorn, Plantagenet?

Plant. Ay, sharp and piercing, to maintain his truth;
Whiles thy consuming canker eats his falsehood.

Som. Well, I'll find friends to wear my bleeding roses,
That shall maintain what I have said is true,
Where false Plantagenet dare not be seen.

Plan. Now, by this maiden blossom in my hand,
I scorn thee and thy fashion[8], peevish boy.

Suf. Turn not thy scorns this way, Plantagenet.

Plan. Proud Poole, I will; and scorn both him and thee.

Suf. I'll turn my part thereof into thy throat.

Som. Away, away, good William De-la-Poole!
We grace the yeoman, by conversing with him.

War. Now, by God's will, thou wrong'st him, Somerset;
His grandfather was Lionel duke of Clarence *,
Third son to the third Edward king of England;

---

7 — *but anger,—that thy cheeks,* &c.] i. e. it is not for fear that my cheeks look pale, but for anger; anger produced by this circumstance, namely, that *thy* cheeks blush, &c. MALONE.

8 *I scorn thee and thy fashion,*] Dr. Warburton understands by *fashion* the badge of the red rose which Somerset said he and his friends should be distinguished by. Mr. Theobald with great probability reads—*faction.* Plantagenet afterwards uses the same word
" —— this pale and angry rose—
" Will I for ever, and my *faction* wear."
In *K. Henry V.* we have *pation* for *paction.* MALONE.
We should undoubtedly read (as I suggested in this note)—and thy *faction.* The old spelling of this word was *faccion,* and hence *fashion* easily crept into the text.
So, in Hale's *Chronicle,* EDWARD IV. fol. xxii. " — whom we ought to believe to be sent from God, and of hym onely to bee provided a kynge, for to extinguish both the *faccions* and *partes* [i. e. parties] of Kyng Henry the VI. and of Kyng Edward the fourth." MALONE.

* *His grandfather was Lionel duke of Clarence.*] The author mistakes. Plantagenet's paternal grandfather was Edmund of Langley, Duke of York. His maternal grandfather was Roger Mortimer, Earl of Marche, who was the son of Philippa the daughter of Lionel Duke of Clarence. That duke therefore was his maternal great great grandfather. MALONE.

Spring

Spring creftlefs yeomen 9 from fo deep a root?

Plan. He bears him on the place's privilege ',
Or durft not, for his craven heart, fay thus.

Som. By him that made me, I'll maintain my words
On any plot of ground in Chriftendom:
Was not thy father, Richard, Earl of Cambridge,
For treafon executed in our late king's days?
And, by his treafon, ftand'ft not thou attainted,
Corrupted, and exempt 2 from ancient gentry?
His trefpafs yet lives guilty in thy blood;
And, till thou be reftor'd, thou art a yeoman.

Plan. My father was attached, not attainted;
Condemn'd to die f
And that I'll prove on better men than Somerfet,
Were growing time once ripen'd to my will.
For your partaker 3 Poole, and you yourfelf,
I'll note you in my book of memory.
To fcourge you for this apprehenfion 4:
Look to it well; and fay you are well warn'd.

Som. Ay, thou fhalt find us ready for thee ftill:
And know us, by thefe colours, for thy foes;
For thefe my friends, in fpite of thee, fhall wear.

Plan. And, by my foul, this pale and angry rofe,
As cognizance of my blood-drinking hate 5,
Will I for ever, and my faction, wear;
Until it wither with me to the grave,
Or flourifh to the height of my degree.

Suf. Go forward, and be chok'd with thy ambition!
And fo farewell, until I meet thee next.   [*Exit.*

9 *Spring* creftlefs *yeomen*—] i. e. thofe who have no right to arms.
WARBURTON.

1 — *on the place's privilege,*] The Temple, being a religious houfe,
was an afylum, a place of exemption, from violence, revenge, and
bloodfhed.   JOHNSON.

2 *Corrupted, and* exempt—] *Exempt,* for *excluded.* WARBURTON.

3 *For your* partaker—] A *partaker* in old language was an accom-
plice; a perfon joined in the fame party with another. MALONE.

4 — *for this* apprehenfion: i. e. opinion. WARBURTON.
Mr. Theobald reads—*reprehenfion.* MALONE.

5 — *this* pale *and angry rofe,*
    As *cognizance of* my blood-drinking *hate,*] So, in *Romeo* and
Juliet:
   " Either my eye-fight fails, or thou look'ft *pale.*—
   " And, truft me, love, in mine eye fo do you:
   " Dry forrow *drinks our blood.*" STEEVENS.

A *badge* is called a *cognifance* à *cognofcendo,* becaufe by it fuch perfons as do wear it upon their fleeves, their fhoulders, or in their hats,
are manifeftly known whofe fervants they are.   In heraldry the *cognifance* is feated upon the moft eminent part of the helmet. TOLLET.

Som.

Som. Have with thee, Poole.—Farewell, ambitious
    Richard.   [*Exit.*

Plan. How I am brav'd, and must perforce endure it!

War. This blot, that they object against your house,
Shall be wip'd out[6] in the next parliament,
Call'd for the truce of Winchester and Gloster:
And, if thou be not then created York,
I will not live to be accounted Warwick.
Mean time, in signal of my love to thee,
Against proud Somerset, and William Poole,
Will I upon thy party wear this rose:
And here I prophesy,—This brawl to-day
Grown to this faction, in the Temple-garden,
Shall send, between the red rose and the white,
A thousand souls to death and deadly night.

    Plan. Good master Vernon, I am bound to you,
That you on my behalf would pluck a flower.

    Ver. In your behalf still will I wear the same.

    Law. And so will I.

    Plan. Thanks, gentle sir[7].
Come, let us four to dinner: I dare say,
This quarrel will drink blood another day.   [*Exeunt.*

S C E N E V.

The same.   A Room in the Tower.

Enter MORTIMER[8], *brought in a chair by two keepers.*

    Mor. Kind keepers of my weak decaying age,

                                          Let

6 *Shall be* wip'd *out*—] Old Copy.—*whip't*. Corrected by the editor
of the second folio. MALONE.

7 — *gentle* sir.] The latter word, which yet does not complete the
metre, was added by the editor of the second folio. MALONE.

8 *Enter* Mortimer.] Mr. Edwards, in his MS notes, observes, that
Shakspeare has varied from the truth of history, to introduce this scene
between Mortimer and Richard Plantagenet. Edmund Mortimer served
under Henry V. in 1422, and died unconfined in Ireland in 1424.
Holinshed says, that Mortimer was one of the mourners at the funeral
of Henry V.

His uncle, Sir John Mortimer, was indeed prisoner in the tower,
and was executed not long before the earl of March's death, being
charged with an attempt to make his escape in order to stir up an insur-
rection in Wales. STEEVENS.

A half-informed *Remarker* on this note seems to think that he has
totally overturned it, by quoting the following passage from Hall's *Chronicle*: " During wh the parliament [held in the third year of Henry VI.
1425.] came to London Peter Duke of Quimber,—whiche of the Duke
of Exeter, &c. was highly fested—. During whych season Edmond
                                       Mortymer,

Let dying Mortimer here reſt himſelf [9].—
Even like a man new haled from the rack,

So

Mortymer, the laſt Erle of Marche of that name, (whiche long tyme
had bene reſtrayned trom hys liberty and finally waxed lame,) diſceaſed
without yſſue, whoſe inheritance deſcended to Lord Richard Plantagenet," &c. as if a circumſtance which Hall has mentioned to mark
the time of Mortimer's death, neceſſarily aſcertained the place where it
happened alſo. The fact is, that this Edmund Mortimer did not die in
London, but at Trim in Ireland. He did not however die in confinement
(as Sandford has erroneouſly aſſerted in his Genealogical Hiſtory. See
K. Henry VI.;) and whether he was ever confined, (except by Owen
Glendower) may be doubted, notwithſtanding the aſſertion of Hall.
Hardyng, who lived at the time, ſays he was treated with the greateſt
kindneſs and care both by Henry IV. (to whom he was a ward,) and
by his ſon Henry V. See his Chronicle, 1543, fol. 229. He was certainly at liberty in the year 1415, having a few days before King Henry
ſailed from Southampton divulged to him in that town the traiterous
intentions of his brother-in-law Richard Earl of Cambridge, by which
he probably conciliated the friendſhip of the young king. He at that
time received a general pardon from Henry, and was employed by him
in a naval enterprize. At the coronation of Queen Catharine he attended
and held the ſceptre.

Soon after the acceſſion of King Henry VI. he was conſtituted by the
Engliſh Regency chief governour of Ireland, an office which he executed
by a deputy of his own appointment. In the latter end of the year 1434
he went himſelf to that country, to protect the great inheritance which
he derived from his grandmother Philippa, (daughter to Lionel Duke of
Clarence) from the incurſions of ſome Iriſh chieſtains, who were aided
by a body of Scottiſh rovers; but ſoon after his arrival died of the plague
in his caſtle at Trim, in January 1624-5.

This Edmond Mortimer was, I believe, confounded by the author of
this play, and by the old hiſtorians, with his kinſman, who was perhaps
about thirty years old at his death. Edmond Mortimer at the time of
his death could not have been above thirty years old; for ſuppoſing that
his grandmother Philippa was married at fifteen, in 1376, his father
Roger could not have been born till 1377; and if he married at the
early age of ſixteen, Edmond was born in 1394.

This family had great poſſeſſions in Ireland, in conſequence of the
marriage of Lionel Duke of Clarence with the daughter of the Earl of
Ulſter, in 1360, and were long connected with that country. Lionel
was for ſome time Viceroy of Ireland, and was created by his father
Edward III. Duke of Clarence, in conſequence of poſſeſſing the honour of
Clare, in the county of Thomond. Edmond Mortimer, Earl of March,
who married Philippa the duke's only daughter, ſucceeded him in the
government of Ireland, and died in his office, at St. Dominick's Abbey
near Cork, in December 1381. His ſon Roger Mortimer was twice
Vicegerent of Ireland, and was ſlain at a place called Kenles in Oſſory,
in 1398. Edmund his ſon, the Mortimer of this play, was, as has been
already mentioned, alſo Chief Governour of Ireland in the years 1623,
and 1624, and died there in 1625. His nephew and heir, Richard
Duke of York (the Plantagenet of this play) was in 1449 conſtituted
Lord Lieutenant of Ireland for ten years, with extraordinary powers;
and his ſon George Duke of Clarence (who was afterwards murdered
in the Tower) was born in the Caſtle of Dublin in 1450. This prince filled

So fare my limbs with long imprifonment :
And thefe grey locks, the purfuivants of death[1],
Neftor-like aged, in an age of care,
Argue the end of Edmund Mortimer.
Thefe eyes,—like lamps whofe wafting oil is fpent,—
Wax dim, as drawing to their exigent[2] :
Weak fhoulders, over-borne with burth'ning grief ;

And

ed the fame office which fo many of his anceftors had poffeffed, being conftituted Chief Governour of Ireland for *life*, by his brother King Edward IV. in the third year of his reign. MALONE.

Since this note was written, I have more precifely afcertained the age of Edmond Mortimer earl of March, uncle to the Richard Plantagenet of this play. He was born in December 1392, and confequently was thirty-two years old when he died. His anceftor, Lionel duke of Clarence, was married to the daughter of the earl of Ulfter, not in 1360, as I have faid, but about the year 1353. He probably did not take his title of *Clarence* from his great Irifh poffeffions (as I have fuggefted) but rather from his wife's mother Elizabeth de Clare, third daughter of Gilbert de Clare earl of Glofter, and fifter to Gilbert de Clare, the laft (of the name) earl of Glofter, who founded Clare Hall in Cambridge.

The errour concerning Edmund Mortimer, brother-in-law to Richard earl of Cambridge, having been " *kept in captivity till he died*," feems to have arifen from the legend of Richard Plantagenet, duke of Yorke, in *The Mirrour for Magiftrates*, 1575, where the following lines are found :

" His curfed fon enfued his cruel path,
" And kept my guiltlefs *coufin* ftrait in *durance*,
" For whom my father hard entreated hath,
" But, living hopelefs of his life's affurance,
" He thought it beft by politick procurance
" To flay the king, and fo reftore his friend ;
" Which brought himfelf to an infamous end,
" For when king Henry, of that name the fift,
" Had tane my father in his confpiracie,
" He, from Sir Edmund all the blame to fhift,
" Was faine to fay, the French king Charles, his ally,
" Had hir'd him this traiterous act to try ;
" For which condemned fhortly he was flain :
" In helping right this was my father's gain." MALONE.

9 *Let dying Mortimer here reft himfelf.*—] I know not whether Milton did not take from this hint the lines with which he opens his tragedy. JOHNSON.

Rather from the beginning of the laft fcene of the third act of the *Phaniffa* of Euripides :

Tirefias. Ἡγῦ πάροιθε, Θύγατερ, ὡς τυφλῷ ποδὶ
Ὀφθαλμὸς εἰ σὺ, ναυβάταισιν ἀστρον ὡς,
Δευς εἰς τὸ λευρὸν πέδον ἴχνος τιθεῖσ' ἱμόν, &c. STEEVENS.

1 —*purfuivants of death*,] Purfuivants. The heralds that, forerunning death, proclaim its approach. JOHNSON.

2 —*as drawing to their* exigent :] Exigent, end. JOHNSON.

So, in *Doctor Dodypoll*, a comedy, 1600 :
" Hath driven her to fome defperate *exigent*. STEEVENS.

And pithlefs arms [3], like to a wither'd vine
That droops his faplefs branches to the ground :—
Yet are thefe feet—whofe ftrengthlefs ftay is numb,
Unable to fupport this lump of clay,—
Swift-winged with defire to get a grave,
As witting I no other comfort have.—
But tell me, keeper, will my nephew come ?

1. Keep. Richard Plantagenet, my lord, will come :
We fent unto the Temple, to his chamber ;
And anfwer was return'd, that he will come.

Mor. Enough ; my foul fhall then be fatisfy'd.—
Poor gentleman ! his wrong doth equal mine.
Since Henry Monmouth firft began to reign,
(Before whofe glory I was great in arms)
This loathfome fequeftration have I had [4] ;
And even fince then hath Richard been obfcur'd,
Depriv'd of honour and inheritance :
But now, the arbitrator of defpairs,
Juft death, kind umpire of men's miferies [5],
With fweet enlargement doth difmifs me hence ;
I would, his troubles likewife were expir'd,
That fo he might recover what was loft.

Enter Richard PLANTAGENET.

1 Keep. My lord, your loving nephew now is come.

Mor. Richard Plantagenet, my friend ? Is he come ?

Plan. Ay, noble uncle, thus ignobly us'd,
Your nephew, late-defpifed Richard, comes.

Mor. Direct mine arms, I may embrace his neck,
And in his bofom fpend my latter gafp :
O, tell me, when my lips do touch his cheeks,
That I may kindly give one fainting kifs.—
And now declare, fweet ftem from York's great ftock,
Why didft thou fay—of late thou wert defpis'd ?

Plan. Firft, lean thine aged back againft mine arm ;
And, in that eafe, I'll tell thee my difeafe [6].

This

---

3 *And pithlefs arms,*] *Pith* was ufed for *marrow*, and figuratively, for
ftrength. JOHNSON.
4 *Since Henry Monmouth firft began to reign,—*
This loathfome fequeftration have I had ;] Here again, the author certainly is miftaken. See p. 38, n. 8. MALONE.
5 —*kind umpire of men's miferies,*] That is, he that terminates or
concludes mifery. The expreffion is harfh and forced. JOHNSON.
6 —*I'll tell thee my difeafe.*] *Difeafe* feems to be here *uneafinefs* or
difcontent. JOHNSON.

E

This day, in argument upon a cafe,
Some words there grew 'twixt Somerfet and me:
Among which terms, he us'd his lavifh tongue,
And did upbraid me with my father's death;
Which obloquy fet bars before my tongue,
Elfe with the like I had requited him:
Therefore, good uncle,—for my father's fake,
In honour of a true Plantagenet,
And for alliance' fake,—declare the caufe
My father, earl of Cambridge, loft his head.

Mor. That caufe, fair nephew, that imprifon'd me,
And hath detain'd me, all my flow'ring youth,
Within a loathfome dungeon, there to pine,
Was curfed inftrument of his deceafe.

Plan. Difcover more at large what that caufe was;
For I am ignorant, and cannot guefs.

Mor. I will; if that my fading breath permit,
And death approach not ere my tale be done,
Henry the fourth, grandfather to this king,
Depos'd his nephew [7] Richard; Edward's fon,
The firft-begotten, and the lawful heir
Of Edward king, the third of that defcent:
During whofe reign, the Percies of the north,
Finding his ufurpation moft unjuft,
Endeavour'd my advancement to the throne:
The reafon mov'd thefe warlike lords to this,
Was—for that (young Richard thus removed,
Leaving no heir begotten of his body,)
1 was the next by birth and parentage;
For by my mother I derived am
From Lionel duke of Clarence, third fon,
To king Edward the Third, whereas he,
From John of Gaunt doth bring his pedigree,
Being but fourth of that heroick line.
But mark; as, in this haughty great attempt [8],
They laboured to plant the rightful heir,   I lo ft

It is fo ufed by other ancient writers, and by Shakfpeare elfewhere.—
Thus likewife in Spenfer's *Faery Queen*, Book III. c. 5:
"But labour'd long in that deep ford with vain *difeafe*."
STEEVENS.

7 — *his* nephew *Richard*;] Thus the old copy. Modern editors
read—his *coufin*—but without neceffity. *Nephew* has fometimes the
power of the Latin *nepos*, and is ufed with great laxity among our ancient Englifh writers. Thus in *Othello*, Iago tells Brabantio—he fhall
"have his *nephews* (i. e. the children of his own daughter) neigh to
him. STEEVENS.

I believe the miftake here arofe from the author's ignorance; and
that he conceived Richard to be Henry's nephew. MALONE.

8 — *in this* haughty *great attempt*,] *Haughty* is *high*. JOHNSON.

I loft my liberty, and they their lives.
Long after this, when Henry the fifth,—
Succeeding his father Bolingbroke,—did reign,
Thy father, earl of Cambridge,—then deriv'd,
From famous Edmund Langley, duke of York,—
Marrying my fifter, that thy mother was,
Again, in pity of my hard diftrefs,
Levied an army* ; weening to redeem,
And have inftall'd me in the diadem :
But, as the reft, to fell that noble earl,
And was beheaded.   Thus the Mortimers,
In whom the title refted, were fupprefs'd.

Plan. Of which, my lord, your honour is the laft.

Mor. True ; and thou feeft, that I no iffue have ;
And that my fainting words do warrant death :
Thou art my heir ; the reft, I wifh thee gather 9 :
But yet be wary in thy ftudious care.

Plan. Thy grave admonifhments prevail with me :
But yet, methinks, my father's execution
Was nothing lefs than bloody tyranny.

Mor. With filence, nephew, be thou politick ;
Strong fixed is the houfe of Lancafter,
And, like a mountain, not to be remov'd.
But now thy uncle is removing hence ;
As princes do their courts, when they are cloy'd
With long continuance in a fettled place.

Plan. O, uncle, 'would fome part of my young years
Might but redeem the paffage of your age * !

Mor. Thou doft then wrong me ; as the flaught'rer doth,
Which giveth many wounds, when one will kill.
Mourn not, except thou forrow for my good ;
Only, give order for my funeral ;

And

---

* *Levied an army* ;] Here is again another falfification of hiftory :
Cambridge levied no army, but was apprehended at Southampton, the
night before Henry failed from that town for France, on the information of this very Edmund Mortimer, Earl of March. MALONE.

9 *Thou art my heir ; the reft I wifh thee gather :*] The fenfe is, I
acknowledge thee to be my heir; the confequences which may be collected from thence, I recommend it to thee to draw. HEATH.

* *O, uncle, 'would fome part of my young years*
Might but redeem, &c.] This thought has fome refemblance to that
of the following lines, which are fuppofed to be addreffed by a married
lady who died very young, to her hufband. The infcription is, I think,
in the church of Trent :

" Immatura peri ; fed tu diuturnior annos
" Vive meos, conjux optime, vive tuos." MALONE.

And so farewel ; and fair be all thy hopes [2] !
And prosperous be thy life, in peace, and war ! [*Dies.*
   Plan. And peace, no war, befall thy parting soul !
In prison haft thou spent a pilgrimage,
And like a hermit over-pass'd thy days.—
Well, I will lock his counsel in my breaft ;
And what I do imagine, let that reft.—
Keepers, convey him hence ; and I myself
Will see his burial better than his life.—
           [*Exeunt Keepers, bearing out* Mortimer.
Here dies the dufky torch of Mortimer,
Chok'd with ambition of the meaner sort [2] :
And, for those wrongs, those bitter injuries,
Which Somerfet hath offer'd to my houfe,—
I doubt not, but with honour to redrefs :
And therefore hafte I to the parliament ;
Either to be reftored to my blood,
Or make my ill [3] the advantage of my good.   [*Exit.*

ACT III. SCENE I.

The fame.   *The Parliament-houfe.*

Flourifb.   *Enter King* HENRY, EXETER, GLOSTER, WAR-
WICK, SOMERSET, *and* SUFFOLK ; *the Bifhop of* Winchefter, Richard PLANTAGENET, *and others.* GLOSTER *offers to put up a bill* ;* WINCHESTER *fnatches it, and
tears it.*

Win. Com'ft thou with deep premeditated lines,

                           With

---

   [2] *—and* fair *be all thy hopes,*] *Fair* is *lucky,* or *profperous.* So we
fay, a *fair* wind, and *fair* fortune. JOHNSON.
   [2] *Chok'd with ambition of the meaner fort :—*] We are to underftand
the fpeaker as reflecting on the ill fortune of Mortimer, in being always
made a tool of by the Percies of the North in their rebellious intrigues ;
rather than in afferting his claim to the crown, in fupport of his own
princely ambition. WARBURTON.
   [3] *—or make my ill—*] i. e. my ill ufage. The old copy has—*will.*
The emendation was made by Mr. Theobald, and has been adopted by
all the fubfequent editors. MALONE.
   4 *The Parliament Houfe.*] This parliament was held in 1426 at Leicef-
ter, though the author of this play has reprefented-it to have been held
in London. King Henry was now in the fifth year of his age. In the
firft parliament which was held at London fhortly after his father's
death, his mother Queen Catharine brought the young king from Windfor to the metropolis, and fat on the throne of the parliament-houfe
with the infant in her lap. MALONE.
   * *—put up a bill ;*] i. e. articles of accufation, for in this fenfe the
                                           word

With written pamphlets ftudioufly devis'd,
Humphry of Glofter? if thou canft accufe,
Or aught intend'ft to lay unto my charge,
Do it without invention fuddenly;
As I with fudden and extemporal fpeech
Purpofe to anfwer what thou canft object.

   Glo. Prefumptuous prieft! this place commands my pa-
      tience,
Or thou fhould'ft find thou haft difhonour'd me.
Think not, although in writing I preferr'd
The manner of thy vile outrageous crimes,
That therefore I have forg'd, or am not able
Verbatim to rehearfe the method of my pen:
No, prelate; fuch is thy audacious wickednefs,
Thy lewd, peftiferous, and diffentious pranks,
As very infants prattle of thy pride.
Thou art a moft pernicious ufurer;
Froward by nature, enemy to peace;
Lafcivious, wanton, more than well befeems
A man of thy profeffion, and degree;
And for thy treachery, What's more manifeft?
In that thou laid'ft a trap to take my life,
As well at London bridge, as at the Tower?
Befide, I fear me, if thy thoughts were fifted,
The king, thy fovereign, is not quite exempt
From envious malice of thy fwelling heart.

   Win. Glofter, I do defy thee —Lords, vouchfafe
To give me hearing what I fhall reply.
If I were covetous, ambitious, or perverfe,
As he will have me, How am I fo poor?
Or how haps it, I feek not to advance
Or raife myfelf, but keep my wonted calling?
And for diffention, Who preferreth peace
More than I do,—except I be provok'd?
No, my good lords, it is not that offends;
It is not that, that hath incen'd the duke:
It is, becaufe no one fhould fway but he;

---

word *bill* was fometimes ufed. To *put up a bill* alfo appears to have
fignified what we now call *bringing in* a bill. So, in Nafhe's *Have with
you to Saffron Walden*, 1596: " That's the caufe we have fo manie
bad workmen now adaies: *put up a bill* againft them next parliament."
                         MALONE.
   I was miftaken in faying that to *put up a bill* fometimes fignified to
bring a bill into parliament. It meant only to prefer a petition to
parliament; and in that fenfe is the phrafe ufed in the paffage quoted
from Nafhe's pamphlet. MALONE.

                                      No

No one, but he, should be about the king;
And that engenders thunder in his breaft,
And makes him roar these accufations forth.
But he shall know, I am as good——

Glo. As good?
Thou baftard of my grandfather [5]!

Win. Ay, lordly fir; For what are you, I pray,
But one imperious in another's throne?

Glo. Am I not protector, faucy prieft?

Win. And am not I a prelate of the church?

Glo. Yes, as an out-law in a caftle keeps,
And ufeth it to patronage his theft.

Win. Unreverent Glofter!

Glo. Thou art reverent
Touching thy fpiritual function, not thy life.

Win. Rome fhall remedy this.

War. Roam thither then [6].

Som. My lord, it were your duty to forbear [7].

War. Ay, fee the bifhop be not over-borne.

Som. Methinks, my lord fhould be religious,
And know the office that belongs to fuch.

War. Methinks, his lordfhip fhould be humbler;
It fitteth not a prelate fo to plead.

Som. Yes, when his holy ftate is touch'd fo near.

War. State holy, or unhallow'd, what of that?
Is not his grace protector to the king?

Plan. Plantagenet, I fee, muft hold his tongue;
Left it be faid, *Speak, firrah, when you fhould;*
Muft your bold verdiEt enter talk with lords?
Elfe would I have a fling at Winchefter.   [*Afide.*

K. Hen. Uncles of Glofter, and of Winchefter,

---

5 *Thou baftard of my grandfather!*—] The bifhop of Winchefter was
an illegitimate fon of John of Gaunt, Duke of Lancafter, by Catharine
Swynford, whom the duke afterwards married. MALONE.

6 Roam *thither then.*] Roam to Rome. To roam is fuppofed to be
derived from the cant of vagabonds, who often pretended a pilgrimage
to Rome. JOHNSON.

The jingle between roam and Rome is common to other writers. So
in Nafh's *Lenten Stuff,* &c. 1599: " — three hundred thoufand people roamed to Rome for purgatorie pills," &c. STEEVENS.

7 Som. *My lord, it were your duty to forbear.*] This line, in the
old copy, is joined to the former hemiftich fpoken by Warwick. The
modern editors have very properly given it to Somerfet, for whom it
feems to have been meant.

   Ay, fee, the bifhop be not over-borne,
was as erroneoufly given in the next fpeech to Somerfet inftead of Warwick, to whom it has been fince reftored. STEEVENS.

The correction was made by Mr. Theobald. MALONE.

The

The special watchmen of our English weal;
I would prevail, if prayers might prevail,
To join your hearts in love and amity.
O, what a scandal is it to our crown,
That two such noble peers as ye, should jar!
Believe me, lords, my tender years can tell,
Civil dissention is a viperous worm,
That gnaws the bowels of the common-wealth.—

        [*A noise within;* Down with the tawny coats!
What tumult's this?

  War. An uproar, I dare warrant,
Begun through malice of the bishop's men.

            [*A noise again,* Stones! Stones!

Enter the Mayor *of* London, *attended.*

  May. O, my good lords,—and virtuous Henry;—
Pity the city of London, pity us!
The bishop and the duke of Gloster's men,
Forbidden late to carry any weapon,
Have fill'd their pockets full of pebble-stones;
And, banding themselves in contrary parts,
Do pelt so fast at one another's pate,
That many have their giddy brains knock'd out:
Our windows are broke down in every street,
And we, for fear, compell'd to shut our shops.

Enter, skirmishing, the retainers of GLOSTER *and* WINCHES-
TER, *with bloody pates.*

  K. Hen. We charge you, on allegiance to ourself,
To hold your slaught'ring hands, and keep the peace.
Pray, uncle Gloster, mitigate this strife.

  1. Serv. Nay, if we be
Forbidden stones, we'll fall to it with our teeth.

  2. Serv. Do what ye dare, we are as resolute.

               [*Skirmish again.*
  Glo. You of my houshold, leave this peevish broil,
And set this unaccustom'd fight [8] aside.

  3. Serv. My lord, we know your grace to be a man
Just and upright; and, for your royal birth,
Inferior to none, but to his majesty:
And, ere that we will suffer such a prince,

---

  [8] — unaccustom'd fight—] Unaccustom'd is unseemly, indecent.
                                  JOHNSON.
                                    So

So kind a father of the common-weal,
To be difgraced by an inkhorn mate [9],
We, and our wives, and children, all will fight,
And have our bodies flaughter'd by thy foes.

1. Serv. Ay, and the very pairing of our nails
Shall pitch a field when we are dead.   [*Skirmifh again.*

Glo. Stay, ftay, I fay!
And, if you love me, as you fay you do,
Let me perfuade you to forbear a while.

K. Hen. O, how this difcord doth afflict my fouL—
Can you, my lord of Winchefter, behold
My fighs and tears, and will not once relent?
Who fhould be pityful, if you be not?
Or who fhould ftudy to prefer a peace,
If holy churchmen take delight in broils?

War. Yield, my lord protector;—yield, Winchefter:—
Except you mean, with obftinate repulfe,
To flay your fovereign, and deftroy the realm.
You fee what mifchief, and what murder too,
Hath been enacted through your enmity:
Then be at peace, except you thirft for blood.

Win. He fhall fubmit, or I will never yield.

Glo. Compaffion on the king commands me ftoop;
Or I would fee his heart out, ere the prieft
Should ever get that privilege of me.

War. Behold, my lord of Winchefter, the duke
Hath banifh'd moody difcontented fury,
As by his fmoothed brows it doth appear:
Why look you ftill fo ftern, and tragical?

Glo Here, Winchefter, I offer thee my hand.

K. Hen. Fie, uncle Beaufort! I have heard you preach,
That malice was a great and grievous fin:
And will not you maintain the thing you teach,
But prove a chief offender in the fame?

War. Sweet king!—the bifhop hath a kindly gird [1].—
For fhame, my lord of Winchefter! relent;
What, fhall a child inftruct you what to do?

Win. Well, duke of Glofter, I will yield to thee;
Love for thy love, and hand for hand I give.

Glo. Ay; but, I fear me, with a hollow heart.—

---

9 — *an inkhorn mate*,] A *bookman.* JOHNSON.
1 — *hath a kindly* gird.—] A kindly *gird* is a *gentle* or *friendly* re-
proof. Falftaff obferves, that—" men of all forts take a pride to *gird*
at him:" and in the *Taming of the Shrew*, Baptifta fays: " — Tranio
hits you now:" to which Lucentio anfwers:
    " I thank thee for that *gird*, good Tranio." STEEVENS.

                              See

See here, my friends, and loving countrymen;
This token serveth for a flag of truce,
Betwixt ourselves, and all our followers:
So help me God, as I dissemble not!

Win. So help me God, as I intend it not!   [*Aside.*

K. Hen. O loving uncle, kind duke of Glofter,
How joyful am I made by this contract!—
Away, my masters! trouble us no more;
But join in friendship, as your lords have done.

1. Serv. Content; I'll to the surgeon's.

2. Serv. And so will I

3. Serv. And I will see what physick the tavern affords.
    [*Exeunt* Servants, Mayor, &c.

War. Accept this scrowl, most gracious sovereign;
Which in the right of Richard Plantagenet
We do exhibit to your majesty.

Glo. Well urg'd, my lord of Warwick;—for, sweet
      prince,
An' if your grace mark every circumstance,
You have great reason to do Richard right:
Especially, for those occasions
At Eltham-place I told your majesty.

K. Hen. And those occasions, uncle, were of force:
Therefore, my loving lords, our pleasure is,
That Richard be restored to his blood.

War. Let Richard be restored to his blood;
So shall his father's wrongs be recompens'd.

Win. As will the rest, so willeth Winchefter.

K. Hen. If Richard will be true, not that alone [2],
But all the whole inheritance I give,
That doth belong unto the house of York,
From whence you spring by lineal descent.

Plan. Thy humble servant vows obedience,
And humble service, till the point of death.

K. Hen. Stoop then, and set your knee against my foot;
And, in reguerdon of that duty done [3],
I girt thee with the valiant sword of York:
Rise, Richard, like a true Plantagenet;
And rise created princely duke of York.

Plan. And so thrive Richard, as thy foes may fall!
And as my duty springs, so perish they
That grudge one thought against your majesty!

---

2 — *that alone,*] By a mistake probably of the transcriber the old
copy reads—that *all* alone. The correction was made by the editor of
the second folio. MALONE.

3 — *reguerdon*—] Recompence, return. JOHNSON.

All. Welcome, high prince, the mighty duke of York !

Som. Perish, base prince, ignoble duke of York ! [*Aside.*

Glo. Now will it best avail your majesty,
To cross the seas, and to be crown'd in France :
The presence of a king engenders love ·
Amongst his subjects, and his loyal friends ;
As it disanimates his enemies.

K. Hen. When Gloster says the word, king Henry goes ;
For friendly counsel cuts off many foes.

Glo. Your ships already are in readiness.

[*Exeunt all but* Exeter.

Exe. Ay, we may march in England, or in France,
Not seeing what is likely to ensue :
This late dissention, grown betwixt the peers,
Burns under feigned ashes of forg'd love [4],
And will at last break out into a flame :
As fester'd members rot but by degrees,
Till bones, and flesh, and sinews, fall away,
So will this base and envious discord breed [5].
And now I fear that fatal prophecy,
Which, in the time of Henry, nam'd the fifth,
Was in the mouth of every sucking babe,—
That Henry, born at Monmouth, should win all ;
And Henry, born at Windsor, should lose all :
Which is so plain, that Exeter doth wish
His days may finish ere that hapless time [6].

[*Exit.*

SCENE II.

France. *Before* Rouen.

Enter La Pucelle *disguis'd, and* Soldiers *dressed like countrymen, with sacks upon their backs.*

Puc. These are the city gates, the gates of Rouen *,
Through which our policy must make a breach :
Take heed, be wary how you place your words ;

4 *Burns under feigned ashes of forg'd love,*]
    Ignes suppositos cineri doloso. Hor. , Malone.
5 *So will this base and envious discord breed.*] That is, so will the malignity of this discord *propagate itself*, and advance. Johnson.
6 *His days may finish,* &c.). The duke of Exeter died shortly after the meeting of this parliament, and the earl of Warwick was appointed governour or tutor to the king in his room. Malone.
* *— the gates of* Rouen,] Here, and throughout the play, in the old copy we have *Roan*, which was the old spelling of *Rouen*. The word, consequently, is used as a monosyllable. Malone.

Talk

Talk like the vulgar sort of market-men,
That come to gather money for their corn.
If we have entrance, (as, I hope, we shall,)
And that we find the slothful watch but weak,
I'll by a sign give notice to our friends,
That Charles the Dauphin may encounter them.

 1. *Sol.* Our sacks shall be a mean to sack the city[7],
And we be lords and rulers over Rouen;
Therefore we'll knock.   [*Knocks.*

 Guard [*within*] *Qui est là*[8]?
 Puc. Païsans, pauvres gens de France :
Poor market-folks, that come to sell their corn.

 Guard. Enter, go in; the market-bell is rung.

           [*opens the gates.*

 Puc. Now, Rouen, I'll shake thy bulwarks to the ground.

     [PUCELLE, &c. *enter the city.*

Enter CHARLES, BASTARD *of* Orleans, ALENÇON, *and
forces.*

 Char. Saint Dennis bless this happy stratagem!
And once again we'll sleep secure in Rouen.

 Bast. Here enter'd Pucelle, and her practisants[9]:
Now she is there, how will she specify
Where is * the best and safest passage in?

 Alen. By thrusting out a torch from yonder tower;
Which, once discern'd, shews, that her meaning is,—
No way to that[1], for weakness, which she enter'd.

Enter LA PUCELLE *on a battlement; holding out a torch
burning.*

 Puc. Behold, this is the happy wedding torch,
That joineth Rouen unto her countrymen;
But burning fatal to the Talbotites.

 Bast. See, noble Charles! the beacon of our friend,

---

7 *Our sacks shall be a mean to sack the city,*] Falstaff has the same quibble, shewing his bottle of *sack* : " Here's that will *sack* a city."
               STEEVENS.

8 *Qui est là ?*] Old Copy—*Che la.* For the emendation I am answerable. MALONE.

9 *Here enter'd Pucelle, and her* practisants :] *Practice,* in the language of that time, was *treachery,* and perhaps in the softer sense *stratagem. Practisants* are therefore *confederates in stratagem.* JOHNSON.

* *Where is—*] Old Copy—*Here is.* Corrected by Mr. Rowe.
               MALONE.

1 *No way to that,*] That is, *no way equal to that,* no way so fit as that. JOHNSON.

The burning torch in yonder turret ſtands.

Char. Now ſhine it like a comet of revenge,
A prophet to the fall of all our foes !

Alen. Defer, no time, Delays have dangerous ends ;
Enter, and cry—*The Dauphin !*—preſently,
And then do execution on the watch. [*They enter.*

Alarums. Enter TALBOT *and certain* Engliſh.

Tal. France, thou ſhalt rue this treaſon with thy tears,
If Talbot but ſurvive thy treachery.—
Pucelle, that witch, that damned ſorcereſs,
Hath wrought this helliſh miſchief unawares,
That hardly we eſcap'd the pride of France [2].
[*Exeunt to the town.*

Alarum : Excurſions. Enter, from the town, BEDFORD,
brought in ſick, in a chair, with TALBOT, BURGUNDY,
and the Engliſh *forces Then, enter on the walls,* LA PU-
CELLE, CHARLES, BASTARD, ALENÇON [3], *and others.*

Puc Good morrow, gallants ! want ye corn for bread ?
I think, the duke of Burgundy will faſt,
Before he'll buy again at ſuch a rate :
'Twas full of darnel ; Do you like the taſte ?

Bur. Scoff on, vile fiend, and ſhameleſs courtezan !
I truſt, ere long to choke thee with thine own,
And make thee curſe the harveſt of that corn.

Char. Your grace may ſtarve, perhaps, before that time.

Red. O, let no words, but deeds, revenge this treaſon !

Puc What will you do, good grey beard ? break a lance,
And run a tilt at death within a chair ?

Tal Foul fiend of France, and hag of all deſpight,
Encompaſs d with thy luſtful paramours !
Becomes it thee to taunt his valiant age,
And twit with cowardice a man half dead ?
Damſel, I'll have a bout with you again,
Or elſe let Talbot periſh with this ſhame.

Puc. Are you ſo hot, Sir ?—Yet, Pucelle, hold thy peace ?
If Talbot do but thunder, rain will follow.—
[TALBOT, *and the reſt, conſult together.*
God ſpeed the parliament ! who ſhall be the ſpeaker ?

---

[2] — *the pride of France.*] Pride ſignifies the *haughty power.*
WARBURTON.

[3] — *Alençon,*] *Alençon* Sir T. Hanmer has replac'd here, inſtead of
Reignier, becauſe Alençon, not Reignier, appears in the enſuing ſcene.
JOHNSON.

Tal.

Tal. Dare ye come forth, and meet us in the field?

Puc. Belike, your lordship takes us then for fools,
To try if that our own be ours, or no.

Tal. I speak not to that railing Hecate,
But unto thee, Alençon, and the rest;
Will ye, like soldiers, come and fight it out?

Alen. Signior, no.

Tal. Signior, hang!—base muleteers of France!
Like peasant foot-boys do they keep the walls,
And dare not take up arms like gentlemen.

Puc. Away, captains: let's get us from the walls;
For Talbot means no goodness, by his looks.—
God be wi' you, my lord! we come but to tell you
That we are here.

        [*Exeunt* LA PUCELLE, *&c. from the walls.*

Tal. And there will we be too, ere it be long,
Or else reproach be Talbot's greatest fame!—
Vow, Burgundy, by honour of thy house,
(Prick'd on by public wrongs, sustain'd in France,)
Either to get the town again, or die:
And I,—as sure as English Henry lives,
And as his father here was conqueror;
As sure as in this late-betrayed town
Great Cœur-de-lion's heart was buried;
So sure I swear, to get the town, or die.

Bur. My vows are equal partners with thy vows.

Tal. But, ere we go regard this dying prince,
The valiant duke of Bedford:—Come, my lord,
We will bestow you in some better place,
Fitter for sickness, and for crazy age.

Bed. Lord Talbot, do not so dishonour me:
Here will I sit before the walls of Rouen,
And will be partner of your weal, or woe.

Bur. Courageous Bedford, let us now persuade you.

Bed. Not to be gone from hence; for once I read,
That stout Pendragon, in his litter [4] sick,
Came to the field, and vanquished his foes:
Methinks, I should revive the soldiers' hearts,
Because I ever found them as myself.

Tal. Undaunted spirit in a dying breast!—
Then be it so:—Heavens keep old Bedford safe!

And

4 — *once I read,*

That stout Pendragon, *in his litter,* &c.] This hero was Uther Pendragon, brother to Aurelius, and father to king Arthur.

Shakspeare has imputed to Pendragon an exploit of Aurelius, who, says Holinshed, " even sicke of a flixe as he was, caused himself to be carried forth in a litter: with whose presence his people were so incouraged,

And now no more ado, brave Burgundy,
But gather we our forces out of hand,
And set upon our boasting enemy.
    [*Exeunt* BURGUNDY, TALBOT, *and forces, leaving* BED-
    FORD, *and others.*

Alarum : Excursions. Enter Sir John FASTOLFE, *and a*
Captain.

    Cap. Whither away, Sir John Fastolfe, in such haste?
    Fast. Whither away ? to save myself by flight [5];
We are like to have the overthrow again.
    Cap. What! will you fly, and leave lord Talbot?
    Fast. Ay,
All the Talbots in the world, to save my life.   [*Exit.*
    Cap. Cowardly knight! ill fortune follow thee!   [*Exit.*

Retreat : Excursions. Enter, from the town LA PUCELLE,
ALENÇON, CHARLES, &c. *and Exeunt flying.*

    Bed. Now, quiet soul, depart when heaven please [6];
For I have seen our enemies' overthrow.
What is the trust or strength of foolish man ?
They, that of late were daring with their scoffs,
Are glad and fain by flight to save themselves.
    [*Dies* [7], *and is carried off in his chair.*

raged, that encountering with the Saxons they wan the victorie." *Hist.*
of Scotland, p. 99.

    Harding, however, in his *Chronicle*, (as I learn from Dr. Gray) gives
the following account of Uther Pendragon :
        " For which the king ordain'd a horse-litter
        " To bear him so then unto Verolame,
        " Where Ocea lay, and Oysa also in fear,
        " That saint Albones now hight of noble fame,
        " Bet downe the walles ; but to him forth they came,
        " Where in battayle Ocea and Oysa were slayn.
        " The fielde he had, and thereof was full fayne." STEEVENS.

    5 —*save myself by flight ;*] I have no doubt that it was the *exagge-*
rated representation of Sir John Fastolfe's *cowardice* which the author
of this play has given, that induced Shakspeare to give the name of
Falstaff to his knight. Sir John Fastolffe did indeed fly at the battle of
Patay in the year 1429; and is reproached by Talbot, in a subsequent
scene, for his conduct on that occasion; but no historian has said that
he fled before Rouen. The change of the name had been already made,
for throughout the old copy of this play this flying general is erroneously
called *Falstaffe.* MALONE.

    6 *Now, quiet soul, depart,* &c.] So in St. Luke, ij. 29. " Lord,
now lettest thou thy servant depart in peace, for mine eyes have seen thy
salvation." STEEVENS.

    7 *Dies,* &c.] The duke of Bedford died at Rouen in September, 1435,
but not in any action before that town. MALONE.

                         Alarum :

Alarum : Enter TALBOT, BURGUNDY, *and Others.*

Tal. Loſt, and recover'd in a day again !
This is a double honour, Burgundy :
Yet, heavens have glory for this victory !
　Bur. Warlike and martial Talbot, Burgundy
Enſhrines thee in his heart ; and there erects
Thy noble deeds, as valour's monument.
　Tal. Thanks, gentle duke.　But where is Pucelle now ?
I think, her old familiar is aſleep :
Now where's the Baſtard's braves, and Charles his gleeks ?
What, all a-mort ? Rouen hangs her head for grief,
That ſuch a valiant company are fled.
Now will we take ſome order in the town,
Placing therein ſome expert officers ;
And then depart to Paris, to the king ;
For there young Henry, with his nobles, lies.
　Bur. What wills lord Talbot, pleaſeth Burgundy.
　Tal. But yet, before we go, let's not forget
The noble duke of Bedford, late deceas'd,
But ſee his exequies fulfill'd in Rouen ;
A braver ſoldier never couched lance,
A gentler heart did never ſway in court :
But kings, and mightieſt potentates, muſt die ;
For that's the end of human miſery.　　　　*[Exeunt.*

SCENE III.

The ſame.　The plains near the city.

Enter CHARLES, *the* Baſtard, ALENÇON, LA PUCELLE,
and forces.

　Puc. Diſmay not, princes, at this accident,
Nor grieve that Rouen is ſo recovered :
Care is no cure, but rather corroſive,
For things that are not to be remedy'd.
Let frantick Talbot triumph for a while,
And like a peacock ſweep along his tail ;
We'll pull his plumes, and take away his train,
If Dauphin, and the reſt, will be but rul'd.
　Char. We have been guided by thee hitherto,
And of thy cunning had no diffidence ;
One ſudden foil ſhall never breed diſtruſt.
　Baſt. Search out thy wit for ſecret policies,
And we will make thee famous through the world;

Alen.

Alen. We'll set thy statue in some holy place,
And have thee reverenc'd like a blessed saint ;
Employ thee then, sweet virgin, for our good.

Puc. Then thus it must be ; this doth Joan devise :
By fair persuasions, mix'd with sugar'd words,
We will entice the duke of Burgundy
To leave the Talbot, and to follow us.

Char Ay, marry, sweeting, if we could do that,
France were no place for Henry's warriors ;
Nor should that nation boast it so with us,
But be extirped [8] from our provinces.

Alen For ever should they be expuls'd from France [9],
And not have title of an earldom here.

Puc. Your honours shall perceive how I will work.,
To bring this matter to the wished end.   [*Drums heard.*
Hark ! by the sound of drum, you may perceive
Their powers are marching unto Paris-ward.

An English *March. Enter and pass over, at a distance,* TAL-
BOT *and his forces.*

There goes the Talbot, with his colours spread ;
And all the troops of English after him.

A French *March. Enter the duke of* BURGUNDY *and forces.*

Now, in the rereward, comes the duke, and his ;
Fortune, in favour, makes him lag behind.
Summon a parley, we will talk with him.   [*A parley sounded.*

Char. A parley with the duke of Burgundy.

Bur. Who craves a parley with the Burgundy ?

Puc. The princely Charles of France, thy countryman.

Bur. What say'st thou, Charles ? for I am marching
hence.

Char. Speak, Pucelle ; and enchant him with thy words.

Puc. Brave Burgundy, undoubted hope of France !
Stay, let thy humble hand-maid speak to thee.

Bur. Speak on ; but be not over-tedious.

---

[8] *But be* exti-ped—] To *extirp* is to root out. So, in Lord Sterline's *Darius,* 1603 :
   " The world shall gather to *extirp* our name." STEEVENS.

   [9] — expuls'd *from France,*] i. e. expelled. So in Ben Jonson's *Se-
janus :*
   " The *expuls'd* Apicata finds them there."
Again, in Drayton's *Muses Elizium :*
   " And if you *expulse* them there,
   " They'll hang upon your braided hair." STEEVENS.

Puc.

Puc. Look on thy country, look on fertile France,
And fee the cities and the towns defac'd
By wafting ruin of the cruel foe!
As looks the mother on her lowly babe [1],
When death doth clofe his tender dying eyes,
See, fee, the pining malady of France;
Behold the wounds, the moft unnatural wounds,
Which thou thyfelf haft given her woful breaft!
O, turn thy edged fword another way;
Strike thofe that hurt, and hurt not thofe that help!
One drop of blood, drawn from thy country's bofom,
Should grieve thee more than ftreams of foreign gore;
Return thee, therefore, with a flood of tears,
And wafh away thy country's ftained fpots

Bur. Either fhe hath bewitch'd me with her words,
Or nature makes me fuddenly relent.

Puc. Befides, all French and France exclaims on thee,
Doubting thy birth and lawful progeny.
Who join'ft thou with, but with a lordly nation,
That will not truft thee, but for profit's fake?
When Talbot hath fet footing once in France,
And fafhion'd thee that inftrument of ill,
Who then, but Englifh Henry, will be lord,
And thou be thruft out, like a fugitive?
Call we to mind,—and mark, but this, for proof;—
Was not the duke of Orleans thy foe?
And was he not in England prifoner?
But, when they heard he was thine enemy,
They fet him free, without his ranfom paid,
In fpite of Burgundy, and all his friends.
See then! thou fight'ft againft thy countrymen,
And join'ft with them will be thy flaughter-men.
Come, come, return; return, thou wand'ring lord;
Charles, and the reft, will take thee in their arms.

Bur. I am vanquifhed; thefe haughty words of hers
Have batter'd me like roaring cannon fhot [2],

---

[1] *— on her lowly babe,*] i. e. lying *low* in death. JOHNSON.

[2] *— thefe haughty words of hers*
Have batter'd me like roaring cannon-fhot,] How thefe lines came
hither I know not; there was nothing in the fpeech of Joan haughty or
violent: it was all foft entreaty and mild expoftulation. JOHNSON.

Haughty here certainly fignifies *high, lofty.* So, in the firft act the
Dauphin fays to La Pucelle:

"Thou haft aftonifh'd me with thy *high* terms."

We have already in this play had the word *haughty* in the fame fenfe.

" But mark; as, in this *haughty* great attempt,—."
Again, in Act IV. fc. i:

" Valiant and virtuous, full of *haughty* courage. MALONE.

And made me almoſt yield upon my knees.—
Forgive me, country, and ſweet countrymen !
And, lords, accept this hearty kind embrace :
My forces and my power of men are yours ;
So, farewell, Talbot ; I'll no longer truſt thee.

  Puc. Done, like a Frenchman ; turn, and turn again [3] !

  Char. Welcome, brave duke ! thy friendſhip makes us
    freſh.

  Baſt. And doth beget new courage in our breaſts.

  Alen. Pucelle hath bravely play'd her part in this,
And doth deſerve a coronet of gold.

  Char. Now let us on, my lords, and join our powers ;
And ſeek how we may prejudice the foe.   [*Exeunt.*

SCENE III.

Paris. *A Room in the Palace.*

Enter King HENRY, GLOSTER, *and other Lords,* VERNON,
  BASSET, *&c. To them* TALBOT, *and ſome of his Officers.*

  Tal. My gracious prince,—and honourable peers,—
Hearing of your arrival in this realm,
I have a while given truce unto my wars,
To do my duty to my ſovereign :
In ſign whereof, this arm—that hath reclaim'd
To your obedience fifty fortreſſes,
Twelve cities, and ſeven walled towns of ſtrength,
Beſides five hundred priſoners of eſteem,—
Lets fall his ſword before your highneſs' feet ;
And, with ſubmiſſive loyalty of heart,
Aſcribes the glory of his conqueſt got,
Firſt to my God, and next unto your grace.

  K. Hen. Is this the lord Talbot, uncle Gloſter,
That hath ſo long been reſident in France ?

  Glo. Yes, if it pleaſe your majeſty, my liege.

  K. Hen. Welcome, brave captain, and victorious lord !
When I was young, (as yet I am not old,)

---

  [3] *Done like a Frenchman ; turn and turn again !*] So afterwards:
    " In France, amongſt a *fickle wavering* nation—." MALONE.
  The inconſtancy of the French was always the ſubject of ſatire. I
have read a diſſertation written to prove that the index of the wind upon
our ſteeples was made in form of a cock, to ridicule the French for their
frequent changes. JOHNSON.

I do remember how my father said*,
A stouter champion never handled sword.
Long since we were resolved of your truth,
Your faithful service, and your toil in war ;
Yet never have you tasted our reward,
Or been reguerdon'd + with so much as thanks,
Because till now we never saw your face :
Therefore, stand up ; and, for these good deserts,
We here create you earl of Shrewsbury ;
And in our coronation take your place.

[*Exeunt King* HENRY, GLO. TAL. *and Nobles.*

Ver. Now, Sir, to you, that were so hot at sea,
Disgracing of these colours that I wear [5]
In honour of my noble lord of York,—
Dar'st thou maintain the former words thou spak'st?

Bas. Yes, sir; as well as you dare patronage
The envious barking of your saucy tongue
Against my lord, the duke of Somerset.

Ver. Sirrah, thy lord I honour as he is.

Bas. Why, what is he ? as good a man as York.

Ver. Hark ye ; not so : in witness, take ye that.

[*Strikes him.*

Bas. Villain, thou know'st, the law of arms is such,
That, who so draws a sword, 'tis present death [6] ;

Or

---

* *I do remember how my father said,*] The author of this play was
not a very correct historian. Henry was but nine months old when his
father died, and he never saw him. MALONE.

4 *Or been* reguerdon'd—] i. e. rewarded. The word was obsolete
even in the time of Shakspeare. Chaucer uses it in the *Boke of Boethius.*
STEEVENS.

5 — *these* colours *that I wear*] This was the badge of a *rose,* and not
an officer's scarf. So, in *Love's Labour's Lost,* Act III. sc. ult.
  " And wear his *colours* like a tumbler's hoop." TOLLET.

6 *That, who so draws a sword, 'tis present death* ;] I believe the line
should be written as it is in the folio :
  That, who so draws a sword—.
i. e. (as Dr. Warburton has observed) with a menace, in the court, or
in the presence-chamber. STEEVENS

Johnson, in his collection of *Ecclesiastical Laws,* has preserved the
following, which was made by Ina, king of the West Saxons, 693. " If
any one fight in the king's house, let him forfeit all his estate, and let the
king deem whether he shall live or not." GREY.

Sir William Blackstone observes, that " by the ancient law, before
the conquest, *fighting in the king's palace,* or before the king's judges,
was punished with death. So too, in the old Gothick constitution, there
were many places privileged by law, *quibus major reverentia et securitas
debetur, ut templa et judicia, quæ sancta habebantur,*—arces et aula
regia,—*denique locus quilibet præsente aut adventante rege.* And at pre-

sent,

Or elfe this blow fhould broach thy deareft blood.
But I'll unto his majefty, and crave ·　.
I may have liberty to venge this wrong ;
When thou fhalt fee, I'll meet thee to thy coft.

　Ver. Well, mifcreant, I'll be there as foon as you ;
And, after, meet you fooner than you would.　　[*Exeunt.*

ACT IV. SCENE I.

The fame.　A Room of ftate.

Enter King HENRY, GLOSTER, EXETER, YORK, SUFFOLK,
　　SOMERSET, WINCHESTER, WARWICK, TALBOT, *the*
　　Governour *of* PARIS, *and Others.*

　Glo. Lord bifhop, fet the crown upon his head.
　Win. God fave king Henry, of that name the fixth !
　Glo. Now, governour of Paris, take your oath,—
　　　　　　　　　　　　[Governour *kneels.*
That you elect no other king but him :
Efteem none friends, but fuch as are his friends ;
And none your foes, but fuch as fhall pretend [7]
Malicious practices againft his ftate :　·
This fhall ye do, fo help you righteous God !
　　　　　　　　　　　[*Exeunt* Gov. *and his train.*

Enter Sir John FASTOLFE.

　Faft. My gracious fovereign, as I rode from Calais,
To hafte unto your coronation,
A letter was deliver'd to my hands,
Writ to your grace from the duke of Burgundy.
　Tal. Shame to the duke of Burgundy, and thee !

fent, with us, by the Stat. 33 Hen. VIII. c. 12. malicious ftriking in
the king's palace, wherein his royal perfon refides, whereby blood is
drawn, is punifhable by perpetual imprifonment and fine, at the king's
pleafure, and alfo with the lofs of the offender's right hand ; the folemn
execution of which fentence is prefcribed in the ftatute at length."—
COMM. IV. 124. " By the ancient common law, before the conqueft,
ftriking in the king's courts of juftice, or drawing a fword therein, was
a capital felony. *Ibid* p 125. REED.
　7 — *fuch as fhall pretend*—] To *pretend* is to *defign,* to *intend.*
　　　　　　　　　　　　　　　　　　　　　　JOHNSON.
　　　　　　　　　　　　　　I vow'd,

I vow'd, bafe knight, when I did meet thee next,
To tear the garter from thy craven's leg, [*plucking it off.*
(Which I have done) becaufe unworthily
Thou waft inftalled in that high degree.—
Pardon me, princely Henry, and the reft :
This daftard, at the battle of Patay [8],—
When but in all I was fix thoufand ftrong,
And that the French were almoft ten to one,—
Before we met, or that a ftroke was given,
Like to a trufty fquire, did run away ;
In which affault we loft twelve hundred men ;
Myfelf, and divers gentlemen befide,
Were there furpriz'd, and taken prifoners.
Then judge, great lords, if I have done amifs ;
Or whether that fuch cowards ought to wear
This ornament of knighthood, yea, or no.

Glo. To fay the truth, this act was infamous,
And ill befeeming any common man ;
Much more a knight, a captain, and a leader.

Tal. When firft this order was ordain'd, my lords,
Knights of the garter were of noble birth ;
Valiant, and virtuous, full of haughty courage [9], .
Such as were grown to credit by the wars ;
Not fearing death, nor fhrinking for diftrefs,
But always refolute in moft extremes.
He then, that is not furnifh'd in this fort,
Doth but ufurp the facred name of knight,
Profaning this moft honourable order ;
And fhould (if I were worthy to be judge)
Be quite degraded, like a hedge-born fwain
That doth prefume to boaft of gentle blood.

[8] *— at the battle of* Patay,—] The old copy has *Poictiers.* The er-
rour was pointed out by Mr. Steevens. MALONE.
The battle of Poictiers was fought in the year 1357, the 31ft of king
Edward III. and the fcene now lies in the 7th year of the reign of king
Henry VI. viz. 1428. This blunder may be juftly imputed to the
players or tranfcribers ; nor can we very well juftify ourfelves for per-
mitting it to continue fo long, as it was too glaring to have efcaped an
attentive reader. The action of which Shakfpeare is now fpeaking, hap-
pened (according to Holinfhed) " neere unto a village in Beauffe called
Pataie," which we fhould read, inftead of *Poictiers.* " From this battell
departed without anie ftroke ftriken, *Sir John Faftolfe,* the fame yeere
by his valiantneffe elected into the order of the garter. But for doubt of
mifdealing at this brunt, the duke of Bedford tooke from him the image
of St. George and his garter," &c. Holinfhed, Vol. II. p. 601.
STEEVENS.
[9] — haughty *courage,*] *Haughty* is here in its original fenfe for *high.*
JOHNSON.

K. Hen.

K. Hen. Stain to thy countrymen ! thou hear'ſt thy doom :
Be packing therefore, thou that waſt a knight ;
Henceforth we baniſh thee, on pain of death.—

                              [Exit FASTOLFE.

And now, my lord protector, view the letter
Sent from our uncle duke of Burgundy.

    Glo. What means his grace, that he hath chang'd his ſtile ?

                    [viewing the ſuperſcription.

No more but, plain and bluntly,—*To the king ?*
Hath he forgot, he is his ſovereign ?
Or doth this churliſh ſuperſcription
Pretend ſome alteration in good will¹ ?
What's here ?—*I have upon eſpecial cauſe,—*   *[Reads.*
   Mov'd with compaſſion of my country's wreck,
   Together with the pitiful complaints
   Of ſuch as your oppreſſion feeds upon,—
   Forſaken your pernicious faction,
   And join'd with Charles, the rightful king of France.
O monſtrous treachery ! Can this be ſo ;
That in alliance, amity, and oaths,
There ſhould be found ſuch falſe diſſembling guile ?

    K. Hen. What ! doth my uncle Burgundy revolt ?

    Glo. He doth, my lord ; and is become your foe.

    K. Hen. Is that the worſt, this letter doth contain ?

    Glo. It is the worſt, and all, my lord, he writes.

    K. Hen. Why then, lord Talbot there ſhall talk with him,
And give him chaſtiſement for this abuſe :—
How ſay you, my lord ? are you not content ?

    Tal. Content, my liege ? Yes ; but that I am prevented ²,
I ſhould have begg'd I might have been employ'd.

    K. Hen. Then gather ſtrength, and march unto him
       ſtraight :
Let him perceive, how ill we brook his treaſon ;
And what offence it is, to flout his friends.

    Tal. I go, my lord ; in heart deſiring ſtill,
You may behold confuſion of your foes.   *[Exit.*

        Enter VERNON, *and* BASSET.

    Ver. Grant me the combat, gracious ſovereign !

    Baſ. And me, my lord, grant me the combat too !

---

1 Pretend *ſome alteration in good will ?*] Thus the old copy. To *pretend* ſeems to be here uſed in its Latin ſenſe, i. e. to *hold out*, to *ſtretch forward.* It may mean, however, as in other places, to. *deſign.* Modern editors read—*portend.* STEEVENS.

2 — *I am* prevented,] *Prevented* is here, *anticipated* ; a Latiniſm.
                              MALONE.
                              York.

York. This is my servant; Hear him, noble prince!

Som. And this is mine; Sweet Henry, favour him!

K. Hen. Be patient, lords, and give them leave to speak.—

Say, gentlemen, What makes you thus exclaim?

And wherefore crave you combat? or with whom?

Ver. With him, my lord; for he hath done me wrong.

Baf. And I with him; for he hath done me wrong.

K. Hen. What is that wrong whereof you both complain?

First let me know, and then I'll answer you.

Baf. Crossing the sea from England into France,

This fellow here, with envious carping tongue,

Upbraided me about the rose I wear;

Saying—the sanguine colour of the leaves

Did represent my master's blushing cheeks,

When stubbornly he did repugn the truth [3],

About a certain question in the law,

Argu'd betwixt the duke of York and him;

With other vile and ignominious terms:

In confutation of which rude reproach,

And in defence of my lord's worthiness,

I crave the benefit of law of arms.

Ver. And that is my petition, noble lord:

For though he seem, with forged quaint conceit,

To set a gloss upon his bold intent,

Yet know, my lord, I was provok'd by him;

And he first took exceptions, at this badge,

Pronouncing—that the paleness of this flower

Bewray'd the faintness of my master's heart.

York. Will not this malice, Somerset, be left?

Som. Your private grudge, my lord of York, will out,

Though ne'er so cunningly you smother it.

K. Hen. Good lord! what madness rules in brain-sick men;

When, for so slight and frivolous a cause,

Such factious emulations shall arise!—

Good cousins both, of York and Somerset,

Quiet yourselves, I pray, and be at peace.

York. Let this dissention first be try'd by fight,

And then your highness shall command a peace.

Som. The quarrel toucheth none but us alone;

Betwixt ourselves let us decide it then.

York. There is my pledge; accept it, Somerset.

---

3 — *did repugn the truth,*] To *repugn* is to resist. The word is used by Chaucer. STEEVENS.

It is found in Bullokar's *English Expositor*, 8vo. 1616. MALONE.

Ver.

Ver. Nay, let it reſt where it began at firſt.

Baſ. Confirm it ſo, mine honourable lord.

Glo. Confirm it ſo ? Confounded be your ſtrife !
And periſh ye, with your audacious prate !
Preſumptuous vaſſals ! are you not aſham'd,
With this immodeſt clamorous outráge
To trouble and diſturb the king and us ?
And you, my lords,—methinks, you do not well,
To bear with their perverſe objections ;
Much leſs, to take occaſion from their mouths
To raiſe a mutiny betwixt yourſelves ;
Let me perſuade you take a better courſe.

   Exe. It grieves his highneſs ;—Good, my lords, be
     friends.

   K. Hen. Come hither, you that would be combatants :
Henceforth, I charge you, as you love our favour,
Quite to forget this quarrel, and the cauſe —
And you, my lords,—remember where we are ;
In France, amongſt a fickle wavering nation :
If they perceive diſſention in our looks,
And that within ourſelves we diſagree,
How will their grudging ſtomachs be provok'd
To wilful diſobedience, and rebel ?
Beſide, What infamy will there ariſe,
When foreign princes ſhall be certify'd,
That, for a toy, a thing of no regard,
King Henry's peers, and chief nobility,
Deſtroy'd themſelves, and loſt the realm of France ?
O, think upon the conqueſt of my father,
My tender years ; and let us not forego
That for a trifle, that was bought with blood !
Let me be umpire in this doubtful ſtrife.
I ſee no reaſon, if I wear this roſe, [*putting on a red roſe.*
That any one ſhould therefore be ſuſpicious
I more incline to Somerſet, than York :
Both are my kinſmen, and I love them both :
As well they may upbraid me with my crown,
Becauſe, forſooth, the king of Scots is crown'd.
But your diſcretions better can perſuade,
Than I am able to inſtruct or teach :
And therefore, as we hither came in peace,
So let us ſtill contiņue peace and love.—
Couſin of York, we inſtitute your grace
To be our regent in theſe parts of France :—
And good my lord of Somerſet, unite
Your troops of horſemen with his bands of foot ;—

                         And,

And, like true fubjects, fons of your progenitors,
Go cheerfully together, and digeft
Your angry choler on your enemies.
Ourfelf, my lord protector, and the reft,
After fome refpite, will return to Calais ;
From thence to England ; where I hope ere long
To be prefented, by your victories,
With Charles, Alençon, and that traiterous rout.

    [*Flourifh. Exeunt King* HENRY, GLO. SOM. WIN. SUF.
    and BASSET.

  War. My lord of York, I promife you, the king
Prettily, methought, did play the orator.

  York. And fo he did ; but yet I like it not,
In that he wears the badge of Somerfet.

  War. Tufh ! that was but his fancy, blame him not ;
I dare prefume, fweet prince, he thought no harm.

  York. And, if I wift, he did [3];—But let it reft ;
Other affairs muft now be mauaged.

    [*Exeunt* YORK, WARWICK, *and* VERNON.

  Exe. Well didft thou, Richard, to fupprefs thy voice :
For, had the paffions of thy heart burft out,
I fear, we fhould have feen decypher'd there
More rancorous fpight, more furious raging broils,
Than yet can be imagin'd or fuppos'd.
But howfoe'er, no fimple man that fees
This jarring difcord of nobility,
This fhould'ring of each other in the court, .
This factious bandying of their favourites,
But that it doth prefage fome ill event [4].
'Tis much [5], when fcepters are in children's hands ;
But more, when envy breeds unkind divifion [6] ;
There comes the ruin, there begins confufion.   [*Exit.*

---

  [3] *And, if* I wift, *he did,*—] The old copy reads—if I wifh.
                                  MALONE.
  I read, I wift. The pret. of the old obfolete verb I wis, which is
ufed by Shakfpeare in *The Merchant of Venice :*
    " There be fools alive, I wis,
    " Silver'd o'er, and fo was this." STEEVENS.
  [4] *— it doth prefage fome ill event.*] That is, it doth prefage *to him*
that fees this difcord, &c. that fome ill event will happen. MALONE.
  'Tis much,—] In our author's time, this phrafe meant—'Tis ftrange,
or wonderful. See *As you like it.* This meaning being included in the
word *much,* the word *ftrange* is perhaps underftood in the next line :
" But more ftrange," &c. The conftruction however may be, But 'tis
much more, when, &c. MALONE.
  [6] *— when envy breeds unkind divifion ;*] Envy in old Englifh writers
frequently means *enmity. Unkind* is unnatural. MALONE.

                                            SCENE

SCENE II.

France. *Before* Bourdeaux.

Enter TALBOT, *with his forces.*

Tal. Go to the gates of Bourdeaux, trumpeter,
Summon their general unto the wall.

Trumpet sounds a parley. Enter, on the walls, the General
of the French *forces, and Others.*

English John Talbot, captains, call you forth,
Servant in arms to Harry king of England ;
And thus he would,—Open your city gates,
Be humble to us ; call my sovereign yours,
And do him homage as obedient subjects,
And I'll withdraw me and my bloody power :
But, if you frown upon this proffer'd peace,
You tempt the fury of my three attendants,
Lean famine, quartering steel, and climbing fire [7] ;
Who, in a moment, even with the earth
Shall lay your stately and air-braving towers,
If you forsake the offer of their love [8].

Gen. Thou ominous and fearful owl of death,
Our nation's terror, and their bloody scourge !
The period of thy tyranny approacheth.
On us thou canst not enter, but by death :
For, I protest, we are well fortify'd,
And strong enough to issue out and fight :
If thou retire, the Dauphin, well appointed,
Stands with the snares of war to tangle thee :
On either hand thee there are squadrons pitch'd,
To wall thee from the liberty of flight ;
And no way canst thou turn thee for redress,

---

[7] *Lean famine, quartering steel, and climbing fire :*] The author of this play followed Hall's *Chronicle:* "The Goddesse of warre, called Bellona—had these three hand-maids ever of necessitie attendynge on her; *Blood, Fyre,* and *Famine*; whiche thre damosels be of that force and strength that every one of them alone is able and sufficient to torment and afflict a proud prince; and they all joyned together are of puissance to destroy the most populous country and most richest region of the world." MALONE.

[8] — their *love.*] Sir T. Hanmer reads—*our* love. "*Their* love" may mean, the peaceable demeanour of my three attendants; their forbearing to injure you. But the expression is harsh. MALONE.

But

But death doth front thee with apparent spoil,
And pale deftruction meets thee in the face.
Ten thoufand French have ta'en the facrament,
To rive their dangerous artillery⁹
Upon no chriftian foul but Englifh Talbot.
Lo! there thou ftand'ft, a breathing valiant man,
Of an invincible unconquer'd fpirit:
This is the lateft glory of thy praife,
That I, thy enemy, due thee withal¹;
For ere the glafs, that now begins to run,
Finifh the procefs of his fandy hour,
Thefe eyes, that fee thee now well coloured,
Shall fee thee wither'd, bloody, pale, and dead.

                              [_Drum afar off._

Hark! hark! the Dauphin's drum, a warning bell,
Sings heavy mufick to thy timorous foul;
And mine fhall ring thy dire departure out.

                    [_Exeunt General, &c. from the walls._

Tal. He fables not², I hear the enemy;—
Out, fome light horfemen, and perufe their wings.—
O, negligent and heedlefs difcipline!
How are we park'd, and bounded in a pale;
A little herd of England's timorous deer,
Maz'd with a yelping kennel of French curs!

---

9 _To rive their dangerous artillery._] _Rive_ their artillery feems to mean charge their artillery fo much as to endanger their burfting. So, in _Troilus and Creffida_, Ajax bids the trumpeter blow fo loud, as to crack his lungs and _fplit_ his brazen pipe. TOLLET.

1 — due _thee withal_;] To _due_ is to _endue_, to _deck_, to _grace._
                                                    JOHNSON.
It means, I think, to honour by giving thee thy _due_, thy merited elogium. _Due_ was fubftituted for _dew_, the reading of the old copy, by Mr. Theobald. _Dew_ was fometimes the old fpelling of _due_, as _Hew_ was of _Hugh_. MALONE.
     The old copy reads—_dew_ thee withal; and perhaps rightly. The _dew of praife_ is an expreffion I have met with in other poets. Shakfpeare ufes the fame verb in _Macbeth:_
        "To _dew_ the fovereign flow'r, and drown the weeds."
Again, in the fecond part of _King Henry VI_:
        " ——— give me thy hand,
     " That I may _dew_ it with my mournful tears." STEEVENS.
     2 _He fables not._] This expreffion Milton has borrowed in his _Mafque at Ludlow Caftle:_
        " She _fables_ not, I feel that I do fear."
It occurs again in the _Pinner of Wakefield_, 1599:
        " ———good father, _fable_ not with him." STEEVENS.

                                                    If

If we be Englifh deer, be then in blood [3] :
Not rafcal-like [4], to fall down with a pinch ;
But rather moody-mad, and defperate ftags,
Turn on the bloody hounds with heads of fteel [5],
And make the cowards ftand aloof at bay :
Sell every man his life as dear as mine,
And they fhall find dear deer of us [6], my friends.—
God, and faint George ! Talbot, and England's right !
Profper our colours in this dangerous fight !　　　*[Exeunt.*

SCENE III.

Plains of Gafcony.

Enter YORK, *with forces ; to him a* Meffenger.

York Are not the fpeedy fcouts return'd again,
That dogg'd the mighty army of the Dauphin ?
Meff. They are return'd, my lord ; and give it out,
That he is march'd to Bourdeaux with his power,
To fight with Talbot : As he march'd along,
By your efpials were difcovered
Two mightier troops than that the Dauphin led ;
Which join'd with him, and made their march for Bour-
　　　deaux.
York. A plague upon that villain Somerfet ;
That thus delays my promifed fupply
Of horfemen, that were levied for this fiege !
Renowned Talbot doth expect my aid ;
And I am lowted [7] by a traitor villain,

　　　　　　　　　　　　　　　　　　　And

3 — *be then* in blood ;] Be in high fpirits, be of true mettle.
　　　　　　　　　　　　　　　　　　　　　JOHNSON.
　　This was a phrafe of the foreft. See *Love's Labour's Loft :* " The
deer was, as you know, *in fanguis, blood,*" Again, in Bullokar's
Englifh Expofitor, 1616 : " Tenderlings. The foft tops of a deere's
horns, when they are *in blood.*" MALONE.
　4 *Not rafcal-like.*] A rafcal deer is the term of chafe for lean poor
deer. JOHNSON.
　5 — *with heads of fteel,*] Continuing the image of the *deer,* he fuppofes the lances to be their horns. JOHNSON.
　6 — *dear deer of us,*] The fame quibble occurs in *K. Henry IV. P. I :*
　　" Death hath not ftruck fo fat a *deer* to-day,
　　" Though many a *dearer,* &c." STEEVENS.
　7 *And I am* lowted—] To *lowt* may fignify to *deprefs,* to *lower,* to
difhonour ; but I do not remember it fo ufed. We may read—*And I
am* flouted. *I am mocked,* and treated with contempt. JOHNSON.
　　　　　　　　　　　　　　　　　　　　　　To

And cannot help the noble chevalier:
God comfort him in this neceffity!
If he mifcarry, farewel wars in France.

Enter Sir William Lucy *.

Lucy. Thou princely leader of the Englifh ftrength,
Never fo needful on the earth of France,
Spur to the refcue of the noble Talbot;
Who now is girdled with a waift of iron,
And hemm'd about with grim deftruction:
To Bourdeaux, warlike duke! to Bourdeaux, York!
Elfe, farewel Talbot, France, and England's honour.

York. O God! that Somerfet—who in proud heart
Doth ftop my cornets—were in Talbot's place!
So fhould we fave a valiant gentleman,
By forfeiting a traitor, and a coward.
Mad ire, and wrathful fury, makes me weep,
That thus we die, while remifs traitors fleep.

Lucy. O, fend fome fuccour to the diftrefs'd lord!

York. He dies, we lofe; I break my warlike word;
We mourn, France fmiles; we lofe, they daily get;
All 'long of this vile traitor Somerfet.

Lucy. Then, God take mercy on brave Talbot's foul!
And on his fon young John; whom, two hours fince,
I met in travel toward his warlike father!
This feven years did not Talbot fee his fon;
And now they meet where both their lives are done².

York. Alas! what joy fhall noble Talbot have,
To bid his young fon welcome to his grave?
Away! vexation almoft ftops my breath,
That funder'd friends greet in the hour of death.—
Lucy, farewel: no more my fortune can,
But curfe the caufe I cannot aid the man.—
Maine, Bloys, Poictiers, and Tours, are won away,
'Long all of Somerfet, and his delay. *[Exit.*

To *but,* in Chaucer, fignifies to *fubmit.* To *fubmit* is to *let down.*
So, Dryden:
"Sometimes the hill *fubmits* itfelf a while,
"In fmall defcents," &c. STEEVENS.
I believe the meaning is, I am treated with contempt, like a *lout,*
or low country fellow MALONE.
* *Enter Sir William Lucy*] In the old copy we have only—"Enter
a Meffenger." But it appears from the fubfequent fcene that the meffenger was Sir William Lucy. MALONE.
² *—are done*] i. e. expended, confumed. The word is yet ufed
in this fenfe in the Weftern counties. MALONE.

Lucy.

Lucy. Thus, while the vulture of sedition [9]
Feeds in the bosom of such great commanders,
Sleeping neglection doth betray to loss
The conquest of our scarce cold conqueror,
That ever-living man of memory,
Henry the fifth :—Whiles they each other cross,
Lives, honours, lands, and all, hurry to loss.   [*Exeunt.*

SCENE IV.

Other Plains of Gascony.

Enter SOMERSET, *with his forces; an* Officer *of* TALBOT'S
with him.

Som. It is too late ; I cannot send them now:
This expedition was by York, and Talbot,
Too rashly plotted ; all our general force
Might with a sally of the very town
Be buckled with : the over-daring Talbot
Hath sullied all his gloss of former honour
By this unheedful, desperate, wild adventure :
York set him on to fight, and die in shame,
That, Talbot dead, great York might bear the name.
Off. Here is sir William Lucy, who with me
Set from our o'er-match'd forces forth for aid.

Enter Sir William LUCY.

Som. How now, sir William ? whither were you sent?
Lucy. Whither, my lord ? from bought and sold lord
     Talbot [1] ;
Who, ring'd about [2] with bold adversity,
Cries out for noble York and Somerset,
To beat assailing death from his weak legions [3].
And whiles the honourable captain there
Drops bloody sweat from his war-wearied limbs,

9 — *the vulture*—] Alluding to the tale of Prometheus. JOHNSON.
1 — *from bought and sold Lord Talbot* ;] i. e. from one utterly ruin'd
by the treacherous practices of others. So, in *K. Richard III.:*
     " Jocky of Norfolk, be not too bold,
     " For Dickon thy master is *bought and sold.*"
The expression appears to have been proverbial. MALONE.
2 —*ring'd about*—] Environ'd, encircled. JOHNSON.
3 — *his weak* legions.] Old Copy—*regions.* Corrected by Mr.
Rowe. MALONE.

           And,

And, in advantage ling'ring [4], looks for rescue,
You, his false hopes, the trust of England's honour,
Keep off aloof with worthless emulation [5].
Let not your private discord keep away
The levied succours that should lend him aid,
While he, renowned noble gentleman,
Yield up his life unto a world of odds:
Orleans the Bastard, Charles, Burgundy,
Alençon, Reignier, compass him about,
And Talbot perisheth by your default.

 Som. York set him on, York should have sent him aid.

 Lucy. And York as fast upon your grace exclaims;
Swearing, that you withhold his levied host;
Collected for this expedition.

 Som. York lies; he might have sent, and had the horse:
I owe him little duty, and less love;
And take foul scorn, to fawn on him by sending.

 Lucy. The fraud of England, not the force of France,
Hath now entrapp'd the noble-minded Talbot:
Never to England shall he bear his life;
But dies, betray'd to fortune by your strife.

 Som. Come, go; I will dispatch the horsemen straight:
Within six hours they will be at his aid.

 Lucy. Too late comes rescue; he is ta'en, or slain:
For fly he could not, if he would have fled;
And fly would Talbot never, though he might.

 Som. If he be dead, brave Talbot then adieu!

 Lucy. His fame lives in the world, his shame in you.

            [*Exeunt.*

SCENE V.

The English *Camp near* Bourdeaux.

Enter TALBOT, *and* John *his son*

 Tal. O young John Talbot! I did send for thee,
To tutor thee in stratagems of war;

---

 4 — *in advantage ling'ring,*] Protracting his resistance by the advantage of a strong post. JOHNSON.

 Or perhaps, endeavouring by every means that he can, with *advantage* to himself, to linger out the action, &c. MALONE.

 5 — *worthless* emulation] In this line *emulation* signifies merely *rivalry*, not struggle for superior excellence. JOHNSON.

 So Ulysses in *Troilus and Cressida* says, that the Grecian chiefs were
    " —— grown to an envious fever.
  " Of pale and bloodless *emulation.*" MASON.

That

That Talbot's name might be in thee reviv'd,
When fapless age, and weak unable limbs,
Should bring thy father to his drooping chair.
But,—O malignant and ill-boding ftars !
Now thou art come unto a feaft of death [6],
A terrible and unavoided [7] danger :
Therefore, dear boy, mount on my fwifteft horfe ;
And I'll direct thee how thou fhalt efcape
By fudden flight : come, dally not, begone.

   John. Is my name Talbot ? and am I your fon ?
And fhall I fly ? O, if you love my mother,
Difhonour not her honourable name,
To make a baftard, and a flave of me :
The world will fay—He is not Talbot's blood,
That bafely fled, when noble Talbot ftood [8].

   Tal. Fly, to revenge my death, if I be flain.

   John. He, that flies fo, will ne'er return again.

   Tal. If we both ftay, we both are fure to die.

   John. Then, let me ftay : and, father, do you fly :
Your lofs is great, fo your regard [9] fhould be ;
My worth unknown, no lofs is known in me.
Upon my death the French can little boaft ;
In yours they will, in you all hopes are loft.
Flight cannot ftain the honour you have won ;
But mine it will, that no exploit have done :
You fled for vantage, every one will fwear ;
But, if I bow, they'll fay—it was for fear.
There is no hope that ever I will ftay,
If, the firft hour, I fhrink, and run away.
Here, on my knee, I beg mortality,
Rather than life preferv'd with infamy.

   Tal. Shall all thy mother's hopes lie in one tomb ?

   John. Ay, rather than I'll fhame my mother's womb.

   Tal. Upon my bleffing I command thee go.

   John. To fight I will, but not to fly the foe.

   Tal. Part of thy father may be fav'd in thee.

---

   [6] — *a feaft of* death,] To a field where *death* will be *feafted* with flaughter. JOHNSON.

   [7] — unavoided—] for *unavoidable.* MALONE.

   [8] — *noble Talbot ftood*] For what reafon this fcene is written in rhyme, I cannot guefs. If Shakfpeare had not in other plays mingled his rhymes and blank verfes in the fame manner, I fhould have fufpect-ed that this dialogue had been a part of fome other poem which was never finifhed, and that being loath to throw his labour away, he in-ferted it here. JOHNSON.

   [9] — *your regard*—] Your care of your own fafety. JOHNSON.

John.

John. No part of him, but will be fhame in me.
Tal. Thou never hadft renown, nor canft not lofe it.
John. Yes, your renowned name; Shall flight abufe it?
Tal. Thy father's charge fhall clear thee from that ftain.
John. You cannot witnefs for me, being flain.
If death be fo apparent, then both fly.
Tal. And leave my followers here, to fight, and die?
My age was never tainted with fuch fhame.
John. And fhall my youth be guilty of fuch blame?
No more can I be fever'd from your fide,
Than can yourfelf yourfelf in twain divide:
Stay, go, do what you will, the like do I;
For live I will not, if my father die.
Tal. Then here I take my leave of thee, fair fon,
Born to eclipfe thy life this afternoon.
Come, fide by fide together live and die;
And foul with foul from France to heaven fly. *[Exeunt.*

SCENE VI.

A field of battle.

Alarm: Excurfions, wherein Talbot's *fon is hemm'd about,
and* Talbot *refcues him.*

Tal. Saint George, and victory! fight, foldiers, fight:
The regent hath with Talbot broke his word,
And left us to the rage of France his fword.
Where is John Talbot?—paufe, and take thy breath;
I gave thee life, and refcu'd thee from death.
John. O twice my father! twice am I thy fon [1]:
The life, thou gav'ft me firft, was loft and done [2];

---

[1] *O twice my father! twice am I thy fon:*] A French epigram, on a child, who being fhipwrecked with his father faved his life by getting on his parent's dead body, turns on the fame thought. After defcrib-ing the wreck, it concludes thus:

             " —— aprez mille efforts,
      " J'apperçus prez de moi flotter des membres morts;
        " Helas! c'etoit mon pere.
        " Je le connus, je l' embraffai,
     " Et fur lui jufq' au port hereufement pouffé,
       " Des ondes et des vents j'evitai la furie.
        " Que ce pere doit m'etre cher,
        " Qui m'a deux fois donné la vie,
       " Une fois fur la terre, et l'autre fur la mer!" MALONE.

[2] *— and done;*] See p. 69, n. 8. MALONE.

Till with thy warlike fword, defpight of fate,
To my determin'd time * thou gav'ft new date.

Tal. When from the Dauphin's creft thy fword ftruck fire,
It warm'd thy father's heart with proud defire
Of bold fac'd victory. Then leaden age,
Quicken'd with youthful fpleen, and warlike rage,
Beat down Alençon, Orleans, Burgundy,
And from the pride of Gallia refcu'd thee.
The ireful baftard Orleans—that drew blood
From thee, my boy; and had the maidenhood
Of thy firft fight:—I foon encountered;
And, interchanging blows, I quickly fhed
Some of his baftard blood; and, in difgrace,
Befpoke him thus: *Contaminated, bafe,*
And mif-begotten blood I fpill of thine,
Mean and right poor; for that pure blood of mine,
Which thou didft force from Talbot, my brave boy:
Here, purpofing the Baftard to deftry,
Came in ftrong refcue. Speak, thy father's care;
Art not thou weary, John? How doft thou fare?
Wilt thou yet leave the battle, boy, and fly,
Now thou art feal'd the fon of chivalry?
Fly, to revenge my death, when I am dead;
The help of one ftands me in little ftead.
O, too much folly is it, well I wot,
To hazard all our lives in one fmall boat.
If I to-day die not with Frenchmen's rage,
To-morrow I fhall die with mickle age:
By me they nothing gain, an if I ftay,
'Tis but the fhort'ning of my life one day:
In thee thy mother dies, our houfhold's name,
My death's revenge, thy youth, and England's fame:
All thefe, and more, we hazard by thy ftay;
All thefe are fav'd, if thou wilt fly away.

John. The fword of Orleans hath not made me fmart,
Thefe words of yours draw life-blood from my heart[3]:
On that advantage[4], bought with fuch a fhame,—

To

---

* — *my determin'd time*—] Time *expir'd*, ended. The word is ftill
ufed in that fenfe by legal conveyancers. MALONE.

3 *The fword of Orleans hath not made me fmart,*
Thefe words of yours draw life-blood from my heart:]
" Are there not poifons, racks, and flames, and *fwords?*
" That Emma thus muft die by Henry's *words?"* PRIOR.
                                                          MALONE.

4 *On that advantage,* &c.] i. e. Before young Talbot fly from his
father, (in order to fave his life while he deftroys his character,) *on,* or
for

To fave a paltry life, and flay bright fame,—
Before young Talbot from old Talbot fly,
The coward horfe, that bears me, fall and die!
And like me to the peafant boys of France⁵;
To be fhame's fcorn, and fubject of mifchance!
Surely, by all the glory you have won,
An if I fly, I am not Talbot's fon:
Then talk no more of flight, it is no boot;
If fon to Talbot, die at Talbot's foot.

Tal. Then follow thou thy defperate fire of Crete,
Thou Icarus; thy life to me is fweet:
If thou wilt fight, fight by thy father's fide;
And, commendable prov'd, let's die in pride.   [*Exeunt.*

SCENE VII.

Another part of the fame.

Alarum: Excurfions. Enter TALBOT *wounded, fupported by a* Servant.

Tal. Where is my other life?—mine own is gone;—
O, where's young Talbot? where is valiant John?
Triumphant death, fmear'd with captivity⁶!
Young Talbot's valour makes me fmile at thee:—
When he perceiv'd me fhrink, and on my knee,
His bloody fword he brandifh'd over me,
And, like a hungry lion, did commence
Rough deeds of rage, and ftern impatience:
But when my angry guardant ftood alone,

for the fake of, *the advantages* you mention, namely, preferving our houfhold's name, &c. may my coward horfe drop down dead! Mr. Theobald reads—*Out* on that *'vantage*—. Sir T. Hanmer and the fubfequent editors read—*O, what* advantage, &c. MALONE.

5 *And like me to the peafant boys of France;*] By " to *like*" I fuppofe the author meant to *make like*, or *reduce to a level with.* JOHNSON.

6 *Triumphant death, fmear'd with captivity!*] That is, death ftained and difhonoured with captivity. JOHNSON.

Death ftained by my being made a captive and dying in captivity. The author when he firft addreffes death, and ufes the epithet *triumphant*, confiders him as a perfon who had triumphed over him by plunging his dart in his breaft. In the latter part of the line, if Dr. Johnfon has rightly explained it, death muft have its ordinary fignification. " I think light of my death, though rendered difgraceful by captivity," &c. Perhaps however the conftruction intended by the poet was—Young Talbot's valour makes *me*, fmeared with captivity, fmile, &c. If fo, there fhould be a comma after *captivity.* MALONE.

E 2   T'end'ring

Tend'ring my ruin 7, and affail'd of none,
Dizzy-ey'd fury, and great rage of heart,
Suddenly made him from my fide to ftart
Into the cluft'ring battle of the French :
And in that fea of blood my boy did drench
His over-mounting fpirit ; and there dy'd
My Icarus, my bloffom, in his pride.

Enter foldiers, bearing the body of John Talbot [8].

Serv. O my dear lord ! lo, where your fon is borne !
Tal. Thou antick death [9], which laugh'ft us here to fcorn,
Anon, from thy infulting tyranny,
Coupled in bonds of perpetuity,
Two Talbots, winged through the lither fky [1],
In thy defpight, fhall 'fcape mortality.—
O thou whofe wounds become hard-favour'd death,
Speak to thy father, ere thou yield thy breath :
Brave death by fpeaking, whether he will, or no ;
Imagine him a Frenchman, and thy foe.—
Poor boy ! he fmiles, methinks ; as who fhould fay—
Had death been French, then death had died to-day.
Come, come, and lay him in his father's arms ;
My fpirit can no longer bear thefe harms.
Soldiers, adieu ! I have what I would have,
Now my old arms are young John Talbot's grave.   [*dies.*
                                                          Alarums.

---

7 *Tend'ring my ruin,*] Watching me with tendernefs in my fall.
                                                          JOHNSON.

I would rather read,—*Tending my ruin,* &c. TYRWHITT.

I adhere to the old reading. So, in *Hamlet*, Polonius fays to Ophe-
lia, "—*Tender* yourfelves more dearly." STEEVENS.

Again, in *K. Henry VI*. P. II.

"I *tender* fo the fafety of my liege—." MALONE.

8 *—the body of John Talbot.*] This John Talbot was the eldeft fon
of the firft earl by his fecond wife, and was Vifcount Lifle, when he was
killed with his father, in endeavouring to relieve Chatillon, after the
battle of Bourdeaux, in the year 1453. He was created Vifcount Lifle
in 1451. John, the earl's eldeft fon by his firft wife, was flain at the
battle of Northampton in 1460. MALONE.

9 *Thou antick death,*] The fool, or *antick* of the play, made fport by
mocking the graver perfonages. JOHNSON.

1 *through the lither fky,*] *Lither* is *flexible* or *yielding.* In much the
fame fenfe Milton fays:

          "——— He with broad fails
          " Winnow'd the *buxom* air."

That is, the obfequious air. JOHNSON.

Lither is the comparative of the adjective *lithe.* So, in *Look about
you,* 1600:

          " I'll bring his *lither* legs in better frame." STEEVENS.

Alarums. Exeunt Sold. *and* Serv. *leaving the two bodies.*
Enter CHARLES, ALENÇON, BURGUNDY, Baſtard, LA
PUCELLE, *and forces.*

Char. Had York and Somerſet brought reſcue in,
We ſhould have found a bloody day of this.

Baſt. How the young whelp of Talbot's raging-wood [2],
Did fleſh his puny ſword in Frenchmen's blood [3] !

Puc. Once I encounter'd him, and thus I ſaid,
Thou maiden youth, be vanquiſh'd by a maid :
But—with a proud, majeſtical high ſcorn,—
He anſwer'd thus ; *Young Talbot was not born*
To be the pillage of a giglot wench [4] :
So, ruſhing in the bowels of the French [5],
He left me proudly, as unworthy fight.

Bur. Doubtleſs, he would have made a noble knight :
See, where he lies inherſed in the arms
Of the moſt bloody nurſer of his harms.

Baſt. Hew them to pieces, hack their bones aſunder ;
Whoſe life was England's glory, Gallia's wonder.

Char. O, no ; forbear : for that which we have fled
During the life, let us not wrong it dead.

Enter Sir William LUCY, *attended ; a French herald*
preceding.

Lucy. Herald,
Conduct me to the Dauphin's tent ; to know
Who hath obtain'd the glory of the day.

Char. On what ſubmiſſive meſſage are you ſent ?

Lucy. Submiſſion, Dauphin ? 'tis a mere French word ;
We

---

[2] *raging-wood,*] That is, raging *mad.* So, in Heywood's *Dialogues,*
containing a number of effectual proverbes, 1562 :
    " She was, as they ſay, horn-*wood.*"
Again, in *The longer thou liveſt the more fool thou art,* 1570 :
    " He will fight as he were *wood.*" STEEVENS.

[3] — *in Frenchmen's blood* !] The return of rhyme where young Talbot is again mentioned, and in no other place, ſtrengthens the ſuſpicion
that thoſe verſes were originally part of ſome other work, and were copied here only to ſave the trouble of compoſing new. JOHNSON

[4] — *of a giglot wench :*] *Giglot* is a *wanton,* or a *ſtrumpet.* JOHNS.
The word is uſed by Gaſcoigne and other authors, though now quite
obſolete. So, in the play of *Orlando Furioſo,* 1599 :
    " Whoſe choice is like that Greekiſh *giglot's* love,
    " That left her lord, prince Menelaus." STEEVENS.

[5] — *in the bowels of the French,*] So, in the firſt part of *Jeronimo,*
1605 :
    " Meet, Don Andrea ! yes, in the *battle's bowels.*" STEEV.

We Englifh warriors wot not what it means.
I come to know what prifoners thou haft ta'en,
And to furvey the bodies of the dead.

   Char. For prifoners afk'ft thou ? hell our prifon is.
But tell me whom thou feek'ft.

   Lucy. Where is the great Alcides * of the field,
Valiant lord Talbot, earl of Shrewfbury ?
Created, for his rare fuccefs in arms,
Great earl of Wafhford [6], Waterford, and Valence ;
Lord Talbot of Goodrig and Urchinfield,
Lord Strange of Blackmere, lord Verdun of Alton,
Lord Cromwell of Wingfield, lord Furnival of Sheffield,
The thrice victorious lord of Falconbridge ;
Knight of the noble order of faint George,
Worthy faint Michael, and the golden fleece ;
Great marefhal to Henry the fixth,
Of all his wars within the realm of France ?

   Puc. Here is a filly ftately ftile, indeed !
The Turk, that two and fifty kingdoms hath [7],
Writes not fo tedious a ftile as this.——
Him, that thou magnify'ft with all thefe titles,
Stinking, and fly-blown, lies here at our feet.

   Lucy. Is Talbot flain ; the Frenchmen's only fcourge,
Your kingdom's terror and black Nemefis ?
O, were mine eye-balls into bullets turn'd,
That I, in rage, might fhoot them at your faces !
O, that I could but call thefe dead to life !
It were enough to fright the realm of France :

Were

---

* *Where is the great Alcides*—Old Copy—*But where's.* Corrected
by Mr. Rowe. The compofitor probably caught the word *But* from the
preceding line. MALONE.

6 *Great earl of* Wafhford,] It appears from Camden's *Britannia* and
Holinfhed's Chronicle of Ireland, that Wexford was anciently called
Weysford. In Crompton's *Manfion of Magnanimitie* it is written as
here, *Wafbford.* This long lift of titles is taken from the epitaph formerly fixed on Lord Talbot's tomb in Rouen in Normandy. Where
this author found it, I have not been able to afcertain, for it is not in
the common hiftorians. The oldeft book in which I have met with it
is the tract above mentioned, which was printed in 1599, pofterior to the
date of this play. Numerous as this lift is, the epitaph has one more,
which, I fuppofe, was only rejected becaufe it would not eafily fall into
the verfe, " Lord Lovetoft of Worfop." It concludes as here,—" Lord
Falconbridge, knight of the noble order of St. George, St. Michael,
and the golden fleece, Great Marfhall to King Henry VI. of his realm
in France, who died in the battle of Bourdeaux, 1453." MALONE.

7 *The Turk,* &c.] Alluding probably to the oftentatious letter of
Sultan Solyman the *Magnificent,* to the emperor Ferdinand, 1562 ; in
which all the *Grand Signior's* titles are enumerated. See Knolles's
Hift. of the Turks, 5th edit. p. 789. GRAY.

Were but his picture left among you here,
It would amaze the proudest of you all.
Give me their bodies ; that I may bear them hence,
And give them burial as beseems their worth.

Puc. I think, this upstart is old Talbot's ghost,
He speaks with such a proud commanding spirit.
For God's fake, let him have 'em [8] ; to keep them here,
They would but stink, and putrefy the air.

Char. Go, take their bodies hence.

Lucy. I'll bear them hence :
But from their ashes * shall be rear'd
A phœnix, that shall make all France afeard.

Char. So we be rid of them, do with 'em what thou wilt.
And now to Paris, in this conquering vein ;
All will be ours, now bloody Talbot's slain.　　　　*[Exeunt.*

ACT V. SCENE I [9].

London. *A Room in the Palace.*

Enter *King* HENRY, GLOSTER, *and* EXETER.

K. Hen. Have you perus'd the letters from the pope,
The emperor, and the earl of Armagnac ?

Glo. I have, my lord ; and their intent is this,——
They humbly sue unto your excellence,
To have a godly peace concluded of,
Between the realms of England and of France.

K. Hen. How doth your grace affect their motion ?

Glo. Well, my good lord ; and as the only means
To stop effusion of our Christian blood,

　　　　　　　　　　　　　　　　　　　　　And

---

[8] —*let him have* 'em;] Old copy—have *him.* So, a little lower,
—do with *him.* The first emendation was made by Mr. Theobald ; the
other by the editor of the second folio. MALONE.

* *But from their ashes,* &c] The defect of the metre shews that
some word of two syllables was inadvertently omitted ; probably an epithet to *ashes.* MALONE.

9 In the original copy, the transcriber or printer forgot to mark the
commencement of the fifth Act ; and has by mistake called this scene
Scene II. The editor of the second folio made a very absurd regulation
by making the act begin in the middle of the preceding scene, (where
the Dauphin, &c. enter, and take notice of the dead bodes of Talbot
and his son,) which was inadvertently followed in subsequent editions.
　　　　　　　　　　　　　　　　　　　　　　　　MALONE.

And 'ſtabliſh quietneſs on every ſide.

   K. Hen. Ay, marry, uncle; for I always thought,
It was both impious and unnatural,
That ſuch immanity [1] and bloody ſtrife
Should reign among profeſſors of one faith.

   Glo. Beſide, my lord,—the ſooner to effect,
And ſurer bind, this knot of amity,—
The earl of Armagnac—near knit to Charles,
A man of great authority in France,—
Proffers his only daughter to your grace
In marriage, with a large and ſumptuous dowry.

   K. Hen. Marriage? uncle, alas! my years are young [*];
And fitter is my ſtudy and my books,
Than wanton dalliance with a paramour.
Yet, call the ambaſſadors ; and, as you pleaſe,
So let them have their anſwers every one :
I ſhall be well content with any choice,
Tends to God's glory, and my country's weal.

Enter a Legate, *and Two Ambaſſadors, with* WINCHESTER *in
a Cardinal's hat.*

   Exe. What ! is my lord of Wincheſter inſtall'd,
And call'd unto a cardinal's degree [2] !
Then, I perceive, that will be verify'd,
Henry the fifth did ſometime propheſy,—
If once he come to be a cardinal,
He'll make his cap co-equal with the crown.

   K. Hen. My lords ambaſſadors, your ſeveral ſuits
Have been conſider'd and debated on.
Your purpoſe is both good and reaſonable :
And, therefore, are we certainly reſolv'd

                      To

---

[1] *— immanity—*] i. e. barbarity, ſavageneſs. STEEVENS.

[*] *— my years are young ;*] His majeſty, however, was twenty-four years old. MALONE.

[2] *What is my lord of Wincheſter inſtall'd,*
   And call'd unto a cardinal's degree!) This (as Mr. Edwards has obſerved in his Mſ. notes) argues a great forgetfulneſs in the poet. In the firſt act Gloſter ſays :
   I'll canvaſs thee in thy broad cardinal's *hat ;*
and it is ſtrange that the duke of Exeter ſhould not know of his advancement. STEEVENS.

   It ſhould ſeem from the ſtage-direction prefixed to this ſcene, and from the converſation between the Legate and Wincheſter, that the author meant it to be underſtood that the biſhop had obtained his cardinal's hat only juſt before his preſent entry. The inaccuracy therefore was in making Gloſter addreſs him by that title in the beginning of the play. He in fact obtained it in the fifth year of Henry's reign. MALONE.

To draw conditions of a friendly peace ;
Which, by my lord of Winchefter, we mean
Shall be tranfported prefently to France.

Glo. And for the proffer of my lord your mafter,——
I have inform'd his highnefs fo at large,
As—liking of the lady's virtuous gifts,
Her beauty, and the value of her dower,——
He doth intend fhe fhall be England's queen.

K. Hen. In argument and proof of which contract,
Bear her this jewel, [*to the* Amb.] pledge of my affection.
And fo, my lord protector, fee them guarded,
And fafely brought to Dover ; where, infhipp'd,
Commit them to the fortune of the fea.

Exeunt K. HEN. *and Train ;* GLO. EXE. *and Ambaf.*

Win. Stay, my lord legate ; you fhall firft receive
The fum of money, which I promifed
Should be deliver'd to his holinefs
For cloathing me in thefe grave ornaments.

Leg. I will attend upon your lordfhip's leifure.

Win. Now Winchefter will not fubmit, I trow,
Or be inferior to the proudeft peer.
Humphrey of Glofter, thou fhalt well perceive,
That, neither in birth [3], or for authority,
The bifhop will be over-borne by thee :
I'll either make thee ftoop, and bend thy knee,
Or fack this country with a mutiny. [*Exeunt.*

SCENE II.

France. *Plains in* Anjou.

Enter CHARLES, BURGUNDY, ALENÇON, LA PUCELLE, *and forces, marching.*

Char. Thefe news, my lords, may cheer our drooping
spirits :
'Tis faid, the ftout Parifians do revolt,
And turn again unto the warlike French.

Alen. Then march to Paris, noble Charles of France,
And keep not back your powers in dalliance.

Puc. Peace be amongft them, if they turn to us ;
Elfe, ruin combat with their palaces !

Enter

3 *That, neither in birth,*] I would read—*for* b'rth: That is, thou
fhalt not rule me though thy birth is legitimate, and thy authority
fupreme. JOHNSON.

Enter a Meſſenger.

Meſſ. Succeſs unto our valiant general,
And happineſs to his accomplices !
  Char. What tidings ſend our ſcouts ? I pr'ythee, ſpeak.
  Meſſ. The Engliſh army, that divided was
Into two parties, is now conjoin'd in one ;
And means to give you battle preſently.
  Char. Somewhat too ſudden, ſirs, the warning is ;
But we will preſently provide for them.
  Bur. I truſt, the ghoſt of Talbot is not there ;
Now he is gone, my lord, you need not fear.
  Puc. Of all baſe paſſions, fear is moſt accurs'd :—
Command the conqueſt, Charles, it ſhall be thine ;
Let Henry fret, and all the world repine.
  Char. Then on, my lords ; and France be fortunate !
                                       [*Exeunt.*

SCENE III.

The ſame, before Angiers.

Alarums : Excurſions. Enter LA PUCELLE:

Puc. The regent conquers, and the Frenchmen fly.—
Now help, ye charming ſpells, and periapts [4] ;
And ye choice ſpirits, that admoniſh me,
And give me ſigns of future accidents !   [*Thunder.*
You ſpeedy helpers, that are ſubſtitutes
Under the lordly monarch of the north [5],

                                Appear,

---

4 — *ye charming ſpells, and periapts* ;] Charms ſow'd up. Ezek.
xiii. 18. "*Woe to them that ſow pillows to all arm holes, to hunt ſouls.*"
                                 POPE.

  Periapts were worn about the neck as preſervatives from diſeaſe or
danger. Of theſe, the firſt chapter of St. John's goſpel was deemed the
moſt efficacious. Whoever is deſirous to know more about them, may
conſult Reginald Scott's *Diſcovery of Witchcraft*, 1584, p. 230, &c.
                              STEEVENS.

  The following ſtory, which is related in *Wits, Fits, and Fancies,*
1595, proves what Mr. Steevens has aſſerted. " A cardinal ſeeing a
prieſt carrying a cudgel under his gown, reprimanded him. His excuſe
was, that he only carried it to defend himſelf againſt the dogs of the
town. Wherefore, I pray you, replied the cardinal, ſerves *St. John's
Goſpel?* Alas, my lord, ſaid the prieſt, theſe curs underſtand no Latin."
                                MALONE.

 5 — *monarch of the north,*] The north was always ſuppoſed to be the
particular habitation of bad ſpirits. Milton therefore aſſembles the rebel
angels in the north. JOHNSON.
                                  The

[Appear, and aid me in this enterprize !

Enter Fiends.

This fpeedy and quick appearance argues proof
Of your accuftomed diligence to me.
Now, ye familiar fpirits, that are cull'd
Out of the powerful regions [6] under earth,
Help me this once, that France may get the field.

　　　　　　　　　　[They walk about and fpeak not.

O, hold me not with filence over-long !
Where.I was wont to feed you with my blood,
I'll lop'a member off, and give it you,
In earneft of a further benefit ;
So you do condefcend to help me now —

　　　　　　　　　　　　[They hang their heads.

No hope to have redrefs ?—My body fhall
Pay recompence, if you will grant my fuit.

　　　　　　　　　　　　[They fhake their heads.

Cannot my body, nor blood-facrifice,
Entreat you to your wonted furtherance ?
Then take my foul ; my body, foul, and all,
Before that England give the French the foil.

　　　　　　　　　　　　[They depart.

See ! they forfake me. Now the time is come,
That France muft vail her lofty-plumed creft,
And let her head fall into England's lap.
My ancient incantations are too weak,
And hell too ftrong for me to buckle with :
Now, France, thy glory droopeth to the duft.　　　*[Exit.*

Alarums. Enter French *and* Englifh *fighting.* La Pucelle
and York *fight hand to hand.* La Pucelle *is taken. The
French fly.*

York. Damfel of France, I think, I have you faft :

The boaft of Lucifer in the xivth chapter of Ifaiah is faid to be, that
he will fit upon the mount of the congregation, in the fides of the north.
　　　　　　　　　　　　　　　　　　Steevens.
6 — *the powerful* regions—] I believe Shakfpeare wrote—*legions.*
　　　　　　　　　　　　　　　　Warburton.
In a former paffage *regions* feems to have been printed inftead of *legions* ; at leaft all the editors from the time of Mr. Rowe have there fubftituted the latter word inftead of the former. The word *cull'd,* a d the
epithet *powerful,* which is applicable to the *fiends* themfelves, but not to
their place of refidence, fhew that it has an equal title to a place in the
text here. So, in *the Tempeft :*
　　" — But one *fiend* at a time,
　　" I'll fight their *legions* o'er. Malone.
The *regions under earth* are the infernal regions. Whence elfe fhould
the forcerefs have felected or fummoned her fiends. Steevens.

Unchain

Unchain your fpirits now with fpelling charms,
And try if they can gain your liberty.—
A goodly prize, fit for the devil's grace!
See, how the ugly witch doth bend her brows,
As if, with Circe, fhe would change my fhape.

Puc. Chang'd to a worfer fhape thou canft not be.

York. O, Charles the Dauphin is a proper man ;
No fhape but his can pleafe your dainty eye.

Puc. A plaguing mifchief light on Charles, and thee !
And may you both be fuddenly furpriz'd
By bloody hands, in fleeping on your beds !

York. Fell, banning hag [7] ! enchantrefs, hold thy tongue.

Puc. I pr'ythee, give me leave to curfe a while.

York. Curfe, mifcreant, when thou comeft to the ftake.

[*Exeunt.*

Alarums. Enter SUFFOLK, *leading in lady* MARGARET.

Suf. Be what thou wilt, thou art my prifoner.

[*gazes on her.*

O faireft beauty, do not fear, nor fly ;
For I will touch thee but with reverent hands,
And lay them gently on thy tender fide.
I kifs thefe fingers [*kiffing her hand*] for eternal peace [8] :
Who art thou ? fay, that I may honour thee

Mar. Margaret my name ; and daughter to a king,
The king of Naples, whofoe'er thou art.

Suf. An earl I am, and Suffolk am I call'd.
Be not offended, nature's miracle,
Thou art allotted to be ta'en by me :

7 *Fell* banning *hag !*] To *ban* is to curfe. STEEVENS.

8 *I kifs thefe fingers for eternal peace :*] In the old copy thefe lines are
thus arranged and pointed :

For I will touch thee but with reverent hands,
I kifs thefe fingers for eternal peace,
And lay them gently on thy tender fide.

by which Suffolk is made to kifs his own fingers, a fymbol of peace of
which there is, I believe, no example. The tranfpofition was made, I
think rightly, by Mr Capel. In the old edition, as here, there is only a
comma after " hands," which feems to countenance the regulation now
made. To obtain fomething like fenfe, the modern editors were obliged
to put a full point at the end of that line.

In confirmation of the tranfpofition here made, let it be remembered
that two lines are in like manner mifplaced in *Troilus* and *Creffida*, Act
1. fol. 1623:

" Or like a ftar dif-orb'd, nay, if we talk of reafon,
" And fly like chidden Mercury from Jove."

Again, in *K. Richard III.* Act IV. fc. iv :

" That reins in galled eyes of weeping fouls,
" That excellent grand tyrant of the earth." MALONE.

So

So doth the fwan her downy cygnets fave,
Keeping them prifoners underneath her wings *.
Yet, if this fervile ufage once offend,
Go, and be free again, as Suffolk's friend.

                                      [*She turns away as going.*

O, ftay !—I have no power to let her pafs ;
My hand would free her, but my heart fays—no.
As plays the fun upon the glaffy ftreams 9,
Twinkling another counterfeited beam,
So feems this gorgeous beauty to mine eyes.
Fain would I woo her, yet I dare not fpeak :
I'll call for pen and ink, and write my mind :
Fie, De la Poole ! difable not thyfelf 1 ;
Haft not a tongue ? is fhe not here ?
Wilt thou be daunted at a woman's fight !
Ay ; beauty's princely majefty is fuch,
Confounds the tongue, and makes the fenfes rough 2.

    Mar. Say, earl of Suffolk,—if thy name be fo,—
What ranfom muft I pay before I pafs ?
For, I perceive, I am thy prifoner.

    Suf. How canft thou tell, fhe will deny thy fuit,
Before thou make a trial of her love ?   [*Afide.*

    Mar. Why fpeak'ft thou not ? what ranfom muft I pay :

    Suf. She's beautiful ; and therefore to be woo'd :
She is a woman ; therefore to be won.   [*Afide.*

    Mar. Wilt thou accept a ranfom, yea, or no ?

    Suf. Fond man ! remember, that thou haft a wife;
Then how can Margaret be thy paramour ?   [*Afide.*

    Mar. I were beft to leave him, for he will not hear.

    Suf. There all is marr'd ; there lies a cooling card 3.

---

   * — her *wings.*] Old Copy—*his.* This manifeft error I only mention becaufe it fupports a note in a former volume of this work,
and juftifies the change there made. Her was formerly fpelt *hir* ; hence
it was oftn confounded with *his.* MALONE.

   9 *As plays the fun upon the glaffy ftreams, &c.*] This comparifon,
made between things which feem fufficiently unlike, is intended to exprefs the foftnefs and delicacy of lady Margaret's beauty, which delighted, but did not dazzle : which was bright, but gave no pain by its luftre.
                                        JOHNSON.

   1 — difable *not thyfelf;*] Do not reprefent thyfelf fo weak. To *difa-*
ble the judgment of another was, in that age, the fame as to deftroy its
credit or authority. JOHNSON.

   So, in *As you like it,* Act V: "—If again, it was not well cut, he
difabled my judgment. STEEVENS.

   2 — *and makes the fenfes*-rough.] The meaning of this word is not
very obvious Sir Thomas Hanmer reads—*crouch.* MALONE.

   3 — *a* cooling card.] So, in *Marius and Sylla,* 1594:
     " I'll have a prefent *cooling card* for you." STEEVENS.

                                              Mar.

Mar. He talks at random; sure, the man is mad.

Suf. And yet a dispensation may be had.

Mar. And yet I would that you would answer me.

Suf. I'll win this lady Margaret. For whom?
Why, for my king: Tush! that's a wooden thing [4].

Mar. He talks of wood: It is some carpenter.

Suf. Yet so my fancy may be satisfy'd,
And peace established between these realms.
But there remains a scruple in that too:
For though her father be the king of Naples,
Duke of Anjou and Maine, yet is he poor,
And our nobility will scorn the match.   [*Aside.*

Mar. Hear ye, captain? Are you not at leisure?

Suf. It shall be so, disdain they ne'er so much:
Henry is youthful, and will quickly yield.—
Madam, I have a secret to reveal.

Mar. What though I be enthrall'd? he seems a knight,
And will not any way dishonour me.

Suf. Lady, vouchsafe to listen what I say.

Mar. Perhaps, I shall be rescu'd by the French;
And then I need not crave his courtesy.   [*Aside.*

Suf. Sweet madam, give me hearing in a cause—

Mar. Tush! women have been captivate ere now. [*Aside.*

Suf. Lady, wherefore talk you so?

Mar. I cry you mercy, 'tis but *quid* for *quo.*

Suf. Say, gentle princess, would you not suppose
Your bondage happy, to be made a queen?

Mar. To be a queen in bondage, is more vile,
Than is a slave in base servility;
For princes should be free.

Suf. And so shall you,
If happy England's royal king be free.

Mar. Why, what concerns his freedom unto me?

Suf. I'll undertake to make thee Henry's queen;
To put a golden scepter in thy hand,
And set a precious crown upon thy head,
If thou wilt condescend to be my—

Mar. What?

Suf. His love.

Mar. I am unworthy to be Henry's wife.

Suf. No, gentle madam; I unworthy am
To woo so fair a dame to be his wife,
And have no portion in the choice myself.

4—*a wooden thing.*] is an *awkward business, an undertaking not
likely to succeed.* So, in Lilly's *Maid's Metamorphosis*, 1600:
  " My master takes but *wooden pains.*" STEEVENS.

How

How say you, madam; are you so content?

Mar. An if my father please, I am content.

Suf. Then call our captains, and our colours, forth :
And, madam, at your father's castle walls
We'll crave a parley, to confer with him.

             [Troops come forward.

    A parley sounded. Enter REIGNIER, *on the walls.*

Suf. See, Reignier, see thy daughter prisoner.

Reig. To whom?

Suf. To me.

Reig. Suffolk, what remedy?
I am a soldier; and unapt to weep,
Or to exclaim on fortune's sickleness.

Suf. Yes, there is remedy enough, my lord :
Consent, (and, for thy honour, give consent,)
Thy daughter shall be wedded to my king ;
Whom I with pain have woo'd and won thereto ;
And this her easy-held imprisonment
Hath gain'd thy daughter princely liberty.

Reig. Speaks Suffolk as he thinks?

Suf. Fair Margaret knows,
That Suffolk doth not flatter, face, or feign [4],

Reig. Upon thy princely warrant, I descend,
To give thee answer of thy just demand

            [Exit, from the walls.

Suf. And here I will expect thy coming.

    Trumpets sounded. Enter REIGNIER, *below.*

Reig. Welcome, brave earl, into our territories ;
Command in Anjou what your honour pleases.

Suf Thanks, Reignier, happy for so sweet a child,
Fit to be made companion with a king :
What answer makes your grace unto my suit?

Reig. Since thou dost deign to woo her little worth [5],
To be the princely bride of such a lord ;
Upon condition I may quietly

---

4 — face, *or feign.*] " To *face* (says Dr. Johnson) is to carry a false
appearance; to play the hypocrite." Hence the name of one of the
characters in Ben Johnson's *Alchymist.* MALONE.

5 *Since thou dost deign to woo her little worth,* &c.] *To woo her little
worth—may mean—to court her small share of merit.* But perhaps the
passage should be pointed thus :

    Since thou dost deign to woo her, little worth
    To be the princely bride of such a lord ;

i. e. little deserving to be the wife of such a prince. MALONE.

                     Enjoy

Enjoy mine own, the county Maine *, and Anjou,
Free from oppreſſion, or the ſtroke of war,
My daughter ſhall be Henry's, if he pleaſe.

Suf. That is her ranſom, I deliver her;
And thoſe two counties, I will undertake
Your grace ſhall well and quietly enjoy.

Reig. And I again,—in Henry's royal name,
As deputy unto that gracious king,—
Give thee her hand, for ſign of plighted faith.

Suf. Reignier of France, I give thee kingly thanks,
Becauſe this is in traffick of a king :
And yet, methinks, I could be well content
To be mine own attorney in this caſe.　　　　　[*Aſide.*
I'll over then to England with this news,
And make this marriage to be ſolemniz'd :
So, farewell, Reignier! Set this diamond ſafe
In golden palaces, as it becomes.

Reig. I do embrace thee, as I would embrace
The Chriſtian prince, king Henry, were he here.

Mar. Farewell, my lord! Good wiſhes, praiſe, and
　　　　　prayers,
Shall Suffolk ever have of Margaret.　　　　　[*going.*

Suf. Farewell, ſweet madam! But hark you, Margaret;
No princely commendations to my king?

Mar. Such commendations as become a maid,
A virgin, and his ſervant, ſay to him.

Suf. Words ſweetly plac'd, and modeſtly [6] directed.
But, madam, I muſt trouble you again,—
No loving token to his majeſty?

Mar. Yes, my good lord; a pure unſpotted heart,
Never yet taint with love, I ſend the king.

Suf. And this withal.　　　　　[*Kiſſes her.*

Mar. That for thyſelf;—I will not ſo preſume,
To ſend ſuch peeviſh tokens to a king [7].

　　　　　[*Exeunt* REIGNIER, *and* MARGARET.

Suf. O, wert thou for myſelf!—But, Suffolk, ſtay,
Thou may'ſt not wander in that labyrinth;
There Minotaurs, and ugly treaſons, lurk
Solicit Henry with her wond'rous praiſe :
Bethink thee on her virtues that ſurmount;

　　　　　　　　　　　　　　　Mad,

* —*the* county *Maine,*] Maine is called a *county* both by Hall and
Holinſhed. The old copy erroneouſly roads—*country* MALONE.
　6 *modeſtly*—] Old Copy—*modeſty.* Corrected by the editor of the ſecond folio. MALONE.
　7 *To ſend ſuch* peeviſh *tokens*—] *Peeviſh* for childiſh. WARBURTON.
See a note in *Cymbeline,* Act I. ſc. vii : "He's ſtrange and *peeviſh.*"
　　　　　　　　　　　　　　　STEEVENS.

Mad, natural graces that extinguiſh art [8] ;
Repeat their ſemblance often on the ſeas,
That, when thou com'ſt to kneel at Henry's feet,
Thou may'ſt bereave him of his wits with wonder. [*Exeunt.*

SCENE IV.

Camp of the Duke of York, *in* Anjou.

Enter YORK, WARWICK, *and others.*

York. Bring forth that ſorcereſs, condemn'd to burn.

Enter LA PUCELLE, *guarded, and a* Shepherd.

Shep. Ah, Joan ! this kills thy father's heart outright !
Have I ſought every country far and near,
And, now it is my chance to find thee out,
Muſt I behold thy timeleſs [9] cruel death ?
Ah, Joan, ſweet daughter Joan, I'll die with thee !

Puc. Decrepit miſer [1] ! baſe ignoble wretch !
I am deſcended of a gentler blood ;
Thou art no father, nor no friend, of mine.

Shep. Out, out !—My lords, an pleaſe you, 'tis not ſo ;
I did beget her, all the pariſh knows :

---

[8] *Mad, natural graces* that extinguiſh art ;] So the old copy. The modern editors have been content to read—*Her* natural graces. By the word *mad,* however, I believe the poet only meant *wild* or uncultivated. In the former of theſe ſignifications he appears to have uſed it in *Othello:* " *he ſhe lov'd prov'd* mad :" which Dr. Johnſon has properly interpreted. We call a wild girl, to this day, a *mad-cap. Mad,* in ſome of the ancient books of gardening, is uſed as an epithet to plants which grow rampant and wild. STEEVENS
Pope had, perhaps, this line in his thought, when he wrote—
" And catch a grace beyond the reach of art."
In *The Two Noble Kinſmen,* 1634, mad is uſed in the ſame manner as in the text :
" Is it not *mad* lodging in theſe wild woods here ?"
Again, in Naſhe's *Have with you to Saffron Walden,* 1596 : "—with manie more *madde* tricks of youth never plaid before." MALONE.

[9] —timeleſs—] is *untimely.* So in Drayton's *Legend of Robert Duke of Normandy:*
" Thy ſtrength was buried in his *timeleſs* death." STEEVENS.

[1] *Decrepit* miſer !] *Miſer* has no relation to avarice in this paſſage, but ſimply means a miſerable creature. So, in Holinſhed, p. 760, where he is ſpeaking of the death of Richard III : " And ſo this *miſer,* at the ſame verie point, had like chance and fortune, &c." Again, p. 951, among the laſt words of lord Cromwell : " — for if I ſhould ſo doo, I were a very wretch and a *miſer.*" STEEVENS.

Her

Her mother liveth yet, can teſtify
She was the firſt-fruit of my bachelorſhip.

War. Graceleſs! wilt thou deny thy parentage?

York. This argues what her kind of life hath been;
Wicked and vile; and ſo her death concludes.

Shep. Fie, Joan! that thou wilt be ſo obſtacle [2]!
God knows, thou art a collop of my fleſh;
And for thy ſake have I ſhed many a tear:
Deny me not, I pr'ythee, gentle Joan.

Puc. Peaſant, avaunt!—You have ſuborn'd this man,
Of purpoſe to obſcure my noble birth.

Shep. 'Tis true, I gave a noble [3] to the prieſt,
The morn that I was wedded to her mother.—
Kneel down and take my bleſſing, good my girl.
Wilt thou not ſtoop? Now curſed be the time
Of thy nativity! I would, the milk
Thy mother gave thee, when thou ſuck'dſt her breaſt,
Had been a little ratſbane for thy ſake!
Or elſe, when thou didſt keep my lambs a-field,
I wiſh ſome ravenous wolf had eaten thee!
Doſt thou deny thy father, curſed drab?
O, burn her, burn her; hanging is too good.   [*Exit.*

York. Take her away; for ſhe hath liv'd too long,
To fill the world with vicious qualities.

Puc. Firſt, let me tell you whom you have condemn'd:
Not me [*] begotten of a ſhepherd ſwain,
But iſſued from the progeny of kings;
Virtuous, and holy; choſen from above,
By inſpiration of celeſtial grace,
To work exceeding miracles on earth.
I never had to do with wicked ſpirits:
But you,—that are polluted with your luſts,
Stain'd with the guiltleſs blood of innocents,
Corrupt and tainted with a thouſand vices,
Becauſe you want the grace that others have,
You judge it ſtraight a thing impoſſible
To compaſs wonders, but by help of devils.

2 — *ſo* obſtacle!] A vulgar corruption of *obſtinate*, which I think has,
oddly laſted ſince our author's time till now. JOHNSON.

The ſame corruption may be met with in Gower, Chapman, and
other writers. STEEVENS.

3 — my noble *birth.*—
'Tis true, I gave a noble—] This paſſage ſeems to corroborate an
explanation, ſomewhat far-fetched, which I have given in *K. Henry IV.*
of the *nobleman* and *royal man.* JOHNSON.

* *Not* me—] I believe the author wrote—Not *one.* MALONE.

No,

No, misconceived [4] ! Joan of Arc hath been
A virgin from her tender infancy,
Chaste and immaculate in very thought ;
Whose maiden blood, thus rigorously effus'd,
Will cry for vengeance at the gates of heaven.

York. Ay, ay ;—away with her to execution.

War. And hark ye, sirs ; because she is a maid,
Spare for no faggots, let there be enough :
Place barrels of pitch upon the fatal stake,
That so her torture may be shortened.

Puc. Will nothing turn your unrelenting hearts ?—
Then, Joan, discover thine infirmity ;
That warranteth by law to be thy privilege.—
I am with child, ye bloody homicides :
Murder not then the fruit within my womb,
Although ye hale me to a violent death.

York. Now heaven forefend ! the holy maid with child ?

War. The greatest miracle, that e'er ye wrought :
Is all your strict preciseness come to this ?

York. She and the Dauphin have been juggling :
I did imagine what would be her refuge.

War. Well, go to ; we will have no bastards live ;
Especially, since Charles must father it.

Puc. You are deceiv'd ; my child is none of his ;
It was Alençon, that enjoy'd my love.

York. Alençon ! that notorious Machiavel [5] !
It dies, an if it had a thousand lives.

Puc. O, give me leave, I have deluded you ;
'Twas neither Charles, nor yet the duke I nam'd,
But Reignier, king of Naples, that prevail'd.

War. A marry'd man ! that most intolerable.

York. Why, here's a girl ! I think she knows not well,
There were so many, whom she may accuse.

4 *No, misconceived!*] i. e. *No, ye misconceivers, ye who mistake me and my qualities.* STEEVENS.

5 — *that notorious* Machiavel !] *Machiavel* being mentioned somewhat before his time, this line is by some of the editors given to the players, and ejected from the text. JOHNSON.
The character of Machiavel seems to have made so very deep an impression on the dramatick writers of this age, that he is many times so prematurely spoken of. So, in the *Valiant Welchman,* 1615, one of the characters bids *Caradoc,* i. e. *Caractacus,*

" —— read *Machiavel :*
" Princes that would aspire, must mock at hell."
Again : " —— my brain
" Italianates my barren faculties
" To *Machiavelian* blackness." STEEVENS.

War. It's sign, she hath been liberal and free.

York. And, yet, forsooth, she is a virgin pure:—
Strumpet, thy words condemn thy brat, and thee:
Use no entreaty, for it is in vain.

Puc. Then lead me hence;—with whom I leave my curse:
May never glorious sun reflex his beams
Upon the country where you make abode!
But darkness and the gloomy shade of death [6]
Environ you; till mischief and despair,
Drive you to break your necks, or hang yourselves [7]!

                          [*Exit, guarded.*

York. Break thou in pieces, and consume to ashes,
Thou foul accursed minister of hell!

     Enter Cardinal BEAUFORT, *attended.*

Car. Lord regent, I do greet your excellence
With letters of commission from the king.
For know, my lords, the states of Christendom,
Mov'd with remorse of these outrageous broils,
Have earnestly implor'd a general peace
Betwixt our nation and the aspiring French;
And see at hand the Dauphin, and his train,
Approacheth, to confer about some matter.

York. Is all our travel turn'd to this effect?
After the slaughter of so many peers,
So many captains, gentlemen, and soldiers,
That in this quarrel have been overthrown,
And sold their bodies for their country's benefit,
Shall we at last conclude effeminate peace?
Have we not lost most part of all the towns,
By treason, falshood, and by treachery,
Our great progenitors had conquered?—
O, Warwick, Warwick! I foresee with grief
The utter loss of all the realm of France.

War. Be patient, York; if we conclude a peace,
It shall be with such strict and severe covenants,
As little shall the Frenchmen gain thereby.

---

6 — *darkness and the gloomy shade of death*—] The expression is scrip-
tural: " Whereby the day-spring from on high hath visited us, to give
light to them that sit *in darkness and the shadow of death.*"—MALONE.

7 — *till mischief and despair,*
    Drives you to break your necks, or hang yourselves! Perhaps Shak-
speare intended to remark in this execration, the frequency of suicide
among the English, which had been commonly imputed to the gloomi-
ness of their air. JOHNSON.

                                            Enter

Enter CHARLES, *attended*; ALENÇON, BASTARD, REIG-
NIER, *and Others.*

Char. Since, lords of England, it is thus agreed,
That peaceful truce shall be proclaim'd in France,
We come to be informed by yourselves
What the conditions of that league must be.
  York. Speak, Winchester; for boiling choler chokes
The hollow passage of my poison'd voice [8],
By sight of these our baleful enemies [9].
  Win. Charles, and the rest, it is enacted thus:
That—in regard king Henry gives consent,
Of meer compassion, and of lenity,
To ease your country of distressful war,
And suffer you to breathe in fruitful peace,—
You shall become true liegemen to his crown:
And, Charles, upon condition thou wilt swear
To pay him tribute, and submit thyself,
Thou shalt be plac'd as viceroy under him,
And still enjoy the regal dignity.
  Alen. Must he be then a shadow of himself?
Adorn his temples with a coronet [1];
And yet, in substance and authority,
Retain but privilege of a private man?
This proffer is absurd and reasonless.
  Char. 'Tis known, already that I am possess'd
With more than half the Gallian territories,
And therein reverenc'd for their lawful king:
Shall I, for lucre of the rest unvanquish'd
Detract so much from that prerogative,
As to be call'd but viceroy of the whole?
No, lord ambassador; I'll rather keep
That which I have, than, coveting for more,
Be cast from possibility of all.

---

[8] *— poison'd voice,]* *Poison'd voice* agrees well enough with *baneful
enemies,* or with *baleful,* if it can be used in the same sense. The modern editors read—*prison'd voice.* JOHNSON.
  Prison'd, was introduced by Mr. Pope. MALONE.
  [9] *— baleful enemies.]* *Baleful* is *sorrowful;* I therefore rather imagine that we should read—*baneful,* hurtful, or mischievous. JOHNSON.
  Baleful had anciently the same meaning as *baneful.* It is an epithet
very frequently bestow'd on poisonous plants and reptiles. So, in *Romeo and Juliet:*
  " With *baleful* weeds, and precious-juiced flowers."
                                                    STEEVENS.
  [1] *— with a coronet:]* *Coronet* is here used for a *crown.* JOHNSON.

York.

York. Infulting Charles! haft thou by fecret means
Us'd interceffion to obtain a league;
And, now the matter grows to compromife,
Stand'ft thou aloof upon comparifon [2] ?
Either accept the title thou ufurp'ft,
Of benefit [3] proceeding from our king,
And not of any challenge of defert,
Or we will plague thee with inceffant wars.

Reig. My lord, you do not well in obftinacy
To cavil in the courfe of this contráct :
If once it be negleſted, ten to one,
We fhall not find like opportunity.

Alen. To fay the truth, it is your policy,
To fave your fubjeſts from fuch maffacre,
And ruthlefs flaughters, as are daily feen
By our proceeding in hoftility :
And therefore take this compaſt of a truce,
Although you break it when your pleafure ferves.
                              [*Afide, to* Charles.

War. How fay'ft thou, Charles ? fhall our condition
      ftand ?
Char. It fhall :
Only referv'd, you claim no intereft
In any of our towns of garrifon.

York. Then fwear allegiance to his majefty ;
As thou art knight, never to difobey,
Nor be rebellious to the crown of England,
Thou, nor thy nobles, to the crown of England.——
                  [Charles, *and the reft, give tokens of fealty.*
So, now difmifs your army when ye pleafe ;
Hang up your enfigns, let your drums be ftill,
For here we entertain a folemn peace.   [*Exeunt.*

SCENE V.

London.   *A Room in the Palace.*

Enter King HENRY, *in conference with* SUFFOLK; GLOS-
      TER *and* EXETER *following.*

K. Hen. Your wond'rous rare defcription, noble earl,

---

2 — *upon comparifon ?*] Do you ftand to compare your prefent ftate,
a ftate which you have neither right or power to maintain, with the
terms which we offer ?   JOHNSON.

3 — *Of* benefit—] *Benefit* is here a term of law.   Be content to live
as the *beneficiary* of our king.   JOHNSON.

                                                  Of

Of beauteous Margaret hath aftonifh'd me :
Her virtues, graced with external gifts,
Do breed love's fettled paffions in my heart :
And like as rigour of tempeftuous gufts
Provokes the mightieft hulk againft the tide ;
So am I driven [4], by breath of her renown,
Either to fuffer fhipwreck, or arrive
Where I may have fruition of her love.

  Suf. Tufh, my good lord ! this fuperficial tale
Is but a preface of her worthy praife :
The chief perfections of that lovely dame,
(Had I fufficient fkill to utter them,)
Would make a volume of enticing lines,
Able to ravifh any dull conceit.
And, which is more, fhe is not fo divine.
So full replete with choice of all delights,
But, with as humble lowlinefs of mind,
She is content to be at your command ;
Command, I mean, of virtuous chafte intents,
To love and honour Henry as her lord.

  K. Hen. And otherwife will Henry ne'er prefume.
Therefore, my lord protector, give confent,
That Margaret may be England's royal queen.

  Glo. So fhould I give confent to flatter fin.
You know my lord, your highnefs is betroth'd
Unto another lady of efteem ;
How fhall we then difpenfe with that contract,
And not deface your honour with reproach ?

  Suf. As doth a ruler with unlawful oaths ;
Or one, that, at a triumph [5] having vow'd
To try his ftrength, forfaketh yet the lifts
By reafon of his adverfary's odds :
A poor earl's daughter is unequal odds,
And therefore may be broke without offence.

  Glo. Why, what, I pray, is Margaret more than that !
Her father is no better than an earl,
Although in glorious titles he excel.

  Suf. Yes, my good lord [*], her father is a king,

---

4 *So am I driven,* &c.] This fimile is fomewhat obfcure; he feems
to mean, that as a fhip is driven againft the tide by the wind, fo he is
driven by love againft the current of his intereft. JOHNSON.

5 — *at a* triumph—] A *triumph* in this author's time fignified an
exhibition of fports, &c. See *A Midfummer Night's Dream.*

                                    MALONE.

* — *my good lord,*] *Good,* which is not in the old copy, was added
for the fake of the metre, in the fecond folio. MALONE.

The king of Naples, and Jerusalem;
And of such great authority in France,
As his alliance will confirm our peace,
And keep the Frenchmen in allegiance.

Glo. And so the earl of Armagnac may do,
Because he is near kinsman unto Charles.

Exe. Beside, his wealth doth warrant a liberal dower;
While Reignier sooner will receive, than give.

Suf. A dower, my lords! disgrace not so your king,
That he should be so abject, base, and poor,
To choose for wealth, and not for perfect love.
Henry is able to enrich his queen,
And not to seek a queen to make him rich:
So worthless peasants bargain for their wives,
As market-men for oxen, sheep, or horse.
Marriage is a matter of more worth,
Than to be dealt in by attorneyship [6];
Not whom we will, but whom his grace affects,
Must be companion of his nuptial bed:
And therefore, lords, since he affects her most,
It most [7] of all these reasons bindeth us,
In our opinions she should be preferr'd.
For what is wedlock forced, but a hell;
An age of discord and continual strife?
Whereas the contrary bringeth bliss [8],
And is a pattern of celestial peace.
Whom should we match with Henry, being a king,
But Margaret, that is daughter to a king?
Her peerless feature, joined with her birth,
Approves her fit for none, but for a king:
Her valiant courage, and undaunted spirit,
(More than in women commonly is seen,)
Will answer our hope in issue of a king;
For Henry, son unto a conqueror,
Is likely to beget more conquerors,
If with a lady of so high resolve,
As is fair Margaret, he be link'd in love.
Then yield, my lords; and here conclude with me,
That Margaret shall be queen, and none but she.

---

6 — *by attorneyship*;] By the intervention of another man's choice; or the discretional agency of another. JOHNSON.

7 It *most*—] The word *It*, which is wanting in the old copy, was inserted by Mr. Rowe. MALONE.

8 *Whereas the* contrary *bringeth bliss*,] *Contrary* is here used as a quadrisyllable; as if it were written *conterary*. So *Henry* is used by our old poets and by our author, as a trisyllable. MALONE.

K. Hen.

K. Hen. Whether it be through force of your report,
My noble lord of Suffolk ; or for that
My tender youth was never yet attaint
With any paffion of inflaming love,
I cannot tell ; but this I am affur'd,
I feel fuch fharp diffention in my breaft,
Such fierce alarums both of hope and fear,
As I am fick with working of my thoughts **9**.
Take, therefore, fhipping ; poft, my lord, to France ;
Agree to any covenants ; and procure
That lady Margaret doth vouchfafe to come
To crofs the feas to England, and be crown'd
King Henry's faithful and anointed queen :
For your expences and fufficient charge,
Among the people gather up a tenth.
Be gone, I fay ; for, till you do return,
I reft perplexed with a thoufand cares.——
And you, good uncle, banifh all offence :
If you do cenfure me by what you were **1**,
Not what you are, I know it will excufe
This fudden execution of my will.
And to conduct me, where from company,
I may revolve and ruminate my grief **2**.   [*Exit.*

Glo. Ay, grief, I fear me, both at firft and laft.
        [*Exeunt* GLOSTER *and* EXETER.

Suf. Thus Suffolk hath prevail'd : and thus he goes,
As did the youthful Paris once to Greece ;
With hope to find the like event in love,
But profper better than the Trojan did.
Margaret fhall now be queen, and rule the king ;
But I will rule both her, the king, and realm **3**.   [*Exit.*

---

9 *As I am fick with working of my thoughts*] So, in Shakfpeare's *King Henry V.*
        " *Work, work your thoughts,* and therein fee a fiege."
                                MALONE.

1 *If you do* cenfure me, &c.] To *cenfure* is here fimply to *judge. If in judging* me you confider the *paft frailties of your own youth.* JOHNSON.

2 — *ruminate my grief.*] *Grief* in the firft line is taken generally for *pain* or *uneafinefs* ; in the fecond fpecially for *forrow.* JOHNSON.

3 Of this play there is no copy earlier than that of the folio in 1623, though the two fucceeding parts are extant in two editions in quarto.—— That the fecond and third parts were publifhed without the firft, may be admitted as no weak proof that the copies were furreptitioufly obtained, and that the printers of that time gave the publick thofe plays not fuch as the author defigned, but fuch as they could get them. That this play was written before the two others is indubitably collected from the feries of events ; that it was written and played before Henry the Fifth

VOL. IX.   F   I S

is apparent, because in the epilogue there is mention made of this play, and not of the other parts:

> Henry the sixth, in infant bands crown'd king,——
> Whose state so many had the managing,
> That they lost France, and made his England bleed:
> Which oft our stage hath shewn.

France is left in this play. The two following contain, as the old title imports, the contention of the houses of York and Lancaster.

Johnson.

That the second and third parts (as they are now called) were printed without the first, is a proof in my apprehension, that they were not written by the author of the first : and the title of *The Contention of the houses of York and Lancaster*, being affixed to the two pieces which were printed in quarto in 1600, is a proof that they were a distinct work, commencing where the other ended, but not written at the same time : and that this play was never known by the name of *The First part of King Henry VI.* till Heminge and Condell gave it this title in their volume, to distinguish it from the two subsequent plays; which, being *altered* by Shakspeare, assumed the new titles of the *Second and Third Parts of King Henry VI* that they might not be confounded with the orininal pieces on which they were formed. This first part was, I conceive, originally called *The historical play of King Henry VI.* See the Essay at the end of these contested pieces. MALONE.

KING HENRY VI.

PART II.

Persons Represented.

King Henry *the Sixth :*
Humphrey, *Duke of* Glofter, *his uncle.*
Cardinal Beaufort, *Bifhop of* Winchefter, *great uncle to the king.*
Richard Plantagenet, *Duke of* York :
Edward *and* Richard, *his fons.*

Duke *of* Somerfet,
Duke *of* Suffolk,
Duke *of* Buckingham,   } *of the king's party.*
Lord Clifford,
Young Clifford, *his fon.*

Earl *of* Salifbury,   } *of the* York *faction.*
Earl *of* Warwick,

Lord Scales, *Governour of the Tower.* Lord Say.
Sir Humphrey Stafford, *and his brother.* Sir John Stanley.
A Sea-captain, Mafter, and Mafter's Mate, and Walter Whitmore.
Two Gentlemen, prifoners with Suffolk.
A Herald. Vaux.
Hume *and* Southwell, *two priefts.*
Bolingbroke, *a Conjuror. A fpirit raifed by him.*
Thomas Horner, *an Armourer.* Peter, *his man.*
Clerk *of* Chatham. *Mayor of* Saint Alban's.
Simpcox, *an Impoftor. Two Murderers.*
Jack Cade, *a Rebel :*
George, John, Dick, Smith, *the Weaver,* Michael, *&c. his followers.*
Alexander Iden, *a Kentifh Gentleman.*

Margaret, *Queen to King* Henry.
Eleanor, *Dutchefs of* Glofter.
Margery Jourdain, *a Witch.*
Wife to Simpcox.

Lords, Ladies, and Attendants ; Petitioners, Aldermen, a Beadle, Sheriff, and Officers ; Citizens, Prentices, Falconers, Guards, Soldiers, Meffengers, &c.

S C E N E, *difperfedly in various parts of* England.

ACT I. SCENE I.

London. *A Room of state in the Palace.*

Flourish of Trumpets : then hautboys. Enter, on one side, king HENRY, *Duke of* GLOSTER, SALISBURY, WARWICK, *and Cardinal* BEAUFORT ; *on the other, Queen* MARGARET, *led in by* SUFFOLK ; YORK, SOMERSET, BUCKINGHAM, *and others, following.*

Suf. As by your high imperial majesty [a]
I had in charge at my depart for France,

As

---

[1] In a note prefixed to the preceding play, I have briefly stated my opinion concerning the drama now before us, and that which follows it; to which the original editors of Shakspeare's works in folio have given the titles of *The Second and Third Parts of King Henry VI.* The *Contention of the two famous houses of Yorke and Lancaster* in two parts, was published in quarto, in 1600 ; and the first part was entered on the Stationers' books, (as Mr. Steevens has observed,) March 12, 1593-4. On these two plays, which I believe to have been written by some preceding author, before the year 1590, Shakspeare formed, as I conceive, this and the following drama ; altering, retrenching, or amplifying, as he thought proper. The reasons on which this hypothesis is founded, I shall subjoin at large at the end of *The Third Part of King Henry VI.* At present it is only necessary to apprize the reader of the method observed in the printing of these plays. All the lines printed in the usual manner, are found in the original quarto plays (or at least with such minute variations as are not worth noticing); and those, I conceive, Shakspeare adopted as he found them. The lines to which inverted commas are prefixed, were, if my hypothesis be well founded, retouched, and greatly improved by him ; and those with asterisks were his own original production ; the embroidery with which he ornamented the coarse stuff that had been aukwardly made up for the stage by some of his contemporaries. The speeches which he new-modelled, he improved, sometimes by amplification, and sometimes by retrenchment. These two pieces, I imagine, were produced in their present form in 1591. See *An Attempt to ascertain the order of Shakspeare's plays,* Vol. I. and the Dissertation at the end of *The Third Part of King Henry VI.* Dr. Johnson observes very justly, that these two parts were not written without a *dependance* on the first. Undoubtedly not ; the old play of *K. Henry VI.* (or, as it is now called, *The first part,*) certainly had been exhibited before these were written in *any form*. But it does not follow from this concession, either that *The Contention of the two houses, &c.* in two parts, was written by the author of the former play, or that Shakspeare was the author of these two pieces as they originally appeared. MALONE.

This

As procurator to your excellence [3],
To marry princefs Margaret för your grace ;
So, in the famous ancient city, Tours,—
In prefence of the kings of France and Sicil,
The dukes of Orleans, Calaber, Bretaigne, and Alençon,
Seven earls, twelve barons, and twenty reverend bifhops,
I have perform'd my tafk, and was efpous'd :
And humbly now upon my bended-knee,
In fight of England and her lordly peers,
Deliver up my title in the queen
To your moft gracious hands, that are [4] the fubftance
Of that great fhadow I did reprefent ;
The happieft gift that ever marquefs gave,
The faireft queen that ever king receiv'd.

   K. Hen. Suffolk, arife.   Welcome, queen Margaret:
I can exprefs no kinder fign of love,
Than this kind kifs.—O Lord, that lends me life,
Lend me a heart replete with thankfulnefs !
For thou haft given me, in this beauteous face,
' A world of earthly bleffings to my foul,
' If fympathy of love unite our thoughts.

   ' *Q. Mar.* Great king of England, and my gracious lord ;

This and *The third part of King Henry VI.* contain that troublefome
period of this prince's reign, which took in the whole contention betwixt
the houfes of York and Lancafter.   The prefent fcene opens with king
Henry's marriage, which was in the twenty third year of his reign
[A. D. 1445] ; and clofes with the firft battle fought at St. Albans,
and won by the York faction, in the thirty-third year of his reign
[1455] : fo that it comprizes the hiftory and tranfactions of ten years.
                                  THEOBALD.
   This play was altered by Crowne, and acted in 1682.   STEEVENS
   [2] *As by our high,* &c]   It is apparent that this play begins where the
former ends, and continues the feries of transactions of which it prefup-
pofes the firft part already known.   This is a fufficient proof that the
fecond and third parts were not written without dependance on the firft,
though they were printed as containing a complete period of hiftory.
                                      JOHNSON.
   [3] *As procurator to your excellence,* &c]   So, in Holinfhed, p. 625:
" The marqueffe of Suffolk, as procurator to king Henrie, efpoufed the
faid ladie in the church of faint Martins.   At the which marriage were
prefent the father and mother of the bride ; the French king himfelf
that was uncle to the hufband, and the French queen alfo that was aunt
to the wife.   There were alfo the dukes of Orleance, of Calabre, of
Alanfon, and of Britaine, feaven earles, twelve barons, twenty bifhops,"
&c.   STEEVENS.
   This paffage Holinfhed tranfcribed *verbatim* from Hall.   MALONE.
   [4] *— that are—*] i. e. to the gracious hands of you, my fovereign,
who are, &c.   In the old play the line ftands :
     Unto your gracious *excellence* that are, &c.   MALONE.

                                     ' The

‘ The mutual conference [5] that my mind hath had—
‘ By day, by night ; waking, and in my dreams ;
‘ In courtly company, or at my beads,—
‘ With you mine alder-lefelt fovereign [6],
‘ Makes me the bolder to falute my king
‘ With ruder terms ; fuch as my wit affords,
‘ And over-joy of heart doth minifter.

‘ *K. Hen.* Her fight did ravifh : but her grace in fpeech,
‘ Her words y-clad with wifdom's majelly,
‘ Makes me, from wondering, fall to weeping joys [7] ;
‘ Such is the fulnefs of my heart's content.—
‘ Lords, with one cheerful voice welcome my love.

All. Long live queen Margaret, England's happinefs !

Q. Mar. We thank you all.   [*Flourifh.*

Suf. My lord protector, fo it pleafe your grace,
Here are the articles of contracted peace,
Between our fovereign and the French king Charles,
‘ For eighteen months concluded by confent.

Glo. [*reads.*] Imprimis, *It is agreed between the French
king, Charles, and William de la Poole, marquefs of Suffolk,
ambaffador for Henry king of England,—that the faid Henry
fhall efpoufe the faid Margaret, daughter unto Reignier king of
Naples, Sicilia, and Jerufalem ; and crown her queen of
England, ere the thirtieth of May next enfuing.—*Item,—*That*

---

5 *The mutual conference—*] I am the bolder to addrefs you, having
already familiarized you t my imagination   JOHNSON.

6 — *mine* alder-lefelt *fovereign,*] *Alder-leveft,* fays Mr. Tyrwhitt,
in his Glos. to Chaucer, fignifies, *deareft of all   Leve* or *lefe,* Sax.
dear; Alder or *Aller,* gen. ca pl. *of all.* MALONE.
The word is ufed by Chaucer, Marfton, and Gafcoigne. STEEVENS.

7 *Makes me, from wondering, fall to* weeping joys;] This *weeping
joy,* of which there is no trace in the original play, Shakfpeare was
extremely fond of; having introduced it in *Much ado about nothing,
K. Richard II. Macbeth,* and *King Lear.* This and the preceding
fpeech ftand thus in the original play in quarto. I tranfcribe them that
the reader may be the better able to udge concerning my hypothefis ;
and fhall quote a few other paffages for the fame purpofe. To exhibit
all the fpeeches that Shakfpeare has altered, would be almoft to print
the two plays twice :
     Queen. The exceffive love I beare unto your grace,
Forbids me to be lavifh of my toi gue,
Lelt I fhould fpeake more than befeems a woman.
Let this fuffice: my blifs is in your liking ;
And nothing can make poor Margaret miferable
Unlefs the frowne of mightie England's king.
     Fr. King. Her lookes did wound, but now her fpeech doth
Lovely Queen Margaret, fit down by my fide ;   [pierce.
And uncle Glofter, and you lordly peers,
With one voice welcome my beloved Queene. MALONE.

th

the duchy of Anjou and the county of Maine*, shall be released and delivered to the king her father—

   K. Hen. Uncle, how now ?

   Glo. Pardon me, gracious lord ;
Some sudden qualm hath struck me at the heart,
And dimm'd mine eyes, that I can read no further.

   K. Hen. Uncle of Winchester, I pray, read on.

   Win. Item,—*It is further agreed between them,—that the dutchies of Anjou and Maine shall be released and delivered over to the king her father ; and she sent over of the king of England's own proper cost and charges, without having dowry.*

   K. Hen. They please us well.—Lord marquess, kneel
      down ;
We here create thee the first duke of Suffolk,
And girt thee with the sword —
Cousin of York, we here discharge your grace
From being regent in the parts of France,
Till term of eighteen months be full expir'd —
Thanks, uncle Winchester, Gloster, York, and Bucking-
      ham,
Somerset, Salisbury, and Warwick ;
We thank you all for this great favour done,
In entertainment to my princely queen.
Come, let us in ; and with all speed provide
To see her coronation be perform'd.

         [*Exeunt* King, Queen, *and* SUFFOLK.

   Glo. Brave peers of England, pillars of the state,
' To you duke Humphrey must unload his grief,
' Your grief, the common grief of all the land.
' What ! did my brother Henry spend his youth,
' His valour, coin, and people, in the wars ?
' Did he so often lodge in open field,
' In winter's cold, and summer's parching heat,
' To conquer France, his true inheritance ?
' And did my brother Bedford toil his wits,
' To keep by policy what Henry got ?
' Have you yourselves, Somerset, Buckingham,

---

  * *and the* county *of Maine*—] So the Chronicles; yet when the Cardinal afterwards reads this article, he says,—" It is further agreed —that the *dutchies* of Anjou and *Maine* shall be released and delivered *over,*" &c. But the words in the instrument could not thus vary, whilst it was passing from the hands of the duke to those of the Cardinal. For this inaccuracy Shakspeare must answer, the author of the original play not having been guilty of it. This kind of inaccuracy is, I believe, peculiar to our poet; for I have never met with any thing similar in any other writer. He has again fallen into the same impropriety in *All's Well that Ends Well.* MALONE.

                          ' Brave

‘ Brave York, Salisbury, and victorious Warwick,
‘ Receiv’d deep scars in France and Normandy?
‘ Or hath mine uncle Beaufort, and myself,
‘ With all the learned council of the realm,
‘ Study’d so long, sat in the council-house,
‘ Early and late, debating to and fro
‘ How France and Frenchmen might be kept in awe?
‘ And hath his highness in his infancy
‘ Been crown’d * in Paris, in despight of foes;
‘ And shall these labours, and these honours, die?
‘ Shall Henry’s conquest, Bedford’s vigilance,
‘ Your deeds of war, and all our counsel, die?
‘ O peers of England, shameful is this league!
‘ Fatal this marriage! cancelling your fame;
‘ Blotting your names from books of memory;
‘ Razing the characters of your renown;
‘ Defacing monuments of conquer’d France;
‘ Undoing all, as all had never been!
    ‘ *Car.* Nephew, what means this passionate discourse?
‘ This peroration with such circumstance 8 ?
‘ For France, ’tis ours; and we will keep it still.
    * *Glo.* Ay, uncle, we will keep it, if we can;
* But now it is impossible we should:
Suffolk, the new-made duke that rules the roast,
* Hath given the dutchies of Anjou and Maine
* Unto the poor king Reignier, whose large style
* Agrees not with the leanness of his purse 9.
    * *Sal.* Now, by the death of him that dy’d for all,
* These counties were the keys of Normandy:—
But wherefore weeps Warwick, my valiant son?
    ‘ *War.* For grief that they are past recovery:
‘ For, were there hope to conquer them again,
‘ My sword should shed hot blood, mine eyes no tears.
‘ Anjou and Maine! myself did win them both;
‘ Those provinces these arms of mine did conquer:
‘ And are the cities, that I got with wounds,

---

* Been *crown’d*—] The word *Been* was supplied by Mr. Steevens.
                                                    MALONE.

; 8 *This peroration with such circumstance?*] This speech crowded
with so many instances of aggravation. JOHNSON.

9 -- *whose large style*
    Agrees not with the leanness of his purse.] So Holinshed: “King
Reigner hir father, for all his *long stile*, had too short a purse to send
his daughter honourably to the king hir spowse.” MALONE.

‘ Deliver’d

' Deliver'd up again with peaceful words ' ?
' Mort Dieu'!

   * *York.* For Suffolk's duke—may he be fuffocate,
* That dims the honour of this warlike ifle!
' France fhould have torn and rent my very heart,
* Before I would have yielded to this league.
' I never read but England's kings have had
' Large fums of gold, and dowries, with their wives :
' And our king Henry gives away his own,
' To match with her that brings no vantages.

   * *Glo.* A proper jeft, and never heard before,
* That Suffolk fhould demand a whole fifteenth,
* For cofts and charges in tranfporting her !
* She fhould have ftaid in France, and ftarv'd in France,
* Before—

   * *Car.* My lord of Glofter, now you grow too hot ;
* It was the pleafure of my lord the king.

   * *Glo.* My lord of Winchefter, I know your mind ;
' 'Tis not my fpeeches that you do miflike,
' But 'tis my prefence that doth trouble you.
' Rancour will out : Proud prelate, in thy face
' I fee thy fury : if I longer ftay,
' We fhall begin our ancient bickerings [2] —
Lordings, farewel : and fay, when I am gone,
I prophefy'd—France will be loft ere long.   [*Exit.*

   Car. So, there goes our protector in a rage.
'Tis known to you, he is mine enemy :
* Nay, more, an enemy unto you all ;
* And no great friend, I fear me, to the king.
* Confider, lords,—he is the next of blood,
* And heir apparent to the Englifh crown :
* Had Henry got an empire by his marriage,
* And all the wealthy kingdoms of the weft [3],

---

1 *And are the cities,* &c.] The indignation of Warwick is natural, and I wifh it had been better expreffed ; there is a kind of jingle intended in *wounds* and *words.* JOHNSON

In the old play the jingle is more ftriking, " And muft that then which we won with our *fwords,* be given away with *words ?*" MALONE.

2 — bickerings.] To *bicker* is to *fkirmifh.* In the ancient metrical romance of *Guy Earl of Warwick,* bl. l no date, the heroes confult whether they fhould *bicker* on the walls, or defcend to battle on the pain *Levi pugna congredior* is the expreffion by which Barret in his *Alvearie,* or *Quadruple Dict.* 1580, explains the verb to *bicker.* STEEVENS.

3 — *of the weft.*] Certainly Shakfpeare wrote—*eaft.* WARBURTON.
There are wealthy kingdoms in the *weft* as well as in the *eaft,* and the weftern kingdoms were more likely to be in the thought of the fpeake. JOHNSON.

              * There's

* There's reafon he fhould be difpleas'd at it.
* Look to it, lords ; let not his fmoothing words
* Bewitch your hearts ; be wife, and circumfpect.
' What though the common people favour him,
' Calling him—*Humphrey, the good duke of Glofter ;*
' Clapping their hands, and crying with loud voice—
' *Jefu maintain your royal excellence!*
' With—*God preferve the good duke Humphrey!*
' I fear me, lords, for all this flattering glofs,
' He will be found a dangerous protector.
  * *Buck* Why fhould he then protect our fovereign,
* He being of age to govern of himfelf?—
' Coufin of Somerfet, join you with me,
' And all together,—with the duke of Suffolk,—
' We'll quickly hoife duke Humphrey from his feat.
  *. *Car.* This weighty bufinefs will not brook delay;
* I'll to the duke of Suffolk prefently.   [*Exit.*
' *Som.* Coufin of Buckingham, though Humphrey's pride,
' And greatnefs of his place be grief to us,
' Yet let us watch the haughty cardinal ;
' His infolence is more intolerable
' Than all the princes in the land befide ;
\' If Glofter be difplac'd, he'll be protector.
  Buck Or thou, or I, Somerfet, will be protector.
*Defpight duke Humphry, or the cardinal.
          ` [*Exeunt* BUCKINGHAM *and* SOMERSET.
  Sal. Pride went before, ambition follows him.
' While thefe do labour for their own preferment,
' Behoves it us to labour for the realm.
' I never faw but Humphrey duke of Glofter
' Did bear him like a noble gentleman.
' Oft have I feen the haughty cardinal—
' More like a foldier, than a man o'the church,
' As ftout, and proud, as he were lord of all,—
' Swear like a ruffian, and demean himfelf
' Unlike the ruler of a common-weal.—
' Warwick my fon, the comfort of my age!
' Thy deeds, thy plainnefs, and thy houfe-keeping,
' Hath won the greateft favour of the commons,
' Excepting none but good duke Humphrey.—
' And, brother York *, thy acts in Ireland,

                                             In

4 *And, brother York,*] Richard Plantagenet, Duke of York, married
Cecely, the daughter of Ralf Nevil, Earl of Weftmoreland: Richard
Nevil, Earl of Salifbury, was fon to the Earl of Weftmoreland by a fecond wife. He married Alice, the only daughter of Thomas Mont.-
cute, Earl of Salifbury, who was killed at the fiege of Orleans ; and
                                             in

‘ In bringing them to civil difcipline * ;
‘ Thy late exploits done in the heart of France,
‘ When thou wert regent for our fovereign,
‘ Have made thee fear'd, and honour'd, of the people :—
‘ Join we together, for the publick good ;
‘ In what we can, to bridle and fupprefs
‘ The pride of Suffolk, and the Cardinal,
‘ With Somerfet's, and Buckingham's ambition ;
‘ And, as we may, cherifh duke Humphrey's deeds,
‘ While they do tend the profit of the land 5.

   * *War.* So God help Warwick, as he loves the land,
* And common profit of his country !

   * *York.* And fo fays York, for he hath greateft caufe.

   Sal. Then let's make hafte away, and look unto the main.

   War. Unto the main ! O father, Maine is loft ;
That Maine, which by main force Warwick did win,
* And would have kept, fo long as breath did laft :
Main chance, father, you meant ; but I meant Maine ;
Which I will win from France, or elfe be flain.

               [*Exeunt* WARWICK *and* SALISBURY.

   York. Anjou and Maine are given to the French ;
* Paris is loft ; the ftate of Normandy
* Stands on a tickle point 6, now they are gone:
* Suffolk concluded on the articles ;
* The peers agreed ; and Henry was well pleas'd,
* To change two dukedoms for a duke's fair daughter.
* I cannot blame them all ; What is't to them ?

in confequence of that alliance obtained the title of Salifbury
in 1428. His eldeft fon Richard, having married the fifter and
heir of Henry Beauchamp Earl of Warwick, was created Earl of Warwick, in 1449. MALONE.

   * — *to civil difcipline;*] This is an anachronifm   The prefent fcene
is in 1445, but Richard Duke of York was not viceroy of Ireland till
1449. MALONE.

   5 — the *profit of the land.*] I think we might read—more clearly—*to*
profit of the land, i. e. to profit themfelves by it ; unlefs *'tends* be
written for *attend.* STEEVENS.

  Perhaps *tend* has here the fame meaning as *tender* in a fubfequent
fcene :
      “ I *tender* fo the fafety of my liege.”
Or it may have been put for *intend* ; while they have the advantage of
the commonwealth as their *object.* MALONE.

   6 — *on a* tickle *point,*] *Tickle* is very frequently ufed for *ticklifh* by
poets contemporary with Shakfpeare. So, in the *Spanifh Tragedy,*
1605 :
      “ Now ftands our fortune on a *tickle* point.”
Again, in *Soliman and Perfeda,* 1599 :
      “ The reft by turning of my *tickle* wheel.” STEEVENS

I   * 'Tis

* 'Tis thine they give away, and not their own.
* Pirates may make cheap pennyworths of their pillage,
* And purchafe friends, and give to courtezans,
* Still revelling, like lords, till all be gone :
* While as the filly owner of the goods
* Weeps over them, and wrings his haplefs hands,
* And fhakes his head, and trembling ftands aloof,
* While all is fhar'd, and all is borne away ;
* Ready to ftarve, and dare not touch his own.
* So York muft fit, and fret, and bite his tongue,
* While his own lands are bargain'd for, and fold.
* Methinks, the realms of England, France, and Ireland,
* Bear that proportion to my fleth and blood,
* As did the fatal brand Althea burn'd [7],
* Unto the prince's heart of Calydon [8].
Anjou and Maine, both given unto the French !
Cold news for me ; for I had hope of France,
Even as I have of fertile England's foil.
A day will come, when York fhall claim his own ;
And therefore I will take the Nevils' parts,
And make a fhew of love to proud duke Humphrey,
And, when I fpy advantage, claim the crown,
For that's the golden mark I feek to hit :
Nor fhall proud Lancafter ufurp my right,
Nor hold the fcepter in his childifh fift,
Nor wear the diadem upon his head,
Whofe church-like humours fit not for a crown.
Then, York, be ftill a while, till time do ferve :
Watch thou, and wake, when others be afleep,
To pry into the fecrets of the ftate ;
Till Henry, furfeiting in joys of love,
With his new bride, and England's dear-bought queen,
And Humphrey with the peers be fall'n at jars :
Then will I raife aloft the milk-white rofe,
With whofe fweet fmell the air fhall be perfum'd ;
And in my ftandard bear the arms of York,
To grapple with the houfe of Lancafter ;
And, force perforce, I'll make him yield the crown,
Whofe bookifh rule hath pull'd fair England down. [Exit.

7 As did the fatal brand Althea burn'd,] According to the fable, Meleager's life was to continue only fo long as a certain firebrand fhould laft. His mother Althea having thrown it into the fire, he expired in great torment. MALONE.

8 — the prince's heart of Calydon. Meleager. STEEVENS.

SCENE

SCENE II.

The fame.   A Room in the duke of Gloſter's *houſe.*

Enter GLOSTER *and the Dutcheſs.*

Dutch. Why droops my lord, like over-ripen'd corn,
Hanging the head at Ceres' plenteous load ?
* Why doth the great duke Humphrey knit his brows,
* As frowning at the favours of the world ?
* Why are thine eyes fix'd to the ſullen earth,
* Gazing on that which ſeems to dim thy ſight ?
' What ſee'ſt thou there ? king Henry's diadem,
* Inchas'd with all the honours of the world ?
* If ſo, gaze on, and grovel on thy face,
* Until thy head be circled with the ſame.
' Put forth thy hand, reach at the glorious gold :——
' What, is't too ſhort ? I'll lengthen it with mine :
* And, having both together heav'd it up,
* We'll both together, lift our heads to heaven ;
* And never more abaſe our ſight ſo low,
* As to vouchſafe one glance unto the ground.
' *Glo.* O Nell, ſweet Nell, if thou doſt love thy lord,
' Baniſh the canker of ambitious thoughts :
' And may that thought, when I imagine ill
' Againſt my king and nephew, virtuous Henry,
' Be my laſt breathing in this mortal world !
' My troublous dream this night doth make me ſad.
' *Dutch.* What dream'd my lord ? tell me, and I'll re-
    quite it
' With ſweet rehearſal of my morning's dream.
' *Glo.* Methought, this ſtaff, mine office-badge in court,
' Was broke in twain ; by whom I have forgot,
' But, as I think, it was by the cardinal ;
' And on the pieces of the broken wand
' Were plac'd the heads of Edmond duke of Somerſet,
' And William de la Poole firſt duke of Suffolk.
' This was my dream ; what it doth bode, God knows.
' *Dutch.* Tut, this was nothing but an argument,
That he, that breaks a ſtick of Gloſter's grove,
' Shall loſe his head for his preſumption.
' But liſt to me, my Humphrey, my ſweet duke :
Methought, I ſat in ſeat of majeſty,
In the cathedral church of Weſtminſter,

                                          And

And in that chair where kings and queens are crown'd ;
Where Henry, and dame Margaret, kneel'd to me,
' And on my head did set the diadem.
   ' *Glo.* Nay, Eleanor, when must I chide outright :
* Presumptuous dame, ill-nurtur'd Eleanor ! †
Art thou not second woman in the realm ;
And the protector's wife, belov'd of him ?
* Haft thou not worldly pleasure at command,
* Above the reach or compass of thy thought ?
And wilt thou still be hammering treachery,
* To tumble down thy husband, and thyself,
* From top of honour to disgrace's feet ?
Away from me, and let me hear no more.
   ' *Dutch.* What, what, my lord ! are you so cholerick
' With Eleanor, for telling but her dream ?
' Next time I'll keep my dreams unto myself,
' And not be check'd.
   ' *Glo.* Nay, be not angry, I am pleas'd again *.

Enter a Messenger.

   · ' *Mess.* My lord protector, 'tis his highness' pleasure,
" You do prepare to ride unto Saint Albans,
' Whereas the king and queen do mean to hawk 9.
   Glo. I go.—Come, Nell, thou wilt ride with us ?
   ' *Dutch.* Yes, my good lord, I'll follow presently.
[*Exeunt* GLOSTER *and* Messenger.
' Follow I must, I cannot go before,
* While Gloster bears this base and humble mind.
* Were I a man, a duke, and next of blood,
* I would remove these tedious stumbling-blocks,
 * And smooth my way upon their headless necks :
* And, being a woman, I will not be slack
* To play my part in fortune's pageant.

<hr>

† — ill-nurtur'd *Eleanor !*] *Ill-nurtur'd* is *ill-educated.* So, in *Venus and Adonis :*
    " Were I hard-favour'd, foul, or wrinkled-old,
    " *Ill-nurtur'd,* crooked, churlish, harsh in voice." MALONE.
  * *Nay, be not angry,* &c.] Instead of this line, we have these two in the old play :
    " Nay, Nell, I'll give no credit to a dream ;
    " But I would have thee to think on no such things." MALONE.
  9 Whereas *the king and queen do mean to hawk.*] *Whereas* is the same as *where* ; and seems to be brought into use only on account of its being a dissyllable. So, in the *Tryal of Treasure,* 1567 :
    " *Whereas* she is resident, I must needes be."
Again, in Daniel's *Tragedy of Cleopatra,* 1594:
    " That I should pass *whereas* Octavia stands
    " To view my misery," &c. STEEVENS.

' Where

' Where are you there ! Sir John [1] ! nay, fear not, man,
' We are alone ; here's none but thee, and I.

Enter HUME.

Hume. Jefu preferve your royal majefty !
' *Dutch.* What fay'ft thou, majefty ! I am but grace.
Hume. But, by the grace of God, and Hume's advice,
' Your Grace's title fhall be multiply'd.

Dutch. What fay'ft thou, man ? haft thou as yet conferr'd
With Margery Jourdain, the cunning witch ;
And Roger Bolingbroke, the conjurer ?
And will they undertake to do me good ?
' *Hume.* This they have promifed,—to fhew your highnefs
A fpirit rais'd from depth of under ground,
' That fhall make anfwer to fuch queftions,
' As by your grace fhall be propounded him.
' *Dutch.* It is enough [2] ; I'll think upon the queftions :
' When from faint Albans we do make return,
' We'll fee thefe things effected to the full.
' Here, Hume, take this reward ; make merry, man,
' With thy confederates in this weighty caufe.

[*Exit* Dutchefs.

* *Hume.* Hume muft make merry with the dutchefs' gold ;
' Marry, and fhall. But, how now, Sir John Hume ?
' Seal up your lips, and give no words but—mum !
' The bufinefs afketh filent fecrecy.
* Dame Eleanor gives gold, to bring the witch :
* Gold cannot come amifs, were fhe a devil.
' Yet have I gold, flies from another coaft :
' I dare not fay, from the rich cardinal,
' And from the great and new-made duke of Suffolk ;

---

1 — *Sir John !*] The title of *Sir* was frequently given to clergymen in ancient times. MALONE.

2 *It is enough*; &c.] This fpeech ftands thus in the old quarto :
" *Elean.* Thanks, good fir John, fome two days hence, I geefs,
" Will fit our time ; then fee that they be here.
" For now, the king is riding to St. Albans,
" And all the dukes and earls along with him.
" When they be gone, then fafely they may come,
" And on the backfide of my orchard here,
" There caft their fpells in filence of the night,
" And fo refolve us of the thing we wifh :—
" Till when, drink that for my fake, and fo farewell."
STEEVENS.

Here we have a fpeech of *ten* lines, with different verfification, and different circumftances, from thofe of the *five* which are found in the folio. What imperfect tranfcript (for fuch the quarto has been called) ever produced fuch a variation ? MALONE.

' Yet

'Yet I do find it so : for, to be plain,
' They, knowing dame Eleanor's aspiring humour,
' Have hired me to undermine the dutchess,
' And buz these conjurations in her brain.'
* They say, A crafty knave does need no broker [3] ;
* Yet am I Suffolk and the cardinal's broker.
* Hume, if you take not heed, you shall go near
* To call them both—a pair of crafty knaves.
* Well, so it stands : And thus, I fear, at last,
* Hume's knavery will be the dutchess' wreck ;
* And her attainture will be Humphrey's fall :
* Sort how it will [4], I shall have gold for all.   [*Exit.*

SCENE III.

The same.   A Room in the palace.

Enter PETER, and Others, with Petitions.

' 1. *Pet.* My masters, let's stand close ; my lord protector
' will come this way by and by, and then we may deliver our
' supplications in the quill [5].
' 2. *Pet.* Marry, the Lord protect him, for he's a good
' man ! Jesu-bless him !

Enter SUFFOLK, and queen MARGARET.

* *Peter.* Here 'a comes, methinks, and the queen with
* him : I'll be the first, sure.

' 2,

---

[3] — *A crafty knave does need no broker :*] This is a proverbial sentence. See Ray's *Collection.* STEEVENS.

[4] Sort *how it will,*] Let the issue be what it will. JOHNSON.
This whole speech is very different in the original play. Instead of the last couplet we find these lines :

   " But whitt, Sir John ; no more of that I trow,
   " For fear you lose your head, before you go." MALONE.

[5] — *in the quill*] Perhaps our supplications *in the quill,* or *in quill,* means no more than our *written* or *penn'd* supplications. We still say, a drawing *in chalk,* for a drawing executed by the use of chalk.
STEEVENS.
In the quill may mean, with great exactness and observance of form, or with the utmost punctilio of ceremony. The phrase seems to be taken from part of the dress of our ancestors, whose ruffs were *quilled.*— While these were wo n, it might be the vogue to say, such a thing is in the *quill,* i. e. in the reigning mode of taste, TOLLET.
To this observation I may add, that after printing began, the similar phrase of a thing being *in print,* was used to express the same circumstance

' 2. *Pet.* Come back, fool ; this is the duke of Suffolk,
' and not my lord protector.

' *Suf.* How now, fellow ? would'st any thing with me ?

' 1. *Pet.* I pray, my lord, pardon me ! I took ye for my
' lord protector..

' *2. Mar.* [reading the superscription.] *To my lord protec-*
' *tor !* are your supplications to his lordship ? Let me see
' them : What is thine ?

' 1. *Pet.* Mine is, an't please your grace, against John
' Goodman, my lord cardinal's man, for keeping my house,
' and lands, and wife and all, from me.

Suf. Thy wife too ? that is some wrong, indeed.—What's
your's ?—What's here ? [*reads*| *Against the duke of Suffolk,*
for enclosing the commons of Melford.—How now, sir knave ?

2. *Pet.* Alas, sir, I am but a poor petitioner of our whole
township.

Peter. [*presenting his petition.*] Against my master, Thomas
Horner, for saying, That the duke of York was the rightful
heir to the crown.

' *2. Mar.* What say'st thou ? Did the duke of York say,
' he was rightful heir to the crown ?

' *Peter.* That my master was [6] ! No, forsooth : my master
' said, That he was ; and that the king was an usurper.

Suf. Who is there ? [*Enter* Servants.]—Take this fellow
in, and send for his master with a pursuivant presently :—
we'll hear more of your matter before the king
[Exeunt Servants, with PETER.

' *2. Mar.* And as for you, that love to be protected
' Under the wings of our protector's grace,
' Begin your suits anew, and sue to him.   [*tears the petitions.*
' Away, base cullions !—Suffolk, let them go.

• *All.* Come, let's be gone.   [*Exeunt* Petitioners.

• *2. Mar.* My lord of Suffolk, say, is this the guise,

stances of exactness " All this" (declares one of the quibbling servants in the *Two Gentlemen of Verona*) " I say *in print,* for in print I
found it." STEEVENS.

6 *That my* master *was !*] The folio reads—That my *mistress* was ;
which has been followed in all subsequent editions. But the context
shews clearly that it was a misprint for *master.* Peter supposes that the
queen had asked, whether the duke of York had said that his *master* (for
so he understands the pronoun *he* in her speech) was rightful heir to the
crown. " That my *master* was heir to the crown ! (he replies) No,
the reverse is the case. My master said, that the duke of York was
heir to the crown." In the *Taming of the Shrew,* mistress and master
are frequently confounded. The mistake arose from these words being
formerly abbreviated in Mss. ; and an M. stood for either one or the
other. MALONE.

• Is

* Is this the fashion in the court of England ?
* Is this the government of Britain's isle,
* And this the royalty of Albion's king?
* What; shall king Henry be a pupil still,
* Under the surly Gloster's governance ?
* Am I a queen in title and in style,
* And must be made a subject to a duke ?
' I tell thee, Poole, when in the city Tours
' Thou ran'st a tilt in honour of my love,
' And stol'st away the ladies' hearts of France ;
' I thought, king Henry had resembled thee,
' In courage, courtship, and proportion :
' But all his mind is bent to holiness, ·
* To number *Ave-Maries* on his beads :
* His champions are—the prophets, and apostles ;
* His weapons, holy saws of sacred writ ;
* His study is his tilt-yard, and his loves
* Are brazen images of canoniz'd saints.
* I would, the college of the cardinals
* Would choose him pope, and carry him to Rome,
* And set the triple crown upon his head ;
* That were a state fit for his holiness.
' *Suf.* Madam, be patient : as I was cause
' Your highness came to England, so will I
' In England work your grace's full content.
* *Q. Mar.* Beside the haught protector, we have Beaufort,
* The imperious churchman ; Somerset, Buckingham,
* And grumbling York : and not the least of these,
* But can do more in England than the king.
* *Suf.* And he of these, that can do most of all,
* Cannot do more in England than the Nevils :
* Salisbury, and Warwick, are no simple peers.
' *Q. Mar.* Not all these lords do vex me half so much,
' As that proud dame, the lord protector's wife.
' She sweeps it through the court with troops of ladies,
' More like an empress, than duke Humphrey's wife ;
Strangers in court do take her for the queen :
* She bears a duke's revenues on her back,
* And in her heart she scorns our poverty :
* Shall I not live to be aveng'd on her ?
* Contemptuous base-born callat as she is,
' She vaunted 'mongst her minions t'other day,
The very train of her worst wearing-gown
Was better worth than all my father's lands,

* Till

* Till Suffolk gave two dukedoms [8] for his daughter.
' *Suf.* Madam, myself have lim'd a bush for her [9];
* And plac'd a quire of such enticing birds,
* That she will light to listen to the lays,
* And never mount to trouble you again.
* So, let her rest: And, madam, list to me;
* For I am bold to counsel you in this.
* Although we fancy not the cardinal,
* Yet must we join with him, and with the lords,
* Till we have brought duke Humphrey in disgrace.
* As for the duke of York,—this late complaint '
* Will make but little for his benefit:
* So, one by one, we'll weed them all at last,
* And you yourself shall steer the happy helm.

Enter king HENRY, YORK, *and* SOMERSET *conversing with him;* Duke *and* Dutchess *of* GLOSTER, *Cardinal* BEAU-FORT, BUCKINGHAM, SALISBURY, *and* WARWICK.

K. Hen. For my part, noble lords, I care not which;
Or Somerset, or York, all's one to me.
York. If York have ill demean'd himself in France,
Then let him be deny'd the regentship.
Som. If Somerset be unworthy of the place,
Let York be regent, I will yield to him.
War. Whether your grace be worthy, yea, or no,
Dispute not that; York is the worthier.
Car. Ambitious Warwick, let thy betters speak.
War. The cardinal's not my better in the field.
Buck. All in this presence are thy betters, Warwick.
War. Warwick may live to be the best of all.
* *Sal.* Peace, son;—and shew some reason, Buckingham,
* Why Somerset should be preferr'd in this.
* *Q. Mar.* Because the king, forsooth, will have it so.
' *Glo.* Madam, the king is old enough himself
' To give his censure [2]: these are no women's matters.

8 — *two dukedoms*—] The duchies of Anjou and Maine, which Henry surrendered to Reignier, on his marriage with Margaret. See Sc. I. MALONE
9 —*lim'd a bush for her;*] In the original play in quarto:
 " I have let lime twigs that will entangle them." MALONE.
1 — *this late complaint*] That is the complaint of Peter the armourer's man against his master, for saying that York was the rightful king. JOHNSON.
2 — *his* censure:] Through all these plays *censure* is used in an indifferent sense, simply for judgment or opinion. JOHNSON.
It is so used by all the contemporaries of Shakspeare. MALONE.

Q. Mar.

' *Q. Mar.* If he be old enough, what needs your grace
' To be protector of his excellence?
' *Glo.* Madám, I am protector of the realm;
' And, at his pleasure, will refign my place.
' *Suf.* Refign it then, and leave thine infolence.
' Since thou wert king, (as who is king, but thou!)
' The commonwealth hath daily run to wreck:
* The Dauphin hath prevail'd beyond the feas;
* And all the peers and nobles of the realm
* Have been as bondmen to thy fovereignty.
* *Car.* The commons haft thou rack'd; the clergy's bags
* Are lank and lean with thy extortions.
* *Som.* Thy fumptuous buildings, and thy wife's attire,
* Have coft a mafs of publick treafury.
* *Buck.* Thy cruelty in execution,
* Upon offenders, hath exceeded law,
* And left thee to the mercy of the law.
' *Q. Mar.* Thy fale of offices, and towns in France,——
* If they were known, as the fufpect is great,——
* Would make thee quickly hop without thy head.

            [*Exit* GLOSTER. *The Queen drops her fan.*
' Give me my fan ³: What, minion! can you not?

                    [*gives the* Dutchefs *a box on the ear.*
' I cry you mercy, madam; Was it you?
' *Dutch.* Was't I? yea, I it was, proud Frenchwoman:
' Could I come near your beauty with my nails,
I'd fet my ten commandments in your face ⁴.

    K. Hen. Sweet aunt, be quiet; 'twas againft her will.
' *Dutch.* Againft her will! good king, look to't in time;
' She'll hamper thee, and dandle thee like a baby:
* Though in this place moft mafter wear no breeches,
She fhall not ftrike dame Eleanor unreveng'd.

                        [*Exit* Dutchefs.⁵
                            * *Buck.*

---

³ *Give me my* fan;] In the original play the queen drops not a *fan,*
but a *glove.*
    "Give me my glove; why minion, can you not fee?"
                                    MALONE.
   4 *I'd fet my* ten commandments *in your face.*] So, in *The Play of
the Four P's,* 1569:
    "Now ten times I befeeche him that hie fits,
    "Thy wives x com. may ferche thy five wits."
Again, in *Selimus Emperor of the Turks,* 1594: "I would fet a tap
abroach, and not live in fear of my wife's *ten commandments.*"
                                  STEEVENS.
  5 *Exit* Dutchefs.] The quarto adds, after the exit of Eleanor, the
following:
    "*King.* Believe me, my love, thou wert much to blame.
                             "I would

* *Buck.* Lord cardinal, I will follow Eleanor,
* And liften after Humphrey, how he proceeds :
* She's tickled now [6]; her fume needs no fpurs,
* She'll gallop faft enough[7] to her deftruction.

[*Exit* BUCKINGHAM.

Re-enter GLOSTER.

* *Glo.* Now, lords, my choler being over-blown
* With walking once about the quadrangle,
* I come to talk of commonwealth affairs.
* As for your fpightful falfe objections,
* Prove them, and I lie open to the law :
* But God in mercy fo deal with my foul,
* As I in duty love my king and country !
* But, to the matter that we have in hand :——
* I fay, my fovereign, York is meeteft man
* To be your regent in the realm of France.

*. *Suf.* Before we make election, give me leave
‘ To fhew fome reafon, of no little force,
‘ That York is moft unmeet of any man.
‘ *York.* I'll tell thee, Suffolk, why I am unmeet.
‘ Firft, for I cannot flatter thee in pride ;
* Next, if I be appointed for the place,
* My lord of Somerfet will keep me here,
* Without difcharge, money, or furniture,
* Till France be won into the Dauphin's hands.
* Laft time, I danc'd attendance on his will,
* Till Paris was befieg'd, famifh'd, and loft.

* *War.* That I can witnefs ; and a fouler fact
* Did never traitor in the land commit.

Suf. Peace, head-ftrong Warwick !
War. Image of pride, why fhould I hold my peace?

Enter Servants of SUFFOLK, *bringing in* HORNER *and*
PETER.

Suf. Becaufe here is a man accus'd of treafon :

“ I would not for a thoufand pounds of gold,
“ My noble uncle had been here in place.——
“ But fee, where he comes! I am glad he met her not.”. STEEV.
[6] *She's* tickled *now* ;] *Tickled* is here ufed as a trifyllable. The editor of the fecond folio, not perceiving this reads—“ her fume *can need* no fpurs ;” in which he has been followed by all the fubfequent editors MALONE.

[7] — faft *enough*—] The folio reads—*farre* enough. Corrected by Mr. Pope. MALONE.

Pray

Pray God, the duke of York excufe himfelf!

   * *York.* Doth any one accufe York for a traitor?

   * *K. Hen.* What mean'ft thou, Suffolk? tell me: What
       are thefe?

   ' *Suf.* Pleafe it your majefty, this is the man

' That doth accufe his mafter of high treafon:

' His words were thefe;—that Richard, duke of York,

' Was rightful heir unto the Englifh crown;

' And that your majefty was an ufurper.

   ' *K. Hen.* Say, man, were thefe thy words?

   Hor. An't fhall pleafe your majefty, I never faid nor
thought any fuch matter: God is my witnefs, I am falfely
accus'd by the villain.

   ' *Pet.* By thefe ten bones[8], my lords, [*holding up his*
 ' *hands*] he did fpeak them to me in the garret one night, as
we were fcouring my lord of York's armour.

   * *York.* Bafe dunghill villain, and mechanical,
 * I'll have thy head for this thy traitor's fpeech:

' I do befeech your royal majefty.

' Let him have all the rigour of the law.

   Hor. Alas, my lord, hang me, if ever I fpake the words.
My accufer is my prentice; and when I did correct him
for his fault the other day, he did vow upon his knees he
would be even with me: I have good witnefs of this; therefore, I befeech your majefty, do not caft away an honeft man
for a villain's accufation.

   K. Hen. Uncle, what fhall we fay to this in law?

   ' *Glo.* This doom, my lord, if I may judge.

' Let Somerfet be regent o'er the French,

' Becaufe in York this breeds fufpicion:

' And let thefe have a day appointed them[9]

                               ' For

---

   8 *By thefe ten bones*, &c.] We have juft heard a dutchefs threaten *to
fet her ten commandments* in the face of a queen. The jefts in this play
turn rather too much on the enumeration of fingers. This adjuration is,
however, very ancient. So, in *The longer thou liveft, the more Fool
thou art,* 1570:
     " By thefe *tenne bones* I will, I have fworne."
   It occurs likewife in the myftery of *Candlemas Day,* in *Hycke Scorner,*
and in *Monfieur Thomas,* 1637. STEEVENS.

   9 *And let them have a day appointed them,* &c.] In the original play,
quarto 1600, the correfponding lines ftand thus:
     The law, my lord, is this. By cafe it refts fufpicious,
     That a day of combat be appointed,
     And thefe to try each other's right or wrong,
     Which fhall be on the thirtieth of this month,
     With ebon ftaves and fandbags combating,
     In Smithfield, before your royal majefty.

                                     An

‘ For fingle combat, in convenient place;
‘ For he hath witnefs of his fervant's malice:
‘ This is the law, and this duke Humphrey's doom ‘.
    Som. I humbly thank your royal majefty.
    Hor. And I accept the combat willingly.
    Pet. Alas, my lord, I cannot fight; * for God's fake,
* pity my cafe! the fpight of man prevaileth againft me.
* O, Lord have mercy upon me! I fhall never be able
* to fight a blow: O Lord, my heart!
    Glo. Sirrah, or you muft fight, or elfe be hang'd.
    ‘ *K. Hen.* Away with them to prifon: and the day
‘ Of combat fhall be the laft of the next month.——
* Come, Somerfet, we'll fee thee fent away.   [*Exeunt.*

An opinion has prevailed that *The whole Contention*, &c. printed in
1600, was an imperfect furreptitious copy of Shakfpeare's play as exhibited in the folio; but what fpurious copy, or imperfect tranfcript
taken in fhort-hand, ever produced fuch variations as thefe? MALONE.
    1 '—— *duke Humphrey's doom*.] After this line, Mr. Theobald introdu-
ced from a longer fpeech in the quarto, the two following lines:
    “ *King.* Then be it fo. My lord of Somerfit,
    “ We make your grace regent over the French.”
The plea urged by Theobald for their introduction was, that otherwife
Somerfet thanks the king before he had declared his appointment; but
Shakfpeare, I fuppofe, thought Henry's affent might be expreffed by a
nod. Somerfet knew that Humphry's *doom* was final; as likewife did the
Armourer, for he, like Somerfet, accepts the combat, without waiting
for the king's confirmation of what Glofter had faid. Shakfpeare therefore not having introduced the following fpeech, which is found in the
firft copy, we have no right to infert it. That it was not intended to
be preferved, appears from the concluding line of the prefent fcene, in
which Henry addreffes Somerfet; whereas in the quarto, Somerfet *goes
out*, on his appointment. This is one of thofe minute circumftances
which may be urged to fhew that thefe plays, however afterwards worked up by Shakfpeare, were *originally* the production of another author,
and that the quarto edition of 1600 was printed from the *copy* originally
written by that author, whoever he was. MALONE.
    After the lines inferted by Theobald, the king continues his fpeech
thus:
    —— over the French:
    And to defend our rights 'gainft foreign foes,
    · And fo do good unto the realm of France.
    Make hafte, my lord; 'tis time that you were gone:
    The time of truce, I think, is full expr'd.
        Som. I humbly thank your royal majefty,
    And take my leave, to poft with fpeed to France.   [*Exit* Som.
        King. Come, uncle Glofter; now let's have our horfe,
    ·For we will to St. Albans prefently.
    Madam, your hawk, they fay, is fwift of flight,
    And we will try how fhe will fly to-day. [*Exeunt.* STEEVENS.

SCENE

SCENE IV.

The same. The Duke of Glofter's *Garden.*

Enter MARGERY JOURDAIN, HUME, SOUTHWELL, *and* BOLINGBROKE [2].

* *Hume.* Come, my mafters; the dutchefs, I tell you,
* expects performance of your promifes.
* *Boiling.* Mafter Hume, we are therefore provided:,
* Will her ladyfhip behold and hear our exorcifms?
* *Hume.* Ay; What elfe? fear you not her courage.
* *Boling.* I have heard her reported to be a woman of
* an invincible fpirit: But it fhall be convenient, mafter
* Hume, that you be by her aloft, while we be bufy be-
* low; and fo, I pray you, go in God's·name, and leave
' us. [*Exit* Hume.] Mother Jourdain, be you proftrate,.and
' grovel on the earth:—* John Southwell,·read you; and
* let us to our work.

Enter Dutchefs, *above.*

* *Dutch.* Well faid, my mafters; and welcome all. To
* this geer; the fooner the better.
* *Boling.* Patience, good lady; wizards know their
times:
Deep night, dark night, the filent of the night [3],

' The

---

2 *Enter*, &c.] The quarto reads:
Enter ELEANOR, *with Sir* John HUM, Roger BOLINGBROKE, *a con-
jurer, and* Margaret JOURDAINE, *a witch.*
   Eleanor. Here, fir John, take this fcroll of paper here,
Wherein is writ the queftions you fhall afk:
And I will ftand upon this tower here,
And hear the fpirit what it fays to you;
And to my queftions write the anfwers down.
        [*She goes up to the tower.*
                STEEVENS.
3 — *the* filent *of the* night,] Silent, though an adjective, is ufed by
Shakfpeare as a fubftantive. So, in *The Tempeft*, the *vaft* of night.is
ufed for the greateft part of it. The old quarto read —*the* filence *of the*
night. The variation between the copies is worth notice.
      Bolingbroke makes a circle.
   Bol. Dark night, dread night, the *filence* of the night,
Wherein the furies mafk in hellifh troops,
Send up, I charge you, from Cocytus' lake

‘ The time of night when Troy was fet on fire ;
‘ The time when fcritch-owls cry, and ban-dogs howl [4],
‘ And fpirits walk, and ghofts break up their graves,
‘ That time beft fits the work we have in hand.
‘ Madam, fit you, and fear not ; whom we raife,
‘ We will make faft within a hallow’d verge.
> [*Here they perform the ceremonies appertaining, and make
> the circle ;* Bolingbroke, *or* Southwell, *reads,* Conjuro
> te, &c. *It thunders and lightens terribly ; then the fpirit
> rifeth.*

* *Spir.* Adfum.
* *M Jourd.* Afmath.
* By the eternal God, whofe name and power
* Thou trembleft at, anfwer that I fhall afk ;
* For, till thou fpeak, thou fhalt not pafs from hence.
> *Spir.* Afk what thou wilt :—That I had faid and done [5] !
> Boling. First, of the king. What fhall of him become [6] ?
> [*Reading out of a paper.*
> Spir.

> The fpirit Afkalen to come to me ;
> To pierce the bowels of this centrick earth,
> And hither come in twinkling of an eye !
> Afkalon, afcend, afcend !"

In a fpeech already quoted from the quarto, Eleanor fays, they have
—caft their fpells in *filence of the night.* STEEVENS.

. 4. — ban dogs howl,] The etymology of the word *ban-dogs* is un-
fettled. They feem, however, to have been defigned by poets to fignify fome terrifick beings whofe office it was *to make night hideous,* like
thofe mentioned in the firft book and eighth fatire of *Horace:*

"———— ferpentes, atque videres
" *Infernas* errare *canes.*" STEEVENS.

Ban-dog is furely a corruption of *band dog;* or rather the firft *d* is
fuppreffed here, as in other compound words. Cole in his Dict. 1679,
renders *ban-dog, canis catenatus.* MALONE.

5 — *That I had faid and done !*] It was anciently believed that fpirits
who were raifed by incantations, remained above ground, and anfwer'd
queftions with reluctance. See both Lucan and Statius. STEEVENS.
So the Apparition fays in *Macbeth,*
" Difmifs me.—Enough."
The words " That I had faid and done !" are not in the old play.

6 — *What fhall of him become ?*] Here is another proof of what has
been already fuggefted. In the quarto, 1600, it is concerted between
Mother Jourdain and Bolingbroke that *he* fhould frame a circle, &c.
and that fhe fhould " fall proftrate on the ground," to " whifper with
the devils below." (Southwell is not introduced in that piece.) Accordingly, as foon as the incantations begin, *Bolingbroke* reads the queftions
out of a paper, as here But our poet has exprefsly laid in the preceding
part of this fcene that Southwell was to read them. Here however he
inadvertently follows his original as it lay before him, forgetting that
confiftently with what he had already written, he fhould have deviated
from

Spir. The duke yet lives, that Henry shall depose;
But him out-live, and die a violent death.

　　　[*As the* Spirit *speaks,* Southwell *writes the answer.*
Boling. What fate awaits the duke of Suffolk?
Spir. By Water shall he die, and take his end.
Boling. What shall befall the Duke of Somerset?
Spir. Let him shun castles?
Safer shall he be upon the sandy plains,
Than where castles mounted stand[7].
‘ Have done, for more I hardly can endure.
　‘ *Boling.* Descend to darkness, and the burning lake:
‘ False fiend, avoid[8]!

　　　　　[*Thunder and lightning.* Spirit *descends.*

Enter YORK, *and* BUCKINGHAM, *hastily, with their guards,
and others.*

‘ *York.* Lay hands upon these traitors, and their trash.
‘ Beldame, I think, we watch'd you at an inch.——
‘ What, madam, are you there? the king and commonweal
‘ Are deeply indebted for this piece of pains;
‘ My lord protector will, I doubt it not,
‘ See you well guerdon'd for these good deserts.
＊ *Dutch.* Not half so bad as thine to England's king,
＊ Injurious duke; that threat'st where is no cause.

from it. He has fallen into the same kind of inconsistency in *Romeo and
Juliet,* by sometimes adhering to and sometimes deserting the poem on
which he formed that tragedy. MALONE.

7 *Than where castles mounted stand.*] I remember to have read this
prophecy in some of our old chronicles, where, I think, it runs thus:
　　　"Safer shall he be on sand,
　　　"Than where mounted castles stand:"
at present I do not recollect where STEEVENS.

8 *False fiend, avoid!*] Instead of this short speech, at the dismission of
the spirit, the old quarto gives us the following:
　　　" Then down, I say, unto the damned pool,
　　　" Where Pluto in his fiery waggon sits,
　　　" Riding, amidst the sing'd and parched smoaks,
　　　" The road of *Dytas,* by the river Styx;
　　　" There howle and burn for ever in those flames:
　　　" Rise, Jordane, rise, and stay thy charming spells:——
　　　" Zounds! we are betray'd!"
Dytas is written by mistake for *Ditis,* the genitive case of *Dis,* which
is used instead of the nominative by more than one ancient author. So,
in Tho. Drant's Translation of the fifth Satire of *Horace,* 1567:
　　　" And by that meanes made manye soles lord *Ditis*' hall to
　　　seeke." STEEVENS.
Here again we have such a variation as never could have arisen from
an imperfect transcript. MALONE.

　　　　　　G 2　　　　　　　　　　　＊ *Buck.*

* *Buck.* True, madam, none at all.   What call you this?
　　　　　　　　　　　　　　　　[*Shewing her papers.*

‘ Away with them ; let them be clapp'd up clofe,
‘ And kept afunder :—You, madam, fhall with us :—
‘ Stafford, take her to thee.——   [*Exit* Dutch. *from above.*
‘ We'll fee your trinkets here all forth-coming ;
‘ All.—Away! [*Exeunt guards, with* SOUTH. BOLING. *&c.*
　　* *York.* Lord Buckingham, methinks, you watch'd her
　　　well [9] :
* A pretty plot, well chofen to build upon !
Now, pray, my lord, let's fee the devil's writ.
What have we here ?　　　　　　　　　　　　　　[*Reads.*
The duke yet lives, that Henry fhall depofe ; .
But him out-live, and die a violent death.

　　* Why, this is juft,
* *Aio te, Æacida, Romanos vincere poffe.*
Well, to the reft :
Tell me*, what fate awaits the duke of Suffolk ?
By Water fhall he die, and take his end.——
What fhall betide the duke of Somerfet ?—— .
Let him fhun caftles ; .
Safer fhall he be upon the fandy plains,
Than where caftles mounted ftand.

* Come, come, my lords ;
* Thefe oracles are hardily attain'd [1],
* And hardly underftood.
‘ The king is now in progrefs towards faint Albans ;
‘ With him, the hufband of this lovely lady :
‘ Thither go thefe news, as faft as horfe can carry them ;

---

　9 *Lord Buckingham, methinks,* &c.] This repetition of the prophecies, which is altogether unneceffary, after what the fpectators had
heard in the fcene immediately preceding, is not to be found in the firft
edition of this play. POPE.
　They are not, it is true, found in this fcene, but they are repeated in
the fubfequent fcene, in which Buckingham brings an account of this
proceeding to the king. This alfo is a *variation* that only could proceed from *various* authors. MALONE.
　* *Tell me,* &c] Yet thefe two words were not in the paper read by
Bolingbroke, which York has now in his hand ; nor are they in the original play. Here we have a fpecies of inaccuracy peculiar to Shakfpeare,
of which he has been guilty in other places. See p. 1103-4, where Glofter
and Winchefter read the fame paper differently, and the note
on that variation, which I had not attended to till that fheet
was worked off. MALONE.
　1 — *are* hardily *attain'd,*] i. e. a great rifque and hazard is run to obtain them. THEOBALD.
　The folio reads—*hardly.* The correction was made by Mr. Theobald, and has been adopted by the fubfequent editors. MALONE.

　　　　　　　　　　　　　　　　　　　　‘ A forry

' A forry breakfaſt for my lord protector.

' *Buck.* Your grace ſhall give me leave, my lord of York,
' To be the poſt, in hope of his reward.

' *York.* At your pleaſure, my good lord.—Who's within there, ho !

Enter a Servant.

Invite my lords of Saliſbury, and Warwick,
' To ſup with me to-morrow night.—Away !   [*Exeunt.*

ACT II. SCENE I.

Saint Albans.

Enter King HENRY, *Queen* MARGARET, GLOSTER, Cardinal, *and* SUFFOLK, *with Falconers hollaing.*

' *Q. Mar.* Believe me, lords, for flying at the brook [2],
' I ſaw not better ſport theſe ſeven years' day :
' Yet, by your leave, the wind was very high ;
And, ten to one, old Joan had not gone out [3].

' *K. Hen.* But what a point, my lord, your falcon made,
' And what a pitch ſhe flew above the reſt* !

' To

---

[2] — *for flying at the brook,*] The falconer's term for hawking at water-fowl. JOHNSON.

[3] — *the wind was very high ;*
And, ten to one, old Joan had not gone out.) I am told by a gentleman better acquainted with falconry than myſelf, that the meaning, however expreſſed, is, that the wind being high, it was ten to one that the old hawk had flown quite away ; a trick which hawks often play their maſters in windy weather. JOHNSON.

The wind was ſo high it was ten to one old Joan would not have taken her flight at the game PERCY.

The ancient books of hawking do not enable me to decide on the merits of ſuch diſcordant explanations. It may yet be remarked, that the terms belonging to this once popular amuſement, were in general ſettled with the utmoſt preciſion ; and I may at leaſt venture to declare, that a miſtreſs might have been kept at a cheaper rate than a falcon. To compound a medicine to cure one of theſe birds of worms, it was neceſſary to deſtroy no fewer animals than a *lamb*, a *culver*, a *pigeon*, a *buck*, and a *cat*. I have this intelligence from the *Booke of Haukinge*, &c. by dame Julyana Bernes, bl. l. no date. STEEVENS.

* *And what a pitch,* &c.] In the old play we find :
" Uncle Gloſter, how high your hawk did ſoar,
" *And on a ſudden ſowe'd the partridge down.*"

The

' To fee how God in all his creatures works !

* Yea, man and birds, are fain of climbing high [4].

Suf. No marvel, an it like your majefty,
My lord protector's hawks do tower fo well;
They know, their mafter loves to be aloft [5],

* And bears his thoughts above his falcon's pitch.

' *Glo* My lord, 'tis but a bafe ignoble mind
' That mounts no higher than a bird can foar.

' *Car.* I thought as much ; he'd be above the clouds.

' *Glo.* Ay, my lord cardinal; How think you by that ?
Were it not good, your grace could fly to heaven ?

* *K. Hen.* The treafury of everlafting joy !

' *Car.* Thy heaven is on earth ; thine eyes and thoughts
⁴ Beat on a crown [6], the treafure of thy heart ;
Pernicious protector, dangerous peer,
That fmooth'ft it fo with king and common-weal !

' *Glo.* What, cardinal, is your priefthood grown perémp-
tory ?

* *Tantæne animis cælestibus iræ ?*

' Churchmen fo hot ? good uncle, hide fuch malice ;

' With fuch holinefs can you do it* ?

' *Suf.* No malice, fir ; no more than well becomes
' So good a quarrel, and fo bad a peer.

Glo. As who, my lord ?

Suf. Why, as you, my lord ;
An't like your lordly lord protectorfhip.

Glo. Why, Suffolk, England knows thine infolence.

Q. Mar. And thy ambition, Glofter.

The variation between thefe lines and thofe in the original play on
which this is founded, is worth notice :

    " Uncle Glofter, how high your hawk d'd foar,

    " *And on a fudden fooc'd the partridge down.*" MALONE.

4 — *are fain of climbing high.*] *Fain,* in this place, fignifies *fond.*
The word (as I am informed) is ftill ufed in Scotland. STEEVENS.

5 — *to be aloft,*] Perhaps alluding to the adage : "High flying hawks
are fit for princes." See Ray's *Collection.* STEEVENS.

6 — *thine eyes and thoughts*
    Beat on *a crown,*] So, in the *Tempeft* :

    " Do not infeft your mind with *beating on*

    " The ftrangenefs of this bufinefs."

Again, in the *Two Noble Kinfmen,* 1634 :

    " This her mind *beats on.*"

I have given thefe inftances of this phrafe, becaufe Dr. Johnfon's Interpretation of it was certainly incorrect. He fuppofed there was an allufion to a hawk's *beating* the wing MALONE.

Again, in Lilly's *Maids Metamorphofis,* 1600 :

    " With him whofe reftlefs *thoughts do beat on* thee." STEEVENS.

* — *can you* do it ?] The old play, quarto 1600, reads more intelli-
gibly,—" Good uncle, can you *doit ?*" MALONE.

                                     K. Hen

K. Hen. I pr'ythee, peace,
Good queen ; and whet not on these furious peers,
For bleſſed 'are the peace-makers on earth.

Car. Let me be bleſſed for the peace I make,
Againſt this proud protector, with my sword !

Glo. Faith, holy uncle, 'would 'twere come to that !
[*Aſide to the* Cardinal.

' *Car.* Marry, when thou dar'ſt. [*Aſide.*

' *Glo.* Make up no factious numbers for the matter,
' In thine own perſon anſwer thy abuſe. [*Aſide.*

' *Car.* Ay, where thou dar'ſt not peep : an if thou dar'ſt,
' This evening, on the eaſt ſide of the grove. [*Aſide.*

' *K. Hen.* How now, my lords ?

' *Car.* Believe me, couſin Gloſter,
' Had not your man put up the fowl ſo ſuddenly,
' We had had more ſport.—Come with thy two-hand ſword.
[*Aſide to* GLO.

Glo. True, uncle.

Car. Are you advis'd ?—the eaſt ſide of the grove 7 ?

Glo. Cardinal, I am with you. [*Aſide.*

K. Hen. Why, how now, uncle Gloſter ?

* *Glo.* Talking of hawking ; nothing elſe, my lord.—
Now, by God's mother, prieſt, I'll ſhave your crown for this,
* Or all my fence ſhall fail 8 [*Aſide.*

* *Car. Medice teipſum ;*
' Protector, ſee to't well, protect yourſelf. } [*Aſid.*

K. Hen. The winds grow high ; ſo do your ſtomachs,
lords 9.

* How irkſome is this muſick to my heart !

* When ſuch ſtrings jar, what hope of harmony ?

7 *Are you* advis'd, &c.] Do you underſtand ?—This line, which in
the old copy is given to Gloſter, was, I think, rightly transferred by Mr.
Theobald to the Cardinal. In the original play the Cardinal deſires Gloſter to bring "his ſword and buckler." The *two-hand ſword* was ſometimes called the *long ſword,* and in common uſe before the introduction
of the rapier. Juſtice Shallow in the *Merry Wives of Windſor* boaſts
of the exploits he had performed in his youth with this inſtrument.
MALONE.

8 — *my fence ſhall fail.*] *Fence* is the art of defence. So, in *Much
Ado about Nothing :*
" Deſpight his nice *fence,* and his active practice." STEEVENS.

9 *The winds grow high, ſo do your ſtomachs, lords.*] This line
Shakſpeare hath injudiciouſly adopted from the old play, changing only
the word *color* [choler] to *ſtomachs.* In the old play the altercation appears not to be concealed from Henry. Here Shakſpeare certainly intended that it ſhould paſs between the Cardinal and Gloſter *aſide* ; and
yet he has inadvertently adopted a line, and added others, that imply
that Henry has heard the appointment they have made. MALONE.

* I pray,

* I pray, my lords, let me compound this ſtrife.

Enter an Inhabitant *of Saint* Albans, *crying,* A Miracle ! *

Glo. What means this noiſe ?
Fellow, what miracle doſt thou proclaim ?
Inhab. A miracle ! a miſacle !
Suf. Come to the king, and tell him what miracle.
Inhab. Forſooth, a blindman at ſaint Alban's ſhrine,
Within this half hour, hath receiv'd his ſight ;
A man, that ne'er ſaw in his life before.
‘ *K. Hen.* Now, God be prais'd ! that to believing ſouls
‘ Gives light in darkneſs, comfort in deſpair !

Enter the Mayor of Saint Albans, *and his brethren ; and* SIMP-
COX, *borne between two perſons in a chair ; his wife and a
great multitude following.*

* *Car.* Here come the townſmen on proceſſion,
* To preſent your highneſs with the man.
* *K. Hen.* Great is his comfort in this earthly vale,
* Although 'by his ſight his ſin be multiply'd.
* *Glo* Stand by, my maſters, bring him near the king,
* His highneſs' pleaſure is to talk with him.
* *K. Hen.* Good fellow, tell us here the circumſtance,
* That we for thee may glorify the Lord.
What, haſt thou been long blind, and now reſtor'd ?
Simp. Born blind, an't pleaſe your grace.
Wife Ay, indeed, was he.
Suf. What woman is this ?
Wife. His wife, an't like your worſhip.
Glo. Had'ſt thou been his mother, thou could'ſt have bet-
　　ter told.
K. Hen. Where wert thou born ?
Simp. At Berwick in the north, an't like your grace.
‘ *K. Henry.* Poor ſoul ! God's goodneſs hath been great
　. to thee :
‘ Let never day nor night unhallow'd paſs,
‘ But ſtill remember what the Lord hath done.
* *2. Mar.* Tell me, good fellow, cam'ſt thou here by
　　chance,
* Or of devotion, to this holy ſhrine ?
‘ *Simp.* God knows, of pure devotion ; being call'd

---

* — *crying, A Miracle !*] This ſcene is founded on a ſtory which Sir
Thomas More has related, and which he ſays was communicated to him
by his father. The impoſtor's name is not mentioned, but he was de-
tected by Humphrey duke of Gloſter, and in the manner here repreſented. See his works, p. 134, edit. 1557. MALONE.

‘ A hundred

‘ A hundred times, and oftner, in my sleep
‘ By good saint Alban; who said,—*Simpcox, come* [1];
‘ *Come, offer at my shrine, and I will help thee.*
 * *Wife.* Most true, forsooth; and many a time and oft
* Myself have heard a voice to call him so.
Car. What, art thou lame?
Simp. Ay, God Almighty help me!
Suf. How cam'st thou so?
Simp. A fall off of a tree.
Wife. A plum-tree, master.
Glo. How long hast thou been blind?
Simp. O, born so, master.
Glo. What, and would'st climb a tree?
Simp. But that in all my life, when I was a youth.
 * *Wife.* Too true; and bought his climbing very dear.
* *Glo.* 'Mass, thou lov'dst plums well, that would'st ven-
 ture so.
‘ *Simp.* Alas, good master, my wife desir'd some dam-
 sons,
‘ And made me climb, with danger of my life.
 * *Glo.* A subtle knave! but yet it shall not serve.—
‘ Let me see thine eyes:—wink now;—now open them:—
‘ In my opinion, yet thou see'st not well.
 ‘ *Simp.* Yes, master, clear as day; I thank God, and
 saint Alban.
Glo. Say'st thou me so? What colour is this cloak of?
Simp. Red, master; red as blood.
Glo. Why, that's well said: what colour is my gown of?
Simp. Black, forsooth; coal-black, as jet.
 K. Hen. Why then, thou know'st what colour jet is of?
Suf. And yet, I think, jet did he never see.
Glo. But cloaks, and gowns, before this day, a many.
* *Wife.* Never, before this day, in all his life.
Glo. Tell me, sirrah, what's my name?
Simp. Alas, master, I know not.
Glo. What's his name?
Simp. I know not.
Glo. Nor his?
Simp. No, indeed, master.

---

1 — Simpcox, *come*;] The old copy has *Simon* Probably *Sim.* only
was set down in the MS. it being a very frequent practice in the dramatick MS. of our author's time to write only the first syllable of proper
names. Mr. Theobald, I find, had made the same emendation, though
it was not followed in the subsequent editions; and an anonymous
writer, I have lately observed, has accounted as I have done for the mistake. MALONE.

Glo.

Glo. What's thine own name?

Simp. Saunder Simpcox, an if it pleafe you, mafter.

Glo. Then Saunder, fit there, the lyingeft knave
In Chriftendom.   If thou hadft been born blind,
Thou might'ft as well have known all our names,
As thus to name the feveral colours we
Do wear.   Sight may diftinguifh of colours;
But fuddenly to nominate them all,
It is impoffible.—
My lords, faint Alban here hath done a miracle;
And would ye not think that cunning * to be great,
That could reftore this cripple to his legs again?

Simp. O, mafter, that you could!

Glo. My mafters of Saint Albans, have you not beadles in
your town, and things call'd whips?

May. Yes, my lord, if it pleafe your grace.

Glo. Then fend for one prefently.

May. Sirrah, go fetch the beadle hither ftraight.
[*Exit an* Attendant.

Glo. Now fetch me a ftool hither by and by.   [*A ftool
brought out.*]   Now, firrah, if you mean to fave yourfelf
from whipping, leap me over this ftool, and run away.

Simp. Alas, mafter, I am not able to ftand alone:
You go about to torture me in vain.

Re-enter Attendant, *with the* Beadle.

Glo. Well, fir, we muft have you find your legs.   Sirrah
beadle, whip him till he leap over that fame ftool.

Bead. I will, my lord.—Come on, firrah; off with your
doublet quickly.

Simp. Alas, mafter, what fhall I do? I am not able to
ftand.

[*After the* Beadle *hath hit him once, he leaps over the
ftool, and runs away; and the people follow, and cry,
A Miracle!*

* *K. Hen.* O God, fee'ft thou this, and bear'ft fo long?

* *Q. Mar.* It made me laugh, to fee the villain run.

* *Glo.* Follow the knave; and take this drab away.

* *Wife.* Alas, fir, we did it for pure need.

Glo. Let them be whipt through every market town till
they come to Berwick, whence they came.
[*Exeunt* Mayor, Beadle, Wife, *&c.*

* —that *cunning*—] Folio—*it* cunning.   Corrected by Mr. Rowe.
That was probably contracted in the Mf. yt.   MALONE.

' *Car.*

‘ *Car.* Duke Humphrey has done a miracle to day.

‘ *Suf.* True ; made the lame to leap, and fly away.

‘. *Glo.* But you have done more miracles than I ;

‘ You made, in a day, my lord, whole towns to fly [2].

Enter BUCKINGHAM.

‘ *K. Hen.* What tidings with our coufin, Buckingham?

‘ *Buck.*· Such as my heart doth tremble to unfold [3].

‘ A fort of naughty perfons, lewdly bent [4],——

‘ Under the countenance and confederacy

‘ Of lady Eleanor, the protector's wife,

‘ The ring-leader and head of this rout,——

‘ Have practis'd dangeroufly againft your ftate,

‘ Dealing with witches, and with conjurers :

‘ Whom we have apprehended in the fact ;

‘ Raifing up wicked fpirits from under ground,

‘ Demanding of king Henry's life and death,

‘ And other of your highnefs' privy council,

‘ As more at large your grace fhall underftand.

‘ *Car.* And fo, my lord protector, by this means

‘ Your lady is forth-coming [5] yet at London.

‘ This news, I think, hath turn'd your weapon's edge ;

‘ ' I is like, my lord, you will not keep your hour.

　　　　　　　　　　　　　　　[*Afide to* GLOSTER.

‘ *Glo.* Ambitious churchman, leave to afflict my heart !

* Sorrow and grief have vanquifh'd all my powers :

---

2 — *whole towns to fly.*] Here in the old play the king adds:
“ Have done, I fay ; and let me hear no more of that ”
　　　　　　　　　　　　　　　　　　MALONE.

3 *Such as my heart doth tremble to unfold,* &c] In the original play the correfponding fpeech ftands thus : and the variation is worth noting :
“ Ill news for fome, my lord, and thus it is,
“ That proud dame Elinor, our protector's wife,
“ Hath plotted treafons 'gainft the king and peers,
“ By witchcraft, forceries, and conjurings :
“ Who by fuch means did raife a fpirit up,
“ To tell her what hap fhould betide the ftate ;
“ But ere they had finifh'd their devilifh drift,
“ By York and myfelf they were all furpriz'd,
“ And here's the anfwer the devil did make to them.”
　　　　　　　　　　　　　　　　　　MALONE.

4 *A* fort — *lewdly bent,*] *Lewdly,* in this place, and in fome others, does not fignify *wantonly,* but *wickedly.* STEEVENS.
The word is fo ufed in old acts of parliament. *A fort* is a company.
　　　　　　　　　　　　　　　　　　MALONE.

5 *Your lady is forth-coming*]— That is, Your lady is in cuftody.
　　　　　　　　　　　　　　　　　　JOHNSON.
　　　　　　　　　　　　　　　　　　* And,

* And, vanquifh'd as I am, I yield to thee,
* Or to the meaneft groom.
   * *K Hen.* O God, what mifchiefs work the wicked ones;
* Heaping confufion on their own heads thereby!
   * *Q Mar.* Glofter, fee here the tainture of thy neft;
* And, look, thyfelf be faultlefs, thou wert beft.
   ' *Glo.* Madam, for myfelf[6], to heaven I do appeal,
' How I have lov'd my king, and common-weal:
' And, for my wife, I know not how it ftands;
' Sorry I am to hear what I have heard:
' Noble fhe is; but, if fhe have forgot
' Honour, and virtue, and convers'd with fuch
' As, like to pitch, defile nobility,
' I banifh her, my bed, and company;
' And give her, as a prey, to law, and fhame,
' That hath difhonour d Glofter's honeft name.
   ' *K. Hen.* Well, for this night, we will repofe us here:
' To-morrow, toward London, back again,
' To look into this bufinefs thoroughly,
' And call thefe foul offenders to their anfwers;
' And poife the caufe in juftice' equal fcales,
' Whofe beam ftands fure, whofe rightful caufe prevails.
                [*Flourifh. Exeunt.*

SCENE II.

London.   *The Duke of* York's *Garden.*

Enter YORK, SALISBURY, *and* WARWICK.

   ' *York.* Now, my good lords of Salifbury and Warwick,
' Our fimple fupper ended, give me leave,
' In this clofe walk, to fatisfy myfelf,
' In craving your opinion of my title,
' Which is infallible[7], to England's crown.

---

6 *Madam for myfelf,* &c.] Thus in the original play:
    " And pardon me, my gracious fovereign,
    " For here I fwear unto your majefty,
    " That I am guiltlefs of thefe heinous crimes,
    " Which my ambitious wife hath falfely done:
    " And or fhe would betray her fovereign lord,
    " I here renounce her from my bed and board;
    " And leave her open for the law to judge,
    " Unlefs fhe clear herfelf of this foul deed." MALONE.
7 *Which is infallible,*] I know not whether he means the opinion or
the title is infallible.   JOHNSON
 Surely he means his *title.* MALONE.

                      * *Sal.*

* *Sal.* My lord, I long to hear it at full.

War. Sweet York, begin: and if thy claim be good,
The Nevils are thy fubjects to command.

York. Then thus:—

' Edward the Third, my lords, had feven fons:
' The firft, Edward the Black Prince, prince of Wales;
' The fecond, William of Hatfield; and the third,
' Lionel, duke of Clarence; next to whom,
' Was John of Gaunt, the duke of Lancafter:
' The fifth, was Edmond Langley [8], duke of York;
' The fixth, was Thomas of Woodftock, duke of Glofter;
' William of Windfor was the feventh, and laft.
' Edward, the Black Prince, dy'd before his father;
' And left behind him Richard, his only fon,
' Who, after Edward the Third's death, reign'd as king;
' Till Henry Bolingbroke, duke of Lancafter,
' The eldeft fon and heir of John of Gaunt,
' Crown'd by the name of Henry the Fourth,
' Seiz'd on the realm; depos'd the rightful king;
' Sent his poor queen to France, from whence fhe came,
' And him to Pomfret; where, as all you know [9],
' Harmlefs Richard was murder'd traiteroufly.

* *War.* Father, the duke hath told the truth;
* Thus got the houfe of Lancafter the crown.

* *York.* Which now they hold by force, and not by right;
* For Richard, the firft fon's heir, being dead,
* The iffue of the next fon fhould have reign'd.

* *Sal.* But William of Hatfield dy'd without an heir.

* *York.* The third fon, duke of Clarence, (from whofe
line
* I claim the crown,) had iffue,—Philippe, a daughter,
* Who married Edmund Mortimer, earl of March.
* Edmund had iffue—Roger, earl of March:
* Roger had iffue—Edmund, Anne, and Eleanor.

' *Sal.* This Edmund, in the reign of Bolingbroke,
' As I have read, laid claim unto the crown;
' And, but for Owen Glendower, had been king,

---

8 *The fifth, was Edmond Langley,* &c.] The author of the original
play has ignorantly enumerated Roger Mortimer, Earl of March, as
Edward's fifth fon; and reprefented the Duke of York as Edward's
fecond fon. MALONE.

9 — *as all you know,*] In the original play the words are, " — as you
both know". This mode of phrafeology, when the fpeaker addreffes
only two perfons, is peculiar to Shakfpeare. In *K. Henry IV.* P. II.
Act III. fc. i. the king addreffing Warwick and Surrey, fays,
" Why then good morrow to you *all,* my lords." MALONE.

' Who

' Who kept him in captivity, till he died '.

* But, to the reft.

'. *York.*

<hr/>

' *Who kept·him in captivity, till he died.*] I have obferved in a former note, that the hiftorians as well as the dramatick poets have been
ftrangely miftaken concerning this Edmond Mortimer, Earl of March,
who was fo far from being " kept in captivity till he died," that he
appears to have been at liberty during the whole reign of King Henry V.
and to have been trufted and employed by him; and there is no proof
that he ever was confined, as a *ftate-prifoner*, by King Henry IV.
Being only fix years of age at the death of his father in 1398. he was
delivered by Henry in ward to his fon Henry Prince of Wales; and
during the whole of that reign, being a minor and related to the family
on the throne, both he and his brother Roger were under the particular
care of the king. At the age of ten years, in 1402, he headed a body
of Herefordfhire men againft Owen Clendower; and they being routed,
he was taken prifoner by Owen, and is faid by Walfingham to have
contracted a marriage with Glendower's daughter, and to have been
with him at the battle of Shrewfbury; but I believe the ftory of his being affianced to Glendower's daughter is a miftake, and that the hiftorian has confounded Mortimer with Lord Gray of Ruthvin, who was
likewife taken prifoner by Glendower, and actually did marry his daughter. Edmond Mortimer Earl of March married Anne Stafford, the
daughter of Edmond Earl of Stafford. If he was at the battle of
Shrewfbury he was probably brought there againft his will, to grace the
caufe of the rebels. The Percies in the Manifefto which they publifhed
a little before that battle, fpeak of him, not as a confederate of Owen's,
but as the rightful heir to the crown, whom Owen had confined, and
whom, finding that the king for political reafons would not ranfom him,
they at their own charges had ranfomed. After that battle, he was
certainly under the care of the king, he and his brother in the feventh
year of that reign having had annuities of two hundred pounds and one
hundred marks allotted to them, for their maintenance during their mi-
norities.

In addition to what I have already faid refpecting the truft repofed
in him during the whole reign of K. Henry V. I may add, that in the
fixth year of that king this Earl of March was with the Earl of Salifbury at the fiege of Frefnes; and foon afterwards with the king himfelf
at the fiege of Melun. In the fame year he was conftituted LIEUTE-
NANT OF NORMANDY. He attended Henry when he had an interview with the French King, &c. at Melun, to treat about a marriage
with Catherine, and he accompanied the queen when fhe returned from
France in 1422, with the corpfe of her hufband.

One of the fources of the miftakes in our old hiftories concerning this
earl, I believe, was this: he was probably confounded with one of his
kinfmen, a Sir John Mortimer, who was confined for a long time in
the Tower, and at laft was executed in 1424. That perfon however,
could not have been his uncle (as has been faid) for he had but one legitimate uncle, and his name was *Edmond.* The Sir John Mortimer,
who was confined in the Tower, was perhaps coufin german to the laft
Edmond Earl of March. the illegitimate fon of his uncle Edmond.

I take this opportunity of correcting an inaccuracy in the note above
referred to. I have faid that Lionel Duke of Clarence was married to
Elizabeth the daughter of the Earl of Ulfter, in 1360. I have fince
learned

‘ *York.* His eldeſt ſiſter, Anne,
‘ My mother, being heir unto the crown,
‘ Married Richard, earl of Cambridge ; who was ſon
‘ To Edmund Langley, Edward the third's fifth ſon.
‘ By her I claim the kingdom : ſhe was heir
‘ To Roger, earl of March ; who was the ſon
‘ Of Edmund Mortimer ; who married Philippe,
‘ Sole daughter unto Lionel, duke of Clarence :
‘ So, if the iſſue of the elder ſon
‘ Succeed before the younger, I am king.
 ‘ *War.* What plain proceedings are more plain than this?
‘ Henry doth claim the crown from John of Gaunt,
‘ The fourth ſon ; York claims it from the third.
‘ Till Lionel's iſſue fails, he ſhould not reign :
‘ It fails not yet ; but flouriſhes in thee,
‘ And in thy ſons, fair ſlips of ſuch a ſtock.—
‘ Then, father Saliſbury, kneel we both together ;
‘ And, in this private plot ², be we the firſt,
‘ That ſhall ſalute our rightful ſovereign
‘ With honour of his birth-right to the crown.
 Both. Long live our ſovereign Richard, England's king !
 ‘ *York.* We thank you, lords. But I am not your king
‘ Till I be crown'd ; and that my ſword be ſtain'd
‘ With heart-blood of the houſe of Lancaſter :
* And that's not ſuddenly to be perform'd ;
* But with advice, and ſilent ſecrecy.
* Do you, as I do, in theſe dangerous days,
* Wink at the duke of Suffolk's inſolence,
* At Beaufort's pride, at Somerſet's ambition,
* At Buckingham, and all the crew of them,
* Till they have ſnar'd the ſhepherd of the flock,
* That virtuous prince, the good duke Humphrey :
* 'Tis that they ſeek ; and they, in ſeeking that,
* Shall find their deaths, if York can propheſy.

learned that he was affianced to her in his tender years ; and conſequently Lionel, having been born in 1338, might have had his daughter
Philippa in 1354. Philippa, I find, was marrie in 1370, at the age of
ſixteen, to Edmond Mortimer Earl of March, who was himſelf born in
1351. Their ſon Roger was born in 1371, and muſt have been married
to Eleanor, the daughter of the Earl of Kent, in the year 13 8 or 1389,
for their daughter Anne, who married Richard Earl of Cambridge, was
born in 1389. Edmond Mortimer, Roger's eldeſt ſon, (the Mortimer
of Shakſpeare's *K. Henry IV.* and the perſon who has given occaſion to
this tedious note,) was born in the latter end of the year 1392 ; and
conſequently when he died in his caſtle at Trim in Ireland, in 1424-5
he was thirty-two years old. MALONE.
 2 — *private plot,*] Sequeſter'd ſpot of ground. MALONE.

           * *Sal.*

* *Sal.* My lord, break we off; we know your mind at full.

' *War.* My heart assures me [3], that the earl of Warwick
' Shall one day make the duke of York a king.

' *York.* And, Nevil, this I do assure myself,—
' Richard shall live to make the earl of Warwick
' The greatest man in England, but the king.   [*Exeunt.*

SCENE III.

The same. A Hall of justice.

Trumpets sounded. Enter King HENRY, *Queen* MARGARET,
GLOSTER, YORK, SUFFOLK, *and* SALISBURY; *the
Dutchess of* GLOSTER, MARGERY JOURDAIN, SOUTH-
WELL, HUME, *and* BOLINGBROKE, *under guard.*

' *K. Hen.* Stand forth, dame Eleanor Cobham, Gloster's
wife:
' In sight of God, and us, your guilt is great;
' Receive the sentence of the law, for sins
' Such as by God's book are adjudg'd to death.—
* You four, from hence to prison back again;

                                        [*to* Jourd. *&c.*

* From thence, unto the place of execution:
* The witch in Smithfield shall be burnt to ashes,
* And you three shall be strangled on the gallows.—
' You, madam, for you are more nobly born, [*to the* Dut.
' Despoiled of your honour in your life,
' Shall, after three days' open penance [4] done,
' Live in your country here, in banishment,
' With sir John Stanley, in the isle of Man.

' *Dutch.* Welcome is banishment, welcome were my
death.

* *Glo.* Eleanor, the law, thou seest, hath judged thee;
* I cannot justify whom the law condemns.—
[*Exeunt the* Dutchess, *and the other prisoners, guarded.*

---

3 *My heart assures me,*] Instead of this couplet, we find in the old
play no less than *ten* lines; so that if we suppose that piece to be an imperfect transcript of this, we must acknowledge the transcriber had a
good *sprag* memory, for he remembered what he never could have
either heard or seen. MALONE.

4 — *after* three *days' open penance*—] In the original play the king
particularly specifies the *mode* of penance. "Thou shalt *two* days do
penance barefoot, in the streets, with a white sheet," &c. MALONE.

' Mine

' Mine eyes are full of tears, my heart of grief.
' Ah, Humphrey, this difhonour in thine age
' Will bring thy head with forrow to the ground !—
'' I befeech your majefty, give me leave to go ;
' Sorrow would folace, and mine age would eafe [2].
   ' *K. Hen.* Stay, Humphrey duke of Glofter : ere thou go,
' Give up thy ftaff ; Henry will to himfelf
' Protector be ; and God fhall be my hope,
' My ftay, my guide, and lantern to my feet ;
' And go in peace, Humphrey ; no lefs belov'd,
' Than when thou wert protector to thy king.
   * *Q. Mar.* I fee no reafon, why a king of years
* Should be to be protected like a child.—
' God and king Henry govern England's realm [3] :
' Give up your ftaff, fir, and the king his realm.
   ' *Glo.* My ftaff ?—here, noble Henry, is my ftaff :
' As willingly do I the fame refign,
' As e'er thy father Henry made it mine ;
And even as willingly at thy feet I leave it,
As others would ambitioufly receive it.
' Farewel, good king : When I am dead and gone,
May honourable peace attend thy throne !   [*Exit.*
   * *Q. Mar.* Why, now is Henry king, and Margaret
       queen ;
* And Humphrey, duke of Glofter, fcarce himfelf,
* That bears fo fhrewd a maim ; two pulls at once,—
* His lady banifh'd, and a limb lopp'd off ;
*Th is ftaff of honour raught [4] :—' There let it ftand
' Where it beft fits to be, in Henry's hand.
   Suf. Thus droops this lofty pine, and hangs his fprays ;
* Thus Eleanor's pride dies in her youngeft days [5].
                         ' *York.*

---

[2] *Sorrow would folace, and my age would eafe.*] That is, Sorrow would have, forrow requires, folace, and age requires eafe. JOHNSON.
[3] *God and king Henry govern England's* realm :] The word *realm* at the end of two lines together is difpleafing ; and when it is confidered that much of this fcene is written in rhyme, it will not appear improbable that the author wrote, *govern England's helm.* JOHNSON
   Dr. Johnfon's emendation undoubtedly fhould be received into the text. So, in *Coriolanus :*
    " —— and you flander
    " The *helms* of the *ftate.*" MALONE.
So, in a preceding fcene of this play :
   And you yourfelf fhall fteer the happy *helm.* STEEVENS.
[4] *This ftaff of honour* raught :— *Raught* is the ancient preterite of the verb *reach,* and is frequently ufed by Spenfer. STEEVENS.
[5] — *in* her *youngeft days.*] Eleanor was certainly not a young woman.

' *York.* Lords, let him go[6].—Pleafe it your majefty.
' This is the day appointed for the combat ;
' And ready are the appellant and defendant,
' The armourer and his man, to enter the lifts,
' So pleafe your highnefs to behold the fight.
  * *Q. Mar* Ay, good my lord ; for purpofely therefore
* Left I the court, to fee this quarrel try'd.
' *K. Hen.* O' God's name, fee the lifts and all things fit ?
' Here let them end it, and God defend the right !
  * *York.* I never faw a fellow worfe befted[7],
* Or more afraid to fight, than is the appellant,
* The fervant of this armourer, my lords.

Enter, on one fide, HORNER, *and his neighbours, drinking to him fo much that he is drunk ; and he enters bearing his ftaff with a fand-bag faftened to it[8] ; a drum before him ; at the other fide,* PETER, *with a drum and a fimilar ftaff ; accompanied by prentices drinking to him.*

1 *Neigh.* Here, neighbour Horner, I drink to you in a cup of fack ; And fear not, neighbour, you fhall do well enough.

2. *Neigh.* And here, neighbour, here's a cup of charneco[9].

3. *Neigh.* And here's a pot of good double beer, neighbour : drink, and fear not your man.

Hor. Let it come, i'faith, and I'll pledge you all ; And a fig for Peter !

man. We muft therefore fuppofe that the pronoun *her* refers to *pride*, and ftands for *its* ;—a licence which Shakfpeare often takes. MASON.

Or the meaning may be, in her, i. e. Eleanor's youngeft days of *power*. But the affertion, which ever way underftood, is untrue. MALONE.

6 *Lords, let him go.*] i. e. Let him pafs out of your thoughts. Duke Humphrey had already left the ftage. STEEVENS.

7 — *worfe befted,*] In a worfe plight. JOHNSON.

8 — *with a fand-bag faftened to it ;*] As, according to the old laws of duels, knights were to fight with the lance and fword ; fo thofe of inferior rank fought with an ebon ftaff or battoon, to the farther end of which was fixed a bag cramm'd hard with fand. To this cuftom Hudibras has alluded in thefe humourous lines :
  " Engag'd with money-bags, as bold
  " As men with *fand-bags* did of old." WARBURTON.
Mr. Sympfon, in his notes on Ben Jonfon, obferves, that a paffage in St. Chryfoftom very clearly proves the great antiquity of this practice. STEEVENS.

9 — *a cup of* charneco.] *Charneco* was, I believe, a fweet wine. It is very often mentioned by old writers, but none of the paffages in which it is mentioned, that I have feen, afcertain either its quality, or the country where it was produced. MALONE.

1. *Pren.*

1. *Pren.* Here, Peter, I drink to thee; and be not afraid.

2. *Pren.* Be merry, Peter, and fear not thy master: fight for credit of the prentices.

Pet. I thank you all: * drink, and pray for me, I pray * you; for, I think, I have taken my last draught in this * world.*—Here, Robin, an if I die, I give thee my apron and, Will, thou shalt have my hammer:—and here, Tom, take all the money that I have.—O Lord, bless me, I pray God! for I am never able to deal with my master, he hath learnt so much fence already.

Sal. Come, leave your drinking, and fall to blows.— Sirrah, what's thy name?

Pet. Peter, forsooth.

Sal. Peter! what more?

Pet. Thump.

Sal. Thump! then see thou thump thy master well.

Hor. Masters, I am come hither, as it were, upon my man's instigation, to prove him a knave, and myself an honest man: * and touching the duke of York;—will take * my death, I never meant him any ill, nor the king, nor the queen; * And therefore, Peter, have at thee with a downright blow, as Bevis of Southampton fell upon Ascapart [1].

* *York.* Dispatch:—this knave's tongue begins to double [2].

* Sound trumpets; alarum to the combatants.

[*Alarum. They fight, and* Peter *strikes down his master.*
Hor. Hold, Peter, hold! I confess, I confess treason.

[*Dies.*
* *York.*

---

[1] *— as Bevis of Southampton fell upon* Ascapart.] I have added this from the old quarto. WARBURTON.

Ascapart—the giant of the story—a name familiar to our ancestors, is mentioned by Dr. Donne.

" Those *Ascaparts*, men big enough to throw
" Charing-cross for a bar," &c. JOHNSON.

The figures of these combatants are still preserved on the gates of Southampton. STEEVENS.

Shakspeare not having adopted these words, according to the hypothesis already stated, they ought perhaps not to be here introduced. However, I am not so wedded to my own opinion, as to oppose it to so many preceding editors, in a matter of so little importance, and therefore I have admitted Dr. Warburton's emendation. MALONE.

[2] *— this knave's tongue begins to double*] So, in Holinshed, whose narrative Shakspeare has deserted, by making the armourer confess treason.—" When he should have come to the field fresh and fasting, his neighbours came to him, and gave him wine and strong drink in such excessive sort, that he was therewith distempered, and reeled as he went; and so was slain without guilt: as for the false servant he lived not long," &c. STEEVENS.

* *York.* Take away his weapon:—Fellow, thank God,
* and the good wine in thy master's way.

' *Pet.* O God! have I overcome mine enemies in this pre-
' sence? O Peter, thou hast prevailed in right!

K. Hen. Go, take hence that traitor from our sight;
For, by his death, we do perceive his guilt *:
And God, in justice, hath reveal'd to us
The truth and innocence of this poor fellow,
Which he had thought to have murder'd wrongfully.—
Come, fellow, follow us for thy reward.   [*Exeunt.*

SCENE IV.

The same. A street.

Enter GLOSTER *and* Servants, *in mourning cloaks.*

* *Glo.* Thus, sometimes, hath the brightest day a cloud;
* And, after summer, evermore succeeds
* Barren winter, with his wrathful nipping cold [3]:
* So cares and joys abound, as seasons fleet [4].—
Sirs, what's o'clock?

Serv. Ten, my lord.

' *Glo.* Ten is the hour that was appointed me,
' To watch the coming of my punish'd dutchess:
' Uneath [5] may she endure the flinty streets,

' To

---

* *For, by his death, we do perceive his guilt.*] According to the ancient usage of the duel, the vanquished person not only lost his life but his
reputation, and his death was always regarded as a certain evidence of
his guilt. We have a remarkable instance of this in an account of the
*Duellum inter Dominum Johannem Hannesly, Militem, & Robertum
Katlenton, Armigerum, in quo Robertus fuit occisus.* From whence,
says the historian, " *magna fuit evidentia qqod militis causa erat vera,
ex quo mors alterius sequebatur.*" A. Murimuth, ad ann. 1380, p. 149.
BOWLE.

3 *Barren* winter, *with his* wrathful *nipping cold:*] So, in Sackville's
Induction:
    " The *wrathful winter* 'proaching on apace—. REED.

4 — *as seasons* fleet.—] To *fleet* is to change. So, in *Antony and
Cleopatra:*
    " ———— now the *fleeting* moon
    " No planet is of mine. STEEVENS.

Dr. Johnson in his Dictionary supposes to *fleet* (as here used) to be
the same as to *flit*; that is, to be in a flux or transient state; to pass
away. MALONE.

5 *Uneath*—] i. e. scarcely. POPE.

Eath is the ancient word for *ease* or *easy.* So, in Spenser's *Faery
Queen,* B. IV c. 6:
    " More *eath* was now impression to receive."

Uneath is commonly used by the same author for *not easily.* STEEVENS.

‘ To tread them with her tender-feeling feet.
Sweet Nell, ill can thy noble mind abrook
The abject people, gazing on thy face,
With envious looks laughing at thy shame ;
That erst did follow thy proud chariot wheels,
When thou didst ride in tiiumph through the streets.
* But, soft! I think, she comes ; and I'll prepare
* My tear-stain'd eyes to see her miseries.

Enter the dutchefs of GLOSTER, *in a white sheet, with papers pinn'd upon her back, her feet bare, and a taper burning in her hand ;* Sir John Stanley, *a sheriff, and officers.*

Serv. So please your grace, we'll take her from the sheriff.
‘ *Glo.* No, stir not for your lives ; let her pass by [6].
Dutch, Come you, my lord, to see my open shame ?
Now thou dost penance too.   Look how they gaze !
‘ See, how the giddy multitude do point,
‘ And nod their heads, and throw their eyes on thee ;
‘ Ah, Glofter, hide thee from their hateful looks ;
‘ And, in thy closet pent up, rue my shame,
And ban thine enemies, both mine and thine.
   Glo. Be patient, gentle Nell ; forget this grief.
   Dutch. Ah, Glofter, teach me to forget myself:
For, whilst I think I am thy marry'd wife,
And thou a prince, protector of this land,
‘ Methinks, I should not thus be led along,
Mail'd up in shame [7], with papers on my back :
* And follow'd with a rabble, that rejoice
* To see my tears, and hear my deep-fet groans.
The ruthlefs flint doth cut my tender feet ;
And, when I start, the envious people laugh,
And bid me be advised how I tread.
‘ Ah, Humphrey, can I bear this shameful yoke ?
* Trow'st thou, that e'er I'll look upon the world ;
* Or count them happy, that enjoy the sun ?
* No ; dark shall be my light, and night my day ;
* To think upon my pomp, shall be my hell.
Sometime I'll say, I am duke Humphrey's wife ;
And he a prince, and ruler of the land :

6 *No, flir not,* &c.] In the original play thus :
  " I charge you for your lives, stir not a foot ;
  " Nor offer once to draw a weapon here,
  " But let them do their office as they should." MALONE.
7 *Mail'd up in shame.*] Wrapped up ; bundled up in disgrace ; alluding to the sheet of penance. JOHNSON.

Yet

Yet so he rul'd, and such a prince he was,
As he stood by, whilst I, his forlorn dutchess,
' Was made a wonder, and a pointing stock,
To every idle rascal follower.
But be thou mild, and blush not at my shame ;
Nor stir at nothing, till the axe of death
Hang over thee, as, sure, it shortly will.
For Suffolk,—he that can do all in all
' With her, that hateth thee, and hates us all,—
And York, and impious Beaufort, that false priest,
Have all lim'd bushes to betray thy wings,
And fly thou how thou canst, they'll tangle thee :
* But fear not thou, until thy foot be snar'd,
* Nor never seek prevention of thy foes.
     * *Glo.* Ah, Nell, forbear ; thou aimest all awry ;
* I must offend, before I be attainted :
* And had I twenty times so many foes.
* And each of them had twenty times their power,
* All these could not procure me any scathe [8],
* So long as I am loyal, true, and crimeless.
' Would'st have me rescue thee from this reproach ?
' Why, yet thy scandal were not wip'd away,
' But I in danger for the breach of law.
' Thy greatest help is quiet [9], gentle Nell :
' I pray thee, sort thy heart to patience ;
' These few days' wonder will be quickly worn.

Enter a Herald.

Her. I summon your grace to his majesty's parliament,
holden at Bury the first of this next month.
     Glo. And my consent ne'er ask'd herein before !
This is close dealing.—Well, I will be there.
[*Exit* Herald.
My Nell, I take my leave :—and, master sheriff,
Let not her penance exceed the king's commission.
     ' *Sher.* An't please your grace, here my commission stays :
' And Sir John Stanley is appointed now
' To take her with him to the isle of Man.
     ' *Glo.* Must you, sir John, protect my lady here ?
     ' *Stan.* So am I given in charge, may't please your grace.

---

8 — *any* scathe,] *Scathe* is harm, or mischief. Chaucer, Spencer,
and all our ancient writers, are frequent in their use of this word.
STEEVENS.
9. *Thy greatest help is quiet,*] The poet has not endeavoured to raise
much compassion for the dutchess, who indeed suffers but what she had
deserved. JOHNSON.

Glo.

Glo. Entreat her not the worſe, in that I pray
You uſe her well : the world may laugh again [1] ;
And I may live to do you kindneſs, if
You do it her.   And ſo, ſir John, farewel.

Dutch. What gone, my lord ; and bid me not farewel ?

‘ *Glo.* Witneſs my tears, I cannot ſtay to ſpeak.

                  [Exeunt GLOSTER *and* Servants.

‘ *Dutch.* Art thou gone too ? * All comfort go with thee!
*. For none abides with me : my joy is—death ;
* Death, at whoſe name I oft have been afear'd,
* Becauſe I wiſh'd this world's eternity,—
‘ Stanley, I pr'ythee, go, and take me hence ;
‘ I care not whither, for I beg no favour,
‘ Only convey me where thou art commanded.

* *Stan.* Why, madam, that is to the iſle of Man ;
* There to be us'd according to your ſtate.

* *Dutch.* That's bad enough, for I am but reproach ;.
* And ſhall I then be us'd reproachfully..?.

* *Stan.* Like to a dutcheſs, and duke Humphrey's lady,
* According to that ſtate you ſhall be us'd.

‘ *Dutch.* Sheriff, farewel, and better than I fare ;
‘ Although thou haſt been conduct of my ſhame * !

‘ *Sher.* It is my office ; and, madam, pardon me.

‘ *Dutch.* Ay, ay, farewel ; thy office is diſcharg'd.—
.‘ Come, Stanley, ſhall we go ?

‘ *Stan.* Madam, your penance done, throw off this ſheet,
‘ And go we to attire you for our journey.

‘ *Dutch.* My ſhame ſhall not be ſhifted with my ſheet :
* No, it will hang upon my richeſt robes,
* And ſhew itſelf, attire me how I can.
* Go, lead the way ; I long to ſee my priſon [2].   *[Exeunt.*

---

   1 *— the world may laugh again* ;] That it, the world may look again,
favourably upon me.   JOHNSON.

   2 *I long to ſee my priſon.*] This impatience of a high ſpirit is very
natural.   It is not ſo dread'ul to be impriſoned, as it is deſirable in a
ſtate of diſgrace to be ſheltered from the ſcorn of gazers.   JOHNSON.

   This is one of thoſe touches which certainly came from the hand of
Shakſpeare ; for theſe words are not in the old play.   MALONE.

   * — conduct *of my ſhame* !] That is, *conductor.*   MALONE.

ACT III. SCENE I.

The Abbey at Bury.

Enter to the Parliament, King HENRY, *Queen* MARGARET,
Cardinal BEAUFORT, SUFFOLK, YORK, BUCKINGHAM,
and Others.

' *K. Hen.* I muse, my lord of Glofter is not come :
' 'Tis not his wont to be the hindmoft man,
' Whate'er occafion keeps him from us now:
' *Q. Mar.* Can you not fee ? or will you not obferve
' The ftrangenefs of his alter'd countenance ?
' With what a majefty he bears himfelf ;
' How infolent of late he is become,
' How proud, how peremptory, and unlike himfelf?
' We know the time, fince he was mild and affable ;
' And, if we did but glance a far-off look,
' Immediately he was upon his knee,
' That all the court admir'd him for fubmiffion :
' But meet him now, and, be it in the morn,
' When every one will give the time of day,
' He knits his brow, and fhews an angry eye,
' And paffeth by with ftiff unbowed knee,
' Difdaining duty that to us belongs.
' Small curs are not regarded, when they grin ;
' But great men tremble, when the lion roars ;
' And Humphrey is no little man in England.
' Firft, note, that he is near you in defcent ;
' And, fhould you fall, he is the next will mount.
' Me feemeth ³ then, it is no policy,—
' Refpecting what a rancorous mind he bears,
' And his advantage following your deceafe,
' That he fhould come about your royal perfon,
' Or be admitted to your highnefs' council.
' By flattery hath he won the commons' hearts ;
' And, when he pleafe to make commotion,
' 'Tis to be fear'd, they all will follow him.
' Now 'tis the fpring, and weeds are fhallow-rooted ;
' Suffer them now, and they'll o'er-grow the garden,

³ *Me feemeth*—] That is, it feemeth to me ; a word more grammatical than *methinks*, which has, I know not how, intruded into its place. JOHNSON.

' And

‘ And choke the herbs for want of husbandry.
‘ The reverent care, I bear unto my lord,
‘ Made me collect these dangers in the duke.
‘ If it be fond*, call it a woman's fear ;
‘ Which fear if better reasons can supplant,
‘ I will subscribe, and say—I wrong'd the duke.
‘ My lord of Suffolk,—Buckingham,—and York,—
‘ Reprove my allegation, if you can ;
‘ Or else conclude my words effectual.

‘ *Suf.* Well hath your highness seen into this duke ;
‘ And, had I first been put to speak my mind,
I think, I should have told your grace's tale 4.
* The dutchess, by his subornation,
* Upon my life, began her devilish practices :
* Or if he were not privy to those faults,
* Yet, by reputing of his high descent 5,
* (As next the king, he was successive heir,)
* And such high vaunts of his nobility,
* Did instigate the bedlam brain-sick dutchess,
* By wicked means to frame our sovereign's fall.
Smooth runs the water, where the brook is deep ;
* And in his simple shew he harbours treason.
The fox barks not, when he would steal the lamb.
No, no, my sovereign ; Gloster is a man
Unsounded yet, and full of deep deceit.

* *Car.* Did he not, contrary to form of law,
* Devise strange deaths for small offences done ?
York. And did he not, in his protectorship,
* Levy great sums of money through the realm,
* For soldiers' pay in France, and never sent it ?
* By means whereof, the towns each day revolted.
* *Buck.* Tut ! These are petty faults to faults unknown,
* Which time will bring to light in smooth duke Humphrey.

* *K. Hen.* My lords, at once : The care you have of us,
* To mow down thorns that would annoy our foot,
* Is worthy praise : But shall I speak my conscience ?
*· Our kinsman Gloster is as innocent
* From meaning treason to our royal person

---

* *If it be fond.*] Idle, foolish MALONE.

4 —*your grace's tale.*] Suffolk uses *highness* and *grace* promiscuously to the queen. *Majesty* was not the settled title till the time of king James the First JOHNSON

5 *Yet, by reputing of his high descent,*] Thus the old copy. The modern editors read—*repeating. Reputing of his high descent,* is *valuing himself upon it.* The same word occurs in the fifth act,:

"· And in my conscience do *repute* his grace," &c. STEEVENS.

* As is the fucking lamb, or harmlefs dove :
* The duke is virtuous, mild ; and too well given,
* To dream on evil, or to work my downfall.
  * _Q. Mar._ Ah, what's more dangerous than this fond affiance !
* Seems he a dove ? his feathers are but borrow'd,
* For he's difpofed as the hateful raven.
* Is he a lamb ? his fkin is furely lent him,
* For he's inclin'd as are the ravenous wolves.
* Who cannot fteal a fhape, that means deceit ?
* Take heed, my lord ; the welfare of us all
* Hangs on the cutting fhort that fraudful man.

Enter SOMERSET.

* _Som._ All health unto my gracious fovereign !
K. Hen. Welcome, lord Somerfet. What news from France ?
' _Som._ That all your intereft in thofe territories
' Is utterly bereft you ; all is loft.
K. Hen. Cold news, lord Somerfet : But God's will be done !
York. Cold news for me ; for I had hope of France,
As firmly as I hope for fertile England [6].
* Thus are my bloffoms blafted in the bud,
* And caterpillars eat my leaves away :
* But I will remedy this gear [7] ere long,
* Or fell my title for a glorious grave.　　　　[_Afide._

Enter GLOSTER.

* _Glo._ All happinefs unto my lord the king !
Pardon, my liege, that I have ftaid fo long.
Suf. Nay, Glofter, know, that thou art come too foon,
' Unlefs thou wert more loyal than thou art :
I do arreft thee of high treafon here.
Glo. Well, Suffolk's duke *, thou fhalt not fee me blufh,
Nor change my countenance for this arreft ;

6 _Cold news for me ;_ &c.] Thefe two lines York had fpoken before in the firft act of this play He is now meditating on his difappointment, and comparing his former hopes with his prefent lofs. STEEVENS.

7 — _this_ gear—] _Gear_ was a general word for things or matters.
　　　　　　　　　　　　　　　　　　　　　　　JOHNSON.

So, in the ftory of _King Darius_, an interlude, 1565 :
　　" Wyll not yet this _gere_ be amended,
　　" Nor your finful acts corrected ?" STEEVENS.

* _Well, Suffolk's duke,_] The folio has—Well. Suffolk, thou,—. The defect of the metre fhews that the word was omitted, which I have fupplied from the old play. MALONE.

　　　　　　　I　　　　　　　　　　　* A heart

* A heart unfpotted is not eafily daunted.
* The pureft fpring is not fo free from mud,
* As I am clear from treafon to my fovereign :
Who can accufe me ?. wherein am I guilty ?

York. 'Tis thought, my lord, that you took bribes of France,
And, being protector, ftay'd the foldiers' pay ;
By means whereof, his highnefs hath loft France.

Glo. Is it but thought fo ? What are they, that think it !
' I never robb'd the foldiers of their pay,
' Nor ever had one penny bribe from France.
' So help me God, as I have watch'd the night,—
' Ay, night by night, in ftudying good for England !
' That doit that e'er I wrefted from the king,
' Or any groat I hoarded to my ufe,
' Be brought againft me at my trial day !
' No ! many a pound of mine own proper ftore,
' Becaufe I would not tax the needy commons,
' Have I difpurfed to the garrifons,
' And never afk'd for reftitution.

  * *Car.* It ferves you well, my lord, to fay fo much.
  * *Glo.* I fay no more than truth, fo help me God !

York. In your protectorfhip, you did devife
Strange tortures for offenders, never heard of,
That England was defam'd by tyranny.

Glo. Why, 'tis well known, that whiles I was protector,
Pity was all the fault that was in me ;
* For I fhould melt at an offender's tears,
* And lowly words were ranfom for their fault.
' Unlefs it were a bloody murderer,
' Or foul felonious thief, that fleec'd poor paffengers,
' I never gave them condign punifhment :
' Murder, indeed, that bloody fin, I tortur'd
' Above the felon, or what trefpafs elfe.

  ' *Suf.* My lord, thefe faults are eafy [8], quickly anfwer'd :
' But mightier crimes are laid unto your charge,
' Whereof you cannot eafily purge yourfelf,
' I do arreft you in his highnefs' name ;
' And here commit you to my lord cardinal
' To keep, until your further time of trial.

  ' *K. Hen.* My lord of Glofter, 'tis my fpecial hope,
' That you will clear yourfelf from all fufpects [9] ;
My confcience tells me, you are innocent.

                         . *Glo.*

---

[8] — *thefe faults are* eafy,—] *Eafy* is flight, inconfiderable, as in other paffages of this author. JOHNSON.

[9] — *from all* fufpects ;] The folio reads—*fufpence.* The emendation

Glo. Ah, gracious lord, thefe days are dangerous !
* Virtue is chok'd with foul ambition,
* And charity chas'd hence by rancour's hand ;
* Foul fubornation is predominant,
* And equity exil'd your highnefs' land.
* I know, their complot is to have my life ;
‘ And, if my death might make this ifland happy,
‘ And prove the period of their tyranny,
‘ I would expend it with all willingnefs :
‘ But mine is made the prologue to their play ;
‘ For thoufands more, that yet fufpect no peril,
‘ Will not conclude their plotted tragedy.
‘ Beaufort's red fparkling eyes blab his heart's malice,
‘ And Suffolk's cloudy brow his ftormy hate ;
‘ Sharp Buckingham unburdens with his tongue
‘ The envious load that lies upon his heart ;
‘ And dogged York, that reaches at the moon,
‘ Whofe over-weening arm I have pluck'd back,
‘ By falfe accufe doth level at my life :—
‘ And you, my fovereign lady, with the reft,
‘ Caufelefs have laid difgraces on my head ;
* And, with your beft endeavour, have ftir'd up
* My liefeft [1] liege to be mine enemy :
* Ay, all of you have laid your heads together,
* Myfelf had notice of your conventicles,
* And all to make away my guiltlefs life :
‘ I fhall not want falfe witnefs to condemn me,
‘ Nor ftore of treafons to augment my guilt ;
‘ The ancient proverb will be well effected,—
A ftaff is quickly found to beat a dog.
* *Car.* My liege, his railing is intolerable :
* If thofe, that care to keep your royal perfon
* From treafon's fecret knife, and traitors' rage,
* Be thus upbraided, chid, and rated at,
* And the offender granted fcope of fpeech,
* 'Twill make them cool in zeal unto your grace.
Suf. Hath he not twit our fovereign lady here,
‘ With ignominious words, though clerkly couch'd,
‘ As if fhe had fuborned fome to fwear

was fuggefted by Mr. Steevens. The correfponding line in the original
play ftands thus :
    " Good uncle, obey to this arreft :
    " I have no doubt but thou fhalt clear thyfelf." MALONE.

  So, in a following fcene :
    " If my *juftce* be falfe, forgive me, God !" STEEVENS.
  — *liefeft*—] is *deareft.* JOHNSON.

                       ‘ Falfe

' Falfe allegations to o'erthrow his ftate ?

' *Q. Mar.* But I can give the lofer leave to chide.

Glo. Far truer fpoke, than meant : I lofe, indeed ;—

' Befhrew the winners, for they play'd me falfe !—

* And well fuch lofers may have leave to fpeak.

Buck. He'll wreft the fenfe, and hold us here all day :—

' Lord cardinal, he is your prifoner.

' *Car.* Sirs, take away the duke, and guard him fure.

Glo. Ah, thus king Henry throws away his crutch,

Before his legs be firm to bear his body :

' Thus is the fhepherd beaten from thy fide,

' And wolves are gnarling who fhall gnaw thee firft.

' Ah ! that my fear were falfe ! ah, that it were !

' For, good king Henry, thy decay I fear [2].

[*Exeunt* Attendants, *with* GLOSTER.

K. Hen. My lords, what to your wifdoms feemeth beft,

Do, or undo, as if ourfelf were here.

Q. Mar. What, will your highnefs leave the parliament ?

K. Hen. Ay, Margaret [3]; my heart is drown'd with grief,

* Whofe flood begins to flow within mine eyes ;

* My body round engirt with mifery ;

* For what's more miferable than difcontent ?—

* Ah, uncle Humphrey ! in thy face I fee

* The map of honour [4], truth, and loyalty ;

* And yet, good Humphrey, is the hour to come,

* That e'er I prov'd thee falfe, or fear'd thy faith.

* What lowring ftar now envies thy eftate, ·

2 *Ah! that my fear were falfe!* &c.] The variation is here worth noting. In the original play, inftead of thefe two lines, we have the following :

" Farewell my fovereign; long may'ft thou enjoy

" Thy father's happy days, free from annoy !" MALONE.

3 *Ay, Margaret,* &c] Of this fpeech the only traces in the quarto are the following lines. In the king's fpeech a line feems to be loft :

Queen. What, will your highnefs leave the parliament ?

King. Yea, Margaret ; my heart is kill'd with grief ;

*   *   *   *   *   *   *

Where I may fit, and figh in endlefs moan,

For who's a traitor, Gloster he is none.

If therefore, according to the conjecture already fuggefted, thefe plays were originally the compofition of another author, the fpeech before us belongs to Shakfpeare. It is obfervable that one of the expreffions in it is found in his *Richard II.* and in the *Rape of Lucrece*; and in perufing the fubfequent lines one cannot help recollecting the trade which his father has by fome been fuppofed to have followed. MALONE.

4 *The map of honour,*—] In *K. Richard II.* if I remember right, we have the fame words. Again, in *The Rape of Lucrece :*

" Shewing life's triumph in the *map* of death." MALONE.

* That

* That thefe great lords, and Margaret our queen,
* Do feek fubverfion of thy harmlefs life ?
* Thou never didft them wrong, nor no man wrong :
* And as the butcher takes away the calf,
* And binds the wretch, and beats it when it ftrays [5],
* Bearing it to the bloody flaughter-houfe ;
* Even fo, remorfelefs, have they borne him hence.
* And as the dam runs lowing up and down,
* Looking the way her harmlefs young one went,
* And can do nought but wail her darling's lofs ;
* Even fo myfelf bewails good Glofter's cafe,
* With fad unhelpful tears ; and with dimm'd eyes
* Look after him, and cannot do him good ;
* So mighty are his vowed enemies.
‘ His fortunes I will weep; and, 'twixt each groan,
‘ Say—Who's a traitor, Glofter he is none.   [Exit.
    * Q. Mar. Free lords, cold fnow melts with the fun's hot
        beams.
* Henry my lord is cold in great affairs,
* Too full of foolifh pity : and Glofter's fhew
* Beguiles him, as the mournful crocodile
* With forrow fnares relenting paffengers ;
* Or as the fnake, roll'd in a flowering bank [7],
* With fhining checker'd flough, doth fting a child,
* That, for the beauty, thinks it excellent
* Believe me, lords, were none more wife than I,
* (And yet, herein, I judge mine own wit good,)
‘ This Glofter fhould be quickly rid the world,
‘ To rid us from the fear we have of him.
    * Car. That he fhould die, is worthy policy ;
* But yet we want a colour for his death :
* 'Tis meet, he be condemn'd by courfe of law.
    * Suf. But, in my mind, that were no policy :

---

5 And as the butcher takes away the calf,
    And binds the wretch, and beats it when it ftrays,] It is common
for butchers to tie a rope or halter about the neck of a calf when they
take it away from the breeder's farm, and to beat it gently if it attempts
to ftray from the direct road. The duke of Glofter is borne away like
the calf, that is, he is taken away upon his feet ; but he is not carried
away as a burthen on horfeback, or upon men's fhoulders, or in their
hands. TOLLET.
    6 Free lords, &c.] By this fhe means (as may be feen by the fequel)
you, who are not bound-up to fuch precife regards of religion as is the
king, but are men of the world, and know how to live. WARBURTON.
    7 — in a flowering bank,] i. e. in the flowers growing on a bank.—
Some of the modern editors read unneceffarily—on a flowering bank.
                                                                    MALONE.
                                                            * The

* The king will labour still to save his life,
* The commons haply rise to save his life ;
* And yet we have but trivial argument,
* More than mistrust, that shews him worthy death.
  * *York.* So that, by this, you would not have him die.
  * *Suf.* Ah, York, no man alive so fain as I.
  * *York.* 'Tis York that hath more reason for his death [8].—
* But, my lord cardinal, and you, my lord of Suffolk,—
* Say as you think, and speak it from your souls,—
* Wer't not all one, an empty eagle were set
* To guard the chicken from a hungry kite,
* As place duke Humphrey for the king's protector?*
  Q. Mar. So the poor chicken should be sure of death.
  ' *Suf.* Madam, 'tis true: and wer't not madness then,
' To make the fox surveyor of the fold ?
' Who being accus'd a crafty murderer.
' His guilt should be but idly posted over,
' Because his purpose is not executed.
' No ; let him die, in that he is a fox,
' By nature prov'd an enemy to the flock,
' Before his chaps be stain'd with crimson blood ;
' As Humphrey, prov'd by reasons, to my liege [9].
' And do not stand on quillets, how to flay him :
' Be it by gins, by snares, by subtilty,
' Sleeping, or waking, 'tis no matter how,
' So he be dead ; for that is good deceit

' Which

[8] *'Tis York that hath more reason for his death.*] Why York had more reason than the rest for desiring Humphrey's death, is not very clear; he had only decided the deliberation about the regency of France in favour of Somerset. JOHNSON.

York had more reason, because duke Humphrey stood between him and the crown, which he had proposed to himself as the termination of his ambitious views. So Act III. sc. v :

For Humphrey being dead as he shall be,
And Henry put apart, the next for me. STEEVENS.

[9] *No ; let him die, in that he is a fox,*
By nature prov'd an enemy to the flock,
Before his chaps be stain'd with crimson blood ;
As Humphrey, prov'd by reasons, to my liege.] The meaning of the speaker is not hard to be discovered, but his expression is very much perplexed. He means that the fox may be lawfully killed, as being known to be by nature an enemy to sheep; even before he has actually killed them ; so Humphrey may be properly destroyed, as being proved by arguments to be the king's enemy, before he has committed any actual crime.

Some may be tempted to read *treasons* for *reasons*, but the drift of the argument is to shew that there may be *reason* to kill him before any *treason* has broken out. JOHNSON.

A 1

' Which mates him firft, that firft intends deceit?'.

    * *Q. Mar.* Thrice-noble Suffolk, 'tis refolutely fpoke.

    * *Suf.* Not refolute, except fo much were done ;

* For things are often fpoke, and feldom meant :

* But, that my heart accordeth with my tongue,—

* Seeing the deed is meritorious,

* And to preferve my fovereign from his foe,—

* Say but the word, and I will be his prieft '.

    * *Car.* But I would have him dead, my lord of Suffolk,

* Ere you can take due orders for a prieft :

* Say, you confent, and cenfure well the deed ',

* And I'll provide his executioner,

* I tender fo the fafety of my liege.

    * *Suf.* Here is my hand, the deed is worthy doing.

    * *Q. Mar.* And fo fay I.

    * *York.* And I: and now we three have fpoke it,

* It fkills not ' greatly who impugns our doom.

Enter a Meffenger.

' *Mef.* Great lords ', from Ireland am I come amain,

                            ' To

As feems to be here ufed for *like*. Sir T. Hanmer reads, with fome probability, As Humphrey's prov'd, &c. In the original play, inftead of thefe lines, we have the following fpeech :

     Suf And to think I, madam; for as you know,
    If our king Henry had fhook hands with death,
    Duke Humphrey then would look to be our king.
    And it may be, by pol cy he works,
    To bring to pafs the thing wh ch now we doubt.
    The fox barks not, when he would fteal the lamb ;
    But if we take him ere he doth the deed,
    We fhould not queftion if that he fhould live.
    No, let him die, in that he is a fox,
    .Left that in living he offend us more. MALONE.

   ' — *for that it good deceit*

Which mates him firft, that firft intends deceit.] *To mate*, I believe, means here as in many other places in our author's plays, to confound or deftroy; from *matar*, Span. to kill. MALONE.

   Mates him means—that the firft puts an end to his moving. To *mate* is a term in chefs, ufed when the king is ftopped from moving, and an end put to the game. PERCY.

   ' — *I will be his prieft.*] I will be the attendant on his laft fcene, I will be the laft man whom he will fee. JOHNSON.

   ' — *and cenfure well the deed*,] That is, approve the deed, judge the deed good. JOHNSON.

   4 *It fkills not*—] It is of no importance. JOHNSON.

   So, in Sir T. More's *Utopia*, tranflated by R. Robinfon, 1624: " I will defcribe to you one or other of them, for *it fkilleth* not greatly which." MALONE.

   5 *Great Lords*, &c.] I fhall fubjoin this fpeech as it ftands in the quarto :

                           " Madam

' To fignify—that rebels there are up.
' And put the Englifhmen unto the fword :
* Send fuccours, lords, and ftop the rage betime,
* Before the wound do grow uncurable ;
* For, being green, there is great hope of help.
   * *Car.* A breach, that craves a quick expedient * ftop!
' What counfel give you in this weighty caufe ?
   ' *York.* That Somerfet be fent as regent thither :
' 'Tis meet, that lucky ruler be employ'd.;
' Witnefs the fortune he hath had in France.
   ' *Som.* If York, with all his far-fet policy,
' Had been the regent there inftead of me,
' He never would have ftaid in France fo long.
   ' *York.* No, not to lofe it all, as thou haft done :
' I rather would have loft my life betimes,
* Than bring a burden of difhonour home,
* By ftaying there fo long, till all were loft.
* Shew me one fcar charac̆ter'd on thy fkin :
* Men's flefh preferv'd fo whole, do feldom win.
   * *Q. Mar.* Nay then, this fpark will prove a raging fire,
* If wind and fuel be brought to feed it with :—
* No more, good York ;—fweet Somerfet, be ftill ;—
* Thy fortune, York, hadft thou been regent there,
* Might happily have prov'd far worfe than his.
   York. What, worfe than naught ? nay, then a fhame take
     all !
   ' *Som.* And, in the number, thee, that wifheft fhame !
   ' *Car.* My lord of York, try what your fortune is.
' The uncivil kerns of Ireland are in arms,
' And temper clay with blood of Englifhmen :
' To Ireland will you lead a band of men,
' Collec̆ted choicely, from each county fome,
' And try your hap againft the Irifhmen ?
   * *York.* I will, my lord, to pleafe his majefty.
   * *Suf.* Why, our authority is his confent ;

   " Madam, I bring you news from Ireland ;
   " The wild Onele, my lord, is up in arms,
   " With troops of Irifh kerns, that uncontroll'd
   " Doth plant themfelves within the Englifh pale,
   " And burn and fpoil the country as they go."

Surely here is not an imperfec̆t exhibition of the lines in the folio, haftily taken down in the theatre by the ear or in fhort-hand, as I once concurred with others in thinking to be the cafe. We have here an original and diftinc̆t draught ; fo, that we muft be obliged to maintain that Shakfpeare wrote *two* plays on the prefent fubjec̆t, a hafty fketch, and a more finifhed performance ; or elfe muft acknowledge, that he formed the piece before us on a foundation laid by another writer. MALONE.

   * — *expedient*—] i. e. expeditious. MALONE.

                                            ' And,

* And, what we do eſtabliſh, he confirms :
* Then, noble York, take thou this taſk in hand.
 ‘ *York.* I am content : Provide me ſoldiers, lords,
 ‘ Whiles I take orders for mine own affairs.’
 ‘ *Suf.* A charge, lord York, that I will ſee perform’d [6].
 ‘ But now return we to the falſe duke Humphrey.
 ‘ *Car.* No more of him ; for I will deal with him,
 ‘ That, henceforth, he ſhall trouble us no more.
 ‘ And ſo break off ; the day is almoſt ſpent :
 ‘ Lord Suffolk, you and I muſt talk of that event.
 ‘ *York.* My lord of Suffolk, within fourteen days,
 ‘ At Briſtol I expect my ſoldiers ;
 ‘ For there I’ll ſhip them all for Ireland.
 ‘ *Suf.* I’ll ſee it truly done, my lord of York.

 [*Exeunt all but* York.

 ‘ *York.* Now, York, or never, ſteel thy fearful thoughts,
 ‘ And change miſdoubt to reſolution :
* Be that thou hop’ſt to be ; or what thou art
* Reſign to death, it is not worth the enjoying :
* Let pale-fac’d fear keep with the mean-born man,
* And find no harbour in a royal heart.
* Faſter than ſpring-time ſhowers, comes thought on thought :
* And not a thought, but thinks on dignity.
* My brain, more buſy than the labouring ſpider,
* Weaves tedious ſnares to trap mine enemies.
* Well, nobles, well ; ’tis politickly done,
* To ſend me packing with an hoſt of men :
* I fear me, you but warm the ſtarved ſnake,
* Who, cheriſh’d in your breaſts, will ſting your hearts.
 ’Twas men I lack’d, and you will give them me :
 ‘ I take it kindly ; yet, be well aſſur’d
 ‘ You put ſharp weapons in a mad man’s hands.
 ‘ Whiles I in Ireland nouriſh a mighty band,
* I will ſtir up in England ſome black ſtorm,
* Shall blow ten thouſand ſouls to heaven, or hell :

---

6 — *that I will ſee perform’d.*] In the old play this office is given to Buckingham :

.   *Queen.* —— my lord of Buckingham,
 Let it be your charge to muſter up ſuch ſoldiers,
 As ſhall ſuffice him in theſe needful wars.
    Buck. Madam, I will ; and levy ſuch a band
 As ſoon ſhall overcome theſe Iriſh rebels :
 But York, where ſhall theſe ſoldiers ſtay for thee ?
    York. At Briſtol I’ll expect them ten days hence.
    Buck. Then thither ſhall they come, and ſo farewell.

 [*Exit* Buck.

 Here again we have a very remarkable variation. MALONE.

 * And

* And this fell tempeſt ſhall not ceaſe to rage
* Until the golden circuit on my head [7],
* Like to the glorious ſun's tranſparent beams,
* Do calm the fury of this mad-bred flaw [8].
' And, for a miniſter of my intent,
' I have ſeduc'd a head-ſtrong Kentiſhman,
' John Cade of Aſhford,
' To make commotion, as full well he can,
' Under the title of John Mortimer.
* In Ireland have I ſeen this ſtubborn Cade
* Oppoſe himſelf againſt a troop of kerns ;
* And fought ſo long, till that his thighs with darts
* Were almoſt like a ſharp-quill'd porcupine :
* And, in the end being reſcu'd, I have ſeen him
* Caper upright like a wild Moriſco [9],
* Shaking the bloody darts, as he his bells.
* Full often, like a ſhag-hair'd crafty kern,
* Hath he converſed with the enemy ;
* And undiſcover'd come to me again,
* And given me notice of their villainies.
* This devil here ſhall be my ſubſtitute ;

7 *Until the* golden circuit *on my head,*] So, in *Macbeth :*
      " All that impedes thee from the g lden *round,*
      " Which fate and metaphyſical-aid doth ſeem
      " To have thee *crown'd* withall."
Again, in *K Henry IV* P. II.
      " —— a ſleep,
      " That from this *golden rigol* hath divorc'd
      " So many Engliſh kings." MALONE.
8 — *mad-bred* flaw.] *Flaw* is a ſudden violent guſt of wind.
                                        JOHNSON.
9 — *a wild Meriſco,*] A Moor in a military dance, now called
Morris, that is, a Mooriſh dance. JOHNSON.
   In *Albion's Triumph,* a maſque, 1631, the ſeventh entry conſiſts of
mimicks or *Mariſcas.*
   The *Morris-dance* was the *Tripudium Mauritanicum,* a kind of horn-
pipe. Junius deſcribes it thus : " — faciem plerumque inficiunt fuli-
gine, et peregrinum veſtium cultum aſſumunt, qui ludicris talibus in-
dulgent, ut Mauri eſſe videantur, aut e longius remota patria credantur
advolaſſe, atque inſolens recreationis genut adveniſſe."
   In the churchwardens' accompts of the pariſh of St. Helen's in
Abington, Berkſhire, from the firſt year of the reign of Philip and
Mary, to the thirty fourth of queen Elizabeth, the *Morrice* bells are
mentioned. Anno 1560, the third of Elizabeth,—" For two doſſin of
Morres bells " As theſe appear to have been purchaſed by the com-
munity, we may ſuppoſe this diverſion was conſtantly practiſed at their
publick feſtivals. See the plate of *Morris-dancers* at the end of the
firſt part of *K. Henry IV.* with Mr. Tollet's remarks annexed to it
                                        STEEVENS
                                        * For

* For that John Mortimer, which now is dead,
* In face, in gait, in speech he doth resemble :
' By this I shall perceive the commons' mind,
' How they affect the house and claim of York.
' Say, he be taken, rack'd, and tortured ;
' I know, no pain, they can inflict upon him,
' Will make him say—I mov'd him to those arms.
' Say, that he thrive, (as 'tis great like he will,)
' Why, then from Ireland come I with my strength,
' And reap the harvest which that rascal sow'd :
' For, Humphrey being dead ², as he shall be,
' And Henry put apart, the next for me.　　　[*Exit.*

S C E N E　II³.

Bury.　*A Room in the Palace.*

Enter certain Murderers, *hastily.*

* 1. *Mur.* Run to my lord of Suffolk ; let him know,
* We have dispatch'd the duke, as he commanded.
* 2. *Mur.* O, that it were to do!—What have we done?
* Didst ever hear a man so penitent?

Enter SUFFOLK.

' 1. *Mur.* Here comes my lord.
' *Suf.* Now, sirs, have you dispatch'd this thing?

2 *For, Humphrey being dead,* &c.] Instead of this couplet we find
in the old play these lines:
　　" And then Duke Humphrey, he well made away,
　　" None that can stop the light to England's crown,
　　" But York can tame, and headlong pull them down."
　　　　　　　　　　　　　　　　　　　MALONE.

3 *Scene II.*] This scene, and the directions concerning it, stand thus
in the quarto edition :
　*Then the curtaines being drawne, Duke Humphrey is discovered in his
bed, and two men lying on his brest, and smothering him in his bed. And
then enter the Duke of Suffolk to them:*
　　Suf. How now, sirs! what have you dispatch'd him?
　　One. Yes, my lord; he's dead, I warrant you.
　　Suf. Then see the cloathes laid smooth about him still,
　That when the king comes, he may perceive
　No other, but that he died of his own accord.
　　2 All things is handsome now, my lord.
　　Suf. Then draw the curtains again, and get you gone,
　And you shall have your firm reward anon.　　[*Exit* Murtherers.
　　　　　　　　　　　　　　　　　　STEEVENS.
' 1 *Mur.*

' 1. *Mur.* Ay, my good lord, he's dead.

' *Suf.* Why, that's well said. Go, get you to my house;
' I will reward you for this venturous deed.
' The king and all the peers are here at hand :—
' Have you laid fair the bed? are all things well,
' According as I gave directions?

' 1. *Mur.* 'Tis, my good lord.

' *Suf.* Away, be gone !   [*Exeunt* Murderers.

Enter King HENRY, *Queen* MARGARET, *Cardinal* BEAU-
FORT, SOMERSET, *Lords, and Others.*

' *K. Hen.* Go, call our uncle to our presence straight :
' Say, we intend to try his grace to-day,
' If he be guilty, as 'tis published.

' *Suf.* I'll call him presently, my noble lord.   [*Exit.*

' *K. Hen.* Lords, take your places ;—And, I pray you
  all,
' Proceed no straiter 'gainst our uncle Gloster,
' Than from true evidence, of good esteem,
' He be approv'd in practice culpable.

* *Q. Mar.* God forbid, any malice should prevail,
* That faultless may condemn a nobleman !
* Pray God, he may acquit him of suspicion !

* *K. Hen.* I thank thee, Margaret [4] ; these words content
  me much.

Re-enter SUFFOLK.

' How now ? why look'st thou pale ? why tremblest thou?
' Where is our uncle ? what is the matter, Suffolk ?

Suf. Dead in his bed, my lord ; Gloster is dead.

* *Q. Mar.* Marry, God forefend !

* *Car.* God's secret judgment :—I did dream to night,
* The duke was dumb, and could not speak a word.
                                        [*The king swoons.*

---

4 *I thank thee,* Margaret ;] The folio reads—I thank thee, *Nell;* and
Mr. Theobald, conceiving that " there can be no reason why the king
should forget his own wife's name," reads—" *Well,* these words," &c.
which the subsequent editors too hastily adopted. Though the king
could not well forget his wife's name, either Shakspeare or the transcriber might. That *Nell* is not a mistake of the press for *Well* is clear
from a subsequent speech of the *queen's* in this scene, where *Eleanor,*
the name of the Dutchess of Gloster, is again *three times* printed instead
of *Margaret.* No reason can be assigned why the proper correction
should be made in all those places, and not here. MALONE.

‘ *2. Mar.* How fares my lord?—Help, lords, the king is
    dead.

* *Som.* Rear up his body; wring him by the nose.

* *2. Mar.* Run, go, help, help!—O, Henry, ope thine
    eyes!

* *Suf.* He doth revive again;—Madam, be patient.

* *K. Hen.* O heavenly God!

* *2. Mar.* How fares my gracious lord?

Suf. Comfort, my sovereign! gracious Henry, comfort!

K. Hen. What, doth my lord of Suffolk comfort me?
Came he right now⁵ to sing a raven's note,
* Whose dismal tune bereft my vital powers;
And thinks he, that the chirping of a wren,
‘ By crying comfort from a hollow breast,
‘ Can chase away the first-conceived sound?
* Hide not thy poison with such sugar'd words.
* Lay not thy hands on me; forbear, I say;
* Their touch affrights me, as a serpent's sting.
Thou baleful messenger, out of my sight!
‘ Upon thy eye-balls murderous tyranny
‘ Sits, in grim majesty, to fright the world.
‘ Look not upon me, for thine eyes are wounding:—
‘ Yet do not go away;—Come, basilisk *,
‘ And kill the innocent gazer with thy sight:
* For in the shade of death I shall find joy;
* In life, but double death, now Gloster's dead.

    2. Mar. Why do you rate my lord of Suffolk thus?
* Although the duke was enemy to him,
* Yet he, most christian-like, laments his death:
* And for myself,—foe as he was to me,
* Might liquid tears, or heart-offending groans,
* Or blood-consuming sighs recall his life,
* would be blind with weeping, sick with groans,
* Look pale as primrose, with blood-drinking sighs⁶,
* And all to have the noble duke alive
‘ What know I how the world may deem of me?
‘ For it is known, we were but hollow friends;
‘ It may be judg'd, I made the duke away:

---

⁵ — *right now*—] Just now, even now. JOHNSON.

* *Come, basilisk, &c.*] So. Mantuanus, a writer very popular at this
time:
    “ Natus in ardente Lydiæ basiliscus arena,
    “ Vulnerat aspectu, luminibusque nocet.” MALONE.

⁶ — *with blood-drinking sighs,*] So, in another of Shakspeare's
plays:
    “ — dry sorrow drinks my blood.” MALONE.

                                    * So

* So shall my name with slander's tongue be wounded,
* And princes' courts be fill'd with my reproach.
* This get I by his death: Ah me, unhappy!
* To be a queen, and crown'd with infamy!
' *K. Hen.* Ah, woe is me for Gloster, wretched man!
  Q Mar. Be woe for me, more wretched than be is [7].
What, dost thou turn away, and hide thy face?
I am no loathsome leper, look on me.
* What, art thou, like the adder, waxen deaf [8]?
* Be poisonous too, and kill thy forlorn queen.
* Is all thy comfort shut in Gloster's tomb?
* Why, then dame Margaret was ne'er thy joy:
* Erect his statue then, and worship it,
* And make my image but an ale-house sign.
Was I, for this, nigh wreck'd upon the sea;
'& And twice by aukward wind [9] from England's bank
' Drove back again unto my native clime?
What boded this, but well-fore-warning wind

---

[7] *Be woe for me,*] That is, Let not woe be to thee for Gloster, but for me. JOHNSON.

[8] *What, art thou, like the adder, waxen deaf?*] This allusion which has been borrowed by many writers from the Proverbs of Solomon, and Psalm lviii. may receive an odd illustration from the following passage in *Gower de Confessione Amantis,* B. I. fol. 1.
  " A serpent whiche that aspidis
  " Is cleped, of his kinde hath this,
  " That he the stone noblest of all,
  " The whiche that men carbuncle call,
  " Bereth in his heed above on hight;
  " For whiche whan that a man by slight
  " (The stone to wynne, and him to dante)
  " With his carecte him wolde enchante,
  " Anone as he perceiveth that,
  " He leyeth downe his one eare all plat
  " Unto the grounde, and halt it fast:
  " And eke that other eare all faste
  " He stoppeth with his taille so sore
  " That be the wordes, lasse or more,
  " Of his enchantement ne bereth:
  " And in this wise him selfe he skiereth,
  " So that he hath the wordes weyved,
  " And thus his eare is nought deceived."
Shakspeare has the same allusion in *Troilus and Cressida:* " Have ears more *deaf* than *adders,* to the voice of any true decision." STEEVENS.

[9] — *aukward wind*—] Thus the old copy. The modern editors read *adverse winds.* STEEVENS.
  The same uncommon epithet is applied to the same subject by Marlowe, in his *King Edward II.*
  " With *aukward* winds, and with sore tempests driven,
  " To fall on shore." MALONE.

Did

Did feem to fay,—Seek not a fcorpion's neft,
* Nor fet no footing on this unkind fhore?
* What did I then, but curs'd the gentle gufts,
* And he that loos'd them from their brazen caves;
* And bid them blow towards England's bleffed fhore,
* Or turn our ftern upon a dreadful rock?
* Yet Æolus would not be a murderer,
* But left that hateful office unto thee:
* The pretty vaulting fea refus'd to drown me;
* Knowing, that thou would't have me drown'd on fhore
* With tears as falt as fea through thy unkindnefs:
* The fplitting rocks cow'r'd in the finking fands ¹,
* And would not dafh me with their ragged fides;
* Becaufe thy flinty heart, more hard than they,
* Might in thy palace perifh Margaret ².
* As far as I could ken thy chalky cliffs,
* When from the fhore the tempeft beat us back,
* I fhood upon the hatches in the ftorm:
* And when the dufky fky began to rob
* My earneft-gaping fight of thy land's view,
* I took a coftly jewel from my neck,—
* A heart it was, bound in with diamonds,—
* And threw it towards thy land; the fea receiv'd it;
* And fo, I wifh'd, thy body might my heart;
* And even with this, I loft fair England's view,
* And bid mine eyes be packing with my heart;
* And call'd them blind and dufky fpectacles,
* For lofing ken of Albion's wifhed coaft.
* How often have I tempted Suffolk's tongue
* (The agent of thy foul inconftancy)
* To fit and witch me ³, as Afcanius did,
* When he to madding Dido, would unfold
* His father's acts, commenc'd in burning Troy?

* Am

---

¹ *The fplitting rocks,* &c.] The fenfe feems to be this—The rocks hid themfelves in the fands, which funk to receive them into their bofom. STEEVENS

² *Might in thy palace perifh Margaret.*] The verb *perifh* is here ufed actively. So, in the *Maid's Tragely,* by Beaumont and Fletcher:
"—— let not my fins
"Perifh your noble youth." STEEVENS.

³ *To fit and witch me,*] The old copy has—*watch me.* The emendation was made by Mr. Theobald, who obferves that the poet forgot the paffage in the Æneid, the hiftory of the deftruction of Troy being related to Dido, not by Afcanius, but Æneas.

Mr. Theobald's emendation is fupported by a line in *K. Henry IV.* P. I. where the fame verb is ufed—
"To *witch* the world with noble horfemanfhip."

It

* Am I not witch'd like her? or thou not false like him?
* Ah me, I can no more! Die, Margaret!
* For Henry weeps, that thou dost live so long.

Noise within. Enter WARWICK, *and* SALISBURY. *The Commons press to the door.*

' *War.* It is reported, mighty sovereign,
' That good duke Humphrey traiterously is murder'd
' By Suffolk and the cardinal Beaufort's means.
' The commons, ' like an angry hive of bees,
' That wants their leader, scatter up and down,
' And care not who they sting in his revenge.
' Myself have calm'd their spleenful mutiny,
' Until they hear the order of his death.
    K. Hen. That he is dead, good Warwick, 'tis too true;
But how he died, God knows, not Henry * :
' Enter his chamber, view his breathless corpse,
' And comment then upon his sudden death.
    War. That I shall do, my liege : Stay, Salisbury,
With the rude multitude, till I return.

    [*Warwick goes into an inner room, and Salisbury retires.*

* *K. Hen.* O thou that judgest all things, stay my thoughts.
* My thoughts, that labour to persuade my soul,
* Some violent hands were laid on Humphrey's life!
* If my suspect be false, forgive me, God;
* For judgment only doth belong to thee!
* Fain would I go to chafe his paly lips
* With twenty thousand kisses, and to drain ⁵
* Upon his face an ocean of salt tears;
* To tell my love unto his dumb deaf trunk,
* And with my fingers feel his hand unfeeling :
* But all in vain are these mean obsequies;
* And, to survey his dead and earthly image,
* What were it but to make my sorrow greater?

It may be remarked, that this mistake was certainly the mistake of Shakspeare, whoever may have been the original author of the first sketch of this play; for this long speech of Margaret's is founded on one in the quarto, consisting only of seven lines, in which there is no allusion to Virgil. MALONE.

4 — *not Henry :*] The poet commonly uses Henry as a word of three syllables. JOHNSON.

5 — *and to drain*—] This is one of our poet's harsh expressions. As when a thing is *drain'd*, drops of water issue from it, he licentiously uses the word here in the sense of *dropping*, or *distilling*. MALONE.

The folding doors of an inner chamber are opened, and GLOSTER *is discovered dead in his bed:* WARWICK *and Others standing by it* [6].

* *War.* Come hither, gracious sovereign, view this body.

* *K. Hen.* That is to see how deep my grave is made :

* For, with his soul, fled all my worldly solace ;

* For seeing him, I see my life in death [7].

' *War.* As surely as my soul intends to live

' With that dread King, that took our state upon him

' To free us from his Father's wrathful curse,

' I do believe that violent hands were laid

' Upon the life of this thrice-famed duke.

Suf. A dreadful oath, sworn with a solemn tongue!

' What instance gives lord Warwick for his vow?

' *War.* See, how the blood is settled in his face !

Oft have I seen a timely-parted-ghost [8],

' Of

---

6 The stage direction I have inserted as best suited to the exhibition. The stage-direction in the quarto is—" Warwick draws the curtaines, [i. e. draws them open] and shews duke Humphry in his bed." In the folio : " A bed with Gloster's body put forth." These are some of the many circumstances which prove, I think, decisively, that the theatres of our author's time were unfurnished with scenes. In those days, as I conceive, curtains were occasionally hung across the middle of the stage on an iron rod, which, being drawn open, formed a second apartment, when a change of scene was required. The direction in the folio, " to put forth a bed," was merely to the property m n to thrust a bed forwards behind those curtains, previous to their be ng drawn open. See the *Account of the ancient Theatres,* Vol. I. MALONE.

7 *For seeing him, I see my life in death.*] I think the meaning is, I see my life in the arms of death : I see my life expiring, or rather expired. The conceit is much in our author's manner. So, in *Macbeth* :
" —the death of each day's life "
Our poet in *K. Richard III.* has a similar play of words, though the sentiment is reversed :
" —— even through the hollow eyes of death
" I spy life peering." MALONE.
The poet's meaning is, *I see my life destroyed or endangered by his death.* PERCY.

8 *Oft have I seen a timely-parted ghost, &c.*] All that is true of the body of a dead man, is here said by Warwick of the soul. I would read : *Oft have I seen a timely parted corse.*
I cannot but stop a moment to observe that this horrible description is scarcely the work of any pen but Shakspeare's. JOHNSON.

A *timely* parted ghost means a body that has become inanimate in the common course of nature ; to which violence has not brought a *timeless* end. The opposition is plainly marked afterwards, by the words—" As guilty of Duke Humphrey's *timeless death.*"

The corresponding lines appear thus in the quarto ; by which, if the notion that has been already suggested be well founded, the reader may

see

‘ Of aſhy ſemblance *, meager, pale, and bloodleſs,
‘ Being all † deſcended to the labouring heart ;
‘ Who, in the conflict that it holds with death,
‘ Attracts the ſame for aidance 'gainſt the enemy ;
‘ Which with the heart there cools, and ne'er returneth
‘ To bluſh and beautify the cheek again.
‘ But, ſee, his face is black, and full of blood ;
‘ His eye-balls further out than when he liv'd,
‘ Staring full ghaſtly like a ſtrangled man :
‘ His hair up-rear'd, his noſtrils ſtretch'd with ſtruggling ;

ſee how much of this deſervedly admired ſpeech is original, and how much ſuper-induced :

" Oft have I ſeen a timely-parted *ghoſt*,
" Of aſhy ſemblance, pale, and bloodleſs :
" But, lo! the blood is ſettled in his face,
" More better coloured than when he liv'd.
" His well proportion'd beard made rough and ſtern ;
" His fingers ſpread abroad, as one that graſp'd
" For life, yet was by ſtrength ſurpriz'd. The leaſt
" Of theſe are probable. It cannot chooſe
" But he was murthered."

In a ſubſequent paſſage, alſo in the original play, which Shakſpeare has not transferred into his piece, the word *ghoſt* is again uſed as here. Young Clifford addreſſing himſelf to his father's *dead body*, ſays,

" O diſmal ſight! ſee, where he breathleſs lies,
" All ſmear'd and welter'd in his luke-warm blood !
" Sweet father, to thy *murder'd ghoſt* I ſwear," &c.

Our author therefore is not chargeable here with any impropriety, or confuſion. He has only uſed the phraſeology of his time. MALONE.

This is not the firſt time that Shakſpeare has confounded the terms that ſignify *body* and *ſoul*, together. So, in *A Midſummer's Night's Dream :*

" ———— damned *ſpirits* all,
" That in croſs-ways and floods have *burial.*"

It is ſurely the *body* and not the *ſoul* that is committed to the earth, or whelm'd in the water. The word *ghoſt*, however, is licentiouſly uſed by our ancient writers In Spenſer's *Faery Queen*, B. II. c. viii. Sir *Guyon* is in a ſwoon, and two knights are about to ſtrip him, when the *Palmer* ſay :

" ———— no knight ſo rude I weene,
" A. to doen outrage to a ſleeping *ghoſt.*"

Again, in the ſhort copy of verſes printed at the concluſion of the three firſt brokes f S, enſer's *Faerie Queen*, 1596 :

" And groanes of *buried' ghoſtes* the heavens did perſe."

Again, in our au hor's *K. Richard II.*

" The *ghoſts* they have depoſ'd."

Again, in *Certain ſecret wonders of nature*, by Edward Fenton, 4to. bl. l. 1569 : " — aſtoniſhed at the view of the mortified *ghoſt* of him that lay dead." STEEVENS.

* —*of aſhy ſemblance*—] So Spenſer, *Ruins of Rome*, 4to. 1591 :
" Ye pallid ſpirits, and ye *aſhy ghoſts*." MALONE.

† *Being all*—] That is the blood being all deſcended, the ſubſtantive being compriſed in the adjective bloodleſs. MASON.

‘ His

' His hands abroad difplay'd *, as one that grafp'd
' And tugg'd for life, and was by ftrength fubdu'd.
' Look on'the fheets, his hair, you fee, is fticking ;
' His well proportion'd beard ⁸ made rough and rugged,
' Like to the fummer's corn by tempeft lodg'd.
' It cannot be, but he was murder'd here ;
' The leaft of all thefe figns were probable.
    ' *Suf.* Why, Warwick, who fhould do the duke to death ?
' Myfelf, and Beaufort, had him in protection ;
' And we, I hope, fir, are no murderers.
    ' *War.* But both of you were vow'd duke Humphrey's
            foes ;
' And you, forfooth, had the good duke to keep :
' 'Tis like, you would not feaft him like a friend ;
' And 'tis well feen, he found an enemy.
    ' *Q. Mar.* Then you, belike, fufpect thefe noblemen
' As guilty of duke Humphrey's timelefs death.
    War. Who finds the heifer dead, and bleeding frefh,
And fees faft by a butcher with an axe,
But will fufpect, 'twas he that made the flaughter ?
Who finds the partridge in the puttock's neft,
But may imagine how the bird was dead,
Although the kite foar with unbloody'd beak ?
Even fo fufpicious is this tragedy.
    ' *Q. Mar.* Are you the butcher, Suffolk ? where's your
            knife ?
Is Beaufort term'd a kite ? where are his talons ?
    Suf. I wear no knife, to flaughter fleeping men ;
But here's a vengeful fword, rufted with eafe,
That fhall be fcoured in his rancorous heart,
That flanders me with murder's crimfon badge :—
Say, if thou dar'ft, proud lord of Warwickfhire,
That I am faulty in duke Humphrey's death.
                    [*Exeunt* Cardinal, Som. *and Others.*
    War. What dares not Warwick, if falfe Suffolk dare him ?
    Q. Mar. He dares not calm his contumelious fpirit,
Nor ceafe to be an arrogant controller,
Though Suffolk dare him twenty thoufand times.
    War. Madam, be ftill ; with reverence may I fay ;

---

* *His hands* abroad *difplay'd,*] i. e. the fingers being widely diftend-
ed. So *adown,* for *down* ; *aweary,* for *weary,* &c. See Peacham's
Complete Gentleman, 1627 : " Herein was the Emperor Domitian fo cunning, that let a boy at a good diftance off hold up his hand and ftretch
his fingers *abroad,* he would fhoot through the fpaces, without touching
the boy's hand or any finger." MALONE.
    ⁸ *His well-proportion'd beard*—] His beard nicely trim'd and adjuft-
ed. MALONE.

                                        For

For every word, you fpeak in his behalf,
Is flander to your royal dignity.
  ‘ *Suf.* Blunt-witted lord, ignoble in demeanour !
If ever lady wrong'd her lord fo much,
Thy mother took into her blameful bed
Some ftern untutor'd churl, and noble ftock
Was graft with crab-tree flip ; whofe fruit thou art,
And never of the Nevils' noble race.
  War. But that the guilt of murder bucklers thee,
And I fhould rob the deathsman of his-fee,
Quitting thee thereby of ten thoufand fhames,
And that my fovereign's prefence makes me mild,
I would, falfe murderous coward, on thy knee
Make thee beg pardon for thy paffed fpeech,
And fay—it was thy mother that thou meant'ft,
That thou thyfelf waft born in baftardy :
And, after all this fearful homage done,
Give thee thy hire, and fend thy foul to hell,
Pernicious blood-fucker of fleeping men !
  Suf. Thou fhalt be waking, while I fhed thy blood,
If from this prefence thou dar'ft go with me.
  War. Away even now, or I will diag thee hence :
* Unworthy though thou art, I'll cope with thee,
* And do fome fervice to duke Humphrey's ghoft.
                              [*Exeunt* SUFFOLK *and* WARWICK.

* *K. Hen* What ftronger breaft-plate than a heart untaint-
        ed ?
* Thrice is he arm'd, that hath his quarrel juft * ;
* And he but naked, though lock'd up in fteel,
* Whofe confcience with injuftice is corrupted.
                              [*A noife within.*
  ℛ. *Mar.* What noife is this ?

Re-enter SUFFOLK *and* WARWICK, *with their weapons
                drawn.*

  K. Hen. Why, how now, lords ? your wrathful weapons
              drawn
‘ Here in our prefence ? dare you be fo bold ?—
‘ Why, what tumultuous clamour have we here ?
  Suf. The traiterous Warwick, with the men of Bury,
Set all upon me, mighty fovereign.

' * *Thrice is he arm'd,* &c.] So, in Marlowe's *Luft's Dominion* :
    “ Come, Moor ; I'm arm'd with more than cómplete *fteel,*
    “ The *juftice* of my *quarrel.*” MALONE.

                                          . *Noife*

Noise of a crowd within. Re-enter SALISBURY.

* *Sal.* Sirs, stand apart ; the king shall know your mind.—
Dread lord, the commons send you word by me,
Unless false Suffolk straight be done to death,
Or banished fair England's territories,
‘ They will by violence tear him from your palace,
* And torture him with grievous lingering death.
They say, by him the good duke Humphrey died ;
‘ They say, in him they fear your highness' death ;
‘ And mere instinct of love, and loyalty,—
‘ Free from a stubborn opposite intent,
‘ As being thought to contradict your liking,—
‘ Makes them thus forward in his banishment.
* They say, in care of your most royal person,
* That, if your highness should intend to sleep,
* And charge—that no man should disturb your rest,
* In pain of your dislike, or pain of death ;
* Yet, notwithstanding such a strait edict,
* Were there a serpent seen, with forked tongue,
* That slily glided towards your majesty,
* It were but necessary you were wak'd ;
* Lest, being suffer'd in that harmful slumber,
* The mortal worm [9] might make the sleep eternal :
* And therefore do they cry, though you forbid,
* That they will guard you, whe'r you will, or no,
* From such fell serpents as false Suffolk is ;
* With whose envenomed and fatal sting,
* Your loving uncle, twenty times his worth,
* They say, is shamefully bereft of life.
    Commons. [*within.*] An answer from the king, my lord of
        Salisbury.
    Suf. 'Tis like, the commons, rude unpolish'd hinds,
Could send such message to their sovereign :
But you, my lord, were glad to be employ'd,
To shew how quaint an orator [1] you are :
But all the honour Salisbury hath won,

---

9 *The mortal worm—*] Serpents in general, were anciently called
worms. So, in the *Devil's Charter*, 1607, Pope Alexander says when
he takes off the aspick from the young princes :
    “ How now, proud *worms ?* how tastes yon prince's blood ?”
                                                STEEVENS.
Mortal is here, as in many other places, *deadly.* MALONE.

1 — *how* quaint *an orator*—] *Quaint* for *dextrous, artificial.* So, in
the *Two Gentlemen of Verona :* “ —a ladder *quaintly* made of cords ”
                                                MALONE.
                                                Is—

Is—that he was the lord ambaffador,
Sent from a fort [2] of tinkers to the king.

   Commons. [*within.*] An anfwer from the king, or we will
    all break in.

  ‘ *K. Hen.* Go, Salifbury, and tell them all from me,
‘ I thank them for their loving tender care :
‘ And had I not been ’cited fo by them,
‘ Yet did I purpofe as they do entreat ;
‘ For, fure, my thoughts do hourly prophefy
‘ Mifchance unto my ftate by Suffolk's means.
‘ And therefore,—by his majefty I fwear,
‘ Whofe far unworthy deputy I am,—
‘ He fhall not breathe infection in this air [3]
‘ But three days longer, on the pain of death.

                    [*Exit* SALISBURY.

  ‘ *Q. Mar.* O Henry, let me plead for gentle Suffolk!
  ‘ *K. Henry.* Ungentle queen, to call him gentle Suffolk.
‘ No more, I fay ; if thou doft plead for him,
‘ Thou wilt but add increafe unto my wrath.
‘ Had I but faid, I would have kept my word ;
‘ But, when I fwear, it is irrevocable :—
* If, after three days' fpace, thou here be'ft found
* On any ground that I am ruler of,
* The world fhall not be ranfom for thy life.—
‘ Come, Warwick, come; good Warwick, go with me ;
‘ I have great matters to impart to thee.

        [*Exeunt* K. HENRY, WARWICK; *Lords, &c.*

  ‘ *Q. Mar.* Mifchance, and forrow, go along with you *!
‘ Heart's difcontent, and four affliction,
‘ Be play-fellows to keep you company !
‘ There's two of you ; the devil make a third !
‘ And three-fold vengeance tend upon your fteps !
  * *Suf.* Ceafe, gentle queen, thefe execrations,
* And let thy Suffolk take his heavy leave.
  ‘ *Q. Mar.* Fie, coward woman, and foft-hearted wretch !
‘ Haft thou not fpirit to curfe thine enemies ?
  Suf. A plague upon them ! wherefore fhould I curfe
    them ?
Would curfes kill, as doth the mandrake's groan [4],

                           ‘ I would

---

   [2] —*a fort*—] Is a company. JOHNSON.
   [3] *He fhall not breathe infection in this air*] That is, he fhall not con-
taminate this air with his infected breath. MALONE.
   * *Mifchance and forrow,* &c.] In the original play the queen is ftill
more violent :
      “ Hell-fire and vengeance go along with you !” MALONE.
   [4] *Would curfes kill, as doth the mandrake's groan,*] The fabulous ac-
                          counts

‘ I would invent as bitter searching terms,
* As curst, as harsh, and horrible to hear,
. Deliver'd strongly through my fixed teeth,
‘ With full as many signs of deadly hate,
As lean-fac'd Envy in her loathsome cave :
My tongue should stumble in mine earnest words ;
Mine eyes should sparkle like the beaten flint ;
My hair be fix'd on end, as one distract ;
Ay, every joint should seem to curse and ban :
And even now my burden'd heart would break,
Should I not curse them.   Poison be their drink [5]!
Gall, worse than gall, the daintiest that they taste !
Their sweetest shade, a grove of cypress trees [6]!
Their chiefest prospect, murdering basilisks !
Their softest touch, as smart as lizards' stings [7]!
Their musick, frightful as the serpent's hiss ;
And boding scritch-owls make the concert full !
All the foul terrors in dark-seated hell—

    2. Mar. Enough, sweet Suffolk ; thou torment'st thy-
self ;
. * And these dread curses—like the sun 'gainst glass,
* Or like an overcharged gun,—recoil,
* And turn the force of them upon thyself.

    Suf. You bade me ban, and will you bid me leave [8] ?
Now, by the ground that I am banish'd from,
Well could I curse away a winter's night,
Though standing naked on a mountain top,
Where biting cold would never let grass grow,
And think it but a minute spent in sport. ·

counts of the plant called a *mandrake* give it an inferior degree of ani-
mal life, and relate, that when it is torn from the ground it groans,
and that this groan being certainly fatal to him that is offering such un-
welcome violence, the practice of those who gather mandrakes is to tie
one end of a string to the plant, and the other to a dog, upon whom the
fatal groan discharges its malignity   Johnson.
  5 — *Poison be their drink !*] Most of these execrations are used, in the
very words of Shakspeare, by Lee, in his *Cæsar Borgia*, Act IV.
                               Steevens.
  6 — *a cypress tree !*] *Cypress* was employed in the funeral rites of
the Romans, and hence is always mentioned as an ill-boding plant.
                               Steevens.
  7 — *murdering* basilisks !—lizard's *stings !*] It has been said of the
basilisk that it had the power of destroying by a single glance of its eye.
A *lizard* has no sting, but is quite inoffensive. Steevens.
  See p. 158, n. *   Malone
  8 *You bade me ban, and will you bid me leave ?*] This inconsistency is
very common in real life. Those who are vexed to impatience are angry to see others less disturbed than themselves ; but when others begin
to rave, they immediately see in them what they could not find in
themselves, the deformity and folly of useless rage. Johnson.

                                     2. Mar.

Q. Mar. O, let me entreát theę ceafe⁹! Give· me thy
      hand,
* That I may dew it with my mournful tears;
* Nor let the rain of heaven wet this place,
* To wafh away my woeful monuments.
* O, could this kifs be printed in thy hand; [*kiffes his hand.*
* That thou might'ft think upon thefe by the feal,
' Through whom a thoufand fighs are breath'd for thee '!
' So, get thee gone, that I may know· my grief;
' 'Tis but furmis'd whilft thou art ftanding by,
* As one that furfeits thinking on a want.
' I will repeal thee, or, be well affur'd,
' Adventure·to· be banifhed myfelf :
* And banifhed I am, if but from thee.
* Go, fpeak not to me; even now be gone —
* O, go not yet !—Even thus two friends condemn'd
* Embrace, and kifs, and take ten thoufand leaves,
* Lother a hundred times to part than die.
* Yet now farewell; and farewell life with thee !
   Suf. Thus is poor Suffolk ten times banifhed,
Once by the king, and three times thrice by thee.
* 'Tis not the land I care for, .wert thou hence ;
* A wildernefs is populous enough,
* So Suffolk had thy heavenly company :
* For where thou art, there is the world itfelf ;
* With every feveral pleafure in the world ;
* And where thou art not, defolation.
* I can no more :—Live thou to joy thy life ;
* Myfelf no joy in nought, but that thou liv'ft.

Enter VAUX.

' *Q. Mar.* Whither goes Vaux fo faft ? what news, I
      pr'ythee?

9 *O, let me entreat thee,* &c.] Inftead of the four firft lines of this
fpeech, we find in the·old play thefe, which Shakfpeare has availed •
- himfelf of elfewhere :
      " No more, fweet Suffolk, hie thee hence to France; ·
      " Or live where thou wilt within this world's globe,
      " I'll have an Irifh [Iris] that fhall find thee out." MALONE.
' *That thou might'ft think upon thefe by the feal,*
      Through whom a thoufand fighs, &c] That by the impreffion of
my kifs for ever remaining on thy hand thou mighteft think on thofe
lips through which a thoufand fighs will be breathed for thee. JOHNSON
   See the fong introduced in *Meafure for Meafure :*
      " But my *kiffes* bring again,
      " *Seals* of love, but feal'd in vain."
Of this image our author appears to have been fond, having introduced
it in feveral places. There is no trace of it in the old play. MALONE.

' *Vaux.* To fignify unto his Majefty,
That cardinal Beaufort is at point of death :
' For fuddenly a grievous ficknefs took him,
' That makes him gafp, and ftare, and catch the air,
' Blafpheming God, and curfing men on earth.
' Sometime, he talks as if duke Humphrey's ghoft
' Were by his fide ; fometime, he calls the king,
And whifpers to his pillow, as to him,
* The fecrets of his over-charged foul [2] :
' And I am fent to tell his Majefty,
' That even now he cries aloud for him.
' *2. Mar.* Go, tell this heavy meffage to the king.
[*Exit* Vaux.

' Ah me ! what is this world ? what news are thefe [2] ?
' But wherefore grieve I at an hour's poor lofs [3],
' Omitting Suffolk's exile, my foul's treafure ?
' Why only, Suffolk, mourn I not for thee,
' And with the fouthern clouds contend in tears ;
' Theirs for the earth's increafe, mine for my forrows ?
' Now, get thee hence : The king, thou know'ft, is coming ;
' If thou be found by me, thou art but dead.

' *Suf.* If I depart from thee, I cannot live :
' And in thy fight to die, what were it elfe,
But like a pleafant flumber in thy lap ?
Here could I breathe my foul into the air,
' As mild and gentle as the cradle-babe,
Dying with mother's dug between its lips :

1 *And whifpers to his pillow, as to him,*

The fecrets, &c.] The firft of thefe lines is in the old play. The
fecond is unqueft onably our author's. The thought appears to have
ftruck him ; for he has introduced it again in *Macbeth* :

" —— Infected minds
" To their deaf pillows will difcharge their fecrets." MALONE.

2 *Ah me ! what is this world ? what news are thefe ?*] Inftead of
this line, the quarto reads :

Oh ! what is worldly pomp ? all men muft die,
And woe am I for Beaufort's heavy end. STEEVENS.

3 —— *at an hour's poor lofs,*] I believe the poet's meaning is, *Wherefore do I grieve that Beaufort has died an hour before his time,* who,
being an old man, could not have had a long time to live ? STEEVENS.

This certainly may be the meaning ; yet I rather incline to think that
the queen intends to fay, " Why do I lament a circumftance, the im-
preffion of which will pafs away in the fhort period of an hour ; while
I neglect to think on the lofs of Suffolk, my affection for whom no time
will efface ?" MALONE.

Where,

Where, from thy fight [4], I fhould be raging mad,
' And cry out for thee to clofe up mine eyes,
' To have thee with thy lips to ftop my mouth ;
' So fhouldft thou either turn my flying foul [5],
' Or I fhould breathe it fo into thy body,
And then it liv'd in fweet Elyfium.
To die by thee, were but to die in jeft ;
From thee to die, were torture more than death :
O, let me ftay, befall what may befall.
' *Q. Mar.* Away ! though parting be a fretful corrofive [6],
' It is applied to a deathful wound.
' To France, fweet Suffolk : Let me hear from thee ;
' For wherefoe'er thou art in this world's globe,
I'll have an Iris [7] that fhall find thee out.
 Suf. I go.
 Q. Mar. And take my heart with thee.
 Suf. A jewel lock'd into the woful'ft cafk
That ever did contain a thing of worth.
Even as a fplitted bark, fo funder we ;
This way fall I to death.
 Q. Mar. This way for me.   [*Exeunt, feverally.*

---

4 Where, *from thy fight,—*] In the preambles of almoft all the ftatutes made during the firft twenty years of queen Elizabeth's reign, the word *where* is ufed inftead of *whereas.* It is fo ufed here. MALONE.

5 —*turn my flying foul,*] Perhaps Mr. Pope was indebted to this paffage in his *Eloifa to Abelard,* where he makes that votarift of exquifite fenfibility fay :
  " See my lips tremble, and my eye-balls roll,
  " Suck my laft breath, and catch my flying foul." STEEV.

6 *Away! though parting be a fretful* corrofive,] This word was generally, in our author's time, written, and, I fuppofe, pronounced, *corfive*; and the metre fhews that it ought to be fo pronounced here. So, in *The Alchymift,* " *corfive* waters." Again, in *The Spanish Tragedy,* 1605:
  " His fon diftreft, a *corfive* to his heart." MALONE.

7 *I'll have an Iris—*] Iris was the meffenger of Juno. JOHNSON.
So, in *All's Well that Ends Well:*
  " —— this diftemper'd meffenger of wet,
  " The many colour'd *Iris,*—" STEEVENS.

I 2   SCENE

SCENE III.

London. *Cardinal* Beaufort's *Bed-chamber.*

Enter King HENRY [8], SALISBURY, WARWICK, *and Others.*
The Cardinal *in bed; Attendants with him.*

K. Hen. How fares my lord [9]? fpeak, Beaufort, to thy
fovereign.

' *Car.* If thou be'ft death, I'll give thee England's treafure [1],

' Enough

---

[8] *Enter* King Henry, *&c.*] The quarto offers the following ftage
directions. *Enter King and Salifbury, and then the curtaines be drawne,
and the cardinal is difcovered in his bed, raving and ftaring as if he
were mad.* STEEVENS.
This defcription did not efcape our author, for he has availed himfelf
of it elfewhere. See the fpeech of Vaux in p. 170. MALONE.

[9] *How fares my lord,* &c.] This fcene, and that in which the dead
body of the duke o Glofter is defcribed, are defervedly admired. Hav-
ing already fubmitted to the reader the lines on which the former fcene
is founded, I fhall now fubjoin thofe which gave rife to that before us:
" *Car.* O death, if thou wilt let me live but one whole year,
" I'll give thee as much gold as will purchafe fuch another ifland.
" *King.* O fee, my lord of Salifbury, how he is troubled,
" Lord Cardinal, remember, Chrift muft have thy foul.
" *Car.* Why, dy'd he not in his bed?
" What would you have me to do then?
" Can I make men live, whether they will or no?
" Sirrah, go fetch me the ftrong poifon, which
" The 'pothecary fent me.
" O, fee where duke Humphrey's ghoft doth ftand,
" And ftares me in the face! Look; look; comb down his hair.
" So now, he's gone again. Oh, oh, oh.
" *Sal.* See how the pangs of death doth gripe his heart.
" *King.* Lord Cardinal, if thou dieft affured of heavenly blifs,
" Hold up thy hand, and make fome fign to me.
[*The Cardinal dies.*
" O fee, he dies, and makes no fign at all.
" O God, forgive his foul!
" *Sal.* So bad an end did never none behold;
" But as his death, fo was his life in all
King. Forbear to judge, good Salfbury, forbear;
" For God will judge us all. Go take him hence,
" And fee his funerals be perform'd " *Exeunt.* MALONE.
[1] *If thou be'ft death, I'll give thee England's treafure,* &c.] The
following paffage in Hall's *Chronicle,* Henry VI. fol. 70, b. fuggefted
the correfponding lines to the author of the old play: " During thefe
doinges, Henry Beaufford, bifhop of Winchefter, and called the riche
Cardynall, departed out of this worlde.—This man was—haut in fto-
mach

‘ Enough to purchafe fuch another ifland,
‘ So thou wilt let me live, and feel no pain.
 * K. Hen. Ah, what a fign it is of evil life,
* When death's approach is feen fo terrible!
 * War Beaufort, it is thy fovereign fpeaks to thee.
 * Car. Bring me unto my trial when you will.
‘ Dy'd he not in his bed? where fhould he die?
‘ Can I make men live, whe'r they will or no² ?—
* O! torture me no more, I will confefs.—
‘ Alive again? then fhew me where he is;
‘ I'll give a thoufand pound to look upon him —
* He hath no eyes, the duft hath blinded them *.—
‘ Comb down his hair; look! look! it ftands upright,
‘ Like lime-twigs fet to catch my winged foul!—
‘ Give me fome drink; and bid the apothecary
‘ Bring the ftrong poifon that I bought of him.
 * K. Hen. O thou eternal Mover of the heavens,
* Look with a gentle eye upon this wretch!
* O, beat away the bufy meddling fiend,
* That lays ftrong fiege unto this wretch's foul,
* And from his bofom purge this black defpair! .
 ‘ War. See, how the pangs of death do make him grin.
 * Sal. Difturb him not, let him pafs peaceably
 * K. Hen. Peace to his foul, if God's good pleafure be!
‘ Lord cardinal, if thou think'ft on heaven's blifs,

mach and hygh in countenance, ryche above meafure of all men, and
to fewe liberal; difdaynful to his kynne, and dread'ul to his lovers.
His covetous infaciable and hope of long lyfe made hym bothe to forget
God, his prynce, and hymfelfe, in his latter days; for Doctor John
Baker, his pryvie counfailer and his chapellayn, wrote, that lying on
his death bed, he faid thefe words. ‘ Why fhould I dye, havyng fo muche
riches? If the whole realme would fave my lyfe, I am able either be
pollicie to get it, or by ryches to bye it. Fye, will not death be hyered
nor will money do nothynge? When my nephew of Bedford died, I
thought my felfe halfe up the whele, but when I fawe myne other
nephew of Gloucefter difceafed, then I thought my felfe able to be
equal with kinges, and fo thought to increafe my treafure in hope to
have worne a trypple croune. But I fe nowe the worlde fayleth me, and
fo I am deceyved; praying you all to pray for me." MALONE
 ² Can I make men live, whe'r they will or no?] So, in King John:
 " We cannot hold mortality's ftrong hand:
 " Why do you bend fuch folemn brows on me?
 " Think you, I bear the fhears of deftiny?
 " Have I commandment on the pulfe of life?" MALONE.
 * He hath no eyes, &c.] So, in Macbeth:
 " Thou haft no fpeculation in thofe eyes,
 " Which thou doft glare with." MALONE.

 ‘ Hold

' Hold up thy hand [3], make signal of thy hope.——
' He dies, and makes no sign; O God, forgive him!
   ' *War.* So bad a death argues a monstrous life.
   ' *K. Hen.* Forbear to judge, for we are sinners all [4].——
' Close up his eyes, and draw the curtain close;
' And let us all to meditation.   [*Exeunt* [5].

ACT IV. SCENE I [6].

Kent. *The Sea-shore near* Dover.

Firing heard at sea [7]. *Then enter from a boat, a* Captain, *a*
Master, *a* Master's-Mate, Walter Whitmore, *and Others;*
with them SUFFOLK, *and other Gentlemen prisoners.*

   * *Cap.* The gaudy, blabbing, and remorseful day [8]
   * Is crept into the bosom of the sea;

                    * And

---

[3] *Hold up thy hand,*] Thus in the old play of *King John,* 1591,
Pandulph sees the king dying, and says:
    " Then, good my lord, if you forgive them all,
    " *Lift up your hand,* in token you forgive."
Again:
    " *Lift up thy hand,* that we may witness here,
    " Thou di'st the servant of our Saviour Christ:——
    " Now joy betide thy soul!" STEEVENS.

[4] *Forbear to judge, for we are sinners all.——*
    " Peccantes culpare cave, nam labimur omnes,
    " Aut sumus, aut fuimus, vel possumus esse quod hic est."
                                  JOHNSON.

[5] *Exeunt.*] This is one of the scenes which have been applauded by
the criticks, and which will continue to be admired when prejudice
shall cease, and bigotry give way to impartial examination. These are
beauties that rise out of nature and of truth; the superficial reader
cannot miss them, the profound can image nothing beyond them.
                                  JOHNSON.

[6] The circumstance on which this scene is founded, is thus related by
Hall in his Chronicle:—" But fortune wold not that this flagitious
person [the Duke of Suffolk, who being impeached by the Commons
was banished from England for five years] shoulde so escape; for when
he shipped in Suffolke, entendynge to be transported into France, he
was encontered with a shippe of warre apperteinyng to the Duke of Ex-
cester, the Constable of the Towre of London, called *the Nicholas of*
the Tower. The capitaine of the same bark with small fight entered
into the duke's shyppe, and perceyving his person present, brought him
to Dover rode, and there on the one syde of a cocke-bote, caused his
head to be stryken of, and left his body with the head upon the sandes of
Dover; which corse was there founde by a chapelayne of his, and conveyed to Wyngfielde college in Suffolke, and there buried." MALONE.

* And now loud-howling wolves arouse the jades
* That drag the tragick melancholy night;
* Who with their drowsy, slow, and flagging wings
* Clip dead men's graves 9, and from their misty jaws
* Breathe foul contagious darkness in the air.
* Therefore, bring forth the soldiers of our prize;
* For, whilst our pinnace anchors in the Downs,
* Here shall they make their ransom on the sand,
* Or with their blood stain this discolour'd shore.—
' Master, this prisoner freely give I thee;—
' And thou that art his mate, make boot of ths;—
' The other [*pointing to* Suffolk.] Walter Whitmore, is thy
    share.
  ' 1. *Gent.* What is my ransom, master? let me know.
  ' *Mast.* A thousand crowns, or else lay down your head.
                     ' *Mate.*

7 *Bring beard at sea.*] Perhaps Ben Jonson was thinking of this play, when he put the following declaration into the mouth of Morose in the *Silent Woman.* " Nay, I would fit out a play that were nothing but *fights at sea*, drum, trumpet, and target." STEEVENS.

8 *The gaudy*, blabbing, *and* remorseful *day*,] The epithet *blabbing* applied to the day by a man about to commit murder, is exquisitely beautiful. Guilt is afraid of light, consi ers darkness as a natural shelter, and makes night the confidante of those actions which cannot be trusted to the *tell-tale day*. JOHNSON.

Remorseful is pityful. So, in the *Two Gentlemen of Verona:*
  " ——— a gentleman,
  " Valiant, wise, *remorseful*, well accomplish'd."
The same idea occurs in *Macbeth:*
    " Scarf up the tender eye of *pityful day.*" STEEVENS.

This speech is an amplification of the following one in the first part of *The Whole Contention*, &c. quarto 1600:
    " Bring forward these prisoners that scorn'd to yield;
    " Unlade their goods with speed, and *sink their ship*.
    " Here master, this prisoner I give to you,
    " This other the master's mate shall have;
    " And Walter Whickmore, thou shalt have this man;
    " And let them pay their ransome ere they pass.
    " *Suff.* Walter!"   [*he starteth*
Had Shakspeare's play been taken down by the ear, or an imperfect copy otherwise obtained, his lines might have been mutilated, or imperfectly represented; but would a new circumstance (like that of *sinking* Suffolk's *ship*) not found in the original, have been *added* by the copyist?—On the other hand, if Shakspeare new modelled the work of another, such a circumstance might well be *omitted*. MALONE.

9 ——— the jades.
  That drag the tragick melancholy night,
  Who with their drowsy, slow, and flagging wings
  Clip dead men's graves,] The wings of the jades that drag night appears an unnatural image, till it is remembered that the chariot of the night is supposed, by Shakspeare, to be drawn by dragons. JOHNSON.

‘ *Mate.* And so much shall you give, or off goes yours.

* *Cap.* What, think you much to pay two thousand crowns,

* And bear the name and port of gentlemen ?—

* Cut both the villains' throats;—for die you shall;

* The lives of those which we have lost in fight,

* Cannot be counter-pois'd [1] with such a petty sum.

* *1. Gent.* I'll give it, sir; and therefore spare my life.

* *2. Gent.* And so will I, and write home for it straight.

‘ *Whit.* I lost mine eye in laying the prize aboard,

‘ And therefore, to revenge it, shalt thou die; [to Suf.

‘ And so should these, if I might have my will.

* *Cap.* Be not so rash; take ransom, let him live.

‘ *Suf.* Look on my George [2], I am a gentleman;

‘ Rate me at what thou wilt, thou shalt be paid.

‘ *Whit.* And so am I; my name is Walter Whitmore.

‘ How now? why star'st thou? what, doth death affright?

‘ *Suf.* Thy name affrights me [3], in whose sound is death.

‘ A cunning man did calculate my birth,

‘ And told me—that by *Water* I should die [4]:

‘ Yet let not this make thee be bloody-minded;

‘ Thy

---

[1] *Cannot be counterpois'd—*] I suspect that a line has been lost, preceding—" The lives of those," &c. and that this speech belongs to *Whitmore*; for it is inconsistent with what the captain says afterwards. The word *cannot* is not in the folio. The old play affords no assistance. The word now added is necessary to the sense, and is a less innovation on the text than what has been made in the modern editions—*Nor can these lives,* &c.

The emendation made in this passage (which was written by Shakspeare, there being no trace of it in the old play,) is supported by another in *Coriolanus,* in which we have again the same expression, and nearly the same sentiments:

" The man I speak of *cannot* in the world

" Be singly *counterpois'd* " MALONE.

[2] *Look on my* George,] In the first edition it is *my ring.* WARBURT. Here we have another proof of what has been already so often observed. A *ring* and a *George* could never have been confounded either by the eye or the ear. So, in the original play the ransom of each of Suffolk's companions is a hundred pounds, but here a thousand crowns. MALONE.

[3] *Thy name affrights me—*] But he had heard his name before, without being startled by it. In the old play, as soon as ever the captain has consigned him to " *Walter Whickmore,*" Suffolk immediately exclaims, *Walter!* Whickmore asks him, why he fears him, and Suffolk replies, " It is thy name affrights me."—Our author has here, as in some other places, fallen into an impropriety, by sometimes following and sometimes deserting his original. MALONE.

[4] *— by* Water—] See the fourth scene of the first act of this play. STEEVENS.

‘ Thy name is—*Gualtier*, being rightly founded.

‘ *Whit.* Gualtier, or *Walter*, which it is, I care not ;

‘ Ne'er yet did bafe difhonour blur our name *,

‘ But with our fword we wip'd away the blot ;

‘ Therefore, when merchant-like I fell revenge,

‘ Broke be my fword, my arms torn and defac'd,

‘ And I proclaim'd a coward through the world!

　　　　　　　　　　　　　　　[*lays hold on* Suffolk.

　‘ *Suf.* Stay, Whitmore ; for thy prifoner is a prince,
The duke of Suffolk, William de la Pole

　‘ *Whit.* The ouke of Suffolk, muffled up in rags!

　Suf. Ay, but thefe rags are no part of the duke :
Jove fometime went difguis'd, And why not I ⁵ ?

　Cap But Jove was never flain, as thou fhalt be.

　‘ *Suf.* Obfcure and lowly fwain ⁶, king Henry's blood,
The honourable blood of Lancafter,

‘ Muft not be fhed by fuch a jaded groom ⁷.
Haft thou not kifs'd thy hand, and held my ftirrop?

‘ Bare-headed plodded by my foot-cloth mule,

‘ And thought thee happy when I fhook my head?

---

* *Ne'er yet did bafe difhonour,* &c] This and the following lines are founded on thefe two in the old play:

　　“ And therefore ere I merchant-like fell blood·for gold,

　　“ Then caft me headlong down into the fea.”

The new image which Shakfpeare has introduced into this fpeech,
“ — my arms torn and de·ac'd,”—is found alfo in *King Richard II:*

　　“ From my own windows *torn my houfehold coat,*

　　“ Raz'd out my imprefs ; leaving me no fign,—

　　“ Save men's opinions, and my living blood,—

　　“ To fhew the world I am a gentleman ” MALONE.

5 *Jove fometime went difguis'd,* &c.] This verfe is omitted in all but the firft old edition, [quarto 1600,] without which what follows is not fenfe. The next line alfo,

　　Obfcure and lowly fwain, king Henry's blood,

was falfely put in the Captain's mouth　PoPE.

6 — lowly *fwain,*] The folio reads.— *owly* fwain. STEEVENS.

The quarto *lowly.* In a fubfequent paffage the folio has the word right:

　　By fuch a *low'y* vaffel as thyfelf.

Lowfy was undoubtedly an error of the prefs. MALONE.

7 — *a* jaded *groom*] I fuppofe he means, a low fellow, fit only to attend upon horfes ; which in our author's time were frequently termed *jades.* The original play has *lady,* which conveys this meaning (the only one that the whole feems to afford,) more clearly, *jaded* being liable to an equivoque.

Jaded groom, however, may mean a groom whom all men treat with contempt ; as worthlefs as the moft paltry kind of horfe. So, in *K. Henry VIII.*

　　“ —— If we live thus tamely,

　　“ To be thus *jaded* by a piece of fcarlet.”—MALONE.

I 5　　　　　　　‘ How

' How often haft thou waited at my cup,
' Fed from my trencher, kneel'd down at the board,
' When I have feafted with queen Margaret?
* Remember it, and let it make thee creft-fall'n;
* Ay, and allay this thy abortive pride [8]:
* How in our voiding lobby haft thou ftood,
* And duly waited for my coming forth?
' This hand of mine hath writ in thy behalf,
' And therefore fhall it charm thy riotous tongue *.
　　*Whit. Speak, captain, fhall I ftab the forlorn fwain?
　　* Cap. Firft let my words ftab him, as he hath me.
　　* Suf. Bafe flave! thy words are blunt, and fo art thou.
　' Cap. Convey him hence, and on our long boat's fide
' Strike off his head.
　　Suf. Thou dar'ft not for thy own.
　　Cap. Yes, Poole.
　　Suf. Poole [9]?
　　Cap. Poole? Sir Poole? lord [1]?
' Ay, kennel, puddle, fink; whofe filth and dirt
' Troubles the filver fpring where England drinks.
' Now will I dam up this thy yawning mouth,
' For fwallowing [9] the treafure of the realm:
' Thy lips, that kifs'd the queen, fhall fweep the ground;

　　　　　　　　　　　　　　　　　　　　　　' And

---

8 — *abortive pride*.] Pride that has had birth too foon, pride iffuing before its time. JOHNSON.

* — charm *thy riotous tongue*.] i. e. reftrain thy licentious talk; compel thee to be filent. See Mr Steevens's note in *Othello*, Act V. Sc. ult where Iago ufes the fame expreffion. It occurs frequently in the books of our author's age. MALONE.

9 Cap *Yes, Poole.*
Suf. *Poole?*] Thefe two little fpeeches are found in the quarto, but not in the folio. It is clear from what follows that thefe fpeeches were not intended to be rejected by Shakfpeare, but accidentally omitted at the prefs. I have therefore reftored them. See p. 177, n. 5.
　　　　　　　　　　　　　　　　　　　　　　　MALONE.
I think the two intermediate fpeeches fhould be inferted in the text, to introduce the captain's repetition of *Poole*, &c. STEEVENS
1 *Poole? Sir Poole? lord?*] The diffonance of this broken line makes it almoft certain that we fhould read with a kind of ludicrous climax:

　　1 *Poole? Sir Poole? lord Poole?*
He then plays upon the name *Poole, kennel, puddle.* JOHNSON.
In the old play the reply of the captain is—
　　" Yes, Poole, puddle, kennell, fink and dirt." MALONE.

9 For *fwallowing*—] He means, perhaps, fo as to prevent thy fwallowing, &c. So, in the *Puritan*, 1607: "—he is now in huckfter's handling for running away." I have met with many other inftances of this kind of phrafeology. The more obvious interpretation, however, may be the true one. MALONE.

' And thou, that fmil'dft at good duke Humphrey's death [*],
' Againſt the fenfeleſs winds ſhalt grin in vain ',
* Who, in contempt, ſhall hiſs at thee again :
* And wedded be thou to the hags of hell,
* For daring to affy [2] a mighty lord
* Unto the daughter of a worthleſs king,
* Having neither ſubject, wealth, nor diadem.
* By deviliſh policy art thou grown great,
* And, like ambitious Sylla, over-gorg'd
* With gobbets of thy mother's bleeding heart.
* By thee, Anjou and Maine were ſold to France:
* The falſe revolting Normans, thorough thee,
* Diſdain to call us lord; and Picardy
* Hath ſlain their governors, ſurpriz'd our forts,
* And ſent the ragged ſoldiers wounded home.
* The princely Warwick, and the Nevils all,—
* Whoſe dreadful ſwords were never drawn in vain,—
* As hating thee, are riſing [3] up in arms:
* And now the houſe of York—thruſt from the crown,
* By ſhameful murder of a guiltleſs king,
* And lofty proud encroaching tyranny,—
* Burns with revenging fire; whoſe hopeful colours
* Advance our half-fac'd ſun [4], ſtriving to ſhine,
* Under the which is writ—_Invitis nubibus._
* The commons here in Kent are up in arms:
* And, to conclude, reproach, and beggary,
* Is crept into the palace of our king,
* And all by thee :—Away! convey him hence.
* _Suf._ O that I were a god, to ſhoot forth thunder

* Upon

---

* _And thou, that fmil'dſt at good duke Humphrey's death, &c._] This enumeration of Suffolk's crimes ſeems to have been ſuggeſted by the _Mirrour of Magiſtrates_, 1575, _Legend of William de la Poile:_
    " And lead me back again to Dover road;
    " Where _unto me recounting all my faults,_—
    " As murthering of duke Humphrey in his bed,
    " And how I had brought all the realm to a pght,
    " Cauſing the king unlawfully to wed.
    " There was no grace, but I muſt loſe my head." MALONE.

[2] — _ſhalt grin in vain,_] From hence to the end of this ſpeech is undoubtedly the original compoſition of Shakſpeare, no traces of it being found in the elder play. MALONE.

[2] — _to affy_—] To affy is to betroth in marriage. STEEVENS.

[3] — _are riſing_—] Old Copy—_and riſing._ Corrected by Mr. Rowe.
    MALONE.

[4] — _whoſe hopeful colours_
    Advance our half-fac'd ſun,] " Edward III bare for his device the rays of the ſun diſperſing themſelves out of a cloud." Camden's _Remains._ MALONE.

* Upon thefe paltry, fervile, abject drudges !

* Small things make bafe men proud : ' this villain here

' Being captain of a pinnace 5, threatens more

' Than Bargulus the ftrong Illyrian pirate 6.

' Drones fuck not eagles' blood, but rob bee-hives.

' It is impoffible, that I fhould die

' By fuch a lowly vaffal as thyfelf.

' Thy words move rage, and not remorfe, in me* :

' I go of meffage from the queen of France ;

' I charge thee, waft me fafely crofs the channel

   ' *Cap.* Walter,—

   ' *Whit.* Come, Suffolk, I muft waft thee to thy death.

   * *Suf. Pene gelidus timor occupat artus* 7 :—'tis thee I
   fear.

Whit.

5 *Being captain of a* pinnace.] A *pinnace* did not anciently fignify, as at prefent, a man of war's boat, but a fhip of fmall burthen So, in *Winwood's Memorials*, Vol III p. 118: " The king (James I.) naming the great fhip, Trade's Increafe; and the prince, a *pinnace* of 250 tons (built to wait upon her) Pepper-corn." STEEVENS.

6 *Than Bargulus the ftrong Illyrian pirate.*] " *Barguius, Illyrius latro, de quo eft apud Theopompum, magnas opes habuit,*" Cicero *de Officiis*, lib. ii. cap. 11. WARBURTON

Dr. Farmer obferves that Shakfpeare might have met with this pirate in two tranflations. Robert Whytinton, 1533, calls him " Bargulus, a pirate upon the fee of Illiry;" and Nicholas Grimald, about twenty-three years afterwards, " Bargulus, the Illyrian robber."

Bargulus does not make his appearance in the quarto, but we meet with another hero in his room. The Captain, fays Suffolk,

   Threatens more plagues than mighty *Abradas,*
   The great Macedonian pirate.

I know nothing more of this *Abradas,* than that he is mentioned by Greene in his *Penelope's Web,* 1601: " *Abradas,* the great Macedonian pirat, thought every one had a letter of mart that bare fayles in the ocean " STEEVENS

Here we fee another proof of what has been before fuggefted.

MALONE.

* *Thy words move rage, and not remorfe in me:*] This line Shakfpeare has injudicioufly taken from the Captain, to whom it is attributed in the original play, and given it to Suffolk; for what *remorfe,* that is, *pity,* could Suffolk be called upon to fhew to his *affailant;* whereas the Captain might with propriety fay to his *captive,*—thy haughty language exafperate me, inftead of exciting my *compaffion.* MALONE.

7 Pene *gelidus timor occupat artus:* The folio, where alone this line is found, reads—*Pine,* &c a corrupt on. I fuppofe of the word that I have fubftituted in its place. I know not what other word could have been intended The editor of the fecond folio, and all the modern editors, have efcaped the difficulty, by fupprefling the word. The meafure is of little confequence, for no fuch line, I believe, exifts in any claffick author. Dr. Grey refers us to " Ovid de Trift. 313, and Metamorph. 247:" a very wide field to range in; however with fome trouble

I found

Whit. Thou fhalt have caufe to fear, before I leave thee.
‘ What, are ye daunted now? now will ye ftoop?
 ‘ 1. *Gent.* My gracious lord, entreat him, fpeak him fair
 ‘ *Suf.* Suffolk's imperial tongue is ftern and rough,
‘ Us'd to command, untaught to plead for favour.'
‘ Far be it, we fhould honour fuch as thefe
‘ With humble fuit: no, rather let my head
‘ Stoop to the block, than thefe knees bow to any.
‘ Save to the God of heaven, and to my king;
‘ And fooner dance upon a bloody pole,
‘ Than ftand uncover'd to the vulgar groom.
* True nobility is exempt from fear:
* More can I bear than you dare execute [8].
 ‘ *Cap.* Hale him away, and let him talk no more.
 ‘ *Suf.* Come, foldiers, fhew what cruelty ye can *,
‘ That this my death may never be forgot!—
‘ Great men oft die by wild bezonians [9]:
‘ A Roman fworder [1] and banditto flave
‘ Murder'd fweet Tully; Brutus' baftard hand [2]
‘ Stabb'd Julius Cæfar; favage iflanders,

‘ Pompey

I found out what he meant. The line is *not* in Ovid; (nor I believe in any other p et;) but in his *D- T.iftibus*, lib. 1. El. iii. 113, we find Navita, conf ffus *gelido* pallore *timo em,*—
and in his *Metamorph* Lib. IV. 247, we meet with thefe lines:
 Ille quidem *gelidos* radiorum viribus *artus,*
 Si queat, in vivum tentat evocare calorem. MALONE.

[8] *More can I bear, than you dare execute.*] So, in *K. Henry VIII.*
 " —— I am able now, methinks,
 " (Out of a fortitude of foul I feel,)
 " To endure more miferies, and greater far,
 " Than my weak hearted enemies dare offer."
Again, in *Othello*:
 " Thou h ft not half that power to do me harm,
 " As I have to be hurt. MALONE.

* *Come, foldiers, fb. w what cruelty ye can*] In the folio this line is given to the Captain by the careleffnefs of the printer or tranfcriber. The prefent regulation was made by Sir Thomas Hanmer, and followed by Dr Warburton See the latte 1 at of note 5, p. 177. MALONE.
 Surely this line belongs to Suffolk No cruelty was medita ed bey nd decollation: and with ut fuch an int oduction, there is an obfcure abruptnefs in the beginning of the reply to the captain STEEVENS

[9] — *bezini nr.*] *Bifognofo,* is a mean low man. So in Markham's *Englifh Hufbandman,* p. 4: " The ordinary tillers o the earth, fuch as we call hufband ren.: in France pelants, in 'paine *befon,ans,* and generally the cl utfhoe " STEEVENS.

[1] *A Roman fworder,* &c.] i. e. Herennius a centurion, and Popilius Laenas, tribune of the foldiers. STEEVENS

[2] *Brutus' baftard band—*] Brutus was the fon of Servilia, a Roman lady, who had been concubine to Julius Cæfar. STEEVENS.

' Pompey the great ³ : and Suffolk dies by pirates.

[Exit Suf. with Whitmore and others.

'Cap. And as for these whose ransom we have set,
It is our pleasure, one of them depart :—
Therefore come you with us, and let him go.

[Exeunt all but the first Gentleman.

Re-enter WHITMORE, with Suffolk's body.

' Whit. There let his head and lifeless body lie,
' Until the queen his mistress bury it ⁴.   [Exit.
' ' 1. Gent. O barbarous and bloody spectacle !
' His body will I bear unto the king :
' If he revenge it not, yet will his friends ;
' So will the queen, that living held him dear.

[Exit, with the body.

³ Pompey the great ;] The poet seems to have confounded the story
of Pompey with some other. JOHNSON.

This circumstance might be advanced as a slight proof, in aid of
many stronger, that our poet was no classical scholar. Such a one could
not easily have forgotten the manner in which the life of Pompey was
concluded. Spenser also abounds with deviations from established history and fable. STEEVENS.

Pompey being killed by Achillas and Septimius at the moment that
the Egyptian fishing-boat in which they were, reached the coast, and his
head being thrown into the sea, (a circumstance which Shakspeare
found in North's translation of Plutarch) his mistake does not appear
more extraordinary than some others which have been remarked in his
works.

It is remarkable that the introduction of Pompey was among Shakspeare's additions to the old play. This may account for the classical
error, into which probably the original author would not have fallen. In
the quarto the lines stand thus :

    " A sworder, and banditti slave
    " Murdered sweet Tully ;
    " Brutus' bastard hand stabb'd Julius Cæsar,
    " And Suffolk dies by pirates on the seas." MALONE.

⁴ There let his head, &c.] Instead of this speech the quarto gives us
the following :

    'Cap. Off with his head, and send it to the queen,
    And ransomless this prisoner shall go free,
    To see it safe deliver'd unto her. STEEVENS.

See p. 180, n. 5, and the notes there referred to. MALONE.

SCENE

SCENE II.

Blackheath.

Enter George Bevis *and* John Holland.

' *Geo.* Come, and get thee a sword [5], though made of a
' lath; they have been up these two days.

' *John.* They have the more need to sleep now then.

' *Geo.* I tell thee [6], Jack Cade the clothier means to dress
' the commonwealth, and turn it, and set a new nap upon it.

John. So he had need, for 'tis thread-bare. Well, I say,
' it was never merry world in England, since gentlemen came
' up.

' *Geo.* O miserable age! Virtue is not regarded in handy-
' crafts-men.

' *John.* The nobility think scorn to go in leather aprons.

' *Geo.* Nay more, the king's council are no good work-
' men.

' *John.* True; And yet it is said,—Labour in thy voca-
' tion: which is as much to say, as,—let the magistrates be
' labouring men; and therefore should we be magistrates.

' *Geo.* Thou hast hit it: for there's no better sign of a
' brave mind, than a hard hand.

' *John.* I see them! I see them! There's Best's son, the
' tanner of Wingham;—

' *Geo.* He shall have the skins of our enemies, to make
' dog's-leather of.

John And Dick the butcher [7],—

' *Geo.* Then is sin struck down like an ox, and iniquity's
' throat cut like a calf.

' *John.* And Smith the weaver:—

---

[5] —*get thee a sword,*] The quarto reads—Come away *Nick*, and
put a long staff in thy pike, &c. STEEVENS.

So afterwards instead of " Cade the *clothier,*" we have in the quarto
" Cade the *dyer of Ashford.*" See the notes above referred to. MALONE.

[6] *I tell thee,*—] In the original play this speech is introduced more
naturally. *Nick* asks George, " Sir a George, what's the matter?" to
which George replies, " Why marry, Jack Cade, the *dyer* of Ashford
here," &c. MALONE.

[7] *And Dick the butcher,*—] In the first copy thus:

" Why there's Dick the butcher, and *Robin the sadler,* and *Will* that
came a wooing to our Nan last Sunday, and Harry and Tom, and *Gregory*
that should have your parnell, and a great sort more, it come from Ro-
chester and from Maidstone, and Canterbury, and all the towns hereta-
bouts, and we must all be lords, or squires, as soon as Jack Cade is king."
MALONE.

' *Geo.*

* *Geo. Argo*, their thread of life is fpun.
* *John.* Come, come, let's fall in with them.

Drum. Enter CADE, DICK *the butcher,* SMITH *the weaver, and others in great number.*

' *Cade* We John Cade, fo term'd of our fuppofed fa-
' ther,—

Dick. Or rather, of ftealing a cade of herrings [8].   [*Afide.*

' *Cade.* —for our enemies fhall fall before us [9], infpired
' with the fpirit of putting down kings and princes,—Com-
' mand filence.

Dick. Silence !

Cade. My father was a Mortimer,—

[8] *a cade of herrings*] That is a barrel of herrings. I fuppofe the word *k g*, which is now ufed, is *cade* corrupted. JOHNSON.

A cade is lefs than a barrel. The quantity it fhould contain is afcer-tained by the account of the Celerefs of the Abbey of Berking "Memorandum, that a *barrel* of herryng fhould contene a thou and herryngs, and a *cade* of herryng fix hundreth, fix fcore to the hundreth." Mon. Ang. '. 83. MALONE.

Nafh fpeaks of naving weighed one of Gabriel Harvey's b oks againft a *cade of herrings*, and fays, " That the rebel Jacke Cade was the firft that devifed to put redde herrings in *cades*, and from h m they have their name." *Praife of the Red Herring*, 1599 STEEVENS.

[9] — *our enemies fhall fall before us*,] He alludes to his name *Cade*, from *cado*, lat. to *fall* He has too much learning for his character
JOHNSON.

We John Cade, &c.] This paffage, I think fhould be regulated thus :
Cade We John Cade, fo term'd of our fuppofed father, for our ene-mies fhall fall before us ,—
Dick Or rather of ftealing a cade of herrings.
Cade Infpired with the fpirit, &c. TYRWHITT.

In the old play the correfponding paffage ftands thus :
Cade. I John Cade, fo named *for* my valiancy,—
Dick Or rather *for* ftealing of a cade of fprats.

The tranfpofition recommended by Mr Tyrwhitt is fo plaufible, that I had once regulated the text accordingly But Dick's quibbling on the word *of* (which is ufed by Cade, according t the phrafeology of our au-thor's t me. for *by*. and as employed by Dick fignifies—*on account of*,) is fo much in Shakfpeare's manner, that no change ought, I think, to be made If the words, " Or rather of ftealing," &c. be poftponed to —" For our enemies fhall fall before us," Dick then, as at prefent, would affert—that Cade is not fo called on account of his enemies *falling* before them, but on account of a particular theft ; which indeed would correfpond fufficiently with the old play ; but the quibble on the word *of*, which appears like a conceit of Shakfpeire, would be deftroyed.— Cade, as the fpeeches ftand in the folio, proceeds to affign the origin of his name without paying any regard to what Dick has faid *Of* is ufed again in *Coriolanus*, in the fenfe which it bears in Cade's fpeech :— " We have been called fo *of* many." i. e. by by many. MALONE.

Dick.

Dick. He was an honeſt man, and a good bricklayer.
　　　　　　　　　　　　　　　　　　[*Aſide.*

‘ *Cade.* My mother a Plantagenet,—

‘ *Dick.* I knew her well, ſhe was a midwife.　　[*Aſide.*

‘ *Cade.* My wife deſcended of the Lacies,—

Dick. She was, indeed, a pedlar's daughter, and ſold many
‘ laces.　　　　　　　　　　　　　　　　　[*Aſide.*

‘ *Smith.* But, now of late, not able to travel with her furr'd
‘ pack [1], ſhe waſhes bucks here at home.　　　[*Aſide.*

‘ *Cade.* Therefore am I of an honourable houſe.

Dick. Ay, by my faith, the field is honourable ; and there
was he born, under a hedge ; for his father had never a houſe,
but the cage [*].　　　　　　　　　　　　　[*Aſide.*

[*] *Cade.* Valiant I am.

[*] *Smith.* 'A muſt needs ; for beggary is valiant.　[*Aſide.*

Cade. I am able to endure much.

Dick. No queſtion of that ; for I have ſeen him whipp'd
three market days together.　　　　　　　　[*Aſide.*

Cade. I fear neither ſword nor fire.

Smith. He need not fear the ſword, for his coat is of
proof [2].　　　　　　　　　　　　　　　　[*Aſide.*

Dick. But, methinks, he ſhould ſtand in fear of fire, being
burnt i'the hand for ſtealing of ſheep.　　　　[*Aſide.*

Cade. Be brave then ; for your captain is brave, and vows
reformation. There ſhall be, in England, ſeven half-penny
loaves ſold for a penny : the three-hoop'd pot ſhall have ten
hoops [3] ; and I will make it felony, to drink ſmall beer : all
the realm ſhall be in common, and in Cheapſide ſhall my
palfry go to graſs. And, when I am king, (as king I will
be)—

All. God ſave your majeſty !

[1] *furr'd pack,*] A wallet or knapſick of ſkin with the hair outward.
　　　　　　　　　　　　　　　　　　　　　　JOHNSON.
In the original play the words are—" and now being not able to
occupy her furred pack,"— under which perhaps " more was meant than
meets the ear." MALONE.

[*] *— but the* cage] A cage was formerly a term for a priſon. See
Minſheu, in v. We yet talk of jail-*birds.* MALONE.

[2] *—for his coat is of* proof.] A quibble between two ſenſes of the
word ; one as being able to reſiſt, the other as being *well tried,* that is,
long worn. HANMER.

[3] *— the* three-hoop'd *pot ſhall have ten* hoops ;] See Naſh's *Pierce
Pennileſſe his Supplication to the Devil,* 1592 : " I believe *hoopes* in
quart pots were invented to that end, that every man ſhould take his
hoope, and no more " It appears from a paſſage in *Cynthia's Revels,*
by Ben Jonſon, that " burning of cans" was one of the offices of a city
magiſtrate. I ſuppoſe he means ſuch as were not of a ſtatutable meaſure. STEEVENS.

　　　　　　　　　　　　　　　　　　　　　　‘ *Cade.*

' *Cade.* I thank you, good people :—there shall be no mo-
' ney [4]; all shall eat and drink on my score; and I will ap-
' parel them all in one livery, that they may agree like bro-
' thers, and worship me their lord.

' *Dick.* The first thing we do, let's kill all the lawyers,

Cade. Nay, that I mean to do. Is not this a lamentable
thing [5], that of the skin of an innocent lamb should be made
parchment? that parchment, being scribbled o'er, should undo a man? Some say, the bee stings : but I say, 'tis the bee's
wax; for I did but seal once to a thing, and I was never mine
own man since. How now? who's there?

Enter some, bringing in the clerk of Chatham.

Smith. The clerk of Chatham : he can write and read, and
cast accompt

Cade. O monstrous!

Smith. We took him setting of boys' copies [*].

Cade. Here's a villain!

Smith. H'as a book in his pocket, with red letters in't.

Cade. Nay, then he is a conjurer.

Dick. Nay, he can make obligations [6], and write court-
hand.

' *Cade.* I am sorry for't : the man is a proper man, on mine
honour; unless I find him guilty, he shall not die.—Come
hither, sirrah, I must examine thee : What is thy name?

Clerk. Emanuel.

Dick. They use to write it on the top of letters [7];—'Twill
go hard with you.

' *Cade.*

4 — *there shall be no money*;] To mend the world by banishing money
is an old contrivance of those who did not consider that the quarrels and
mischief which arise from money, as the sign or ticket of riches, and
must, if money were to cease, arise immediately from riches themselves,
and could never be at an end till every man was contented with his own
share of the goods of life. JOHNSON.

5 *Is not this a lamentable thing,* &c.] This speech was transposed by
Shakspeare, it being found in the old play in a subsequent scene.
MALONE.

* *We took him,* &c.] We must suppose that Smith had taken the Clerk
some time before, and left him in the custody of those who now bring
him in. In the old play *Will* the *weaver* enters with the Clerk,
though he has not long before been conversing with Cade. Perhaps it
was intended that Smith should go out after his speech—ending, " for
his coat is of proof:" but no *Exit* is marked in the old copy. It is a
matter of little consequence.—It is, I think, most probable that *Will*
was the true name of this character, as in the old play, (so Dick, George,
John, &c.) and that *Smith*, the name of some low actor, has crept into
the folio by mistake. MALONE.

6 — *obligations,*] That is, *bonds.* MALONE.

7 — *on the top of letters*:] i. e. of letters missive, and such like
publick acts. See Mabillon's *Diplomata.* WARBURTON.
                                                         In

' *Cade.* Let me alone :—Doſt thou uſe to write thy
' name ? or haſt thou a mark to thyſelf, like an honeſt plain-
' dealing man ?

Clerk. Sir, I thank God, I have been ſo well brought up,
that I can write my name.

' *All.* He hath confeſs'd : away with him ; he's a villain
' and a traitor.

' *Cade.* Away with him, I ſay : hang him with his pen
' and inkhorn about his neck.

[*Exeunt ſome with the* Clerk.

Enter MICHAEL.

' *Mich.* Where's our general ?

' *Cade.* Here I am, thou particular fellow.

' *Mich.* Fly, fly, fly ! Sir Humphrey Stafford and his
' brother are hard by, with the king's forces.

' *Cade.* Stand, villain, ſtand, or I'll fell thee down : He
' ſhall be encounter'd with a man as good as himſelf : He is
' but a knight, is 'a ?

' *Mich.* No.

' *Cade.* To equal him, I will make myſelf a knight preſent-
' ly ; Riſe up ſir John Mortimer. Now have at him [8].

Enter Sir Humphrey STAFFORD, *and* William *his brother,
with drum and forces.*

* *Staf.* Rebellious hinds, the filth and ſcum of Kent,
* Mark'd for the gallows,—lay your weapons down,
* Home to your cottages, forſake this groom ;—
* The king is merciful, if you revolt.

* *W. Staf.* But angry, wrathful, and inclin'd to blood,
* If you go forward : therefore yield, or die.

Cade. As for theſe ſilken-coated ſlaves, I paſs not [9] ;

In the old anonymous play, called *The famous Victories of Henry V.
containing the honourable Battell of Agincourt,* I find the ſame circumſtance. The archbiſhop of Burges (i. e Bruges) is the ſpeaker, and
addreſſes himſelf to king Henry :

" I beſeech your grace to deliver me your ſafe
" Conduct, under your broad ſeal *Emanuel,*"

The king in anſwer ſays :

" ———— deliver him ſafe conduct
" Under our broad ſeal *Emanuel.*" STEEVENS.

[8] —*have at him:*] After this ſpeech the old play has the following
words :

—Is there any more of them that be knights ?
Tom. Yea, his brother.
Cade. Then kneel down, Dick Butcher ; riſe up ſir Dick
Butcher. Sound up the drum.
See p. 176, n. 2 ; and p. 180, n. 6. MALONE.

[9] —*I paſs not ;*] I pay them no regard. JOHNSON.
So, in Drayton's *Queſt of Cynthia :*
" Transform me to what ſhape you can,
" I paſs not what it be." STEEVENS.

It

It is to you, good people that I speak,
* O'er whom, in time to come, I hope to reign;
* For I am rightful heir unto the crown.
    ' Staf. Villain, thy father was a plaisterer;
' And thou thyself a shearman. Art thou not?
    Cade. And Adam was a gardener.
    ' W. Stof. And what of that?
    Cade. Marry, this:—Edmund Mortimer, earl of March,
Married the duke of Clarence' daughter; Did he not?
    ' Staf. Ay, sir.
    Cade. By her he had two children at one birth.
    W. Staf. That's false.
    ' Cade. Ay, there's the question; but, I say, 'tis true:
' The elder of them being put to nurse,
' Was by a beggar-woman stol'n away;
' And, ignorant of his birth and parentage,
' Became a bricklayer, when he came to age:
' His son am I; deny it, if you can.
    Dick. Nay, 'tis too true; therefore he shall be king.
    Smith. Sir, he made a chimney in my father's house, and
the bricks are alive at this day to testify it; therefore, deny it
not.
    * Staf. And will you credit this base drudge's words,
* That speaks he knows not what?
    * All. Ay, marry, will we; therefore get ye gone.
    W. Staf. Jack Cade, the duke of York hath taught you
this.
    * Cade. He lies, for I invented it myself. [Aside.]—Go
to, sirrah, Tell the king from me, that—for his father's sake,
Henry the fifth, in whose time boys went to span-counter for
French crowns,—I am content he shall reign; but I'll be protector over him.
    ' Dick. And, furthermore, we'll have the lord Say's head,
' for selling the dukedom of Maine.
    ' Cade. And good reason; for thereby is England maim'd[1],
' and fain to go with a staff, but that my puissance holds it up.
' Fellow kings, I tell you, that that lord Say hath gelded the
' common-wealth[2], and made it an eunuch: and more than
' that, he can speak French, and therefore he is a traitor.
    ' Staf. O gross and miserable ignorance!
    ' Cade. Nay, answer, if you can: The Frenchmen are
                                                    ' our

1 — is England maim'd,] The folio has—main'd. The correction
was made from the old play. I am not; however, sure that a blunder
was not intended Daniel has the same conceit; C. W. 1595:
    " Anjou and Maine, the main that foul appears—." MALONE.
2 — hath gelded the common-wealth,] Shakspeare hath here trans-
                                                    gressed

‘ our enemies : go to then, I aſk but this ; Can he, that
‘ ſpeaks with the tongue of an enemy, be a good counſellor, or
‘ no ?

* *All.* No, no; and therefore we'll have his head.

* *W. Staf.* Well, ſeeing gentle words will not prevail,
* Aſſail them with the army of the king.

‘ *Staf.* Herald, away : and throughout every town,
‘ Proclaim them traitors that are up with Cade ;
‘ That thoſe, which fly before the battle ends,
‘ May, even in their wives' and childrens ſight,
‘ Be hang'd up for example at their doors :—
‘ And you, that be the king's friends, follow me.

         [Exeunt the two STAFFORDS, *and forces.*

* *Cade.* And you, that love the commons, follow me.—
* Now ſhew yourſelves men, 'tis for liberty.
* We will not leave one lord, one gentleman :
* Spare none, but ſuch as go in clouted ſhoon ;
* For they are thrifty honeſt men, and ſuch
* As would (but that they dare not) take our parts.

* *Dick.* They are all in order, and march towards us.

* *Cade.* But then are we in order, when we are moſt out
* of order. Come, march forward [3].   *[Exeunt.*

SCENE III.

Another part of Blackheath.

*Alarums. The two parties enter, and fight, and both the
Staffords are ſlain.*

‘ *Cade.* Where's Dick, the butcher of Aſhford ?
‘ *Dick.* Here, ſir.
‘ *Cade.* They fell before thee like ſheep and oxen, and
‘ thou behav'ſt thyſelf as if thou haſt been in thy own ſlaugh-

---

greſſed a rule laid down by Tully, *De Oratore: Nolo morte dici Afri-
cani caſtratam* eſſe rempublicam." The character of the ſpeaker, however, may countenance ſuch indelicacy. In other places our author,
leſs excuſeably, talks of *gelding* purſes, patrimonies, and continents
                     STEEVENS.

This peculiar expreſſion is Shakſpeare's own, not being found in the
old play. In *King Richard II.* Roſs ſays that Henry of Bolingbroke has
been—
      " Bereft and *gelded of* his patrimony."
So Cade here ſays, that the commonwealth is *bereft of* what it before
poſſeſſed, namely, certain provinces in France. MALONE.

  3 *Come, march forward.*] In the firſt copy, inſtead of this ſpeech, we
have only—Come, Sirs, *St. George for us, and Kent.* MALONE.

                         ter houſe:

‘ ter-house : therefore thus will I reward thee,—The Lent
‘ shall be as long again as it is [4] ; and thou shalt have a licence
‘ to kill for a hundred lacking one.

‘ *Dick.* I desire no more.

* *Cade.* And to speak truth, thou deserv’st no less. This
* monument of the victory will I bear [5] ; and the bodies shall
* be dragg’d at my horse’ heels, till I do come to London,
* where we will have the mayor’s sword borne before us.

* *Dick.* If we mean to thrive and do good, break open the
* gaols, and let out the prisoners.

* *Cade.* Fear not that, I warrant thee. Come, let’s march
* towards London.   [*Exeunt.*

SCENE IV.

London,   *A Room in the Palace.*

Enter King HENRY, *reading a supplication ; the duke of* BUCK-
INGHAM, *and lord* SAY *with him : at a distance,* Queen
MARGARET, *mourning over* SUFFOLK’*s head.*

* *Q. Mar.* Oft have I heard—that grief softens the mind,
* And makes it fearful and degenerate ;
* Think therefore on revenge, and cease to weep.
* But who can cease to weep, and look on this ?
* Here may his head lie on my throbbing breast :
* But where’s the body that I should embrace ?

‘ *Buck.* What answer makes your grace to the rebels’ sup-
‘ plications [6] ?

* *K. Hen.* I’ll send some holy bishop to entreat [7] :

‘ For God forbid, so many simple souls
                                                   ‘ Should

---

4 — *as long again as it is ;*] The word *again*, which was certainly
omitted in the folio by accident, was restored from the old play, by Mr.
Steevens, on the suggestion of Dr. Johnson. MALONE

5 *This monument of the victory will I bear ;*] Here Cade must be supposed to take off Stafford’s armour. So, Holinshed :

“ Jack Cade, upon victory against the Staffords, apparelled himself
in Sir Humphrey’s brigandine, set full of gilt nails, and so in some glory
returned again toward London.” STEEVENS.

6 — *to the rebels’ supplication ?*] “ And to the entent that the cause
of this glorious capitaynes comyng thither might be shadowed from the
king and his counsayll, he sent to him an humble *supplication*,—affirm-
yng his commyng not to be against him, but against divers of his coun-
sayl,” &c. H.II, Henry VI. fol. 77. MALONE.

7 *I’ll send some holy bishop to entreat :*] Here, as in some other places, our author has fallen into an inconsistency, by sometimes following
                                                                      and

' Should perish by the sword ! And I myself,
' Rather than bloody war shall cut them short,
' Will parly with Jack Cade their general.—
' But stay, I'll read it over once again.

* *Q. Mar.* Ah, barbarous villains ! hath this lovely
	face
* Rul'd, like a wandering planet [8], over me ;
* And could it not enforce them to relent,
* That were unworthy to behold the same ?

' *K. Hen.* Lord Say, Jack Cade hath sworn to have thy
	head.
' *Say.* Ay, but I hope, your highness shall have his.
K. Hen. How now, madam ? Still
Lamenting, and mourning for Suffolk's death ?
I fear, my love [*], if that I had been dead,
Thou wouldest not have mourn'd so much for me.
Q. Mar. No, my love, I should not mourn, but die for
	thee.

Enter a Messenger.

* *K. Hen.* How now ! what news ? Why com'st thou in
	such haste ?
' *Mes.* The rebels are in Southwark ; Fly, my lord !
' Jack Cade proclaims himself lord Mortimer,
' Descended from the duke of Clarence' house ;
' And calls your grace usurper, openly,
' And vows to crown himself in Westminster.

and sometimes deserting his original. In the old play, the king says not
a word of sending any *bishop* to the rebels ; but says, he will himself
come and parly with them, and in the mean while orders *Clifford* and
Buckingham to gather an army and to go to them. See p. 192, n. 9.—
Shakspeare, in new modelling this scene, found in Holinshed's Chronicle the following words : " — to whome [Cade] were sent from the
king, the *Archbishop* of *Canterburie* and Humphrey duke of Buckingham, to common with him of his griefs and requests " This gave birth
to the line before us: which our author afterwards forgot, having introduced in scene viii. only Buckingham and Clifford, *conformably to the
old play.* MALONE.

	8 *Rul'd, like a wandering planet,*] Predominated irresistibly over my
passions, as the planets over the lives of those that are born under their
influence. JOHNSON

	The old play led Shakspeare into this strange exhibition ; a queen
with the head of her murdered paramour on her bosom, in the presence
of her husband! MALONE.

	* *I fear, my love,*] The folio has here—I fear me, love, which is cer-
tainly sense ; but as we find " my love" in the old play, and these lines
were adopted without retouching, I suppose the transcriber's ear deceived him. MALONE.

' His

‘ His army is a ragged multitude.
‘ Of hinds and peafants, rude and mercilefs :
‘ Sir Humphrey Stafford and his brother's death
‘ Hath given them heart and courage to proceed :
‘ All fcholars, lawyers, courtiers, gentlemen,
‘ They call—falfe caterpillars, and intend their death.
   * *K. Hen.* O gracelefs men ! they know not what they.
      do [9].
   ‘ *Buck.* My gracious lord, retire to Kenelworth,
‘ Until a power be rais'd to put them down.
   * *Q. Mar.* Ah ! were the duke of Suffolk now alive,
* Thefe Kentifh rebels would be foon appeas'd.
   ‘ *K. Hen.* Lord Say, the traitors hate thee,
‘ Therefore away with us to Kenelworth.
   ‘ *Say.* So might your grace's perfon be in danger ;
‘ The fight of me is odious in their eyes :
‘ And therefore in this city will I ftay,
‘ And live alone as fecret as I may.

Enter another Meſſenger.

   * 2. *Mef.* Jack Cade hath gotten London-bridge ; the ci-
      tizens
* Fly and forfake their houfes :
* The rafcal people, thirfting after prey,
* Join with the traitor ; and they jointly fwear,
* To fpoil the city, and your royal court.
   * *Buck.* Then linger not, my lord ; away, take horfe.
   * *K. Hen.* Come, Margaret ; God, our hope, will fuccour us.
   * *Q. Mar.* My hope is gone, now Suffolk is deceas'd.
   * *K. Hen.* Farewel, my lord ; [*to lord* Say.] truft not
      the Kentifh rebels.
   * *Buck.* Truft no body, for fear you be betray'd [1].
   ‘ *Say.* The truft I have is in mine innocence,
‘ And therefore am I bold and refolute.   [*Exeunt.*

SCENE V.

The fame. The Tower.

Enter Lord Scales, *and Others, on the walls. Then enter
certain* Citizens, *below.*

Scales. How now ? is Jack Cade flain ?
   1. *Cit.* No, my lord, nor likely to be flain ; for they have

---

9 — *what they do.*] Inftead of this line, in the old copy we have—
     " Go, bid Buckingham and Clifford gather
     " An army up, and meet with the rebels   MALONE.
1 — *be betray'd.*] *Be,* which was accidentally omitted in the old
copy, was fupplied by the editor of the fecond folio. MALONE.

WON

won the bridge, killing all those that withstand them : The lord mayor craves aid of your honour from the tower, to defend the city from the rebels.

Scales. Such aid as I can spare, you shall command ;
But I am troubled here with them myself,
The rebels have assay'd to win the Tower.
But get you to Smithfield, and gather head,
And thither I will send you Matthew Gough :
Fight for your king, your country, and your lives ;
And so farewel, for I must hence again.   [*Exeunt.*

SCENE VI.

The same. Cannon-street.

Enter Jack Cade, *and his followers. He strikes his staff on London-stone.*

Cade. Now is Mortimer lord of this city. And here, sitting upon London-stone, I charge and command, that, of the city's cost, the pissing-conduit run nothing but claret wine this first year of our reign. And now, henceforward, it shall be treason for any that calls me other than—lord Mortimer.

Enter a Soldier, *running.*

Sol. Jack Cade ! Jack Cade !
Cade. Knock him down there².   [*They kill him.*
• *Smith.* If this fellow be wise, he'll never call you Jack
• Cade more ; I think, he hath a very fair warning.
Dick. My lord, there's an army gather'd together in Smithfield.
Cade. Come then, let's go fight with them : But first, go and set London-bridge on fire³; and, if you can, burn down the Tower too. Come, let's away.   [*Exeunt.*

---

² *Knock him down there.*] So, Holinshed, p. 634 : " He also put to execution in Southwark diverse persons, some for breaking his ordinance, and other being his old acquaintance, lest they should bewraie his base linage, disparaging him for his usurped name of Mortimer." STEEVENS.
³ — *set* London-bridge *on fire;*] At that time *London bridge* was made of wood. " After that, (says Hall) he entered London and cut the ropes of the *draw* bridge:" The houses on London-bridge were in this rebellion burnt, and many of the inhabitants perished. MALONE.

O

SCENE VII.

The same. Smithfield.

Alarum. Enter, on one side, CADE, *and his company ; on the other, Citizens, and the king's forces, headed by* Matthew Gough. *They fight ; the citizens are routed, and* Matthew Gough [4] *is slain.*

Cade. So, firs :—Now go fome and pull down the Savoy ; others to the inns of court ; down with them all.

Dick. I have a fuit unto your lordfhip.

Cade. Be it a lordfhip, thou fhalt have it for that word.

‘ *Dick.* Only, that the laws of England may come out of ‘ your mouth [5].

‘ *John.* Mafs, 'twill be fore law then ; for he was thruft in ‘ the mouth with a fpear, and 'tis not whole yet.   [*Afide.*

‘ *Smith.* Nay, John, it will be ftinking law ; for his breath ‘ ftinks with eating toafted cheefe.   [*Afide.*

‘ *Cade.* I have thought upon it, it fhall be fo. Away, burn ‘ all the records of the realm ; my mouth fhall be the parlia- ‘ ment of England.

* *John.* Then we are like to have biting ftatutes, unlefs his * teeth be pulled out.   [*Afide.*

* *Cade.* And henceforward all things fhall be in common.

Enter a Meffenger.

‘ *Mef.* My lord, a prize, a prize ! here's the lord Say, * which fold the towns in France ; * he that made us pay one * and twenty fifteens [6], and one fhilling to the pound, the laft * fubfidy.

4 — *Matthew Gough*—] “ A man of great wit and much experience in feats of chivalrie, the which in continuall warres had fpent his time in fervice of the king and his father.” Holinfhed, p. 635. STEEVENS.

5 — *that the laws of England may come out of your mouth.*] This alludes to what Holinfhed has related of *Wat Tyler*, p. 432. “ It was reported indeed, that he fhould faie with great pride. putting his hands to his lips, that within four daies *all the lawes of England fhould come foorth of his mouth.*” TYRWHITT.

6 — *one and twenty fifteens,*] “ This capteine [Cade] affured them —if either by force or policie they might get the king and queene into their hands, he would caufe them to be honourably ufed, and take fuch order for the punifhing and reforming of the mifdemeanours of their bad counfellours, that neither *fifteens* fhould hereafter be demanded, nor anie impofitions or taxes be fpoken of.” Holinfhed, Vol. II. p. 632. A *fifteen* was the fifteenth part of all the moveables or perfonal property of each fubject. MALONE.

E nt

O

Enter George Bevis, *with the Lord* SAY.

'*Cade.* Well, he shall be beheaded for it ten times.—Ah,
' thou say, thou serge [7], nay, thou buckram lord! now art
' thou within point-blank of our jurisdiction regal.   What
' canst thou answer to my majesty, for giving up of Normandy
' unto mounsieur Basimecu [8], the dauphin of France? Be it
' known unto thee by these presence, even the presence of
' lord Mortimer, that I am the besom that must sweep the court
' clean of such filth as thou art.   Thou hast most traiterously
' corrupted the youth of the realm, in erecting a grammar-
'school: and whereas, before, our fore-fathers had no other
' books but the score and the tally, thou hast caused printing
' to be used [9]; and, contrary to the king, his crown, and

---

7 — *thou say, thou serge,*]. It appears from Minshew's DICT. 1617,
that *say* was a kind of serge It is made entirely of wool.   There is a
considerable manufactory of *say* at Sudbury near Colchester.   This stuff
is frequently dyed green, and is yet used by some mechanics in aprons.
MALONE.

\ 8 — *mounsieur* Basimecu,] Shakspeare probably wrote *Baisermycu,* or,
by a designed corruption, *Basemycu,* in imitation of his original, where
also we find a word half French, half English,—" Monsier *Bussmineca*."
MALONE.

9 — *Printing to be used;*] Shakspeare is a little too early with this ac-
cusation. JOHNSON.

Shakspeare might have been led into this mistake by Daniel, in the
fifth book of his *Civil Wars,* who introduces *printing* and *artillery* as
contemporary inventions:

  " Let there be found two fatal instruments,
  " The one to publish, th' other to defend
  " Impious contention, and proud discontents;
  " Make that *inflamped characters* may send
  " Abroad to thousands thousand men's intents;
  " And, in a moment, may dispatch much more
  " Than could a world of pens perform before."

Shakspeare's absurdities may always be countenanced by those of writer
nearly his contemporaries.
  In the tragedy of *Herod and Antipater,* by Gervase Markham and
William Sampson, who were both scholars, is the following passage:
  " Though *cannons* roar, yet you must not be deaf."
  Spenser mentions *cloth* made at Lincoln during the ideal reign of K.
Arthur, and has adorn'd a castle at the same period " with cloth of
Arras and of *Toure* " Chaucer introduces *guns* in the time of Antony
and Cleopatra, and (as Warton has observed) Salvator Rosa places a
cannon at the entrance of the tent of Holofernes. STEEVENS.
  Mr. Meerman in his *Origines Typographicæ* hath availed himself of
this passage in Shakspeare, to support his hypothesis, that printing was
introduced into England (before the time of Caxton) by Frederick Cor-
fellis, a workman from Haerlem, in the time of Henry VI
BLACKET NE.
' dignity,

' dignity *, thou haſt built a paper-mill. It will be proved to
' thy face, that thou haſt men about thee, that uſually talk of a
' noun, and a verb; and ſuch abominable words, as no
' chriſtian ear can endure to hear. Thou haſt appointed
' juſtices of peace, to call poor men before them about matters
' they were not able to anſwer ¹. Moreover thou haſt put
' them in priſon; and, becauſe they could not read, thou haſt
' hang'd them ²; when, indeed, only for that cauſe they have
' been moſt worthy to live. Thou doſt ride on a foot-cloth ³,
' doſt thou not ?

Say. What of that ?

Cade. Marry, thou ought'ſt not to let thy horſe wear a
cloak ⁴, when honeſter men than thou go in their hoſe and
doublets.

* *Dick.* You men of Kent,—

Dick. What ſay you of Kent ?

' *Say.* Nothing but this : 'Tis *bona terra, mala gens* ⁵.

' *Cade.* Away with him, away with him ! he ſpeaks
' Latin.

* *Say.* Hear me but ſpeak, and bear me where you will.

' Kent, in the commentaries Cæſar writ,

' Is term'd the civil'ſt place of all this iſle ⁶ :

' Sweet is the country, becauſe full of riches ;

' The

---

* *—cintrary to the king, his crown, &c.*] " Againſt the peace of
the ſaid lord the now king, his crown, and dignity," is the regular language of indictments. MALONE.

¹ *— to call poor men before them about matters they were not able to
anſwer.*] The old play reads, with more humour,—" to hang honeſt
men that ſteal for their living. MALONE.

² *— becauſe they could not read, thou haſt hang'd them ;*] That is,
they were hanged becauſe they cou'd not claim the benefit of clergy.
                                                            JOHNSON.

³ *Thou doſt ride on a* footcloth,] A *foot-cloth* was a kind of houſing,
which covered the body of the horſe, and almoſt reached the ground.
It was ſometimes made of velvet, and bordered with gold lace.
                                                            MALONE.

⁴ *— to let thy horſe wear a cloak,*] This is a reproach truly charac-
teriſtical. Nothing gives ſo much offence to the lower ranks of mankind
as the ſight of ſuperfluities merely oſtentatious. JOHNSON.

⁵ *— bona terra, mala gens.*] After this line the quarto proceeds
thus :

  " *Cade.* Bonum terrum, what's that?
  " *Dick.* He ſpeaks French.
  " *Will.* No, 'tis Dutch.
  " *Nick.* No, 'tis Outalian : I know it well enough "
Holinſhed has likewiſe ſtigmatized the Kentiſh men, p. 677. " The
Kentiſh-men, in this ſeaſon (whoſe minds be ever moveable at the
change of princes) came," &c. STEEVENS.

⁶ *Is term'd the civil'ſt place of all this iſle :*] So, in Cæſar's Comment.
B V. " Ex his omnibus ſunt humaniſſimi qui *Cantium* incolunt." The
                                                            paſſage

' The people liberal, valiant, active, wealthy ;
' Which makes me hope you are not void of pity.
' I fold not Maine, I loft not Normandy ;
* Yet, to recover them, † would lofe my life.
* Juftice with favour have I always done ;
* Prayers and tears have mov'd me, gifts could never,
* When have I aught exacted at your hands,
* Kent to maintain, the king, the realm, and you ?
* Large gifts have I beftow'd on learned clerks,
* Becaufe my book preferr'd me to the king 7 :
* And—feeing ignorance is the curfe of God,
* Knowledge the wing wherewith we fly to heaven,—
* Unlefs you be poffefs'd of devilifh fpirits,
* You cannot but forbear to murder me.
* This tongue hath parley'd unto foreign kins
* For your behoof,—

* Cade.

passage is thus tranflated by Arthur Golding, 1590. " Of all the inhabitants of this ifle, the civileft are the Kentifhfolke." STEEVENS.

So, in Lilly's *Euphues and his England*, 1580, a book which the author of the *Whole Contention*, &c. probably, and Shakfpeare certainly, had read : '· Of all the inhabitants of this ifle the Kentifhmen are the civileft." MALONE.

† *Yet to recover them*, &c.] I fufpect that here, as in a passage in *King Henry V*. Yet was mifprinted for *Tea*. MALONE.

7 *When have I aught exacted at your hands,*
Kent to maintain, the king, the realm, and you ?
Large gifts have I beftow'd on learned clerk,
Becaufe my book preferr'd me to the king.] This passage I know not well how to explain It is pointed [in the old copy] fo as to make Say declare that he preferred clerks to maintain Kent and the king.— This is not very clear; and befides he gives in the following line another reafon of his bounty, that learning raifed him, and therefore he fupported learning. I am inclined to think Kent flipped into this passage by chance, and would read :

When have I aught exacted at your hands,
But to maintain the king, the realm, and you? JOHNSON.

I concur with Dr Johnson in believing the word *Kent* to have been fhuffled into the text by accident. Lord Say, as the passage ftands [in the folio], not only declares he had preferred men or learning *to maintain* Kent, *the king, the realm,* but adds tautologically *you*; for it fhould be remembered that they are Kentifh' men to whom he is now fpeaking. I would read, *Bent* to maintain, &c. i. e. *ftrenuoufly refolved to the utmoft*; to, &c: STEEVENS.

The punctuation to which Dr. Johnfon alludes, is that of the folio :

When have I aught exacted at your hands?
Kent to maintain, the king, the realm, and you,
Large gifts, have I beftow'd on learned clerks, &c.

I have pointed the passage differently, the former punctuation appearing to me to render it nonfenfe. I fufpect, however, with the preceding editors, that the word *Kent* is a corruption. MALONE.

* *Cade.* Tut! when ftruck'ft thou one blow in the field?

* *Say.* Great men have reaching hands : oft have I ftruck
* Thofe that I never faw, and ftruck them dead.

* *Geo.* O monftrous coward! what, to come behind folks!

* *Say.* Thefe cheeks are pale for watching for your good [8].

* *Cade.* Give him a box o'er the ear, and that will make
'em red again.

e *Say.* Long fitting to determine poor men's caufes
* Hath made me full of ficknefs and difeafes.

* *Cade.* Ye fhall have a hempen caudle then, and the help
of a hatchet [9].

' *Dick* Why doft thou quiver, man [1]?

' *Say.* The palfy, and not fear, provokes me?

' *Cade* Nay, he nods at us; as who fhould fay, I'll be
' even with you. I'll fee if his head will ftand fteadier on a
' pole, or no: Take him away, and behead him.

* *Say.* Tell me, wherein have I offended moft?
* Have I affected wealth, or honour; fpeak?
* Are my chefts fill'd up with extorted gold?
* Is my apparel fumptuous to behold?
* Whom have I injur'd, that ye feek my death?
* Thefe hands are free from guiltlefs blood-fhedding [2],
* This breaft from harbouring foul deceitful thoughts.
* O, let me live!

* *Cade.* I feel remorfe in myfelf with his words : but I'll
* bridle it; he fhall die, an it be but for pleading fo well for

---

[8] — for *watching*—] This is, in confequence of watching. So Sir
John Davies:
   " And fhuns it ftill, although *for* thirft fhe die."
The fecond folio and all the modern editions read—*with* watching.
         MALONE.

[9] — *and the help of a hatchet.*] I fuppofe, to cut him down after he
has been hanged, or perhaps to cut off his head. The article (*a* hatchet)
was fupplied by the editor of the fecond folio. MALONE.

[1] *Why doft thou quiver, man?* &c] Otway has borrowed this
thought in *Venice Preferved:*
   " *Spinofa* You are trembling, fir.
   " *Renault.* 'Tis a cold night indeed, and I am aged,
   " Full of decay and natural infirmities." STEEVENS.

[2] *Thefe hands are free from guiltlefs blood-fhedding,*] I formerly imagined that the word *guiltlefs* was mifplaced, and that the poet wrote—
   Thefe hands are guiltlefs, free from blood-fhedding.
But change is unneceffary. *Guiltlefs* is not an epithet to *blood fhedding,*
but to *blood.* Thefe hands are free from fhedding *guiltlefs* or *innocent*
blood. So, in *K. Henry VIII:*
   " For then my *guiltlefs blood* muft cry againft them." MALONE.

                         * his

* his life³. Away with him! he has a familiar under his
* tongue⁴; he speaks not o'God's name. Go, take him
' away, I say, and strike off his head presently; and then
' break into his son-in-law's house, Sir James Cromer, and
' strike off his head, and bring them both upon two poles
' hither.

' *All.* It shall be done.

* *Say.*.Ah, countrymen! if when you make your prayers,
* God should be so obdurate as yourselves,
* How would it fare with your departed souls?
* And therefore yet relent, and save my life.
* *Cade.* Away with him, and do as I command ye.

[*Exeunt some, with Lord,* Say.

' The proudest peer in the realm shall not wear a head on his
' shoulders, unless he pay me tribute; there shall not a maid
' be married, but she shall pay to me her maiden-head ere
' they have it⁵: Men shall hold of me *in capite*⁶; and we
' charge and command, that their wives be as free as heart
' can wish, or tongue can tell*.

---

3 — *he shall die, as it be but for pleading so well for his life.*] This
sentiment is not merely designed as an expression of ferocious triumph,
but to mark the eternal enmity which the vulgar bear to those of more
liberal education and superior rank. The vulgar are always ready to
depreciate the talents which they behold with envy, and insult the
eminence which they despair to reach. STEEVENS.

4 — *a familiar under his tongue;*] A *familiar* is a dæmon who was
supposed to attend at call. So, in *Love's Labour Lost* :
   " Love is a *familiar*; there is no angel but love." STEEVENS.

5 —*shall pay to me her maidenhead,* &c.] Alluding to an ancient
usage on which B. and Fletcher have founded their play called the *Custom
of the Country.* See Mr. Seward's note at the beginning of it. STEEV.
   See Blount's GLOSSOGRAPHY, 8vo. 1681, in v. *Marcheta.* Hector
Boethius and Skene both mention this custom as existing in Scotland till
the time of Malcolm the Third, A. D. 1057. MALONE.
   Blount's account of this custom has received the sanction of several
eminent antiquaries; but a learned writer, Sir David Dalrymple, con-
troverts the fact, and denies the actual existence of the custom. See
Annals of Scotland. Judge Blackstone, in his *Commentaries,* is of opini-
on it never prevailed in *England,* though he supposes it certainly did in
Scotland. REED.

6 — *in* capite;] This equivoque, for which the author of the old play
is answerable, is too learned for Cade. MALONE.

* *or tongue can tell.*] After this, in the old play, Robin enters to
inform Cade that London bridge is on fire and Dick enters with a serjeant; i. e a bailiff; and there is a dialogue consisting of seventeen lines,
of which Shakspeare has made no use whatsoever. MALONE.

Dick.

' *Dick.* My lord, when fhall we go to Cheapfide, and take
up commodities upon our bills [7] ?

' *Cade.* Marry, prefently.

' *All.* O brave !

Re-enter Rebels, *with the heads of Lord* SAY *and his fon-in-law.*

' *Cade.* But is not this braver ?—Let them kifs one an-
' other [8] ; for they loved well, when they were alive. Now
' part them again, left they confult about the giving up of
' fome more towns in France. Soldiers, defer the fpoil of the
' city until night : for with thefe borne before us, inftead of
' maces, will we ride through the ftreets ; and, at every cor-
' ner, have them kifs.—Away !   [*Exeunt.*

SCENE VIII.

Southwark.

Alarum.   Enter CADE, *and all his rabblement.*

' * *Cade.* Up Fifh-ftreet ! down faint Magnus' corner ! kill

---

7 — *take up commodities upon our* bills ?] Perhaps this is an equivoque
alluding to the *brown bills*, or halberds, with which the commons were
anciently armed. PERCY.

Thus, in the original play :
   " *Nick.* But when fhall we take up thofe commodities which
   " you told of us ?
   " *Cade.* Marry, he that will luftily ftand to it, fhall take up
   " thefe commodities following : Item, a gown, a kirtle, a petti-
   " coat, and a fmocke."

. If the *Whole Contention*, &c. printed in 1600, was an imperfect tranfcript of Shakfpeare's Second and Third Part of *K. Henry VI.* (as it
has hitherto been fuppofed to be,) we have here another extraordinary
proof of the *inventive* faculty of the tranfcriber.—It is obfervable that
the equivoque which Dr. Percy has taken notice of, is *not* found in the
old play, but *is* found in Shakfpeare's *Much ado about Nothing :*
   " *Her.* We are likely to prove a goodly *commodity*, being taken
   " up of thefe men's *bills.*
   " *Con.* A *commodity* in queftion, I warrant you." MALONE.

8 *Let them kifs one another ;*] This is from the *Mirrour for Magi-
ftrates*, in the legend of *Jack Cade :*
   " With thefe two heads I made a pretty play,
   " For pight on poles I bore them through the ftrete,
   " And for my fport made *each kiffe other* fwete " FARMER.

Is likewife found in Holinfhed, p 634 : " — and as it were in a
fpite caufed them in every ftreet *to kiffe* together." STEEVENS.

So alfo in Hall, Henry VI. folio 78. MALONE.

                                              * and

* and knock down.! throw them into Thames!—

[*A parley sounded, then a retreat.*

* What noise is this I hear? Dare any be so bold to sound re-
* treat or parley, when I command them kill?

Enter BUCKINGHAM, *and old* CLIFFORD, *with forces.*

' *Buck.* Ay, here they be that dare, and will disturb thee:
' Know, Cade, we come ambassadors from the king
' Unto the commons whom thou hast misled;
' And here pronounce free pardon to them all,
' That will forsake thee, and go home in peace.
' *Clif.* What say ye, countrymen [9]? will ye relent,
' And yield to mercy, whilst 'tis offer'd you?
' Or let a rabble lead you to your deaths?
' Who loves the king, and will embrace his pardon,
' Fling up his cap, and say—God save his majesty!
' Who hateth him, and honours not his father,
' Henry the fifth, that made all France to quake,
' Shake he his weapon at us, and pass by.
' *All.* God save the king! God save the king!
' *Cade.* What, Buckingham, and Clifford, are ye so
' brave?—And you, base peasants, do ye believe him? will
' you needs be hang'd with your pardons about your necks?
' Hath my sword therefore broke through London gates,
' that you should leave me at the White-hart in South-
' wark? I thought, ye would never have given out these
' arms, till you had recover'd your ancient freedom: but
' you are all recreants, and dastards; and delight to live in
' slavery to the nobility. Let them break your backs with
' burdens, take your houses over your heads, ravish your

---

9 *Clif What say ye, countrymen,* &c.] The variation in the original.
play is worth noting:
 " Why countrymen, and warlike friends of Kent,
 " What means this mutinous rebellion;
 " That you in troops do muster thus yourselves,
 " Under the conduct of this traitor, Cade?
 " To rise against your sovereign lord and king,
 " Who mildly hath this pardon sent to you,
 " If you forsake this monstrous rebel here.
 " If honour be the mark whereat you aim,
 " Then haste to France, that our fore others won,
 " And win again that thing which now is lost,
 " And leave to seek your country's overthrow.
 " *All.* A Clifford, a Clifford. [*They forsake Cade*
Here we have precisely the same versification which we find in all
the tragedies and historical dramas that were written before the time of
Shakspeare. MALONE.

' wives and daughters before your faces: For me,—I will
' make shift for one; and so—God's curse 'light upon you
' all!

' *All.* We'll follow Cade, we'll follow Cade.

' *Clif.* Is Cade the son of Henry the fifth,
' That thus you do exclaim—you'll go with him?
' Will he conduct you through the heart of France,
' And make the meanest of you earls and dukes?
' Alas, he hath no home, no place to fly to;
' Nor knows he how to live, but by the spoil,
' Unless by robbing of your friends, and us.
' Wer't not a shame, that, whilst you live at jar,
' The fearful French, whom you late vanquished,
' Should make a start o'er seas, and vanquish you?
' Methinks, already, in this civil broil,
' I see them lording it in London streets,
' Crying—*Villageois* * ! unto all they meet,
' Better, ten thousand base-born Cades miscarry,
' Than you should stoop unto a Frenchman's mercy.
' To France, to France, and get what you have lost;
' Spare England, for it is your native coast:
' Henry hath money [1], you are strong and manly;
' God on our side, doubt not of victory.

' *All.* A Clifford! a Clifford! we'll follow the king, and
' Clifford.

' *Cade.* Was ever feather so lightly blown to and fro, as
' this multitude? the name of Henry the fifth hales them to
' an hundred mischiefs, and makes them leave me desolate.
' I see them lay their heads together, to surprize me: my
' sword make way for me [2], for here is no staying.—In de-
' spight of the devils and hell, have through the very midst
' of you! and heavens and honour be witness, that no want
' of resolution in me, but only my followers' base and igno-
' minious treasons, makes me betake me to my heels. [*Exit.*

' *Buck.* What, is he fled? go some, and follow him;

---

* —*Villageois!*] Old Copy—*Villiage.* Corrected by Mr. Theobald.
MALONE.

[1] *Henry hath* money,] Dr. Warburton reads—Henry hath *mercy*,
but he does not seem to have attended to the speaker's drift, which is
to lure them from their present design by the hope of French plunder.
He bids them spare England, and go to France, and encourages them
by telling them that all is ready for their expedition; that they have
strength, and the king has *money*. JOHNSON.

[2] — *my sword make way for me*,] In the original play Cade employs
a more vulgar weapon: " My *staff* shall make way through the midst of
you, and so a pox take you all!" MALONE.

' And

‘ And he, that brings his head unto the king,
‘ Shall have a thousand crowns for his reward.——
[Exeunt some of them.

‘ Follow me, soldiers ; we'll devise a mean
‘ To reconcile you all unto the king. [Exeunt.

SCENE IX.

Kenelworth Castle.

Enter King HENRY, Queen MARGARET, and SOMERSET,
on the terrace of the Castle.

* K. Hen. Was ever king, that joy'd an earthly throne,
* And could command no more content than I ?
* No sooner was I crept out of my cradle,
* But I was made a king, at nine months old ³ :
* Was never subject long'd to be a king,
* As I do long and wish to be a subject ⁴.

Enter BUCKINGHAM, and CLIFFORD.

* Buck. Health, and glad tidings, to your majesty !
* K. Hen. Why, Buckingham, is the traitor Cade sur-
      priz'd ?
* Or is he but retir'd to make him strong ?

Enter, below, a great number of Cade's followers, with halters about their necks.

‘ Clif. He's fled, my lord, and all his powers do yield ;

---

3 —— I was made a king at nine months old :] So all the historians agree.
And yet in Part I king Henry is made to say:
      " I do remember how my father said,"——
a plain proof that the whole of that play was not written by the same
hand as this. BLACKSTONE.
4 —— to be a subject.] In the original play before the entry of Buckingham and Clifford, we have the following short dialogue, of which
Shakspeare has made no use :
      " King. Lord Somerset, what news hear you of the rebel Cade ?
      " Som. This, my gracious lord, that the lord Say is done to
" death ; and the city is almost sack'd.
      " King. God's will be done ; for as he hath decreed,
" So it must be ; and be it as he please,
" To stop the pride of these rebellious men.
      " Queen. Had the noble duke of Suffolk been alive,
      " The rebel Cade had been suppress'd ere this,
      " And all the rest that do take part with him "
This sentiment he has attributed to the queen in sc. iv. MALONE.
‘ And

‘ And humbly thus with halters on their necks
‘ Expect your highness' doom, of life, or death.
   ‘ *K. Hen.* Then, heaven, set ope thy everlasting gates [5],
‘ To entertain my vows of thanks and praise!——
‘ Soldiers, this day have you redeem'd your lives,
‘ And shew'd how well you love your prince and country:
‘ Continue still in this so good a mind,
‘ And Henry, though he be unfortunate,
‘ Assure yourselves, will never be unkind:
‘ And so, with thanks, and pardon to you all,
‘ I do dismiss you to your several countries.
   All. God save the king! God save the king!

Enter a Messenger.

   * *Mes.* Please it your grace to be advertised,
* The duke of York is newly come from Ireland:
* And with a puissant and a mighty power,
* Of galloglasses, and stout kerns [6],
* Is marching hitherward in proud array;
* And still proclaimeth, as he comes along,
* His arms are only to remove from thee
* The duke of Somerset, whom he terms a traitor.
   * *K. Hen.* Thus stands my state, 'twixt Cade and York
       distress'd;
* Like to a ship, that, having 'scap'd a tempest,
* Is straitway calm, and boarded with a pirate [7]:

                                    * But

---

5 *Then, heaven,* &c.] Thus, in the original play:
    “ *King.* Stand up, you simple men, and give God praise,
    “ For you did take in hand you know not what;
    “ And go in peace, obedient to your king;
    “ And live as subjects; and you shall not want,
    “ Whilst Henry lives and wears the English crown.
    “ *All.* God save the king, God save the king ” MALONE.

6 *Of* galloglasses, *and stout* kerns,] These were two orders of foot soldiers among the Irish. See Dr. Warburton's note on the second scene of the first act of *Macbeth.* STEEVENS.

“ The *galloglasse* useth a kind of pollax for his weapon. These men are grim of countenance, tall of stature, big of limme, lusty of body, wel and strongly timbered. The *kerne* is an ordinary souldier, using for weapon his sword and target, and sometimes his piece, being commonly good markmen. Kerne {Kigheyren} signifieth a shower of hell, because they are taken for no better than for rake-hells, or the devils blacke garde.” Stanihurst's *Description of Ireland,* Ch. 8. f. 28.
                                              BOWLE.

7 *Is straitway* calm, *and boarded with a pirate:*] Thus the first folio, where alone this passage is found. The editor of the second folio, who appears to have been wholly unacquainted with Shakspeare's phraseology, changed *calm* to *claim'd.* The editor of the third folio changed
                                          claim'd

* But now [8] is Cade driven back, his men dispers'd;
* And now is York in arms, to second him.——
* I pray thee, Buckingham, to go and meet him;
* And ask him, what's the reason of these arms.
* Tell him, I'll send duke Edmund to the Tower;——
* And, Somerset, we will commit thee thither,
* Until his army be dismiss'd from him.
　* *Som.* My lord,
* I'll yield myself to prison willingly,
* Or unto death, to do my country good.
　* *K. Hen.* In any case, be not too rough in terms;
* For he is fierce, and cannot brook hard language.
*　*Buck.* I will, my lord; and doubt not so to deal,
* As all things shall redound unto your good.
　* *K. Hen.* Come, wife, let's in [9], and learn to govern
　　　better;
* For yet may England curse my wretched reign. [*Exeunt.*

SCENE X.

Kent. Iden's *Garden* [1].

Enter CADE.

* *Cade.* Fie on ambition! fie on myself; that have a
　　　　　　　　　　　　　　　　　　　　　　　* sword

claim'd to calm'd; and the latter word has been adopted, unnecessarily in my apprehension, by the modern editors. Many words were used in this manner in our author's time, and the import is precisely the same as if he had written *calm'd.* So, in *King Henry IV.* "— what a *candy* deal of courtesy," which Mr. Pope altered improperly to—" what a deal of *candy'd* courtesy."

By *my state* Henry, I think, means, *his realm*; which had recently become quiet and peaceful by the defeat of Cade and his rabble. " *With* a pirate," agreeably to the phraseology of Shakspeare's time, means, " *by* a pirate." MALONE.

I believe *calm'd* (not *claim'd*] is right. The commotion raised by Cade was over, and the mind of the king was subsiding into a *calm*, when York appeared in arms, to raise fresh disturbances, and deprive it of its momentary peace. STEEVENS.

8 But *now* —] *But* is here not adversative.—It was only *just now*, says Henry, that Cade and his followers were routed. MALONE.

9 *Come, wife, let's in,* &c.] In the old play the king concludes the scene thus:

　　" Come, let us haste to London now with speed,
　　" That solemn processions may be sung,
　　" In laud and honour of the God of heaven,'
　　" And triumph of this happy victory." MALONE.

1 *Kent. Iden's garden.*] Holinshed, p. 635, says: " — a gentleman of Kent, named Alexander Eden, awaited so his time, that he
　　　　　　　　　　　　　　　　　　　　　　　　　　　　tooke

* sword, and yet am ready to famish! These five days have
* I hid me in these woods; and durst not peep out, for all
* the country is lay'd for me; but now am I so hungry,
* that if I might have a lease of my life for a thousand years,
* I could stay no longer. Wherefore, on a brick-wall have I
* climb'd into this garden; to see if I can eat grass, or pick
* a sallet another while, which is not amiss to cool a man's
* stomach this hot weather. And, I think, this word sallet
* was born to do me good: for, many a time, but for a
* sallet, my brain-pan ² had been cleft with a brown bill;
* and, many a time, when I have been dry, and bravely march-
* ing, it hath served me instead of a quart-pot to drink in;
* and now the word sallet must serve me to feed on.

Enter IDEN, with Servants.

' Iden. Lord, who would live turmoiled in the court,
' And may enjoy such quiet walks as these?
' This small inheritance, my father left me,
' Contenteth me, and is worth a monarchy.
' I seek not to wax great by others' waining ³ ;
' Or gather wealth, I care not with what envy ⁴ ;

' Sufficeth,.

tooke the said Cade in a garden in *Suffex*, so that there he was slaine at Hothfield, &c."

Instead of the soliloquy with which the present scene begins, the quarto has only this stage-direction. *Enter Jack Cade at one doore, and at the other M. Alexander Eyden and his men, and Jack Cade lies down picking of herbs, and eating them.* STEEVENS.

² — but for a sallet, my brain-pan, &c.] A *sallet* is a helmet. Minshieu conjectures that it is derived a "*salut*, Gal. because it keepeth the head whole from breaking." He adds, "alias *salade* dicitur, a G. *salade*, idem; utrumque vero *celando*, quod caput tegit."

The word undoubtedly came to us from the French In the Stat. 4. and 5 Ph. and Mary, ch 2. we find—"twentie haquebuts, and twentie morians or *salets*." MALONE.

So, in Sir Thomas North's translation of *Plutarch:* "—One of the company seeing Brutus athirst also, he ran to the river for water, and brought it in his *sallet*." STEEVENS.

Brain-pan for *skull*, occurs, I think, in Wickliff's translation of Judges, xix. 53. WHALLEY.

³ — by others' waining ;] The folio reads—*warning*. Corrected by Mr. Pope. *Is* in the preceding line was supplied by Mr. Rowe.
MALONE.

4 *Or gather wealth, I care not with what* envy ;] Or accumulate riches, without regarding the odium I may incur in the acquisition, however great that odium may be. *Envy* is often used in this sense by our author and his contemporaries. It may, however, have here its more ordinary acceptation.

This

‘ Sufficeth, that I have maintains my ſtate,
‘ And ſends the poor well pleaſed from my gate.

‘ *Cade.* Here's the lord of the foil come to ſeize me for a
‘ ſtray, for entering his fee-ſimple without leave. Ah, vil-
‘ lain, thou wilt betray me, and get a thouſand crowns of
‘ the king for carrying my head to him ; but I'll make thee
‘ eat iron like an oſtridge, and ſwallow my ſword like a great
‘ pin, ere thou and I part.

‘ *Iden.* Why, rude companion, whatſoe'er thou be,
‘ I know thee not ; Why then ſhould I betray thee ?
‘ Is't not enough, to break into my garden,
‘ And, like a thief, to come and rob my grounds,
‘ Climbing my walls in ſpight of me the owner,
‘ But thou wilt brave me with theſe ſaucy terms ?

. *Cade.* Brave thee ? ay, by the beſt blood that ever was
broach'd, and beard thee too. Look on me well : I have
eat no meat theſe five days ; yet, come thou and thy five
men, and if I do not leave you all as dead as a door-nail [5],
I pray God, I may never eat graſs more.

‘ *Iden.* Nay, it ſhall ne'er be ſaid, while England ſtands,
That Alexander Iden, an eſquire of Kent,
Took odds to combat a poor famiſh'd man.
‘ Oppoſe thy ſtedfaſt-gazing eyes to mine [6],
. ‘ See if thou canſt out-face me with thy looks.
‘ Set limb to limb ; and thou art far the leſſer :
‘ Thy hand is but a finger to my fiſt ;
‘ Thy leg a ſtick, compared with this truncheon ;
‘ My foot ſhall fight with all the ſtrength thou haſt ;
‘ And if mine arm be heaved in the air,

This ſpeech in the old play ſtands thus :
“ Good Lord, how pleaſant is this country life !
“ This little land my father left me here,
“ With my contented mind, ſerves me as well,
“ As all the pleaſures in the court can yield,
“ Nor would I change this pleaſure for the court.”
Here ſurely we have not a haſty tranſcript of our author's lines, but
the diſtinct compoſition of a preceding writer. The verſification muſt at
once ſtrike the ear of every perſon who has peruſed any of our old
dramas MALONE.

5 — *as dead as a door-na l*,] See *K. Henry IV.* P. II. Act V. ſc. iii.
STEEVENS.

6 *Oppoſe thy ſtedfaſt-gazing eyes to mine*, &c.] This and the follow-
ing nine lines are an amplification by Shakſpeare on theſe three of the
old play :
“ Look on me, my limbs are equal unto thine,
“ And every way as big : then hand to hand
“ I'll combat with thee. Sirra, fetch me weapons,
“ And ſtand you all aſide.” MALONE.

‘ Thy

' Thy grave is digg'd already in the earth.

' As for words, whose greatness answers words,

' Let this, my sword report what speech forbears [7].

* *Cade.* By my valour, the most complete champion that
* ever I heard.—' Steel, if thou turn the edge, or cut not
' out the burly-boned clown in chines of beef ere thou sleep
' in thy sheath, I beseech God [8] on my knees, thou may'st
' be turn'd to hobnails. [*They fight. Cade falls.*] O, I
' am slain! famine, and no other, hath slain me: let ten
' thousand devils come against me, and give me but the ten
' meals I have lost, and I'd defy them all. Wither, garden;
' and be henceforth a burying-place to all that do well in this
' house, because the unconquer'd soul of Cade is fled.

' *Iden.* Is't Cade that I have slain, that monstrous traitor?

' Sword, I will hallow thee for this thy deed,

' And hang thee o'er my tomb, when I am dead. [9] :

         * Ne'er

---

[7] *As for words, whose greatness answers words,*

Let this, my sword report what speech forbears.] *For more words,*
whose pomp and tumour may answer words, and only words, I shall
forbear them, *and refer the rest to my sword.* JOHNSON.

So, in the third part of *K. Henry VI:*

     " I will not bandy with thee, word for word,

     " But buckle with thee blows, twice two for one."

More (As for *more* words) was an arbitrary and unnecessary addition
made by Mr Rowe. MALONE

[8] — *I beseech* God—] The folio reads—I beseech *Jove.* This hea-
then deity, with whom Cade was not likely to be much acquainted,
was undoubtedly introduced by the editor of the folio to avoid the
penalty of the statute, 3 Jac. I ch 21. In the old play 1600, he says,
" I beseech *God* thou might'st fall into some *smith's hand*, and be
turned to hobnails." This the editor of the *second* edition of the quarto
play, no date, but printed in 1619, changed (from the same apprehension) to " I *would* thou might'st fall." &c. These alterations fully confirm my note on *King Henry V.*—Contrary to the general rule which I
have observed in printing this play, I have not adhered in the present
instance to the reading of the folio; because I am confident that it proceeded not from Shakspeare, but his editor, who, for the reason already
given, makes Falstaff say to Prince Henry—" I knew ye as well as he
that made ye," instead of—" *By the Lord*, I knew ye," &c.

                MALONE.

[9] — *when I am dead*:] How Iden was to hang a sword over his own
tomb, after he was dead, it is not easy to explain. The sentiment is
more correctly expressed in the quarto :

     Oh sword, I honour thee for this, and in my chamber

     Shalt thou hang, as a monument to after age,

     For this great service thou hast done to me. STEEVENS.

Here again we have a single thought considerably amplified, Shakspeare in new moulding this speech, has used the same mode of expression that he has employed in the *Winter's Tale:* " If thou'lt see a

             thing

* Ne'er shall this blood be wiped from thy point;
* But thou shalt wear it as a herald's coat,
* To emblaze the honour that thy master got.

' *Cade.* Iden, farewell; and be proud of thy victory: Tell
' Kent from me, she hath lost her best man, and exhort all
' the world to be cowards; for I, that never fear'd any, am
' vanquish'd by famine, not by valour. [*Dies.*

* *Iden.* How much thou wrong'st me', heaven be my
judge.
* Die, damned wretch, the curse of her that bare thee!
* And as I thrust thy body in with my sword,
* So wish I, I might thrust thy soul to hell'.

---

thing to *talk on*, when *thou art dead* and rotten come hither." i. e, for people to talk of. So again, in a subsequent scene of this play before us; " And *dead men's cries* do fill the empty air."

Which of our author's plays does not exhibit expressions equally bold as " I will hang thee," to express " I will have thee hung?"

I must just observe, that most of our author's *additions* are strongly characteristick of his manner. The making Iden's sword wear the stains of Cade's blood on its point, and comparing those stains to a herald's coat, declare at once the pen of Shakspeare. MALONE.

' *How much thou wrong'st me,*] That is, in supposing that I am proud of my victory. JOHNSON.

An anonymous writer suggests that the meaning may be, that Cade wrongs Iden by undervaluing his prowess, and declaring that he was subdued by famine, not by the valour of his adversary.—I think Dr. Johnson's is the true interpretation. MALONE.

' *So wish I, I might thrust thy soul to hell.*] Not to dwell upon the wickedness of this horrid wish, with which Iden debases his character, the whole speech is wild and confused. To draw a man by the heels, headlong, is somewhat difficult; nor can I discover how the dunghill would be his grave, if his trunk were left to be fed upon by crows. These I conceive not to be the faults of corruption but negligence, and therefore do not attempt correction. JOHNSON.

The quarto is more favourable both to Iden's morality and language. It omits this savage wish, and makes him only add, after the lines I have just quoted:

I'll drag him hence, and with my sword
Cut off his head, and bear it with me.

The player editors seem to have preferred want of humanity and common sense, to fewness of lines, and defect of versification. STEEVENS.

By *headlong* the poet undoubtedly meant, with his head trailed along the ground. By saying, " the dunghill shall be thy grave," Iden means, the dunghill shall be the place where thy *dead body shall be laid:* the dunghill shall be the *only* grave which thou shalt have. Surely in poetry this is allowable. So, in *Macbeth:*

" ———— our monuments
" Shall be the maws of kites."

After what has been already stated, I fear it must be acknowledged, that this faulty *amplification* was owing rather to our author's desire to expand a scanty thought of a preceding writer, than to any want of judgment in the player editors. MALONE.

' Hence

' Hence will I drag thee headlong by the heels
' Unto a dunghill, which ſhall be thy grave,
' And there cut off thy moſt ungracious head ;
' Which I will bear in triumph to the king,
' Leaving thy trunk for crows to feed upon.

         [*Exit, dragging out the body.*

ACT V. SCENE I.

The ſame. Fields between Dartford *and* Blackheath.

The King's Camp on one ſide. On the other, enter YORK *attended, with drum and colours : his forces at ſome diſtance.*

' *York.* From Ireland thus comes York, to claim his
     right,
' And pluck the crown from feeble Henry's head :
' Ring, bells, aloud ; burn, bonfires, clear and bright,
' To entertain great England's lawful king.
Ah, *ſanĉta majeſtas !* who would not buy thee dear ?
' Let them obey, that know not how to rule ;
' This hand was made to handle nought but gold :
' I cannot give due aĉtion to my words,
' Except a ſword, or ſcepter, balance it ³.
' A ſcepter ſhall it have, have I a ſoul ⁴ ;
' On which I'll toſs the flower-de-luce of France.

---

3 — *balance it.*] That is, Balance my hand. Johnson.

4 *A ſcepter ſhall it have, have I a ſoul ;*] I read :
     A ſcepter ſhall it have, have I a ſword.
York obſerves that his hand muſt be employed with a ſword or ſcepter; he then naturally obſerves, that he has a ſword, and reſolves that if he has a ſword he will have a ſcepter. Johnson.

I rather think York means to ſay—If I have a ſoul, my hand ſhall not be without a ſcepter. Steevens.

This certainly is a very natural interpretation of theſe words, and being no friend to alteration merely for the ſake of improvement, we ough't, I think, to acquieſce in it. But ſome difficulty will ſtill remain ; for if we read, with the old copy, ſoul, York threatens to " toſs the flower-de-luce of France on his ſcepter," which ſounds but oddly. To toſs it on his ſword, was a threat very natural for a man who had already triumphed over the French. So, in *K Henry VI. P. III.*

     " The ſoldiers ſhould have toſs'd me on their pikes.".

However, in the licentious phraſeology of our author, York may mean, that he will *wield his ſceptre*, (that is, exerciſe his royal power,) when he obtains it, ſo as to abaſe and deſtroy the French.—The following line alſo in *King Henry VIII.* adds ſupport to the old copy :

     " Si., *as I have a ſoul*, ſhe is an angel." Malone.

               Enter

Enter BUCKINGHAM.

‘ Whom have we here? Buckingham to diſturb me?
‘ The king hath ſent him, ſure: I muſt diſſemble.
 ‘ *Buck.* York, if thou meaneſt well, I greet thee well.
 ‘ *York.* Humphrey of Buckingham, I accept thy greet-
  ing.
‘ Art thou a meſſenger, or come of pleaſure?
 ‘ *Buck.* A meſſenger from Henry, our dread liege,
‘ To know the reaſon of theſe arms in peace;
‘ Or why, thou—being a ſubject as I am [5],—
‘ Againſt thy oath and true allegiance ſworn,
‘ Should’ſt raiſe ſo great a power without his leave.
‘ Or dare to bring thy force ſo near the court.
 ‘ *York.* Scarce can I ſpeak, my choler is ſo
  great [6].
‘ O, I could hew up rocks, and fight with flint,
‘ I am ſo angry at theſe abject terms;
‘ And now like Ajax Telamonius,
‘ On ſheep or oxen could I ſpend my fury!
‘ I am far better born than is the king;
‘ More like a king, more kingly in my thoughts:
‘ But I muſt make fair weather yet a while,
‘ Till Henry be more weak, and I more ſtrong.—
‘ O Buckingham [7], I pr’ythee, pardon me,
‘ That I have given no anſwer all this while;
‘ My mind was troubled with deep melancholy.
‘ The cauſe why I have brought this army hither,
‘ Is—to remove proud Somerſet from the king,
‘ Seditious to his grace, and to the ſtate.
 ‘ *Buck.* That is too much preſumption on thy part:
‘ But if thy arms be to no other end,

Aſide.

---

5 — *being a ſubject as I am*,] Here again in the old play we have the
ſtyle and verſification of our author’s immediate predeceſſors:
 “ Or that thou, being a ſubject as I am,
 “ *Should’ſt thus approach ſo near with colours ſpread*,
 “ *Whereas the perſon of the king doth keepe.*” MALONE.

6 *Scarce can I ſpeak*, &c.] The firſt nine lines of this ſpeech are
founded on the following in the old play:
 “ A ſubject as he is:
 “ O, how I hate theſe ſpiteful abject terms!
 “ But York diſſemble, *till thou meet thy ſonnes*,
 “ Who now in arms expect thy father’s fight,
 “ And not far hence I know they cannot be.” MALONE.

7 O *Buckingham*,] O, which is not in the authentick copy, was
added, to ſupply the metre, by the editor of the ſecond folio. MALONE.

I

          ‘ The

' The king hath yielded unto thy demand;
' The duke of Somerſet is in the Tower.

York. Upon thine honour, is he priſoner?

Buck. Upon mine honour, he is priſoner.

' *York.* Then, Buckingham, I do diſmiſs my powers:—
' Soldiers, I thank you all; diſperſe yourſelves;
' Meet me to-morrow in ſaint George's field,
' You ſhall have pay, and every thing you wiſh.—
* And let my ſovereign, virtuous Henry,
* Command my eldeſt ſon,—nay, all my ſons,
* As pledges of my fealty and love,
* I'll ſend them all as willing as I live;
* Lands, goods, horſe, armour, any thing I have
* Is his to uſe, ſo Somerſet may die.

' *Buck.* York, I commend this kind ſubmiſſion:
' We twain will go into his highneſs' tent [8].

Enter King HENRY attended.

' *K. Hen.* Buckingham, doth York intend no harm to us,
' That thus he marcheth with thee arm in arm?

' *York.* In all ſubmiſſion and humility,
* York doth preſent himſelf unto your highneſs.

' *K. Hen.* Then what intend theſe forces thou doſt bring?

' *York.* To heave the traitor Somerſet from hence [9];
' And fight againſt that monſtrous rebel, Cade,
' Who ſince I hear'd to be diſcomfited.

Enter IDEN, with Cade's head.

' *Iden.* If one ſo rude, and of ſo mean condition,
' May paſs into the preſence of a king,
' Lo, I preſent your grace a traitor's head,
' The head of Cade, whom I in combat ſlew.

---

8 *We twain will go into his highneſs' tent.*] Shakſpeare has here deviated from the original play without much propriety.—He has followed it in making Henry come to Buckingham and York, inſtead of their going to him:—yet without the introduction found in the quarto, where the lines ſtand thus:

    Buck. Come, York, thou ſhalt go ſpeak unto the king;—
    But ſee, his grace is coming to meet with us MALONE.

9 York. *To heave the traitor Somerſet from hence;*] The corresponding ſpeech to this is given in the old play to Buckingham who acquaints the king with the plea that York had before made to him for his riſing : " To heave the duke of Somerſet, &c. This variation could never have ariſen from copyiſts, ſhort-hand writers, or printers. MALONE.

    ' *K. Hen.*

‘ *K. Hen.* The head of Cade * ?—Great God, how juſt
art thou !—

‘ O, let me view his viſage being dead,
‘ That living wrought me ſuch exceeding trouble.
‘ Tell me, my friend, art thou the man that ſlew him ?
‘ *Iden.* I was, an't like your majeſty.
‘ *K. Hen.* How art thou call'd ? and what is thy degree ?
‘ *Iden.* Alexander Iden, that's my name ;
‘ A poor eſquire of Kent, that loves his king.
* *Buck.* So pleaſe it you, my lord, 'twere not amiſs
* He were created knight for his good ſervice.
‘ *K. Hen.* Iden, kneel down ; [*he kneels.*] Riſe up a
knight.
‘ We give thee for reward a thouſand marks ;
‘ And will, that thou henceforth attend on us.
‘ *Iden.* May Iden live to merit ſuch a bounty,
‘ And never live but true unto his liege ¹ !
‘ *K. Hen.* See, Buckingham ! Somerſet comes with the
queen ;
‘ Go, bid her hide him quickly from the duke.

Enter Queen MARGARET, *ana* SOMERSET.

‘ *Q. Mar.* For thouſand Yorks he ſhall not hide his head,
‘ But boldly ſtand, and front him to his face.
‘ *York.* How now ! is Somerſet at liberty ² ?

---

* *The head of Cade ?*] The ſpeech correſponding to this in the firſt
part of the *Whole Contention*, &c. 1600, is alone ſufficient to prove that
piece the work of another poet :

> *King.* Firſt, thanks to heaven, and next, to thee, my friend,
> That haſt ſubdu'd that wicked traitor thus.
> O, let me ſee that head, that in his life
> Did work me and my land ſuch cruel ſpight.
> *A viſage ſtern, coal-black his curled locks ;*
> *Deep trenched furrows in his frowning brow,*
> *Preſageth warlike humours in his life.*
> Here take it hence, and thou for thy reward
> Shalt be immediately created knight :
> Kneel down, my friend, and tell me what's thy name. MALONE.

¹ *May Iden,* &c.] Iden has ſaid before :
> *Lord ! who would live turmoiled in a court,*
> *And may enjoy,* &c.

Shakſpeare mak s Iden rail at thoſe enjoyments which he ſuppoſes to be
out of his reach ; but no ſooner are they offered to him but he readily
accepts them. ANONYMOUS.

In Iden's eulogium on the happineſs of rural life, and his acceptance
of the honours beſtowed by his majeſty, Shakſpeare has merely followed the old play. MALONE.

² *How now !* &c.] This ſpeech is greatly amplified, and in other reſ-
pects very different from the original, which conſiſts but of ten lines.
MALONE.

‘ Then,

‘ Then, York, unloose thy long imprison’d thoughts,
‘ And let thy tongue be equal with thy heart.
‘ Shall I endure the fight of Somerset ?—
‘ False king! why haft thou broken faith with me,
‘ Knowing how hardly I can brook abuse ?
‘ King did I call thee? no, thou art not king ;
‘ Not fit to govern and rule multitudes,
‘ Which dar’ft not, no, nor canft not rule a traitor.
‘ That head of thine doth not become a crown ;
‘ Thy hand is made to grasp a palmer’s ftaff,
‘ And not to grace an awful princely fcepter.
‘ That gold muft round engirt these brows of mine ;
‘ Whose smile and frown, like to Achilles’ fpear,
‘ Is able with the change to kill and cure [3].
‘ Here is a hand to hold a fcepter up,
‘ And with the same to act controlling laws.
‘ Give place ; by heaven, thou fhalt rule no more
‘ O’er him, whom heaven created for thy ruler.

　‘ *Som.* O monftrous traitor !—I arreft thee, York,
‘ Of capital treason ’gainft the king and crown :
* Obey, audacious traitor ; kneel for grace.

　　* *York.* Would’ft have me kneel? firft let me afk of
　　　　thefe [4],
* If they can brook I bow a knee to man.——
* Sirrah, call in my fons to be my bail ;　　[*Exit an* Attend.
* I know, ere they will have me go to ward,
* They’ll pawn their fwords for my enfranchifement.

　　‘ *Q. Mar.* Call hither Clifford ; bid him come amain,
　　　　　　　　　　　　　　[*Exit* BUCKINGHAM.

3 —— *like to Achilles’ fpear.*
　　Is able with the change to kill and cure.]
　　Myfus et Æmonia Juvenis qua cufpide vulnus
　Senferat, hac ipfa cufpide fenfit opem. PROPERT Lib. II. El. 1.
Greene in his *Orlando Fariofo,* 1594, has the fame allufion :
　　‘ Where I took hurt, there was I heal’d myfelf :
　　‘ As those that with Achilles’ launce were wounded,
　　‘ Fetch’d help at felf-fame pointed fpeare.’ MALONE.

4 —— *firft let me afk of thefe,*] By *thefe* Mr. Tyrwhitt fuppofes York
means his knees, “ on which he lays his hands, or at leaft points to
them.” I have no doubt that York means either his fons, whom he
mentions in the next line, or his troops, to whom he may be fuppofed
to point. Dr. Warburton transpofed the lines, placing that which is
now the middle line at the beginning of the fpeech. But, like many of
his emendations, it appears to have been unneceffary. The folio reads
—of *thee.* The emendation was made by Mr. Theobald. *Sens* was
fubftituted for *fen* by the editor of the fecond fo’io. The correction is
juftified both by the context and the old play. “ Fer my enfranchifement,” inftead of—*of my,* &c. was likewife his correction. MALONE.

* To

* To fay, if that the baftard boys of York
* Shall be the furety for their traitor father.
  * *York.* O blood-befpotted Neapolitan,
* Out-caft of Naples, England's bloody fcourge!
' The fons of York, thy betters in their birth,
' Shall be their father's bail ; and bane to thofe
' That for my furety will refufe the boys.

Enter EDWARD *and* RICHARD PLANTAGENET, *with forces,
at one fide ; at the other, with forces alfo, old* CLIFFORD
and his fon.

* See, where they come ; I'll warrant, they'll make it good.
  * *Q. Mar.* And here comes Clifford, to deny their bail.
  ' *Clif.* Health and all happinefs to my lord the king!
                                   [*kneels.*
  ' *York.* I thank thee, Clifford : Say, what news with
     thee ?
' Nay, do not fright us with an angry look :
' We are thy fovereign, Clifford, kneel again ;
' For thy miftaking fo, we pardon thee.
  Clif. This is my king, York, I do not miftake ;
' But thou miftak'ft me much, to think I do :——
' To Bedlam with him ! is the man grown mad ?
  ' *K. Hen.* Ay, Clifford ; a bedlam and ambitious hu-
    mour [5]
' Makes him oppofe himfelf againft his king.
  ' *Clif.* He is a traitor ; let him to the Tower,
' And chop away that factious pate of his.
  Q. Mar. He is arrefted, but will not obey ;
' His fons, he fays, fhall give their words for him.
  ' *York.* Will you not, fons ?
  Edw. Ay, noble father, if our words will ferve.
  ' *Rich.* And if words will not, then our weapons fhall.
  * *Clif.* Why, what a brood of traitors have we here !
  * *York.* Look in a glafs, and call thy image fo ;
* I am thy king, and thou a falfe-heart traitor.——
 « Call hither to the ftake my two brave bears [6],

    [5] —*a bedlam and ambitious humour*—] The word *bedlam* was not
ufed in the reign of king Henry the Sixth, nor was Bethlehem Hofpital
(vulgarly called Bedlam) converted into a houfe or hofpital for lunaticks
till the reign of king Henry the Eighth, who gave it to the city of London for that purpofe. GREY.
  Shakfpeare was led into this anachronifm by the author of the elder
play. MALONE.
   [6] *Call hither to the ftake my two brave bears,*—
    Bid Salifbury and Warwick come—] The Nevils, earls of War-
wick, had a *bear and ragged ftaff* for their cognizance. SIR J HAWK.
                                     * That

* That, with the very shaking of their chains,
* They may astonish these fell lurking curs [7];
* Bid Salisbury, and Warwick, come to me [8].

Drums.   Enter WARWICK *and* SALISBURY, *with forces.*

' *Clif.* Are these thy bears ? we'll bait thy bears to death,
' And manacle the bear-ward in their chains,
' If thou dar'st bring them to the baiting-place.
  * *Rich.* Oft have I seen a soft o'er-weening cur
* Run back and bite, because he is withheld [9];
* Who, being suffer'd * with the bear's fell paw,
* Hath clapp'd his tail between his legs, and cry'd :
* And such a piece of service will you do,
* If you oppose yourself to match lord Warwick.
  * *Clif.* Hence, heap of wrath, foul indigested lump,
* As crooked in thy manners as thy shape !
  * *York.* Nay, we shall heat you thoroughly anon.
  * *Clif.* Take heed, lest by your heat you burn yourselves.
  * *K. Hen.* Why, Warwick, hath thy knee forgot to bow ?—
* Old Salisbury,—shame to thy silver hair,
* Thou mad mis-leader of thy brain-sick son !—
* What, wilt thou on thy death-bed play the ruffian,
* And seek for sorrow with thy spectacles ?—
* O, where is faith ? O, where is loyalty ?
* If it be banish'd from the frosty head,
* Where shall it find a harbour in the earth ?—
* Wilt thou go dig a grave to find out war,
* And shame thine honourable age with blood ?
* Why art thou old, and want'st experience ?
* Or wherefore dost abuse it, if thou hast it ?
* For shame ! in duty bend thy knee to me,

7 — fell lurking *curs :*] Curs who are at once a compound of *cruelty* and *triachery.* STEEVENS.

8 *Bid Salisbury, and Warwick, come to me.*] Here in the old play the following lines are found :
    King. Call Buckingham, and bid him arm himself.
    York. Call Buckingham and all the friends thou hast ;
Both then and they shall curse this fatal hour.
Buckingham accordingly enters immediately with his forces. Shakspeare, we see, has not introduced him in the present scene, but has availed himself of those lines below. MALONE.

9 *Oft have I seen,* &c] Bear-baiting was anciently a royal sport — See Stow's Account of Queen Elizabeth's amusements of this kind ; and Langham's *Letter concerning that Queen's Entertainment at Knelworth Castle.* PERCY.

* — *being* suffer'd—] Being suffer'd to approach to the bear's fell paw. Such may be the meaning. I am not however sure but the poet meant, being in a state of *sufferance* or pain. MALONE.

* That bows unto the grave with mickle age.

 * *Sal.* My lord, I have confider'd with myfelf
* The title of this moft renowned duke ;
* And in my confcience do repute his grace
* The rightful heir to England's royal feat.

 * *K. Hen.* Haft thou not fworn allegiance unto me ?

 * *Sal.* I have

 * *K. Hen.* Canft thou difpenfe with heaven for fuch an oath ?

 * *Sal.* It is great fin, to fwear unto a fin [1] ;
* But greater fin, to keep a finful oath.
* Who can be bound by any folemn vow
* To do a murderous deed, to rob a man,
* To force a fpotlefs virgin's chaftity,
* To reave the orphan of his patrimony,
* To wring the widow from her cuftom'd right ;
* And have no other reafon for this wrong,
* But that he was bound by a folemn oath ?

 * *Q. Mar.* A fubtle traitor needs no fophifter.

 ' *K. Hen.* Call Buckingham, and bid him arm himfelf.

 ' *York.* Call Buckingham, and all the friends thou haft,
' I am refolv'd for death, or dignity [2].

 ' *Clif.* The firft I warrant thee, if dreams prove true.

 ' *War.* You were beft to go to bed, and dream again,
To keep thee from the tempeft of the field.

 Clif. I am refolv'd to bear a greater ftorm,
Than any thou canft conjure up to-day ;
And that I'll write upon thy burgonet [3],
Might I but know thee by thy houfhold badge [4].

 War. Now by my father's badge, old Nevil's creft,
The rampant bear chain'd to the ragged ftaff,
This day I'll wear aloft my burgonet,
(As on a mountain top the cedar fhews,
That keeps his leaves in fpight of any ftorm,)
Even to affright thee with the view thereof.

---

[1] *It is great fin, to fwear unto a fin* ;] We have the fame fentiment in *Love's Labour's Loft* :

  " It is religion, to be thus forfworn."
Again, in *King John* :
  " It is religion that doth make vows kept ;
  " But thou doft fwear only to be forfworn ;
  " And moft forfworn to keep what thou doft fwear." MALONE.

 [2] — *for death, or dignity.*] The folio read—*and* dignity. The emendation was made by Mr. Pope. MALONE.

 [3] — *burgonet,*] is a *helmet.* JOHNSON.

 [4] — *thy houfhold badge.*] The folio has *houfed* badge, owing probably to the tranfcriber's ear deceiving him. The true reading is found in the old play. MALONE.

Clif. And from thy burgonet I'll rend thy bear,
And tread it under foot with all contempt,
' Defpight the bear ward that protects the bear.
  ' *Y. Clif.* And fo to arms, victorious father,
' To quell the rebels, and their 'complices.
  Rich. Fie! charity, for fhame! fpeak not in fpight,
For you will fup with *Jefu Chrift* to-night.
  ' *Y. Clif.* Foul ftigmatick⁵, that's more than thou canft
    tell.
  ' *Rich.* If not in heaven, you'll furely fup in hell.

[Exeunt feverally.

SCENE II.

Saint Albans.

Alarums; Excurfions. **Enter WARWICK.**

War. Clifford of Cumberland, 'tis Warwick calls!
And if thou doft not hide thee from the bear,
Now,—when the angry trumpet founds alarm,
And dead men's cries do fill the empty air,—
Clifford, I fay come forth and fight with me!
Proud northern lord, Clifford of Cumberland,
Warwick is hoarfe with calling thee to arms.

Enter YORK.

' How now, my noble lord? what, all a-foot?
  ' *York.* The deadly-handed Clifford flew my fteed;
' But match to match I have encounter'd him,
' And made a prey for carrion kites and crows
' Even of the bonny beaft he lov'd fo well⁶.

Enter CLIFFORD.

' *War.* Of one or both of us the time is come.
  York. Hold, Warwick, feek thee out fome other chace,
For I myfelf muft hunt this deer to death.
  ' *War.* Then, nobly, York; 'tis for a crown thou fight'ft.—

---

⁵ *foul ftigmatick,*] A *ftigmatick* is one on whom nature has fet a mark of deformity, a ftigma. STEEVENS.

This certainly is the meaning here. A *ftigmatick* originally and properly fignified a perfon who had been branded with a hot iron for fome crime. See Bulkar's *Eng'fh Expofitor*, 1616. MALONE.

⁶ *Even of the bonny beaft be lov'd fo well*] In the old play:
. " The bonnieft gray, that e'er was bred in North." MALONE.

' **As**

' As I intend, Clifford, to thrive to-day,
It grieves my foul to leave thee unaſſail'd.   [*Exit* WARWICK.

  ' *Clif.* What feeſt thou in me, York[7]? why doſt thou
      pauſe ?

  ' *York.* With thy brave bearing ſhould I be in love,
' But that thou art ſo faſt mine enemy.

  ' *Clif.* Nor ſhould thy proweſs want praiſe and eſteem,
' But that 'tis ſhewn ignobly, and in treaſon.

  ' *York.* So let it help me now againſt thy ſword,
' As I in juſtice and true right expreſs it !

  ' *Clif.* My ſoul and body on the action both !—

  ' *York.* A dreadful lay[8] !—addreſs thee inſtantly.

                 [*They fight, and* Clifford *falls.*

  ' Clif. *La fin couronne les oeuvres*[9].   .   [*Dies*[1].

  ' *York.* Thus war hath given thee peace, for thou art ſtill.
' Peace with his ſoul, heaven, if it be thy will !   [*Exit.*

---

7 *What ſee'ſt thou in me, York ?* &c.] Inſtead of this and the ten following lines, we find theſe in the old play, and the variation is worth
noting :

    York. Now, Clifford, ſince we are ſingled here a'one,
    Be this the day of doom to one of us ;
    For now my heart hath ſworn immortal hate
    To thee and all the houſe of Lancaſter
      Clif. And here I ſtand, and pitch my foot to thine,
    Vowing ne'er to ſtir till thou or I be ſlain ;
    For never ſhall my heart be ſafe at reſt,
    Till I have ſpoil'd the hateful houſe o' York.
          [*Alarums, and they fight, and* York *kills* Clifford.
    York. Now Lancaſter, ſit ſure ; thy ſinews ſhrink.
    Come, fearful Henry, groveling on thy face,
    Yield up the crown unto the prince of York.   .[*Exit* York.
                            MALONE.

  '8 *A dreadful lay !*] A dreadful wager ; a tremendous ſtake.
                                  JOHNSON.

9 *La fin couronne les oeuvres.*] The players read:
    La fin corrone les eumenes. STEEVENS.
Corrected by the editor of the ſecond folio. MALONE.

  1 *Dies.*] Our author, in making Clifford fall by the hand of York,
has departed from the truth of hiſtory. a practice not uncommon to
him when he does his utmoſt to make his characters conſiderable. This
circumſtance however ſerves to prepare the reader or ſpectator for thee
vengeance afterwards taken by Clifford's ſon on York and Rutland.

  It is remarkable, that at the beginning of the third part of this hiſtorical play, the poet has forgot this occurrence, and there repreſent
Clifford's death as it really happened :

    " *Lord Clifford and Lord Stafford all abreaſt.*
    " *Charg'd our main battle's front ; and breaking in,*
    " *Were by the ſwords of common ſoldiers ſlain.*"   PERCY.

  For this inconſiſtency the elder poet muſt anſwer ; for theſe lines are
in the *True tragedie of Richard duke of York,* &c on which, as I conceive, the third part of *King Henry VI.* was founded. MALONE.

                                   Enter

Enter young CLIFFORD.

* *Y. Clif.* Shame and confusion ! all is on the rout [2] ;
* Fear frames disorder, and disorder wounds
* Where it should guard   O war, thou son of hell,
* Whom angry heavens do make their minister,
* Throw in the frozen bosoms of our part
* Hot coals of vengeance !—Let no soldier fly :
* He, that is truly dedicate to war,
* Hath no self-love ; nor he, that loves himself,
* Hath not essentially, but by circumstance,
* The name of valour.—O, let the vile world end.

> [*Seeing his dead father.*

* And the premised flames [3] of the last day
* Knit earth and heaven together !
* Now let the general trumpet blow his blast,
* Particularities and petty sounds
* To cease [4] !—Wast thou ordain'd, dear father,
* To lose thy youth in peace, and to atchieve [5]
* The silver livery of advised age [6] ;
* And, in thy reverence [7], and thy chair-days, thus

2 *Shame and confusion ! all is on the rout* :] Instead of this long speech, we have the following lines in the old play :

> Y Clif Father of Cumberland !
> Where may I seek my aged father forth ?
> O dismal sight ! see where he breathless lies,
> All smear'd and welter'd in his luke warm blood !
> Ah, aged pillar of all Cumberland's true house !
> Sweet father, to thy murder'd ghost I swear
> Immortal hate unto the house of York ;
> Nor never shall I sleep secure one night,
> Till I have curiously reveng'd thy death,
> And left not one of them to breathe on earth.
>
> [*He takes him up on his back.*
>
> And thus as old Anchises' son did bear
> His aged father on his manly back,
> *And fought with him against the bloody Greeks,*
> Even so will I ;—but stay, here's one of them,
> To whom my soul hath sworn mortal hate. MALONE.

3 *And the premised flames*—] *Premised,* for sent before their time. The sense is, let the flames reserved for the last day be sent now.
WARBURTON.

4 *To* cease !] is to *stop,* a verb active. So, in *Timon of Athens :*
" ——— be not ceas'd
" With slight denial—." STEEVENS.

5 — *to* atchieve] is, to obtain. JOHNSON.

6 *of* advised *age* :] *Advised* is wise, experienced. MALONE.

7 *And, in thy* reverence,] In that period of life, which is entitled to the reverence of others. Our author has used the word in the same manner in *As you like it,* where the younger brother says to the elder, (speaking of their father,) " thou art indeed nearer to his *reverence* "
MALONE.

* To

* To die in ruffian battle ?—Even at this fight,
* My heart is turn'd to ftone * : and, while 'tis mine,
* It fhall be ftony.   York not our old men fpares ;
* No more will I their babes : tears virginal
* Shall be to me even as the dew to fire ;
* And beauty, that tne tyrant oft reclaims,
* Shall to my flaming wrath be oil and flax ³.
* Henceforth, I will not have to do with pity :
* Meet I an infant of the duke of York,
* Into as many gobbets will I cut it,
* As wild Medea young Abfyrtus did † :
* In cruelty will I feek out my fame.
' Come, thou new ruin of old Clifford's houfe ;

                            [Taking up the body.

' As did Æneas old Anchifes bear,
' So bear I thee upon my manly fhoulders ⁹ ;
* But then Æneas bare a living load,
* Nothing fo heavy as thefe woes of mine.   *[Exit.*

Fnter RICHARD PLANTAGENET *and* SOMERSET, *fighting,*
    and SOMERSET *is killed.*

  Rich. So, lie thou there ;—

   * *My heart is turn'd to ftone :*] So, in *Othello :* " — my heart is turn'd
to ftone ; I ftrike it, and it hurts my hand." MALONE.
   ³ — *to my flaming wrath be oil and flax.*] So, in *Hamlet :*
     " To flaming youth let virtue be as wax,
     " And melt in her own fire." STEEVENS.
  † *As wild Medea,* &c] When Medea fled with Jafon from Colchos,
fhe murdered her brother Abfyrtus, and cut his body into feveral pieces,
that her father might be prevented for fome time from purfuing her.—
See Ovid, *Trift.* Lib III. El. 9.
     — divellit, divulfaque membra per agros
     Diffipat, in multis invenienda locis :—
     Ut genitor luctuque novo tardetur, et artus
     Dum legit extinctos, trifte moretur iter. MALONE.
  9 The quarto copy has thefe lines :
     Even fo will I.—But ftay, here's one of them,
     To whom my foul hath fworn immortal hate.
⌐*Enter* Richard, *and then* Clifford *lays down his father, fights with him,*
    and Richard *flies away again.*
     Out, crook-back'd villain, get thee from my fight !
     But I will after thee, and once again
     (When I have borne my father to his tent)
     I'll try my fortune better with thee yet.
                [Exit young Clifford, *with his father.*
                           STEEVENS.
  This is to be added to all the other circumftances which have been
urged to fhew that the quarto play was the production of an elder writer
than Shakfpeare. The former defcription of Æneas is different. See
p. 220, n. 2. MALONE.
                                  ' For,

' For, underneath an ale-houfe' paltry fign ¹,
The caftle in faint Albans, Somerfet
Hath made the wizard famous in his death ².—
* Sword, hold thy temper; heart, be wrathful ftill :
* Priefts pray for enemies, but princes kill.　　[*Exit.*

Alarums. Excurfions. Enter King Henry, *Queen* Margaret, *and others, retreating.*

' *Q. Mar.* Away, my lord ³, you are flow; for fhame,
　　away !

* *K. Hen.* Can we out-run the heavens ? good Margaret,
　　ftay.

* *Q. Mar* What are you made of ? you'll not fight nor
　　fly :

* Now is it manhood, wifdom, and defence,

---

¹ *For, underneath an ale-houfe' paltry fign.*] Dr. Johnfon juftly ob-
ferves that the particle *for* feems to be u ed here without any apparent
inference. The correfponding paffage in the old play induces me to be-
lieve that a line has been omitted, perhaps of this import :
　　" *Behold the prophecy is come to pafs ;*
　　" *For, underneath—*" &c.
We have already two fimilar omiffions in this play.　Malone.
　　Thus the paffage ftands in the quarto:
　　Rich. So lie thou there, and tumble in thy blood !
　Whats here ? tne fign of the Caftle ?
　Then the prophecy is come to pafs ;
　For Somerfet was forewarned of caftles,
　The which he always did obferve ; and now,
　Behold, under a paltry ale-houfe fign,
　The Caftle in faint Albans, Somerfet
　Heth made the wizard famous by his death.　Steevens.
　　² —*famous in his death.*—] The death of Somerfet here accom-
plifhes that equivocal prediction given by Jourdain, the witch, concern-
ing this duke ; which we meet with at the clofe of the firft act of this
play :
　　Let him fhun caftles :
　　Safer fhall be be upon the fandy plains,
　　Than where caftles, mounted, ftand.
i. e. the reprefentation of a *caftle*, mounted for a *fign*.　Theobald.
　　³ *Away, my lord,* &c] Thus in the old play :
　　Queen. Away, my lord, and fly to London ftraight ;
　　Make hafte, for vengeance comes along with them ;
　　Come, ftand not to expoftulate : let's go.
　　King. Come then, fair queen, to London let us hafte,
　　And fummon a parliament with fpeed,
　　To ftop the fury of thefe dire events. [*Exeunt* King *and* Queen.
　Previous to the entry of the king and queen, there is the following
ftage-direction :
　　" *Alarums again, and then enter three or four bearing* the duke of
Buckingham wounded to his tent. *Alarums ftill, and then enter the king
and queen.*" Malone.

　　　　　　　　　　　　　　　　　　　* To

* To give the enemy way ; and to fecure us
* By what we can, which can no more but fly.

[*Alarum afar off.*

* If you be ta'en, we then fhould fee the bottom
* Of all our fortunes 4 : but if we haply fcape,
* (As well we may, if not through your neglect,)
* We fhall to London get ; where you are lov'd ;
* And where this breach, now in our fortunes made,
* May readily be ftopp'd.

Enter young CLIFFORD.

* *Y. Clif.* But that my heart's on future mifchief fet,
* I would fpeak blafphemy ere bid you fly ;
* But fly you muft ; uncurable difcomfit
* Reigns in the hearts of all our prefent parts 5.
* Away, for your relief ! and we will live
* To fee their day, and them our fortune give :
* Away, my lord, away !

[*Exeunt.*

4 *If you be ta'en, we then fhould* fee the bottom
Of all our fortunes :] Of this expreffion, which is undoubtedly
Shakfpeare's, he appears to have been fond. So, in *K. Henry IV. P. I.*
"   ―――― for therein fhould we read
"   The very *bottom* and the foul of hope,
"   The very lift, the ve y utmoft bound
"   *Of all our fortunes.*"
Again, in *Romeo and Juliet :*
"   Which *fees into the bottom* of my grief."
Again, in *Meafure for Meafure :*
"   To *look* into *the bottom* of my place."   MALONE.
5 ― *all our prefent* parts.] Should we not read ?―*party.* TYRWITT.
The text is undoubtedly right.   So, before:
"   Throw in the frozen bofoms of our *part*
"   Hot coals of vengeance."
I think I have met with *part* for *party* in other books of that time.
So, in the proclamation for the apprehenfion of John Cade, Stowe's
Chronicle, p. 646, edit. 1605: "― the which John Cade alfo, after
this, was worne to the French *parts*, and owel ed with them;" &c.
Again, in Hall's Chronicle, *King Henry VI.* fol. 101: "― in con-
clufion king Edward fo courageoufly comforted his men, refrefhing the
weary, and helping the wounded, that the other *part* [i e the adverfe
army] was difcomforted and overcome.   See alfo a preceding extract
from the fame Chronicle in p. 647.
Again, in *Coriolanus:*
"   ―――― if I cannot perfuade thee
"   Rather to fhew a noble grace to both *parts*,
"   Than feek the one,"―
In Plutarch the correfponding paffage runs thus: " For if I cannot
perfuade thee rather to do good unto both *parties*, &c."   MALONE.

SCENE

SCENE III.

Fields near Saint Albans.

Alarum. Retreat. Flourish; then enter YORK, RICHARD
PLANTAGENET, WARWICK, *and soldiers, with drum and
colours.*

' *York.* Of Salisbury, who can report of him [6];
* That winter lion, who, in rage, forgets
* Aged contusions and all brush of time [7];
* And, like a gallant in the brow of youth [8],
* Repairs him with occasion? this happy day
* Is not itself, nor have we won one foot,
* If Salisbury be lost.
' *Rich.* My noble father,
' Three times to-day I holp him to his horse,
' Three times bestrid him [9], thrice I led him off,
' Persuaded him from any further act :

---

[6] *Of Salisbury, &c.*] The corresponding speeches to this and the fol-
lowing, are these, in the original play :
    York. How now, boys! fortunate this fight hath been,
I hope to us and ours, for England's good,
And our great honour, that so long we lost,
Whilst faint-hearted Henry did usurp our rights.
But did you see old Salisbury, since we
With bloody minds did buckle with the foe ?
I would not for the loss of this right hand
That aught but well betide this good old man.
    Rich. My lord, I saw in the thickest throng,
Charging his launce with his old weary arms ;
And thrice I saw him beaten from his horse,
And thrice this hand did set him up again ;
And still he fought with courage 'gainst his foes ;
The boldest-spirited man that e'er mine eyes beheld. MALONE.

[7] — *brush of time* ,] The gradual detrition of time. So, in *Timon of
Athens :* " — one winter's *brush*—." STEEVENS.

[8] — *gallant in the* brow *of* youth,] The *brow of youth* is the *height*
of youth, as the *brow* of a hill is its summit. So, in *Othello :*
    " —— the head and *front* of my offending."
Again, in *K. John :*
    " Why here walk I in the black *brow* of night." STEEVENS.

[9] *Three times* bestrid *him*,] That is, Three times I saw him fallen,
and, striding over him, defended him till he recovered. JOHNSON
    Of this act of friendship, which Shakspeare has frequently noticed in
other places, no mention is made in the old play, as the reader may find
in n. 6. of this page ; and its introduction here is one of the numerous minute circumstances, which when united form almost a decisive proof that the piece before us was constructed on foundations laid by
a preceding writer. MALONE.

    ' But

' But ftill, where danger was, ftill there I met him ;
* And like rich hangings in a homely houfe,
* So was his will in his old feeble body.
* But, noble as he is, look where he comes.

Enter SALISBURY.

' *Sal* Now, by my fword, well haft thou fought to-day [1];
' By the mafs, fo did we all.—I thank you, Richard:
' God knows how long it is I have to live ;
' And it hath pleas'd him, that three times to-day
' You have defended me from imminent death.—
* Well, lords, we have not got that which we have [2];
* 'Tis not enough our foes are this time fled,
* Being oppofites of fuch repairing nature [3].
' *York.* I know, our fafety is to follow them ;
' For, as I hear, the king is fled to London,
' To call a prefent court of parliament [4].
' Let us purfue him, ere the writs go forth :—
' What fays lord Warwick, fhall we after them ?
War. After them ! nay, before them, if we can.

—[1] *Well haft thou fought,* &c.] The variation between this fpeech and that in the originil play deferves to be noticed:

> *Sal* Well haft thou fought this day, thou valiant duke ;
> And thou brave bud of York's increafing houfe,
> The fmall remainder of my weiiy life,
> I hold for thee, for with thy warl.ke arm
> Three times this day thou haft prefeiv'd my life. MALONE.

[2] *Well, lords, we have not got that which we have* ;] i. e. we have not fecured, we are not fure of retaining, that which we have acquired. In our author's *Rape of Lucrece,* a poem very nearly contemporary with the prefent piece, we meet with a fimilar expreffion :

> " That oft they nave not that whi.h they poffe's." MALONE.

[3] *Being oppofites of fuch repairing nature.*] Being enemies that are likely fo loin to rally and recover them'elves from this defeat.
To *repair* in our author's laug .age i , *to renovate.* So, in *Cymbeline.*

> " O, difloyal thi g !
> " That fhould'ft *repair* my youth,—."

Again, in *All's well that ends well :*

> " It much *repairs* me,
> " To talk of your good father." MALONE.

[4] *To call a prefent court of parliament.*] The king and queen left the ftage only juft as York entered, and have not faid a word about calling a parliament. Where then could York hear this ?—The fact is, as we have feen, that in the old play the king does fay, " he will call a parliament," but our author has omitted the lines. He has, therefore, here as in fome other places, fallen into an impropriety, by fometimes following and at others deferting his original. MALONE.

Now by my faith [5], lords, 'twas a glorious day :
Saint Albans' battle, won by famous York,
Shall be eterniz'd in all age to come.——
Sound, drums and trumpets ;——and to London all :
And more such days as these to us befall!   [*Exeunt.*

[5] *Now by my* faith,] The first folio reads—Now by my *hand.* This undoubtedly was one of the many alterations made by the editors of that copy, to avoid the penalty of the Stat. 3 Jac. l. c. 21.   See p. 208, n. 8.   The true reading I have restored from the old play.   MALONE.

KING HENRY VI.

PART III.

Perfons Reprefented.

King Henry *the Sixth*:
Edward, *Prince of* Wales, *his fon.*
Lewis XI. *King of* France.
Duke of Somerfet, }
Duke of Exeter, }
Earl of Oxford, } *Lords on King* Henry's *fide.*
Earl of Northumberland, }
Earl of Weftmoreland, }
Lord Clifford, }
Richard Plantagenet, *Duke of* York.
Edward, *Earl of* March, *afterwards King* }
   Edward IV. }
Edmund, *Earl of* Rutland, } *his fons.*
George, *afterwards Duke of* Clarence, }
Richard, *afterwards Duke of* Glocefter, }
Duke of Norfolk, }
Marquis of Montague, }
Earl of Warwick, } *of the Duke of* York's *party.*
Earl of Pembroke, }
Lord Haftings, }
Lord Stafford, }
Sir John Mortimer, } *uncles to the Duke of* York.
Sir Hugh Mortimer, }
Henry, *Earl of* Richmond, *a Youth.*
Lord Rivers, *brother to lady* Grey. *Sir* William Stanley.
Sir John Montgomery. *Sir* John Somerville.
Tutor to Rutland. *Mayor of* York. *Lieutenant of the* Tower.
A Nobleman. Two Keepers. A Huntfman.
A fon that has killed his father.
A father that has killed his fon.

Queen Margaret.
Lady Grey, *afterwards Queen to* Edward IV.
Bona, *fifter to the* French *queen.*

Soldiers, and other Attendants on King Henry *and* King Edward, *Meffengers, Watchmen, &c.*

S C E N E, *during part of the third act, in* France; *during all the reft of the play, in* England.

THIRD PART OF
KING HENRY VI[1].

ACT I. SCENE I.

London. *The Parliament-House.*

Drums. Some Soldiers of York's *party break in. Then, Enter the Duke of* YORK, EDWARD, RICHARD, NORFOLK, MONTAGUE, WARWICK, *and Others, with white roses in their hats.*

War. I wonder, how the king escap'd our hands.
York. While we pursu'd the horsemen of the north,

He

---

[1] The action of this play (which was at first printed under this title, *The true Tragedy of Richard Duke of York, and the good King Henry the Sixth; or, The Second Part of the Contention of York and Lancaster)* opens just after the first battle at Saint Albans, [May 23, 1455,] wherein the York faction carried the day; and closes with the murder of king Henry VI. and the birth of prince Edward, afterwards king Edward V. [November 4, 1471.] So that this history takes in the space of full sixteen years. THEOBALD.

I have never seen the quarto copy of the *Second part* of THE WHOLE CONTENTION, &c printed by *Valentine Simmes,* for Thomas Millington 1600; but the copy printed by W. W. for Thomas Millington, 1600, is now before me, and it is not precisely the same with that described by Mr. Pope and Mr. Theobald, nor does the undated edition (printed in fact, in 1519) correspond with their description. The title of the piece printed in 1600, by W. W is as follows: *The true Tragedie of Richarde Duke of Yorke, and the death of good King Henrie the Sext: With the whole contention betweene the two houses Lancaster and Yorke: as it was sundry times acted by the Right Honourable the Earle of Pembrooke his Servants. Printed at London by W. W for Thomas Millington, and are to be sold at his shoppe under St. Peter's Church in Cornewall, 1600."* On this piece Shakspeare, as I conceive, in 1591 formed the drama before us. See the Essay at the end of this play MALONE.

The present historical drama was altered by Crowne, and brought on the stage in the year 1680, under the title of *The Miseries of Civil War.* Surely the works of Shakspeare could have been little read at that period; for Crowne in his prologue, declares the play to be entirely his own composition:

" For by his feeble skill 'tis built alone,
" The divine Shakspeare *did not lay one stone.*"

whereas

He flily ſtole away, and left his men :
Whereat the great lord of Northumberland,
Whoſe warlike ears could never brook retreat,
' Chear'd up the drooping army ; and himſelf,
' Lord Clifford, and lord Stafford, all a-breaſt,
' Charg'd our main battle's front, and, breaking in,
' Were by the ſwords of common ſoldiers ſlain [2].
    Edw. Lord Stafford's father, duke of Buckingham,
' Is either ſlain, or wounded dangerous :
I cleft his beaver with a downright blow ;
' That this is true, father, behold his blood.
                      [ſhewing his bloody ſword.
    Mont. And, brother, here's the earl of Wiltſhire's blood,
                [to York, *ſhewing his.*
Whom I encounter'd as the battles join'd.
    Rich. Speak thou for me, and tell them what I did. *
        [throwing down the duke of Somerſet's *head.*
  * *York.* Richard hath beſt deſerv'd of all my ſons.——

whereas the very firſt ſcene is that of Jack Cade copied almoſt verbatim from the ſecond part of *K. Henry VI.* and ſeveral others from this
third part, with as little variation. STEEVENS

  This play is only divided from the former for the convenience of exhibition ; for the ſeries of action is continued without interruption, nor
are any two ſcenes of any play more cloſely connected than the fiſt
ſcene of this play with the laſt of the former. JOHNSON.

  2 *Were by the ſwords of common ſoldiers ſlain.*] Dr. Percy in a note
on the preceding play, (p. 219, n. 1.) has pointed out the inconſiſtency
between this account, and the repreſentation there, Clifford being killed on the ſtage by the duke of York, the preſent ſpeaker. Shakſpeare
was led into this inconſiſtency by the author of the original plays : if
indeed there was but one author, for this circumſtance might lead us
to ſuſpect that the *firſt* and *ſecond* part of *The Contention*, &c. were not
written by the ſame hand.—However, this is not deciſive ; for the
author, whoever he was, might have been inadvertent, as we find
Shakſpeare undoubtedly was. MALONE.

  * *Speak thou for me, and tell them what I did.*] Here, as Mr.
Elderton of Saliſbury has obſerved to me, is a groſs anachroniſm. At
the time of the firſt battle of Saint Albans, at which Richard is repreſented in the laſt ſcene of the preceding play to have fought, he was,
according to that gentleman's calculation, not one year old, having (as
he conceives) been born at Fotheringay caſtle, October 21, 1454. At
the time to which the third ſcene of the firſt act of this play is referred,
he was, according to the ſame gentleman's computation, but ſix years
old ; and in the fifth act, in which Henry is repreſented as having been
killed by him in the Tower, not more than ſixteen and eight months.

  For this anachroniſm the author or authors of the old plays on which
our poet founded theſe two parts of King Henry the Sixth, are anſwerable. MALONE.

                                         What,

What, is your grace ³ dead, my lord of Somerset?

Norf. Such hope have all the line of John of Gaunt!

Rich. Thus do I hope to shake king Henry's head.

War. And so do I.—Victorious prince of York,

Before I see thee seated in that throne

Which now the house of Lancaster usurps,

I vow by heaven, these eyes shall never close.

This is the palace of the fearful king,

' And this the regal seat : possess it, York ;

For this is thine, and not king Henry's heirs'.

York. Assist me then, sweet Warwick, and I will ;

' For hither we have broken in by force.

Norf. We'll all assist you ; he, that flies, shall die.

York. Thanks, gentle Norfolk,—Stay by me, my lords ;—

' And, soldiers, stay, and lodge by me this night.

War. And, when the king comes, offer him no violence,

' Unless he seek to thrust you out by force.   [*They retire.*

✱ *York.* The queen, this day, here holds her parliament ;

✱ But little thinks, we shall be of her counsel :

✱ By words, or blows, here let us win our right.

Rich. Arm'd as we are, let's stay within this house.

War. The bloody parliament shall this be call'd,

Unless Plantagenet, duke of York, be king ;

And bashful Henry depos'd, whose cowardice

Hath made us by-words to our enemies.

' *York.* Then leave me not, my lords ; be resolute ;

I mean to take possession of my right.

War. Neither the king, nor he that loves him best,

' The proudest he that holds up Lancaster,

Dares stir a wing, if Warwick shake his bells ⁴.

'—I'll plant Plantagenet, root him up who dares :—

Resolve thee, Richard ; claim the English crown.

[Warwick *leads* York *to the throne, who seats himself.*

Flourish. Enter *King* HENRY, CLIFFORD, NORTHUM-
BERLAND, WESTMORELAND, EXETER, *and Others,
with red roses in their hats.*

K. Hen. My lords, look where the sturdy rebel sits,

Even in the chair of state! belike, he means,

---

3 What, *is your grace*—] The folio reads—*But* is your grace, &c.
It was evidently a mistake of the transcriber, the word in the old play
being *What*, which suits sufficiently with York's exultation ; whereas
But affords no sense whatsoever. MALONE.

4 — *if Warwick shake his bells.*] The allusion is to falconry. The
hawks had sometimes little bells hung upon them, perhaps to *dare* the
birds ; that is, to fright them from rising. JOHNSON.

(Back'd

(Back'd by the power of Warwick, that falſe peer,)
To aſpire unto the crown, and reign as king.—
Earl of Northumberland, he ſlew thy father ;—
And thine, lord Clifford ; and you both have vow'd re-
   venge
On him, his ſons, his favourites, and his friends.
 ' *North.* If I be not, heavens, be reveng'd on me!
 Clif. The hope thereof makes Clifford mourn in ſteel.
 Weſt. What, ſhall we ſuffer this ? let's pluck him down :
' My heart for anger burns, I cannot brook it.
 K. Hen. Be patient, gentle earl of Weſtmoreland.
 Clif. Patience is for poltroons, ſuch as he :
He durſt not ſit there had your father liv'd.
My gracious lord, here in the parliament
Let us aſſail the family of York.
 North. Well haſt thou ſpoken, couſin ; be it ſo.
 K. Hen. Ah, know you not, the city favours them,
And they have troops of ſoldiers at their beck ?
 Exe. But, when [5] the duke is ſlain, they ll quickly fly.
 K. Hen. Far be the thought of this from Henry's heart.
To make a ſhambles of the parliament-houſe !
Couſin of Exeter, frowns, words, and threats,
Shall be the war that Henry means to uſe.— ·
         [*They advance to the duke.*
Thou factious dukè of York, deſcend my throne,
And kneel for grace and mercy at my feet ;
I am thy ſovereign.
 York. Thou art deceiv'd [6], I am thine.
 Exe. For ſhame, come down ; he made thee duke of.
  York.
 York. 'Twas my inheritance, as the earldom was [7].

---

 5 Exe. *But when,* &c.] This line is by the miſtake of the compoſitor given to Weſtmoreland. The king's anſwer ſhews that it belongs to
Exeter, to whom it is aſſigned in the old play. MALONE.
 6 *Thou art deceiv'd,*] Theſe words, which are not in the folio, were
reſtored from the old play. The defect of the metre in the folio, makes
it probable that they were accidentally omitted The meaſure is, however, ſtill faulty. MALONE.
 7 *'Twas my inheritance, as the* earldom *was.*] York means, I ſuppoſe, that the dukedom of York was his inheritance from his fath r,
as the earldom of March was his inheritance from his mother, Anne
Mortimer, the wife of the earl of Cambridge ; and by naming the earldom, he covertly aſſerts his right to the crown; for his title to the crown
was not as duke of York, but earl of March.
 In the original play the line ſtands thus :
  " 'Twas my inheritance, as *the kingdom is,*"—
and why Shakſpeare altered it, it is not eaſy to ſay ; for the new line
only exhibits the ſame meaning more obſcurely. MALONE.
                Exe.

Exe. Thy father was a traitor to the crown,

War. Exeter, thou art a traitor to the crown,
In following this ufurping Henry.

Clif. Whom fhould he follow, but his natural king?

War. True, Clifford; and that's Richard [8], duke of
York.

‘ *K Hen.* And fhall I ftand, and thou fit in my throne?

‘ *York.* It muft and fhall be fo. Content thyfelf.

War. Be duke of Lancafter, let him be king.

Weft. He is both king and duke of Lancafter;
And that the lord of Weftmoreland fhall maintain.

War. And Warwick fhall difprove it. You forget,
That we are thofe, which chas'd you from the field,
And flew your fathers, and with colours fpread
March'd through the city to the palace-gates.

‘ *North.* Yes, Warwick, I remember it to my grief;
And, by his foul, thou and thy houfe fhall rue it.

‘ *Weft.* Plantagenet, of thee, and thefe thy fons,
Thy kinfmen, and thy friends, I'll have more lives,
Than drops of blood were in my father's veins.

Clif. Urge it no more; left that, inftead of words,.
I fend thee, Warwick, fuch a meffenger,
As fhall revenge his death, before I ftir.

‘ *War.* Poor Clifford! how I fcorn his worthlefs threats!

York. Will you, we fhew our title to the crown?
‘ If not, our fwords fhall plead it in the field.

K. Hen. What title haft thou, traitor, to the crown?
Thy father was, as thou art, duke of York [9];
Thy grandfather, Roger Mortimer, earl of March:
I am the fon of Henry the fifth [1],
Who made the Dauphin and the French to ftoop,
And feiz'd upon their towns and provinces

War. Talk not of France, fith thou haft loft it all.

K Hen. The lord protector loft it, and not I;
When I was crown'd, I was but nine months old.

8 — and *that's Richard,*] The word *and,* which was accidentally omitted in the firft folio, is found in the old play MALONE.

9 *Thy father was, as thou art, duke of York;*] This is a miftake, into which Shakfpeare was led by the author of the old play The father of Richard duke of York was earl of Cambridge, and was never duke of York, being beheaded in the life time of his elder brother Edward duke of York, who fell in the battle of Agincourt The folio, by an evident error of the prefs, reads—*My* father. The true reading was furnifhed by the old play. MALONE.

¹ *I am the fon of Henry the fifth,*] The military reputation of Henry the Fifth is the fole fupport of his fon. The name of Henry the Fifth difperfed the followers of Cade. JOHNSON.

Rich.

Rich. You are old enough now, and yet, methinks, you lose:—

Father, tear the crown from the usurper's head.

Edw. Sweet father, do so; set it on your head.

Mont. Good brother, [*to* York.] as thou lov'st and honour'st arms,

Let's fight it out, and not stand cavilling thus.

Rich. Sound drums and trumpets, and the king will fly.

York Sons, peace!

K. Hen. Peace thou! and give king Henry leave to speak.

War. Plantagenet shall speak first:—hear him, lords;

And be you silent and attentive too,

For he, that interrupts him, shall not live.

' *K. Hen.* Think'st thou, that I will leave my kingly throne [2],

Wherein my grandsire, and my father, sat?

No: first shall war unpeople this my realm;

' Ay, and their colours—often borne in France;

And now in England, to our heart's great sorrow,—

Shall be my winding-sheet.—Why faint you, lords?

' My title's good, and better far than his.

War. Prove it, Henry, and thou shalt be king [3].

K. Hen. Henry the fourth by conquest got the crown,

York. 'Twas by rebellion against his king

K. Hen. I know not what to say; my title's weak.

Tell me, may not a king adopt an heir?

Yor. What then?

K. Hen. An if he may, then am I lawful king:

' For Richard, in the view of many lords,

Resign'd the crown to Henry the fourth;

Whose heir my father was, and I am his.

York. He rose against him, being his sovereign,

And made him to resign his crown perforce

War. Suppose, my lords, he did it unconstrain'd,

---

[2] *Think'st thou,* &c.] The old play here exhibits four lines that are not in the folio. They could not have proceeded from the *imagination* of the transcriber, and therefore they must be added to the many other circumstances that have been already urged, to shew that these plays were not *originally* the production of Shakspeare:

" Ah Plantagenet, why seek'st thou to depose me?

" Are we not both Plantagenets by birth,

" And from two brothers lineally descent?

" Suppose by right and equity thou be king,

" Think'st thou," &c. MALONE.

[3] *Prove it,* Henry, &c.] *Henry* is frequently used by Shakspeare and his contemporaries as a word of three syllables. MALONE.

Think

Think you, 'twère prejudicial to his crown [4]?

Exe. No; for he could not fo refign his crown,
But that the next heir fhould fucceed and reign.

K. Hen. Art thou againſt us, duke of Exeter?

Exe His is the right, and therefore pardon me.

* *York.* Why whiſper you, my lords, and anſwer not?

Exe. My conſcience tells me, he is lawful king.

K. Hen. All will revolt from me, and turn to him.

North. Plantagenet, for all the claim thou lay ſt,
Think not, that Henry fhall be fo depos'd.

' *War.* Depos'd he fhall be, in deſpight of all.

North. Thou art deceiv'd: 'tis not thy ſouthern power,
' Of Eſſex, Norfolk, Suffolk, nor of Kent,—
Which makes thee thus preſumptuous and proud,—
Can fet the duke up, in deſpight of me.

Clif. King Henry, be thy title right or wrong,
Lord Clifford vows to fight in thy defence:
May that ground gape, and ſwallow me alive [5],
' Where I fhall kneel to him that flew my father!

· ' *K. Hen.* O Clifford, how thy words revive my heart!

York. Henry of Lancaſter, refign thy crown:—
What mutter you, or what conſpire you, lords?

War. Do right unto this princely duke of York;
Or I will fill the houſe with armed men,
And, o'er the chair of ſtate, where now he fits,
Write up his title with uſurping blood.

[*He ſtamps, and the ſoldiers ſhew themſelves.*

' *King.* My lord of Warwick, hear but one word [6];—
' Let me, for this my life-time, reign as king.

York. Confirm the crown to me, and to mine heirs,
And thou fhalt reign in quiet while thou liv'ſt.

K. Hen. I am content: Richard Plantagenet,
Enjoy the kingdom after my deceaſe [7].

---

4 — *prejudicial to his crown?*] Detrimental to the general rights of
hereditary royalty. JOHNSON.

5 *May that* ground gape, *and ſwallow me alive,*] So, in Phaer's
Tranſlation of the fourth Æneid:
   " But rather would I wiſh the ground to gape for me below."
                                                    STEEVENS.

6 —hear *but one word;*] *Hear* is in this line, as in ſome other
places, uſed as a diſſyllable. The editor of the third folio, and all the
ſubſequent editors, read—hear *me* but one word. MALONE.

7 *I am* content: *&c.*] Inſtead of this ſpeech the old play has the fol-
lowing lines:
   " *King.* Convey the ſoldiers hence, and then I will.
   " *War.* Captaine, conduct them into Tuthilfields." MALONE.
                                                    Clif.

Clif. What wrong is this unto the prince your son ?

War. What good is this to England, and himself ?

West. Base, fearful, and despairing Henry !

‘ *Clif.* How hast thou injur'd both thyself and us ?

West. I cannot stay to hear these articles.

North. Nor I.

Clif. Come, cousin, let us tell the queen these news.

* *West.* Farewell, faint-hearted and degenerate king,

* In whose cold blood no spark of honour bides.

North. Be thou a prey unto the house of York,

‘ And die in bands for this unmanly deed !

Clif. In dreadful war may'st thou be overcome !

Or live in peace, abandon'd, and despis'd !

       [*Exeunt* NORTHUMBERLAND, CLIFFORD, *and*
         WESTMORELAND.

* *War.* Turn this way, Henry, and regard them not.

Exe. They seek revenge [8], and therefore will not yield.

K. Hen. Ah, Exeter !

War. Why should you sigh, my lord ?

K. Hen. Not for myself, lord Warwick, but my son,

Whom I unnaturally shall disinherit.

But, be it as it may :—I here entail

‘ The crown to thee, and to thine heirs for ever ;

Conditionally, that here thou take an oath

To cease this civil war, and, whilst I live,

To honour me as thy king and sovereign ;

* And neither [9] by treason, nor hostility,

* To seek to put me down, and reign thyself.

York. This oath I willingly take, and will perform.

               [*coming from the throne.*

War. Long live king Henry !—Plantagenet, embrace him.

‘ *K. Hen.* And long live thou, and these thy forward
    sons !

York. Now York and Lancaster are reconcil'd.

Exe. Accurs'd be he, that seeks to make them foes !

          [*Senet. The lords come forward.*

---

8 *They seek revenge,*] They go away, not because they doubt the justice of this determination, but because they have been conquered, and seek to be revenged. They are not influenced by principle, but passion. JOHNSON

9 *And* neither—] *Neither, either, whether, brother, rather,* and many similar words, were used by Shakspeare as monosyllables. So, in *A Midsummer's Night's Dream* :

    " *Either* death or you I'll find immediately."

The editor of the second folio, who appears to have been entirely ignorant of our author's metre and phraseology, not knowing this, omitted the word *And.* MALONE.

                   ‘ *York.*

'*York.* Farewel, my gracious lord ; I'll to my caſtle [1].

War And I'll keep London with my ſoldiers.

Norf. And I to Norfolk, with my followers.

Mont. And I unto the ſea, from whence I came.

[*Exeunt* YORK, *and his* ſons, WARWICK, NOR-
FOLK, MONTAGUE, *Soldiers, and Attendants.*

K. Hen. And I, with grief and ſorrow, to the court.

Enter Queen MARGARET, *and the prince of* Wales.

Exe. Here comes the queen, whoſe looks bewray her anger:

I'll ſteal away.

K. Hen. Exeter, ſo will I.   [*going.*

'*Q. Mar.* Nay, go not from me; I will follow thee.

K. Hen. Be patient, gentle queen, and I will ſtay.

'*Q. Mar.* Who can be patient in ſuch extremes ?

* Ah, wretched man ! 'would I had died a maid,

* And never ſeen thee, never borne thee ſon,

* Seeing thou haſt prov'd ſo unnatural a father ;

* Hath he deſerv'd to loſe his birth right thus ?

* Hadſt thou but lov'd him half ſo well as I ;

* Or felt that pain which I did for him once ;

* Or nouriſh'd him, as I did with my blood ;

* Thou wouldſt have left thy deareſt heart-blood there,

* Rather than have made [2] that ſavage duke thine heir,

* And diſinherited thine only ſon.

* *Prince.* Father, you cannot diſinherit me :

* If you be king, why ſhould not I ſucceed ?

* *K. Hen.* Pardon me, Margaret ;—pardon me, ſweet
ſon ;—

* The earl of Warwick, and the duke, enforc'd me.

* *Q. Mar.* Enforc'd thee ! art thou king, and wilt be·
forc'd ?

I ſhame to hear thee ſpeak.   Ah, timorous wretch !

Thou haſt undone thyſelf, thy ſon, and me ;

'·And given unto the houſe of York ſuch head,

* As thou ſhalt reign but by their ſufferance.

* To entail him and his heirs unto the crown,

* What is it, but to make thy ſepulchre [3],

[1] — *I'll to my caſtle.*] Sandal Caſtle near Wakefield, in Yorkſhire.
                                                        MALONE.

[2] Rather *than have made*—] *Rather* is here uſed as a monoſyllable.
See p. 236, n. 9 MALONE.

[3] *What is it, but to make thy ſepulchre,*] The queen's reproach is
founded on a poſition long received among politicians, that the loſs of a
king's power is ſoon followed by loſs of life. JOHNSON.

* And

* And creep into it far before thy time ?
* Warwick is Chancellor, and the lord of Calais ;
Stern Faulconbridge commands the narrow seas ;
The duke is made protector of the realm ;
' And yet shalt thou be safe ? * such safety finds
* The trembling lamb, environed with wolves.
' Had I been there, which am a silly woman,
' The soldiers should have toss'd me on their pikes,
' Before I would have granted to that act.
* But thou preferr'st thy life before thine honour :
' And, seeing thou dost, I here divorce myself,
' Both from thy table, Henry, and thy bed,
' Until that act of parliament be repeal'd,
' Whereby my son is disinherited +.
The northern lords, that have forsworn thy colours,
Will follow mine, if once they see them spread :
' And spread they shall be ; to thy foul disgrace,
' And utter ruin of the house of York.
' Thus do I leave thee :—Come, son, let's away ;
' Our army's ready ; come, we'll after them.

    K. Hen. Stay, gentle Margaret, and hear me speak.
    Q. Mar. Thou hast spoke too much already ; get thee
        gone.
    K. Hen. Gentle son Edward, thou wilt stay with me ?
    Q. Mar. Ay, to be murder'd by his enemies.
    Prince. When I return with victory from the field [5],
I'll see your grace : till then, I'll follow her.
    Q. Mar. Come, son, away ; we may not linger thus.
            [*Exeunt Queen* MARGARET, *and the* Prince.
' *K. Hen* Poor queen ! how love to me, and to her son,
' Hath made her break out into terms of rage !
' Reveng'd may she be on that hateful duke ;
* Whose haughty spirit, winged with desire,
* Will cost my crown [6], and, like an empty eagle,
* Tire on the flesh of me [7], and of my son !

---

4 *Whereby my son is disinherited.*] The corresponding line in the old
play is this. The variation is remarkable.
    " Wherein th u y eldest to the house o' York." MALONE.
    5 — from *the field.*] Folio—*to* the field. The true reading is found
in the old play. MALONE
    6 *Will cost my crown*] i. e. will cost *me* my crown ; will induce on
me the expence or loss of my crown. MALONE.
    7 *Tire on th flesh of me,*] To *tire* is to fasten, to fix the talons, from
the French *tirer.* JOHNSON.
    To *tire* is to *peck.* So, in Decker's *Match me in London,* 1631 :
        " —— the vulture *tires*
        " Upon the eagle's heart." STEEVENS.
                              * The

*   The lofs of thofe three lords 8 torments my heart :
*   I'll write unto them, and entreat them fair ;—
*   Come, coufin, you fhall be the meffenger 9.
    *   *Exe.* And I, I hope, fhall reconcile them all.

[*Exeunt.*

SCENE II.

A Room in Sandal *Caftle, near* Wakefield, *in* Yorkfhire.

Enter EDWARD, RICHARD, *and* MONTAGUE.

' *Rich.* Brother, though I be youngeft, give me leave.
Edw. No, I can better play the orator.
Mont. But I have reafons ftrong and forcible.

Enter YORK.

' *York.* Why, how now, fons, and brother ¹, at a ftrife?
' What is your quarrel? how began it fiift?
' *Edw.* No quarrel, but a flight contention.

8 — *thofe three lords*—] That is, of Northumberland, Weftmorland, and Clifford who had left him in difguft. JOHNS N.

9 — *you fhall be the meffenger.*] Inftead of the fix laft lines of this fpeech, the fiift copy prefents thefe:

' Come, coufin of Exeter, ftay thou here,
' For Clifford and thofe northern lords be gone,
' I fear towards Wakefield, to difturb the duke.' MALONE.

¹ —*fons and brother,*]'I believe we fhould read—*coufin* inftead of *broth r,* unlefs *brother* be ufed by Shakfpeare as a term expreffive of endearment, or becaufe they embarked like brothers, in one caufe.— Montague was only coufin to York, and in the quarto he is fo called.— Shakfpeare ufes the expreffion, *brother of the war,* in *King Lear.*

STEEVENS.

It fhould be, fons and *brothers*; my *fons*, and *brothers* to each other.

JOHNSON.

The third folio reads as Dr. Johnfon advifes But as York again in this fcene addreffes Montague by the title of *brother,* and Montague ufes the fame to York, Dr. J hnfon's conjecture cannot be right Shakfpeare certainly fuppofed them to be brothers-in law. MALONE.

Brother is ight. In the two fucceeding page York calls Montague *brother* This may be in refpect to their being *brothers of the war,* as Mr. Steevens obferves, or of the fame council as in *King Henry VIII.* who fays to Cranmer, " You are a *brother* of us." Montague was brother to Warwick; Warwick's daughter was married to a fon of York : therefore York and Montague were brothers. But as this alliance did not take place during the life of York, I embrace Mr. Steevens's interpretation rather than fuppofe that Shakfpeare made a miftake about the time of the marriage. TOLLET.

York.

York. About what ?

' *Rich.* About that which concerns your grace, and us ;
' The crown of England, father, which is yours.

' *York.* Mine, boy ? not till king Henry be dead.

* *Rich.* Your right depends not on his life, or death.

* *Edw.* Now you are heir, therefore enjoy it now :
* By giving the house of Lancaster leave to breathe,
* It will outrun you, father, in the end.

' *York.* I took an oath, that he should quietly reign.

' *Edw.* But, for a kingdom, any oath may be broken :
' I'd break a thousand oaths, to reign one year.

' *Rich.* No ; God forbid[2], your grace should be forsworn.

' *York.* I shall be, if I claim by open war.

' *Rich.* I'll prove the contrary, if you'll hear me speak.

' *York.* Thou canst not, son ; it is impossible.

' *Rich.* An oath is of no moment[3], being not took
' Before a true and lawful magistrate,
' That hath authority over him that swears :
' Henry had none, but did usurp the place ;
' Then, seeing 'twas he that made you to depose,
' Your oath, my lord, is vain and frivolous.
' Therefore, to arms   * And, father, do but think,
* How sweet a thing it is to wear a crown ;
* Within whose circuit is Elysium,
* And all that poets feign of bliss and joy.
* Why do we linger thus ? I cannot rest,
* Until the white rose, that I wear, be dy'd
* Even in the lukewarm blood of Henry's heart.

2 *Rich. No ; God forbid*, &c.] Instead of this and the three following speeches, the old play has these lines:

 Rich. An if it please your grace to give me leave,
  I'll shew your grace the way to save your oath,
  And dispossess king Henry from the crown.

 York. I pr'ythee, Dick, let me hear thy devise. MALONE.

3 *An oath is of no moment,*] The obligation of an oath is here eluded
by very despicable sophistry. A lawful magistrate alone has the power
to exact an oath, but the oath derives no part of its force from the magistrate. The plea against the obligation of an oath obliging to maintain an usurper, taken from the unlawfulness of the oath itself in the
foregoing play, was rational and just JOHNSON

This speech is formed on the following one in the old play :

 Rich. Then thus, my lord.   An oath is of no moment,
  Being not sworn before a lawful magistrate ;
  Henry is none, but doth usurp your right ;
  And yet your grace stands bound to him by oath :
  Then, noble father,
  Resolve yourself, and once more claim the crown. MALONE.

       ' *York.*

' *York.* Richard, enough; I will be king, or die.—
' Brother, thou shalt to London presently [4],
' And whet on Warwick to this enterprize.—
' Thou, Richard, shalt to the duke of Norfolk,
' And tell him privily of our intent.—
' You, Edward, shall unto my lord Cobham,
With whom the Kentishmen will willingly rise :
' In them I trust; for they are soldiers,
' Witty, courteous [5], liberal, full of spirit.—
' While you are thus employ'd, what resteth more,
' But that I seek occasion how to rise ;
' And yet the king not privy to my drift,
' Nor any of the house of Lancaster ?

Enter a Messenger [6].

' But, stay; What news? Why com'st thou in such post ?
' *Mes.* The queen, with all the northern earls and lords [7],
' Intend here to besiege you in your castle :

' She

---

[4] *Brother, thou shalt to London presently,*] Thus the original play :
Edward, thou shalt to Edmond Brooke, lord Cobham,
With whom the Kentishmen will willingly rise.
Thou, cousin Montague, shalt to Norfolk straight,
And bid the duke to muster up his soldiers,
And come to me to Wakefield presently.
And Richard, thou to London straight shalt post,
And bid Richard Nevill Earl of Warwick
To leave the city, and with his men of war
To meet me at St Alban's ten days hence.
My self here in Sandall castle will provide
Both men and money, to further our attempts. MALONE.

[5] *Witty, courteous,*] *Witty* anciently signified, of sound judgment.—
The poet calls Buckingham " the deep-revolving, *witty* Buckingham."
STEEVENS.

[6] *Enter a* Messenger.] In the folio, we have here by inadvertence,
" Enter *Gabriel*." Gabriel was the actor who played this inconsidera-
ble part. He is mentioned by Heywood in his *Apology for actors*, 1612.
The correction has been made from the old play. MALONE.

[7] *The queen, with all,* &c.] I know not whether the author intended any moral instruction, but he that reads this has a striking admoni-
tion against the precipitancy by which men often use unlawful means to
do that which a little delay would put honestly in their power. Had
York staid but a few moments, he had saved his cause from the stain of
perjury. JOHNSON.

In October 1460, when it was established in parliament that the duke
of York should succeed to the throne after Henry's death, the duke and
his two sons, the earl of March and the earl of Rutland, took an oath to
do no act whatsoever that might " sound to the abridgment of the natural life of King Henry the Sixth, or diminishing of his reign or dignity
royal." Having persuaded the king to send for the queen and the prince
of

‘ She is hard by with twenty thousand men ;
‘ And therefore fortify your hold, my lord.
  * *York.* Ay, with my sword.   What ! think’st thou, that
            we fear them ?—
‘ Edward and Richard, you shall stay with me ;—
‘ My brother Montague shall post to London :
* Let noble Warwick, Cobham, and the rest,
* Whom we have left protectors of the king,
* With powerful policy strengthen themselves,
* And trust not simple Henry, nor his oaths.
  * *Mont.* Brother, I go ; I’ll win them, fear it not :
* And thus most humbly I do take my leave.   [*Exit.*

Enter Sir John *and Sir* Hugh MORTIMER.

  York. Sir John, and Sir Hugh Mortimer, mine uncles !
‘ You are come to Sandal in a happy hour ;
‘ The army of the queen mean to besiege us.
  Sir John. She shall not need, we’ll meet her in the field.
‘ *York.* What, with five thousand men ?
  Rich. Ay, with five hundred, father, for a need.
A woman’s general ; What should we fear ?

                                      [*A march afar off.*
‘ *Edw.* I hear their drums ; let’s set our men in order ;—
‘ And issue forth, and bid them battle straight.
‘ *York.* Five men to twenty [9] !—though the odds be great,
‘ I doubt not, uncle, of our victory.
‘ Many a battle have I won in France,
‘ When as the enemy hath been ten to one ;

of Wales, (who were then in York) and finding that she would not obey
his requisition, he on the second of December set out for his castle in
Yorkshire, with such military power as he had, a messenger having been
previously dispatched to the earl of March, to desire him to follow his
father with all the forces he could procure. The duke arrived at Sandal castle on the 24th of December, and in a short time his army amounted to five thousand men. An anonymous remarker, however, very
confidently asserts, that “ this scene, so far as respects York’s *oath* and
his resolution to break it, proceeds entirely from the author’s imagination.” His oath is on record ; and what his *resolution* was when he
marched from London at the head of a large body of men, and sent the
message above stated to his son, it is not very difficult to conjecture.
                                                    MALONE.

9 *Five men to twenty !* &c.] Thus in the old play:
      York. Indeed many brave battles have I won
    In Normandy, whereas the enemy
    Hath been ten to one, and why should I now
    Doubt of the like success. I am resolv’d.
    Come, let us go.
      Edw. Let us march away. I hear their drums.   MALONE.
                                                    ‘ Why

'Why fhould I not now have the like fuccefs?

[*Alarum. Exeunt.*

SCENE III.

Plains near Sandal Caftle.

Alarums. Excurfions. Enter RUTLAND, *and his* Tutor.

' *Rut.* Ah, whither ' fhall I fly, to 'fcape their hands!
Ah, tutor! look, where bloody Clifford comes!

Enter CLIFFORD, *and Soldiers.*

Clif. Chaplain, away! thy priefthood faves thy life.
As for the brat of this accurfed duke,—
Whofe father [2] flew my father,—he fhall die.
 Tut. And I, my lord, will bear him company.
 Clif. Soldiers, away with him.
' *Tut.* Ah, Clifford! murder not this innocent child,
' Left thou be hated both of God and man.

[*Exit, forced off by Soldiers.*

 Clif. How now! is he dead already? Or, is it fear,
That makes him clofe his eyes [3]?—I'll open them.
' *Rut.* So looks the pent-up lion o'er the wretch [4]

' [1] *Ah, whither,* &c.] This fcene in the old play opens with thefe lines:

 Tutor Oh, fly my lord, let's leave the caftle,
 And fly to Wakefield ftraight. MALONE.

[2] *Whofe father—*] i. e. the father of which brat, namely the duke of York. MALONE.

[3] —— *is he dead already? Or is it fear,
That makes him clofe his eyes?*] This circumftance is taken from Hall: " Whilft this battail was in fighting, a prieſte called Sir Robert Aſpall, chappelaine and fchole-mafter to the young erle of Rutlande, ii fonne to the above named duke of Yorke, fcarce of the age of xii yeres, a faire gentleman and a maydenlike perfon, perceyving that flight was more fafe gard than tarrying, bothe for hym and his mafter, fecretly conveyd therfe out of the felde, by the lord Cliffordes bande, toward the towne; but or he could entre into a boufe, he was by the fayd Lord Clifford efpied, folowed, and taken, and by refon of his apparell, de-maunded what he was. The yong gentleman difmayed, had not a worde to fpeake, but kneled on his knees, imploring mercy, and de-firyng grace, both with holding up his handes, and making dolorous countenance, *for his fpeache was gone with feare.*" MALONE.

[4] *So looks the pent up lion—*] That is, The lion that hath been long confined without food, and is let out to devour a man condemned

JOHNSON.

M 2

' That

‘ That trembles under his devouring paws :
And so he walks, insulting o’er his prey ;
‘ And so he comes, to rend his limbs asunder.—
‘ Ah, gentle Clifford, kill me with thy sword,
And not with such a cruel threat’ning look.
Sweet Clifford, hear me speak before I die ;—
I am too mean a subject for thy wrath,
Be thou reveng’d on men, and let me live.

   Clif. in vain thou speak’st, poor boy ; my father’s blood
Hath stopp’d the passage where thy words should enter.

   Rut. Then let my father’s blood open it again ;
He is a man, and, Clifford, cope with him.

   Clif. Had I thy brethren here, their lives, and thine,
Were not revenge sufficient for me :
No, if I digg’d up thy forefathers’ graves,
And hung their rotten coffins up in chains,
It could not slake mine ire, nor ease my heart.
The sight of any of the house of York
Is as a fury to torment my soul ;
‘ And till I root out their accursed line,
‘ And leave not one alive, I live in hell.
Therefore—   [*Lifting up his hand.*

   Rut. O, let me pray before I take my death :
To thee I pray ; Sweet Clifford, pity me !
   Clif. Such pity as my rapier’s point affords.
   ‘ *Rut.* I never did thee harm ; Why wilt thou slay me ?
   Clif. Thy father hath.
   Rut. But ’twas ere I was born [5].
Thou hast one son, for his sake pity me ;
Lest, in revenge thereof,—sith God is just,—
He be as miserably slain as I.
Ah, let me live in prison all my days ;
And when I give occasion of offence,
Then let me die, for now thou hast no cause.
   Clif. No cause ?
Thy father slew my father ; therefore die.   [*Clif. stabs him.*
   Rut. Dii faciant, laudis summa fit ista tuæ [6] !   [*Dies.*

---

[5] *But ’twas ere I was born*] The author of the original play appears
to have been as incorrect in his chronology as Shakspeare. Rutland was
born, I believe, in 1443 ; according to Hall in 1448 ; and Clifford’s father was killed at the battle of St. Alban’s, in 1455. Consequently
Rutland was then at least seven years old ; more probably twelve —
The same observation has been made by an anonymous writer. MALONE.

[6] This line is in Ovid’s *Epistle from Phillis to Demophoon.* I find the
same quotation in *Have with you to Saffron-Walden, or Gabriel Harvey’s
hunt is up,* 1596. STEEVENS.

                                                     Clif.

Clif. Plantagenet! I come, Plantagenet!
And this thy fon's blood, cleaving to my blade,
Shall ruſt upon my weapon, till thy blood,
Congeal'd with this, do make me wipe off both. [*Exit.*

SCENE IV.

The Same.

Alarum. Enter YORK.

'   *York.* The army of the queen hath got the field:
' My uncles both are ſlain in reſcuing me [1];
' And all my followers to the eager foe
' Turn back, and fly, like ſhips before the wind,
' Or lambs purſu'd by hunger-ſtarved wolves.
' My fons—God knows, what hath bechanced them:
But this I know,—they have demean'd themſelves
Like men born to renown, by life, or death.
' Three times did Richard make a lane to me;
And thrice cry'd,—*Courage, father! fight it out!*
' And full as oft came Edward to my ſide,
With purple faulchion, painted to the hilt
' In blood of thoſe that had encounter'd him:
' And when the hardieſt warriors did retire,
' Richard cry'd,—*Charge! and give no foot of ground!*
' And cry'd—*A crown, or elſe a glorious tomb!*
' *A ſcepter, or an earthly ſepulchre!*
With this, we charg'd again: but, out, alas!
' We bodg'd again [2]; as I have ſeen a ſwan
' With bootleſs labour ſwim againſt the tide,

---

[1] *My uncles both are ſlain in reſcuing me;*] Theſe were two baſtard uncles by the mother's ſide, ſir John and ſir Hugh Mortimer. See Grafton's *Chronicle,* p. 649. PERCY.

[2] *We bodg'd again;*] I find *bodgery* uſed by Naſhe in his *Apologie of Pierce Pennileſs,* 1593, for *botckery.* " Do you know your own miſbegotten *bodgery?*" To *bodge* might therefore mean, (as to *botch* does now) to do a thing imperfectly and aukwardly; and thence to *fail* or *miſcarry* in an attempt. Cole in his Latin Dictionary, 1679, renders —" to botch or bungle, *opus cirrumpere, diſperdere.*"

I ſuſpect, however, with Dr. Johnſon, that we ſhould read—We *budg'd* again. " To *budge*" Cole renders, *pedem riſerre,* to retreat: the preciſe ſenſe required here. So Coriolanus, ſpeaking of his army who had *fled* from their adverſaries:

" The mouſe ne'er ſhunn'd the cat) as they did *budge* " From raſcals worſe than they." MALONE.

' And

‘ And fpend her ftrength with over-matching waves.

[*A fhort alarum within.*

‘ Ah, hark ! the fatal followers do purfue ;

‘ And I am faint, and cannot fly their fury :

‘ And, were I ftrong, I would not fhun their fury :

‘ The fands are number’d, that make up my life ;

‘ Here muft I ftay, and here my life muft end.

Enter Queen MARGARET, CLIFFORD, NORTHUMBERLAND, *and Soldiers.*

‘ Come, bloody Clifford,—rough Northumberland,—

‘ I dare your quenchlefs fury to more rage ;

‘ I am your butt, and I abide your fhot.

North. Yield to our mercy, proud Plantagenet.

Clif. Ay, to fuch mercy, as his ruthlefs arm,

With downright payment, fhew’d unto my father.

Now Phaeton hath tumbled from his car,

And made an evening at the noon-tide prick [3].

York. My afhes, as the phœnix, may bring forth

‘ A bird that will revenge upon you all :

‘ And, in that hope, I throw mine eyes to heaven,

Scorning whate’er you can afflict me with.

‘ Why come you not ? what ! multitudes, and fear ?

Clif. So cowards fight, when they can fly no further ;

‘ So doves do peck the faulcon’s piercing talons ;

So defperate thieves, all hopelefs of their lives,

Breathe out invectives ’gainft the officers.

York O, Clifford, but bethink thee once again,

‘ And in thy thought o’er-run my former time :

* And, if thou canft for blufhing, view this face ;

And bite thy tongue, that flanders him with cowardice,

‘ Whofe frown hath made thee faint and fly ere this.

Clif. I will not handy with thee word for word ;

But buckle with thee blows, twice two for one.   [*Draws.*

Q. Mar. Hold, valiant Clifford ! for a thoufand caufes,

I would prolong a while the traitor’s life :—

Wrath makes him deaf : fpeak thou, Northumberland.

North. Hold, Clifford ; do not honour him fo much,

To prick thy finger, though to wound his heart :

What valour were it, when a cur doth grin,

For one to thruft his hand between his teeth,

When he might fpurn him with his foot away ?

---

3 — *noon-tide prick.*] Or, noon-tide point on the dial. JOHNSON.

It

It is war's prize [4] to take all vantages ;
' And ten to one is no impeach of valour.

[*They lay hands on* York, *who ſtruggles.*

Clif. Ay, ay, ſo ſtrives the woodcock with the gin.

North. So doth the coney ſtruggle in the net.

[*York is taken priſoner.*

York. So triumph thieves upon their conquer'd booty ;
So true men yield [5], with robbers ſo o'er-match'd.

North. What would your grace have done unto him now ?

Q. Mar. Brave warriors, Clifford, and Northumberland,
Come make him ſtand upon this mole-hill here ;
' That raught [6] at mountains with out-ſtretched arms,
Yet parted but the ſhadow with his hand.——
* What ! was it you, that would be England's king ?
Was't you, that revell'd in our parliament,
And made a preachment of your high deſcent ?
Where are your meſs of ſons, to back you now ?
The wanton Edward, and the luſty George ?
' And where's that valiant crook-back prodigy,
Dicky your boy, that, with his grumbling voice,
Was wont to cheer his dad in mutinies ?
Or, with the reſt, where is your darling Rutland ?
Look, York ; I ſtain'd this napkin [7] with the blood
That valiant Clifford, with his rapier's point,
Made iſſue from the boſom of the boy :
And, if thine eyes can water for his death,
I give thee this to dry thy cheeks withal.
' Alas, poor York ! but that I hate thee deadly,
I ſhould lament thy miſerable ſtate.
I pr'ythee grieve, to make me merry, York ;
Stamp, rave, and fret, that I may ſing and dance [8].
What, hath thy fiery heart ſo parch'd thine entrails,
That not a tear can fall for Rutland's death ?
* Why art thou patient, man ? thou ſhouldſt be mad ;

4 *It is war's prize*—] All 'vantages are in war lawful prize ; that is,
may be lawfully taken and uſed. JOHNSON.
—— dolu·, an virtus, quis in hoſte requirat ? VIRG. MALONE.
5 *So true men yield,*] A true man has been already explained to be an
honeſt man; as oppoſed to a thief. MALONE.
6 *That raught*—] i. e. That reach'd. The ancient preterite and
participle paſſive of *reach.* So, Shakſpeare in another place :
"The hand of death has *raught* him." STEEVENS.
7 — *this napkin*—] A napkin is a handkerchief. JOHNSON.
8 *Stamp, rave, and fret,* &c.] I have placed this line as it ſtands in
the old play. In the folio it is introduced, I believe, by the careleſſneſs
of the tranſcriber, ſome lines lower, after the words—" do mock thee
thus ;" where it appears to me out of its place. MALONE.

* And

* And I, to make thee mad, do mock thee thus.
Thou would'ft be fee'd, I fee, to make me fport ;
York cannot fpeak, unlefs he wear a crown.—
A crown for York ;—and, lords, bow low to him —
Hold you his hands, whilft I do fet it on.—

[Putting a paper crown on his head .*

Ay, marry, fir, now looks he like a king !
Ay, this is he that took king Henry's chair ;
And this is he was his adopted heir.—
But how is it, that great Plantagenet
Is crown'd fo foon, and broke his folemn oath ?
As I bethink me, you fhould not be king,
Till our king Henry had fhook hands with death '.
And will you pale ² your head in Henry's glory,
And rob his temples of the diadem,
Now in his life, againft your holy oath ?
O, 'tis a fault too too unpardonable !—
Off with the crown ; and, with the crown, his head ;
And, whilft we breathe, take time to do him dead *.

Clif. That is my office, for my father's fake.

Q. Mar. Nay, ftay ; let's hear the orifons he makes.

---

9 *Putting a paper crown on his head.*] Shakfpeare has on this occafion deviated from hiftory, if fuch of our *Englifh* chronicles as I have been able to procure, may be believed. According to them the paper crown was not placed on the duke of York's head till after it had been cut off. Rutland likewife was not killed by Clifford till after his father's death.

STEEVENS.

According to Hall the paper crown was not placed on York's head till after he was dead ; but Holinfhed after giving Hall's narration of this bufinefs almoft *verbatim*, adds —" Some write, that the duke was taken alive, and in derifion caufed to ftand upon a *mole hill*, on whofe heade they put a garlande inftead of a crowne, which they had fafhioned and made of fegges or bulrufhes, and having fo crowned him with that garlande, they kneeled downe afore him, as the Jewes did to Chrifte in fcorne, faying to him, hayle king without rule, hayle king without heritage, hayle duke and prince without people or poffeffions And at length having thus fcorned him with thefe and dyverfe other the like defpitefull woordes, they ftroke off his heade, which (as yee have heard) they prefented to the queen."
Both the chroniclers fay, that the earl of Rutland was killed by Clifford *during* the battle of Wakefield ; but it may be prefumed that his father had firft fallen. The earl's tutor probably attempted to fave him as foon as the rout began. MALONE.

¹ *Till our king Henry had fhook hands with death.*] On York's return from Ireland, at a meeting of parliament it was fettled, that Henry fhould enjoy the throne during his life, and that York fhould fucceed him. See Hall, Henry VI. fol. 98. MALONE.

² *And will you pale*—] i. e. impale, encircle with a crown.

MALONE.

* — *to do him dead.*] To kill him. MALONE.

York.

York. She-wolf of France, but worfe than wolves of
 France,'
' Whofe tongue more poifons than the adder's tooth !
How ill-befeeming is it in thy fex,
To triumph, like an Amazonian trull,
' Upon their woes, whom fortune captivates ?
But that thy face is, vizor-like, unchanging,
Made impudent with ufe of evil deeds,
I would affay, proud queen, to make thee blufh :
To tell thee whence thou cam'ft, of whom deriv'd,
Were fhame enough to fhame thee, wert thou not fhame-
 lefs.
Thy father bears the type of king of Naples,
Of both the Sicils, and Jerufalem ;
Yet not fo wealthy as an Englifh yeoman.
Hath that poor monarch taught thee to infult ?
It needs not, nor it boots thee not, proud queen ;
Unlefs the adage muft be verify'd,—
That beggars, mounted, run their horfe to death.
'Tis beauty, that doth oft make women proud :
But, God he knows, thy fhare thereof is fmall :
'Tis virtue, that doth make them moft admir'd ;
The contrary doth make thee wonder'd at :
'Tis government, that makes them feem divine [3] ;
The want thereof makes thee abominable :
Thou art as oppofite to every good,
As the Antipodes are unto us,
Or as the fouth to the feptentrion.
O, tyger's heart, wrapp'd in a woman's hide [*] !
How could'ft thou drain the life-blood of the child,
To bid the father wipe his eyes withal,
And yet be feen to bear a woman's face ?
Women are foft, mild, pitiful, and flexible ;
' Thou ftern, obdurate, flinty, rough, remorfelefs.
' Bid'ft thou me rage ? why, now thou haft thy wifh :
' Would'ft have me weep ? why, now thou haft thy will :
' For raging wind blows up inceffant fhowers,
And, when the rage allays, the rain begins [5].

          Thefe

[3] *'Tis government that makes them feem divine ;*] *Government*, in the
language of that time, fignified evenness of temper, and decency of
manners. JOHNSON.

[*] *O, tyger's heart, wrapp'd in a woman's hide !*] We find almoft the
fame line in *Acolaftus his Afterwitte*, 1600:

  " *O woolvifh heart, wrapp'd in a woman's hide !*" MALONE.
[5] *Would'ft have me* weep ? *why, now thou haft thy will :*
 For raging wind blows up inceffant fhowers,

These tears are my sweet Rutland's obsequies;
' And every drop cries vengeance for his death,—
' 'Gainst thee, fell Clifford,—and thee, false French-woman.

North. Beshrew me, but his passions move me so,
That hardly can I check my eyes from tears.

York. That face of his the hungry cannibals
Would not have touch'd, would not have stain'd with blood:
But you are more inhuman, more inexorable,—
O, ten times more,—than tygers of Hyrcania.
See ruthless queen, a hapless father's tears:
This cloth thou dipp'dst in blood of my sweet boy,
And I with tears do wash the blood away.
Keep thou the napkin, and go boast of this:
                                   [*He gives back the handkerchief.*
And, if thou tell'st the heavy story right,
Upon my soul, the hearers will shed tears;
Yea, even my foes will shed fast-falling tears,
And say,—Alas, it was a piteous deed!—
There, take the crown, and, with the crown, my curse;
And, in thy need, such comfort come to thee,
As now I reap at thy too cruel hand!—
Hard-hearted Clifford, take me from the world;
My soul to heaven, my blood upon your heads!

North. Had he been slaughter-man to all my kin,
' I should not for my life but weep with him,
To see how inly sorrow gripes his soul.

Q. Mar. What, weeping-ripe, my lord Northumberland?
Think but upon the wrong he did us all,
And that will quickly dry thy melting tears.

Clif. Here's for my oath, here's for my father's death.
                                   [*stabbing him.*

Q. Mar. And here's to right our gentle-hearted king.
                                   [*stabbing him.*

And when the rage allays, the rain begins.] We meet with the
same thought in our author's *Rape of Lucrece :*
    " This *windy tempest, till it blows up rain,*
    " Held back his sorrow's tide, to make it more;
    " At last it rains, and busy winds give o'er.
    " Then son and father weep with equal strife,
    " Who should weep most for daughter or for wife.
Again, in *Macbeth :*
    " ———— that *tears* shall *drown* the *wind.*"
Again, in *Troilus and Cressida :*
    " Where are my *tears?* Rain, rain, to *lay* this *wind.*"
Again, in *King John :*
    " This shower, blown up by tempest of the soul,—," MALONE.
— *inceffant showers,*] Thus the folio. The quartos read:
    " For raging winds blow up a *storm of tears.*" STEEVENS.
                                             York

York. Open thy gate of mercy, gracious God !
' My foul flies through thefe wounds to feek thee out. [*Dies.*
Q. Mar. Off with his head, and fet it on York gates ;
So York may overlook the town of York [6].   [*Exeunt.*

ACT II. SCENE I.

A plain near Mortimer's *crofs in* Herefordfhire.

Drums. Enter EDWARD, *and* RICHARD, *with their forces, marching.*

* *Edw.* I wonder, how our princely father 'fcap'd ;
* Or whether he be 'fcap'd away, or no,
* From Clifford's and Northumberland's purfuit ;
* Had he been ta'en, we fhould have heard the news ;
* Had he been flain, we fhould have heard the news ;
* Or, had he 'fcap'd, methinks we fhould have heard
* The happy tidings of his good efcape.—

[6] *So York may overlook,* &c] This gallant nobleman fell by his own imprudence, in confequence of leading an army of only five thoufand men to engage with twenty thoufand, and not waiting for the arrival of his fon the earl of March, with a large body of Welchmen. He and Cicely his wife, with his fon Edmond earl of Rutland, were originally buried in the chancel of Foderingay church ; and (as Peacham informs us in his *Complete Gentleman,* 4to, 1627,) " when the chancel in that furie of knocking churches and facred monuments in the head, was alfo felled to the ground," they were removed into the church-yard ; and afterwards lapped in lead they were buried in the church by the commandment of Queen Elizabeth ; and a mean monument of plaifter wrought with the trowel erected over them, very homely, and far unfitting fo noble princes."

" I remember, (adds the fame writer,) Mafter Creufe, a gentleman and my worthy friend, who dwelt in the college at the fame time, told me, that their coffins being opened, their bodies appeared very plainly to be difcerned, and withall that the dutchefs Cicely had about her necke, hanging in a filke ribband, a pardon from Rome, which, penned in a very fine Roman hand, was as faire and frefh to be read, as it had been written yefterday." This *pardon* was probably a difpenfation which the duke procured, from the oath of allegiance that he had fworn to Henry in St. Paul's church on the 10th of March, 1452. MALONE.

' How

' How fares my brother[7]? why is he so sad?

Rich. I cannot joy, until I be resolv'd
Where our right valiant father is become.
' I saw him in the battle range about;
' And watch'd him, how he singled Clifford forth.
' Methought, he bore him[8] in the thickest troop,
As doth a lion in a herd of neat:
* Or as a bear, encompass'd round with dogs;
* Who having pinch'd a few, and made them cry,
* The rest stand all aloof, and bark at him.
* So far'd our father with his enemies;
' So fled his enemies my warlike father;
' Methinks, 'tis prize enough to be his son[9].
See, how the morning opes her golden gates,
And takes her farewel of the glorious sun[1]!
* How well resembles it the prime of youth,
* Trimm'd like a yonker, prancing to his love?

Edw. Dazzle mine eyes, or do I see three suns[2]?

Rich. Three glorious suns, each one a perfect sun;

---

[7] *How fares our brother?*] This scene, in the old quartos, begins thus:

" After this dangerous fight and hapless war,
" How doth my noble brother Richard fare?"

Had the author taken the trouble to revise this play, he hardly would have begun the first act and the second with almost the same exclamation, expressed in almost the same words. Warwick opens the scene with—

I *wonder how the king escaped our hands.* STEEVENS.

[8] *Methought, he bore him*—] i. e. he demeaned himself. So, in *Measure for Measure:*

" How I may formally in person *bear me*—." MALONE.

[9] *Methinks, 'tis prize enough to be his son.*] The old quarto reads,—*pride,* which is right, for *ambition,* i. e. We need not aim at any higher glory than this. WARBURTON.

I believe *prize* is the right word. Richard's sense is, though we have missed the *prize* for which we fought, we have yet an honour left that may content us. JOHNSON.

Prize, if it be the true reading, I believe, here means *privilege.*—So, in the former act:

" It is war's *prize* to take all 'vantages?" MALONE.

[1] *And takes her farewel of the glorious sun!*] Aurora takes for a time her farewel of the sun, when she dismisses him to his diurnal course.

JOHNSON.

[2] —*do I see* three suns?] This circumstance is mentioned both by Hall and Holinshed: " — at which tyme the *son* (as some write) appeared to the earle of March like *three sunnes,* and sodainely joyned altogither in one, uppon whiche sight hee tooke suche courage, that he fiercely setting on his enemyes put them to flight; and for this cause menne ymagined that he gave the sun in his full bryghtnesse for his badge or cognisance." These are the words of Holinshed. MALONE.

Not

Not separated with the racking clouds [3],
But sever'd in a pale clear-shining sky.
See, see! they join, embrace, and seem to kiss,
As if they vow'd some league inviolable :
Now are they but one lamp, one light, one sun.
In this the heaven figures some event.

    * *Edw.* 'Tis wondrous strange, the like yet never heard
        of.
I think, it cites us, brother, to the field ;
That we, the sons of brave Plantagenet,
' Each one already blazing by our meeds [4],
Should, notwithstanding, join our lights together,
' And over-shine the earth, as this the world.
' Whate'er it bodes, henceforward will I bear
Upon my target three fair shining suns.

    * *Rich.* Nay, bear three daughters ;—by your leave I
       speak it,
    * You love the breeder better than the male.

Enter a Messenger.

' But what art thou, whose heavy looks foretel
' Some dreadful story hanging on thy tongue ?
    Mes. Ah, one that was a woeful looker on,
When as the noble duke of York was slain,
    * Your princely father, and my loving lord.
    ' *Edw.* O, speak no more [5]! for I have heard too much.
    ' *Rich.* Say how he dy'd, for I will hear it all.
    ' *Mes.* Environed he was with many foes [6] ;

                              * And

---

3 —*the* racking *clouds,*] i. e. the clouds which fleet with a quick motion. So, in our author's 32d Sonnet :
     " Anon permit the basest *clouds* to ride
     " With ugly *rack* on his celestial face." MALONE.

4 —*blazing by our* meeds,] *Meed* is *merit.* JOHNSON.
So, in the fourth act the king says,
     " My *meed* hath got me fame."
And in *Timon of Athens* the word is used in the same sense :
     " —— No *meed* but he repays
     " Seven-fold above itself." MASON.

5 O, *speak no . more !*] The generous tenderness of Edward, and savage fortitude of Richard, are well distinguished by their different reception of their father's death. JOHNSON.

6 *Environed he was with many foes* ;] Thus, in the old play:
     Oh, one that was a woeful looker on,
     When as the noble duke of York was slain,—
     When as the noble duke was put to flight,
     . And then pursude by Clifford and the queene,
     And many soldiers moe, who all at once

* And ſtood againſt them, as the hope of Troy *
* Againſt the Greeks that would have enter'd Troy.
* But Hercules himſelf muſt yield to odds ;
* And many ſtrokes, though with a little axe,
* Hew down and fell the hardeſt-timber'd oak.
' By many hands your father was ſubdu'd ;
' But only ſlaughter'd by the ireful arm
' Of unrelenting Clifford, and the queen :
' Who crown'd the gracious duke, in high deſpight ;
' Laugh'd in his face ; and, when with grief he wept,
' The ruthleſs queen gave him, to dry his cheeks,
' A napkin ſteeped in the harmleſs blood
' Of ſweet young Rutland, by rough Clifford ſlain :
' And, after many ſcorns, many foul taunts,
' They took his head, and on the gates of York
' They ſet the ſame ; and there it doth remain,
' The ſaddeſt ſpectacle that e'er I view'd.
    Edw. Sweet duke of York, our prop to lean upon ;
' Now thou art gone, we have no ſtaff, no ſtay !—
* O Clifford, boiſt'rous Clifford, thau haſt ſlain
* The flower of Europe for his chivalry ;
* And treacherouſly haſt thou vanquiſh'd him,
* For, hand to hand, he would have vanquiſh'd thee !—
Now my ſoul's palace is become a priſon :
' Ah, would ſhe break from hence ! that this my body
' Might in the ground be cloſed up in reſt :
' For never henceforth ſhall I joy again,
' Never, O never, ſhall I ſee more joy.
    ' _Rich._ I cannot weep ; for all my body's moiſture
Scarce ſerves to quench my furnace-burning heart :
* Nor can my tongue unload my heart's great burden ;
* For ſelf ſame wind, that I ſhould ſpeak withal,
* Is kindling coals, that fire all my breaſt,

Let drive at him, and forſt the duke to yield ;
And then they ſet him on a moul hill there,
And crown'd the gracious duke in high deſpight ;
Who then with tears began to wail his fall.
The ruthleſſe queene perceiving he did weepe,
Gave him a handkerchief to wipe his eyes,
Dipt in the bloud of the ſweete young Rutland, by
Rough Clifford ſlaine ; who weeping tooke it up :
Then through his breſt they thruſt their bloudie ſwords,
Who like a lambe fell at the butcher's feate.
Then on the gates of Yorke they ſet his head,
And there it doth remaine the piteous ſpectacle
That ere mine eyes beheld. MALONE.

* — _the hope of Troy_—] Hector. MALONE.

* And

* And burn me up with flames, that tears would quench.
* To weep [7], is to make lefs the depth of grief :
* Tears, then, for babes.; blows, and revenge, for me!——
‘ Richard, I bear thy name, I'll venge thy death,
‘ Or die renowned by attempting it.

    Edw. His name that valiant duke hath left with thee ;
‘ His dukedom and his chair with me is left.

    Rich. Nay, if thou be that princely eagle's bird,
Shew thy defcent by gazing 'gainft the fun [8] :
For chair and dukedom, throne and kingdom fay ;
Either that is thine, or elfe thou wert not his.

March. Enter WARWICK, *and* MONTAGUE, *with forces.*

    War. How now, fair lords ? What fare ? what news
      abroad ?

‘ *Rich.* Great lord of Warwick, if we fhould recount
Our baleful news, and, at each word's deliverance,
Stab poniards in our flefh, till all were told,
The words would add more anguifh than the wounds.
O valiant lord, the duke of York is flain.

    Edw. O Warwick! Warwick! that Plantagenet,
Which held thee dearly, as his foul's redemption,
Is by the ftern lord Clifford done to death [9].

    War. Ten days ago I drown'd thefe news in tears :
And now, to add more meafure to your woes,
I come to tell you things fince then befall'n.
After the bloody fray at Wakefield fought,
Where your brave father breath'd his lateft gafp,
Tidings, as fwiftly as the pofts could run,
Were brought me of your lofs, and his depart.
I then in London, keeper of the king,
Mufter'd my foldiers, gather'd flocks of friends,
And very well appointed, as I thought [1],
March'd towards faint Alban's to intercept the queen,
Bearing the king in my behalf along :

    7 *To weep,* &c.] Here, in the original play, inftead of thefe two
lines, we have——
      “ I cannot joy, till this white rofe be dy'd.
      “ Even in the heart-bloud of the houfe of Lancafter.” MALONE.
    8 *Shew thy defcent by gazing 'gainft the fun :*] So, in Spenfer's *Hymn
of Heavenly Beauty :*
      “ —— like the native brood of eagle's kind,
      “ On that bright fun of glory fix thine eyes.” STEEVENS.
    9 — *done to death.*] *Done to death* for *killed,* was a common expref-
fion long before Shakfpeare's time. GREY.
    1 *And very well,* &c.] This line I have reftored from the old quar-
tos. STEEVENS.

For

For by my scouts I was advertised,
That she was coming with a full intent
To dash our late decree in parliament,
‘ Touching king Henry's oath, and your succession,
Short tale to make,—we at saint Alban's met,
Our battles join'd, and both sides fiercely fought :
But, whether 'twas the coldness of the king,
Who look'd full gently on his warlike queen,
That robb'd my soldiers of their hated spleen ;
Or whether 'twas report of her success ;
Or more than common fear of Clifford's rigour,
‘ Who thunders to his captives [2]—blood and death,
I cannot judge : but, to conclude with truth,
Their weapons like to lightning came and went ;
Our soldiers'—like the night-owl's lazy flight [3];
‘ Or like a lazy thresher with a flail,—
Fell gently down, as if they struck their friends.
I cheer'd them up with justice of our cause,
With promise of high pay, and great rewards :
But all in vain ; they had no heart to fight,
And we, in them, no hope to win the day,
So that we fled ; the king, unto the queen ;
Lord George your brother, Norfolk, and myself,
In haste, post haste, are come to join with you ;
For in the marches here, we heard, you were,
Making another head to fight again.

‘ *Edw.* Where is the duke of Norfolk, gentle Warwick ?
And when came George from Burgundy to England ?

‘ *War.* Some six miles off the duke is with the soldiers :
And for your brother,—he was lately sent
From your kind aunt, dutchess of Burgundy [4],   ‘ With

---

2 — *to his* captives—] So the folio. The old play reads—*captaines.*
                                                MALONE.

3 — *like the night-owl's lazy flight.*] This image is not very congruous to the subject, nor was it necessary to the comparison, which is happily enough completed by the thresher. JOHNSON.
   Dr. Johnson objects to this comparison as incongruous, but I think unjustly. Warwick compares the languid blows of his soldiers to the lazy strokes which the wings of the owl give the air in its flight, which is remarkably slow. MASON.
   In the subsequent line the old play more elegantly reads—Or like an idle thresher, &c. MALONE.

4 —— *he was lately sent*
   From your kind aunt, dutchess of Burgundy, &c.] This circumstance is not warranted by history. Clarence and Glocester (as they were afterwards created) were sent into Flanders immediately after the battle of Wakefield, and did not return till their brother Edward got possession of the crown. Besides, Clarence was not now more than twelve years old.

                                                Isabel

‘ With aid of foldiers to this needful war.

Rich. 'Twas odds, belike, when valiant **Warwick** fled :
Oft have I heard his praifes in purfuit,
But ne'er, till now, his fcandal of retire.

War. Nor now my fcandal, Richard, doft thou hear:
For thou fhalt know, this ftrong right hand of mine
Can pluck the diadem from faint Henry's head,
And wring the awful fcepter from his fift ;
Were he as famous and as bold in war,
As he is fam'd for mildnefs, peace, and prayer.

Rich. I know it well, lord Warwick : blame me not ;
'Tis love, I hear thy glories, makes me fpeak.
But, in this troublous time, what's to be done ?
Shall we go throw away our coats of fteel,
And wrap our bodies in black mourning gowns,
Numb'ring our Ave-Maries with our beads ?
Or fhall we on the helmets of our foes
Tell our devotion with revengeful arms;
If for the laft, fay—Ay, and to it, lords.

War. Why, therefore Warwick came to feek you out;
And therefore comes my brother Montague.
Attend me, lords. The proud infulting queen,
With Clifford, and the haught Northumberland [5],
And, of their feather, many more proud birds,
Have wrought the eafy-melting king, like wax [6].
He fwore confent to your fucceffion,
His oath enrolled in the parliament ;
And now to London all the crew are gone,
To fruftrate both his oath, and what befide
May make againft the houfe of Lancafter.

‘ Their power, I think, is thirty thoufand ftrong [7] :

Ifabel dutchefs of Burgundy, whom Shakfpeare calls the duke's aunt, was daughter of John I. king of Portugal by Philippa of Lancafter, eldeft daughter of John of Gaunt. They were therefore no more than their coufins. ANONYMOUS.

[5] — haught *Northumberland*,] So, Grafton in his *Chronicle* fays, p. 417: " — the lord Henry Percy, whom the Scottes for his *haut* and valiant courage called Sir Henry Hotfpurie." PERCY.
The word is common to many writers; *Marlow, Kyd,* &c.
STEEVENS.

[6] — *the ealy-melting king, like* wax.] So, again in this play, of the Lady Grey :
" As red as fire; nay, then her *wax* muft melt." JOHNSON.

[7] — *is* thirty *thoufand ftrong :*] Thus the folio. The old play reads—
" Their power, I guefs them *fiftie* thoufand ftrong."
A little lower the fame piece has—*eight and forty thoufand.*
MALONE.
Now,

Now, if the help of Norfolk, and myfelf,
With all the friends that thou, brave earl of March,
Amongft the loving Welfhmen canft procure,
‘ Will but amount to five and twenty thoufand,
Why, *Via!* to London will we march amain ;
And once again beftride our foaming fteeds,
‘ And once again cry—Charge upon our foes !
But never once again turn back, and fly.
   Rich. Ay, now, methinks, I hear great Warwick fpeak :
Ne’er may he live to fee a fun-fhine day,
‘ That cries—Retire, if Warwick bid him ftay.
   Edw. Lord Warwick, on thy fhoulder will I lean ;
‘ And when thou fail’ft, (as God forbid the hour !)
Muft Edward fall, which peril heaven forefend !
   War. No longer earl of March, but duke of York ;
‘ The next degree is, England’s royal throne :
For king of England fhalt thou be proclaim’d
In every borough as we pafs along ;
And he, that throws not up his cap for joy,
‘ Shall for the fault make forfeit of his head.
King Edward,—valiant Richard,—Montague,—
Stay we no longer dreaming of renown,
‘ But found the trumpets, and about our tafk.
   * *Rich.* Then, Clifford, were thy heart as hard as fteel,
* (As thou haft fhewn it flinty by thy deeds,)
* I come to pierce it,—or to give thee mine.
   * *Edw.* Then ftrike up, drums ;—God, and faint George,
      for us !

         Enter a Meffenger.

   War. How now ? what news ?
   Mef. The duke of Norfolk fends you word by me,
The queen is coming with a puiffant hoft ;
And craves your company for fpeedy counfel.
   ‘ *War.* Why then it forts *, brave warriors ; Let’s away.
                      [*Exeunt.*

---

  * *Why then it* forts,] Why then things are as they fhould be.
                             JOHNSON.
   So, in Greene’s *Card of Fancy,* 1608 : “ — thy love fhall *fort* to
fuch happy fuccefs as thou thyfelf doft feek for.” STEEVENS.

                                 SCENE

SCENE II.

Before York.

Enter King HENRY, *Queen* MARGARET, *the Prince of* Wales, CLIFFORD, *and* NORTHUMBERLAND, *with forces.*

Q. Mar. Welcome, my lord, to this brave town of York.
Yonder's the head of that arch-enemy,
That fought to be encompass'd with your crown :
' Doth not the object cheer your heart, my lord?

   ' *K. Hen.* Ay, as the rocks cheer them that fear their
       wreck ;—
To see this fight, it irks my very soul.—
Withhold revenge, dear God ! 'tis not my fault,
Nor wittingly have I infring'd my vow.

   Clif. My gracious liege, this too much lenity
And harmful pity, must be laid aside.
To whom do lions cast their gentle looks?
Not to the beast that would usurp their den.
Whose hand is that, the forest bear doth lick?
Not his, that spoils her young before her face.
Who 'scapes the lurking serpent's mortal sting ?
Not he, that sets his foot upon her back.
The smallest worm will turn, being trodden on ;
' And doves will peck in safeguard of their brood.
Ambitious York did level at thy crown,
Thou smiling, while he knit his angry brows :
He, but a duke, would have his son a king,
And raise his issue, like a loving sire ;
Thou, being a king, blest with a goodly son,
Didst yield consent to disinherit him,
' Which argued thee a most unloving father.
Unreasonable creatures feed their young :
And though man's face be fearful to their eyes,
Yet, in protection of their tender ones,
Who hath not seen them (even with those wings
' Which sometime they have us'd with fearful flight).
Make war with him that climb'd unto their nest;
Offering their own lives in their young's defence?
For shame, my liege, make them your precedent !
Were it not pity, that this goodly boy
Should lose his birth-right by his father's fault;

And long hereafter fay unto his child,—
What my great grand-father and grandfire got,
My carelefs father fondly gave away?
Ah, what a fhame were this! Look on the boy;
And let his manly face which promifeth
Succefsful fortune, fteel thy melting heart,
To hold thine own, and leave thine own with him.

   K. Hen. Full well hath Clifford play'd the orator,
Inferring arguments of mighty force.
' But, Clifford, tell me, didft thou never hear,—
That things ill got had ever bad fuccefs?
And happy always was it for that fon,
Whofe father for his hoarding went to hell[9]?
I'll leave my fon my virtuous deeds behind;
And 'would, my father had left me no more!
For all the reft is held at fuch a rate,
' As brings a thoufand fold more care to keep,
' Than in poffeffion any jot of pleafure.—
Ah, coufin York! 'would thy beft friends did know,
' How it doth grieve me that thy head is here!

   ' *Q. Mar.* My lord, cheer up your fpirits; our foes are
     nigh,
' And this foft courage makes your followers faint.
' You promis'd knighthood to our forward fon;
' Unfheath your fword, and dub him prefently.—
Edward, kneel down.

   K. Hen. Edward Plantagenet, arife a knight;
And learn this leffon,—Draw thy fword in right.

   Prince. My gracious father, by your kingly leave,
I'll draw it as apparent to the crown,
And in that quarrel ufe it to the death.

   Clif. Why, that is fpoken like a toward prince.

Enter a Meffenger.

   Mef. Royal commanders, be in readinefs:
' For, with a band of thirty thoufand men,
Comes Warwick, backing of the duke of York;
And, in the towns as they do march along,
Proclaims him king, and many fly to him:
' Darraign[1] your battle, for they are at hand.

---

9 *Whofe father*, &c.] Alluding to a common proverb:
   Happy the child whofe father went to the devil. Johnson.
1 *Darraign—*] That is, *Range* your hoft, put your hoft in order,
                             Johnson.
  Chaucer, Skelton, and Spenfer, ufe this word. The quartos read
—*Prepare your battles*, &c. Steevens.

Clif.

Clif. I would, your highnefs would depart the field;
The queen hath beft fuccefs when you are abfent[2].

Q. Mar. Ay, good my lord, and leave us to our fortune.

K. Hen. Why, that's my fortune too; therefore I'll ftay.

North. Be it with refolution then to fight.

Prince. My royal father, cheer thefe noble lords,
And hearten thofe that fight in your defence: —
Unfheath your fword, good father, cry, *Saint George!*

March. Enter EDWARD, GEORGE, RICHARD, WAR-
WICK, NORFOLK, MONTAGUE, *and Soldiers.*

' *Edw.* Now, perjur'd Henry! wilt thou kneel for grace,
' And fet thy diadem upon my head;
* Or bide the mortal fortune of the field?

Q. Mar. Go rate thy minions, proud infulting boy!
' Becomes it thee to be thus bold in terms,
' Before thy fovereign, and thy lawful king?

Edw. I am his king, and he fhould bow his knee:
I was adopted heir by his confent[3]:
Since when[4], his oath is broke; for, as I hear,
You—that are king, though he do wear the crown,—
Have caus'd him, by new act of parliament,
' To blot out me, and put his own fon in.

' *Clif.* And reafon too;

---

[2] *— when you are abfent.*] So, Hall: "Happy was the queene in
her two battayls, but unfortunate was the king in all his enterprifes;
for where his perfon was prefent, the victorie fledde ever from him to
the other parte." Henry VI. fol. C. MALONE.

[3] *I am his king, and he fhould bow his knee;*
I was adopted heir by his confent:
Since when, his oath is broke;] Edward's argument is founded on the
following article in the compact entered into by Henry and the duke of
York, which the author found in Hall's Chronicle, but which I believe
made no part of that agreement: "Provided alwaye, that if the king
did clofely or apertly ftudye or go about to breake or alter this agreement, or to compafs or imagine the death or diftruction of the fayde
duke or his bloud, then he *to forfet the crowne*, and the duke of Yorke
to take it." If this had been one of the articles of the compact, the
duke having been killed at Wakefield, his eldeft fon would have now a
title to the crown. MALONE.

[4] *Since when,* &c.] The quartos give the remainder of this fpeech to
Clarence, and read:
To blot our brother *out*, &c. STEEVENS.
Here is another variation of the fame kind with thofe which have
been noticed in the preceding play, which could not have arifen from
a tranfcriber or printer.—Though Shakfpeare gave the whole of this
fpeech to Edward by fubftituting *me* for *brother*, the fame divifion which
is found in the quarto, is inadvertently retained in the folio. MALONE.

Who

Who should succeed the father, but the son?

' *Rich.* Are you there, butcher?—O, I cannot speak!

' *Clif.* Ay, crook-back; here I stand, to answer thee,

' Or any he the proudest of thy sort.

Rich. 'Twas you that kill'd young Rutland, was it not?

Clif. Ay, and old York, and yet not satisfy'd.

Rich. For God's sake, lords, give signal to the fight.

War. What say'st thou, Henry, wilt thou yield the
        crown?

' *Q. Mar.* Why, how now, long-tongu'd Warwick? dare
        you speak?

When you and I met at saint Alban's last,

Your legs did better service than your hands [5].

War. Then 'twas my turn to fly, and now 'tis thine.

Clif. You said so much before, and yet you fled.

War. 'Twas not your valour, Clifford, drove me thence.

' *North.* No, nor your manhood, that durst make you stay,

Rich. Northumberland, I hold thee reverently;—

Break off the parley; for scarce I can refrain

The execution of my big-swoln heart

Upon that Clifford, that cruel child-killer.

Clif. I slew thy father; Call'st thou him a child?

Rich. Ay, like a dastard, and a treacherous coward,

As thou didst kill our tender brother Rutland;

But, ere sun-set, I'll make thee curse the deed.

' *K. Hen.* Have done with words, my lords, and hear me
        speak.

Q. Mar. Defy them then, or else hold close thy lips.

K. Hen. I pr'ythee, give no limits to my tongue;

I am a king, and privileg'd to speak.

Clif. My liege, the wound, that bred this meeting here,

Cannot be cur'd by words; therefore be still.

Rich. Then, executioner, unsheath thy sword:

By him that made us all, I am resolv'd [6],

' That Clifford's manhood lies upon his tongue.

' *Edw.* Say, Henry, shall I have my right, or no?

A thousand men have broke their fasts to-day,

That ne'er shall dine, unless thou yield the crown.

War. If thou deny, their blood upon thy head;

For York in justice puts his armour on

' *Prince.* If that be right, which Warwick says is right,

There is no wrong, but every thing is right.

---

5 *Your legs did better service than your hands*] An allusion to the
proverb, " One pair of heel's is worth two pair of hands." STEEVENS.

6 — *I am resolv'd,*] It is my firm persuasion; I am no longer in
doubt. JOHNSON.

Rich.

Rich. Whoever got thee *, there thy mother ſtands ;
For, well I wot, thou haſt thy mother's tongue.

Q. Mar. But thou art neither like thy ſire, nor dam?
But like a foul miſ-ſhapen ſtigmatick [7],
Mark'd by the deſtinies to be avoided,
' As venom toads, or lizards' dreadful ſtings [8].

Rich. Iron of Naples, hid with Engliſh gilt [9],
Whoſe father bears the title of a king,
(As if a channel ſhould be call'd the ſea [1],)
' Sham'ſt thou not, knowing whence thou art extraught,
' To let thy tongue detect thy baſe-born heart [2]?

Edw. A wiſp of ſtraw [3] were worth a thouſand crowns,

---

* Rich *Whoever got thee,* &c.] In the folio this ſpeech is erroneouſly aſſigned to Warwick. The anſwer ſhews that it belongs to Richard,
to whom it is attributed in the old play. MALONE.

7 — *miſhapen* ſtigmatick,] See p. 218, n. 5. MALONE.

8 *lizards' dreadful ſtings.*] Thus the folio. The quartos have this
variation :—*or lizards' fainting looks.*

This is the ſecond time that Shakſpeare has armed the lizard (which
in reality has no ſuch defence) with a ſting ; but great powers ſeem to
have been imputed to its looks. So, in *Noah's Flood,* by Drayton :
   " The *lizard* ſhuts up his *ſharp-ſighted eyes,*
   " Amongſt the ſerpents, and there ſadly lies. STEEVENS.

Shakſpeare is here anſwerable for the introduction of the lizard's
ſting ; but in a preceding paſſage, the author of the old play has
fallen into the ſame miſtake. MALONE.

9 — gilt,] *Gilt* is a ſuperficial covering of gold. STEEVENS.

1 *(As if a channel ſhould be called the ſea,)*] A *channel* in our author's
time ſignified what we now call a *kennel.* So, in Stowe's *Chronicle,*
quarto, 1605, p. 1148 : " — ſuch a ſtorme of raine happened at London, as the like of long time could not be remembered ; whereth-ough,
the *channels* of the citie ſuddenly riſing," &c. Again, in *K. Henry IV.*
P. II " — quoit him into the *channel.*" MALONE.

2 *To let thy tongue,* &c.] To ſhew thy meanneſs of birth by the inde-
cency of language with which thou raileſt at my deformity. JOHNSON.

Inſtead of this line, the old play has—
   To parly thus with England's lawful heirs. MALONE.

3 *A wiſp of ſtraw*—] It appears from the following paſſage in Thomas Drant's tranſlation of the ſeventh ſatire of *Horace,* 1567, that a
wiſpe was the puniſhment of a ſcold :
   " So perfyte and exacte a ſcoulde, that women mighte geve place,
   " Whoſe rattling tongues had won a *wiſhe,*" &c. STEEVENS.

See alſo Naſhe's *Apology of Pierce Pennileſſe,* 1593 : " Why, thou
errant butter whore, thou cotquean and ſcrattop of *ſcolds,* wilt thou
never leave afflicting a dead carcaſſe? continually read the rhetorick
lecture of Ramme-Alley ? a *wiſpe,* a *wiſpe,* you kitchen-ſtuffe wrang-
ler." Again, in *A Dialogue between John and Jone ſtriving who ſhall
wear the Breeches,*—PLEASURES OF POETRY bl. l. no date :
   " Good gentle Jone, with holde thy hands,
   " This once l t me entreat thee,
   " And make me promiſe, never more
   " That thou ſhalt mind to beat me :
   " For feare *thou weare the wiſpe,* good wife,
   " And make our neighbours ride—". MALONE.

I

To make this shameless callet know herself [4].——
* Helen of Greece was fairer far than thou,
* Although thy husband may be Menelaus.;
* And ne'er was Agamemnon's brother wrong'd
* By that false woman, as this king by thee.
' His father revell'd in the heart of France,
And tam'd the king, and made the Dauphin stoop;
And, had he match'd according to his state,
He might have kept that glory to this day:
But, when he took a beggar to his bed,
And grac'd thy poor sire with his bridal day;
' Even then that sun-shine brew'd a shower for him,
' That wash'd his father's fortunes forth of France,
'And heap'd sedition on his crown at home.
For what hath broach this tumult, but thy pride?
Hadst thou been meek, our title still had slept;
And we, in pity of the gentle king,
Had slipp'd our claim until another age.
    ' *Geo.* But, when we saw our sun-shine made thy spring.
' And that thy summer bred us no increase [5],
We set the axe to thy usurping root:
And though the edge hath something hit ourselves,
' Yet, know thou, since we have begun to strike,
' We'll never leave, till we have hewn thee down,
Or bath'd thy growing with our heated bloods.
    Edw. And, in this resolution, I defy thee;
Not willing any longer conference,
Since thou deny'st the gentle king to speak.——
Sound trumpets!—let our bloody colours wave!——
And either victory, or else a grave.
    Q. Mar. Stay, Edward.
    Edw. No, wrangling woman, we'll no longer stay:
These words will cost ten thousand lives to-day   [*Exeunt.*

---

4 *To make this shameless* callet *know herself.*] Callet, a lewd woman, a drab, perhaps so called from the French *calote*, which was a sort of head dress worn by country girls. See *Gloss.* to *Urry's Chaucer.* GREY

5 — *we saw our sunshine made thy spring,*
    And that thy summer bred us no increase,] When we saw that by favouring thee we made thee grow in fortune, but that we received no advantage from thy fortune flourishing by our favour, we then resolved to destroy thee, and determine to try some other means, though our first efforts have failed. JOHNSON.
    The quartos read:
      But when we saw our summer brought thee gain,
      And that the harvest brought us no increase. STEEVENS.

SCENE

SCENE III.

A field of battle between Towton *and* Saxton *in* Yorkshire.

Alarums. Excurfions. Enter WARWICK.

' *War.* Forfpent with toil, as runners with a race;
I lay me down a little while to breathe :
For ftrokes receiv'd, and many blows repaid,
Have robb'd my ftrong-knit finews of their ftrength,
' And, fpight of fpight, needs muft I reft a while.

Enter EDWARD, *running.*

Edw. Smile, gentle heaven ! or ftrike, ungentle death [6] !
' For this world frowns, and Edward's fun is clouded.
War. How now, my lord ? what hap ? what hope of
good ?

Enter GEORGE.

* *Geo.* Our hap is lofs, our hope but fad defpair [7];
' Our ranks are broke, and ruin follows us :
' What counfel give you ? whither fhall we fly ?
' *Edw.* Bootlefs is flight, they follow us with wings ;
' And weak we are, and cannot fhun purfuit.

Enter RICHARD.

' *Rich.* Ah, Warwick, why haft thou withdrawn thyfelf ?
' Thy brother's blood the thirfty earth hath drunk [8],

' Broach'd

---

6 *Smile, gentle heaven !* &c.] Thus the folio. Inftead of thefe
lines, the quartos give the following :
Smile, gentle heavens, or ftrike, ungentle death,
That we may die unlefs we gain the day !
What fatal ftar malignant frowns from heaven,
Upon the harmlefs line of York's fair houfe ? STEEVENS.
7 *Our hap is lofs,* our hope but fad defpair ;] Milton is faid to have
copied this line :
" —— Thus repuls'd, our final hope
" Is flat defpair." MALONE.
Our hap is lofs, &c.] Thus the folio. The quarto thus :
Come, brother, come, let's to the field again,
And yet there's hope enough to win the day :
Then let us back to cheer our fainting troops,
Left they retire now we have left the field.
War. How now, my lords ? what hap ? what hope of good ?"
STEEVENS.
8 *Thy brother's blood the thirfty earth hath drunk,*] The old play (as
Theobald

' Broach'd with the steely point of Clifford's lance :
' And, in the very pangs of death, he cry'd—
' Like to a dismal clangor heard from far,—
' *Warwick, revenge ! brother, revenge my death !* . . . .
' So, underneath the belly of their steeds,
' That stain'd their fetlocks in his smoking blood,
' The noble gentleman gave up the ghost.

War. Then let the earth be drunken with our blood :
I'll kill my horse, because I will not fly [9].

Theobald has observed) applies this description to the death of Salisbury,
contrary to the truth of history, for that nobleman was taken prisoner at
the battle of Wakefield, and afterwards beheaded at Pomfret. But
both Hall and Holinshed, in nearly the same words, relate the circumstance on which this speech as exhibited in the *folio*, is founded ; and
from the latter our author undoubtedly took it. "The Lord Fitzwalter
[who had been stationed to keep the pass of Ferry-bridge] hearing the
noise [made by Lord Clifford and a body of light-horsemen, who attack-
ed by surprize the party stationed at the bridge,] sodainely rose out of
his bedde, and unarmed, with a pollax in his hande, thinking that it
had bin a fraye amongst his men, came downe to appease the same, but
ere he knew what the matter ment, he was slaine, and with him the
bastard of Salisbury, *brother to the erle of Warwick*, a valiant young
gentleman, and of great audacitie." Holinshed, p 664 In this action at Ferrybridge, which happened on the 24th of March, 1461, the
day before the great battle of Towton, Lord Clifford was killed The
author of this play has blended the two actions together. MALONE.

Thy brother's blood, &c] Instead of this speech, which is printed,
like almost all the rest of the play, from the folio, the quartos give the
following :
> Thy noble *father* in the thickest throngs
> Cry'd still for Warwick, his thrice valiant son ;
> · Until with thousand swords he was beset,
> And many wounds made in his aged breast.
> ·And, as he tottering sat upon his steed,
> He waft his hand to me, and cried aloud,
> Richard, commend me to my valiant son :
> And still he cried, Warwick, revenge my death !
> And with these words he tumbled off his horse ;
> And so the noble Salisbury gave up the ghost. STEEVENS.

Thy brother's blood the thirsty earth hath drunk.] In this line, of which
there is no trace in the original play, Shakspeare had probably the sacred
writings in his thoughts : " And now art thou cursed from the *earth*,
which hath *opened her mouth* to receive *thy brother's* blood." GENESIS,
iv. 11 MALONE.

9 *I'll kill my horse, because I will not fly*] From H II, Henry VI. p.
102 : " When the Earle of Warwick was informed of this feate, he,
lyke a man desperate, mounted on his hackeney, and came blowing to
king Edward, saying, Syr, I pray God have mercy of their soules,
which in the beginning of your enterprize hath lost their lives ; and because I see no succours of the world, I remit the vengeance and punish-
ment to God, our creator and redemer ; and with that lighted downe,
and *slew his horse with his sworde*, saying, let him flee that wyl, for
surely I wil tarye with him that will tarye with me ; and kissed the
crosse of his sworde." MALONE.

* Why

* Why ſtand we like ſoft-hearted women here.
* Wailing our loſſes, whiles the foe doth rage ;
* And look upon *, as if the tragedy
* Were play'd in jeſt by counterfeiting actors?
‘ Here on my knee I vow to God above,
‘ I'll never pauſe again, never ſtand ſtill,
‘ 'Till either death hath clos'd theſe eyes of mine,
‘ Or fortune given me meaſure of revenge.
 Edw. O Warwick, I do bend my knee with thine ;
‘ And, in this vow, do chain my ſoul to thine ¹.—
* And, ere my knee riſe from the earth's cold face,
* I throw my hands, mine eyes, my heart to thee,
Thou ſetter up and plucker down of kings !
‘ Beſeeching thee ², —if with thy will it ſtands,
‘ That to my foes this body muſt be prey,—
‘ Yet that thy brazen gates of heaven may ope,
‘ And give ſweet paſſage to my ſinful ſoul !—
‘ Now, lords, take leave until we meet again,
Where-e'er it be, in heaven, or on earth.
 ‘ *Rich.* Brother, give me thy hand ;—and, gentle War-
  wick,
‘ Let me embrace thee in my weary arms :—
‘ I, that did never weep, now melt with woe,
‘ That winter ſhould cut off our ſpring-time ſo.

---

* *And* look upon,] And are mere ſpectators. So, in *the Winter's Tale*, where I idly ſuſpected ſome corruption in the text.:
 ‘‘ And *look on* alike.'' MALONE.
¹ *And in this vow do chain my ſoul to thine.*—] Thus the folio. The quarto as follows :
  ‘‘ And in *that* vow *now join* my ſoul to *thee*.'' STEEVENS.
² *Beſeeching* thee,—] That is, beſeeching the divine power. Shakſpeare in new-forming this ſpeech may ſeem, at the firſt view of it, to have made it obſcure, by placing this line immediately after,—‘‘ Thou ſetter up,'' &c.
 What I have now obſerved is founded on a ſuppoſition that the words ‘‘ *Thou ſetter up*,'' &c. are applied to Warwick, as they appear to be in the old play. However, our author certainly intended to deviate from it, and to apply this deſcription to the deity ; and this is another ſtrong confirmation of the obſervation already made relative to the variations between theſe pieces and the elder dramas on which they were formed. In the old play the ſpeech runs thus :
  Lord Warwick, I do bend my knees with thine,
  And in that vow now join my ſoul to thee,
  Thou ſetter-up and puller-down of kings :—
  Vouchſafe a gentle victory to us,
  Or let us die before we loſe the day !
 The laſt two lines are certainly here addreſſed to the deity ; but the preceding line, notwithſtanding the anachroniſm, ſeems to be addreſſed to Warwick. MALONE.

             ‘ *War.*

‘ _War._ Away, away! Once more, sweet lords, farewel. ·
‘ _Geo._ Yet let us all together to our troops : ·
‘ And give them leave to fly that will not stay ;
And call them pillars, that will stand to us ;
‘ And, if we thrive, promise them such rewards
‘ As victors wear at the Olympian games :
‘ This may plant courage in their quailing breasts ;
‘ For yet is hope of life, and victory.——
‘ Fore-flow no longer [3], make we hence amain [4].

[_Exeunt._

SCENE IV.

The same. Another part of the field.

Excursions. _Enter_ RICHARD _and_ CLIFFORD.

‘ _Rich._ Now, Clifford, I have singled thee alone [5]:
‘ Suppose, this arm is for the duke of York,
‘ And this for Rutland ; both bound to revenge,
‘ Wert thou environ’d with a brazen wall.

---

[3] Fore-flow _no longer_,] To _fore-flow_ is to be dilatory, to loiter, So,
in the _Battle of Alcazar_, 1594 :
    “ Why, king Sebastian, wilt thou now _foreslow ?_”
Again, in Marlowe’s _Edward II_ 1598 :
    “ _Foreslow_ no time ; sweet Lancaster, let’s march.”
                                                        STEEVENS.

[4] — _make we hence amain._] Instead of this and the two preceding
speeches, we have in the old play the following :
    Geo. Then let us haste to cheare the souldiers’ hearts,
    And call them pillers that will stand to us,
    And highly promise to remunerate
    Their trustie service in these dangerous warres.
    Rich. Come, come away, and stand not to debate,
    For yet is hope of fortune good enough,
    Brothers, give me your handes, and let us part,
    And take our leaves untill we meete againe ;
    Where ere it be, in heaven or in earth.
    Now I that never wept, now melt in woe,
    To see these dire mishaps continue so.
    Warwick, farewell,
    War. Away, away ; once more, sweet lords, farewell.
                                                        MALONE.

[5] _Now, Clifford, I have singled thee alone :_ &c] Thus the folio.
The quartos thus :
    Now, Clifford, for York and young Rutland’s death,
    This thirsty sword that longs to drink thy blood,
    Shall lop thy limbs, and slice thy cursed heart,
    For to revenge the murders thou hast made. STEEVENS.

Clif.

Clif. Now, Richard. I am with thee here alone:
This is the hand, that ſtabb'd thy father Yòrk;
And this the hand, that ſlew thy brother Rutland;
And here's the heart that triumphs in their death,
And cheers theſe hands, that ſlew thy ſire and brother,
To execute the like upon thyſelf;
And ſo, have at thee.

    [*They fight.* Warwick *enters;* Clifford *flies.*

' *Rich.* Nay, Warwick, ſingle out ſome other chace;
' For I myſelf will hunt this wolf to death [6]. [*Exeunt.*

SCENE V.

Another part of the field.

Alarum. Enter King HENRY.

* *K. Hen.* This battle fares like to the morning's war [7],
* When dying clouds contend with growing light;
* What time the ſhepherd, blowing of his nails [8],
* Can neither call it perfect day, nor night.
' Now ſways it this way, like a mighty ſea,

---

[6] *Nay, Warwick, &c.*] We have had two very ſimilar lines in the preceding play, (See alſo p. 218 of this vol. for a like repetition.)
 " Hold, Warwick, ſeek thee out ſome other chace;
 " For I myſelf muſt hunt this deer to death." MALONE.
[7] *This battle fares like to the morning's war, &c.*] Inſtead of this intereſting ſpeech, the quartos exhibit only the following:
  Oh gracious God of heaven, look down on us,
  And ſet ſome ends to theſe inceſſant griefs!
  How like a maſtleſſ ſhip upon the ſeas,
  This woeful battle doth continue ſtill
  Now leaning this way, now to that ſide driven;
  And none doth know to whom the day will fall
  Oh, would my death might ſtay theſe *civil* jars[*]!
  Would I had never reign'd, nor ne'er been king!
  Margaret and Clifford chide me from the field,
  Swearing they had beſt ſucceſs when I was thence.
  Would God that I were dead, ſo all were well;
  Or, would my crown ſuffice, I were content
  To yield it them, and live a private life!
The leading thought in both theſe ſoliloquies is borrowed from Holinſhed, p 665:—" This deadly conflict continued ten hours in doubtful ſtate of victorie, uncertainte weaving and ſetting on both ſides." &c. STEEVENS.
[8] *— the ſhepherd, blowing of his nails,*] So, in *Love's Labour's Loſt*:
 " When icicles hang by the wall,
 " And Dick the *ſhepherd blows his nail,*—." MALONE.
[*] The quarto 1600, printed by W. W. reads—*cruel* jars.

           Forc'd

'Forc'd by the tide to combat with the wind;
'Now sways it that way, like the self-same sea
'Forc'd to retire by fury of the wind:
'Sometime, the flood prevails; and then, the wind;
'Now, one the better; then, another best;
'Both tugging to be victors, breast to breast,
'Yet neither conqueror, nor conquered:
'So is the equal poise of this fell war.
* Here on this mole-hill will I sit me down.
* To whom God will, there be the victory!
' For Margaret my queen, and Clifford too,
'Have chid me from the battle; swearing both,
'They prosper best of all when I am thence.
'Would I were dead! if God s good will were so:
'For what is in this world, but grief and woe?
* O God! methinks, it were a happy life[9],
To be no better than a homely swain;
* To sit upon a hill, as I do now,
* To carve out dials quaintly, point by point,
* Thereby to see the minutes how they run:
* How many make the hour full complete[1],
* How many hours bring about the day,
* How many days will finish up the year,
* How many years a mortal man may live.
* When this is known, then to divide the times:
* So many hours must I tend my flock;
* So many hours must I take my rest;
* So many hours must I contemplate;
* So many hours must I sport myself;
* So many days my ewes have been with young;
* So many weeks ere the poor fools will yean[2];

9 — *methinks, it were a happy life*,] This speech is mournful and soft, exquisitely suited to the character of the king, and makes a pleasing interchange, by affording, amidst the tumult and horror of the battle, an unexpected glimpse of rural innocence and pastoral tranquillity. JOHNSON.
This speech strongly confirms the remark made by Sir Joshua Reynolds in a passage in *Macbeth*. MALONE.

1 *Thereby to see the* minutes *how they run*;
How many make the hour full complete,] So, in our author's *Rape of Lucrece*:
"Stuff up his lust, *as minutes fill up hours*." MALONE.

2 — *ere the* poor fools *will yean*;] *Poor fool*; it has already been observed, is an expression of tenderness, often used by our author.
MALONE.

* So

* So many years ere I ſhall ſheer the fleece [3] :
* So minutes, hours, days, months, and years,
* Paſt over to the end they were created,
* Would bring white hairs unto a quiet grave.
* Ah, what a life were this! how ſweet! how lovely!
* Gives not the hawthorn buſh a ſweeter ſhade
* To ſhepherds, looking on their ſilly ſheep,
* Than doth a rich embroider'd canopy
* To kings, that fear their ſubjects' treachery?
* O, yes, it doth; a thouſand fold it doth.
* And to conclude,—the ſhepherd's homely curds,
* His cold thin drink out of his leather bottle,
* His wonted ſleep under a freſh tree's ſhade,
* All which ſecure and ſwectly he enjoys,
* Is far beyond a prince's delicates,
* His viands ſparkling in a golden cup,
* His body couched in a curious bed,
* When care, miſtruſt, and treaſon wait on him.

Alarum. *Enter a* Son *that has killed his Father, dragging in the dead body* [4].

Son. Ill blows the wind, that profits no-body.—
' This man, whom hand to hand I ſlew in fight,
' May be poſſeſſed with ſome ſtore of crowns :
* And I, that haply take them from him now,
* May yet ere night yield both my life and them
* To ſome man elſe, as this dead man doth me.—
' Who's this?—O God! it is my father's face,
' Whom in this conflict I unwares have kill'd.
' O heavy times, begetting ſuch events!
' From London by the king was I preſs'd forth;
' My father, being the earl of Warwick's man,
' Came on the part of York, preſs'd by his maſter;
' And I, who at his hands receiv'd my life,
' Have by my hands of life bereaved him.—

3 *So many years ere I ſhall ſheer the fleece:*] i. e. the years which muſt elapſe between the time of the yeaning of the ewes, and the lambs arriving to ſuch a ſtate as to admit of being ſhorn. Mr. Rowe changed *years* to *months*; which was followed by the ſubſequent editors; and in the next line inſerted the word *weeks*, not obſerving that *hours* is uſed there, and throughout this ſpeech, as a diſſyllable. *Years* is in that line likewiſe uſed as a word of two ſyllables MALONE.

4 *Enter a* Son, *&c.*] Theſe horrible incidents are ſelected to ſhew the innumerable calamities of civil war. JOHNSON.

In the battle of Conſtantine and Maxentius, by Raphael, the ſecond of theſe incidents is introduced on a ſimilar occaſion. STEEVENS.

' Pardon

' Pardon me, God, I knew not what I did!—
And pardon, father, for I knew not thee!—
* My tears shall wipe away these bloody marks;
* And no more words, till they have flow'd their fill.

' *K. Hen.* O piteous spectacle! O bloody times⁵!
Whilst lions war, and battle for their dens,
' Poor harmless lambs abide their enmity —
* Weep, wretched man, I'll aid thee tear for tear;
* And let our hearts, and eyes, like civil war,
* Be blind with tears, and break o'ercharg'd with grief⁶.

Enter a Father, *who has killed his Son, with the body in his*
arms.

' *Fath.* Thou that so stoutly hast resisted me,
' Give me thy gold, if thou hast any gold;
' ' For I have bought it with a hundred blows.—
' But let me see:—is this our foeman's face?
' Ah, no, no, no, it is mine only son!—
* Ah, boy, if any life be left in thee,
* Throw up thine eye; see, see, what showers arise⁷,
* Blown with the windy tempest of my heart,
* Upon thy wounds, that kill mine eye and heart!—
' O pity, God, this miserable age!—
' What stratagems, how fell, how butcherly⁸,

                                        ' Erroneous,

---

⁵ *O piteous spectacle!* &c.] In the old play the king does not speak,
till both the son and the father have appeared, and spoken, and then
the following words are attributed to him, out of which Shakspeare has
formed two distinct speeches:
          Woe above woe! grief more than common grief!
          Whilst lions war, and battle for their dens,
          Poor lambs do feel the rigour of their wraths.
          The red rose and the white are on his face,
          The fatal colours of our striving houses.
          Wither one rose, and let the other perish,
          For, if you strive, ten thousand lives must perish. MALONE.
⁶ *And let our hearts and eyes, like civil war,*
     Be blind with tears, and break o'ercharg'd with grief. The mean-
ing is here inaccurately expressed. The king intends to say that the state
of their *hearts and eyes* shall be like that of the kingdom in a *civil war*,
all shall be destroyed by power formed within themselves. JOHNSON.
     ⁷ — *what showers arise,*
     Blown with the windy tempest of my heart,] This image had oc-
curred in the preceding act:
     " *For raging wind blows up incessant showers.*" STEEVENS.
     ⁸ *What stratagems, how fell, how butcherly,*] *Stratageme.* A policie
or subtle device in *warre,* whereby the enemie is often vanquished."—
Bullokar's *English Expositor,* octavo, 1616. Florio in his Italian *Dict.*
                                                  1598,

' Erroneous, mutinous, and unnatural,
' This deadly quarrel daily doth beget !—
' O boy, thy father gave thee life too foon [9],
' And hath bereft thee of thy life too late [1] !

K. Hen. Woe above woe ! grief more than common grief !
' O, that my death would ftay thefe ruthlefs deeds !—
* O pity, pity, gentle heaven, pity !—
The red rofe and the white are on his face,
The fatal colours of our ftriving houfes :
* The one, his purple blood right well refembles ;
* The other, his pale cheeks, methinks, prefent :
Wither one rofe, and let the other flourifh !
' If you contend, a thoufand lives muft wither [1].

Son How will my mother, for a father's death,
Take on with me *, and ne'er be fatisfy'd ?

Fath. How will my wife, for flaughter of my fon,
' Shed feas of tears, and ne'er be fatisfy'd ?

K. Hen. How will the country [2], for thefe woeful chances,
' Mif-think

1598, defines *Stratagema*, "a policie, a wile, or wittie fhift in *warre*."
This was undoubtedly its ordinary fenfe in our author's time, though
then and afterwards it was occafionally ufed for *any* fubtle device or policy. Here it has unqueftionably its ordinary fignification. MALONE

9 *O boy! thy father gave thee life too foon,*] Becaufe had he been born
later, he would not now have been of years to engage in this quarrel.
WARBURTON.

1 *And hath bereft thee of thy life too* late 1] Too *late*, without doubt,
means *too recently*. The memory of thy virtues and thy hap'efs end is
too *recent*, to be thought of without the deepeft anguifh. The fame
quaint expreffion is found in our author's *Rape of Lucrece* :
"O, quoth Lucretius, I d'd give that life,
"Which fhe too early and *too late* hath fpill'd."
Here *late* clearly means *lately*. Again, in this third part of *King
Henry VI*.
"Where fame, *late* entering at his heedful ears."
Again, as Mr. Tollet has obferved, in *King Richard III*:
"Too *late* he died, that might have kept that title."
In the old play this and the preceding line ftand thus :
"*Poor* boy, thy father gave thee life too *late*,
"And hath bereft thee of thy life too *foon*." MALONE.

1 — *muft* wither.] The old play has—muft *perifh*, and I think the
word *wither* is more likely to have been inadvertently repeated by the
tranfcriber, than fubftituted by Shakfpeare for the former word.
MALONE.

* Take on *with me*,] Be enraged at me. So, in a pamphlet by T.
Nafhe, 1592 : "Some will *take on*, like a madman, &c. MALONE.

2 *How will the country*, &c] So, the folio. The quartos thus :
How will the country now mifdeem their king !
Oh, would my death their minds could fatisfy !
To *mif-think* is to think ill, unfavourably. STEEVENS.
This word, which Shakfpeare fubftituted for *mifdeem*, he has again
ufed in *Antony and Cleopatra* :
"Be

‘ Miſ-think the king, and not be ſatisfy’d ?
  ‘ *Son.* Was ever ſon, ſo ru’d a father’s death ?
  ‘ *Fath.* Was ever father, ſo bemoan’d his ſon [3] ?
  ‘ *K. Hen.* Was ever king, ſo griev’d for ſubjects’ woe ?
‘ Much is your ſorrow ; mine, ten times ſo much.
  ‘ *Son.* I’ll bear thee hence, where I may weep my fill [4],
                 [*Exit with the body.*

* *Fath.* Theſe arms of mine ſhall be thy winding ſheet ;
* My heart, ſweet boy, ſhall be thy ſepulchre ;
* For from my heart thine image ne’er ſhall go.
* My ſighing breaſt ſhall be thy funeral bell ;
* And ſo obſequious will thy father be [5],
* Sad for the loſs of thee [5], having no more,
*-As Priam was for all [6] his valiant ſons
I’ll bear thee hence ; and let them fight that will,
For I have murder’d where I ſhould not kill.
                 [*Exit, with the body.*

  ‘ *K. Hen.* Sad-hearted men, much overgone with care,
‘ Here ſits a king more woeful than you are.

Alarums. Excurſions. Enter Queen MARGARET, *Prince of*
          Wales, *and* EXETER.

  ‘ *Prince.* Fly, father, fly ! for all your friends are fled,
‘ And Warwick rages like a chafed bull :
‘ Away ! for death doth hold us in purſuit.
  ‘ *Q. Mar.* Mount you, my lord, towards Berwick poſt
    amain :
‘ Edward and Richard, like a brace of greyhounds
‘ Having the fearful flying hare in ſight,
‘ With firy eyes, ſparkling for very wrath,

    “ Be it known, that we the greateſt are *miſ-thought,*
    “ For things that others do.” MALONE.
  3 *Was ever ſon, ſo ru’d a father’s death ?*
    Was ever father, ſo bemoan’d his ſon ?] The variation is here
worth remarking, for in the old play the corresponding lines are :
    Was ever ſon ſo *rude,* his father’s blood to ſpill ?
    Was ever father ſo unnatural, his ſon to kill ? MALONE.
  4 *I’ll bear thee hence,* &c.] Thus the folio. The old play thus :
    I’ll bear thee hence from this accurſed place,
    For woe is to me, to ſee my father’s face. MALONE.
  5 *And ſo* obſequious *will thy father be,*] Obſequious is here careful of
obſequies, or of funeral rites. JOHNSON.
  In the ſame ſenſe it is uſed in *Hamlet :*
    “ —— to do *obſequious* ſorrow ” STEEVENS.
  5 Sad *for the loſs of thee,*] The old copy reads—*Men* for the loſs, &c.
Mr. Rowe made the alteration. STEEVENS.
  6 *As Priam was for all*—] I having but one ſon, will grieve as much
for that one, as Priam, who had many, could grieve for many.
                         JOHNSON.
                                ‘And

And bloody steel grasp'd in their ireful hands,
Are at our backs ; and therefore hence amain.
   Exe. Away ! for vengeance comes along with them :
' Nay, stay not to expostulate, make speed ;
Or else come after, I'll away before.
   ' *K. Hen.* Nay, take me with thee, good sweet Exeter ;
' Not that I fear to stay, but love to go
' Whither the queen intends. Forward ; away !   [*Exeunt.*

SCENE VI.

The Same.

A loud alarum. Enter CLIFFORD *wounded* [7].

   ' *Clif.* Here burns my candle out, ay, here it dies,
Which, while it lasted, gave king Henry light.
O, Lancaster ! I fear thy overthrow,
More than my body's parting with my soul.
My love, and fear, glew'd many friends to thee ;
' And, now I fall, thy tough commixtures melt [8].
Impairing Henry, strength'ning mis-proud York,
The common people swarm like summer flies [9] :
And whither fly the gnats, but to the sun ?
And who shines now, but Henry's enemies ?
O Phœbus ! hadst thou never given consent [1]
That Phaeton should check thy firy steeds,
Thy burning car never had scorch'd the earth :

---

  7 *Enter Clifford, wounded*] The quarto adds, *with an arrow in his neck.* In ridicule of this B. and Fletcher have introduced *Ralph*, the grocer's prentice, in the *Knight of the Burning Pestle*, with a *forked arrow through his head.* It appears, however, from Holinshed, p. 664, that this circumstance has some relation to the truth : " The lord Clifford, euher for heat or paine, putting off his gorget suddenlie, with an *arrow* (as some saie) without a head, was striken into the *throte*, and immediately rendered his spirit." STEEVENS.

  8 *Thy tough commixtures melt.*] Perhaps better, *the tough commixture* JOHNSON.

  The quartos read—" *that* tough commixture *melts.*" STEEVENS.

  9 *The common people swarm like summer flies :*] This line, which is not in the f lio, was recovered from the old play by Mr. Theobald.— The context shews, that like a line in the second part of *K. Henry VI.* it was omitted by the negligence of the transcriber or compositor.
                               MALONE.

  9 *O, Phœbus ! hadst thou never given consent*—] The duke of York had been entrusted by Henry with the reins of government both in Ireland and France ; and hence perhaps was taught to aspire to the throne.
                                 MALONE.

And,

And, Henry, hadft thou fway'd as kings fhould do,
Or as thy father, and his father did,
Giving no ground unto the houfe of York,
* They never then had fprung like fummer flies;
' I, and ten thoufand in this lucklefs realm,
Had left no mourning widows for our death,
And thou this day hadft kept thy chair in peace.
For what doth cherifh weeds, but gentle air ?
' And what makes robbers bold, but too much lenity ?
Bootlefs are plaints, and curelefs are my wounds;
' No way to fly, nor ftrength to hold out flight [2]:
The foe is mercilefs, and will not pity;
For, at their hands, I have deferv'd no pity.
' The air hath got into my deadly wounds,
And much effufe of blood doth make me faint :——
Come, York, and Richard, Warwick, and the reft;
' I ftabb'd your fathers' bofoms, fplit my breaft.   [He faints.

Alarum and retreat. *Enter* EDWARD, GEORGE, RICHARD,
MONTAGUE, WARWICK, *and foldiers.*

' *Edw.* Now breathe we, lords [3]; good fortune bids us
    paufe,
' And fmooth the frowns of war with peaceful looks.——
* Some troops purfue the bloody-minded queen;——
' That led calm Henry, though he were a king,
' As doth a fail, fill'd with a fretting guft,
' Command an argofy to ftem the waves.
' But think you, lords, that Clifford fled with them ?
    War. No, 'tis impoffible he fhould efcape :
For, though before his face I fpeak the words,

---

[2] *No way to fly, nor ftrength to hold out flight :*] i. e. No way to fly,
nor with ftrength fufficient left to fuftain myfelf in flight, if there were.
STEEVENS.
[3] *Now breathe we, lords;* &c.] This battle, in which the houfe of
York was victorious, was fought on a plain between Towton and Saxton,
on the 29th of March, (Palm Sunday) 1461. The royal army confifted,
according to Hall, of about forty thoufand men; and the young duke of
York's forces were 48,760. In this combat, which lafted fourteen
hours, and in the actions of the two following days, thirty-fix thoufand
feven hundred and feventy-fix perfons are faid to have been killed, the
greater part of whom were undoubtedly Lancaftrians. MALONE.
Inftead of this fpeech, the quartos have the following :
    Thus far our fortune, keep an upward courfe,
    And we are grac'd with wreaths of victory.
    Some troops purfue the bloody-minded queen,
    That now towards Berwick doth poft amain :——
    But think you that Clifford is fled away with them ? STEEVENS.

Your

Your brother Richard mark'd him for the grave :
‘ And, wherefoe'er he is, he's furely dead.

　　　　　　　　　　　　　　[Clifford *groans, and dies.*
Edw. Whofe foul [4] is that which takes her heavy leave ?
Rich. A deadly groan, like life and death's departing [5]
Edw. See who it is : and, now the battle's ended,
If friend, or foe, let him be gently us'd:
‘ *Rich.* Revoke that doom of mercy, for 'tis Clifford ;
‘ Who not contented that he lopp'd the branch
‘ In hewing Rutland when his leaves put forth [6],
‘ But fet his murdering knife unto the root
‘ From whence that tender fpray did fweetly fpring,
‘ I mean our princely father, duke of York.

War. From off the gates of York fetch down the head,
Your father's head, which Clifford placed there :
‘ Inftead whereof, let this fupply the room ;
Meafure for meafure muft be anfwered.

Edw. Bring forth that fatal fcritch-owl to our houfe,
‘ That nothing fung but death to us and ours :
‘ Now death fhall ftop his difmal threatening found,
‘ And his ill-boding tongue no more fhall fpeak.

　　　　　　　　　[*Attendants bring the body forward.*
War. I think his underftanding is bereft :—
Speak, Clifford, doft thou know who fpeaks to thee ?—
Dark cloudy death o'erfhades his beams of life,

---

4 Edw *Whofe foul,* &c.] I have diftinguifhed this and the two following fpeeches according to the authority of the quarto. The folio gave all
to Richard, except the laft line and half. STEEVENS.

　I have alfo followed the original regulation, becaufe it feems abfurd
that Richard fhould firft fay to his brother, or to one of the foldiers,
“ See who it is ;”—and then, himfelf declare that it is Clifford ; and
therefore I fuppofe the variation in the folio arofe, not from Shakfpeare,
but from fome negligence or inaccuracy of a compofitor or tranfcriber.
　　　　　　　　　　　　　　　　　　　　　MALONE.
5 — *like life and death's* departing.] Departing for *feparation.* MALONE.
“ Till death us *depart*” was the expreffion in the old *Marriage Service.* FARMER.
6 *In hewing Rutland when his leaves put forth.*] It is manifeft from
this and many other paffages, that the author of the old play, where the
correfponding line ftands thus—
　　“ Who killed our *tender* brother Rutland—”
imagined that Rutland was younger than George and Richard ; whereas
he was in fact older than them both, being the Duke of York's eldeft
fon ; in confequence of which he bore a title by courtefy : and a particular ftipulation was made in the compact entered into between Henry and
the duke of York, that Rutland, as well as his elder brother Edward
earl of March, fhould fwear to the due obfervance of the agreement.—
Shakfpeare has, we fee, fallen into the fame error ; as have Habington
in his nervous and elegant *Hiftory of Edward IV.* and feveral other hiftorians. MALONE.

　　　　　　　　　　　　　　　　　　　　　　　　And

And he nor fees, nor hears us what we fay.

    Rich. O, 'would he did! and fo, perhaps, he doth;
‘ 'Tis but his policy to counterfeit,
‘ Becaufe he would avoid fuch bitter taunts
‘ Which in the time of death he gave our father.

    Geo. If fo thou think'ft, vex him with eager words [8].

    Rich. Clifford, afk mercy, and obtain no grace.

    Edw. Clifford, repent in bootlefs penitence.

    War. Clifford, devife excufes for thy faults.

    Geo. While we devife fell tortures for thy faults.

    ‘ *Rich.* Thou didft love York, and I am fon to York.

    Edw. Thou pitied'ft Rutland, I will pity thee.

    Geo. Where's captain Margaret, to fence you now?

    War. They mock thee, Clifford! fwear as thou waft
        wont.

    ‘ *Rich.* What, not an oath? nay, then the world goes
        hard,
‘ When Clifford cannot fpare his friends an oath :—
I know by that, he's dead; And, by my foul,
‘ If this right hand would buy two hours' life,
That I in all defpight might rail at him,
‘ This hand fhould chop it off; and with the iffuing blood
Stifle the villain, whofe unftanched thirft
York and young Rutland could not fatisfy.

    War. Ay, but he's dead: Off with the traitor's head,
And rear it in the place your father's ftands.—
And now to London with triumphant march,
There to be crowned England's royal king
‘ From whence fhall Warwick cut the fea to France,
And afk the lady Bona for thy queen :
So fhalt thou finew both thefe lands together;
‘ And, having France thy friend, thou fhalt not dread
The fcatter'd foe, that hopes to rife again;
For though they cannot greatly fting to hurt,
Yet look to have them buz, to offend thine ears.
Firft, will I fee the coronation;
‘ And then to Britany I'll crofs the fea [9],
To effect this marriage, fo it pleafe my lord.

    Edw. Even as thou wilt, fweet Warwick, let it be:
‘ For on thy fhoulder do I build my feat;

---

    8 — eager *words.*] Sour words; words of afperity. JOHNSON.
    So, in *Hamlet :* “ It is a nipping and an *eager* air. STEEVENS.
    9 *And then to Britany I'll crofs the fea,*] Thus the folio. The quartos thus :
        And afterward I'll crofs the feas to France. STEEVENS.

                          * And

* And never will I undertake the thing,

* Wherein thy counfel and confent is wanting.—

‘ Richard, I will create thee duke of Glofter;—

‘ And George, of Clarence;—Warwick, as ourfelf,

‘ Shall do, and undo, as him pleafeth beft.

    Rich. Let me be duke of Clarence; George, of Glof-
ter;

For Glofter's dukedom is too ominous ¹.

    War. Tut, that's a foolifh obfervation;
Richard, be duke of Glofter: Now to London,
To fee thefe honours in poffeffion.   [*Exeunt.*

ACT III. SCENE I.

A Chace in the North of England.

Enter two Keepers ², *with crofs-bows in their hands.*

‘ 1. *Keep.* Under this thick-grown brake we'll fhroud ourfelves;

‘ For through this laund ³ anon the deer will come;

‘ And in this covert will we make our ftand,

‘ Culling the principal of all the deer.

* 2. *Keep.* I'll ftay above the hill, fo both may fhoot.

---

¹ *For Glofter's dukedom is too ominous*] The author of the original
play, in which this line is found, probably had here a paffage in Hall's
Chronicle in his thoughts: " It feemeth to many men that the name
and title of Gloucefter hath bene unfortunate and unluckie to diverfe,
whiche for their honor have bene erected by creation of princes to that
ftile and dignitie: as 'Hugh Spencer, Thomas of Woodftocke, fon to
kynge Edwarde the third, and this duke Humphrey, [who was killed at
Bury;] whiche three perfons by miferable death finifhed their daies;
and after them king Richard the iii. alfo duke of Gloucefter, in civil
warre was flaine and confounded; fo that this name of Gloucefter is
taken for an unhappie and unfortunate ftile, as the proverb fpeaketh
of Sejanes horfe, whofe ryder was ever unhorfed, and whofe poffeffer
was ever brought to miferie " MALONE.

² — *two Keepers*—] In the folio, inftead of *two keepers*, we have,
through negligence, the names of the perfons who reprefented thefe
characters; *Sinklo,* and *Humphrey* MALONE.

³ — *this* laund—] *Laund* means the fame as *lawn*; a plain extended between woods. So, in the play of *Orlando Furiofo*, 1591:

" And that they trace the fhady *lawnds*," &c. STEEVENS.

          * 1. *Keep.*

* 1. *Keep.* That cannot be ; the noise of thy cross-bow [4]
* Will scare the herd, and so my shoot is lost.
* Here stand we both, and aim we at the best :
* And, for the time shall not seem tedious,
● I'll tell thee what befell me on a day,
● In this self-place where now we mean to stand.

  ‘ 2. *Keep.* Here comes a man, let's stay till he be past.

   Enter King HENRY, *disguised, with a prayer-book.*

  K. Hen. From Scotland am I stol'n, even of pure love,
‘ To greet mine own land with my wishful sight [5].
‘ No, Harry, Harry, 'tis no land of thine ;
* Thy place is fill'd, thy scepter wrung from thee,
* Thy balm wash'd off, wherewith thou wast anointed [6] :
No bending knee will call thee Cæsar now,
‘ No humble suitors press to speak for right,
● No, not a man comes for redress of thee ;
For how can I help them, and not myself?

  ‘ 1 *Keep.* Ay, here's a deer whose skin's a keeper's fee :
‘ This is the *quondam* king ; let's seize upon him.

  * *K. Hen.* Let me embrace these four adversities [7] ;
● For wise men say, it is the wisest course.

  * 2. *Keep.* Why linger we ? let us lay hands upon him.

  * 1. *Keep.* Forbear a while ; we'll hear a little more.

  ‘ *K. Hen.* My queen, and son, are gone to France for
    aid ;
And, as I hear, the great commanding Warwick
‘ Is thither gone, to crave the French king's sister

---

  4 — *the noise of thy cross-bow*—] The poet appears not to have forgot the secrets of his former profession. So, in the *Merry Devil of Edmonton*, 1626: "—Did I not hear a *bow* go off, and the buck bray?" STEEVENS.

  5 *To greet mine own land with my wishful sight.*] So, the folio. The quartos perhaps better thus :
    And thus disguis'd to greet my native land. STEEVENS.

  6 *Thy balm wash'd off,*] This is an image very frequent in the works of Shakspeare. So again, in this scene :
    I was anointed king.
It is common in these plays to find the same images, whether jocular or serious, frequently recurring. JOHNSON.
  So, in *King Richard II:*
    " Not all the water in the rough rude sea
    " Can wash the balm from an anointed king."
  It is observable that this line is one of those additions to the original play, which are found in the folio, and not in the quarto. MALONE.

  7 — these *four* adversities ;] The old copy reads—*the sewre adversaries.* STEEVENS.
  Corrected by Mr. Pope. MALONE.

                                  ‘ To

' To wife for Edward : If this news be true,
' Poor queen, and fon, your labour is but loſt ;
' For Warwick is a fubtle orator,
' And Lewis a prince foon won with moving words.
' By this account, then, Margaret may win him ;
' For ſhe's a woman to be pity'd much :
* Her ſighs will make a battery in his breaſt ;
* Her tears will pierce into a marble heart :
* The tyger will be mild, while ſhe doth mourn ;
* And Nero will be tainted with remorſe [8],
* To hear, and fee, her plaints, her briniſh tears.
* Ay, but ſhe's come to beg ; Warwick, to give :
She, on his left ſide, craving aid for Henry ;
He, on his right, aſking a wife for Edward.
She weeps, and ſays—her Henry is depos'd ;
He ſmiles, and ſays—his Edward is inſtall'd ;
* That ſhe, poor wretch, for grief can ſpeak no more :
* Whiles Warwick tells his title, ſmooths the wrong,
* Inferreth arguments of mighty ſtrength [9] ;
* And, in concluſion, wins the king from her,
* With promiſe of his ſiſter, and what elſe,
* To ſtrengthen and ſupport king Edward's place.
* Margaret [1], thus 'twill be ; and thou, poor ſoul,
* Art then forſaken, as thou went'ſt forlorn.
   2. *Keep.* Say, what art thou, that talk'ſt of kings and
        queens ?
   ' *K. Hen.* More than I feem, and leſs than I was born to :
' A man at leaſt, for leſs I ſhould not be [2] ;
And men may talk of kings, and why not I ?
   ' 2. *Keep.* Ay, but thou talk'ſt as if thou wert a king.

---

[8] And *Nero will*—] Perhaps we might better read—*A Nero will*—
                                    STEEVENS.
  [9] *Inferreth arguments of mighty ſtrength* ;] In the former act was the
fame line :
    Inferring arguments of mightie force. JOHNSON.
  This repetition, like many others in theſe two plays, feems to have
ariſen from Shakſpeare's firſt copying his original as it lay before him,
and afterwards in ſubfequent paſſages (added to the old matter) introducing expreſſions which had ſtruck him in preceding ſcenes. In the
old play the line occurs but once. MALONE.
  [1] *O Margaret*, &c.] The piety of Henry ſcarce intereſts us more for
his misfortunes, than this his conſtant ſolicitude for the welfare of his
deceitful queen. STEEVENS.
  [2] *More than I feem*, &c.] Thus, in the old play :
    More than I feem, for leſs I ſhould not be ;
    A man at leaſt, and more I cannot be. MALONE.
                                   ' K. Hen.

' *K. Hen.* Why, ſo I am, in mind* ; and that's enough.

2. *Keep.* But, if thou be a king, where is thy crown?

K. Hen. My crown is in my heart, not on my head ;

* Not deck'd with diamonds, and Indian ſtones,

* Nor to be ſeen : ' my crown is call'd, content ;

' A crown it is, that ſeldom kings enjoy.

' 2. *Keep.* Well, if you be a king crown'd with content,
Your crown content, and you, muſt be contented

' To go along with us : for, as we think,

' You are the king, king Edward hath depos'd ;

' And we his ſubjeᵃs ³, ſworn in all allegiance,

' Will apprehend you as his enemy.

* *K. Hen.* But did you never ſwear, and break an oath?

* 2. *Keep.* No, never ſuch an oath ; nor will not now.

* *K. Hen.* Where did you dwell, when I was king of
  England?

* 2. *Keep.* Here in this country, where we now remain.

* *K. Hen.* I was anointed king at nine months old ;

* My father, and my grandfather, were kings ;

* And you were ſworn true ſubjeᵈts unto me :

* And, tell me then, have you not broke your oaths?

* 1. *Keep.* No ; for we were ſubjeᵈts, but while you were
  king.

* *K. Hen.* Why, am I dead? do I not breathe a man?

* Ah, ſimple men, you know not what you ſwear.

* Look, as I blow this feather from my face,

* And as the air blows it to me again *,

* Obeying with my wind when I do blow,

* And yielding to another when it blows,

* Commanded always by the greater guſt ;

* Such is the lightneſs of you common men.

* But do not break your oaths ; for, of that ſin

* My mild entreaty ſhall not make you guilty.

* Go where you will the king ſhall be commanded ;

* And be you kings ; command, and I'll obey.

---

* — *but thou talk'ſt as if thou wert a* king.

Why, ſo I am, in mind ;] There ſeems to be an alluſion to a line
in an old ſong quoted in *Every Man out of bis Humour* :

  " My *mind* to me a *kingdom* is." MALONE.

3 *And we his ſubjeᵈts,* &c.] So, the folio. The quarto thus ;

  And therefore we charge you in God's name, and the king's,

  To go along with us unto the officers. STEEVENS.

* *Look, as I blow this feather from my face,*

  And as the air blows it to me again, &c] So, in the *Winter's Tale,*

  " I am a feather for each wind that blows." MALONE.

           * 1 *Keep.*

* 1. *Keep.* We are true subjects to the king, king Edward.

* *K. Hen.* So would you be again to Henry,
* If he were seated as king Edward is.

1. *Keep.* We charge you, in God's name, and the king's,
To go with us unto the officers.

' *K. Hen.* In God's name, lead; your king's name be
        obey'd :

* And what God will, that let your king perform;
* And what he will, I humbly yield unto.   [*Exeunt.*

SCENE II.

London.   *A Room in the Palace.*

Enter King EDWARD, GLOSTER, CLARENCE, *and Lady*
GREY.

' *K. Edw.* Brother of Gloster, at saint Albans' field
' This lady's husband, sir John Grey⁴, was slain,
His lands then seiz'd on by the conqueror:
Her suit is now, to repossess those lands ;
·' Which we in justice cannot well deny,
· Because in quarrel of the house of York
' The worthy gentleman did lose his life⁵.

                                                Glo.

---

4 — *Sir John Grey,*] Vid. Hall, 3d Year of Edward IV. folio 5. It
was hitherto falsly printed *Richard.* POPE.

    Sir John Grey was slain at the second battle of St. Albans, fighting
on the side of King Henry. MALONE.

    5 *His lands then* seiz'd on by the conqueror:
    Her suit is now, to repossess those lands;
    Which we in justice cannot well deny,
    Because in quarrel of the house of York.
    The worthy gentleman did lose his life.] This is in every particular
a falsification of history. Sir John Grey, as has been already observed,
fell in the second battle of Saint Albans, which was fought on Shrove-
Tuesday, Feb. 17, 1460-1, fighting on the side of king *Henry.*; and so
far is it from being true that his lands were seized by the conqueror,
(Queen Margaret,) that they were in fact seized by the very person who
now speaks, after his great victory at Towton, on the 29th of March,
1461. The present scene is laid in 1464.

    Shakspeare in new moulding this play followed implicitly his author,
(for these five lines, with only a slight variation in the third, and fifth,
are found in the old play,) without giving himself the trouble to examine the history; but a few years afterwards, when he had occasion
to write his *Richard III.* and was not warped by a preceding misre-
presentation of another writer, he stated from the chronicles this
                                                                matter

Glo. Your highnefs fhall do well, to grant her fuit;
It were difhonour, to deny it her.

K. Edw. It were no lefs ; but yet I'll make a paufe.

'*Glo.* Yea ! is it fo [a] ? 　　　　　　　　[*Afide* to Clar.
I fee the lady hath a thing to grant,
Before the king will grant her humble fuit.

Clar. He knows the game; How true he keeps the wind ?
　　　　　　　　　　　　　　　　　　[*Afide.*

Glo. Silence !　　　　　　　　　　　　　[*Afide.*

K. Edw Widow, we will confider of your fuit [7];
' And come fome other time, to know our mind.

'*L Grey.* Right gracious lord, I cannot brook delay :
' May it pleafe your highnefs to refolve me now ;
' And what your pleafure is, fhall fatisfy me.

'*Glo.* [*Afide.*] Ay, widow ? then I'll warrant you all
　　　your lands,
An if what pleafes him, fhall pleafure you.
' Fight clofer, or, good faith, you'll catch a blow.

Clar. I fear her not, unlefs fhe chance to fall.　[*Afide.*

Glo. God forbid that I for he'll take vantages.　[*Afide.*

'*K. Edw.* How many children haft thou, widow? tell
　　me.

Clar. I think, he means to beg a child of her.　[*Afide.*

Glo. Nay, whip me then ; he'll rather give her two.
　　　　　　　　　　　　　　　　　　[*Afide.*

L. Grey. Three, my moft gracious lord.

Glo. You fhall have four, if you'll be rul'd by him.
　　　　　　　　　　　　　　　　　　[*Afide.*

'*K. Edw.* 'Twere pity, they fhould lofe their father's
　　land.

---

matter truly as it was; and this is one of the numerous circumftances
that prove inconteftably, in my apprehenfion, that he was not the ori-
ginal author of this and the preceding play.
　　In *King Richard III.* Act I. fc. iii. Richard addreffing himfelf to
Queen Elizabeth, (the lady Grey of the prefent fcene,) fays,
　　　　" In all which time you, and your hufband *Grey,*
　　　　" Were factious *for the houfe of Lancafter* ;—
　　　　" (And Rivers fo were you :)—was not your hufband
　　　　" In *Margaret's battle* at Saint Albans fl..in?"
He calls it *Margaret's battle,* becaufe fhe was there victorious.
　　　　　　　　　　　　　　　　　　　　　　　MALONE.

6 *Glo. Yea, is it fo?* &c:] So the folio. The quartos read with the
following variations:
　　Glo. I, Is the wind in that door ?
　　Clarence. I fee the lady, &c. STEEVENS.

7 *Widow, we will confider*—] This is a very lively and fpritely dialogue; the reciprocation is quicker than is common in Shakfpeare.
　　　　　　　　　　　　　　　　　　　　　　　JOHNSON.

　　　　　　　　　　　　　　　　　　　　　　　L. Grey.

L. Grey. Be pitiful, dread lord, and grant it them.

K. Edw. Lords, give us leave; I'll try this widow's
wit.

Glo. Ay, good leave have you; for you will have leave,
' Till you take leave, and leave you to the crutch:

[*Gloster and Clarence retire to the other side.*

* *K. Edw.* Now tell me, madam, do you love your children?

* *L. Grey.* Ay, full as dearly as I love myself.

K. Edw. And would you not do much to do them good?

* *L. Grey.* To do them good, I would sustain some harm.

* *K. Edw.* Then get your husband's lands, to do them
good

* *L. Grey.* Therefore I come unto your majesty.

K. Edw. I'll tell you how these lands are to be got.

* *L. Grey.* So shall you bind me to your highness' service.

* *K. Edw.* What service wilt thou do me, if I give them?

* *L. Grey.* What you command that rests in me to do.

* *K. Edw.* But you will take exceptions to my boon.

* *L. Grey.* No, gracious lord, except I cannot do it.

* *K Edw.* Ay, but thou canst do what I mean to ask.

* *L. Grey.* Why, then I will do what your grace commands.

* *Glo.* He plies her hard; and much rain wears the marble.   [*Aside.*

* *Clar.* As red as fire! nay, then her wax must melt.
                                                             [*Aside.*

L. Grey. Why stops my lord? shall I not hear my task?

K Edw. An easy task; 'tis but to love a king.

L. Grey. That's soon perform'd, because I am a subject.

K. Edw. Why then, thy husband's lands I freely give
thee.

L. Grey. I take my leave, with many thousand thanks.

Glo. The match is made; she seals it with a court'sy.

' *K. Edw.* But stay thee, 'tis the fruits of love I mean.

* *L. Grey.* The fruits of love I mean, my loving liege.

* *K. Edw.* Ay, but, I fear me, in another sense.
What love, think'st thou, I sue so much to get?

' *L. Grey.* My love till death, my humble thanks, my
prayers;

' That love, which virtue begs, and virtue grants [8]:

8 *My love till death,* &c.] The variation is here worth noting. In
the old play we here find—
      My humble service, such as subjects owe,
      And the laws command. MALONE.

K. Edw.

K. Edw. No, by my troth, I did not mean such love.

L. Grey. Why, then you mean not as I thought you did.

K. Edw. But now you partly may perceive my mind.

L. Grey. My mind will never grant what I perceive Your highness aims at, if I am aright.

K. Edw. To tell thee plain, I aim to lie with thee.

L Grey. To tell you plain, I had rather lie in prison.

K. Edw. Why, then thou shalt not have thy husband's lands.

L. Grey. Why, then mine honesty shall be my dower; For by that loss I will not purchase them.

' *K. Edw.* Therein thou wrong'st thy children mightily.

L. Grey. Herein your highness wrongs both them and me.
But, mighty lord, this merry inclination
' Accords not with the sadness of my suit;
Please you dismiss me, either with ay, or no.

K. Edw. Ay; if thou wilt say ay, to my request:
No; if thou dost say no, to my demand.

L. Grey. Then, no, my lord. My suit is at an end.

' *Glo.* The widow likes him not, she knits her brows.
[*Afide.*

Clar. He is the bluntest wooer in Christendom. [*Afide.*

' *K. Edw.* [*Afide.*] Her looks do argue her replete with modesty [9] ;

* Her words do shew her wit incomparable;

* All her perfections challenge sovereignty:
One way, or other, she is for a king;
And she shall be my love, or else my queen.—
Say, that king Edward take thee for his queen?

L. Grey. 'Tis better said than done, my gracious lord:
I am a subject fit to jest withal,
But far unfit to be a sovereign.

K. Edw. Sweet widow, by my state I swear to thee,
I speak no more than what my soul intends;
And that is, to enjoy thee for my love.

L. Grey. And that is more than I will yield unto:
' I know, I am too mean to be your queen;

---

9 *Her looks do argue her replete with modesty:*] So, the folio. The quartos read:
Her looks *are all* replete with *majesty*. STEEVENS.

And yet too good to be your concubine [1].

K. Edw. You cavil, widow; I did mean, my queen.

L. Grey. 'Twill grieve your grace, my fons fhould call
you—father.

K. Edw. No more, than when my daughters call thee
mother.

Thou art a widow [2], and thou haft fome children;
And, by God's mother, I, being but a bachelor,
Have other fome: why, 'tis a happy thing
To be the father unto many fons.

' Anfwer no more, for thou fhalt be my queen.

Glo. The ghoftly father now hath done his fhrift. [*Afide.*

Clar. When he was made a fhriver, 'twas for fhift.
[*Afide.*

K. Edw. Brothers, you mufe what chat we two have had.

* *Glo.* The widow likes it not, for fhe looks very fad.

K. Edw. You'd think it ftrange, if I fhould marry her.

Clar. To whom, my lord?

K. Edw. Why, Clarence, to myfelf.

Glo That would be ten day's wonder, at the leaft.

Clar. That's a day longer than a wonder lafts.

' *Glo.* By fo much is the wonder in extremes.

K. Edw. Well, jeft on, brothers; I can tell you both,
Her fuit is granted for her hufband's lands.

Enter a Nobleman.

Nob. My gracious lord, Henry your foe is taken,
' And brought your prifoner to your palace gate.

' *K. Edw.* See, that he be convey'd unto the Tower:—
' And go we, brothers to the man that took him,
' To queftion of his apprehenfion.—

[1] *I know, I am too mean to be your queen;*
And yet too good to be your concubine.] Thefe words, which are
found in the old play, (except that we there have *bad*, inftead of *mean*,)
were taken by the author of that piece from Hall's *Chronicle*:
"— whiche demaund fhe fo wyfely and with fo covert fpeeche aun-
fwered and repugned, affyrmyng that as fhe was for his honour far unable to be his fpoufe and bedfellowe, fo for her awne poor honeftie fhe
was too good to be either his concubine, or fovereigne lady; that where
he was a littell before heated with the dart of Cupido, he was nowe,"
&c. MALONE.

[2] *Thou art a widow, &c*] This is part of the king's reply to his
mother in Stowe's *Chronicles* " That fhe is a widow and hath already
children; by God's bleffed lady I am a batchelor, and have fome too,
and fo each of us hath a proofe that neither of us is like to be bar-
rain;" &c. STEEVENS.

' Widow,

' Widow, go you along ;—Lords, use her honourable.

    [*Exeunt* K. Edw. *Lady* Grey, Clar. *and Lord.*

   Glo. Ay, Edward will use women honourably.

'Would he were wasted, marrow, bones, and all,

' That from his loins no hopeful branch may spring,

' To cross me from the golden time I look for !

' And yet, between my soul's desire, and me,

* (The lustful Edward's title buried)

' Is Clarence, Henry, and his son young Edward,

' And all the unlook'd-for issue of their bodies,

' To take their rooms, ere I can place myself :

A cold premeditation for my purpose !

* Why, then I do but dream on sovereignty ;

* Like one that stands upon a promontory,

* And spies a far-off shore where he would tread,

* Wishing his foot were equal with his eye ;

* And chides the sea that sunders him from thence,

* Saying—he'll lade it dry to have his way :

* So do I wish the crown, being so far off ;

* And so I chide the means that keep me from it ;

* And so I say—I'll cut the causes off,

* Flattering me with impossibilities.—

* My eye's too quick, my heart o'erweens too much,

* Unless my hand and strength could equal them.

* Well, say there is no kingdom then for Richard ;

* What other pleasure can the world afford ?

' I'll make my heaven in a lady's lap [3],

' And deck my body in gay ornaments,

And witch sweet ladies with my words and looks.

' O miserable thought ! and more unlikely,

' Than to accomplish twenty thousand crowns !

Why, love forswore me in my mother's womb [4] :

' And, for I should not deal in her soft laws,

' She did corrupt frail nature with some bribe

' To shrink mine arm up like a wither'd shrub ;

' To make an envious mountain on my back,

Where sits deformity to mock my body ;

' To shape my legs of an unequal size ;

* To disproportion me in every part,

3 *I'll make my heaven,* &c.] Thus the folio. The quartos alter and transpose the two lines, as follow :

    I will go clad my body in gay ornaments,

    And lull myself within a lady's lap. Steevens.

4 — *love forswore me in my mother's womb* :] This line is found also in a play entitled *Wily Beguiled.* The earliest edition that I have seen of that piece, was printed in 1606 ; but it had been exhibited on the stage soon after the year 1590. Malone.

                                * Like

* Like to a chaos, or an unlick'd bear-whelp [5],
* That carries no impreſſion like the dam.
And am I then a man to bebelov'd?
' O, monſtrous fault, to harbour ſuch a thought!
* Then, ſince this earth affords no joy to me,
* But to command, to check, to o'erbear ſuch
* As are of better perſon than myſelf [6],
* I'll make my heaven—to dream upon the crown:
* And, whiles I live, to account this world but hell,
* Until my miſ-ſhap'd trunk that bears this head,
* Be round impaled [7] with a glorious crown.
* And yet I know not how to get the crown,
* For many lives ſtand between me and home:
* And I,—like one loſt in a thorny wood,
* That rents the thorns, and is rent with the thorns;
* Seeking a way, and ſtraying from the way;
* Not knowing how to find the open air,
* But toiling deſperately to find it out,—
* Torment myſelf to catch the Engliſh crown:
* And from the torment I will free myſelf,
* Or hew my way out with a bloody axe.
Why, I can ſmile, and murder while I ſmile;
' And cry, content, to that which grieves my heart;
* And wet my cheeks with artificial tears,

---

5 — *unlick'd bear whelp*,] It was an opinion which, in ſpite of its abſurdity, prevailed long, that the bear brings forth only ſhapeleſs lumps of animated fleſh, which ſhe licks into the form of bears. It is well known that the whelps of the bear are produced in the ſame ſtate, with thoſe of other creatures. JOHNSON.

6 — *to o'erb ar ſuch*
As are of better perſon than myſelf.] Richard ſpeaks here the language of nature. Whoever is ſtigmatized with deformity has a conſtant ſource of envy in his mind, and would counter balance by ſome other ſuperiority thoſe advantages which he feels himſelf to want. Bacon remarks that the deformed are commonly daring; and it is almoſt proverbially obſerved that they are ill-natured. The truth is, that the deformed, like all other men, are diſpleaſed with inferiority, and endeavour to gain ground by good or bad means, as they are virtuous or corrupt.
JOHNSON.

1   2   3   4   5   6   7   8

7 *Until my miſ-ſhap'd trunk that bears this head,*
Be round impaled, &c.] Impaled is encircled.—A tranſpoſition ſeems to be neceſſary:

1   2   8   5   7   3   4   6

Until my head, that this miſ-ſhap'd trunk bears.—
Otherwiſe the *trunk that bears the head* is to be encircled with the crown, and not the *head* itſelf. STEEVENS.

Sir T. Hanmer reads as Mr Steevens recommends. I believe our author is anſwerable for this inaccuracy. MALONE.

* And frame my face to all occasions.
* I'll drown more sailors than the mermaid shall.;
* I'll slay more gazers than the basilisk ;
* I'll play the orator as well as Nestor,
* Deceive more slily than Ulysses could,
* And, like a Sinon, take another Troy :
I can add colours to the cameleon ;
' Change shapes, with Proteus, for advantages,
' And set the murd'rous Machiavel to school 8.
Can I do this, and cannot get a crown ?
* Tut ! were it further off, I'll pluck it down.　　　[*Exit.*

SCENE III.

France. *A Room in a Palace.*

Flourish. Enter Lewis *the* French *King, and Lady* Bona, *attended ; the King takes his state. Then enter Queen* Margaret, *Prince* Edward *her son, and the Earl of* Oxford.

K. Lew. Fair queen of England 9, worthy Margaret,
　　　　　　　　　　　　　　　　　　[*Rising.*
* Sit down with us ; it still befits thy state,
* And birth, that thou should'st stand, while Lewis doth sit.

---

8 *And set the murd'rous Machiavel to school.*] As this is an anachronism, and the old quarto reads :
　　And set the aspiring Cataline *to school.*
I don't know why it should not be preferred. WARBURTON.

Cataline first occurred to the author of the old play, who was probably a scholar ; and *Machiavel,* who is mentioned in various books of our author's age, as the great exemplar of profound politicians, naturally was substituted by Shakspeare in his room.

In *K. Edward II.* Marlowe, who was probably the author of *The True Tragedie of Richarde duke of Yorke,* in like manner introduces Catiline :
　　" Spencer, the father of that wanton Spencer,
　　" That like the lawless *Cataline* of Rome,
　　" Revell'd in England's wealth, and treasury." MALONE.

9 *Fair queen of England,* &c.] Thus the folio. The quartos give the following :
　　Welcome, queen Margaret, to the court of France.
　　It fits not Lewis to sit, while thou dost stand.
　　Sit by my side ; and here I vow to thee,
　　Thou shalt have aid to re-possess thy right,
　　And beat proud Edward from his usurped seat,
　　And place king Henry in his former rule. STEEVENS.

* 2. Mar.

* *Q. Mar.* No, mighty king of France [1]; now Margaret
* Muſt ſtrike her ſail, and learn a while to ſerve,
* Where kings command. I was, I muſt confeſs,
* Great Albion's queen in former golden days :
* But now miſchance hath trod my title down,
* And with diſhonour laid me on the ground ;
* Where I muſt take like ſeat unto my fortune,
* And to my humble ſeat conform myſelf.

* *K. Lew.* Why, ſay, fair queen, whence ſprings this
deep deſpair ?

* *Q. Mar.* From ſuch a cauſe as fills mine eyes with tears,
* And ſtops my tongue, while heart is drown'd in cares.

* *K. Lew.* Where'er it be, be thou ſtill like thyſelf,
* And ſit thee by our ſide : yield not thy neck

[*Seats her by him.*

* To fortune's yoke, but let thy dauntleſs mind
* Still ride in triumph over all miſchance.
* Be plain, queen Margaret, and tell thy grief ;
* It ſhall be eas'd, if France can yield relief.

* *Q. Mar.* Thoſe gracious words revive my drooping
thoughts,
* And give my tongue ty'd ſorrows leave to ſpeak.
* Now, therefore, be it known to noble Lewis,—
* That Henry, ſole poſſeſſor of my love,
* Is, of a king, become a baniſh'd man,
* And forc'd to live in Scotland a forlorn ;
* While proud ambitious Edward, duke of York,
* Uſurps the regal title, and the ſeat
* Of England's true-anointed lawful king.
* This is the cauſe, that I, poor Margaret,—
* With this my ſon, prince Edward, Henry's heir,—
* Am come to claim thy juſt and lawful aid ;
' And, if thou fail us, all our hope is done :
* Scotland hath will to help, but cannot help ;
* Our people and our peers are both miſ-led,
* Our treaſure ſeiz'd ; our ſoldiers put to flight,
* And as thou ſee'ſt, ourſelves in heavy plight.

* *K. Lew.* Renowned queen, with patience calm the
ſtorm,
* While we bethink a means to break it off.

* *Q. Mar.* The more we ſtay, the ſtronger grows our
foe.

1 *No, mighty king of France* ; &c.] Inſtead of this ſpeech the quartos only ſupply the following :

Queen. I humbly thank your royal majeſty,
And pray the God of heaven to bleſs thy ſtate,
Great king of France, that thus regard'd our wrongs. STEEVENS.

* *K. Lew.*

* *K. Lew.* The more I ſtay, the more I'll ſuccour thee.
* *Q. Mar.* O, but impatience waiteth on true ſorrow :
* And ſea, where comes the breeder of my ſorrow.

Enter WARWICK *attended.*

' *K. Lew.* What's he, approacheth boldly to our preſence ?

Q. Mar. Our earl of Warwick, Edward's greateſt friend.

K. Lew. Welcome, brave Warwick ! What brings thee
  to France ?

     [*deſcending from his ſtate.*   *Queen* Mar. riſes.

* *Q. Mar.* Ay, now begins a ſecond ſtorm to riſe ;
* For this is he, that moves both wind and tide.

' *War.* From worthy Edward, king of Albion,
My lord and ſovereign, and thy vowed friend,
I come,—in kindneſs,' and unfeigned love,—
Firſt, to do greetings to thy royal perſon ;
And, then, to crave a league of amity ;
And, laſtly, to confirm that amity
With nuptial knot, if thou vouchſafe to grant
That virtuous lady Bona, thy fair ſiſter,
To England's king in lawful marriage.

' *Q. Mar.* If that go forward, Henry's hope is done [2].

War. And, gracious madam, [*to Bona.*] in our king's be-
  half,
' I am commanded, with your leave and favour,
Humbly to kiſs your hand, and with my tongue
To tell the paſſion of my ſovereign's heart :
Where fame, late entering at his heedful ears,
Hath plac'd thy beauty's image, and thy virtue.

Q. Mar. King Lewis,—and lady Bona,—hear me ſpeak,
' Before you anſwer Warwick   His demand [3]
* Springs not from Edward's well-meant honeſt love,
* But from deceit, bred by neceſſity :
* For how can tyrants ſafely govern home,

---

[2] — *Henry's hope is done.*] So, the folio. The quartos read—*all our*
hope is done. STEEVENS.
  We have had nearly the ſame line in Margaret's former ſpeech in the
preceding page. The line having made an impreſſion on Shakſpeare,
he introduced it in that ſpeech, which appears except in this inſtance)
to have been entirely his own production ; and afterwards inadvertently
ſuffered t with a ſlight variation to remain here, where only it is found
in the old play. MALONE.
  [3] *His demand,* &c.] Inſtead of the remainder of this ſpeech the old
play has the following lines :
        —— hear me ſpeak,
  Before you anſwer Warwick, or his words,
  For he it is hath done us all theſe wrongs. MALONE.

               * Unleſs

* Unlefs abroad they purchafe great alliance?
* To prove him tyrant, this reafon may fuffice,—
* That Henry liveth ftill : but were he dead,
* Yet here prince Edward ftands, king Henry's fon.
* Look, therefore, Lewis, that by this league and marriage
* Thou draw not on thy danger and difhonour :
* For though ufurpers fway the rule a while,
* Yet heavens are juft, and time fuppreffeth wrongs.

War. Injurious Margaret!

Prince. And why not queen?

War. Becaufe thy father Henry did ufurp ;
And thou no more art prince, than fhe is queen.

Oxf. Then Warwick difannuls great John of Gaunt,
Which did fubdue the greateft part of Spain;
And, after John of Gaunt, Henry the fourth,
' Whofe wifdom was a mirror to the wifeft ;
And, after that wife prince, Henry the fifth,
Who by his prowefs conquered all France :
From thefe our Henry lineally defcends.

War. Oxford, how haps it, in this fmooth difcourfe,
You told not, how Henry the fixth hath loft
All that which Henry the fifth had gotten ?
Methinks, thefe peers of France fhould fmile at that.
But for the reft,—You tell a pedigree
Of threefcore and two years ; a filly time
To make prefcription for a kingdom's worth.

' *Oxf.* Why, Warwick, can'ft thou fpeak againft thy liege,
' Whom thou obey'dft thirty and fix years [4],
And not bewray thy treafon with a blufh ?

War. Can Oxford, that did ever fence the right,
Now buckler falfhood with a pedigree ?
For fhame, leave Henry, and call Edward king.

' *Oxf.* Call him my king, by whofe injurious doom
' My elder brother, the lord Aubrey Vere,
Was done to death ? and more than fo, my father,
Even in the downfall of his mellow'd years,
' When nature brought him to the door of death [5] ?

---

4 — *thirty and fix years.*] So, the folio. The quartos, *thirty and eight* years. STEEVENS.

The number in the old play is right. The alteration, however, is of little confequence. MALONE.

5 *When nature brought him to the door of death ?*] Thus the folio.—
The quartos : When *age did call him* to the door of death. STEEVENS.

This paffage unavoidably brings before the mind that admirable image of *old age* in Sackville's *Induction :*

" His withered fift ftill *knocking at deathe's dore,*" &c. FARMER.

No, Warwick, no ; while life upholds this arm,
This arm upholds the houſe of Lancaſter.

War. And I the houſe of York.

K. Lew. Queen Margaret, prince Edward, and Oxford,
‘ Vouchſafe, at our requeſt, to ſtand aſide,
‘ While I uſe further conference with Warwick.

* *Q. Mar.* Heavens grant, that Warwick's words bewitch him not !

[*retiring with the* Prince *and* Oxf.

K. Lew. Now, Warwick, tell me, even upon thy con-
ſcience,
‘ Is Edward your true king ? for I were loth,
‘ To link with him that were not lawful choſen [6].

War. Thereon I pawn my credit and mine honour.

K. Lew. But is he gracious in the people's eye ?

War. The more, that Henry was unfortunate [7].

‘ *K. Lew.* Then further,—all diſſembling ſet aſide,
‘ Tell me for truth the meaſure of his love
‘ Unto our ſiſter Bona.

War. Such it ſeems,
As may beſeem a monarch like himſelf.
Myſelf have often heard him ſay, and ſwear,—
That this his love was an eternal plant [8] ;
Whereof the root was fix'd in virtue's ground,
The leaves and fruit maintain'd with beauty's ſun ;
Exempt from envy, but not from diſdain [9],

[6] — *that were not lawful choſen.*] Thus the folio. The quartos:
—*that is not lawful heir.* STEEVENS.

Here we have another inſtance of an impropriety into which Shakſpeare has fallen by ſometimes following and ſometimes deſerting his
original. After Lewis has aſked in the old play whether Henry was
lawful heir to the crown of England, and has been anſwered in the
affirmative ; he next inquires whether he is *gracious*, that is, a fav urite
with the people. Shakſpeare has preſerved this latter queſtion, though
he made a variation in the former; not adverting that after a man has
been *choſen* by the voices of the people to be their king, it is quite ſu-
perfluous to aſk whether he is popular or no.—Edward was in fact *choſen*
king, both by the parliament and by a large body of the people aſſem-
bled in St. John's fields. See Fabian, who wrote about fifty years after the time, p. 472, and Stowe, p 688, edit. 1605. MALONE.

[7] — *that Henry was unfortunate.*] He means, that Henry was unſuc-
ceſsful in war, having loſt his dominions in France, &c MALONE.

[8] —*was an eternal plant ;*] The folio reads—an *external* plant; but
as that word ſeems to afford no meaning, and as Shakſpeare has adopted
every other part of this ſpeech as he found it in the old play, without
alteration, I ſuppoſe *external* was a miſtake of the tranſcriber or printer, and have therefore followed the reading of the quarto. The poet,
ſays Dr. Warburton, alludes to the plants of para iſe. MALONE.

[9] *Exempt from envy, but not from diſdain,*] I believe *envy* is in this
place, as in many others, put for *malice* or *hatred.* His ſituation places
him above theſe, though it cannot ſecure him from female diſdain.
STEEVENS.

Unleſs

Unlefs the lady Bona quit his pain.

K. Lew. Now, fifter, let us hear your firm refolve.

Bona. Your grant, or your denial, fhall be mine :—
Yet I confefs, [*to* War.] that often ere this day,
When I have heard your king's defert recounted,
Mine ear hath tempted judgment to defire. .

* *K. Lew.* Then, Warwick, thus,—Our fifter fhall be
                    Edward's ;
* And now forthwith fhall articles be drawn
* Touching the jointure that the king muft make,
* Which with her dowry fhall be counterpois'd :—
Draw near, queen Margaret ; and be a witnefs,
That Bona fhall be wife to the Englifh king.

Prince. To Edward, but not to the Englifh king.

* *Q. Mar.* Deceitful Warwick ! it was thy device
* By this alliance to make void my fuit ;
* Before thy coming, Lewis was Henry's friend.

* *K. Lew.* And ftill is friend to him and Margaret :
* But if your title to the crown be weak,—
* As may appear by Edward's good fuccefs,—
* Then, 'tis but reafon, that I be releas'd
* From giving aid, which late I promifed.
* Yet fhall you have all kindnefs at my hand.
* That your eftate requires, and mine can yield.

War. Henry now lives in Scotland, at his eafe ;
Where having nothing, nothing he can lofe.
And as for you yourfelf, our *quondam* queen,—
You have a father able to maintain you [1] ;
And better 'twere, you troubled him than France,

* *Q. Mar.* Peace, impudent and fhamelefs Warwick ;
* Proud fetter-up and puller-down of kings * !
* I will not hence, till with my talk and tears,
* Both full of truth, I make king Lewis behold
* Thy fly conveyance [2], and thy lord's falfe love ;
* For both of you are birds of felf-fame feather.

[*A horn founded within.*

K. Lew. Warwick, this is fome poft to us, or thee.

Enter a Meffenger.

Mef. My lord ambaffador, thefe letters are for you ;

---

[1] *You have a father able,* &c.] This feems ironical. The poverty of
Margaret's father, is a very frequent topick of reproach. JOHNSON.

* *Proud fetter-up and puller down of kings !*] This line, with a flight
variation has occurred before. See p. 267, n. 2. The repetition has been
already accounted for, in p. 281, n. 9. and p. 292, n. 2. MALONE.

[2] *Thy fly conveyance,*] Conveyance is *juggling,* and thence is taken
for artifice and fraud. JOHNSON.

Sent

Sent from your brother, marquis. Montague.——,
These from our king unto your majesty.——
And, madam, these for you ; from whom, I know not.
　　　　　[To Margaret. *They all read their letters.*
　Oxf. I like it well, that our fair queen and mistress
Smiles at her news, while Warwick frowns at his.
　Prince. Nay, mark, how Lewis stamps as he were net-
　　tled :
* ' hope all's for the best.
　' *K. Lew.* Warwick, what are thy news ? and your's fair
　　queen?
　Q. Mar. Mine, such as fill my heart with unhop'd joys.
　War. Mine, full of sorrow and heart's discontent.
　K. Lew. What! has your king marry'd the lady Grey ?.
' And now, to sooth your forgery and his [5],
' Sends me a paper to persuade me patience ?
' Is this the alliance that he seeks with France ?
' Dare he presume to scorn us in this manner ?
　* *Q. Mar.* I told your majesty as much before :
This proveth Edward's love, and Warwick's honesty.
　War. King Lewis, I here protest,——in sight of heaven,
And by the hope I have of heavenly bliss,——
That I am clear from this misdeed of Edward's ;
No more my king, for he dishonours me ;
But most himself, if he could see his shame.——
Did I forget, that by the house of York
My father came untimely to his death ? *
Did I let pass the abuse done to my niece [6]?

---

5 — *to* sooth *your forgery and his,*] To soften it, it makes it more endurable : or perhaps, to sooth us, and to prevent our being exasperated by your forgery and his. MALONE.

　* *Did I forget, that by the house of York*
　My father came untimely to his death ?] Warwick's father came untimely to his death, being taken at the battle of Wakefield, and beheaded at Pomfret. But the author of the old play imagined he fell at the action at Ferry-bridge, and has in a former scene, to which this line refers, described his death as happening at that place. See p. 265, n. 8. Shakspeare very properly rejected that description of the death of the earl of Salisbury, of whose death no mention is made in his play, as it now stands; yet he has inadvertently retained this line which alludes to a preceding description that he had struck out; and this is another proof of his falling into inconsistencies, by sometimes following, and sometimes deserting, his original. MALONE.

　[6] *Did I let pass the abuse done to my niece ?*] Thus Holinshed, p. 668 : " King Edward did attempt a thing once in the earles house, which was much against the earles honestie, (whether he would have defloured his daughter or his niece, the certaintie was not for both their honors revealed) for surely such a thing was attempted by king Edward."
　　　　　　　　　　　　　　　　　　STEEVENS,
　　　　　　　　　　　　　　　　　　　　Did

Did I impale him with the regal crown ?
Did I put Henry from his native right ;
‘ And am I guerdon'd at the laſt with ſhame ?
* Shame on himſelf ! for my deſert is honour.
* And, to repair my honour loſt for him,
* I here renounce him, and return to Henry :
‘ My noble queen, let former grudges paſs,
And henceforth I am thy true ſervitor ;
I will revenge this wrong to lady Bona,
And replant Henry in his former ſtate.
   ‘ Q. Mar. Warwick, theſe words have turn'd my hate to
       love ;
‘ And I forgive and quite forget old faults,
‘ And joy that thou becom'ſt king Henry's friend.
   War. So much his friend, ay, his unfeigned friend,
That, if king Lewis vouchſafe to furniſh us
With ſome few bands of choſen ſoldiers,
I'll undertake to land them on our coaſt,
And force the tyrant from his ſeat by war.
'Tis not his new-made bride ſhall ſuccour him :
* And as for Clarence,—as my letters tell me,
* He's very likely now to fall from him ;
* For matching more for wanton luſt than honour,
* Or than for ſtrength and ſafety of our country.
   * Bona Dear brother, how ſhall Bona be reveng'd,
* But by thy help to this diſtreſſed queen ?
   * Q. Mar. Renowned prince, how ſhall poor Henry live,
* Unleſs thou reſcue him from foul deſpair ?
   * Bona. My quarrel, and this Engliſh queen's, are one.
   * War. And mine, fair lady Bona, joins with yours.
   * K. Lew. And mine, with hers, and thine, and Mar
       garet's.
Therefore, at laſt, I firmly am reſolv'd,
You ſhall have aid.
   * Q. Mar. Let me give humble thanks for all at once.
   K. Lew. Then England's meſſenger, return in poſt ;
And tell falſe Edward, thy ſuppoſed king,—
That Lewis of France is ſending over maſkers,
To revel it with him and his new bride :
* Thou feeſt what's paſt, go fear thy king withal [7].
   Bona. Tell him, in hope he'll prove a widower ſhortly,
I'll wear the willow garland for his ſake.
   Q. Mar. Tell him, My mourning weeds are laid aſide,
And I am ready to put armour on [8].

                                   War.

---

7 —go fear thy king—] That is fright thy king. JOHNSON.
8 —to put armour on.] It was once no unuſual thing for queen them-
                        O 5   ſelve.

War. Tell him from me, That he hath done me wrong ;
And therefore I'll uncrown him, ere't be long,
There's thy reward [9]; be gone.   *[Exit Mef.*

   K. Lew. But, Warwick ;
Thou, and Oxford, with five thousand men,
Shall cross the seas, and bid false Edward battle [1] :
* And, as occasion serves, this noble queen
* And prince shall follow with a fresh supply.
' Yet ere thou go, but answer me one doubt ;—
' What pledge have we of thy firm loyalty ?—
 War. This shall assure my constant loyalty ;—
That if our queen and this young prince agree,
I'll join mine eldest daughter [2], and my joy,
To him forthwith in holy wedlock bands.
  ' *Q. Mar.* Yes, I agree [3], and thank you for your mo-
    tion :—

selves to appear in armour at the head of their forces. The suit which
Elizabeth wore when she rode through the lines at Tilbury to encourage
the troops, on the approach of the armada, may be still seen in the
Tower. STEEVENS

  9 — *thy reward* ;] Here we are to suppose that, according to ancient
custom, Warwick makes a present to the herald or messenger, whom
the original copies call—a *Post*. STEEVENS.

  1 —*and* bid *false Edward battle* :] This phrase is common to many
of our ancient writers. So, in the *Misfortunes of Arthur,* a dramatick
performance, 1587:
     " ———— my flesh abhors
     " To bid the battle to my proper blood." STEEVENS.

  2 *I'll join mine* eldest *daughter*.] This is a departure from the truth
of history, for Edward prince of Wales (as Mr. Theobald has observed)
was married to Anne, the *second* daughter of the earl of Warwick. But
notwithstanding this, his reading [*youngest* daughter] has, I think,
been improperly adopted by the subsequent editors; for though in fact
the duke of Clarence married Isabella, the *eldest* daughter of Warwick,
in 1468, and Edward prince of Wales married Anne, his *second* daughter, in 1470; neither of his daughters was married at the time when
Warwick was in France negotiating a marriage between Lady Bona and
his king: so that there is no inconsistency in the present proposal. Supposing, however, that the original author of this play made a mistake,
and imagined that the *youngest* daughter of Warwick was married to
Clarence, I apprehend, he, and not his editor, ought to answer for it.
  This is one of the numerous circumstances which prove that Shakspeare was not the *original* author of this play; for though here, as in a
former passage, (p. 283, n. 5.) he has followed the old drama, when he
afterwards wrote his *K. Richard III.* and found it necessary to consult
the ancient historians, he represented Lady Anne, as she in fact was, the
widow of Edward, prince of Wales, and the *youngest* daughter of the
earl of Warwick. MALONE.

  3 *Yes, I agree,* &c.] Instead of this speech, the quarto has only the
following:
    With all my heart; I like this match full well.
    Love her, son Edward; she is fair and young;
    And give thy hand to Warwick, for his love. STEEVENS.

                             ' Son

' Son Edward, she is fair and virtuous,
' Therefore delay not, give thy hand to Warwick;
' And, with thy hand, thy faith irrevocable,
' That only Warwick's daughter shall be thine.
　* *Prince.* Yes, I accept her, for she well deserves it;
* And here, to pledge my vow, I give my hand.
　　　　　　　　　[*He gives his hand to* Warwick

　' *K. Lew.* Why stay we now? These soldiers shall be
　　　levy'd,
' And thou, lord Bourbon [4], our high admiral,
' Shall waft them over with our royal fleet.——
' I long, till Edward fall by war's mischance,
' For mocking marriage with a dame of France.
　　　　　　　　　　Exeunt all but Warwick.

War. I came from Edward as ambassador,
But I return his sworn and mortal foe:
Matter of marriage was the charge he gave me,
But dreadful war shall answer his demand.
Had he none else to make a stale, but me?
Then none but I shall turn his jest to sorrow.
I was the chief that rais'd him to the crown,
And I'll be chief to bring him down again:
Not that I pity Henry's misery,
But seek revenge on Edward's mockery.　　　[*Exit.*

---

4 *And thou, lord Bourbon,* &c.] Instead of this and the three following
lines, we have these in the old play:
　　And you, lord Bourbon, our high admiral,
　　Shall waft them *safely to the English coasts*;
　　And chase proud Edward *from his slumb'ring trance,*
　　For mocking marriage with the name of France. MALONE.

A C T

ACT IV. SCENE I.

London.   *A Room in the Palace.*

Enter GLOSTER, CLARENCE, SOMERSET, MONTAGUE,
and Others.

' *Glo.* Now tell me, brother Clarence ⁵, what think you
' Of this new marriage with the lady Grey ? '
* Hath not our brother made a worthy choice ?
  * *Clar.* Alas, you know, 'tis far from hence to France ;
* How could he ftay till Warwick made return ?
  * *Som.* My lords, forbear this talk ; here comes the king.

Flourifh. Enter King Edward, *attended ;* Lady Grey, *as
queen ;* PEMBROKE, STAFFORD, HASTINGS, *and Others*⁶.

  * *Glo.* And his well-chofen bride.
  * *Clar.* I mind to tell him plainly what I think.
  ' *K. Edw.* Now, brother of Clarence, how like you our
        choice,
' That you ftand penfive, as half malecontent ?
  ' *Clar.* As well as Lewis of France, or the earl of War-
        wick ;
' Which are fo weak of courage, and in judgment,
ẻ That they'll take no offence at our abufe.
  ' *K. Edw.* Suppofe, they take offence without a caufe,
' They are but Lewis and Warwick ; I am Edward,
' Your king and Warwick's, and muft have my will.

⁵ *Now tell me, brother Clarence,*] In the old play the king enters here
along with his brothers, not after them, and opens the fcene thus :
        Edw Brothers of Clarence and of Gloce{ter,
    What think you of our marriage with the lady Grey ?
        Glo. My lord, we think as Warwick and Lewis,
    That are fo flack in judgment that they'll take
    No offence at this fudden marriage.
        Edw. Suppofe they do, they are but Lewis and Warwick ;
    And I am your king and Warwick's ; and will be
    Obey'd.
        Glo And fhall, becaufe you are our king ;
    But yet fuch fudden marriages feldom proveth well.
        Edw. Yes, brother Richard, are you againft us too ?
                                                    MALONE.
⁶ The ftage direction in the folio, [*Four ftand on one fide, and four
on the other.*] is fufficient proof that the play, as exhibited there, was
printed from a ftage copy. I fuppofe thefe *eight* important perfonages
are attendants. STEEVENS.
                                                    ' *Glo.*

' *Glo.* And fhall have your will, becaufe our king:

' Yet hafty marriage feldom proveth well.

K. Edw. Yea, brother Richard, are you offended too?

' *Glo.* Not I:

' No; God forbid, that I fhould wifh them fever'd

' Whom God hath join'd together: ay, and 'twere pity,

To funder them that yoke fo well together.

' *K. Edw.* Setting your fcorns, and your miflike, afide,

' Tell me fome reafon, why the lady Grey

' Should not become my wife, and England's queen:——

' And you too, Somerfet [7], and Montague,

' Speak freely what you think.

' *Clar.* Then this is my opinion [8],—that king Lewis

' Becomes your enemy, for mocking him

' About the marriage of the lady Bona.

' *Glo.* And Warwick, doing what you gave in charge,

' Is now difhonoured by this new marriage.

' *K. Edw.* What, if both Lewis and Warwick be ap-
            peas'd,

' By fuch invention as I can devife?

Mont. Yet to have join'd with France in fuch alliance,

Would more have ftrengthen'd this our commonwealth

'Gainft foreign ftorms, than any home-bred marriage.

' *Haft.* Why, knows not Montague, that of itfelf

' England is fafe, if true within itfelf [9]?

* *Mont.* But the fafer, when it is back'd with France.

* *Haft.* 'Tis better ufing France, than trufting France:

* Let us be back'd with God, and with the feas [1],

* Which he hath given for fence impregnable,

---

7 *And you too,* Somerfet, &c.] In the old play Somerfet does not appear in this fcene. MALONE.

8 Clar. *Then this is my opinion,*—&c.] Inftead of this and the following fpeech, the quartos read thus:

    Clar. My lord, then this is my opinion;

    That Warwick, being difhonour'd in hisembaffage,

    Doth feek revenge, to quit hisinjuries.

    Glo. And Lewis in regard of his fifter's wrongs,

    Doth join with Warwick to fupplant your ftate. STEEVENS.

9 *Why, knows not Montague, that of itfelf*

    England is fafe, if true within itfelf?] In the old play thefe lines
ftand thus:

    Let England be true within itfelf,

    We need not France nor any alliance with them.

It is obfervable that the firft of thefe lines occurs in the old play of
King John, 1591, from which our author borrowed it, and inferted it
with a flight change in his own play with the fame title. MALONE.

1 — *with the feas,*] This has been the advice of every man who in
any age underftood and favoured the intereft of England. JOHNSON.

* And

* And with their helps only defend ourfelves ;
* In them, and in ourfelves, our fafety lies. ,

   Clar. For this one fpeech, lord Haftings well deferves
To have the heir of the lord Hungerford.

   ‘ *K. Edw.* Ay, what of that ? it was my will, and grant ;
* And, for this once, my will fhall ftand for law.

   ‘ *Glo.* And yet, methinks [2], your grace hath not done
      well,
‘ To give the heir and daughter of lord Scales
‘ Unto the brother of your loving bride ;
‘ She better would have fitted me, or Clarence :
‘ But in your bride you bury brotherhood.

   ‘ *Clar.* Or elfe you would not have beftow’d the heir [3]
‘ Of the lord Bonville on your new wife’s fon,
‘ And leave your brothers to go fpeed elfewhere.

   K. Edw. Alas, poor Clarence ! is it for a wife,
‘ That thou art malecontent ? I will provide thee.

   ‘ *Clar.* In choofing for yourfelf, you fhew’d your judg-
      ment :
‘ Which being fhallow, you fhall give me leave
‘ To play the broker in mine own behalf ;
‘ And, to that end, I fhortly mind to leave you.

   ‘ *K. Edw.* Leave me, or tarry, Edward will be king,
‘ And not be ty’d unto his brother’s will.

   ‘ *Q. Eliz.* My lords, before it pleas’d his majefty
‘ To raife my ftate to title of a queen,
‘ Do me but right, and you muft all confefs
‘ That I was not ignoble of defcent *,
* And meaner than myfelf have had like fortune.
* But as this title honours me and mine,
* So your diflikes, to whom I would be pleafing,

---

   2 *And yet, methinks,* &c.] The quartos vary from the folio, as follows :
      Clar. Ay, and for fuch a thing too, the lord Scales
      Did well deferve at your hands, to have the
      Daughter of the lord Bonfield ; and left your
      Brothers to go feek elfewhere ; but in your madnefs
      You bury brotherhood. STEEVENS.
   3 — *you would not have beftow’d the heir*—] It muft be remembered,
that till the Reftoration, the heireffes of great eftates were in the ward-
fhip of the king, who in their minority gave them up to plunder, and
afterwards matched them to his favourites. I know not when liberty
gained more than by the abolition of the court of wards. JOHNSON.
   * — *I was not ignoble of defcent,*] Her father was Sir Richard Widville, knight, afterwards earl of Rivers ; her mother, Jaqueline,
Dutchefs dowager of Bedford, who was daughter to Peter of Luxem-
burgh, earl of Saint Paul, and widow of John duke of Bedford, brother
to king Henry V. MALONE.

                                * Do

* Do cloud my joys with danger and with forrow.

‘ *K. Edw.* My love, forbear to fawn upon their frowns [4]:
‘ What danger, or what forrow can befall thee,
‘ So long as Edward is thy conftant friend,
‘ And their true fovereign, whom they muft obey?
‘ Nay, whom they fhall obey, and love thee too,
‘ Unlefs they feek for hatred at my hands :
‘ Which if they do, yet will I keep thee fafe,
‘ And they fhall feel the vengeance of my wrath.

* *Glo.* I hear, yet fay not much, but think the more.

                                   [*Afide.*

Enter a Meffenger.

‘ *K. Edw.* Now, meffenger, what letters, or what news,
From France?

‘ *Mef.* My fovereign liege, no letters ; and few words,
‘ But fuch as I, without your fpecial pardon,
Dare not relate.

‘ *K. Edw.* Go to, we pardon thee : therefore, in brief,
‘ Tell me their words as near as thou canft guefs them.
‘ What anfwer makes king Lewis to our letters ?

Mef. At my depart, thefe were his very words ;
Go tell falfe Edward, thy fuppofed king,—
That Lewis of France is fending over mafkers,
To revel it with him and his new bride.

K. Edw. Is Lewis fo brave ? belike, he thinks me Henry.
‘ But what faid lady Bona to my marriage ?

Mef. Thefe were her words, utter’d with mild difdain :
Tell him, in hope he’ll prove a widower fhortly,
I’ll wear the willow garland for his fake.

‘ *K. Edw.* I blame not her, fhe could fay little lefs ;
‘ She had the wrong. But what faid Henry’s queen ?
‘ For I have heard, that fhe was there in place [5].

Mef. *Tell him,* quoth fhe, *my mourning weeds are done* [6],

---

4 *My love, forbear,* &c.] Inftead of this and the following fpeech,
the old play has only thefe lines :

    Edw Forbear, my love, to fawn upon their frowns,
    For thee they muft obey, nay, fhall obey,
    And if they look for favour at my hands.
    Ment My lord, here is the meffenger return’d from Fraunce.
                            MALONE.

5 —*fhe was there* in place] This expreffion, fignifying, fhe was
there *prefent,* occurs frequently in old Englifh writers. MALONE.

6 —*are done,* i. e. are confumed, thrown off. The word is often
ufed in this fenfe by the writers of our author’s age. So, in his *Rape of
Lucrece :*

    “ And if poffefs’d, as foon decay’d and *done*
    “ As is the morning’s filver-melting dew.” MALONE.

                                       And

And I am ready to put armour on.

' *K. Edw.* Belike, she minds to play the Amazon.
But what said Warwick to these injuries?

' *Mes.* He, more incens'd against your majesty
' Than all the rest, discharg'd me with these words;
Tell him from me, that he hath done me wrong,
And therefore I'll uncrown him, ere't be long.

' *K. Edw.* Ha! durst the traitor breathe out so proud
      words?

' Well, I will arm me, being thus forewarn'd:
' They shall have wars, and pay for their presumption.
' But say, is Warwick friends with Margaret?

' *Mes.* Ay, gracious sovereign; they are so link'd in
      friendship,

' That young prince Edward marries Warwick's daughter.
  Clar. Belike, the elder; Clarence will have the younger[7].

' Now, brother king, farewel, and sit you fast,
' For I will hence to Warwick's other daughter;
' That, though I want a kingdom, yet in marriage
' I may not prove inferior to yourself —
You, that love me and Warwick follow me[8].

      [*Exit* CLARENCE, *and* SOMERSET *follows.*

7 *Belike the elder, Clarence will have the younger.*] Clarence having in fact married Isabella, the *elder* daughter of Warwick, Mr.
Theobald made *elder* and *younger* change places in this line; in which
he has been followed, I think, improperly, by the subsequent editors:
The author of the old play, where this line is found, might from ignorance or intentionally have deviated from history, in his account of the
person whom Clarence married. See a former note, p. 298, n. 2.
                               MALONE.

8 *You, that love me and Warwick, follow me*] That Clarence should
make this speech in the king's hearing is very improbable, yet I do not
see how it can be palliated. The king never goes out, nor can Clarence be talking to a company apart, for he answers immediately to that
which the post says to the king. JOHNSON.

You, that love me, and Warwick, follow me.] When the earl of
Essex attempted to raise a rebellion in the city, with a design, as was
supposed, to storm the queen's palace, he ran about the streets with
his sword drawn, crying out, " They that love me, follow me "
                               STEEVENS.

Clarence certainly speaks in the hearing of the king, who immediately after his brother has retired, exclaims, that he is gone to join
with Warwick.

  This line is in the old quarto play. One nearly resembling it is like-
wise found in *the Battle of Alcazar*, 1594:
         " Myself will lead the way,
     " And make a passage with my conquering sword,
     " Knee-deep in blood of these accursed Moors;
     " *And they that love my honour, follow me.*"
So also, in our author's *King Richard III:*
     " The rest that love me, rise, and follow me." MALONE.

                                * *Glo.*

* *Glo.* Not I [9]

* My thoughts aim at a further matter; I

* Stay not for the love of Edward, but the crown.   [*Aside.*

K. Edw. Clarence and Somerset both gone to Warwick!

* Yet I am arm'd against the worst can happen;

* And haste is needful in this desperate case.—

' Pembroke, and Stafford, you in our behalf [2]

' Go levy men, and make prepare for war;

' They are already, or quickly will be landed:

' Myself in person will straight follow you.

                    [*Exeunt* Pembroke *and* Stafford.

' But, ere I go, Hastings,—and Montague,—

' Resolve my doubt.   You twain, of all the rest,

' Are near to Warwick, by blood, and by alliance:

' Tell me, if you love Warwick more than me?

' If it be so, then both depart to him;

' I rather wish you foes, than hollow friends:

' But if you mind to hold your true obedience,

' Give me assurance with some friendly vow,

' That I may never have you in suspect.

Mon. So God help Montague, as he proves true!

Hast. And Hastings, as he favours Edward's cause!

' *K. Edw.* Now brother Richard, will you stand by us?

Glo. Ay, in despight of all that shall withstand you.

' *K. Edw.* Why so; then am I sure of victory.

' Now therefore let us hence; and lose no hour,

' Till we meet Warwick with his foreign power.   [*Exeunt.*

9 *Glo. Not I:*] After Clarence goes out, we have in the old play the following dialogue; part of which Shakspeare rejected, and transposed the rest:

> *Edw.* Clarence and Somerset fled to Warwick!
> What say you, brother Richard, will you stand to us?
>   *Glo.* Ay, my lord, in despight of all that shall withstand you;
> For why hath nature made me halt downright,
> But that I should be valiant and stand to it?
> For if I would, I cannot run away. MALONE.

1 *Pembroke, and Stafford,* &c] The quarto give the passage thus:

> Pembroke, go raise an army presently;
> Pitch up my tent; for in the field this night
> I mean to rest; and, on the morrow morn,
> I'll march to meet proud Warwick, ere he land
> Those straggling troops which he hath got in France.
> But ere I go, Montague and Hastings, you
> Of all the rest are nearest ally'd in blood
> To Warwick; therefore tell me if you favour
> Him more than me, or not; speak truly, for
> I had rather have you open enemies,
> Than hollow friends. STEEVENS.

SCENE

SCENE II.

A Plain in Warwickſhire.

Enter WARWICK *and* OXFORD, *with* French *and other* forces.

War. Truſt me, my lord, all hitherto goes well ;
The common people by numbers ſwarm to us.

Enter CLARENCE *and* SOMERSET.

But, ſee, where Somerſet and Clarence come ;
Speak ſuddenly, my lords, are we all friends ?
  Clar. Fear not that, my lord.
  War. Then, gentle Clarence, welcome unto Warwick ;
And welcome, Somerſet :—I hold it cowardice,
To reſt miſtruſtful where a noble heart
Hath pawn'd an open hand in ſign of love ;
Elſe might I think, that Clarence, Edward's brother,
Were but a feigned friend to our proceedings :
But welcome, ſweet Clarence ; my daughter ſhall be thine.
And now what reſts, but, in night's coverture,
Thy brother being careleſly encamp'd,
His ſoldiers lurking in the towns about [2],
And but attended by a ſimple guard,
We may ſurprize and take him at our pleaſure ?
Our ſcouts have found the adventure very eaſy [3] :
* That as Ulyſſes, and ſtout Diomede,
* With ſleight and manhood ſtole to Rheſus' tents,
* And brought from thence the Thracian fatal ſteeds ;
* So we, well cover'd with the night's black mantle,
* At unawares may beat down Edward's guard,
* And ſeize himſelf ; I ſay not—ſlaughter him,
* For I intend but only to ſurprize him —
' You, that will follow me to this attempt,

---

2 — towns *about*,] Old Copies—*town*. Corrected by Dr. Thirlby.
See the next ſcene :
  " ——— but why commands the king,
  " That his chief followers lodge in *towns* about him ?"
                                      MALONE.
3 — *very eaſy* :] Here the quartos conclude this ſpeech, adding only
the following lines :
  Then cry king Henry with reſolved minds,
  And break we preſently into his tent. STEEVENS.
                                        ' Applaud

' Applaud the name of Henry, with your leader.
                                [*They all cry* Henry!
Why, then, let's on our way in filent fort:
For Warwick and his friends, God and faint George⁴!
                                        [*Exeunt.*

SCENE III.

Edward's *Camp, near* Warwick.

Enter certain Watchmen, *to guard the king's tent.*

* 1. *Watch.* Come on, my mafters, each man take his
    fland;
* The king, by this, is fet him down to fleep.
* 2 *Watch.* What, will he not to bed?
* 1. *Watch.* Why, no: for he hath made a folemn vow,
* Never to lie and take his natural reft,
* 'Till Warwick, or himfelf, be quite fuppreft.
* 2. *Watch.* To-morrow then, belike, fhall be the day,
* If Warwick be fo near as men report.
* 3. *Watch.* But fay, I pray, what nobleman is that,
* That with the king here refteth in his tent?
* 1. *Watch.* 'Tis the lord Haftings, the king's chiefeft
    friend.
* 3. *Watch* O, is it fo? But why commands the king,
* That his chief followers lodge in towns about him,
* While he himfelf keeps in the cold field?
* 2. *Watch.* 'Tis the more honour, becaufe more dange-
    rous
* 3. *Watch.* Ay; but give me worfhip, and quietnefs,
* I like it better than a dangerous honour.
* If Warwick knew in what cftate he ftands,
* 'Tis to be doubted, he would waken him.
* 1. *Watch.* Unlefs our halberds did fhut up his paffage.
* 2. *Watch.* Ay; wherefore elfe guard we his royal tent.
* But to defend his perfon from night-foes?

4 — *and faint George!*] After the two concluding lines of this fcene,
which in the old are given not to Warwick but to Clarence, we there
find the following fpeeches, which Shakfpeare has introduced in a fubfequent place:
        War. This is his tent; and fee where his guard doth ftand.
    Courage, my foldiers; now or never.
    But follow me now, and Edward fhall be ours.
    All. A Warwick, a Warwick!   MALONE.

                                        Enter

Enter WARWICK, CLARENCE, OXFORD, SOMERSET,
and forces.

‘ *War.* This is his tent; and see, where stand his guard.
‘ Courage, my masters: honour now, or never!
‘ But follow me, and Edward shall be ours.
   1. *Watch.* Who goes there?
  * 2. *Watch.* Stay, or thou diest.
    [Warwick, *and the rest, cry all—*Warwick! War-
    wick! *and set upon the guard; who fly, crying—*
    Arm! Arm! Warwick, *and the rest, following*
    them.

The drum beating, and trumpets sounding, Re-enter WARWICK,
and the rest, bringing the king out in a gown, sitting in a
chair: GLOSTER *and* HASTINGS *fly.*

  ‘ *Som* What are they that fly there?
  ‘ *War.* Richard, and Hastings: let them go, here’s the
      duke.
  K. Edw. The duke! why, Warwick, when, we parted
      last[5],
Thou call’dst me King?
  War. Ay, but the case is alter’d:
‘ When you disgrac’d me in my embassade,
‘ Then I degraded you from being king,
And come now to create you duke of York.
Alas! how should you govern any kingdom,
That know not how to use ambassadors;
Nor how to be contented with one wife;
Nor how to use your brothers brotherly;
* Nor how to study for the people’s welfare;
Nor how to shroud yourself from enemies?
   * *K. Edw.* Yea, brother[6] of Clarence, art thou here
      too?
* Nay, then I see, that Edward needs must down.—
‘ Yet, Warwick, in despight of all mischance,
‘ Of thee thyself, and all thy complices,
‘ Edward will always bear himself as king:

5 — *when we parted* last,] The word *last*, which is found in the old
play, was inadvertently omitted in the folio. MALONE.
  6 *Yea, brother,* &c] In the old play this speech consists of only these
two lines:
    Well, Warwick, let fortune do her worst,
    Edward in mind will bear himself a king.
Henry has made the same declaration in a former scene. MALONE.
                  * Though

* Though fortune's malice overthrow my ftate,
* My mind exceeds the compafs of her wheel.
  War. Then, for his mind, be Edward England's king:

[*Takes off his crown.*

But Henry now fhall wear the Englifh crown,
* And be true king indeed; thou but the fhadow.—
' My lord of Somerfet, at my requeft,
' See that forthwith duke Edward be convey'd
' Unto my brother, archbifhop of York.
' When I have fought with Pembroke and his fellows,
' I'll follow you, and tell what anfwer
' Lewis, and the lady Bona, fend to him:—
Now, for a while, farewel, good duke of York.
  * *K. Edw.* What fates impofe, that men muft needs abide;
* It boots not to refift both wind and tide.

[*Exit King* Edward, *led out;* Somerfet *with him.*

* *Oxf.* What now remains?, my lords, for us to do,
* But march to London with our foldiers?
  War. Ay, that's the firft thing that we have to do;
' To free king Henry from imprifonment,
And fee him feated in the regal throne.

[*Exeunt.*

SCENE IV.

London. *A Room in the Palace.*

Enter *Queen* ELIZABETH *and* RIVERS [8].

' *Riv.* Madam, what makes you in this fudden change?
' *Q. Eliz.* Why, brother Rivers, are you yet to learn,

' What

---

7 *What new remains,* &c.] Inftead of this and the following fpeech, the quartos have:

Clar. What follows now? all hitherto goes well;
But we muft difpatch fome letters into France,
To tell the queen of our happy fortune;
And bid her come with fpeed to join with us.
  War. Ay, that's the firft thing that we have to do,
And free king Henry from imprifonment,
And fee him feated on the regal throne.
Come, let's away; and having paft thefe cares,
  I'll poft to York, and fee how Edward fares. STEEVENS.

8 *Enter Rivers,* &c.] Throughout this fcene the quartos vary in almoft every fpeech from the folio. The variations however are hardly fuch as to deferve notice. STEEVENS.

They are, however, fo marked, as to prove decifively, I think, that either Shakfpeare wrote two diftinct pieces on this fubject at different periods, or that the play as exhibited in the folio was his, and that in

quarto

What late misfortune is befall'n king Edward?

Riv. What, loſs of ſome pitch'd battle againſt Warwick?

' *Q. Eliz.* No, but the loſs of his own royal perſon.

' *Riv.* Then is my ſovereign ſlain?

' *Q. Eliz.* Ay, almoſt ſlain, for he is taken priſoner;

' Either betray'd by falſhood of his guard,

' Or by his foe ſurpriz'd at unawares :

' And, as I further have to underſtand,

' Is new committed to the biſhop of York,

' Fell Warwick's brother, and by that our foe.

' *Riv.* Theſe news, I muſt confeſs, are full of grief:

' Yet, gracious madam, bear it as you may;

' Warwick may loſe, that now hath won the day.

* *Q. Eliz.* Till then, fair hope muſt hinder life's decay.

* And I the rather wean me from deſpair,

* For love of Edward's offspring in my womb:

* This is it that makes me bridle paſſion,

* And bear with mildneſs my misfortune's croſs;

* Ay, ay, for this I draw in many a tear,

* And ſtop the riſing of blood-ſucking ſighs,

* Leſt with my ſighs or tears I blaſt or drown

' King Edward's fruit, true heir to the Engliſh crown.

* *Riv.* But, madam, where is Warwick then become?

' *Q. Eliz.* I am informed, that he comes towards London,

* To ſee the crown once more on Henry's head:

* Gueſs thou the reſt; king Edward's friends muſt down.

' But, to prevent the tyrant's violence,

' (For truſt not him that hath once broken faith,)

' I'll hence forthwith unto the ſanctuary,

' To ſave at leaſt the heir of Edward's right;

' There ſhall I reſt ſecure from force, and fraud.

' Come therefore, let us fly, while we may fly;

' If Warwick take us, we are ſure to die. [*Exeunt.*

quarto the production of a preceding writer. Let the ſecond ſpeech of
Rivers be read with this view :

    What loſſe? of ſome pitcht battaile againſt Warwicke?

    Tuſh, feare not, faire queene, caſt theſe cares aſide.

    King Edward's noble mind his honour doth diſplay,

    And Warwick may loſe, though then he got the day.

See alſo the ſpeech of Clarence quoted in the laſt note. MALONE.

SCENE -

SCENE V[9].

A Park near Middleham *Caſtle in* Yorkſhire.

Enter GLOSTER, HASTINGS, *Sir* William Stanley, *and Others.*

' *Glo.* Now, my lord Haſtings [1], and ſir William Stanley,

' Leave off to wonder why I drew you hither,
' Into the chiefeſt thicket of the park.
' Thus ſtands the caſe: You know, our king, my brother,
' Is priſoner to the biſhop here, at whoſe hands
' He hath good uſage and great liberty;
' And often, but attended with weak guard,
' Comes hunting this way to diſport himſelf.
' I have advertis'd him by ſecret means,
' That if, about this hour, he make this way,
' Under the colour of his uſual game,
' He ſhall here find his friends, with horſe and men,
' To ſet him free from his captivity.

Enter King EDWARD, *and a* Huntſman.

' *Hunt.* This way, my lord; for this way lies the game.
' *K. Edw.* Nay, this way, man; ſee, where the huntſ-
men ſtand.——
' Now, brother of Gloſter, lord Haſtings, and the reſt,
' Stand you thus cloſe to ſteal the biſhop's deer?

---

9 *Scene V.*] In new forming theſe pieces Shakſpeare tranſpoſed not
only many lines and ſpeeches, but ſome of the ſcenes. This ſcene in
the original play precedes that which he has made the fourth ſcene of
this act. MALONE.

1 *Now, my lord Haſtings,* &c.] I ſhall inſert the ſpeech correſponding to this in the old play, as the compariſon will ſhew the reader in
what manner Shakſpeare proceeded, where he merely retouched and expanded what he found in the elder drama, without the addition of any
new matter:

  Glo. Lord Haſtings and Sir William Stanley,
 Know that the cauſe I ſent for you is this.
 I look my brother with a ſlender train
 Should come a hunting in this foreſt here.
 The biſhop of York befriends him much,
 And lets him uſe his pleaſure in the chaſe.
 Now I have privily ſent him word
 How I am come with you to reſcue him;
 And ſee where the huntſman and he doth come. MALONE.

                 Glo.

' *Glo.* Brother, the time and cafe requireth hafte;
' Your horfe ftands ready at the park-corner.

' *K. Edw.* But whither fhall we then?

' *Haft.* To Lynn, my lord; and fhip² from thence to
　　Flanders.

' *Glo.* Well guefs'd, believe me: for that was my mean-
　　ing.

' *K. Edw.* Stanley, I will requite thy forwardnefs.

* *Glo.* But wherefore ftay we? 'tis no tim to talk.

' *K. Edw.* Huntfman, what fay'ft thou? wilt thou go
　　along?

' *Hunt.* Better do fo, than tarry and be hang'd.

* *Glo.* Come then, away; let's have no more ado.

' *K. Edw.* Bifhop, farewel: fhield thee from Warwick's
　　frown;

And pray that I may repoffefs the crown.　　.　　[*Exeunt.*

SCENE VI.

A Room in the Tower.

Enter King HENRY, CLARENCE, WARWICK, SOMERSET,
　young RICHMOND, OXFORD, MONTAGUE, Lieutenant
of the Tower, and Attendants.

* *K. Hen.* Mafter lieutenant, now that God and friends

* Have fhaken Edward from the regal feat;

* And turn'd my captive ftate to liberty,

* My fear to hope, my forrows unto joys;

* At our enlargement what are thy due fees?

* *Lieu.* Subjects may challenge nothing of their fovereigns;

* But, if an humble prayer may prevail,

* I then crave pardon of your majefty.

' *K. Hen.* For what, lieutenant? for well ufing me?

* Nay, be thou fure, I'll well requite thy kindnefs,

* For that it made my imprifonment a pleafure:

* Ay, fuch a pleafure as incaged birds

* Conceive, when, after many moody thoughts,

* At laft, by notes of houfhold harmony,

* They quite forget their lofs of liberty.——

* But, Warwick, after God, thou fet'ft me free,

* And chiefly therefore I thank God, and thee;

---

² — *and* fhip—] The firft folio has *fhipt*. The correction was made
by the editor of the fecond folio. MALONE.

I

* He

* He was the author, thou the inftrument.
* Therefore, that I may conquer fortune's fpight,
* By living low, where fortune cannot hurt me;
* And that the people of this bleffed land
* May not be punifh'd with my thwarting ftars;
' Warwick, although my head ftill wear the crown,
' I here refign my government to thee,
'' For thou art fortunate in all thy deeds.
    * *War.* Your grace hath ftill been fam'd for virtuous;
* And now may feem as wife as virtuous,
* By fpying, and avoiding, fortune's malice,
* For few men rightly temper with the ftars[3]:
* Yet in this one thing let me blame your grace,
* For choofing me, when Clarence is in place.
    * *Clar.* No, Warwick, thou art worthy of the fway,
* To whom the heavens, in thy nativity,
* Adjudg'd an olive branch, and laurel crown,
* As likely to be bleft in peace and war;
* And therefore I yield thee my free confent.
    * *War.* And I choofe Clarence only for protector
    * *K. Hen.* Warwick, and Clarence, give me both your
       hands;
* Now join your hands, and, with your hands, your hearts,
* That no diffention hinder government:
' I make you both protectors of this land;
' While I myfelf will lead a private life,
' And in devotion fpend my latter days,
' To fin's rebuke, and my Creator's praife.
    Wor. What anfwers Clarence to his fovereign's will?
    * *Clar.* That he confents, if Warwick yield confent;
* For on thy fortune I repofe myfelf.
    * *War.* Why then, though loth, yet muft I be content:
* We'll yoke together, like a double fhadow
* To Henry's body, and fupply his place;
* I mean, in bearing weight of government,
* While he enjoys the honour, and his eafe.
* And, Clarence, now then it is more than needful,
* Forthwith that Edward be pronounc'd a traitor,
* And all his lands and goods be confifcate[4].

3 — *few men rightly* temper *with the ftars:*] I fuppofe the meaning
is, that few men conform their *temper* to their deftiny, which king
Henry did, when finding himfelf unfortunate he gave the management
of publick affairs to more profperous hands. JOHNSON.
    4 *And all his lands and goods* be *confifcate*] For the infertion of the
word *be,* which the defect of the metre proves to have been accidentally
omitted in the old copy, I am anfwerable. MALONE.

             Clar.

Clar. What elfe ? and that fucceffion be determin'd.

* *War.* Ay, therein Clarence fhall not want his part.

* *K. Hen.* But, with the firft of all your chief affairs,

* Let me entreat, (for I command no more,)

* That Margaret your queen, and my fon Edward,

* Be fent for, to return from France with fpeed :

* For, till I fee them here, by doubtful fear

* My joy of liberty is half eclips'd.

* *Clar.* It fhall be done, my fovereign, with all fpeed.

' *K. Hen.* My lord of Somerfet, what youth is that,

' Of whom you feem to have fo tender care ?

' *Som.* My liege, it is young Henry, earl of Richmond.

' *K. Hen.* Come hither, England's hope : If fecret
    powers   [*Lays his hand on his head.*

' Suggeft but truth to my divining thoughts,

' This pretty lad ⁵ will prove our country's blifs.

' His looks are full of peaceful majefty ;

' His head by nature fram'd to wear a crown,

' His hand to wield a fcepter ; and himfelf.

⁵ *This pretty lad—*] He was afterwards Henry VII, a man who put
an end to the civil war of the two houfes, but not otherwife remarkable
for virtue. Shakfpeare knew his trade. Henry VII was grandfather
to queen Elizabeth, and the king from whom James inherited.

             JOHNSON

Shakfpeare only copied this particular, together with fome others,
from Holinfhed : " —whom when the king had a good while beheld,
he faid to fuch princes as were with him: Lo, fuerlie this is he, to
whom both we and our adverfaries leaving the poffeffion of all things,
fhall hereafter give room and place." p. 678. STEEVENS.

Holinfhed tranfcribed this paffage almoft *verbatim* from Hall, whom
the author of the old play, as I conceive, copied. This fpeech originally flood thus :

   Come hither, pretty lad. If heavenly powers
   Do aim aright, to my divining foul,
   Thou, pretty boy, fhalt prove this country's blifs ;
   Thy head is made to wear a princely crown;
   Thy locks are all replete with majefty :
   Make much of him, my lords, &c.

Henry earl of Richmond was the fon of Edmond earl of Richmond,
and Margaret, daughter to John the firft duke of Somerfet Edmond
earl of Richmond was half brother to king Henry the Sixth, being the
fon of that king's mother queen Catherine, by her fecond hufband Owen
Teuther or Tudor, who was taken prifoner at the battle of Mortimer's
Crofs, and foon afterwards beheaded at Hereford.

Henry the Seventh, to fhew his gratitude to Henry the Sixth for this
early prefage in his favour, folicited Pope Julius to canonize him as a
faint ; but either Henry would not pay the money demanded, or, as
Bacon fuppofes, the Pope refufed. left, " as Henry was reputed in the
world abroad but for a fimple man, the eftimation of that kind of honour might be diminifhed, if there were not a diftance kept between
innocents and faints. MALONE.

               ' Likely,

'Likely, in time, to bless a regal throne.
Make much of him, my lords; for this is he,
'Must help you more than you are hurt by me.

Enter a Messenger.

War. What news, my friend ?
Mes. That Edward is escaped from your brother,
And fled, as he hears since, to Burgundy.
War. Unsavoury news : But how made he escape ?
Mes. He was convey'd by Richard duke of Gloster,
And the lord Hastings, who attended him
In secret ambush on the forest side,
And from the bishop's huntsmen rescued him ;
For hunting was his daily exercise.
War. My brother was too careless of his charge.—
But let us hence, my sovereign, to provide
A salve for any sore that may betide.
            [*Exeunt king* HENRY, WAR. CLA. Lieu. *and All.*

Som. My lord, I like not of this flight of Edward's :
For, doubtless, Burgundy will yield him help ;
And we shall have more wars, before't be long.
As Henry's late presaging prophecy
Did glad my heart, with hope of this young Richmond ;
So doth my heart misgive me, in these conflicts
What may befall him, to his harm, and ours :
Therefore, lord Oxford, to prevent the worst,
Forthwith we'll send him hence to Britany,
Till storms be past of civil enmity.
Oxf. Ay ; for, if Edward re-possess the crown,
'Tis like, that Richmond with the rest shall down.
Som. It shall be so ; he shall to Britany.
Come therefore, let's about it speedily.   [*Exeunt.*

P 2   SCENE

SCENE VII.

Before York.

Enter King EDWARD, GLOSTER, HASTINGS, *and forces.*

' *K. Edw.* Now, brother Richard [7], lord Haftings, and
the reft [8] ;
' Yet thus far fortune maketh us amends,
' And fays—that once more I fhall enterchange
' My wained ftate for Henry's regal crown.
' Well have we pafs'd, and now repafs'd the feas,
' And brought defired help from Burgundy :
' What then remains, we being thus arriv'd
' From Ravenfpurg haven before the gates of York,
' But that we enter, as into our dukedom ?
' *Glo.* The gates made faft !—Brother, I like not this ;
* For many men, that ftumble at the threfhold,
* Are well foretold—that danger lurks within.
* *K. Edw.* Tufh, man ! abodements muft not now af-
fright us :
* By fair or foul means we muft enter in,
* For hither will our friends repair to us.
* *Haft.* My liege, I'll knock once more, to fummon them.

Enter, on the walls, the Mayor *of* York, *and his brethren.*

' *May.* My lords, we are fore-warned of your coming,
' And fhut the gates for fafety of ourfelves ;
' For now we owe allegiance unto Henry.

---

6 *SCENE VII*] This fcene in the old play precedes that which
Shakfpeare has made the fixth of the prefent act. MALONE.

7 *Now, brother Richard,* &c.] Inftead of this and the three following
fpeeches, the quartos read only :
Enter Edward and Richard, *with a troop of Hollanders.*
Edw. Thus far from Belgia have we paft the feas,
And march'd from Raun'pur-haven unto York :
But foft ! the gates are fhut ; I like not this.
Rich. Sound up the drum, and call them to the walls.
STEEVENS.

8 — lord *Haftings, and the reft* ;] " Leave out the word *lord,*" fays
one of our author's commentators. If we do not clofely attend to his
phrafeology and metre, and fhould think ourfelves at liberty to fubfti-
tute modern phrafeology and modern metre, almoft every line in his
plays might be altered.—*Brother,* like many fimilar words, *(rather,
whether, either,* &c.) is here ufed by Shakfpeare, as a monofyllable, and
the metre was to his ear perfect. MALONE.

I   K. *Edw.*

' *K. Edw.* But, mafter mayor, if Henry be your king,
' Yet Edward, at the leaft, is duke of York.
' *May.* True, my good lord; I know you for no lefs.
' *K. Edw.* Why, and I challenge nothing but my duke-
        dom ;
* As being well content with that alone.
' *Glo.* But, when the fox hath once got in his nofe,
' He'll foon find means to make the body follow.   [*Afide.*
' *Haft.* Why, mafter mayor, why ftand you in a doubt ?
Open the gates, we are king Henry's friends.
' *May.* Ay, fay you fo ? the gates fhall then be open'd.
                                    [*Exeunt, from above.*
' *Glo.* A wife ftout captain, and foon perfuaded !
* *Haft.* The good old man would fain that all were well [9],
* So 'twere not 'long of him : but, being enter'd,
* I doubt not, I, but we fhall foon perfuade
* Both him, and all his brothers, unto reafon.

               Re-enter the Mayor *and two* Aldermen, *below.*

' *K. Edw.* So, mafter mayor : thefe gates muft not be
        fhut,
' But in the night, or in the time of war.
' What ! fear not, man, but yield me up the keys ;
                                    [*Takes his keys.*
' For Edward will defend the town, and thee,
' And all thofe friends that deign to follow me.

               Drum. Enter MONTGOMERY, *and forces, marching.*

Glo. Brother, this is fir John Montgomery,
Our trufty friend, unlefs I be deceiv'd.
' *K. Edw.* Welcome, fir John ! But why come you in
        arms ?
Mont. To help king Edward in his time of ftorm,
As every loyal fubject ought to do.
' *Edw.* Thanks, good Montgomery : But we now for-
        get
' Our title to the crown ; and only claim
' Our dukedom, till God pleafe to fend the reft.
' *Mont.* Then fare you well, for I will hence again ;
I came to ferve a king, and not a duke.—
' Drummer, ftrike up, and let us march away.
                                    [*A march begun.*

9 *The good old man would fain that all were well;*] The mayor is
willing that we fhould enter, fo he may not be blamed.   JOHNSON.
                                    ' *K. Edw.*

‘ *K. Edw.* Nay, ſtay, ſir John, a while; and we'll de-
    bate,
‘ By what ſafe means the crown may be recover'd.
    ‘ *Mont.* What talk you of debating ? in few words,
‘ If you'll not here proclaim yourſelf our king,
‘ I'll leave you to your fortune ; and be gone,
To keep them back that come to ſuccour you :
Why ſhould we fight, if you pretend no title ?
    ‘ *Glo.* Why, brother, wherefore ſtand you on nice points ?
* *K. Edw.* When we grow ſtronger, then we'll make our
    claim :
* Till then, 'tis wiſdom to conceal our meaning.
    * *Haſt.* Away with ſcrupulous wit ! now arms muſt rule.
    * *Glo.* And fearleſs minds climb ſooneſt unto crowns.
‘ Brother, we will proclaim you out of hand ;
* The bruit thereof¹ will bring you many friends.
    * *K. Edw.* Then be it as you will ; for 'tis my right,
* And Henry but uſurps the diadem.
Mont. Ay, now my ſovereign ſpeaketh like himſelf ;
And now will I be Edward's champion.
    Haſt. Sound, trumpet ; Edward ſhall be here pro-
    claim'd :——
* Come, fellow-ſoldier, make thou proclamation.
                    [*gives him a paper. Flouriſh.*
    Sold. [*reads*] *Edward the fourth, by the grace of God, king
of England and France, and lord of Ireland,* &c.
    Mont. And whoſoe'er gainſays king Edward's right,
By this I challenge him to ſingle fight.
                    [*thrown down his gauntlet.*
    Ail. Long live Edward the fourth !
    ‘ *K Edw.* Thanks, brave Montgomery ² ;—and thanks
    unto you all.

¹ *The* bruit *whereof—*] The word *bruit* is found in Bullokar's *Eng-*
liſh Expoſitor, 8vo. 1616, and is defined " a reporte ſpread abroad."
                    MALONE.

So, in Preſton's *Cambyſes :*
    " —— Whoſe many acts do fly
    " By *bruit* of fame." STEEVENS.
    The French word *bruit* was very early made a denizon of our lan-
guage : " Behold the noiſe of the *bruit* is come." Jeremiah X. 22.
                    WHALLEY
² *Thanks, brave Montgomery ;* &c.] Inſtead of this ſpeech, the quartos have only the following :
    Edw. We thank you all: lord mayer, lead on the way.
    For this night we will harbour here in York;
    And then as early as the morning ſun
    Lifts up his beams above this horizon,
    We'll march to London to meet with Warwick,
    And pull falſe Henry from the regal throne. STEEVENS.
                    ‘ If

' If fortune serve me, I'll requite this kindness.
' Now, for this night, let's harbour here in York :
' And, when the morning fun shall raise his car
' Above the border of this horizon,
' We'll forward towards Warwick, and his mates ;
' For, well I wot, that Henry is no soldier.—
* Ah, froward Clarence !—how evil it beseems thee,
* To flatter Henry, and forsake thy brother !
* Yet, as we may, we'll meet both thee and Warwick.—
* Come on, brave soldiers ; doubt not of the day ;
* And, that once gotten, doubt not of large pay.

[*Exeunt.*

SCENE VIII³.

London. *A Room in the Palace.*

Enter King HENRY, WARWICK, CLARENCE, MONTAGUE, EXETER, *and* OXFORD.

War. What counsel, lords ? Edward from Belgia,
With hasty Germans, and blunt Hollanders,
Hath pass'd in safety through the narrow seas,
And with his troops doth march amain to London ;
' And many giddy people flock to him.
 * *Oxf.* Let's levy men, and beat him back again⁴.

Clar.

---

§ *SCENE VIII*] This scene in the original play follows immediately after Henry's observation on young Richmond, which is in the sixth scene of the present play. MALONE.
 4 *Let's levy men, and beat them back again.*] This line is given in the folio to the king, to whom it is so unsuitable, that I have no doubt it was merely a printer's error. I have not however assigned it to Warwick, and the preceding speech to Henry, as Dr. Johnson proposes in the subsequent note, because it appears to me safer to take the old play as a guide ; in which, as in Shakspeare's piece, the first speech is attributed to Warwick. The second speech is given to *Oxford*, and stands thus:

> *Oxf.* 'Tis best to look to this betimes ;
> For if this fire do kindle any further;
> It will be hard for us to quench it out.

Shakspeare, in new-modelling this scene, probably divided this speech between Oxford and Clarence, substituting the line before us in the room of the words—" 'Tis best to look to this betimes." I have therefore given this line to Oxford. It might with equal, or perhaps with more propriety, be assigned to Warwick's brother, Montague. MALONE.
 ·This line expresses a spirit of war so unsuitable to the character of

Henry,

Clar. A little fire is quickly trodden out ;
Which, being suffer'd, rivers cannot quench.

War. In Warwickshire I have true-hearted friends,
Not mutinous in peace, yet bold in war :
Those will I muster up :—and thou, son Clarence,
' Shalt stir up in Suffolk, Norfolk, and in Kent,
' The knights and gentlemen to come with thee :—
' Thou, brother Montague, in Buckingham,
' Northampton, and in Leicestershire, shalt find
' Men well inclin'd to hear what thou command'st :—
And thou, brave Oxford, wondrous well belov'd,
In Oxfordshire shalt muster up thy friends.—
My sovereign, with the loving citizens,—
* Like to his island, girt in with the ocean,
* Or modest Dian, circled with her nymphs,—
Shall rest in London, till we come to him.—
Fair lords, take leave, and stand not to reply.—
Farewel, my sovereign.

K. Hen. Farewel, my Hector, and my Troy's true
hope [5].

* *Clar.* In sign of truth, I kiss your highness' hand.
* *K. Hen.* Well-minded Clarence, be thou fortunate !
* *Mont.* Comfort, my lord ;—and so I take my leave.
* *Oxf.* And thus [*kissing* Henry's *hand.*] I seal my truth,
and bid adieu.
* *K. Hen.* Sweet Oxford, and my loving Montague,
* And all at once, once more a happy farewel.

Wur. Farewel, sweet lords ; let's meet at Coventry.

[*Exeunt* WAR. CLAR. OXF. *and* MONT.

Henry, that I would give the first cold speech to the king, and the brisk
answer to Warwick. This line is not in the old quarto ; and when
Henry said nothing, the first speech might be as properly given to Warwick as to any other. JOHNSON.
    Every judicious reader must concur in this opinion. STEEVENS.

    5 — *my Hector, and my Troy's true hope.*] This line having probably
made an impression on our author, when he read over the old play, he
has applied the very same expression to the duke of York, where his
overthrow at Wakefield is described, and yet suffered the line to stand
here as he found it :

    Environed he was with many foes,
    And stood against them, *as the hope of Troy*
    Against the Greeks.

    The two latter lines, as the reader may find in p. 255, were new,
no trace of them being *there* found in the old play. Many similar repetitions may be observed in this third part of *King Henry VI.* from the
same cause. MALONE.

*K. Hen.

K. Hen. Here at the palace will I rest a while.
Cousin of Exeter, what thinks your lordship?
Methinks, the power, that Edward hath in field,
Should not be able to encounter mine.

Exe. The doubt is, that he will seduce the rest.

K. Hen. That's not my fear, my meed hath got me fame [6].
I have not stopp'd mine ears to their demands,
Nor posted off their suits with slow delays;
My pity hath been balm to heal their wounds,
My mildness hath allay'd their swelling griefs,
My mercy dry'd their water-flowing tears:
I have not been desirous of their wealth,
Nor much oppress'd them with great subsidies,
Nor forward of revenge, though they much err'd;
Then why should they love Edward more than me?
No, Exeter, these graces challenge grace:
And, when the lion fawns upon the lamb,
The lamb will never cease to follow him.

Shout within. A Lancaster! *A* Lancaster [7]!

Exe. Hark, hark, my lord! What shouts are these?

Enter King EDWARD, GLOSTER, *and Soldiers.*

K. Edw. Seize on the shame-fac'd Henry, bear him hence,
And once again proclaim us king of England.—
You are the fount, that makes small brooks to flow;
Now stops thy spring; my sea shall suck them dry,
And swell so much the higher by their ebb.—
Hence with him to the Tower; let him not speak.

[*Exeunt some with king* Henry.

And, lords, towards Coventry bend we our course,
Where peremptory Warwick now remains [8]:

'The

6 — *my* meed *hath got me fame.*] *Meed* means *merit.* So, before [p. 253, n. 4]:
"Each one already blazing by our *meeds.*" MASON.

7 *Shout within. A* Lancaster!] Surely the shouts that ushered king Edward should be, A York! A York! I suppose the author did not write the marginal directions, and the players confounded the characters. JOHNSON.

We may suppose the shouts to have come from some of Henry's guard, on the appearance of Edward. MALONE.

8 *And lords, towards Coventry bend we our course,*
Where peremptory Warwick now remains:] Warwick, as Mr. Mason has observed, has but just left the stage, declaring his intention to go to Coventry. How then could Edward know of that intention? Our

‘ The fun fhines hot, and, if we ufe delay, ’
‘ Cold biting winter mars our hop’d-for hay [9].
　* *Glo.* Away betimes, before his forces join,
　* And take the great-grown traitor unawares :
　* Brave warriors, march amain towards Coventry.

[Exeunt.

ACT V. SCENE I.

Coventry.

Enter, upon the walls, WARWICK, *the Mayor of* Coventry,
two Meffengers, *and others.*

War. Where is the poft, that came from valiant Oxford ?
How far hence is thy lord, mine honeft fellow ?
　‘ 1. *Mef.* By this at Dunfmore [1], marching hitherward.
　War. How far off is our brother Montague ?—
Where is the poft that came from Montague ?
　‘ 2. *Mef.* By this at Daintry [2], with a puiffant troop.

Enter Sir John SOMERVILLE.

　‘ *War.* Say, Somerville, what fays my loving fon ?
‘ And, by thy guefs, how nigh is Clarence now ?
　‘ *Som.* At Southam I did leave him with his forces,

author was led into this impropriety by the old play, where alfo Edward
fays,

　　And now towards Coventry let’s bend our courfe,
　　To meet with Warwick and his confederates.
　Some of our old writers feem to have thought, that all the perfons of
the drama muft know whatever was known to the writers them'elves, or
to the audience. MALONE
　9 *The fun fhines hot*, &c.] Thefe lines are formed on two others
wh'ch are found in the old play in a fubfequent fcene in the next act,
being fpoken by Edward, after the battle of Barnet, and juft before he
fets out for Tewkfbury.
　　—— Come, let us go ;
　　For if we flack their fair bright fummers day,
　　Sharp winters fhowers will mar our hope, for haie.
　I fufpect, *haie* was inadvertently written in the manufcript inftead of
eye, and that Shakfpeare was thus led to introduce an idea different
from that intended to be conveyed by the original author. MALONE.

　1 —*at Dunfmore,*] The quartos read—at Daintry. STEEVENS.
　2 —*at Daintry*· The quartos read—at Dunfmore. STEEVENS.

‘ And

' And do expect him here some two hours hence.

[Drum heard.

' War. Then Clarence is at hand, I hear his drum.

* Som It is not his, my lord ; here Southam lies ;

* The drum your honour hears, marcheth from Warwick.

* War. Who should that be ? belike, unlook'd-for
    friends.

* Som. They are at hand, and you shall quickly know.

Drums. Enter King Edward, Gloster, and forces
marching.

* K. Edw. Go, trumpet, to the walls, and sound a
    parle.

' Glo. See, how the surly Warwick mans the wall.

War. O, unbid spight ! is sportful Edward come ?
Where slept our scouts, or how are they seduc'd,
That we could hear no news of his repair ?

* K. Edw. Now, Warwick, wilt thou ope the city
    gates,

' Speak gentle words, and humbly bend thy knee ?—

' Call Edward—king, and at his hands beg mercy,

' And he shall pardon thee these outrages.

' War. Nay, rather, wilt thou draw thy forces hence,
Confess who set thee up and pluck'd thee down ?—
Call Warwick—patron, and be penitent,
And thou shalt still remain the duke of York.

    Glo. I thought, at least he would have said—the king ;
Or did he make the jest against his will ?

* War. Is not a dukedom, sir, a goodly gift?

* Glo. Ay, by my faith, for a poor earl to give ;

* I'll do thee service for so good a gift.

' War. 'Twas I, that gave the kingdom to thy brother.

    K. Edw. Why, then 'tis mine, if but by Warwick's
    gift.

' War. Thou art no Atlas for so great a weight :
And, weakling, Warwick takes his gift again ;
And Henry is my king, Warwick his subject.

* K. Edw. But Warwick's king is Edward's prisoner :

' And, gallant Warwick, do but answer this,—
What is the body when the head is off ?

' Glo. Alas, that Warwick had no more fore-cast,
But, whiles he thought to steal the single ten,

' The

' Theking was flily finger'd from the deck ³ !
You left poor Henry at the bifhop's palace ⁴,
And, ten to one; you'll meet him in the Tower.
   K. Edw. 'Tis even fo ; yet you are Warwick ftill ⁵.
   * *Glo.* Come, Warwick, take the time, kneel down,
      kneel down.
  * Nay, when ? ftrike now, or elfe the iron cools.
  * *War* I had rather chop this hand off at a blow,
  * And with the other fling it at thy face,
  * Than bear fo low a fail, to ftrike to thee.
    * *K. Edw.* Sail how thou canft, have wind and tide thy
      friend ;
  * This hand, faft wound about thy coal-black hair,
  * Shall, whiles thy head is warm, and new cut off,
  * Write in the duft this fentence with thy blood,—
' *Wind-changing* Warwick *now can change no more.*

    Enter OXFORD, *with drum and colours.*

  * *War.* O cheerful colours ! fee, where Oxford comes !
Oxf. Oxford, Oxford, for Lancafter !
         [OXF. *and his forces enter the city.*

  ' *Glo.* The gates are open, let us enter too ⁶,
  ' *K. Edw.* So other foes may fet upon our backs.
  * Stand we in good array ; for they, no doubt,
  * Will iffue out again, and bid us battle :
  ' If not, the city being but of fmall defence,
  ' We'll quickly rouze the traitors in the fame.
  * *War.* O, welcome, Oxford ! for we want thy help.

3 — flily *from the* deck l] The quartos read—*finely* finger'd—. *Finely*
is fubtily. So, in Holinfhed's reign of K. Henry VI. p. 640. " — in
his way he took by *fine* force a tower"
    A pack of cards was anciently termed a *deck* of cards or a *pair* of
cards. It is ftill, as I am informed, fo called in Ireland. So, in *King
Edward I* 1593 : " — as it were, turned, as with duces and trays, out
of the *deck.*" STEEVENS.

    4 — *the bifhop's palace*,] The palace of the bifhop of London.
                                  MALONE.
    5 — *yet you are Warwick ftill*] Thus the folio. The old play reads
— ' *and yet you are* ould Warwick ftill." MALONE.

    6 *The gates are open,* &c.] Thus the folio. The quartos read :
      Edw The gates are open ; fee, they enter in ;
      Let's follow them, and bid them battle in the ftreets.
      Gl. No : fo fome o her might fet upon our backs,
      We'll ftay till all be enter'd, and then follow them. STEEVENS.
                                   Enter

Enter MONTAGUE, *with drum and colours.*

Mont. Montague, Montague, for Lancaster !
                    [*He and his forces enter the city.*
' *Glo.* Thou and thy brother both shall buy this treason
'· Even with the dearest blood your bodies bear.
K. Edw. The harder match'd, the greater victory ;
* My mind presageth happy gain, and conquest.

Enter SOMERSET, *with drums and colours.*

Som. Somerset, Somerset, for Lancaster !
                    [*He and his forces enter the city.*
Glo. Two of thy name, both dukes of Somerset,
Have sold their lives unto the house of York [7] ;
And thou shalt be the third, if this sword hold.

Enter CLARENCE, *with drums and colours.*

War. And lo, where George of Clarence sweeps along,
Of force enough to bid his brother battle [8] ;
* With whom an upright zeal to right prevails,
* More than the nature of a brother's love :—
* Come, Clarence, come ; thou wilt, if Warwick calls.
Clar. Father of Warwick, know you what this means ?
                    [*taking his red rose out of his hat.*
' Look here, I throw my infamy at thee :
I will not ruinate my father's house,
Who gave his blood to lime the stones [9] together,
' And set up Lancaster. Why, trow'st thou, Warwick,

---

7 *Two of thy names, both dukes of Somerset,*
    Have sold their lives unto the house of York ;] Edmond Beaufort,
duke of Somerset, who married Eleanor the daughter of Richard Beauchamp earl of Warwick, was slain at the first battle of Saint Alban's.
    His eldest son, Henry, was taken prisoner at the battle of Hexham, in
1463, and soon afterwards beheaded. MALONE.
    8 — *to bid his brother battle ;*] Here the quartos conclude this speech,
and add the following :
        Clar. Clarence, Clarence, for Lancaster !
        Edw. Et tu Brute ! wilt thou stab Cæsar too ?
    A parly, sirra, to George of Clarence. STEEVENS.
    This line of the old play, *Et tu Brute,* &c. is found also in *Acolastus
his Afterwitte,* a poem by S. Nicholson, 1600 ; and the Latin words,
though not retained here, were afterwards transplanted by Shakspeare
into his *Julius Cæsar,* Act III. MALONE.
    9 — *to lime the stones*—] That is, To cement the stones. Lime makes
mortar. JOHNSON.

                                                ' That'

' That Clarence is fo.harſh; ſo blunt [1], unnatural,
' To bend the fatal inſtruments of war
' Againſt his brother, and his lawful king [2]?
* Perhaps, thou wilt object my holy oath:
* To keep that oath, were more impiety
* Than Jepthah's, when he ſacrific'd his daughter.
* I am ſo ſorry for my treſpaſs made,
* That, to deſerve well at my brother's hands,
* I here proclaim myſelf thy mortal foe ;
* With reſolution, whereſoe'er I meet thee,
* (As I will meet thee, if thou ſtir abroad,)
* To plague thee for thy foul miſ-leading me.
And ſo, proud-hearted Warwick, I defy thee,
And to my brother turn my bluſhing cheeks.——
' Pardon me, Edward, I will make amends ;
' And, Richard, do not frown upon my faults,
' For I will henceforth be no more unconſtant.
  ' *K. Edw.* Now welcome more, and ten times more be-
        lov'd,
Than if thou never had'ſt deſerv'd our hate.
  ' *Glo.* Welcome, good Clarence ; this is brother-like ;
  War. O paſſing traitor [3], perjur'd, and unjuſt !
  . *K. Edw.* What, Warwick, wilt thou leave the town, and
        fight ?
Or ſhall we beat the ſtones about thine ears ?
  ' *War.* Alas, I am not coop'd here for defence :
' I will away towards Barnet preſently,
And bid thee battle, Edward, if thou dar'ſt.
  K. Edw. Yes, Warwick, Edward dares, and leads the
        way :
Lords, to the field ; ſaint George, and victory !
                              [*March. Exeunt.*

1 — *ſo blunt,*] Stupid. inſenſible of paternal fondneſs. JOHNSON.
2 *To bend the fatal inſtruments of war*
    Againſt his brother and his lawful king ?] Thus the folio. The
old play thus :
        To liſt his ſword againſt his brother's life ? MALONE.
3 *O paſſing traitor,*] Eminent, egregious ; traiterous beyond the common track of treaſon. JOHNSON.

                                        S.C.E.N.E

SCENE II.

A field of battle near Barnet.

Alarums, and Excursions. Enter king EDWARD, *bringing in* WARWICK *wounded.*

* *K. Edw.* So, lie thou there : die thou, and die our
    fear ;
* For Warwick was a bug, that fear'd us all 4.—
* Now, Montague, fit faft ; I feek for thee,
* That Warwick's bones may keep thine company.   [*Exit.*
    War. Ah, who is nigh ? come to me, friend or foe,
And tell me, who is victor, York, or Warwick ?
Why afk I that ? my mangled body fhows,
* My blood, my want of ftrength, my fick heart fhows,
That I muft yield my body to the earth,
And, by my fall, the conqueft to my foe.
Thus yields the cedar to the axe's edge,
Whofe arms gave fhelter to the princely eagle,
Under whofe fhade the ramping lion flept 5 ;
Whofe top branch over-peer'd Jove's fpreading tree,
.* And kept low fhrubs from winter's powerful wind.
* Thefe eyes, that now are dimm'd with death's black veil,
* Have been as piercing as the mid-day fun,
* To fearch the fecret treafons of the world :
The wrinkles in my brows, now fill'd with blood,
Were liken'd oft to kingly fepulchres ;
For who liv'd king, but I could dig his grave ?
And who durft fmile, when Warwick bent his brow ?

4 — *a bug that fear'd us all.*—] *Bug* is a bugbear, a terrific being.
                                  JOHNSON.
So, in *Cymbeline :*
  " —————— are become
  " The mortal *bugs* of the field."
  Again, in Stephen Goffon's *Schoole of Abafe,* 1579: " Thefe *bugs*
are fitter to *fear* babes than to move men." STEEVENS.
  To *fear* in old language frequently fignifies, to *terrify.* MALONE.

    5 *Thus yields the cedar to the axe's edge,*
      Whofe arms gave fhelter to the princely eagle,
      Under whofe fhade the ramping lion flept; &c.] It has been ob-
ferved to me that the 31ft chapter of the prophet *Ezechiel* fuggefted
thefe images to Shakfpeare. " All the fowls of heaven made their nefts
in his boughs, and under his branches did all the beafts of the field
bring forth their young." STEEVENS.

                                            Lo,

Lo, now my glory smear'd in dust and blood !
My parks, my walks, my manors that I had [6],
Even now forsake me; and, of all my lands,
Is nothing left me, but my body's length [7] !
Why, what is pomp, rule, reign, but earth and dust [8] ?
And live we how we can, yet die we must.

Enter OXFORD *and* SOMERSET.

' *Som.* Ah, Warwick, Warwick ! wert thou as we are [9],
' We might recover all our loss again !
' The queen from France hath brought a puissant power ;
' Even now we heard the news : Ah, could'st thou fly !
    ' *War.* Why, then I would not fly.—Ah, Montague,
' If thou be there, sweet brother, take my hand,
' And with thy lips keep in my soul a while !

6 *My parks, &c.*]
    Cedes coemptis saltibus, et domo,
    Villâque. HOR.
This mention of his *parks* and *manors* diminishes the pathetick effect of
the foregoing lines.   JOHNSON.
    7 — *and, of all my lands,*
    Is nothing left me but my body's length !]
    —— *Mars sola fatetur*
    Quantula sint hominum corpuscula.   JUV.
Camden mentions in his *Remains,* that Constantine, in order to dif-
suade a person from covetousness, drew out with his lance the length
and breadth of a man's grave, adding, " this is all thou shalt have when
thou art dead, if thou canst happily get so much."   MALONE.
    8 — *what is pomp, &c.*] This and the following line make no part
of this speech in the old play ; but were transposed by Shakspeare from
a subsequent speech, addressed by Warwick to Somerset.   MALONE.
    9 *Ah, Warwick, Warwick !* &c.] These two speeches stand thus
in the quartos :
        Oxf. Ah, Warwick, Warwick ! chear up thyself, and live ;
    For yet there's hope enough to win the day.
    Our warlike queen with troops is come from France,
    And at Southampton landed hath her train ;
    And, might'st thou live, then would we never fly.
        War. Why, then I would not fly, nor have I now ;
    But Hercules himself must yield to odds :
    For many wounds receiv'd, and many more repaid,
    Hath robb'd my strong-knit sinews of their strength,
    And spite of spites needs must I yield to death.   STEEVENS.
One of these lines, " But Hercules," &c. Shakspeare has transposed
and inserted in the Messenger's account of the death of the duke of
York. See p. 254.   Not being aware of this, I inadvertently marked
that line as our author's, which I ought not to have done. The three
following lines have already been spoken by Warwick in a former
scene (see p. 265.) and therefore were here properly rejected by Shakspeare.   MALONE.

* Thou

* Thou lov'st me not ; for, brother, if thou didst,
* Thy tears would wash this cold congealed blood,
* That glews my lips, and will not let me speak.
* Come quickly, Montague, or I am dead.
' *Som.* Ah, Warwick, Montague hath breath'd his last ;
' And to the latest gasp, cry'd out for Warwick,
' And said—Commend me to my valiant brother.
' And more he would have said ; and more he spoke,
' Which sounded like a cannon in a vault,
' That might not be distinguish'd [1] ; but, at last,
' I well might hear deliver'd with a groan,—
' O, farewel, Warwick !

   War. Sweet rest his soul !—fly, lords, and save your-
    selves ;
For Warwick bids you all farewel, to meet in heaven. [*Dies.*
   Oxf. Away, away [2], to meet the queen's great power !
              [*Exeunt, bearing off* Warwick's *body.*

SCENE III.

Another part of the field.

Flourish. Enter King EDWARD *in triumph ; with* CLARENCE,
   GLOSTER, *and the rest.*

' *K. Edw.* Thus far our fortune keeps an upward course,

[1] *Which sounded like a* cannon *in a vault,*
  That might not be distinguish'd ;] That is, like the *noise* of a cannon
in a vault, *which,* &c. Shakspeare's alteration here is perhaps not so
judicious as many others that he has made. In the old play, instead of
cannon, we have *clamour,* and the speech stands thus :
     Thy brother Montague hath breath'd his last,
     And at the pangs of death I heard him cry,
     And say, commend me to my valiant brother ;
     And more he would have said, and more he said,
     Which sounded like a *clamour* in a vault,
     That could not be distinguish'd for the sound ;
     And so the valiant Montague gave up the ghost. MALONE.
[2] *Away, away,* &c] Instead of this line, the quartos have the following :
     Come, noble Somerset, let's take our horse,
     And cause retreat be sounded through the camp ;
     That all our friends remaining yet alive
     May be forewarn'd, and save themselves by flight,
     That done, with them we'll post unto the queen,
     And once more try our fortune in the field. STEEVENS,
  It is unnecessary to repeat here an observation that has already been
more than once made I shall therefore only refer to former notes.—
See p. 251, n. 9. MALONE.

                  ' And

'And we are grac'd with wreaths of victory [3];
'But, in the midſt of this bright-ſhining day,
'I ſpy a black, ſuſpicious, threat'ning cloud,
'That will encounter with our glorious ſun,
'Ere he attain his eaſeful weſtern bed ;
'I mean, my lords,—thoſe powers [4], that the queen
'Hath rais'd in Gallia, have arriv'd our coaſt [5],
'And, as we hear, march on to fight with us.

   Clar. A little gale will ſoon diſperſe that cloud,
'And blow it to the ſource from whence it came :
'Thy very beams will dry thoſe vapours up ;
'For every cloud engenders not a ſtorm.

   Glo. The queen is valu'd thirty thouſand ſtrong,
'And Somerſet, with Oxford, fled to her ;
'If ſhe have time to breathe, be well aſſur'd,
Her faction will be full as ſtrong as ours.

   K. Edw. We are advertis'd by our loving friends,
That they do hold their courſe toward Tewkſbury ;
'We, having now the beſt at Barnet field,
'Will thither ſtraight, For willingneſs rids way ;
'And as we march, our ſtrength will be augmented
In every county as we go along.—
Strike up the drum ; cry—Courage! and away [6]. [*Exeunt.*

3 *Thus far our fortune keeps an upward courſe,*
   And we are grac'd with wreaths of victory.] Thus the folio, the quartos thus :
     Thus ſtill our fortune gives us victory,
     And girts our temples with triumphant joys.
     The big-bon'd traitor Warwick hath breath'd his laſt,
     And heaven this day hath ſmil'd upon us all. STEEVENS.
   It is obſervable that the expreſſion which Shakſpeare had ſubſtituted for " *temples engirt with triumphal joys*;" occurs again in *King Richard III.*
     " Now are our brows bound with victorious wreaths,—"
Again, in his *Rape of Lucrece* :
     " Made glorious by his manly chivalry,
     " With bruiſed arms and *wreaths of victory.*" MALONE.
   4 *I mean, my lords,—thoſe powers,* &c.] Thus the folio. The old play thus :
     I meane thoſe powers which the queen hath got in France,
     Are landed, and meane once more to menace us. MALONE.
   5 — *have arriv'd our coaſt,*] Milton uſes the ſame ſtructure, *Par. Loſt,* B. II :
     " ——— ere he arrive
     " The happy iſle." STEEVENS.
   6 *Strike up the drum ; cry—Courage! and away.*] Thus the folio.— The quartos have the following couplet :
     Come, let's go ;
     For if we ſlack this faire bright ſummer's day,
     Sharp winter ſhowers will mar our hope for haie. STEEVENS.
   See p. 322, n. 9. MALONE.

                            SCENE

SCENE IV.

Plains near Tewkſbury.

March. Enter Queen MARGARET, *Prince* EDWARD, SO-
MERSET, OXFORD, *and* Soldiers.

* *Q. Mar.* Great lords [7], wiſe men ne'er ſit and wail
            their loſs,
* But cheerly ſeek how to redreſs their harms.
' What though the maſt be now blown over-board,
' The cable broke, the holding anchor loſt,
' And half our ſailors ſwallow'd in the flood ?
' Yet lives our pilot ſtill : It's meet, that he.
' Should leave the helm, and like a fearful lad,
* With tearful eyes add water to the ſea,
* And give more ſtrength to that which hath too much [8] ;
* Whiles, in his moan, the ſhip ſplits on the rock,

                                           * Which

7 *Great lords,* &c.] This ſpeech in the old play ſtands thus :
      Queen. Welcome to England, my loving friends of France,
    - And welcome Somerſet, and Oxford too.
      Once more have we ſpread our ſails abroad ;
      And though our tackling be almoſt conſumde,
      And Warwick at our main-maſt overthrowne,
      Yet, warlike lordes, raiſe you that ſturdie poſt
      That bears the ſailes to bring us unto reſt.
      And Ned and I, as willing pilots ſhould,
      For once, with careful mindes, guide on the ſterne,
      To beare us through that dangerous gulfe,
      That heretofore hath ſwallowed up our friends.
    There is perhaps no ſpeech that proves more deciſively than the above,
that *the Firſt part of the Contention of the two houſes of Yorke and Lancaſter,* &c. and *The True tragedie of the duke of Yorke,* &c. printed in
1600, were the production of ſome writer who preceded Shakſpeare ;
and that what are now called *The ſecond and third parts of K. Henry VI.*
were only a *revival* and *amplification* of thoſe pieces.
    Here we have a thought which in the original play is expreſſed in
eleven lines, expanded by our author into thirty ſeven lines. MALONE.

8 *With tearful eyes add water to the ſea,*
    And give more ſtrength to that which hath too much.] So, in our
author's *Lover's Complaint* :
      " Upon whoſe weeping margent ſhe was ſet,
      " Like uſury, *applying wet to wet.*"
    Again, in *As You like it* :
      " —— Thou mak'ſt a teſtament
      " As worldlings do, *giving the ſum of more*
      " *To that which hath too much.*"

                                           Again,

* Which induſtry and courage might have ſav'd ?
* Ah, what a ſhame ! ah, what a fault were this !
‘ Say, Warwick was our anchor ; What of that ?
‘ And Montague our top-maſt ; What of him ?
‘ Our ſlaughter'd friends the tackles ; What of theſe ?
‘ Why, is not Oxford here another anchor ?
‘ And Somerſet another goodly maſt ?
‘ The friends of France our ſhrouds and tacklings ?
‘ And, though unſkilful, why not Ned and I
‘ For once allow'd the ſkilful pilot's charge ?
‘ We will not from the helm, to ſit and weep ;
* But keep our courſe, though the rough wind ſay—no,
* From ſhelves and rocks that threaten us with wreck.
* As good to chide the waves, as ſpeak them fair.
* And what is Edward, but a ruthleſs ſea ?
* What Clarence, but a quick-ſand of deceit ?
* And Richard, but a ragged fatal rock ?
* All theſe the enemies to our poor bark.
* Say, you can ſwim ; alas, 'tis but a while :
* Tread on the ſand ; why, there you quickly ſink :
* Beſtride the rock ; the tide will waſh you off,
* Or elſe you famiſh, that's a threefold death.
* This ſpeak I, lords, to let you underſtand,
* In caſe ſome one of you would fly from us,
* That there's no hop'd-for mercy with the brothers ;
* More than with ruthleſs waves, with ſands, and rocks,
* Why, courage, then ! what cannot be avoided,
’Twere childiſh weakneſs to lament, or fear.
　* *Prince.* Methinks, a woman [9] of this valiant ſpirit

Again, in *Romeo and Juliet :*
　　“ With tears augmenting the freſh morning dew.”
So alſo Spenſer, in his *Shepherds Calendar,* 1679 :
　　“ Thou, plenteous ſpring, haſt lull'd me oft aſleep,
　　“ Whoſe ſtreames my tickling tears did oft augment ”
Of this thought, which we ſee Shakſpeare has ſo often expreſſed, there is no trace in the old play. See the preceding note. MALONE.
　9 *Methinks, a woman,* &c.] In this ſpeech there is much and important variation in the quarto :
　　　Prince. And if there be (as God forbid they ſhould)
　　’Mongſt us a timorous or fearful man,
　　Let him depart before the battle join ;
　　Leſt he in time of need entice another,
　　And ſo withdraw the ſoldiers' hearts from us.
　　I will not ſtand aloof, and bid you fight,
　　But with my ſword preſs in the thickeſt throngs,
　　And ſingle Edward from his ſtrongeſt guard,
　　And hand to hand enforce him for to yield,
　　Or leave my body, as witneſs of my thoughts. STEEVENS.
　Our author has availed himſelf of theſe lines in former ſcenes of theſe plays. MALONE.
　　　　　　　　　　　　　　　* Should,

* Should, if a coward heard her speak these words,
* Infuse his breast with magnanimity,
* And make him, naked, foil a man at arms.
‘ I speak not this, as doubting any here:
‘ For, did I but suspect a fearful man,
‘ He should have leave to go away betimes ;
‘ Lest, in our need, he might infect another,
‘ And make him of like spirit to himself.
‘ If any such be here, as God forbid !
‘ Let him depart, before we need his help.

‘ Oxf. Women and children of so high a courage !
And warriors faint ! why, 'twere perpetual shame.—
‘ Oh, brave young prince ! thy famous grandfather
Doth live again in thee ; Long may'st thou live,
To bear his image, and renew his glories !

‘ Som. And he, that will not fight for such a hope,
‘ Go home to bed, and, like the owl by day,
‘ If he arise, be mock'd and wonder'd at [1].

* Q. Mar. Thanks, gentle Somerset ;—sweet Oxford, thanks.

* Prince. And take his thanks, that yet hath nothing else.

Enter a Messenger.

‘ Mes. Prepare you, lords [2], for Edward is at hand,
‘ Ready to fight ; therefore be resolute.
‘ Oxf. I thought no less : it is his policy,
‘ To haste thus fast, to find us unprovided.
Som. But he's deceiv'd, we are in readiness.
Q. Mar. This cheers my heart, to see your forwardness.
Oxf. Here pitch our battle, hence we will not budge.

March. Enter, at a distance, King EDWARD, CLARENCE, GLOSTER, *and forces.*

‘ K. Edw. Brave followers [3], yonder stands the thorny wood,

‘ Which

[1] *If he arise, be* mock'd *and* wonder'd *at.*] So the folio. The old play thus :
Be hiss'd and wonder'd at, if he arise. MALONE.
[2] *Prepare you, lords, &c*] In the old play these speeches stand thus :
Mes. My lordes, duke Edward with a mightie power
Is marching hitherward to fight with you.
Oxf. I thought it was his policy to take us unprovided,
But here will we stand, and fight it to the death. MALONE.
[3] K. Edw. Brave followers, &c.] This scene is ill-contrived, in which

' Which, by the heavens' affiftance, and your ftrength,

' Muft by the roots be hewn up yet ere night.

* I need not add more fuel to your fire,

* For, well I wot, ye blaze to burn them out :

* Give fignal to the fight, and to it, lords.

    Q. Mar. Lords, knights, and gentlemen, what I fhould
        fay,

' My tears gainfay [4] ; for every word I fpeak,

' Ye fee, I drink the water of my eyes [5].

' Therefore, no more but this :—Henry, your fovereign [6],

' Is prifoner to the foe ; his ftate ufurp'd,

' His realm a flaughter-houfe, his fubjects flain,

' His ftatutes cancell'd, and his treafure fpent ;

' And yonder is the wolf, that makes this fpoil.

' You fight in juftice : then, in God's name, lords,

' Be valiant, and give fignal to the fight.

                [Exeunt both armies.

SCENE V.

Another part of the fame.

*Alarums ; Excurfions ; and afterwards a Retreat. Then En-
ter King* EDWARD, CLARENCE, GLOSTER, *and forces ;
with Queen* MARGARET, OXFORD, *and* SOMERSET, *prifoners.*

  ' *K. Edw.* Now, here a period of tumultuous broils.

                          Away

which the king and queen appear at once on the ftage at the head of oppofite armies. It had been eafy to make one retire before the other entered. JOHNSON.

  4 *My tears* gainfay ;] To *gainfay* is to unfay, to deny, to contradict.
                              STEEVENS.

  5 *Ye fee I drink the water of my eyes.*] So, in our author's *Venus
and Adonis :*

      " 'Doft thou *drink tears,* that thou provok'ft fuch weeping ?'"

  Thefe paffages were probably recollected by Rowe, when he wrote
in his *Jane Shore :*

    " Feed on my fighs, and *drink my falling tears.*"

  So, alfo Pope, in the *Epiftle from Eloifa to Abelard :*

    " And drink the falling tears each other fhed."

  The folio has—*eye* ; but I imagine it was rather an error in the tranfcriber than an alteration by Shakfpeare. The old play reads—*eyes.*

                          MALONE.

  6 *Henry, your fovereign,* &c.] Inftead of this and the following lines,
the original play has thefe :

                                 Henry

Away with Oxford to Hammes' caſtle 7 ſtraight :
For Somerſet 8, off with his guilty head.
‘ Go, bear them hence ; I will not hear them ſpeak.
  Oxf. For my part, I'll not trouble thee with words.
‘ *Som.* Nor I, but ſtoop with patience to my fortune.

     [*Exeunt* OXFORD *and* SOMERSET, *guarded.*

* *Q. Mar.* So part we ſadly in this troublous world,
* To meet with joy in ſweet Jeruſalem.
* *K. Edw.* Is proclamation made,—that, who finds Edward,
* Shall have a high reward, and he his life ?
* *Glo.* It is ; and, lo, where youthful Edward comes.

Enter *ſoldiers,* with *Prince* EDWARD.

* *K. Edw.* Bring forth the gallant, let us hear him ſpeak :
* What ! can ſo young a thorn begin to prick ?—
‘ Edward, what ſatisfaction canſt thou make,
‘ For bearing arms, for ſtirring up my ſubjects,
* And all the trouble thou haſt turn'd me to 9 ?
  Prince. Speak like a ſubject, proud ambitious York!
Suppoſe, that I am now my father's mouth ;
Reſign thy chair, and, where I ſtand, kneel thou,
Whilſt I propoſe the ſelf-ſame words to thee,
Which, traitor, thou would'ſt have me anſwer to.
  Q. Mar. Ah, that thy father had been ſo reſolv'd !
‘ *Glo.* That you might ſtill have worn the petticoat,
And ne'er have ſtolen the breech from Lancaſter.

    Henry your king is priſoner in the Tower ;
    His land and all our friends are quite diſtreſt,
    And yonder ſtands the wolfe that makes all this,
    Then in God's name, lords, together crie ſaint George.

  7 — *to Hammes' caſtle*—] A caſtle in Picardy, where Oxford was confined many years. MALONE.

  8 *For Somerſet*—] Edmond Beaufort, duk of Somerſet, the ſecond ſon of Edmond duke of Somerſet who was killed at the battle of Saint Albans. See p. 308, n. 7. MALONE.

  9 *And all the* trouble thou haſt turn'd me to] This line was one of Shakſpeare's additions to the original play. We have almoſt the ſame words in the *Tempeſt :*
    " ———— O, my heart bleeds,
    " To think of *the teen* [i. e. trouble] *that I have turn'd you to.*"
In the old play Prince Edward is not brought forth as here, but enters with his mother ; and after Oxford and Somerſet are carried off, he is thus addreſſed by the king :
    " Now, Edward, what ſatisfaction canſt thou make,
    " For ſtirring up my ſubjects to rebellion ?" MALONE.

Prince

Prince. Let Æsop fable [1] in a winter's night;
His currish riddles fort not with this place.

Glo. By heaven, brat, I'll plague you for that word.

Q. Mar. Ay, thou waſt born to be a plague to men;

Glo. For God's ſake, take away this captive ſcold.

Prince. Nay, take away this ſcolding crook-back rather.

K. Edw. Peace, wilful boy, or I will charm your
tongue [2]

Clar. Untutor'd lad, thou art too malapert.

Prince. I know my duty, you are all undutiful :
Laſcivious Edward,—and thou perjur'd George,—.
And thou miſhapen Dick,—I tell ye all,
I am your better, traitors as ye are ;—
* And thou uſurp'ſt my father's right and mine.

K. Edw. Take that, the likeneſs of this railer here [3].
　　　　　　　　　　　　　　　　　　　　　　[*Stabs him.*

* *Glo.* Sprawl'ſt thou? take that, to end thy agony.
　　　　　　　　　　　　　　　　　　　　[*Glo. ſtabs him.*

Clar. And there's for twitting me with perjury.
　　　　　　　　　　　　　　　　　　　[*Clar. ſtabs him.*

Q. Mar. O, kill me too !

Glo. Marry, and ſhall.　　　　　　　[*Offers to kill her.*

K. Edw. Hold, Richard, hold, for we have done too
much.

Glo. Why ſhould ſhe live, to fill the world with words ?

K. Edw. What ! doth ſhe ſwoon ? uſe means for her re-
covery.

Glo. Clarence, excuſe me to the king my brother;
I ll hence to London on a ſerious matter :
Ere ye come there, be ſure to hear ſome news.

_____

1 *Let Æſop, &c.*] The prince calls Richard, for his crookedneſs,
Æſop ; and the poet, following nature, makes Richard highly incenſed
at the reproach.　JOHNSON.

2 —*charm your tongue.*] The quarto reads—*tame* your tongue. The
former is beſt.　STEEVENS.

The expreſſion which our author ſubſtituted, is one that he has often
uſed. See p. 178, n *. The meaning is, I will compel you to be as
ſilent, as you would be, if you were *charm'd*, if you were deprived of
ſpeech by the power of enchantment.　MALONE.

3 —*the likeneſs of this railer here*] That is, *thou who art* the likeneſs, &c. Mr. Rowe and the other modern editors read—*thou* likeneſs,
and ſo we ſhould now write ; but the other was the phraſeology of
Shakſpeare's time. So, in *Julius Cæſar :*

　"*The* laſt of all the Romans fare thee well."

In that paſſage, as in the preſent, Mr. Rowe ſubſtituted *thou* for *the*,
though Shakſpeare has employed the very words he found in North's
Tranſlation of Plutarch.　MALONE.

　— *the likeneſs of ibis railer here.*] Thou that reſemb'eſt thy railing
mother.　JOHNSON.

　　　　　　　　　　　　　　　　　　　　　　　　　　Clar.

Clar. What? what?

' *Glo.* The Tower, the Tower [4].   [*Exit.*

' *Q. Mar.* O, Ned, sweet Ned! speak to thy mother,
        boy!

' Canst thou not speak?—O, traitors! murderers!—
They, that stabb'd Cæsar, shed no blood at all,
Did not offend, nor were not worthy blame,

* If this foul deed were by, to equal it.

' He was a man; this, in respect, a child;
And men ne'er spend their fury on a child;

' What's worse than murderer, that I may name it?

* No, no; my heart will burst, an if I speak:—

* And I will speak, that so my heart may burst.—

* Butchers and villains, bloody cannibals!

* How sweet a plant you have untimely cropp'd!

' You have no children, butchers [5]; if you had,

' The thought of them would have stirr'd up remorse:

' But, if you ever chance to have a child,
Look in his youth to have him so cut off,

' As deathsmen! you have rid this sweet young prince [6].

' *K. Edw.* Away with her; go, bear her hence perforce.

Q. Mar. Nay, never bear me hence, dispatch me here;
Here sheath thy sword, I'll pardon thee my death:
What! wilt thou not?—then, Clarence, do it thou.

Clar. By heaven, I will not do thee so much ease.

' *Q. Mar.* Good Clarence, do; sweet Clarence, do thou
        do it [7].

Clar. Didst thou not hear me swear, I would not do it?

---

4 *The Tower, the Tower!*] The quarto adds—*I'll root them out*; but,
perhaps, injudiciously. STEEVENS.

5 *You have no children, butchers;*] The original play reads:
        You have no children, *devils*; if you had,
        The thought of them would *then have stopped your rage.*
This thought occurring also (as Sir William Blackstone has observed)
in *Macbeth,* may perhaps be urged as a proof of Shakspeare's being the
author of the first draught, as well as o the alterations and additions to
it. But how many thoughts and even expressions has he borrowed from
preceding writers? Having (as I suppose) greatly enlarged, and almost
new-written, this and the preceding play, the thoughts they contain,
whether found in the first copy, or his amplification of it, were as likely
to recur in a future piece, as any of those which he employed in one
originally written by himself. In his original plays he frequently borrowed from himself. MALONE.

6 —*you have rid this sweet young prince.*] The condition of this warlike queen would move compassion, could it be forgotten that she gave
York, to wipe his eyes in his captivity, a handkerchief stained with his
young child's blood. JOHNSON.

7 —*do thou do it.*] The old play reads—kill me too. MALONE.

Q. Mar. Ay, but thou ufeſt to forſwear thyſelf;
'Twas ſin before [8], but now 'tis charity.
' What ! wilt thou not ? where is that devil's butcher [9],
Hard-favour'd Richard ? Richard, where art thou ?
Thou art not here : Murder is thy alms-deed ;
Petitioners for blood thou ne'er put'ſt back.
' *K. Edw.* Away, I ſay ; I charge ye, bear her hence.
Q. Mar. So come to you, and yours, as to this prince !
          [*Exit, led out forcibly.*
' *K. Edw.* Where's Richard gone ?
' *Clar.* To London, all in poſt ; and, as I gueſs,
To make a bloody ſupper in the Tower.
 K. Edw. He's ſudden, if a thing comes in his head.
' Now march we hence : diſcharge the common ſort
' With pay and thanks, and let's away to London,
' And ſee our gentle queen how well ſhe fares ;
' By this, I hope, ſhe hath a ſon for me. [*Exeunt.*

SCENE VI.

London. *A Room in the Tower.*

King HENRY *is diſcovered ſitting with a book in his hand, the* Lieutenant *attending.* Enter GLOSTER.

Glo. Good day, my lord ! What, at your book ſo hard ?
 K Hen. Ay, my good lord : My lord, I ſhould ſay ra-
  ther ;
'Tis ſin to flatter, good was little better :
Good Gloſter, and good devil, were alike,
* And both prepoſterous ; therefore, not good lord.
 * *Glo.* Sirrah, leave us to ourſelves : we muſt confer.
          [*Exit* Lieutenant.

 * *K. Hen.* So flies the reckleſs ſhepherd from the wolf :
* So firſt the harmleſs ſheep doth yield his fleece,
* And next his throat unto the butcher's knife.—

[8] *'Twas ſin before,*] She alludes to the deſertion of Clarence.
              JOHNSON.
 [9] *— where is that devil's butcher,*] *Devil's butcher* is a butcher ſet on by the devil. JOHNSON.
 The folio adds, at the end of this line, the word—*Richard.* But both the metre and the old play ſhew that it was an accidental repetition by the tranſcriber, or compoſitor. MALONE.

               What

What scene of death hath Roscius now to act [1] ?

Glo. Suspicion always haunts the guilty mind;
The thief doth fear each bush an officer.

' *K. Hen.* The bird, that hath been limed in a bush,
' With trembling wings misdoubteth every bush [2] :
And I, the hapless male to one sweet bird,
Have now the fatal object in my eye,
Where my poor young was lim'd, was caught, and kill'd.

' *Glo.* Why, what a peevish fool [3] was that of Crete,
' That taught his son the office of a fowl?
' And yet, for all his wings, the fool was drown'd.[4]

K. Hen.

---

[1] *What scene of death hath Roscius now to act ?*] So, in *Acolastus his Afterwitte*, a poem, 1600:
" What bloody scene hath cruelty to act ?"

Dr. Warburton reads *Richard*, instead of *Roscius*, because Roscius was a comedian. That he is right in this assertion, is proved beyond a doubt by a passage in Quintilian, cited by W. R. [probably Sir Walter Rawlinson] in the *Gentleman's Magazine*, Vol. LIV. P. II. p. 886. "Roscius citatior, Æsopus gravior fuit, quod *ille comœdias*, hic tragœdias egit." QUINTIL. Lib. XI. c. 3 —But it is not in Quintilian or in any other ancient writer we are to look in order to ascertain the text of Shakspeare. Roscius was called a *tragedian* by our author's contemporaries, as appears from the quotations in the next note: and this was sufficient authority to him, or rather to the author of the original play, for there this line is found. MALONE.

Shakspeare has occasion to compare Richard to some player about to represent a scene of murder, and took the first or only name of antiquity that occurred to him, without being very scrupulous about its propriety. Nash, in *Pierce Pennilesse's Supplication to the Devil*, 1592, says, " Not *Roscius* nor *Æsope*, those admired *tragedians*, that have lived ever since before Christ was born, could ever performe more in action than famous Ned Allen.' Again, in *Acolastus his Afterwitte*, 1600 :
" Through thee each murthering *Roscius* is appointed
" To *act strange scenes of death* on God's anointed."
Again, in *Certaine Satyres*, 1598 :
" Was penn'd by *Roscio* the *tragedian*." STEEVENS.

[2] — misdoubteth *every bush* :] To *misdoubt* is to suspect danger, to fear. So, in *Humour out of Breath*, a comedy by John Day, 1608 :
" *Hip.* Doubt and *misdoubt* ! what difference is there here ?
" *O.J.* Yes, much: when men *misdoubt*, 'tis said they *fear*."
STEEVENS.

[3] — *peevish fool*—] As *peevishness* is the quality of children, *peevish* seems to signify *childish*, and by consequence *silly*. *Peevish* is explained by *childish*, in a former note of Dr. Warburton. JOHNSON.

Shakspeare employs the word *peevish* in the same sense in *Cymbeline* where the reader will find many instances of this use of it. STEEVENS.

This epithet which Shakspeare has so frequently employed, was one of his additions to the original play.

The ordinary signification of *peevish* in our poe 's time was *foolish*.— See Minsheu's Dict. 1617. in v. MALONE.

[4] — *the office of a fowl?*

Q 1

'*K. Hen.* I, Dædalus ; my poor boy, Icarus ;
Thy father, Minos, that deny'd our courfe ;
' The fun, that fear'd the wings of my fweet boy,
' Thy brother Edward ; and thyfelf, the fea,
' Whofe envious gulph did fwallow up his life.
* Ah, kill me with thy weapon, not with words !
' My breaft can better brook thy dagger's point,
Than can my ears that tragick hiftory.—
* But wherefore doft thou come ? is't for my life ?
'*Glo.* Think'ft thou, I am an executioner ?
K. Hen. A perfecutor, I am fure, thou art ;
'If murdering innocents be executing,
' Why, then thou art an executioner.
'*Glo.* Thy fon I kill'd for his prefumption.
K. Hen. Hadft thou been kill'd, when firft thou didft pre-
　　　fume,
Thou hadft not liv'd to kill a fon of mine.
' And thus I prophefy,—that many a thoufand,
' Which now miftruft no parcel of my fear⁵ ;
' And many an old man's figh, and many a widow's,
' And many an orphan's water-ftanding eye,—
' Men for their fons, wives for their hufbands' fate,
' Orphans for their parents' timelefs death⁶.—
' Shall rue the hour that ever thou waft born.
The owl fhriek'd at thy birth, an evil fign ;
' The night crow cry'd, aboding lucklefs time ;
Dogs howl'd, and hideous tempefts fhook down trees ;
The raven rook'd her ⁷ on the chimney's top,
And chattering pyes in difmal difcords fung.
Thy mother felt more than a mother's pain,
And yet brought forth lefs than a mother's hope ;

And yet, for all his wings, the fool was drown'd.] The old play
reads : — the office of a *bird* ?
　　And yet for all *that* the poor *fowl* was drown'd. MALONE.

5 *Which now miftruft no parcel of my fear* ;] Who fufpect no part of
what my fears prefage. JOHNSON.

6 *Men for their fons, wives for their hufbands' fate,*
　　Orphans for their parents' timelefs death,] The word *fate* was fupplied by the editor of the fecond folio. MALONE.

7 *The raven rook'd her*—] To *rook,* or rather to *ruck,* is a north-
country word, fignifying to *fquat down,* or *lodge* on any thing. So, in
Stanyhurft's tranflation of *Virgil,* 1582, Book the Fourth :
　　" Alfo on the turrets the fkrich howle, &c.
　　" —— doth *ruck,*" &c.
Again in Warner's *Albion's England,* 1602, B. VII. c. 37 :
　　" Have lazy wings, be ever lean, in fullen corners *ruck.*'"
　　　　　　　　　　　　　　　　　　　　STEEVENS.
　　　　　　　　　　　　　　　　　　　　　　' To

‘ To wit,—an indigeſt deformed lump [8],
Not like the fruit of ſuch a goodly tree.
Teeth hadſt thou in thy head, when thou waſt born,
To ſignify,—thou cam'ſt to bite the world :
And, if the reſt be true which I have heard,
‘ Thou cam'ſt [9]—

   Glo. I'll hear no more ;—Die, prophet, in thy ſpeech ;
                                   [Stabs him.
For this, amongſt the reſt, was I ordain'd.
   K. Hen. Ay, and for much more ſlaughter after this.
O God! forgive my ſins, and pardon thee !   *[Dies.*
   Glo. What, will the aſpiring blood of Lancaſter
Sink in the ground ? I thought it would have mounted.
See, how my ſword weeps for the poor king's death !
‘ O, may ſuch purple tears be always ſhed
‘ From thoſe that wiſh the downfal of our houſe !—
‘ If any ſpark of life be yet remaining,
Down, down to hell ; and ſay—I ſent thee thither;
                                 [Stabs him again.
I, that have neither pity, love, nor fear.—
Indeed, 'tis true, that Henry told me of [1];
For I have often heard my mother ſay,
I came into the world with my legs forward :
Had I not reaſon, think ye, to make haſte,
‘ And ſeek their ruin that uſurp'd our right ?
The midwife wonder'd ; and the women cry'd,
O, Jeſus bleſs us, he is born with teeth !
‘ And ſo I was ; which plainly ſignify'd—

<hr>

[8] — *an* indigeſt—] The folio his—*indigeſted.* But the metre and
the old play ſhew that it was a miſprint. Shakſpeare uſes the word *indi-*
geſt in *King John.* MALONE.
   9 *Thou cam'ſt*—] Thus the folio. The old play as follows :
     Thou cam'ſt *into the world*—
     Glo. Die prophet in thy ſpeech;—I'll hear no more. MALONE.
   [1] — *that Henry told me of* ;] Namely, that my birth was attended
with ſingular circumſtances.—Theobald, grounding himſelf on this and
the two following lines, reads in a former paſſage—
     Thou cam'ſt *into the world with thy legs forward.*
for " how, (ſays he,) can Richard ſay, " Indeed 'tis true that Henry
told me of," &c. unleſs we ſuppoſed that King Henry reproached him
with his prepoſterous birth ?" But ſurely Henry *has* done ſo in the laſt
ten lines of his ſpeech, though he is at length prevented by the fatal ſtab
from mentioning a *farther* proof of Richard's being born for the deſtruc-
tion of mankind. Theobald's addition therefore to that line, has, I
think, been adopted too haſtily by the ſubſequent editors, and the interruption in the midſt of Henry's ſpeech appears to me not only pre-
ferable, as warranted by the old copies, and by Gloſter's ſubſequent
words, [Die, prophet, *in thy ſpeech* ;] but more agreeable to nature.
                                    MALONE.
                                 That

That I fhould fnarl, and bite, and play the dog.
' Then, fince the heavens have fhap'd my body fo,
Let hell make crook'd my mind, to anfwer it [1].
I have no brother, I am like no brother :
' And this word—love, which grey-beards call divine,
Be refident in men like one another,
And not in me ; I am myfelf alone.—
Clarence, beware ; thou keep'ft me from the light ;
But I will fort a pitchy day for thee [3] :
For I will buz abroad fuch prophecies,
' That Edward fhall be fearful of his life [4] ;
And then, to purge his fear, I'll be thy death.
' King Henry, and the prince his fon, are gone :
' Clarence, thy turn is next ; and then the reft ;
Counting myfelf but bad, till I be beft.—
' I'll throw thy body in another room,
And triumph, Henry, in thy day of doom.   , [*Exit.*

SCENE VII.

The fame. A Room in the Palace.

King Edward *is difcovered fitting on his throne;* Queen
Elizabeth *with the infant Prince,* Clarence, Gloster, Hastings, *and Others, near him.*

K. Edw. Once more we fit in England's royal throne,
Re-purchas'd with the blood of enemies.

[1] *Let hell,* &c.] This line Dryden feems to have thought on in his
Oedipus:
    " It was thy crooked mind hunch'd out thy back,
    " And wander'd in thy limbs." Steevens.
After this line, we find in the old play the following :
    I have no father, I am like no father.
It might have been omitted in the folio merely by accident, (as fome
lines in the fecond part of *King Henry VI.* certainly were,) but its reftoration is not neceffary, for the fenfe is complete without it. Malone.
[3] *But I will* fort *a pitchy day for thee :*] But I will choofe out an
hour whofe gloom fhall be as fatal to you. To *fort* is to *felect.*
                                                        Steevens.

[4] *For I will* buz *abroad fuch prophecies,*
    That Edward fhall be fearful of his life;] The quartos add a line
between thefe :
    ——*fuch prophecies,*
    Under pretence of outward feeming ill,
    That, &c. Steevens.
    This line is not in the quarto printed by W. W. 1600 ; but it is in the
undated quarto, which in fact was printed in 1619, from that printed in
1600 by V. S. Malone.

                                                        What

What valiant foe-men, like to autumn's corn,
Have we mow'd down, in tops of all their pride?
Three dukes of Somerset, threefold renown'd
For hardy and undoubted champions:
Two Cliffords, as the father and the son,
And two Northumberlands; two braver men
Ne'er spur'd their coursers at the trumpet's sound:
'With them, the two brave bears, Warwick and Montague,
That in their chains fetter'd the kingly lion,
And made the forest tremble when they roar'd.
Thus have we swept suspicion from our seat,
And made our footstool of security.—
Come hither, Bess, and let me kiss my boy:—
Young Ned, for thee, thine uncles, and myself,
Have in our armours watch'd the winter's night;
'Went all afoot in summer's scalding heat,
That thou might'st repossess the crown in peace;
And of our labours thou shalt reap the gain.

Glo. I'll blast his harvest, if your head were lay'd;
For yet I am not look'd on in the world.
This shoulder was ordain'd so thick, to heave;
And heave it shall some weight, or break my back:—
Work thou the way,—and thou shalt execute [5].   [*Aside.*

K. Edw. Clarence, and Gloster, love my lovely queen;
And kiss your princely nephew, brothers both.

Clar. The duty, that I owe unto your majesty,
I seal upon the lips of this sweet babe.

K. Edw. Thanks, noble Clarence; worthy brother,
          thanks.

'*Glo.* And, that I love the tree from whence thou
          sprang'st,
'Witness the loving kiss I give the fruit:—
To say the truth, so Judas kiss'd his master;   ⎫
'And cry'd—all hail! when as he meant—all   ⎬ [*Aside.*
     harm.   ⎭

[5] *Work thou the way, and thou shalt execute.*] This is the reading of the old play. The folio reads—and *that* shalt execute. But as the word *shalt* is preserved, the other must have been an error of the transcriber or composer. MALONE.

I believe we should read—and *this* shall execute.

Richard laying his hand on his forehead says: *Work thou the way*—then bringing down his hand, and beholding it,—*and this shall execute.* Though *that* may stand, the arm being included in the shoulder.
                                                      JOHNSON.

The quartos read—*and thou shalt execute.*
I suppose he speaks this line, first *touching* his *head*, and then *looking* on his *hand*. STEEVENS.

K. Edw. Now am I seated as my soul delights,
Having my country's peace, and brothers' loves.

Clar. What will your grace have done with Margaret?
Reignier, her father, to the king of France
Hath pawn'd the Sicils and Jerusalem,
And hither have they sent it for her ransom.

K. Edw. Away with her, and waft her hence to France.
And now what rests, but that we spend the time
With stately triumphs [6], mirthful comick shows,
Such as befit the pleasures of the court?—
Sound, drums and trumpets!—farewel, four annoy!
For here, I hope, begins our lasting joy.   [*Exeunt.*

---

[6] *With stately* triumphs,] By *triumphs* are meant masques, revels,
processions, &c. MALONE.

⁎ THE following SUMMARY ACCOUNT of the times and places
of the several battles fought between the two houses of York and Lancaster, and of the numbers killed on both sides, is given by Trussel, at
the end of his *History of England,* a book of little value, but in matters
of this kind tolerably correct. I have compared his account with our
earliest historians, and in some places corrected it by them.

1. THE BATTLE OF SAINT ALBANS, fought on the 23d of May
1455, between Richard Plantagenet, duke of York, and King Henry
VI. In this battle the duke of York was victorious, and Henry was
taken prisoner.

KILLED, on the royal side 5041, (among whom were Edmond duke
of Somerset, Henry earl of Northumberland, Humphry earl of Stafford,
and Thomas lord Clifford;) on the side of the duke of York, 600.
TOTAL—5641.

2 THE BATTLE OF BLOARHEATH in Shropshire, fought on the
30th of September 1459, between James lord Audley on the part of
King Henry, and Richard Nevil earl of Salisbury on the part of the
duke of York, in which battle lord Audley was slain, and his army defeated.

KILLED—2411.

3. THE BATTLE OF NORTHAMPTON, 10th of July, 1460, between
Edward Plantagenet, earl of March, eldest son to the duke of York,
and Richard Nevil earl of Warwick, on the one side, and King Henry
on the other; in which the Yorkists were victorious.

KILLED—1035, among whom were John Talbot earl of Shrewsbury, Humphrey duke of Buckingham, and Sir William Lucy.

4. THE BATTLE OF WAKEFIELD, December 30, 1460, between
Richard duke of York and Queen Margaret; in which the duke of York
was defeated.

KILLED—2801, among whom were the duke of York, Edmond
earl of Rutland his second son, Sir John and Sir Hugh Mortimer, his
base uncles, and the earl of Shrewsbury. Richard Nevil earl of
Salisbury was in this battle taken prisoner, and afterwards beheaded at
Pomfret.

5 THE BATTLE OF MORTIMER's CROSS, in Herefordshire, on
Candlemas-day, 1460-1, between Edward duke of York, on the one
side, and Jasper earl of Pembroke, and James Butler earl of Wiltshire,
on the other; in which the duke of York was victorious.

KILLED,

KILLED, 3800, among whom was Sir Owen Tuther or Tudor, who married Queen Catharine, the widow of King Henry V.

6. THE SECOND BATTLE OF SAINT ALBANS, February 17, 1460-1, between Margaret on one side, and the duke of Norfolk and the earl of Warwick on the other; in which the queen obtained the victory.

KILLED—2303; among whom was Sir John Gray, a Lancastrian, whose widow, Lady Gray, afterwards married King Edward the Fourth.

7. THE ACTION AT FERRYBRIDGE, in Yorkshire, May 28, 1461, between lord Clifford on the part of King Henry, and the lord Fitzwalter on the part of the duke of York.

KILLED—230, among whom were lord Fitzwalter, John lord Clifford, and the bastard son of the earl of Salisbury.

8. THE BATTLE OF TOWTON, four miles from York, Palm-Sunday, March 29, 1461, between Edward duke of York and King Henry; in which King Henry was defeated.

KILLED—37,046; among whom were Henry Percy earl of Northumberland, the earl of Shrewsbury, and the lords Nevil, Beaumond, Willoughby, Wells, Roos, Gray, Dacres, and Fitzhugh. The earl of Devonshire was taken prisoner; and soon afterwards beheaded at York.

9. THE BATTLE OF HEDGELEY MOOR, in Northumberland, April 29, 1463, between John Nevil Viscount Montague, on the part of King Edward IV. and the lords Hungerford and Roos on the part of King Henry VI. in which the Yorkists were victorious.

KILLED—108, among whom was Sir Ralph Percy.

10. THE BATTLE OF HEXHAM, May 15, 1463, between viscount Montague and King Henry, in which he was defeated.

KILLED—2024. Henry Beaufort, duke of Somerset, and the lords Roos and Hungerford, fighting on the side of King Henry, were taken prisoners, and soon afterwards beheaded.

11. THE BATTLE OF HEDGECOTE, four miles from Banbury, July 25, 1469, between William Herbert earl of Pembroke, on the part of King Edward, and the lords Fitzhugh and Latimer, and Sir John Conyers, on the part of King Henry; in which the Lancastrians were defeated.

KILLED—5009. The earl of Pembroke and his brothers, Richard Widville earl of Rivers, father to King Edward's queen, Sir John Widville, John Tiptoft earl of Worcester, the lords Willoughby, Stafford and Wells, were taken prisoners, and soon afterwards beheaded.

13 THE BATTLE OF STAMFORD, in Lincolnshire, October 1, 1469, between Sir Robert Wells and King Edward; in which the former was defeated and taken prisoner. The vanquished who fled, in order to lighten themselves threw away their coats, whence the place of combat was called Losecoatfield.

KILLED—10,000.

14. THE BATTLE OF BARNET, on Easter-Sunday, April 14, 1471, between King Edward on one side, and the earl of Warwick, the marquis of Montague and the earl of Oxford on the part of King Henry VI. in which the Lancastrians were defeated.

KILLED—" more than a thousand;" among whom were the earl of Warwick, the marquis of Montague, the lord Cromwell, and the son and heir of lord Say.

15. THE BATTLE OF TEWKSBURY, May 3, 1471, between King Edward and Queen Margaret, in which the queen was defeated, and she and her son Prince Edward were taken prisoners.

Q 5

On

of the ſame kind; yet many of the characters are well diſcriminated, King Henry, and his queen, king Edward, the duke of Glouceſter, and the earl of Warwick, are very ſtrongly and diſtinctly painted.

The old copies of the two latter parts of *King Henry VI.* and of *King Henry V.* are ſo apparently imperfect and mutilated, that there is no reaſon for ſuppoſing them the firſt draughts of Shakſpeare. I am inclined to believe them copies taken by ſome auditor who wrote down, during the repreſentation, what the time would permit, then perhaps filled up ſome of his omiſſions at a ſecond or third hearing, and when he had by this method formed ſomething like a play, ſent it to the printer. JOHNSON.

So, Heywood, in the Preface to his *Rape of Lucrece*, (fourth impreſſion) 1630:

" — for though ſome have uſed a double ſale of their labours, firſt to the ſtage and after to the preſs, for my own part I here proclaim myſelf ever faithful to the firſt, and never guilty of the laſt: yet ſince ſome of my plays have (unknown to me, and without any of my direction) accidentally come into the printer's hands, and therefore ſo corrupt and mangled *(copied only by the ear)*, that I have been as unable to know them as aſhamed to challenge them, this therefore I was the willinger," &c. COLLINS.

I formerly coincided with Dr. Johnſon on this ſubject, at a time when I had examined the two old plays publiſhed in quarto under the title of *The Whole Contention of the two famous houſes of York and Lancaſter*, in two parts, with leſs attention than I have lately done. That dramas were ſometimes imperfectly taken down in the theatre, and afterwards publiſhed in a very mutilated ſtate, is proved deciſively by the prologue to a play entitled *If you knew not me you knew Nobody*, by Thomas Heywood, 1623:

" ———— 'Twas ill nurſt,
" And yet receiv'd as well perform'd at firſt;
" Grac'd and frequented; for the cradle age
" Did throng the ſeats, the boxes, and the ſtage,
" So much, that ſome by *ſtenography* drew
" The plot, *put it in print*, ſcarce one word true:
" And in that lameneſs it has limp'd ſo long,
" The author now, to vindicate that wrong,
" Hath took the pains upright upon its feet
" To teach it walk;—ſo pleaſe you, ſit and ſee it."

But the old plays in quarto, which have been hitherto ſuppoſed to be imperfect repreſentations of the ſecond and third parts of *K. Henry VI.* are by no means mutilated and imperfect. The ſcenes are as well connected, and the verſification as correct, as that of moſt of the other dramas of that time. The fact therefore, which Heywood's prologue aſcertains, throws no light upon the preſent conteſted queſtion. Such obſervations as I have made upon it, I ſhall ſubjoin in a diſtinct Eſſay on the ſubject. MALONE.

There is another circumſtance which may ſerve to ſtrengthen Dr. Johnſon's ſuppoſition, viz. moſt of the fragments of Latin verſes omitted in the quartos, are to be found in the folio; and when any of them are inſerted in the former, they are ſhamefully corrupted and miſ-ſpelt. The auditor, who underſtood Engliſh, might be unſkill'd in any other language. STEEVENS.

I have already given ſome reaſons, why I cannot believe, that theſe plays were *originally* written by Shakſpeare. The queſtion, who did write them? is at beſt, but an argument: *ad ignorantiam.* We muſt remember,

remember, that very many old plays are *anonymous*; and that *play-writing* was scarcely yet thought reputable: nay, some authors expres for it great horrors of repentance.—I will attempt, however, at some future time, to answer this question: the disquisition of it would be too long for this place.

One may at least argue, that the plays were not written by Shakspeare, from Shakspeare himself. The *Chorus*, at the end of *K. Henry V.* addresses the audience.

> "———— for their sake,
> " In your fair minds let *this* acceptance take."

But it could be neither agreeable to the poet's judgment, or his modesty, to recommend his new play from the merit and success of *King Henry VI*—His claim to indulgence is, that, though *bending* and unequal to the task, he has ventured to *pursue the story*: and this sufficiently accounts for the connection of the whole, and the allusions of particular passages. FARMER.

It is seldom that Dr. Farmer's arguments fail to enforce conviction; but here, perhaps, they may want somewhat of their usual weight. I think that Shakspeare's bare mention of these pieces, is a sufficient proof they were his. That they were so, could be his only motive for inferring benefit to himself from the spectator's recollection of their past success. For the sake of three historical dramas of mine which have already afforded you entertainment, let me (says he) intreat your indulgence to a fourth. Surely this was a stronger plea in his behalf than any arising from the kind reception which another might have already met with in the same way of writing. Shakspeare's claim to favour is founded on his having previously given pleasure in the course of three of those histories; because he is a *bending*, supplicatory author, and not a literary bully like Ben Jonson; and because he has ventured to exhibit a series of annals in a suite of plays, an attempt which till then had not received the sanction of the stage.

I hope Dr. Farmer did not wish to exclude the three dramas before us, together with the *Taming of a Shrew*, from the number of those produced by our author, on account of the Latin quotations to be found in them. His proofs of Shakspeare's want of learning are too strong to stand in need of such a support; and yet *Venus and Adonis*, "the first heire of his invention," is usher'd into the world with a Latin motto:

> Vilia miretur vulgus; mihi flavus Apollo.
> Pocula Castalia plena ministrat aqua. STEEVENS.

Though the objections, which have been raised to the genuineness of the *three plays of Henry the sixth*, have been fully considered and answered by Dr. Johnson, it may not be amiss to add here, from a contemporary writer, a passage, which not only points at Shakspeare as the author of them, but also shews, that, however meanly we may now think of them in comparison with his latter productions, they had, at the time of their appearance, a sufficient degree of excellence to alarm the jealousy of the older playwrights. The passage, to which I refer, is in a pamphlet, entitled, *Greene's Groatsworth of Witte*, supposed to have been written by that voluminous author, Robert Greene, M. A. and said, in the title page to be *published at his dying request*; probably, about 1592. The conclusion of this piece is an address to his brother-poets, to dissuade them from writing any more for the stage, on account of the ill treatment which they were used to receive from the players. It begins thus: *To those gentlemen, his quondam acquaintance, that spend their wits in making playes, R. G. wisheth a better exercise, &c.* After having addrest himself particularly to *Christopher Marlowe*

Marlowe and *Thomas Lodge*, (as I guess from circumstances, for their names are not mentioned; he goes on to a third (perhaps *George Peele*;) and having warned him against *depending on so meane a stay* as the players, he adds: *Yes, trust them not: for there is an upstart crow beautified with our feathers, that with his* tygres head wrapt in a players hide, *supposes hee is as well able to bombaste out a blanke verse as the best of you; and being an absolute* Johannes fac totum *is, in his own conceit, the onely* Shake-scene *in a country*. There can be no doubt, I think, that *Shake-scene* alludes to *Shakspeare*; or that *tygres head wrapt in a players hyde* is a parodie upon the following line of York's speech to Margaret, *Third Part of King Henry the Sixth*, A&t I. sc. iv.

" Oh *tygres* heart, *wrapt in a* woman's *hide*. TYRWHITT.

DISSERTATION

ON

THE THREE PARTS

OF

KING HENRY VI.

THE CONTENTS.

THE subject stated. The inferior parts in these three plays being of a different complexion from the inferior parts of Shakspeare's undoubted performances, a proof that they were not written *originally* and *entirely* by him, p. 357.—The editor's hypothesis   *The* First *Part of K. Henry VI* not written by Shakspeare, or a very small part of it written by him.— *The* Second *and* Third *Part of K. Henry VI.* formed by Shakspeare on two elder plays, the one entitled *The first part of the Contention of the two famous houses of Yorke and Lancaster, with the death of the good duke Humphrey,* &c. the other, *The true Tragedie of Richarde duke of Yorke, and the death of good King Henrie the Sixt.* p. 358.

THE FIRST PART OF K. HENRY VI.

The diction, versification, and allusions, of this piece all different from the diction, versification, and allusions of Shakspeare, and corresponding with those of the dramatists that preceded him, p 358—365. Date of this play some years before 1592 ; p 365. Other internal evidence (beside the diction, &c.) that this piece was not written by Shakspeare ; nor by the author of *The first part of the Contention of the two houses,* &c. nor by the author of *The true tragedie of Richarde duke of Yorke,* p 366—367. Presumptive proof that this play was not written by Shakspeare, from its not containing any familiarities of thought to his undisputed plays, nor of expression, (except in a single instance,) and from its general paucity of rhymes, p. 368.

THE SECOND AND THIRD PART OF K. HENRY VI.

I. EXTERNAL EVIDENCE. 1. The entry of *The first part of the Contention of the two houses,* &c. at Stationers' Hall in 1594, *anonymous.* 2. That piece, and *The true tragedie of Richard duke of Yorke,* printed in 1600, *anonymously.* Shakspeare's name afterwards fraudulently affixed to these pieces, and why. The same artifice practised with respect to other plays

C O N T E N T/S.

plays *on which he had conftructed dramas*, p. 369—370. 3. Thefe two old plays performed by Lord Pembroke's fervants, by whom *Titus Andronicus*, and *The old Taming of a Shrew* were performed, and by whom not one of Shakfpeare's undifputed plays were reprefented, p. 371. 4. Reafons affigned for fuppofing Robert Greene, or George Peele, or both, the author or authors of the old plays, p. 371—372. Thefe pieces *new-modelled* and *re-written* by Shakfpeare, with great additions, which in the prefent edition are diftinguifhed by a peculiar mark, p. 372. The mode taken by Shakfpeare, p: 372—376. 6. The fraud of Pavier the bookfeller, who in the year 1619, after the death of Shakfpeare, affixed his name to thefe two old plays, accounted for, p. 376—377. 7. Thefe two old pieces being printed and re-printed, and *The firft part of K. Henry VI.* not being printed, in Shakfpeare's life time, a prefumptive proof that he new-modelled the former, and had little or no concern with the latter, p. 378.

II. INTERNAL EVIDENCE. 1. The VARIATIONS between the two old plays in quarto, and the correfponding pieces in the folio edition of our author's dramatic works, of fo peculiar a nature, as to mark *two diftinct* hands. Several paffages and circumftances found in the old plays, of which there is no trace in Shakfpeare's new modification of them; others materially varying. Thefe infertions and variations could not have arifen from unfkilful copyifts or fhort-hand-writers, who fometimes curtail and mutilate, but do not invent and amplify, p. 378—383. 2. The RESEMBLANCES between certain paffages in Shakfpeare's *Second and Third Part of K. Henry VI.* and his undifputed works, a proof that he wrote a large portion of thofe plays; and 3. the DISCORDANCIES between them and his undifputed plays, a proof that he did not write the whole; thefe refemblances being found *only* in the folio, that is, in the plays as new-modelled by Shakfpeare; and thefe difcordancies being found in the old quarto plays, from whence it muft be prefumed that they were adopted through careleffnefs or hafte, p. 383.—386. 4. The peculiar INACCURACIES of Shakfpeare; and 5. his peculiar PHRASEOLOGY, which are found in *The Second* and *Third Part of K. Henry VI.* as exhibited in folio, and not in the old quarto plays printed in 1600, prove that there were two diftinct hands in thefe pieces; p. 387—388. So alfo do, 6. the TRANSPOSITIONS, p. 389; and 7. the REPETITIONS, p. 390; and 8. the INCONSISTENCIES arifing from fometimes following, and fometimes departing from, an original

ginal

CONTENTS.

ginal model, p. 391. 9. Hall the historian on whose Chronicle the old plays in quarto were constructed, but Holinshed and not Hall, Shakspeare's historian, p. 392—393.

The old plays on which Shakspeare formed his *Second* and *Third Parts of K. Henry VI.* probably written by the author of *King John*, printed in 1591, whoever he was ; p. 394. An attempt made to account for *The First Part of K. Henry VI.* being printed in the first folio edition of our poet's dramatick works, p. 395. Objections of Dr. Johnson and others, enumerated. Recapitulation, p. 396. A considerable part of the English history dramatized before the time of Shakspeare ; and many of his historical and other plays formed on those of preceding writers. Conclusion, p. 397.

A

DISSERTATION

ON

THE THREE PARTS

OF

KING HENRY VI,

TENDING TO SHEW

That thofe Plays were *not* written ORIGINALLY by
SHAKSPEARE.

SEVERAL paffages in *The* Second *and* Third *Part of King Henry VI.* appearing evidently to be of the hand of Shakfpeare, I was long of opinion that the *three* hiftorical dramas which are the fubject of the prefent difquifition, were properly afcribed to him ; not then doubting that the whole of thefe plays was the production of the fame perfon. But a more minute inveftigation of the fubject, into which I have been led by the prefent revifion of all our author's works, has convinced me, that though the premifes were true, my conclufion was too haftily drawn ; for though the hand of Shakfpeare is unqueftionably found in the two latter of thefe plays, it does not therefore neceffarily follow, that they were *originally* and *entirely* compofed by him. My thoughts upon this point have already been intimated in the foregoing notes :— but it is now neceffary for me to ftate my opinion more particularly, and to lay before the reader the grounds on which, after a very careful inquiry, it has been formed.

What at prefent I have chiefly in view is, to account for the vifible *inequality* in thefe pieces ; many traits of Shakfpeare being clearly difcernible in them, while the inferior parts are not merely unequal to the reft, (from which no certain conclufion can be drawn,) but of quite a different complexion from the inferior parts of our author's undoubted performances.

My hypothefis then is, that *The* Firft *Part of K. Henry VI.*

VI. as it now appears, (of which no quarto copy is extant,) was the entire or nearly the entire production of some ancient dramatist ; that *The Whole Contention of the two Houses of York and Lancaster,* &c. written probably before the year 1590, and printed in quarto, in 1600, was also the composition of some writer who preceded Shakspeare; and that from this piece, which is in two parts, (the former of which is entitled, *The first Part of the Contention of the two famous Houses of Yorke and Lancaster, with the death of the good duke Humphrey,* &c. and the latter, *The true Tragedie of Richard duke of Yorke, and the death of good King Henrie the Sixt,)* our poet formed the two plays, entitled *The Second and* Third *Parts of K. Henry VI.* as they appear in the first folio edition of his works.

Mr. Upton has asked, " How does the painter distinguish copies from originals but by manner and style? And have not authors their peculiar style and manner, from which a true critick can form as unerring a judgment as a painter?" Dr. Johnson, though he has shewn, with his usual acuteness, that " this illustration of the critick's science will not prove what is desired," acknowledges in a preceding note, that " dissimilitude of style and heterogeneousness of sentiment may sufficiently shew that a work does not really belong to the reputed author. But in these plays (he adds) no such mark of spuriousness are found. The diction, the versification, and the figures are Shakspeare's."—By these criteria then let us examine *The* First *Part of King Henry VI.* (for I choose to consider that piece separately ;) and if the diction, the figures, or rather the allusions, and the versification of that play, (for these are our surest guides) shall appear to be different from the other two parts, *as they are exhibited in the folio,* and from our author's other plays, we may fairly conclude that he was not the writer of it.

I. With respect to the diction and allusions, which I shall consider under the same head, it is very observable that in *The* First *Part of K. Henry VI.* there are more allusions to mythology, to classical authors, and to ancient and modern history, than I believe, can be found in any one piece of our author's written on an English story ; and that these allusions are introduced very much in the same manner as they are introduced in the plays of Greene, Peele, Lodge, and other dramatists who preceded Shakspeare ; that is, they do not naturally arise out of the subject, but seem to be inserted merely to shew the writer's learning. Of these the following are the most remarkable.

1. Mars his true moving, even as in the heavens,
   So in the earth, to this day is not known.

2. A

2. A far more glorious ftar thy foul will make
   Than Julius Cæfar, or bright—

This blank, Dr. Johnſon with the higheſt probability conjectures, ſhould be filled up with " Berenice;" a word that
the tranſcriber or compoſitor probably could not make out.—
In the ſame manner he left a blank in a ſubſequent paſſage for
the name of " Nero, as is indubitably proved by the following line, which aſcertains the omitted word. See N°. 6.

3. Was Mahomet inſpired with a dove?
4. Helen, the mother of Great Conſtantine,
   Nor yet Saint Philip's daughters, were like thee.
5. Froiſard, a countryman of ours, records, &c.
6. ——— and, like thee, [Nero,]
   Play on the lute, beholding the towns burning.

[In the original copy there is a blank where the word *Nero*
is now placed]

7. The ſpirit of deep prophecy ſhe hath,
   Exceeding the nine Sybils of old Rome.
8. A witch, by fear, not force, like Hannibal,
   Drives back our troops—
9. Divineſt creature, Aſtræ's daughter—.
10. ——— Adonis' gardens,
    That one day bloom'd, and fruitful were the next.
11. A ſtatelier pyramis to her I'll rear,
    Than Rhodope's, or Memphis', ever was.
12. ——— an urn more precious
    Than the rich-jewel'd coffer of Darius.
13. I ſhall as famous be by this exploit,
    As Scythian Thomyris, by Cyrus' death.
14. I thought I ſhould have ſeen ſome Hercules,
    A ſecond Hector, for his grim aſpect.
15. Neſtor-like aged, in an age of care.
16. Then follow thou thy deſperate ſire of Crete,
    Thou Icarus.
17. Where is the great Alcides of the field ?
18. Now am I like that proud inſulting ſhip,
    That Cæſar and his fortune bare at once.
19. Is Talbot ſlain; the Frenchman's only ſcourge,
    Your kingdom's terror, and black Nemeſis ?
20. Thou may'ſt not wander in that labyrinth ;
    There Minotaurs, and ugly treaſons lurk.
21. See, how the ugly witch doth bend her brows,
    As if, with Circe, ſhe would change my ſhape.
22. ——— thus he goes,

As

As did the youthful Paris once to Greece ;
With hope to find the like event in love.

Of particular expreffions there are many in this play, that
feem to me more likely to have been ufed by the authors already named, than by Shakfpeare; but I confefs, with Dr.
Johnfon, that fingle words can conclude little. However,
I will juft mention that the words *proditor* and *immanity*, which
occur in this piece, are not, I believe, found in any of Shakfpeare's undifputed performances: not to infift on a direct
Latinifm, *pile-efteemed*, which I am confident was the word
intended by the author, though, being a word of his own
formation, the compofitor has printed—*pil'd-efteem'd*, inftead of it[1].

The verfification of this play appears to me clearly of a
different colour from that of all our author's genuine dramas,
while at the fame time it refembles that of many of the plays
produced before the time of Shakfpeare.

In all the tragedies written before his time, or juft when he
commenced author, a certain ftately march of verfification is
very obfervable. The fenfe concludes or paufes almoft uni-
formly at the end of every line ; and the verfe has fcarcely
ever a redundant fyllable. As the reader may not have any
of thefe pieces at hand, (by the poffeffion of which, however,
his library would not be much enriched,) I fhall add a few
inftances,—the firft that occur :

" Moft loyal lords, and faithful followers,
" That have with me, unworthy general,
" Paffed the greedy gulph of Ocean,
" Leaving the confines of fair Italy,
" Behold, your Brutus draweth nigh his end,
" And I muft leave you, though againft my will.
" My finews fhrink, my numbed fenfes fail,
" A chilling cold poffeffeth all my bones ;
" Black ugly death, with vifage pale and wan,
" Prefents himfelf before my dazzled eyes,
" And with his dart prepared is to ftrike."

Locrine, 1595.

" My lord of Gloucefter, and lord Mortimer,
" To do you honour in your fovereign's eyes,
" That, as we hear, is newly come aland,
" From Paleftine, with all his men of war,
" (The poor remainder of the royal fleet,
" Preferv'd by miracle in Sicil road,)

---

[1] See *K. Henry VI.* P. I. p. 21, n.

" Go

" Go mount your courfers, meet him on the way :
" Pray him to fpur his fteed, minutes and hours,
" Until his mother fee her princely fon,
" Shining in glory of his fafe return."

Edward I. by George Peele, 1593.

" Then go thy ways, and clime up to the clouds,
" And tell Apollo that Orlando fits
" Making of verfes for Angelica.
" And if he do deny to fend me down
" The fhirt which Deianira fent to Hercules,
" To make me brave upon my wedding day,
" Tell him I'll pafs the Alps, and up to Meroe,
" (I know he knows that watry lakifh hill)
" And pull the harp out of the minftrels hands,
" And pawne it unto lovely Proferpine,
" That fhe may fetch the faire Angelica."

Orlando Furiofo, by Robert Greene, printed
in 1599 ; written before 1592.

" The work that Ninus rear'd at Babylon,
" The brazen walls fram'd by Semiramis,
" Carv'd out like to the portal of the funne,
" Shall not be fuch as rings the Englifh ftrand
" From Dover to the market place of Rye."

*   *   *

" To plain our queftions, as Apollo did."

*   *   *

" Facile and debonaire in all his deeds,
" Proportion'd as was Paris, when in gray,
" He courted Oenon in the vale by Troy."

*   *   *

" Who dar'd for Edward's fake cut through the feas,
" And venture as Agenor's damfel through the deepe."

*   *   *

" England's rich monarch, brave Plantagenet,
" The Pyren mountains fwelling above the clouds,
" That ward this wealthy Caftile in with walls,
" Could not detain the beauteous Eleanor ;
" But hearing of the fame of Edward's youth,
" She dar'd to brave Neptunus' haughty pride,
" And brave the brunt of froward Eolus."

" Daphne, the damfel that caught Phœbus faft,
" And lock'd him in the brightnefs of her looks,
" Was not fo beauteous in Apollo's eyes,
" As is fair Margaret, to the Lincoln earl."

*　　　*　　　*

" We muft lay plots for ftately tragedies,
" Strange comic fhews, fuch as proud Rofcius
" Vaunted before the Roman emperours."

*　　　*　　　*

" Lacy, thou can'ft not fhrowd thy traiterous thoughts,
" Nor cover, as did Caffius, all his wiles;
" For Edward hath an eye that looks as far,
" As Lynceus from the fhores of Greecia."

*　　　*　　　*

" Pardon, my lord : If Jove's great royalty
" Sent me fuch prefents as to Danae ;
" If Phœbus tied to Latona's webs,
" Came courting from the beauty of his lodge ;
" The dulcet tunes of frolick Mercurie,
" Nor all the wealth heaven's treafury affords,
" Should make me leave lord Lacy or his love."

*　　　*　　　*

" What will thou do ?—
" Shew thee the tree leav'd with refined gold,
" Whereon the fearful dragon held his feate,
" That watch'd the garden call'd Hefperides,
" Subdued and wonne by conquering Hercules."

*

" ———— Margaret,
" That overfhines our damfels, as the moone
" Darkens the brighteft fparkles of the night."

*　　　*　　　*

" Should Paris enter in the courts of Greece,
" And not lie fettered in fair Helen's looks ?
" Or Phœbus fcape thofe piercing amorifts,
" That Daphne glanced at his deitie ?
" Can Edward then fit by a flame and freeze,
" Whofe heat puts Helen and fair Daphne down ?

The honourable Hiflorie of Friar Bacon, &c. by Robert
Greene; written before 1592, printed in 1598.

" *King.* Thus far, ye Englifh peers, have we difplay'd
" Our waving enfigns with a happy war ;
" Thus nearly hath our furious rage reveng'd

" My

" My daughter's death upon the traiterous Scot :
" And now before Dunbar our camp is pitch'd,
" Which if it yield not to our compromife,
" The place fhall furrow where the palace ftood,
" And fury fhall envy' fo high a power,
" That mercy fhall be banifh'd from our fword.
  " *Doug.* What feeks the Englifh king ?
  " *King.* Scot, ope thefe gates, and let me enter in.
" Submit thyfelf and thine unto my grace,
" Or I will put each mother's fon to death,
" And lay this city level with the ground."

James IV. by Robert Greene, printed in
1598 ; written before 1592.

  " Valeria, attend ; I have a lovely bride
" As bright as is the heaven chryftaline ;
" As faire as is the milke white way of Jove,
" As chafte as Phœbe in her fummer fports,
" As foft and tender as the azure downe
" That circles Citherea's filver doves ;
" Her do I meane to make my lovely bride,
" And in her bed to breathe the fweet content
" That I, thou know'ft, long time have aimed at."

The Taming of a Shrew, written before 1594.

  " *Pol.* Faire Emilia, fummers bright fun queene,
" Brighter of hew than is the burning clime
" Where Phœbus in his bright equator fits,
" Creating gold and pretious minerals,
" What would Emilia doe, if I were fond
" To leave fair Athens, and to range the world ?
  " *Emil.* Should thou affay to fcale the feate of Jove,
" Mounting the fubtle airie regions,
" Or be fnatcht up, as erft was Ganimede,
" Love fhould give wings unto my fwift defires,
" And prune my thoughts, that I would follow thee,
" And fall and perifh as did Icarus." *Ibid.*

  " Barons of England, and my noble lords,
" Though God and fortune have bereft from us
" Victorious Richard, fcourge of infidels,
" And clad this land in ftole of difmal hue,
" Yet give me leave to joy, and joy you all,
" That from this wombe hath fprung a fecond hope,
" A king that may in rule and virtue both
" Succeed his brother in his emperie."

The troublefome raigue of King John, 1591.

" —— as fometimes Phaeton,
" Miftrufting filly Merops for his re——." *Ibid.*

" As curfed Nero with his mother did,
" So I with you, if you refolve me not." *Ibid.*

* * *

" Peace, Arthur, peace! thy brother. makes thee wings,
" To foar with. peril after Icarus." *Ibid.*

* * *

" How doth Alecto whifper in my ears,
" Delay not, Philip, kill the villaine ftraight." *Ibid.*

* * *

" *Philippus atavis edite regibus,*
" What faift thou, Philip, fprung of ancient kings,—
" *Quo me rapit tempeftas?*" *Ibid.*

* * *

" Morpheus, leave here thy filent Ebon cave,
" Befiege his thoughts with difmal phantafies;
" And ghaftly objects of pale threatning Mors,
" Affright him every minute with ftern looks." *Ibid.*

* * *

" Here is the ranfome that allaies his rage,
" The firft freehold that Richard left his fonne,
" With which I fhall furprize his living fpies,
" As Hector's ftatue did the fainting Greeks." *Ibid.*

* * *

" This curfed country, where the traitors breathe,
" Whofe perjurie (as proud Briareus)
" Beleaguers all the fky with mifbelief." *Ibid.*

* * *

" Muft Conftance fpeak? let tears prevent her talk.
" Muft I difcourfe? let *Dido* figh, and fay,
" She weeps again to hear the wrack of Troy." *Ibid.*

* * *

" John, 'tis thy fins that make it miferable.
" *Quicquid delirant reges, plectuntur, Achivi.*" *Ibid.*

* * *

" *King.* Robert of Artoys, banifh'd though thou be,
" From France, thy native country, yet with us
" Thou fhalt retain as great a figniorie,
" For we create thee earl of Richmond here:
" And now go forwards with our pedigree;
" Who next fucceeded Philip of Bew?
" *Art.* Three fonnes of his, which, all fuccefsfully,
" Did fit upon their father's regal throne;
" Yet died, and left no iffue of their loynes.
" *King.* But was my mother fifter unto thefe?

" *Art.*

" *Art.* She was, my lord; and only Ifabel
" Was all the daughters that this Philip had."
                    The raigne of King Edward III. 1596.

The tragedies of *Marius and Sylla*, by T. Lodge, 1594,
A Looking-Glafs for London and England, by T. Lodge and
R. Greene, 1598, *Solyman and Perfeda*, written before
1592, *Selimus Emperor of the Turks*, 1594, *The Spanifh Tragedy*, 1592, and *Titus Andronicus*, will all furnifh examples
of a fimilar verfification ; a verfification fo exactly correfponding with that of *The firft Part of King Henry VI.* and *The
Whole Contention of the two Houfes of Torke and Lancafter*,
&c. as it originally appeared, that I have no doubt thefe
plays were the production of fome one or other of the authors
of the pieces above quoted or enumerated.

A paffage in a pamphlet written by Thomas Nafhe, an in-
timate friend of Greene, Peele, &c. fhews that The *firft* part
of *King Henry VI.* had been on the ftage before 1592 ; and
his favourable mention of this piece inclines me to believe
that it was written by a friend of his. " How would it have
joyed brave Talbot, (fays Nafhe in *Pierce Pennileffe his Supplication to the Devil*, 1592,) the terror of the French, to
thinke that after he had lyen two hundred yeares in his tombe,
he fhould triumph again on the ftage ; and have his bones
new embalmed with the teares of ten thoufand fpectators at
leaft, (at feveral times) who in the tragedian that reprefents
his perfon behold him frefh bleeding "

This paffage was feveral years ago pointed out by my friend
Dr. Farmer, as a proof of the hypothefis which I am now
endeavouring to eftablifh. That it related to the old play of
K. Henry VI. or, as it is now called, *The firft Part of King
Henry VI.* cannot, I think, be doubted. *Talbot* appears in
the *firft* part, and not in the *fecond* or *third* part ; and is exprefsly fpoken of in the play, (as well as in Hall's Chronicle)
as " the terror of the French." Holinfhed, who was
Shakfpear's guide, omits the paffage in Hall, in which Talbot is thus defcribed ; and this is an additional proof that this
play was not our author's. But of this more hereafter.

The firft part of King Henry VI. (as it is now called) fur-
nifhes us with other *internal* proofs alfo of its not being the
work of Shakfpeare.

1. The author of that play, whoever he was, does not
feem precifely to have known how old Henry the Sixth was
at the time of his father's death. He opens his play indeed
with the funeral of Henry the Fifth, but no where mentions
exprefsly the young king's age. It is clear, however, from
                                                        one

one paſſage, that he ſuppoſed him to have paſſed the ſtate of
infancy before he loſt his father, and even to have remembered ſome of his ſayings. In the fourth act, ſc iv. ſpeaking
of the famous Talbot, he ſays,

> When *I was young*, (as yet I am not old,)
> *I do remember how my father ſaid,*
> A ſtouter champion never handled ſword.

But Shakſpeare, as appears from two paſſages, one in the *ſecond,* and the other in the *third,* part of *King Henry VI.*
knew that that king could not poſſibly remember any thing
his father had ſaid ; and therefore Shakſpeare could not have
been the author of the *firſt* part.

> No ſooner was I crept out of my cradle,
> But I was made a king at *nine months old.*
> > *K. Henry VI. P. II. Act. IV. ſc. ix.*
> When I was crown'd, I was but *nine months old.*
> > *K. Henry VI. P III. Act I. ſc. i.*

The firſt of theſe paſſages is found in the folio copy of The
ſecond part of *King Henry VI.* and not in *The firſt Part of the
Contention,* &c. printed in quarto ; and according to my hypotheſis, was one of Shakſpeare's additions to the old play.—
This therefore does not prove that the *original* author, whoever
he was, was not likewiſe the author of the *firſt* part of *King
Henry VI.* but, what is more material to our preſent queſtion,
it proves that *Shaſpeare* could not be the author of that play. The
ſecond of theſe paſſages is found in *The true Tragedie of Richard
duke of Yorke,* &c. and is a deciſive proof that The *firſt* part
of *King Henry VI.* was written *neither* by the author of that
tragedy, nor by Shakſpeare.

2 A ſecond internal proof that Shakſpeare was not the author of the *firſt* part of theſe three plays, is furniſhed by that
ſcene, (Act II. ſc. v. p. 38) in which it is ſaid, that the
earl of Cambridge *raiſed an army* againſt his ſovereign. But
Shakſpeare in his play of *King Henry V.* has repreſented the
matter truly as it was ; the earl being in the ſecond act of
that hiſtorical piece condemned at Southampton for conſpiring
to *aſſaſſinate* Henry.

3. I may likewiſe add, that the author of The *firſt* part of
K. Henry VI knew the pronunciation of the word *Hecate,*
and has uſed it as it is uſed by the Roman writers :

> I ſpeak not to that railing *Heca-te."*

But Shakſpeare in his *Macbeth* always uſes *Hecate* as a diſſyllable ; and therefore could not have been the author of the
other piece [2].   **Having**

---

[2] It may perhaps appear a minute remark, but I cannot help obſerving that the ſecond ſpeech in this play aſcertains the writer to have been
very converſant with Hall's Chronicle :

"*What*

Having now, as I conceive, vindicated Shakſpeare from being the writer of The *firſt* part of *King Henry VI.* it may
ſeem unneceſſary to inquire who was the author; or whether
it was the production of the ſame perſon or perſons who
wrote the two pieces, entitled, *The firſt Part of the Contention
of the two Houſes,* &c. and *The true Tragedie of Richard
duke of Yorke,* &c. However, I ſhall add a word or two on
that point.

We have already ſeen that the author of the play laſt named
could not have written *The firſt Part of K. Henry VI.* The
following circumſtances prove that it could not have been
written by the author of *The firſt Part of the Contention,* &c.
ſuppoſing for a moment that piece, and *The true Tragedie of
the duke of Yorke,* &c. to have been the works of different
hands.

1. The writer of *The firſt Part of the Contention,* &c.
makes Saliſbury ſay to Richard duke of York, that the perſon from whom the duke derived his title, (he means his maternal uncle Edmund Mortimer, though he ignorantly gives
him a different appellation,) was " done to death by that
monſtrous rebel Owen Glendower;" and Shakſpeare in this
has followed him :

> *Sal.* This Edmund, in the reign of Bolingbroke,
> As I have read, laid claim unto the crown ;
> And, but for Owen Glendower, had been king,
> Who kept him in captivity, till he died.

On this falſe aſſertion the duke of York makes no remark.
But the author of *The Firſt Part of K. Henry VI.* has repreſented this Edmund Mortimer, not as put to death, or kept
in captivity to the time of his death, by Owen Glendower,
(who himſelf died in the ſecond year of *King Henry V.* but as
a *ſtate* priſoner, who died in the Tower in the reign of *King
Henry VI.* in the preſence of this very duke of York, who
was then only Richard Plantagenet [3].

2. A correct ſtatement of the iſſue of King Edward the
Third, and of the title of Edmund Mortimer to the crown, is
given in *The Firſt Part of King Henry VI.* But in *The firſt
Part of the Contention,* &c. we find a very incorrect and falſe

---

" *What ſhould I ſay?* his deeds exceed all ſpeech."
This phraſe is introduced on almoſt every occaſion by that writer
when he means to be eloquent. Holinſhed and not Hall, was Shakſpeare's hiſtorian (as has been already obſerved); this therefore is an
additional proof that this play was not our author's.

[3] See the firſt part of King Henry VI. p. 39; and the ſecond part p.
134.

ſtatement

ſtatement of Edward's iſſue, and of the title of Mortimer, whoſe father Roger Mortimer, the author of that piece ignorantly calls the *fifth ſon* of that monarch Theſe two plays therefore could not have been the work of one hand.

On all theſe grounds it appears to me clear, that neither Shakſpeare, nor the author of *The firſt Part of the Contention,* &c. or *The true Tragedie of Richard duke of Yorke,* &c. could have been the author of *The* Firſt *Part of King Henry VI.*

It is obſervable that in The *Second* and *Third* Part of *King Henry VI.* many thoughts and many modes of expreſſion are found, which likewiſe occur in Shakſpeare's other dramas: but in the *Firſt* Part I recollect but one marked expreſſion, that is alſo found in one of his undiſputed performances:

" As I am ſick with *working of my thoughts.*"

So, in *K. Henry V:*

" *Work, work your thoughts,* and therein ſee a ſiege."

But ſurely this is too ſlight a circumſtance to overturn all the other circumſtances that have now been urged to prove this play not the production of our author. The co-incidence might be accidental, for it is a co-incidence not of thought but of language;—or the expreſſion might have remained in his mind in conſequence of his having often ſeen this play; (we know that he has borrowed many other expreſſions from preceding writers;)—or laſtly, this might have been one of the very few lines that he wrote on reviſing this piece; which, however few they were, might, with other reaſons, have induced the firſt publiſhers of his works in folio to print it with the *ſecond* and *third* part, and to aſcribe it to Shakſpeare.

Before I quit this part of the ſubject, it may be proper to mention one other circumſtance that renders it very improbable that Shakſpeare ſhould have been the author of The *Firſt* Part of *K. Henry VI.* In this play, though one ſcene is entirely in rhyme, there are very few rhymes diſperſed through the piece, and no alternate rhymes; both of which abound in our author's undiſputed *early* plays. This obſervation indeed may likewiſe be extended to the *ſecond* and *third* part of theſe hiſtorical dramas; and perhaps it may be urged, that if this argument has any weight, it will prove that he had no hand in the compoſition of thoſe plays. But there being no alternate rhymes in thoſe plays may be accounted for, by recollecting that in 1591, Shakſpeare had not written his *Venus and Adonis,* or his *Rape of Lucrece;* the meaſures of which perhaps inſenſibly led him to employ a ſimilar kind of metre occaſion-

ally

ally in the dramas that he wrote fhortly after he had compofed thofe poems.   The paucity of regular rhymes muft be accounted for differently.   My folution is, that working up
the materials which were furnifhed by a preceding writer, he
naturally followed his mode : and in the original plays from
which thefe two were formed very few rhymes were found.
Nearly the fame argument will apply to the *firft* part ; for
its date alfo, were that piece Shakfpeare's, would account
for the want of alternate rhymes.   The paucity of regular
rhymes indeed cannot be accounted for by faying that here
too our author was following the track of another poet ; but
the folution is unneceffary ; for from the beginning to the
end of that play, except perhaps in fome fcenes of the fourth
act, there is not a fingle print of the footfteps of Shakfpeare.

I have already obferved that it is highly improbable that
*The firft Part of the Contention of the two Houfes of York and
Lancafter,* &c. and *The true Tragedie of Richard duke of
Yorke,* &c. printed in 1600, were written by the author of
The firft part of K. Henry VI.   By whom thefe two plays
were written, it is not here neceffary to inquire ; it is fufficient, if probable reafons can be produced for fuppofing this two-
part piece not to have been the compofition of Shakfpeare, but
the work of fome preceding writer, on which he formed thefe
two plays which appear in the firft folio edition of his works,
comprehending a period of twenty-fix years, from the time of
Henry's marriage to that of his death.

II. I now therefore proceed to ftate my opinion concerning *The* Second and Third *Part of K. Henry VI.*

" A book entituled, *The Firft Part of the Contention of the
two famous Houfes of Yorke and Lancafter, with the death of
the good duke Humphrie, and the banifhment and deathe of the
duke of York, and the tragical end of the proude Cardinall
of Winchefter, with the notable rebellion of Jack Cade, and the
duke of Yorke's firft claime unto the crowne,"* was entered at
Stationer's Hall, by Thomas Millington, March 12, 1593-4.
—This play, however, (on which *The* Second *Part of King
Henry VI.* is formed) was not then printed ; nor was *The
true Tragedie of Richard duke of Yorke, and the deathe of good
King Henrie the Sixt, &c.* (on which Shakfpeare's *Third* Part
of King Henry VI. is founded) entered at Stationers' Hall at
the fame time ; but they were both printed for T. Millington
in 1600 [4]

4 They were probably printed in 1600, becaufe Shakfpeare's alterations of them were then popular, as *King Lear and his three daughters*
was printed in 1605, becaufe our author's play was probably at that
time firft produced.

R 5   Th

The firſt thing that ſtrikes us in this entry is, that *the name of Shakſpeare is not mentioned ;* nor, when the two plays were publiſhed in 1600, did the printer aſcribe them to our author in the title-page, (though his reputation was then at the high-eſt,) as ſurely he would have done, had they been his compo-ſitions.

In a ſubſequent edition indeed of the ſame pieces, printed by one Pavier, without date, but in reality in 1619, after our great poet's death, the name of Shakſpeare appears ; but this was a bookſeller's trick, founded upon our author's cele-brity ; on his having new modelled theſe plays ; and on the proprietors of the Globe and Blackfriars' theatre not having publiſhed Shakſpeare's *Second and Third Parts of King Henry VI.* The very ſame deception was practiſed with reſpect to *King John.* The old play (written perhaps by the ſame per-ſon who was the author of *The Contention of the two famous Houſes, &c*) was printed in 1591, like that piece, anony-mouſly. In 1611, (Shakſpeare's *King John,* founded on the ſame ſtory, having been probably often acted and admired,) the old piece in two parts was reprinted ; and, in order to de-ceive the purchaſer, was ſaid in the title-page to be written by *W Sh* A ſubſequent printer in 1622 grew more bold, and affixed Shakſpeare s name to it at full length.

It is obſervable that Millington the bookſeller, by whom *The firſt Part of the Contention of the two famous Houſes, &c.* was entered at Stationers' Hall, in 1593-4, and for whom that piece and *The Tragedie of the duke of Yorke, &c.* were printed in 1600, was not the proprietor of any one of Shak-ſpeare's undiſputed plays, except *King Henry V.* of which he publiſhed a *ſpurious* copy, that, I think, muſt have been im-perfectly taken down in ſhort-hand in the play houſe.

The next obſervable circumſtance with reſpect to theſe two quarto plays, is, that they are ſaid in their title pages to have been " ſundry times acted by the earle of Pembrooke his ſer-vantes." *Titus Andronicus* and *The* old *Taming of a Shrew* were acted by the ſame company of Comedians ; but not *one* of our author's plays is ſaid in its title-page to have been acted by any but the Lord Chamberlain's, or the Queen's, or King's ſervants. This circumſtance alone, in my opinion, might de-cide the queſtion.

This much appears on the firſt ſuperficial view of theſe pie-ces ; but the paſſage quoted by Mr. Tyrwhitt from an old pamphlet, entitled *Greene's Groatſworth of Witte,* &c. affords a ſtill more deciſive ſupport to the hypotheſis that I am endea-vouring to maintain ; which indeed that pamphlet ſuggeſted to me. As this paſſage is the chief hinge of my argument,
. though

though it has already been printed in a preceding page, it is necessary to lay it again before the reader.—" Yes," says the writer, Robert Greene, (addressing himself, as Mr. Tyrwhitt conjectures with great probability, to his poetical friend George Peele,) " trust them [the players] not ; for there is an upstart crowe BEAUTIFIED WITH OUR FEATHERS, that with his *tygers heart wrapped in a players hide* supposes hee is as well able to bombaste out a blank verse as the best of you ; and being an absolute *Johannes fac totum*, is, in his own conceit, the only *Shake-scene* in a country."—" O tyger's heart, wrapt in a woman's hide !" is a line of the old quarto play, entitled *The first part of the Contention of the two houses*, &c.

That Shakspeare was here alluded to, cannot, I think, be doubted. But what does the writer mean by calling him " *a crow beautified with our feathers ?*" My solution is, that GREENE and PEELE were the joint-authors of the two quarto plays, entitled *The first part of the Contention of the two famous houses of Yorke and Lancaster*, &c. and *The true Tragedie of Richarde duke of Yorke*, &c. or that Greene was the author of one, and Peele of the other. Greene's pamphlet, from whence the foregoing passage is extracted, was written recently before his death, which happened in September 1592. How long he and Peele had been dramatick writers, is not precisely ascertained. Peele took the degree of Master of Arts at Oxford, in 1579: Greene took the same degree in Cambridge in 1583. Each of them has left four or five plays, and they wrote several others which have not been published. The earliest of Peele's printed pieces, *The Arraignment of Paris*, appeared in 1584 ; and one of Greene's pamphlets was printed in 1583. Between that year and 1591 it is highly probable that the two plays in question were written. I suspect they were produced in 1588 or 1589. We have undoubted proofs that Shakspeare was not above working on the materials of other men. His *Taming of the Shrew*, his *King John*, and other plays, render any arguments on that point unnecessary. Having therefore probably not long before the year 1592, when Greene wrote this dying exhortation to his friend, new-modelled and amplified these two pieces, and produced on the stage what in the folio edition of his Works are called *The* Second *and* Third *Part of King Henry VI.* and having acquired considerable reputation by them, Greene could not conceal the mortification that he felt at his own fame and that of his associate, both of them old and admired play-wrights, being eclipsed by a new *upstart* writer, (for so he calls our great poet,) who had then first perhaps attracted

the

the notice of the publick by exhibiting two plays, formed upon old dramas written by them, confiderably enlarged and improved. He therefore in direct terms charges him with having acted like the crow in the fable, *beautified himfelf with their feathers ;* in other words, with having acquired fame *furtivis coloribus,* by new-modelling a work originally produced by them : and wifhing to depreciate our author, he very naturally quotes a line from one of the pieces, which Shakfpeare had thus *re-written ;* a proceeding which the authors of the original plays confidered as an invafion both of their literary property and character. This line with many others Shakfpeare adopted without any alteration. The very term that Greene ufes,—" to *bombaft* out a blank verfe," exactly correfponds with what has been now fuggefted. This new poet, fays he, knows as well as any man how to *amplify* and fwell out a blank verfe. *Bumlaft* was a foft ftuff of a loofe texture, by which garments were rendered more fwelling and protuberant.

Several years after the death of Boiardo, Francefco Berni undertook to new verfify Boiardo's poem, entitled ORLANDO INNAMORATO. Berni (as Baretti obferves) " was not fatisfied with merely making the verfification of that poem better ; he interfperfed it with many ftanzas of his own, and changed almoft all the beginnings of the cantos, introducing each of them with fome moral reflection arifing from the canto foregoing." What Berni did to Boiardo's poem after the death of its author, and more, I fuppofe Shakfpeare to have done to *The firft part of the Contention of the two Houfes of Yorke and Lancafter,* &c. and *The true Tragedie of Richarde duke of Yorke,* &c. in the life time of Greene and Peele, their literary parents ; and this *Rifacimento* (as the Italians call it) of thefe two plays I fuppofe to have been executed by Shakfpeare, and exhibited at the Globe and Blackfriars theatre, in the year 1591.

I have faid Shakfpeare did what Berni did, and more. He did not content himfelf with writing new beginnings to the acts ; he new-verfified, he new-modelled, he tranfpofed many of the parts, and greatly amplified and improved the whole.— Several lines, however, and even whole fpeeches which he thought fuffciently polifhed, he accepted, and introduced into his own work, without any, or with very flight, alterations.

In the prefent edition, all thofe lines which he adopted without any alteration, are printed in the ufual manner ; thofe fpeeches which he altered or expanded, are diftinguifhed by inverted commas ; and to all the lines entirely compofed

by

by himself afterisks are prefixed. The total number of lines in our author's *Second* and *Third Part* of *K. Henry VI.* is Six Thousand and Forty-three : of these, as I conceive, 1771 lines were written by some author who preceded Shakspeare ; 2373 were formed by him on the foundation laid by his predecessors ; and 1899 lines were entirely his own composition.

That the reader may have the whole of the subject before him, I shall here transcribe the fourth scene of the fourth act of *The* Third *Part* of *King Henry VI.* (which happens to be a short one,) together with the corresponding scene in the original play ; and also a speech of Queen Margaret in the fifth act, with the original speech on which it is formed. The first specimen will serve to shew the method taken by Shakspeare, where he new-polished the language of the old play, rejecting some part of the dialogue, and making some slight additions to the part which he retained ; the second is a striking proof of his facility and vigour of composition, which has happily expanded a thought comprized originally in a very short speech, into thirty seven lines, none of which appear feeble or superfluous.

The true Tragedie of Richarde buke of Yorke, &c. Sign. F. 4. edit. 1600.

Enter the Queen, and the Lord Rivers.

Riv. Tell me, good madam,
Why is your grace so passionate of late ?
Queene. Why, brother Rivers, heare you not the news
Of that success king Edward had of late ?
Riv. What ? losse of some pitcht battaile against War-
      wick ?
Tush ; fear not, faire queen, but cast these cares aside.
King Edwards noble minde his honours doth display ;
And Warwicke may lose, though then he got the day.
Queene. If that were all, my griefes were at an end ;
But greater troubles will, I fear, befall.
Riv. What ? is he taken prisoner by the foe,
To the danger of his royal person then ?
Queene. I, there's my griefe ; king Edward is surprisde,
And led away as prisoner unto Yorke.
Riv. The newes is passing strange, I must confesse ;
Yet comfort yourselfe, for Edward hath more friends
Than Lancaster at this time must perceive,—
That some will set him in his throne againe.

    i
                                          Queene.

Queene. God grant they may ! but gentle brother, come,
And let me leane upon thine arm a while,
Untill I come unto the fanctuarie ;
There to preferve the fruit within my womb,
King Edwards feed, true heir to Englands crowne.

Exeunt.

KING HENRY VI. PART III. ACT. IV. SCENE IV.

Enter the QUEEN, and RIVERS.

Riv. Madam, what makes you in this fudden change ?
Queen. Why, brother Rivers, are you yet to learn,
What late misfortune is befall'n king Edward ?
Riv. What, lofs of fome pitch'd battle againft Warwick ?
Queen. No, but the lofs of his own royal perfon.
Riv. Then is my fovereign flain ?
Queen. Ay, almoft flain, for he is taken prifoner :
Either betray'd by falfehood of his guard,
Or by his foe furpriz'd at unawares :
And, as I further have to underftand,
Is now committed to the bifhop of York,
Fell Warwick's brother, and by that our foe.
Riv. Thefe news, I muft confefs, are full of grief :
Yet gracious madam, bear it as you may ;
Warwick may lofe, that now hath won the day.
Queen. Till then, fair hope muft hinder life's decay.
And I the rather wean me from defpair,
For love of Edward's offspring in my womb :
That is it that makes me bridle paffion,
And bear with mildnefs my misfortune's crofs ;
Ay, ay, for this I draw in many a tear,
And ftop the rifing of blood-fucking fighs,
Left with my fighs or tears I blaft or drown
King.Edward's fruit, true heir to the Englifh crown.
Riv. But, madam, where is Warwick then become ?
Queen. I am informed, that he comes towards London
To fet the crown once more on Henry's head :
Guefs thou the reft ; king Edward's friends muft down.
But, to prevent the vilant's violence,
(For truft not him that once hath broken faith,)
I'll hence forthwith unto the fanctuary,
To fave at leaft the heir of Edward's right ;
There fhall I left fecure from force and fraud.
Come therefore, let us fly, while we may fly ;
If Warwick takes us, we are fure to die.

[*Exeunt.*

THE TRUE TRAGEDIE OF RICHARDE DUKE OF YORK, &c.
Sign. G 4. edit. 1600.

Enter the Queene, Prince Edward, Oxford, Somerset, with
drumme and souldiers.

Queene. Welcome to England, my loving friends of France;
And welcome Somerset and Oxford too.
Once more have we spread our failes abroad ;
And though our tackling be almost confumde,
And Warwick as our main-mast overthrowne,
Yet, warlike lords, raise you that sturdie post,
That bears the failes to bring us unto rest ;
And Ned and I, as willing pilots should,
For once with careful mindes guide on the sterne,
To bear us thorough that dangerous gulfe,
That heretofore hath swallowed up our friendes.

KING HENRY VI. PART III. ACT V. SCENE IV.

March. Enter Queen MARGARET, *Prince* EDWARD,
SOMERSET, OXFORD, *and Soldiers.*

Q. Mar. Great lords, wise men ne'er sit and wail their
           lofs,
But cheerly seek how to redress their harms.
What though the mast be now blown over-board,
The cable broke, the holding anchor lost,
And half our failors swallow'd in the flood ?
Yet lives our pilot still : Is't meet, that he
Should leave the helm, and, like a fearful lad,
With tearful eyes add water to the sea,
And give more strength to that which hath too much ;
Whiles, in his moan, the ship splits on the rock,
Which industry and courage might have fav'd ?
Ah, what a shame ! ah, what a fault were this !
Say, Warwick was our anchor ; What of that ?
And Montague our top mast ; What of him ?
Our slaughter'd friends the tackles ; What of these ?
Why, is not Oxford here another anchor ?
And Somerset another goodly mast ?
The friends of France our shrouds and tacklings ?
And, though unfkilful, why not Ned and I
For once allow'd the skilful pilot's charge ?
We will not from the helm, to sit and weep ;

But

But keep our courſe, though the rough wind ſay—no,
From ſhelves and rocks that threaten us with wreck.
As good to chide the waves, as ſpeak them fair,
And what is Edward, but a ruthleſs ſea?
What Clarence, but a quick-ſand of deceit?
And Richard, but a ragged fatal rock?
All theſe the enemies to our poor bark.
Say, you can ſwim; alas, 'tis but a while:
Tread on the ſand; why, there you quickly ſink:
Beſtride the rock; the tide will waſh you off,
Or elſe you famiſh, that's a threefold death.
This ſpeak I, lords, to let you underſtand,
In caſe ſome one of you would fly from us,
That there's no hop'd for mercy with the brothers,
More than with ruthleſs waves, with ſands, and rocks.
Why, courage, then! what cannot be avoided,
'Twere childiſh weakneſs to lament, or fear [5].

If the reader wiſhes to compare *The firſt Part of the Conten-*
tion of the two Houſes, &c. with *The* Second *Part of King*
Henry VI. which was formed upon it, he will find variou-
paſſages quoted from the elder drama in the notes on thats
play. The two celebrated ſcenes, in which the dead body
of the duke of Gloſter is deſcribed, and the death of Cardinal Beaufort is repreſented, may be worth examining with
this view; and will ſufficiently aſcertain how our author proceeded in new-modelling that play; with what expreſſion,
animation, and ſplendour of colouring he filled up the outline
that had been ſketched by a preceding writer [6].

Shakſpeare having thus given celebrity to thoſe two old
dramas, by altering and writing ſeveral parts of them over
again, the bookſeller, Millington, in 1593-4, to avail himſelf of the popularity of the new admired poet, got, perhaps
from Peele, who was then living, or from the author, whoever he was, or from ſome of the comedians belonging to the
earl of Pembroke, the *original* play on which *The* Second
Part of K. Henry VI. was founded; and entered it on the
Stationers' books, certainly with an intention to publiſh it.—

[5] Compare alſo the account of the death of the duke of York (p. 253)
and King Henry's Soliloquy (p. 269) with the old play as quoted in the
notes.—Sometimes our author new-verſified the old, without the addition of any new, matter. See p. 311, n. 1.

[6] See p. 162, n. 8; and p 172, n. 9. Compare alſo Clifford's
ſpeech to the rebels in p. 201, Buckingham's addreſs to King Henry in
p. 203, and Iden's ſpeech in p. 206, With the old play, as quoted in the
notes.

Why

Why it did not then appear, cannot be now afcertained. But both that, and the other piece on which *The* Third *Part of King Henry VI.* was formed, was printed by the fame book-feller in 1600, either with a view to lead the common reader to fuppofe that he fhould purchafe two plays *as altered,* and new-modelled by Shakfpeare, or, without any fuch fraudulent intention, to derive a profit from the exhibition of a work that fo great a writer had thought proper to retouch, and form into thofe dramas which for feveral years before 1600 had without doubt been performed with confiderable applaufe. In the fame manner *The* old *Taming of a Shrew,* on which our author formed a play, had been entered at Stationers' Hall in 1594, and was printed in 1607, without doubt with a view to pafs it on the public as the production of Shakfpeare.

When William Pavier republifhed *The Contention of the two Houfes,* &c. in 1619[7], he omitted the words in the original title page,—" *as it was acted by the earl of Pembroke his fervantes* ;"—juft as, on the republication of *King John* in two parts, in 1611, the words,—" *as it was acted in the honourable city of London,*"—were omitted ; becaufe the omitted words in both cafes marked the refpective pieces not to be the production of Shakfpeare[8]. And as in *King John* the letters *W. Sh.* were added in 1611 to deceive the purchafer, fo in the republication of *The whole Contention,* &c Pavier, having difmiffed the words above mentioned, inferted thefe :— " *Newly* CORRECTED *and* ENLARGED *by William Shakfpeare* ;" knowing that thefe two pieces had been made the ground work of two other plays ; that they had in fact been *corrected* and *enlarged,* (though not in that copy which Pavier printed, which is a mere republication from the edition of 1600,) and exhibited under the titles of *The* Second *and* Third *Part of K. Henry VI.;* and hoping that this new edition of the *original* plays would pafs for thofe *altered* and *augmented* by Shakfpeare, which were then unpublifhed.

If Shakfpeare had originally written thefe three plays of *King Henry VI.* would they not probably have been found by the bookfeller in the fame Mf.? Would not the three

[7] Pavier's edition has no date, but it is afcertained to have been printed in 1619, by the fignatures ; the *laft* of which is Q. The play of *Pericles* was printed in 1619, for the fame bookfeller, and its *firft* fignature is R. The undated copy, therefore, of *The Whole Contention,* &c. and *Pericles,* muft have been printed at the fame time.

[8] See *An Attempt to afcertain the order of Shakfpeare's plays,* Vol. I. Article *King John.*

parts have been procured, whether furreptitiouſly or otherwiſe, *all together?* Would they not in the Mſ. have borne
the titles of the *Firſt* and *Second* and *Third* Part of *King
Henry VI.?* And would not the bookſeller have entered them
on the Stationers' books, and publiſhed ſuch of them as he
did publiſh, under thoſe titles, and *with the name of Shakſpeare?* On the other hand, if that which is now diſtinguiſhed by the name of *The* Firſt *Part of King Henry VI.*
but which I ſuppoſe in thoſe times was only called " *The
hiſtorical play of King Henry VI.*" if this was the production
of ſome old dramatiſt, if it had appeared on the ſtage ſome
years before 1501, (as from Naſhe's mention of it ſeems
to be implied,) perhaps in 1587 or 1588, if its popularity
was in 1594 in its wane, and the attention of the publick
was entirely taken up by Shakſpeare's alteration of two
other plays which had likewiſe appeared before 1591, would
not the ſuperior popularity of theſe two pieces, altered by
ſuch a poet, attract the notice of the bookſellers? and finding themſelves unable to procure them from the theatre,
would they not gladly ſeize on the *originals* on which this
new and admired writer had worked, and publiſhed them as
ſoon as they could, neglecting entirely the preceding old
play, or *Firſt Part of King Henry VI.* (as it is now called)
which Shakſpeare had not embelliſhed with his pen?—
Such, we have ſeen, was actually the proceſs; for Thomas
Millington, neglecting entirely *The Firſt Part of K. Henry VI.*
entered the ORIGINAL of *The Second Part of K. Henry VI.*
at Stationers' Hall in 1593-4, and publiſhed the ORIGI-
NALS of both that and *The Third Part* in 1600. When
Heminge and Condell printed theſe three pieces in folio, they
were neceſſarily obliged to name the old play of *King Henry
VI.* the *firſt* part, to diſtinguiſh it from the two following
hiſtorical dramas, founded on a later period of the ſame king's
reign.

Having examined ſuch external evidence as time has left
us concerning theſe two plays, now denominated *The* Second
and Third *Parts of King Henry VI.* let us ſee whether we
cannot by internal marks aſcertain how far Shakſpeare was
concerned in their compoſition.

It has long been a received opinion that the two quarto
plays, one of which was publiſhed under the title of *The
Firſt Part of the Contention of the two Houſes of York and Lancaſter,* &c. and the other under the title of *The true Tragedie
of Richard duke of Yorke,* &c. were ſpurious and imperfect
copies of Shakſpeare's *Second* and *Third Part of King
Henry VI.;* and many paſſages have been quoted in the
notes

notes to the late editions of Shakfpeare, as containing
merely the various readings of the quartos and the folio;
the paffages being fuppofed to be in fubftance the fame, only
varioufly exhibited in different copies. The variations have
been accounted for, by fuppofing that the imperfect and fpurious quarto copies (as they were called) were taken down
either by an unfkilful fhort-hand writer, or by fome auditor
who picked up " during the reprefentation what the time
would permit, then filled up fome of his omiffions at a fecond
or third hearing, and when he had by this method formed
fomething like a play, fent it to the printer. To this opinion, I with others for a long time fubfcribed : two of Heywood's pieces furnifhed indubitable proofs that plays in the
time of our author were fometimes imperfectly copied during the reprefentation, by the ear, or by fhort-hand writers [9]. But a minute examination of the two pieces in
queftion, and a careful comparifon of them with Shakfpeare's
Second and *Third Part of King Henry VI.* have convinced
me that this could not have been the cafe with refpect to them.
No fraudulent copyift or fhort-hand writer would invent circumftances *totally different* from thofe which appear in Shakfpeare's new-modelled draughts as exhibited in the firft folio;
or infert *whole fpeeches*, of which fcarcely a trace is found in
that edition. In the courfe of the foregoing notes many of
thefe have been particularly pointed out. I fhall now bring
into one point of view all thofe internal circumftances which
prove in my apprehenfion decifively, that the quarto plays
were not fpurious and imperfect copies of Shakfpeare's pieces,
but elder dramas on which he formed his *Second* and *Third
Part of King Henry VI.*

1. In fome places a fpeech in one of thefe quartos confifts of ten or twelve lines. In Shakfpeare's folio the fame
fpeech confifts of perhaps only half the number [1]. A copyift
by the ear, or an unfkilful fhort-hand writer, might mutilate
and exhibit a poet's thoughts or expreffions imperfectly; but
would he dilate and amplify them, or introduce totally new
matter? Affuredly he would not.

2 Some circumftances are mentioned in the old quarto
plays, of which there is not the leaft trace in the folio; and
many minute variations are found between them and the
folio, that prove the pieces in quarto to have been original and
diftinct compofitions.

9 See p. 331.
1 See p. 112, n. 2; p. 133, n. 8; p. 213, n. *; p. 309, n. 7; and
p. 312, n. 2.

In

In the laſt act of the *Firſt Part of the Contention*, &c. the duke of Buckingham after the battle of Saint Albans, is brought in wounded, and carried to his tent; but in Shakſpeare's play he is not introduced on the ſtage after that battle.

In one of the *original* ſcenes between Jack Cade and his followers, which Shakſpeare has made the ſeventh ſcene of the fourth act of his *Second Part of King Henry VI.* Dick Butcher drags a ſerjeant, that is, a catch-pole, on the ſtage, and a dialogue conſiſting of ſeventeen lines paſſes between Cade, &c. at the concluſion of which it is determined that the ſerjeant ſhall be " brain'd with his own mace." Of this not one word appears in our author's play[2]. In the ſame piece Jack Cade, hearing that a knight, called Sir Humphrey Stafford, was coming at the head of an army againſt him, to put himſelf on a par with him makes himſelf a knight; and finding that Stafford's brother was alſo a knight, he dubs Dick Butcher alſo. But in Shakſpeare's play the latter circumſtance is omitted.

In the old play Somerſet goes out immediately after he is appointed regent of France. In Shakſpeare's *Second Part of King Henry VI.* he continues on the ſtage with Henry to the end of the ſcene (Act I. ſc. iii) and the king addreſſes him as they go out.

In the old play, the dutcheſs of Gloſter enters with Hume, Bolinbroke, and Margery Jourdain, and after ſome converſation with them, tells them that while they perform their rites, ſhe will go to the top of an adjoining tower, and there write down ſuch anſwers as the ſpirits, that they are to raiſe, ſhall give to her queſtions. But in Shakſpeare's play, Hume, *Southwell*, (who is not introduced in the elder drama) and Bolingbroke, &c. enter without the dutcheſs; and after ſome converſation the dutcheſs appears above, (that is, on the tower,) and encourages them to proceed[3].

In Shakſpeare's play, when the duke of York enters, and finds the dutcheſs of Gloſter, &c. and her co-adjutors performing their magick rites, (p. 123,) the duke ſeizes the paper in which the anſwers of the ſpirit to certain queſtions are written down, and reads them aloud. In the old play the anſwers are not here recited by York; but in a ſubſequent ſcene Buckingham reads them to the king; (ſee p. 124, n. 9, and p. 131, n. 3.) and this is one of the many tran-

---

[2] See p. 159, n. *; and *The Firſt Part of the Contention*, &c. 1600, ſign. G. 3.

[3] See p. 121, n. 2.

positions that Shakspeare made in new-modelling these pieces of which I shall speak more fully hereafter.

In the old play, when the king pronounces sentence on the dutchess of Gloster, he particularly mentions the mode of her penance; and the sentence is pronounced in prose. "Stand forth dame Eleanor Cobham, dutchess of Gloster, and hear the sentence pronounced against thee for these treasons that thou hast committed against us, our state and peers. First, for thy haynous crimes thou shalt *two* daies in London do penance *barefoot in the streets, with a white sheete about thy bodie, and a wax taper burning in thy hand:* that done, thou shalt be banished for ever into the Isle of Man, there to end thy wretched daies; and this is our sentence irrevocable.—Away with her." But in Shakspeare's play, (p. 136) the king pronounces sentence in *verse* against the dutchess *and her confederates* at the same time; and only says in general, that "after *three* days open penance, she shall be banished to the Isle of Man."

In Shakspeare's play, (p. 153) when the duke of York undertakes to subdue the Irish rebels, if he be furnished with a sufficient army, *Suffolk* says, that he "will see that charge performed." But in the old play the queen enjoins *the duke of Buckingham* to attend to this business, and he accepts the office.

In our author's play Jack Cade is described as a *clothier,* in the old play he is "the *dyer* of Ashford." In the same piece, when the king and Somerset appear at Kenelworth, a dialogue passes between them and the queen, of which not one word is preserved in the corresponding scene in *The Second Part of King Henry VI.* (p. 203) In the old play, Buckingham states to the king the grounds on which York had taken up arms; but in Shakspeare's piece, (p. 241,) York himself assigns his reasons for his conduct.

In the old play near the conclusion, young Clifford, when he is preparing to carry off the dead body of his father, is assaulted by Richard, and after putting him to flight, he makes a speech consisting of four lines. But in Shakspeare's play (p. 221) there is no combat between them, nor is Richard introduced in that scene. The four lines therefore above mentioned are necessarily omitted.

In the old play the queen drops her glove, and finding that the dutchess of Gloster makes no attempt to take it up, she gives her a box on the ear:

"Give me my *glove;* why, minion, can you not *see?*"

But

But in Shakfpeare's play, (p. 117,) the queen drops not a glove, but a *fan*:

    " Give me my *fan: What*, minion, can you not?"

In Shakfpeare's *Second Part of King Henry VI.* (p. 176,) Suffolk difcovers himfelf to the captain who had feized him, by fhewing his *George.* In the old play he announces his quality by a *ring*, a feal-ring we may fuppofe, exhibiting his arms. In the fame fcene of Shakfpeare's play, he obferves that the captain threatens more

    " Than *Bargulus*, the ftrong *Illyrian* pirate."

But in the elder drama Suffolk fays, he

    " Threatens more plagues than mighty *Abradas*,
    " The great *Macedonian* pirate."

In the fame fcene of the original play the captain threatens to *fink* Suffolk's fhip; but no fuch menace is found in Shakfpeare's play.

In *The True Tragedie of Richarde duke of York*, &c. Richard (afterwards duke of Glofter) informs Warwick that his *father* the earl of Salifbury was killed in the action which he defcribes, and which in fact took place at Ferrybridge in Yorkfhire. But Shakfpeare in his *Third Part of King Henry VI.* (p. 266) formed upon the piece above-mentioned, has rightly deviated from it, and for *father* fubftituted *brother*, it being the natural brother of Warwick, (the baftard fon of Salifbury) that fell at Ferrybridge. The earl of Salifbury, Warwick's father, was beheaded at Pomfret.

In the fame old play a fon is introduced who has killed his father, and afterwards a father who has killed his fon. King Henry, who is on the ftage, fays not a word till they have both appeared, and fpoken; he then pronounces a fpeech of feven lines. But in Shakfpeare's play (p. 271) this fpeech is enlarged, and two fpeeches formed on it: the firft of which the king fpeaks after the fon has appeared, and the other after the entry of the father.

In our author's play, (p. 300,) after Edward's marriage with Lady Grey, his brothers enter, and converfe on that event. The king, queen, &c. then join them, and Edward afks Clarence how he approves his choice. In the elder play there is no previous dialogue between Glofter and

Clarence;

Clarence ; but the scene opens with the entry of the king, &c. who defires the opinion of his brothers on his recent marriage.

In our author's play (p. 290,) the following line is found :

    " And fet the *murderous Machiavel* to fchool."

This line in *The true Tragedie of Richarde duke of York,* &c. ftood thus :

    " And fet the *afpiring Cataline* to fchool.

Cataline was the perfon that would naturally occur to Peele or Greene, as the moft fplendid *claffical* example of inordinate ambition ; but Shakfpeare, who was more converfant with Englifh books, fubftituted Machiavel, whofe name was in fuch frequent ufe in his time that it became a fpecifick term for a confummate politician [4] ; and accordingly he makes his hoft in *The Merry Wives of Windfor,* when he means to boaft of his own fhrewdnefs, exclaim, 'Am I fubtle ? am I a *Machiavel ?*"

Many other variations befide thofe already mentioned might be pointed out ; but that I may not weary the reader, I will only refer in a note to the moft ftriking diverfities that are found between Shakfpeare's *Second* and *Third Part of King Henry VI.* and the elder dramas printed in quarto [5].

The fuppofition of imperfect or fpurious copies cannot account for fuch numerous variations in the *circumftances* of thefe pieces ; (not to infift at prefent on the *language* in which they are clothed ;) fo that we are compelled (as I have already obferved) to maintain, either that Shakfpeare wrote *two* plays on the ftory which forms his *Second Part of King Henry VI.* a hafty fketch, and an entirely diftinct and more finifhed performance ; or elfe we muft acknowledge that he formed that piece on a foundation laid by another writer, that is, upon the quarto copy of *The Firft Part of the Contention of the Houfes of Yorke and Lancafter,* &c.—And the fame argument precifely applies to *The Third Part of King*

---

4 See p. 91, n. 5. of this volume.

5 See p. 112, n. 2 ; p. 120, n. 1 ; p. 121, n. 3 ; p. 123. n. 8 ; p. 149, n. 2 ; p. 152, n. 5 ; p. 156, n. 2 ; p. 175, n. 8 ; p. 176, n. 2 ; p. 180, n. 6 ; p. 200, n. 7 ; p. 203, n. 4 ; p. 212, n. 9 and 213, n. * ; p. 214, n. 6 ; p. 232, n. 7 ; p. 234, n. 2 ; p. 235, n. 7 ; p. 239, n. 9 ; p. 240, n. 2 ; p. 241, n. 4 ; p. 243, n. 4 ; p. 265, n. 8 ; p. 268, n. 4 ; p. 272, n. 5 ; p. 290, n. 9 ; p. 299, n. 4 ; p. 304, n. 8, and 305, n. 9 ; p. 309, n. 8.

                                      Henry

Henry VI. which is founded on *The true Tragedie of Richard duke of Yorke*, &c. printed in quarto 1600.

Let us now advert to the *Refemblances* that are found in thefe pieces as exhibited in the folio, to paffages in our author's undifputed plays; and alfo to the *Inconfiftencies* that may be traced between them; and, if I do not deceive myfelf, both the one and the other will add confiderable fupport to the foregoing obfervations.

In our author's genuine plays, he frequently borrows from himfelf, the fame thoughts being found in nearly the fame expreffions in different pieces. In *The* Second *and* Third *Part of King Henry VI.* as in his other dramas, thefe coincidencies with his other works may be found[6]; and this was one of the circumftances that once weighed much in my mind, and convinced me of their authenticity. But a collation of thefe plays with the old pieces on which they are founded, has fhewn me the fallacy by which I was deceived; for the paffages of thefe two parts of *K. Henry VI.* which correfpond with others in our author's undifputed plays, exift *only* in the *folio* copy, and not in the *quarto*; in other words, in thofe parts of thefe new-modelled pieces, which were of Shakfpeare's writing, and not in the originals by another hand, on which he worked. This, I believe, will be found invariably the cafe, except in three inftances.

The firft is, " You have no children, butchers;" which is, it muft be acknowledged, in *The true Tragedie of Richarde duke of Yorke*, &c. 1600; (as well as in *The* Third *Part of King Henry VI.*) and is alfo introduced with a flight variation in *Macbeth.*

Another inftance is found in *K. John.* That king, when charged with the death of his nephew, afks,

" Think you, I bear the fhears of deftiny?

" Have I commandment on the pulfe of life?"

which bears a ftriking refemblance to the words of Cardinal Beaufort in *The firft part of the Contention of the two houfes*, &c. which Shakfpeare has introduced in his *Second Part of King Henry VI.*

" —— Died he not in his bed?

" Can I make men live whe'r they will or no?"

The third inftance is found in *The true Tragedie of Richarde duke of Yorke*, &c. In that piece are the following lines, which

5 See p. 112, n. 2; p. 120, n. 1; p. 121, n. 3; p. 123. n. 8; p. 149, n. 2; P. 152, n. 5; P. 156, n. 2; p. 175, n. 8; p. 176, n. 2; p. 180, n. 6; p. 200, n. 7; p. 203, n. 4; p. 212, n. 9; and 213, n. *;
P. 224,

which Shakſpeare adopted with a very ſlight variation, and inſerted in his *Third Part of King Henry VI.*

" —— doves will peck in reſcue of their brood.——
" Unreaſonable creatures feed their young ;
" And though man's face be fearful to their eyes,
" Yet, in protection of their tender ones,
" Who hath not ſeen them even with thoſe ſame wings
" Which they have ſometimes uſed in fearful flight,
" Make war with him that climb'd unto their neſt,
" Offering their own lives in their young's defence ?"

So, in our author's *Macbeth :*

" —— the poor wren——
" The moſt diminutive of birds, will fight,
" Her young ones in the neſt, againſt the owl." .

But whoever recollects the various thoughts that Shakſpeare has borrowed from preceding writers, will not be ſurpriſed that in a *ſimilar* ſituation, in *Macbeth*, and *King John*, he ſhould have uſed the expreſſions of an old dramatiſt, with whoſe writings he had been particularly converſant; expreſſions too, which he had before embodied in former plays: nor can, I think, theſe three inſtances much diminiſh the force of the foregoing obſervation. That it may have its full weight, I have in the preſent edition diſtinguiſhed by aſteriſks all the lines in *The Second* and *Third Part of King Henry VI.* of which there is no trace in the old quarto plays, and which therefore I ſuppoſe to have been written by Shakſpeare. Though this has not been effected without much trouble, yet, if it ſhall tend to ſettle this long-agitated queſtion, I ſhall not conſider my labour as wholly thrown away.

Perhaps a ſimilar coincidency in *The* Firſt *Part of King Henry VI.* may be urged in oppoſition to my hypotheſis relative to that play. " Lean famine, quartering ſteel, and climbing fire," are in that piece called the attendants on the brave lord Talbot; as in Shakſpeare's *King Henry V.* " famine, ſword, and fire, are leaſh'd in like hounds, crouching under the martial Henry for employment." If this image had proceeded from our author's imagination, this coincidency might perhaps countenance the ſuppoſition that he had ſome hand at leaſt in that ſcene of *The* Firſt *Part of King Henry VI.* where theſe attendants on war are perſonified. But that is not the caſe: for the fact is, that Shakſpeare was furniſhed with this imagery by a paſſage in *Holinſhed*, as the author of the old play of *King Henry VI.* was by *Hall's* Chronicle: " The Goddeſſe of warre, called Bellonas—hath thefe three hand-maides ever of neceffitie attending on her; *bloud, fyre.* and *famine* [8]."

In our prefent inquiry, it is undoubtedly a very ftriking circumftance that *almoft* all the paffages in The *Second* and *Third Part of King Henry VI.* which refemble others in Shakfpeare's undifputed plays, are not found in the original pieces in quarto, but in his *Rifacimento* publifhed in folio. As thefe *Refemblances* to his other plays, and a peculiar Shakfpearian phrafeology, afcertain a *confiderable portion* of thefe difputed dramas to be the production of Shakfpeare, fo on the other hand certain paffages which are *difcordant* (in matters of fact) from his other plays, are proved by this *Difcordancy*, not to have been compofed by him; and thefe difcordant paffages, being found in the original quarto plays, prove that thofe pieces were compofed by another writer.

Thus, in *The Third Part of King Henry VI.* (p. 283,) Sir John Grey is faid to have loft " his life in quarrel of the houfe of ·*York*; and king Edward ftating the claim of his widow, whom he afterwards married, mentions, that his lands after the battle of Saint Albans (February 17, 1760-1) " were feized on by the conqueror." Whereas in fact they were feized on by Edward himfelf after the battle of Towton, (in which he was conqueror,) March 29, 1461. The conqueror at the fecond battle of Saint Albans, the battle here meant, was Queen Margaret This ftatement was taken from the old quarto play; and, from carelefsnefs was adopted by Shakfpeare without any material alteration. But at a fubfequent period when he wrote his *King Richard III.* he was under a neceffity of carefully examining the Englifh chronicles; and in that play, Act I fc. iii. he has reprefented this matter truly as it was:

> " In all which time, you, and your hufband Grey,
> " Were *factious for the houfe of ·Lancafter*;—
> " (And, Rivers, fo were you;)—Was not your hufband
> " In Margaret's battle at Saint Albans flain?'

It is called " Margaret's battle," becaufe fhe was there victorious.

An equally decifive circumftance is furnifhed by the fame play. In *The* Third *Part of King Henry VI.* (p. 296.) Warwick propofes to marry his eldeft daughter *(Ifabella)* to Edward prince of Wales, and the propofal is accepted by Edward; and in a fubfequent fcene Clarence fays, he will marry the *younger* daughter *(Ann)*. In thefe particulars

---

[8] Hall's *Chron.* Henry VI. fol. xxix.

Shakfpeare

Shakfpeare has implicitly followed the elder drama. But the fact is, that the prince of Wales married Anne the *younger* daughter of the earl of Warwick, and the duke of Clarence married the *elder*, Ifabella. Though the author of *The true Tragedie of the duke of Yorke*, &c. was here inaccurate, and though Shakfpeare too negligently followed his fteps,—when he wrote his *King Richard III.* he had gained better information; for there Lady ANNE is rightly reprefented as the widow of the prince of Wales, and the *youngeft* daughter of the earl of Warwick:

" Which done, God take king Edward to his mercy,
" And leave the world to me to buftle in.
" For then I'll marry Warwick's *youngeft* daughter;
" What though I kill'd her hufband, and her father," &c.

i. e. Edward prince of Wales, and king Henry VI.
King Richard III. Act I. fc. 1.

I have faid that certain paffages in *The Second and Third Part of King Henry VI.* are afcertained to be Shakfpeare's by a peculiar phrafeology. This peculiar phrafeology, without a fingle exception, diftinguifhes fuch parts of thefe plays as are found in the folio, and not in the *elder* quarto dramas, of which the phrafeology, as well as the verfification, is of a different colour. This obfervation applies not only to the new original matter produced by Shakfpeare, but to his alteration of the old. Our author in his undoubted compofitions has fallen into an inaccuracy, of which I do not recollect a fimilar inftance in the works of any other dramatift. When he has occafion to quote the fame paper twice, (not from memory, but *verbatim*,) from negligence he does not always attend to the words of the paper which he has occafion to quote, but makes one of the perfons of the drama recite them with variations, though he holds the very paper quoted before his eyes. Thus, in *All's well that ends well*, Act V fc. iii. Helena fays,

" — here's your letter; This it fays:
" *When from my finger you can get this ring,*
" *And are by me with child*,"—

Yet, as I have obferved in another place, Helena in Act III. fc. ii. *reads* this very letter aloud, and there the words are different, and in plain profe: " When thou canft get the ring from my finger, which never fhall come off, and fhew me a child begotten of thy body," &c. In like manner, in the firft fcene of *The Second Part of King*

Henry.

Henry VI. Suffolk prefents to the duke of Glofter, protector of the realm, the articles of peace concluded between France and England. The protector begins to read the articles, but when he has proceeded no further than thefe words,—" Item, that the *dutchy* of Anjou and the *county* of Maine fhall be releafed and delivered to the king her father," —he is fuddenly taken ill, and rendered incapable of proceeding: on which the bifhop of Winchefter is called upon to read the remainder of the paper. He accordingly reads the whole of the article, of which the duke of Glofter had only read a part: " Item, *It is further agreed between them,* that *the dutchies of Anjou and Maine* fhall be releafed and delivered *over* to the king her father, and fhe fent," &c Now though Maine in our old chronicles is fometimes called a county, and fometimes a dutchy, yet words cannot thus change their form under the eyes of two readers: nor do they in the original play, entitled *The firft part of the Contention of the two houfes,* &c. for there the article as recited by the protector correfponds with that recited by the bifhop, without the moft minute variation. " Item, It is further agreed between them, that the *dutchies of Anjou and of Maine* fhall be releafed and delivered *over* to the king her father, and fhe fent," &c. Thus in the old play fays the duke, and fo fays the cardinal after him. This one circumftance, in my apprehenfion, is of fuch weight, that though it ftood alone, it might decide the prefent queftion. Our author has fallen into a fimilar inaccuracy in the fourth fcene of the fame act, where the duke of York recites from a paper the queftions that had been put to the Spirit, relative to the duke of Suffolk, Somerfet [9], &c.

Many minute marks of Shakfpeare's hand may be traced in fuch parts of the old plays as he has new modelled. I at prefent recollect one that muft ftrike every reader who is converfant with his writings. He very frequently ufes adjectives adverbially; and this kind of phrafeology, if not peculiar to him, is found more frequently in his writings than thofe of any of his contemporaries. Thus,—" I am myfelf *indifferent* honeft;"—" as *difhonourable* ragged as an old faced ancient;"—*equal* ravenous;"—" leaves them *invifible;*" &c. In *The true Tragedie of the duke of Yorke,* &c. the king, having determined to marry Lady Grey, injoins his brothers to ufe her *honourably.* But in Shakfpeare's play the words are,—" ufe her *honourable.*" So, in *Julius Cæfar:*

9 See p. 124, n *.

" Young

" Young man, thou could'ſt not die more *honourable*."

In like manner, in *The Third Part of King Henry VI.*
we find this line :

" Is either ſlain, or wounded *dangerous*."

but in the old play the words are—" wounded *danger-
ouſly*."

In the ſame play the word *handkerchief* is uſed ; but in the
correſponding ſcene in *The Third Part of King Henry VI.*
(p. 254.) Shakſpeare has ſubſtituted the northern term *napkin*,
which occurs ſo often in his works, in its room.   -

The next circumſtance to which I wiſh to call the attention
of thoſe who do not think the preſent inveſtigation wholly in-
curious, is, the *Tranſpoſitions* that are found in theſe plays.
In the preceding notes I have frequently obſerved that not
only ſeveral lines, but ſometimes whole ſcenes [1], were tranſpoſed by Shakſpeare.

In p. 253, 254, a Meſſenger, giving an account of the
death of the duke of York, ſays,

" Environed he was with many foes ;
" And ſtood againſt them, as the hope of Troy
" Againſt the Greeks, that would have enter'd Troy.
" But Hercules himſelf muſt yield to odds ;"—

When this paſſage was printed, not finding any trace of the
laſt three lines in the correſponding part of the old play, I
marked them inadvertently as Shakſpeare's original compoſition ; but I afterwards found that he had borrowed them
from a ſubſequent ſcene on a quite different ſubject, in which
Henry, taking leave of Warwick, ſays to him,

" Farewell my Hector, and *my Troy's true hope !*"

and the laſt line, " But Hercules," &c. is ſpoken by Warwick near the concluſion of the piece, after he is mortally
wounded in the battle of Barnet.

So, in *The true Tragedie of Richard duke of Yorke*, &c.
after the duke has ſlain Clifford, he ſays,

" *Now, Lancaſter, ſit ſure :*—thy ſinews ſhrink."

Shakſpeare has not made uſe of that line in that place, but
availed himſelf of it afterwards, where Edward brings forth
Warwick wounded ; *King Henry VI.* P. III. Act V. ſc. ii.

" *Now*, Mountague, *ſit faſt :* I ſeek for thee," &c.

---

[1] See p. 311, n. 9 ; p. 316, n. 6 ; p. 320, n. 5.

Many

Many other tranfpofitions may be traced in thefe plays, to which I fhall only refer in a note [2].

Such tranfpofitions as I have noticed, could never have arifen from any careleffnefs or inaccuracy of tranfcribers or copyifts; and therefore are to be added to the many other circumftances which prove that *The Second and Third Parts of King Henry VI.*, as exhibited in the folio, were formed from the materials of a preceding writer.

It is alfo obfervable, that many lines are *repeated* in Shakfpeare's *Second and Third Part of King Henry VI.*[3], but no fuch repetitions are found in the old quarto plays. The repetition undoubtedly arofe from Shakfpeare's not always following his original ftrictly, but introducing expreffions which had ftruck him in other parts of the old plays; and afterwards, forgetting that he had before ufed fuch expreffions, he fuffered them to remain in their original places alfo.

Another proof that Shakfpeare was not the author of *The Contention of the two houfes*, &c. is furnifhed by the inconfiftencies into which he has fallen, by fometimes adhering to, and fometimes deviating from, his original: an inaccuracy which may be fometimes obferved in his undifputed plays.

One of the moft remarkable inftances of this kind of inconfiftency is found in *The Second Part of King Henry VI.* p. 190, where he makes Henry fay,

    " I'll fend fome holy bifhop to entreat,' &c.

a circumftance which he took from Holinfhed's Chronicle; whereas in the old play no mention is made of a bifhop on this occafion. The king there fays, he will himfelf come and parley with the rebels, and in the mean time he orders Clifford and Buckingham to gather an army. In a fubfequent fcene, however, Shakfpeare forgot the new matter which he had introduced in the former; and *Clifford* and *Buckingham* only parley with Cade, &c. *conformably to the old play* [4].

In *Romeo and Juliet* he has fallen into a fimilar inaccuracy. In the poem on which that tragedy is founded, Romeo, in his interview with the Friar, after fentence of banifhment has been pronounced againft him, is defcribed as paffionately lamenting his fate in the following terms:

---

2 See p. 169, n. 9; p. 186, n. 5; p. 216, n 8; p. 307, n. 4; p 309, n. 8, and n 9; p. 322, n. 9.
3 See p 269, n. 6; p 281, n. 9; p. 292, n. 2; p 295, n. *.
4 See alfo p. 122, n. 6; p. 294, n 6; and p. 295, n. *.

                                   " Firft

" Firſt *nature* did he blame, the *author of his life,*

" In which his joys had been ſo ſcant, and ſorrows aye
　　ſo riſe;

" The time and place of *birth* he fiercely did reprove;

" He cry'd out with open mouth againſt *the ſtars
　　above.—*

" On *fortune* eke he *rail'd,* &c.

The friar afterwards reproves him for want of patience.
In forming the correſponding ſcene Shakſpeare has omitted
Romeo's invective againſt his fate, but inadvertently copied
the friar's remonſtrance *as it lay before him:*

" Why *rail'ſt* thou on thy birth, the heaven, and earth?"

If the following ſhould be conſidered as a trifling circumſtance, let it be remembered, that circumſtances which, ſepa-
rately conſidered, may appear unimportant, ſometimes ac-
quire ſtrength, when united to other proofs of more efficacy:
in my opinion, however, what I ſhall now mention is a
circumſtance of conſiderable weight. It is obſervable that
the prieſt concerned with Eleanor Cobham Dutcheſs of Glo-
ceſter, in certain pretended operations of magick, for which
ſhe was tried, is called by Hall, John *Hum.* So is he named
in *The firſt part of the Contention of the two Houſes of Yorke,*
&c. the original, as I ſuppoſe, of *The* Second *Part of K.
Henry VI.* Our author probably thinking the name harſh or
ridiculous, ſoftened it to *Hume;* and by that name this prieſt
is called in *his* play printed in folio. But in Holinſhed he is
named *Hun;* and ſo undoubtedly, or perhaps for ſoftneſs,
Hune, he would have been called in the original quarto play
juſt mentioned, if Shakſpeare had been the author of it; for
Holinſhed and not Hall was his guide, as I have ſhewn in-
conteſtably in a note on *King Henry V.* But Hall was
undoubtedly the hiſtorian who had been conſulted by the
original writer of *The Contention of the two Houſes of Yorke
and Lancaſter;* as appears from his having taken a line
from thence, " That *Alexander Iden, an eſquire of Kent* [6],"
and from the ſcene in which Cardinal Beaufort is exhibited
on his death-bed. One part of the particular deſcription of
the Cardinal's death and dying words, in the old quarto play,
is founded on a paſſage in Hall, which Holinſhed, though in
general a ſervile copyiſt of the former chronicler, has omitted.
The paſſage is this. " Dr. John Baker, his pryvie coun-
ſailer and hys chapellayn, wrote, that lying on his death bed

---

6 See Hall, Heury V. fol. lxxix. Holinſhed ſays, " a gentleman of
Kent, named Alexander Iden, awaited ſo his time," &c.

he [Cardinal Beaufort] faid thefe words: ' Why fhould I
dye, havyng fo much riches? If the whole realme would
fave my life, I am able either by pollicie to get it, or by
ryches to bye it. Fye! will not death be hyered, nor will
money do nothynge? From this the writer of the old play
formed thefe lines:

O death, if thou will let me live
But one whole year, I'll give thee as much gold
As will purchafe fuch another ifland.

which Shakfpeare new-modelled thus:

If thou be'ft death, I'll give thee England's treafure,
Enough to purchafe fuch another ifland,
So thou wilt let me live, and feel no pain.

If Shakfpeare had been the author of *The firft part of the
Contention*, &c finding in his Holinfhed the name *Hun*, he
would either have preferved it, or foftened it to *Hune*.
Working on the old play, where he found the name of *Hum*,
which founded ridiculous to his ear, he changed it to *Hume*.
But whoever the original writer of the old play was, having
ufed the name of *Hum*, he muft have formed his play on
Hall's Chronicle, where *alone* that name is found Shakfpeare therefore having made Holinfhed, and not Hall; his
guide, could not have been the writer of it.

It may be remarked, that by the alteration of the prieft's
name he has deftroyed a rhyme intended by the author of
the original play, where Sir John begins a foliloquy with
this jingling line:

" Now, Sir John *Hum*, no word but *mum*:
" Seal up your lips, for you muft filent be."

which Shakfpeare has altered thus:

" — But how now, Sir John *Hume*?
" Seal up your lips, and give no words but *mum*.

Lines rhiming in the middle and end, fimilar to that above
quoted, are often found in our old Englifh plays, (previous to
the time of Shakfpeare,) and are generally put into the
mouths of priefts and friars.

It has already been obferved, that in the original play on
which *The* Second *Part of King Henry VI.* is founded,
" *Abradas*, the *Macedonian* pirate," is mentioned. This
hero does not appear in Shakfpeare's new-modelled play,
" *Bargulus*, the ftrong *Illyrian* pirate," being introduced in
his room. *Abradas* is fpoken of (as Mr. Steevens has remarked) by Robert Greene, the very perfon whom I fuppofe
to have been one of the joint authors of the original plays, in
a pamphlet,

a pamphlet, entitled *Penelope's Web*, 1598 :—" *Abradas*, the great *Macedonean pirate*, thought every one had a letter of mart that bare fayles in the ocean." Of this pirate or his atchievements, however celebrated he may have been, I have not found the flightest trace in *any book* whatfoever, except that above quoted : a fingular circumftance, which appears to me ftrongly to confirm my hypothefis on the prefent fubject ; and to fupport my interpretation of Greene's words in his *Groatfworth of Witte*, in a former part of the prefent difquifition.

However this may be, there are certainly very good grounds for believing that *The firft part of the Contention of the two houfes of Yorke and Lancafter*, &c. and *The true Tragedie of Richarde duke of Yorke*, &c. were written by the author or authors of the old *King John*, printed in 1591.

In *The true Tragedie*, &c. we find the following lines:

" *Let England be true within itfelf,*
" We need not France, nor any alliance with her."

The firft of thefe lines is found, with a very minute variation, in the old *King John*, where it runs thus :

" Let England *live but* true within itfelf,—".

Nor is this the only coincidence   In the defervedly admired fcene in which Cardinal Beaufort's death is reprefented, in the original play, (as well as in Shakfpeare's *Second Part of King Henry VI.)* he is called upon to hold up his hand, as a proof of his confidence in God :

" Lord Cardinal,
" If thou dieft affured of heavenly bliffe,
" Hold up thy hand, and make fome fign to us.
                              [*The Cardinal dies.*
" O fee, he dies, and makes no fign at all :
" O God, forgive his foule !"

I quote from the original play.—It is remarkable that a fimilar proof is demanded in the old play of *King John* alfo, when that king is expiring :

" Then, good my lord, if you forgive them all,
" Lift up your hand, in token you forgive."

Again :
" —— in token of thy faith,
" And figne thou dieft the fervant of the Lord,

                                       " Lift

" Lift up thy hand, that we may witneffe here
" Thou dieft the fervant of our Saviour Chrift.—
" Now joy betide thy foul !"

This circumftance appears to me to add confiderable fupport to my conjecture.

One point only remains. It may be afked, if *The* Firft *Part of King Henry VI.* was not written by Shakfpeare, why did Heminge and Condell print it with the reft of his works? The only way that I can account for their having done fo, is by fuppofing, either that their memory at the end of thirty years was not accurate concerning our author's pieces, (as appears indeed evidently from their omitting *Troilus and . Creffida*, which was not recollected by them, till the whole . of the firft folio, and even the table of contents, (which is always the laft work of the prefs,) had been printed ; or, that they imagined the infertion of this hiftorical drama was neceffary to underftanding the two pieces that follow it ; or laftly, that, Shakfpeare, for the advantage of his own theatre, having written a few lines in *The* Firft *Part of King Henry VI.* after his own *Second* and *Third* Part had been played, they conceived this a fufficient warrant for attributing it, along with the others, to him, in the general collection of his works. If Shakfpeare was the author of any part of this play, perhaps the fecond and the following fcenes of the fourth act were his ; which are for the moft part written in rhyme, and appear to me fomewhat of a different complexion from the reft of the play.   Nor is this the only inftance of their proceeding on this ground ; for is it poffible to conceive that they could have any other reafon for giving *Titus Andronicus* a place in their edition of Shakfpeare's works, than his having written twenty or thirty lines in that piece, or having retouched a few verfes of it, if indeed he did fo much ?

Shakfpeare's referring in the Epilogue to *K. Henry V.* which was produced in 1599, to thefe three parts of *King Henry VI.* of which the firft, by whom foever it was written, appears from the teftimony of a contemporary to have been exhibited with great applaufe ; and the two latter, having been, as I conceive, eight years before new-modelled and almoft re-written by our author, we may be confident were performed with the moft brilliant fuccefs ; his fupplicating the favour of the audience to his new play of *King Henry V.* " *for the fake*" of thefe old and *popular* dramas, which were fo clofely connected with it, and in the compofition of which, as they had for many years been exhibited, he had fo confi-

derable

derable a fhare; the connection between the laft fcene of
King Henry VI. and the firft fcene of *K. Richard III.* the
Shakfpearian diction, verfification, and figures, by which the
Second and *Third Part of K. Henry VI.* are diftinguifhed;
" the eafinefs of expreffion and the fluency of numbers,"
which, it is acknowledged, are found here, and were poffeffed by no other author of that age; all thefe circumftances
are accounted for by the theory now ftated, and all the objections [8] that have been founded upon them, in my apprehenfion,
vanifh away.

On the other hand, the entry on the Stationers' books of
the old play, entitled *The firft part of the Contention of the two
houfes of Yorke and Lancafter,* &c. without the name of the
author; that piece, and *The true Tragedie of Richarde duke
of Yorke,* &c. being printed in 1600, anonymoufly; their
being founded on the Chronicle of *Hall,* who was not Shakfpeare's hiftorian, and reprefented by the fervants of lord
Pembroke, by whom none of his unconteſted dramas were reprefented; the colour, diction, and verfification of thofe old
plays; the various circumftances, lines, and fpeeches, that
are found in them, and not in our author's new-modification
of them, as publifhed in folio by his original editors; the refemblances that have been noticed between his other works
and fuch parts of thefe dramas as are *only* exhibited in their
folio edition: the difcordances (in matters of fact) between
certain parts of the old plays printed in quarto and Shakfpeare's undoubted performances; the tranfpofitions that he
has made in thefe pieces; the repetitions, and the peculiar
Shakfpearian inaccuracies, and phrafeology, which may be
traced in the folio, and not in the old quarto plays; thefe
and other circumftances, which have been ftated in the foregoing pages, form, when united, fuch a body of arguments
and proofs, in fupport of my hypothefis, as appears to me,
(though I will not venture to affert that " the probation bears
no hinge nor loop to hang a doubt on,") to lead directly to the
door of *truth.*

It is obfervable that feveral portions of the Englifh Hiftory
had been dramatized *before* the time of Shakfpeare. Thus,
we have *King John* in two parts, by an anonymous writer;
Edward I. by George Peele; *Edward II.* by Chriftopher
Marlowe; *Edward III.* anonymous; *Henry IV.* containing the depofition of *Richard II.* and the acceffion of *Henry*
to the crown, anonymous; *Henry V.* and *Richard III.*

---

[8] See thefe feveral objections ftated by Dr. Johnfon in the notes at
the end of *The Third Part of King Henry VI.*

both

both by anonymous authors [9]. Is it not then highly probable, that the *whole* of the ſtory of *Henry VI.* had alſo been brought upon the ſcene ? and that the firſt of the plays now in queſtion, formerly (as I believe) called *The hiſtorical play of king Henry VI.* and now named *The Firſt Part of king Henry VI.* as well as *The firſt part of the Contention of the two houſes of Yorke and Lancaſter*, &c. and *The true Tragedie of Richard duke of Yorke*, &c. (which three pieces comprehend the entire reign of that king from his birth to his death,) were the compoſition of ſome of the authors, who had produced ſome of the hiſtorical dramas above enumerated ?

In conſequence of a haſty and inconſiderate opinion formed by Mr. Pope, without any minute examination of the ſubject, *K. John* in two parts, printed in 1591, and *The old Taming of a Shrew*, which was entered at Stationers' Hall in 1594, and printed in 1607, paſſed for half a century for the compoſitions of Shakſpeare. Further inquiries have ſhown that they were the productions of earlier writers ; and perhaps a more profound inveſtigation of this ſubject than I have been able to make, may hereafter prove deciſively, that the *firſt* of the three *Henries* printed in folio, and both the parts of *The Whole Contention of the two famous Houſes of York and Lancaſter*, as exhibited in quarto, and printed in 1600, ought to be claſſed in the ſame predicament with the two old plays above mentioned. For my own part, if it ſhould ever be thought proper to reprint the old dramas on which Shakſpeare founded ſome of his plays, which were publiſhed in two volumes a few years ago, I have no doubt that *The firſt part of the Contention of the two houſes of Yorke and Lancaſter*, &c and *The true Tragedie of the duke of Yorke*, &c. ſhould be added to the number.

Gildon ſomewhere ſays, that " in a converſation between Shakſpeare and Ben Jonſon, Ben aſked him the reaſon why he wrote his hiſtorical plays." Our author (we are told) replied, that " finding the nation generally very ignorant of hiſtory, he wrote them in order to inſtruct the people in that particular." This anecdote, like many other traditional ſtories, ſtands on a very weak foundation ; or to ſpeak more juſtly, it is certainly a fiction. The malignant Ben does indeed, in his *Devil's an Aſs*, 1616, ſneer at our author's hiſtorical pieces, which for twenty years preceding had been in high reputation, and probably were *then* the only hiſtorical dramas that had poſſeſſion of the theatre; but from the liſt above given, it is clear that Shakſpeare was not the *firſt* who

9 Entered on the Stationers' books in 1594.

dramatized

dramatized our old chronicles ; and that the principal events of the Englifh Hiftory were familiar to the ears of his audience, before he commenced a writer for the ftage [1] : though undoubtedly at this day whatever knowledge of our annals is difperfed among the people, is derived from the frequent exhibition of our author's hiftorical plays.

He certainly did not confider writing on fables that had already been formed into dramas, as any derogation from his fame ; if indeed fame was ever an object of his thoughts. We know that plays on the fubjects of *Meafure for Meafure*, *The Taming of the Shrew*, *The Merchant of Venice*, *King John*,

---

[1] This point is eftablifhed not only by the lift referred to, but by a paffage in a pamphlet already quoted, entitled *Pierce Pennileffe his Supplication to the Devil*, written by Thomas Nafhe, quarto, 1592 :— " Whereas the afternoone being the eldeft time of the day, wherein men that are their owne mafters (as gentlemen of the Court, the Innes of Court, and the number of captaines and foldiers about London) do wholly beftow themfelves upon pleafure, and that pleafure they divide (how virtuoufly it fkilles not,) into gaming, following of harlots, drinking, or *feeing a play* ; is it not then better, fince of foure extreames all the world cannot keepe them but they will choofe one, that they fhould betake them to the leaft, which is *Playes ?* Nay, what if I prove playes to be no extreame, but a rare exercife of vertue ?— Firft, for the *fubject* of them ; *for the moft part it is borrowed* out of our ENGLISH CHRONICLES, wherein our fore-fathers' valiant actes, that have been long buried in ruftic braffe and worm-eaten bookes, are revived, and they themfelves raifed from the grave of oblivion, and brought to plead their aged honours in open prefence ; than which, what can be a fharper reproofe to thefe degenerate dayes of ours ?"

After an eulogium on the brave Lord Talbot, and on the actor who had perfonated him in a popular play of that time, " before ten thoufand fpectators at the leaft ;" (which has already been printed in a former page,) and after obferving " what a glorious thing it is to have King Henry the Fifth reprefented on the ftage, leading the French king prifoner, and forcing both him and the Dolphin to fwear fealty,"— the writer adds thefe words :

" In playes, all coufenages, all cunning drifts, over-guilded with outward holineffe, all ftratagems of warre, all canker-wormes that breed in the ruft of peace, are moft lively anatomized. They fhew the ill fucceffe of treafon, the fall of hafty climbers, *the wretched end of ufurpers, the miferie of civil diffention*, and how juft God is evermore in punifhing *murder*. And to prove every one of thefe allegations, could I propound the circumftances *of this play and that*, if I meant to handle this theme otherwife than *obiter*."

It is highly probable that the words, " *the miferie of civil diffention*," allude to the very plays which are the fubjects of the prefent difquifition, *The firft part of the Contention of the two houfes*, &c. and *The true Tragedie of Richarde duke of Yorke* ; as, by " the wretched end of Ufurpers," and the juftice of God in " *punifhing murder*," old plays on the fubject of *King Richard III.* and that of *Hamlet*, prior to thofe of Shakfpeare, were, I believe, alluded to.

King Richard II. King Henry IV. King Henry V. King Richard III. King Lear, Antony and Cleopatra, and, I strongly suspect, on those of *Hamlet, Timon of Athens, and Julius Cæsar* [2], existed before he commenced a dramatick author ; and perhaps in process of time it may be found, that many of the fables of his *other* plays also had been unskilfully treated, and produced upon the stage, by preceding writers.

Such are the only lights that I am able to throw on this very dark subject. The arguments which I have stated have entirely satisfied my own mind ; whether they are entitled to bring conviction to the minds of others, I shall not presume to determine. I produce them, however, with the more confidence, as they have the approbation of one who has given such decisive proofs of his taste and knowledge, by ascertaining the extent of *Shakspeare's learning,* that I have no doubt his thoughts on the present question also, will have that weight with the publick to which they are undoubtedly entitled. It is almost unnecessary to add, that I mean my friend Dr. Farmer; who many years ago delivered it as his opinion, that these plays were not written *originally* by Shakspeare

MALONE.

[2] See *An Attempt to ascertain the order of Shakspeare's Plays,* Vol. I.

END OF VOL. IX.